EVERYMAN, I will go with thee,

and be thy guide,

In thy most need to go by thy side

ROBERT BROWNING

Born in Camberwell in 1812. First visit to
Italy in 1834; married Elizabeth Barrett, 1846;
lived in Italy, except for brief intervals, from
1846 to 1861, when he settled in London.
Died at Venice on 16th December 1889.

The five-volume Everyman edition
of Browning's poems and plays

Robert Browning's Poems and Plays

IN FIVE VOLUMES

VOLUME ONE: 1833–1844

Introduction by
JOHN BRYSON, M.A.

DENT: LONDON
EVERYMAN'S LIBRARY
DUTTON: NEW YORK

NO. 41

ISBN: 0 460 00041 1

INTRODUCTION

I

A REVIVED interest in the Victorian writers is a marked
feature of current literary taste. We recognize and admire
Tennyson's supreme poetic artistry; we are enlightened and
encouraged by Arnold's approach to the moral and intel-
lectual problems of his time; we assess the Pre-Raphaelite
achievement with sympathy and critical understanding.
Yet one author awaits rediscovery. Till recently Browning
has been denied the attention given to his equals and even
to far lesser figures than himself. The author of *The Ring
and the Book* is naturally not refused the tribute of a distant
and awed respect, but has any one of his major poems
gained such a hold on our affections as have *In Memoriam*
and *The Scholar Gipsy*? It is worth considering why this
undeniably great poet is less read than others. Is it his
fault or ours?

It is not surprising that we have first of all turned back
to the Victorian writers of discontent, to those who question
the easy acceptance of traditional belief and who anticipate
something of the doubts and uncertain values of our own
time. Browning, at least on a superficial acquaintance, is
not one of those. He troubled himself little with social and
political problems; his concern was with the relations of
men and women, because (as he wrote to his friend Milsand)
'little else is worth study save incidents in the development
of a soul.' It was only with a profound conviction that
man must discover

> By the means of Evil that Good is best,
> And through earth and its noise, what is heaven's serene,

that he was willing to confess himself 'one who in the world,
both lives and likes life's way.' The common accusation of
facile optimism and unquestioning belief is easy enough to
make when the evidence for it rests on nothing more solid
than a memory of Pippa's song, or a recollection of the
opening lines of *Rabbi Ben Ezra*. But Browning is not to
be known thus in snatches or single poems; he reveals his
range and depth in a wide variety of subject and in the
ample leisured planning of his canvas. To realize his
quality one must know him well.

He found in dramatic method his true means of self-expression, and achieved with it a success which is all his own. His poems are 'the utterances of so many imaginary persons, not mine,' and it is through the eyes of men and women in many ages and settings that he attains his own vision of truth. This is far from an impersonal vision though it is revealed by indirect and shifting lights. He is indeed a poet who rarely lays bare the secrets of his heart in personal confession; his horror of those who would pry into the artist's private life is expressed in the contrasting pair of poems, *House* and *Shop*;

> A peep through my window, if folk prefer;
> But, please you, no foot over threshold of mine.

In another late poem, *At the 'Mermaid,'* speaking for Shakespeare he is again speaking for himself:

> Here's my work, does work discover—
> What was rest from work—my life.
> Did I live man's hater, lover?
> Leave the world at peace, at strife?
>
> Blank of such a record, truly,
> Here's the work I leave, this scroll,
> Yours to take or leave: as duly,
> Mine remains the unproffered soul.

Consequently he has little to offer to the reader who is more interested in a man than in his work. No sane literary criticism will deny the value of biography, but Browning's reticence, though extreme, is not unrefreshing when one thinks of how much attention has been devoted to the tragedy of Ruskin's private life and how little to the great body of his prose. Browning saw to it that there were no skeletons left in his cupboard for the curious to find.

We have inherited a belief that Browning is a difficult philosophical writer; it is a legacy from the Browning Society of the eighties, and it should not have survived the delicate mockery of Max Beerbohm's drawing of a worldly poet, top-hatted and lemon-gloved, taking tea with the earnest early members of that society. In searching for his 'message' they were only too likely to miss the true appeal of his poetry, which is moral and imaginative rather than speculative. He is not an easy poet, but whatever the difficulties of its expression the message itself is never obscure; however complex the detail and diverse the material there is seldom complexity in the theme. With an unshaken trust in a personal immortality Browning preaches the doctrine of effort; through study of character balked of perfection he becomes convinced that failure here is redeemed in the hereafter. The faith on which this belief is based is far from an unquestioning, unexamined faith. He pondered those problems of good and evil which troubled his contemporaries, and if he arrived at a different solution from theirs it was not by way of conventional Christianity or sentimental optimism. The poet whose faith in human nature survived the creation of Sludge the Medium and Guido Franceschini was no facile optimist; it was no weak sentimentalist who with Pompilia succeeded in making real an ideal of womanhood in portraying which nearly every other Victorian fails. Though his own heart is ever with the burning warrior saints, yet, like the aged Pope pondering judgment in solitary vigil through the length of that grey winter day in the chill and silent Vatican, he too is profoundly aware of

> That sad obscured sequestered state
> Where God unmakes but to remake the soul
> He else made first in vain; which must not be.

He goes deep in his analysis of the workings of the human soul and he is far more often concerned with failure than with success. The range of his sympathies, the ability to project himself into so many different types of individual give rich humanity to his poetry. The indomitable optimism, despite irritating lapses into buoyant jocularity, can in the end antagonize only those who set an absolute value on doubt.

Browning's obscurity is largely a matter of style and expression. Swinburne noted the speed of his thought, and in a letter to Ruskin Browning himself makes, if not a convincing defence, at least an illuminating comment on his method of writing and makes it in the language of the mountains Ruskin knew so well:

You ought, I think, to keep pace with the thought tripping from ledge to ledge of my 'glaciers' as you call them; not stand poking your alpenstock into the holes and demonstrating that no foot . could have stood there;—suppose it sprang over there? . . . In asking for more *ultimates* you must accept less *mediates*, nor expect that a Druid stone-circle will be traced for you with as few breaks to the eye as the North Crescent and South Crescent that go together so cleverly in many a suburb.

His grammar—with its parentheses and absolute clauses, omission of relative pronouns, and docking of the smaller parts of speech for staccato effect—is a swift grammar of sense rather than the slow grammar of logical development. This manner satisfies the needs of the dramatic monologue, where, as Elton has well said, he is often writing in a conversational way, which though it does not exclude poetry does not exactly encourage it. This impatient breathless utterance by trying to cram much into little space often congests the meaning, and it was a generous gift to Calverley and the other parodists. But when the imagination fires in lyrical and descriptive passages the utterance clears and the language can glow with concentrated passion:

> He with a 'look you' vents a brace of rhymes,
> And in there breaks the sudden rose herself,
> Over us, under, round us every side.

Browning does not possess Tennyson's or Arnold's verbal magic; unlike them he cared little for surface and 'texture' in the painter's sense; when a phrase or line remains in the memory it does so more for force and truth of content than for word music.

There is another difficulty. Browning was all his life a wide and curious reader, and it is therefore not surprising that his poetry should be charged with learned allusion. Readers who have not the patience to discover that this type of obscurity yields to study will never come to friendly terms with him. Just as he delighted to shock with the grotesque rhyme when it suited his purpose, so he will on occasion pursue freakish byways of scholarship for their own sake; but the body of his learning is not there for display, nor is it merely remote and academic. What Browning read he experienced imaginatively and he used his reading to illuminate and enrich his verse. *The Grammarian's Funeral* and *The Bishop orders his Tomb at St Praxed's Church*, for instance, are vivid re-creations of two contrasting aspects of the Renaissance, written by one who had felt his way into the very heart of the period and who was not content to see it through the spectacles of books alone. It may be remarked in passing that the

austere church of San Prassede, with its ninth-century
mosaics and pillar of the Flagellation, seems an odd and
Browningesque choice for the last resting place of a bishop
who is the very embodiment of a new paganism. The
long residence in Italy allowed him to take for granted
much that was unfamiliar to the average insular Englishman of his time. He moves with equal ease among the
unknown Florentine primitives, and through the streets and
churches of Baroque Rome. With our increasing knowledge of Italian art and with our taste for the *Seicento* we
should to-day more easily appreciate this aspect of Browning's poetry than did an earlier generation. He was a
friend of the contemporary painters and sculptors resident
in Rome, frequenting their studios and even practising
drawing in an amateur way himself; gifted with a strong
visual sense he always writes understandingly of art and
artists, and always superbly of the Italian scene. His
fondness for music enabled him to write more convincingly
of the sister art than any of our poets since Milton. He
evokes eighteenth-century Venice through the echo of a
tune of Galuppi he heard on his first visit to Italy in 1838,
and in another mood, contrapuntal harmonies of the organ
under the hands of an imaginary Hugues of Saxe-Gotha.
One who knew and loved Italy as well as Browning could
not confine himself to her historic past. The Risorgimento
has left deep, and sometimes unsuspected, marks on
English literature. Clough, watching from the Pincio,
drafted his most famous lyric as Garibaldi's guns were
firing into Rome in 1849. Other poets wrote nobly from
afar. Browning alone saw the struggle for liberty not in
terms of political and moral ideals but through his understanding of human character and situation. In poems like
De Gustibus and *The Italian in England* he gets to the very
heart of the Italian patriot and peasant.

II

Browning's great poetic period extends roughly from his
meeting with Elizabeth Barrett in 1845 to the publication of
The Ring and the Book in 1868, seven years after her death.
During these twenty odd years appeared the *Dramatic*

Romances and Lyrics, Men and Women, Dramatis Personae,
and the great verse novel. Before he met his future wife
Browning was already a poet of repute, and she had, in
Lady Geraldine's Courtship, paid his works a charming
tribute:

Or at times a modern volume, Wordsworth's solemn-thoughted
    idyl,
Howitt's ballad-verse, or Tennyson's enchanted reverie,—
Or from Browning some 'Pomegranate,' which, if cut deep down
    the middle,
Shows a heart within blood-tinctured, of a veined humanity.

It would be sentimental to say that the romantic engagement and marriage made him a poet, but in giving him full
emotional experience, happiness, and stability, it did change
him into a great and mature one. The earlier poetry in
the first two volumes of this edition (derivative as much of
it is) is not negligible, especially in descriptive passages;
and a recent biographer has shown how important it is
for a study of his personality.[1] Much of it, however, is
obscure without the strength which is compensation for
the difficulty of the later work. The impenetrability of
Sordello is notorious. These early poems are long drawn
out; a tendency, indeed, to outrun the legitimate bounds of
his subject was always one of Browning's dangers. There
is justice in Matthew Arnold's criticism of a 'confused
multitudinousness.' His dramatic gift was to find its
true medium of expression later, not in following up the
early attempts at extended play of character in action on
the stage, but in the dramatic monologue.

  The poetry of the last twenty years of his life appears in
the final volume of this collection of his work. Some of the
very greatest Browning is there alongside poems where he
is now content to utter his naked argumentative thoughts,
no longer 'draping them in sights and sounds.' This is the
abrupt and noisy voice of the man of the world who was so
familiar and puzzling a figure in the London drawing-
rooms of the seventies; and when he speaks the verse sinks
to pedestrian level. Yet the trunk of the tree is sound as
ever, though with age the branches gnarl into wilful fantastic shapes.

        While, treading down rose and ranunculus,
        You *Tommy-make-room-for-your-uncle* us!

---

[1] *Robert Browning: a Portrait*, by Betty Miller, 1952.

There is still in the late poems the old lively play of intellect and the unquenched interest in human conduct; and some of his finest intensest lyrics were written in the later years. At the end of a long poetic career both Tennyson and Browning made their *confessio fidei* in a noble lyric; it is characteristic that the one puts out to sea on a quiet note of resignation and hope, while the other marches forward to greet the unseen with a cheer of assurance.

Of all the Victorians Browning had the strongest dramatic sense. After early experiments with stage drama he discovered the right form for this gift in the narrower scope of the dramatic monologue, the form he has made peculiarly his own. The greatest of the monologues are to be found in the volumes of the middle years. In them he analyses the workings of the human soul in some testing revealing situation. His dramatic lyrics and monologues are more than mere art of soliloquy; the scene is set, the tone and colour are indicated, and the background of the tiny stage is alive with characters who have no speaking part. Flaring torches throw into strong light and shade the faces of the watch who surround Fra Lippo Lippi. It is Andrea del Sarto that speaks, but his wife Lucrezia is there silent in the twilight shadow and we know what she will say. Over the bishop's wine Gigadibs is no less clearly presented than Blougram. Exotic sights and sounds of the magic island provide the setting for Caliban's meditation on Setebos. In *A Death in the Desert* the goatherd keeps watch while the fierce sun blazes outside the lonely cave, in the cool depths of which the aged Saint John lies dying. Men and women in their infinite variety people this poetry. They are chosen from all ages, and the setting is as vivid as the people who play out their parts against it.

The Ring and the Book might seem no more than a collection of separate monologues grouped round a central theme. It is more than that. This vast poem, 'of a proportional monstrous magnificence' (as Henry James described it), is an architectural whole carefully planned on the grand scale, albeit the poet allows himself a wealth of detail and freedom of treatment which is more Baroque than Classic. Pompilia, his most moving and tender portrait of a woman, is the dramatic centre. It is essential to the conception that she in the helplessness of her innocence and purity and ignorance—a flower sprung from the

Roman gutter—should change the lives of all the chief characters; even Guido's, witness that last despairing cry of terror:

> Abate,—Cardinal,—Christ,—Maria,—God, . . .
> Pompilia, will you let them murder me?

This is a theme he had already handled in *Pippa Passes*, but it is developed now with the wisdom and tragic awareness of mature experience. Each book views the crime from a different standpoint and throws some fresh light on motive; the infinitely complex nature of truth is slowly revealed, and the seemingly static subject is carried forward with the movement and mounting excitement of a detective story. The scale of the immense canvas, packed with the teeming life of seventeenth-century Rome, provincial Arezzo, and Browning's own Florence, allows for change of rhythm, reiteration, and seeming excrescence. In perspective even the legal technicalities of Dominus Hyacinthus and Doctor Bottinus fall into place in the scheme as a whole, and justify themselves as more than mere display of pedantry. Wagner too knew the value of such contrast in a large-scale lyrical plan, when he allowed Beckmesser his exposition of the academic rules of song in the first act of *Die Meistersinger*. The novel in verse was a favourite form with the later nineteenth-century poets, usually in their lighter vein. Changing its subject from contemporary sentiment to the reconstruction of a long forgotten crime, Browning made it the vehicle for his profoundest exploration of truth and of the mystery of good and evil. Much has been written about this poem, but nothing with more subtle understanding than Henry James's essay on 'The novel in *The Ring and the Book*.'

In the love poetry which is a large part of Browning's output passionate feeling unites with sensitive and exact observation of external nature. He is subtle in his analysis of passion and it is remarkable how often he explores it from the woman's point of view. There was in his nature (and more than one contemporary observed it) a feminine strain beneath the virile exterior, and this enabled him to succeed with poems like *James Lee's Wife* and *Any Wife to Any Husband*, where it is the woman who speaks. Though frail human beings may fail in this as in other fields of experience, it is through love, above all else, that they can conjecture a world outside and beyond themselves. In Browning's view 'the gain of earth must be Heaven's gain too.' He could often write harshly on unattractive unpromising themes, but to set off against those in a true estimate of his achievement there is the quiet evening music of *Love among the Ruins*, the suspended stillness of *Two in the Campagna*, and the reflective musing on his own happiness in *By the Fireside*, where he gives us a rare intimate glimpse of the Casa Guidi interior:

> And to watch you sink by the fire-side now
>   Back again, as you mutely sit
> Musing by fire-light, that great brow
>   And the spirit-small hand propping it
> Yonder, my heart knows how.

Here he is writing greatly in the great tradition of English lyric poetry.

It is not the philosophy or the metaphysics that will bring us back to Browning, but his essential sanity, normality, and warmth of heart. He is a poet for whom the visible world exists, his genius is firmly rooted in real life, and the range of his creations is evidence of the breadth of his interests and understanding. The characters express his own consistent view of life, but dramatic imagination makes them convincing as individuals in their own right and in their own time and place. Among the questioning or doubting voices of the Victorian age he strikes the note of assurance; and even when it is strident his voice is still the voice of a poet. He succeeds in the difficult combination of argument and poetry, for just when it looks as if reasoning had gained the upper hand there comes 'the sunset touch,' 'the chorus-ending from Euripides,' to prove that the poet is in control. Despite audacities of grammar, rhythm, and rhyme he remains a master of his instrument; metrically his verse takes the rough with the smooth in its stride, and he was experimenting with new measures to the end. There is much in Browning's way of writing that anticipates the poetic manner of to-day, with its colloquialism, its high demands on intelligence as well as emotion, and its refusal to be limited by literary convention. The size of the man demands that he shall be judged as a whole in his strength and his weakness. If, in conclusion, we are to look for something that will indicate the best of him—the warmth, the courage, the delight in life lived to the full, and the confidence and the faith—it may be found not only in the familiar 'Epilogue' to *Asolando* but in *Prospice*, the poem he wrote after his wife's death.

> I was ever a fighter, so,—one fight more,
> The best and the last!
> I would hate that death bandaged my eyes, and forbore,
> And bade me creep past.
> No! let me taste the whole of it, fare like my peers
> The heroes of old,
> Bear the brunt, in a minute pay glad life's arrears
> Of pain, darkness and cold.
> For sudden, the worst turns best to the brave,
> The black minute's at end,
> And the elements' rage, the fiend-voices that rave,
> Shall dwindle, shall blend,
> Shall change, shall become first a peace, then a joy,
> Then a light, then thy breast,
> O thou soul of my soul! I shall clasp thee again,
> And with God be the rest!

JOHN BRYSON.

1955.

Note on the Text

In the collected editions which appeared during his lifetime Browning made considerable changes in the order, grouping and text of his poems. The final arrangement and revised text is that of the collected edition of 1888–9 in seventeen volumes. Everyman's Library does not follow this arrangement. *Dramatic Romances and Lyrics* are given as they appeared in the 1849 collected edition. The poems from *Men and Women* (1855) onwards are printed from the first editions. Two poems—*Ben Karshook's Wisdom* and *Sonnet*—which appeared in periodicals but were not reprinted by Browning, are included. For detailed information about order of composition, sources and textual revision the reader is referred to *A Browning Handbook* by W. C. de Vane.

SELECT BIBLIOGRAPHY

WORKS. *Pauline*, 1833; *Paracelsus*, 1835; *Strafford*, 1837; *Sordello*, 1840; *Bells and Pomegranates*: No. 1, *Pippa Passes*, 1841; No. 2, *King Victor and King Charles*, 1842; No. 3, *Dramatic Lyrics*, 1842; No. 4, *The Return of the Druses* (a Tragedy), 1843; No. 5, *A Blot in the 'Scutcheon* (a Tragedy), 1843; No. 6, *Colombe's Birthday* (a Play), 1844; No. 7, *Dramatic Romances and Lyrics*, 1845; No. 8, *Luria*; and *A Soul's Tragedy*, 1846; *Christmas Eve and Easter Day*, 1850; *Cleon*, 1855; *The Statue and the Bust*, 1855; *Men and Women*, 1855; *Gold Hair : A Legend of Pornic*, 1864; *Dramatis Personae*, 1864; *The Ring and the Book*, 1868; *Balaustion's Adventure*, 1871; *Prince Hohenstiel-Schwangau*, 1871; *Fifine at the Fair*, 1872; *Red-cotton Nightcap Country*, 1873; *Aristophanes' Apology* with *A Transcript from Euripides* and *Last Adventure of Balaustion*, 1875; *The Inn Album*, 1875; *Pacchiarotto*, 1876; *The Agamemnon of Aeschylus*, 1877; *La Saisiaz: The Two Ports of Croisic*, 1878; *Dramatic Idylls*: 1st series, 1879: 2nd Series, 1880; *Jocoseria*, 1883; *Ferishtah's Fancies*, 1884; *Parleyings with Certain People of Importance in their Day*, 1887; *Essay on Shelley* (Introductory Essay to Volume of Shelley's letters (suppressed), 1852), 1888; *Asolando*, 1890 (1889).

In the Browning Society's Papers are published poems which appeared in various magazines, and were not reprinted in any of the above-named works.

First Collected Edition, 1849; 2nd, 1863; 3rd, 1868; Complete Edition, 1889-90; *Poetry and Prose*, ed. S. Nowell Smith (Reynard Library), 1950.

Letters of Robert Browning and Elizabeth Barrett, 1845-6, 2 vols., 1899; *Letters*, collected by T. J. Wise, ed. T. L. Hood, 1933; *New Letters of Robert Browning*, ed. W. C. de Vane and R. L. Knickerbocker, 1951.

BIOGRAPHY AND CRITICISM. Alexandra Orr: *A Handbook to the Works of Robert Browning*, 1902; G. K. Chesterton: *Robert Browning*, 1903; E. Dowden: *Life of Robert Browning*, 1904 (Everyman's Library, 1915); Stopford A. Brooke: *The Poetry of Robert Browning*, 1905; A. Symons: *An Introduction to the Study of Browning*, 1906; W. Hall Griffin and H. C. Minchin: *Life of Robert Browning*, 1910; Henry James: 'The Novel in *The Ring and the Book*' (in *Notes on Novelists*, 1914); A. K. Cook: *A Commentary on Browning's 'The Ring and the Book*,' 1920; O. Elton: *The Brownings*, 1924; Paul de Reul: *The Art and Thought of Robert Browning*, 1926; D. C. Somervell: 'The Reputation of Robert Browning' (in *Essays and Studies*, 1929); A. A. Brockington: *Browning and the Twentieth Century*, 1932; O. Burdett: *The Brownings*, 1933; W. C. de Vane: *A Browning Handbook*, 1935; B. G. McCarthy: *The Psychology of a Genius*, 1936; H. B. Charlton: *Browning as a Dramatist*, 1939; D. Kenmare: *Browning and Modern Thought*, 1939; B. Groom: *On the Diction of Tennyson, Browning, and Arnold*, 1939; J. M. Cohen: *Robert Browning*, 1952; Betty Miller: *Robert Browning: a Portrait*, 1952; H. C. Duffin: *Amphibian: a Reconsideration of Browning*, 1956; P. Honan: *Browning's Characters: a Study in Poetic Technique*, 1961; J. Bryson: *Robert Browning* (Writers and their Work, revised ed.), 1963; B. Litzinger and K. L. Knickerbocker: *The Browning Critics*, 1965; B. Melchiori: *Browning's Poetry of Reticence*, 1968; R. D. Altick and J. F. Loucks: *Browning's Roman Murder Story*, 1968; M. Ward: *Robert Browning and his World*, 2 vols., 1968-9; B. Litzinger and D. Smalley (eds.): *Robert Browning*, 1970; P. Drew: *Critical Introduction to the Poetry of Browning*, 1970.

CONTENTS

Volume I

Volume II

PAGE

Contents

PAGE

PAGE

Contents

PAULINE

A FRAGMENT OF A CONFESSION

Plus ne suis ce que j'ai été,
Et ne le sçaurois jamais être.—Marot.

Non dubito, quin titulus libri nostri raritate suâ quamplurimos alliciat ad legendum: inter quos nonnulli obliquæ opinionis, mente languidi, multi etiam maligni, et in ingenium nostrum ingrati accedent, qui temerariâ suâ ignorantiâ, vix conspecto titulo clambunt: Nos vetita docere, hæresium semina jacere: piis auribus offendiculo, præclaris ingeniis scandalo esse: . . . adeò conscientiæ suæ consulentes, ut nec Apollo, nec Musæ omnes, neque Angelus de cœlo me ab illorum execratione vindicare queant: quibus et ego nunc consulo, ne scripta nostra legant, nec intelligant, nec meminerint: nam noxia sunt, venenosa sunt: Acherontis ostium est in hoc libro, lapides loquitur, caveant, ne cerebrum illis excutiat. Vos autem, qui æquâ mente ad legendum venitis, si tantam prudentiæ discretionem adhibueritis, quantam in melle legendo apes, jam securi legite. Puto namque vos et utilitatis haud parùm et voluptatis plurimûm accepturos. Quod si qua repereritis, quæ vobis non placeant, mittite illa, nec utimini. Nam et ego vobis illa non Probo, sed Narro. Cætera tamen propterea non respuite. . . . Ideo, si quid liberius dictum sit, ignoscite adolescentiæ nostræ, qui minor quam adolescens hoc opus composui.— *H. Cor. Agrippa, De Occult. Phil.*

London, January, 1833,
V. A. XX.

Browning reprinted *Pauline* with reluctance in the 1868 collected edition with the following note: 'The first piece in the series, I acknowledge and retain with extreme repugnance, indeed purely of necessity; for not long ago I inspected one, and am certified of the existence of other transcripts, intended sooner or later to be published abroad; by forestalling these, I can at least correct some misprints.'

PAULINE

A FRAGMENT OF A CONFESSION

PAULINE, mine own, bend o'er me—thy soft breast
Shall pant to mine—bend o'er me—thy sweet eyes,
And loosened hair, and breathing lips, and arms
Drawing me to thee—these build up a screen
To shut me in with thee, and from all fear,
So that I might unlock the sleepless brood
Of fancies from my soul, their lurking place,
Nor doubt that each would pass, ne'er to return
To one so watched, so loved, and so secured.
But what can guard thee but thy naked love?
Ah, dearest! whoso sucks a poisoned wound
Envenoms his own veins,—thou art so good,
So calm—if thou should'st wear a brow less light
For some wild thought which, but for me, were kept
From out thy soul, as from a sacred star.
Yet till I have unlocked them it were vain
To hope to sing; some woe would light on me;
Nature would point at one, whose quivering lip
Was bathed in her enchantments—whose brow burned
Beneath the crown, to which her secrets knelt;
Who learned the spell which can call up the dead,
And then departed, smiling like a fiend
Who has deceived God. If such one should seek
Again her altars, and stand robed and crowned
Amid the faithful: sad confession first,
Remorse and pardon, and old claims renewed,
Ere I can be—as I shall be no more.

I had been spared this shame, if I had sate
By thee for ever, from the first, in place
Of my wild dreams of beauty and of good,
Or with them, as an earnest of their truth.
No thought nor hope, having been shut from thee,

No vague wish unexplained—no wandering aim
Sent back to bind on Fancy's wings, and seek
Some strange fair world, where it might be a law;
But doubting nothing, had been led by thee,
Thro' youth, and saved, as one at length awaked,
Who has slept thro' a peril.   Ah! vain, vain!

Thou lovest me—the past is in its grave,
Tho' its ghost haunts us—still this much is ours,
To cast away restraint, lest a worse thing
Wait for us in the darkness.   Thou lovest me,
And thou art to receive not love, but faith,
For which thou wilt be mine, and smile, and take
All shapes, and shames, and veil without a fear
That form which music follows like a slave;
And I look to thee, and I trust in thee,
As in a Northern night one looks alway
Unto the East for morn, and spring and joy.
Thou seest then my aimless, hopeless state,
And resting on some few old feelings, won
Back by thy beauty, would'st that I essay
The task, which was to me what now thou art:
And why should I conceal one weakness more?

Thou wilt remember one warm morn, when Winter
Crept aged from the earth, and Spring's first breath
Blew soft from the moist hills—the black-thorn boughs,
So dark in the bare wood; when glistening
In the sunshine were white with coming buds,
Like the bright side of a sorrow—and the banks
Had violets opening from sleep like eyes—
I walked with thee, who knew not a deep shame
Lurked beneath smiles and careless words, which sought
To hide it—till they wandered and were mute;
As we stood listening on a sunny mound
To the wind murmuring in the damp copse,
Like heavy breathings of some hidden thing
Betrayed by sleep—until the feeling rushed
That I was low indeed, yet not so low
As to endure the calmness of thine eyes;
And so I told thee all, while the cool breast
I leaned on altered not its quiet beating;
And long ere words, like a hurt bird's complaint,

Bade me look up and be what I had been,
I felt despair could never live by thee.
Thou wilt remember:—thou art not more dear
Than song was once to me; and I ne'er sung
But as one entering bright halls, where all
Will rise and shout for him. Sure I must own
That I am fallen—having chosen gifts
Distinct from theirs—that I am sad—and fain
Would give up all to be but where I was;
Not high as I had been, if faithful found—
But low and weak, yet full of hope, and sure
Of goodness as of life—that I would lose
All this gay mastery of mind, to sit
Once more with them, trusting in truth and love.
And with an aim—not being what I am.
Oh, Pauline! I am ruined! who believed
That tho' my soul had floated from its sphere
Of wide dominion into the dim orb
Of self—that it was strong and free as ever:—
It has conformed itself to that dim orb,
Reflecting all its shades and shapes, and now
Must stay where it alone can be adored.
I have felt this in dreams—in dreams in which
I seemed the fate from which I fled; I felt
A strange delight in causing my decay;
I was a fiend, in darkness chained for ever
Within some ocean-cave; and ages rolled,
Till thro' the cleft rock, like a moonbeam, came
A white swan to remain with me; and ages
Rolled, yet I tired not of my first joy
In gazing on the peace of its pure wings.
And then I said, " It is most fair to me,
" Yet its soft wings must sure have suffered change
" From the thick darkness—sure its eyes are dim—
" Its silver pinions must be cramped and numbed
" With sleeping ages here; it cannot leave me,
" For it would seem, in light, beside its kind,
" Withered—tho' here to me most beautiful."
And then I was a young witch, whose blue eyes,
As she stood naked by the river springs,
Drew down a god—I watched his radiant form
Growing less radiant—and it gladdened me;
Till one morn, as he sat in the sunshine

Upon my knees, singing to me of heaven,
He turned to look at me, ere I could lose
The grin with which I viewed his perishing.
And he shrieked and departed, and sat long
By his deserted throne—but sunk at last,
Murmuring, as I kissed his lips and curled
Around him, " I am still a god—to thee."
Still I can lay my soul bare in its fall,
For all the wandering and all the weakness
Will be a saddest comment on the song.
And if, that done, I can be young again,
I will give up all gained as willingly
As one gives up a charm which shuts him out
From hope, or part, or care, in human kind.
As life wanes, all its cares, and strife, and toil,
Seem strangely valueless, while the old trees
Which grew by our youth's home—the waving mass
Of climbing plants, heavy with bloom and dew—
The morning swallows with their songs like words,—
All these seem clear and only worth our thoughts.
So aught connected with my early life——
My rude songs or my wild imaginings,
How I look on them—most distinct amid
The fever and the stir of after years!

I ne'er had ventured e'en to hope for this,
Had not the glow I felt at His award,
Assured me all was not extinct within.
HIM whom all honor—whose renown springs up
Like sunlight which will visit all the world;
So that e'en they who sneered at him at first,
Come out to it, as some dark spider crawls
From his foul nets, which some lit torch invades,
Yet spinning still new films for his retreat.—
Thou didst smile, poet,—but, can *we* forgive?

Sun-treader—life and light be thine for ever;
Thou art gone from us—years go by—and spring
Gladdens, and the young earth is beautiful,
Yet thy songs come not—other bards arise,
But none like thee—they stand—thy majesties,
Like mighty works which tell some Spirit there
Hath sat regardless of neglect and scorn,

Till, its long task completed, it hath risen
And left us, never to return: and all
Rush in to peer and praise when all in vain.
The air seems bright with thy past presence yet,
But thou art still for me, as thou hast been
When I have stood with thee, as on a throne
With all thy dim creations gathered round
Like mountains,—and I felt of mould like them,
And creatures of my own were mixed with them,
Like things half-lived, catching and giving life.
But thou art still for me, who have adored,
Tho' single, panting but to hear thy name,
Which I believed a spell to me alone,
Scarce deeming thou wert as a star to men—
As one should worship long a sacred spring
Scarce worth a moth's flitting, which long grasses cross,
And one small tree embowers droopingly,
Joying to see some wondering insect won,
To live in its few rushes—or some locust
To pasture on its boughs—or some wild bird
Stoop for its freshness from the trackless air,
And then should find it but the fountain-head,
Long lost, of some great river—washing towns
And towers, and seeing old woods which will live
But by its banks, untrod of human foot,
Which, when the great sun sinks, lie quivering
In light as some thing lieth half of life
Before God's foot—waiting a wondrous change
—Then girt with rocks which seek to turn or stay
Its course in vain, for it does ever spread
Like a sea's arm as it goes rolling on,
Being the pulse of some great country—so
Wert thou to me—and art thou to the world.
And I, perchance, half feel a strange regret,
That I am not what I have been to thee:
Like a girl one has loved long silently,
In her first loveliness, in some retreat,
When first emerged, all gaze and glow to view
Her fresh eyes, and soft hair, and lips which bleed
Like a mountain berry. Doubtless it is sweet
To see her thus adored—but there have been
Moments, when all the world was in his praise,
Sweeter than all the pride of after hours.

Yet, Sun-treader, all hail!—from my heart's heart
I bid thee hail!—e'en in my wildest dreams,
I am proud to feel I would have thrown up all
The wreathes of fame which seemed o'erhanging me,
To have seen thee, for a moment, as thou art.

And if thou livest—if thou lovest, spirit!
Remember me, who set this final seal
To wandering thought—that one so pure as thou
Could never die. Remember me, who flung
All honor from my soul—yet paused and said,
" There is one spark of love remaining yet,
" For I have nought in common with him—shapes
" Which followed him avoid me, and foul forms
" Seek me, which ne'er could fasten on his mind;
" And tho' I feel how low I am to him,
" Yet I aim not even to catch a tone
" Of all the harmonies which he called up,
" So one gleam still remains, altho' the last."
Remember me—who praise thee e'en with tears,
For never more shall I walk calm with thee;
Thy sweet imaginings are as an air,
A melody, some wond'rous singer sings,
Which, though it haunt men oft in the still eve,
They dream not to essay; yet it no less,
But more is honored. I was thine in shame,
And now when all thy proud renown is out,
I am a watcher, whose eyes have grown dim
With looking for some star—which breaks on him,
Altered and worn, and weak, and full of tears.

Autumn has come—like Spring returned to us,
Won from her girlishness—like one returned
A friend that was a lover—nor forgets
The first warm love, but full of sober thoughts
Of fading years; whose soft mouth quivers yet
With the old smile—but yet so changed and still!
And here am I the scoffer, who have probed
Life's vanity, won by a word again
Into my old life—for one little word
Of this sweet friend, who lives in loving me,
Lives strangely on my thoughts, and looks, and words,
As fathoms down some nameless ocean thing

Its silent course of quietness and joy
O dearest, if indeed, I tell the past,
May'st thou forget it as a sad sick dream;
Or if it linger—my lost soul too soon
Sinks to itself, and whispers, we shall be
But closer linked—two creatures whom the earth
Bears singly—with strange feelings, unrevealed
But to each other; or two lonely things
Created by some Power, whose reign is done,
Having no part in God, or his bright world,
I am to sing; whilst ebbing day dies soft,
As a lean scholar dies, worn o'er his book,
And in the heaven stars steal out one by one,
As hunted men steal to their mountain watch.
I must not think—lest this new impulse die
In which I trust. I have no confidence,
So I will sing on—fast as fancies come
Rudely—the verse being as the mood it paints.

I strip my mind bare—whose first elements
I shall unveil—not as they struggled forth
In infancy, nor as they now exist,
That I am grown above them, and can rule them,
But in that middle stage when they were full,
Yet ere I had disposed them to my will;
And then I shall show how these elements
Produced my present state, and what it is.

I am made up of an intensest life,
Of a most clear idea of consciousness
Of self—distinct from all its qualities,
From all affections, passions, feelings, powers;
And thus far it exists, if tracked in all,
But linked in me, to self-supremacy,
Existing as a centre to all things,
Most potent to create, and rule, and call
Upon all things to minister to it;
And to a principle of restlessness
Which would be all, have, see, know, taste, feel, all—
This is myself; and I should thus have been,
Though gifted lower than the meanest soul.

And of my powers, one springs up to save
From utter death a soul with such desires

Confined to clay—which is the only one
Which marks me—an imagination which
Has been an angel to me—coming not
In fitful visions, but beside me ever,
And never failing me; so tho' my mind
Forgets not—not a shred of life forgets—
Yet I can take a secret pride in calling
The dark past up—to quell it regally.

A mind like this must dissipate itself,
But I have always had one lode-star; now,
As I look back, I see that I have wasted,
Or progressed as I looked toward that star—
A need, a trust, a yearning after God,
A feeling I have analysed but late,
But it existed, and was reconciled
With a neglect of all I deemed his laws,
Which yet, when seen in others, I abhorred.
I felt as one beloved, and so shut in
From fear—and thence I date my trust in signs
And omens—for I saw God every where;
And I can only lay it to the fruit
Of a sad after-time that I could doubt
Even his being—having always felt
His presence—never acting from myself,
Still trusting in a hand that leads me through
All dangers; and this feeling still has fought
Against my weakest reason and resolves.

And I can love nothing—and this dull truth
Has come the last—but sense supplies a love
Encircling me and mingling with my life.

These make myself—for I have sought in vain
To trace how they were formed by circumstance,
For I still find them—turning my wild youth
Where they alone displayed themselves, converting
All objects to their use—now see their course!

They came to me in my first dawn of life,
Which passed alone with wisest ancient books,
All halo-girt with fancies of my own,
And I myself went with the tale,—a god,

Wandering after beauty—or a giant,
Standing vast in the sunset—an old hunter,
Talking with gods—or a high-crested chief,
Sailing with troops of friends to Tenedos;—
I tell you, nought has ever been so clear
As the place, the time, the fashion of those lives.
I had not seen a work of lofty art,
Nor woman's beauty, nor sweet nature's face,
Yet, I say, never morn broke clear as those
On the dim clustered isles in the blue sea:
The deep groves, and white temples, and wet caves—
And nothing ever will surprise me now—
Who stood besides the naked Swift-footed,
Who bound my forehead with Proserpine's hair.
An' strange it is, that I who could so dream,
Should e'er have stooped to aim at aught beneath—
Aught low, or painful, but I never doubted;
So as I grew, I rudely shaped my life
To my immediate wants, yet strong beneath
Was a vague sense of power folded up—
A sense that tho' those shadowy times were past,
Their spirit dwelt in me, and I should rule.

Then came a pause, and long restraint chained down
My soul, till it was changed. I lost myself,
And were it not that I so loathe that time,
I could recall how first I learned to turn
My mind against itself; and the effects,
In deeds for which remorse were vain, as for
The wanderings of delirious dream; yet thence
Came cunning, envy, falsehood, which so long
Have spotted me—at length I was restored,
Yet long the influence remained; and nought
But the still life I led, apart from all,
Which left my soul to seek its old delights,
Could e'er have brought me thus far back to peace.
As peace returned, I sought out some pursuit:
And song rose—no new impulse—but the one
With which all others best could be combined.
My life has not been that of those whose heaven
Was lampless, save where poesy shone out;
But as a clime, where glittering mountain-tops,
And glancing sea, and forests steeped in light,

Give back reflected the far-flashing sun;
For music, (which is earnest of a heaven,
Seeing we know emotions strange by it,
Not else to be revealed) is as a voice,
A low voice calling Fancy, as a friend,
To the green woods in the gay summer time.
And she fills all the way with dancing shapes,
Which have made painters pale; and they go on
While stars look at them, and winds call to them,
As they leave life's path for the twilight world,
Where the dead gather. This was not at first,
For I scarce knew what I would do. I had
No wish to paint, no yearning—but I sang.

And first I sang, as I in dream have seen,
Music wait on a lyrist for some thought,
Yet singing to herself until it came.
I turned to those old times and scenes, where all
That's beautiful had birth for me, and made
Rude verses on them all; and then I paused—
I had done nothing, so I sought to know
What mind had yet achieved. No fear was mine
As I gazed on the works of mighty bards,
In the first joy at finding my own thoughts
Recorded, and my powers exemplified,
And feeling their aspirings were my own.
And then I first explored passion and mind;
And I began afresh; I rather sought
To rival what I wondered at, than form
Creations of my own; so much was light
Lent back by others, yet much was my own.

I paused again—a change was coming on,
I was no more a boy—the past was breaking
Before the coming, and like fever worked.
I first thought on myself—and here my powers
Burst out. I dreamed not of restraint, but gazed
On all things: schemes and systems went and came,
And I was proud (being vainest of the weak),
In wandering o'er them, to seek out some one
To be my own; as one should wander o'er
The white way for a star.

On one, whom praise of mine would not offend,
Who was as calm as beauty—being such
Unto mankind as thou to me, Pauline,
Believing in them, and devoting all
His soul's strength to their winning back to peace;
Who sent forth hopes and longings for their sake,
Clothed in all passion's melodies, which first
Caught me, and set me, as to a sweet task,
To gather every breathing of his songs,
And woven with them there were words, which seemed
A key to a new world; the muttering
Of angels, of some thing unguessed by man.
How my heart beat, as I went on, and found
Much there! I felt my own mind had conceived,
But there living and burning; soon the whole
Of his conceptions dawned on me; their praise
Is in the tongues of men; men's brows are high
When his name means a triumph and a pride;
So my weak hands may well forbear to dim
What then seemed my bright fate: I threw myself
To meet it. I was vowed to liberty,
Men were to be as gods, and earth as heaven.
And I—ah! what a life was mine to be,
My whole soul rose to meet it. Now, Pauline,
I shall go mad if I recall that time.

.   .   .   .   .

O let me look back, e'er I leave for ever
The time, which was an hour, that one waits
For a fair girl, that comes a withered hag.
And I was lonely—far from woods and fields,
And amid dullest sights, who should be loose
As a stag—yet I was full of joy—who lived
With Plato—and who had the key to life.
And I had dimly shaped my first attempt,
And many a thought did I build up on thought,
As the wild bee hangs cell to cell—in vain;
For I must still go on: my mind rests not.

'Twas in my plan to look on real life,
Which was all new to me; my theories
Were firm, so I left them, to look upon
Men, and their cares, and hopes, and fears, and joys;

And, as I pondered on them all, I sought
How best life's end might be attained—an end
Comprising every joy. I deeply mused.

And suddenly, without heart-wreck, I awoke
As from a dream—I said, 'twas beautiful,
Yet but a dream; and so adieu to it.
As some world-wanderer sees in a far meadow
Strange towers, and walled gardens, thick with trees,
Where singing goes on, and delicious mirth,
And laughing fairy creatures peeping over,
And on the morrow, when he comes to live
For ever by those springs, and trees, fruit-flushed
And fairy bowers—all his search is vain.
Well I remember . . .
First went my hopes of perfecting mankind,
And faith in them—then freedom in itself,
And virtue in itself—and then my motives' ends,
And powers and loves; and human love went last.
I felt this no decay, because new powers
Rose as old feelings left—wit, mockery,
And happiness; for I had oft been sad,
Mistrusting my resolves: but now I cast
Hope joyously away—I laughed and said,
" No more of this "—I must not think; at length
I look'd again to see how all went on.

My powers were greater—as some temple seemed
My soul, where nought is changed, and incense rolls
Around the altar—only God is gone,
And some dark spirit sitteth in his seat!
So I passed through the temple: and to me
Knelt troops of shadows; and they cried, " Hail, king!
" We serve thee now, and thou shalt serve no more!
" Call on us, prove us, let us worship thee! "
And I said, " Are ye strong—let fancy bear me
" Far from the past."—And I was borne away
As Arab birds float sleeping in the wind,
O'er deserts, towers, and forests, I being calm;
And I said, " I have nursed up energies,
" They will prey on me."   And a band knelt low,
And cried, " Lord, we are here, and we will make
" A way for thee—in thine appointed life

" O look on us! "   And I said, " Ye will worship
" Me; but my heart must worship too."   They shouted,
" Thyself—thou art our king! "   So I stood there
  Smiling * * * * * *

And buoyant and rejoicing was the spirit
With which I looked out how to end my days;
I felt once more myself—my powers were mine;
I found that youth or health so lifted me,
That, spite of all life's vanity, no grief
Came nigh me—I must ever be light-hearted;
And that this feeling was the only veil
Betwixt me and despair: so if age came,
I should be as a wreck linked to a soul
Yet fluttering, or mind-broken, and aware
Of my decay.   So a long summer morn
Found me; and e'er noon came, I had resolved
No age should come on me, ere youth's hopes went,
For I would wear myself out—like that morn
Which wasted not a sunbeam—every joy
I would make mine, and die; and thus I sought
To chain my spirit down, which I had fed
With thoughts of fame.   I said, the troubled life
Of genius seen so bright when working forth
Some trusted end, seems sad, when all in vain—
Most sad, when men have parted with all joy
For their wild fancy's sake, which waited first,
As an obedient spirit, when delight
Came not with her alone, but alters soon,
Coming darkened, seldom, hasting to depart,
Leaving a heavy darkness and warm tears.

But I shall never lose her; she will live
Brighter for such seclusion—I but catch
A hue, a glance of what I sing; so pain
Is linked with pleasure, for I ne'er may tell
The radiant sights which dazzle me; but now
They shall be all my own, and let them fade
Untold—others shall rise as fair, as fast.
And when all's done, the few dim gleams transferred,—
(For a new thought sprung up—that it were well
To leave all shadowy hopes, and weave such lays
As would encircle me with praise and love;

So I should not die utterly—I should bring
One branch from the gold forest, like the night
Of old tales, witnessing I had been there,)—
And when all's done, how vain seems e'en success,
And all the influence poets have o'er men!
'Tis a fine thing that one, weak as myself,
Should sit in his lone room, knowing the words
He utters in his solitude shall move
Men like a swift wind—that tho' he be forgotten,
Fair eyes shall glisten when his beauteous dreams
Of love come true in happier frames than his.
Ay, the still night brought thoughts like these, but morn
Came, and the mockery again laughed out
At hollow praises, and smiles, almost sneers;
And my soul's idol seemed to whisper me
To dwell with him and his unhonoured name—
And I well knew my spirit, that would be
First in the struggle, and again would make
All bow to it; and I would sink again.

    .   .   .

And then know that this curse will come on us,
To see our idols perish—we may wither,
Nor marvel—we are clay; but our low fate
Should not extend them, whom trustingly
We sent before into Time's yawning gulf,
To face what e'er may lurk in darkness there—
To see the painter's glory pass, and feel
Sweet music move us not as once, or worst,
To see decaying wits ere the frail body
Decays. Nought makes me trust in love so really,
As the delight of the contented lowness
With which I gaze on souls I'd keep for ever
In beauty—I'd be sad to equal them;
I'd feed their fame e'en from my heart's best blood,
Withering unseen, that they might flourish still

    .   .   .

Pauline, my sweet friend, thou dost not forget
How this mood swayed me, when thou first wert mine,
When I had set myself to live this life,
Defying all opinion. Ere thou camest
I was most happy, sweet, for old delights

Had come like birds again; music, my life,
I nourished more than ever, and old lore
Loved for itself, and all it shows—the king
Treading the purple calmly to his death,
—While round him, like the clouds of eve, all dusk,
The giant shades of fate, silently flitting,
Pile the dim outline of the coming doom,
—And him sitting alone in blood, while friends
Are hunting far in the sunshine; and the boy,
With his white breast and brow and clustering curls
Streaked with his mother's blood, and striving hard
To tell his story ere his reason goes,
And when I loved thee, as I've loved so oft,
Thou lovedst me, and I wondered, and looked in
My heart to find some feeling like such love,
Believing I was still what I had been;
And soon I found all faith had gone from me,
And the late glow of life—changing like clouds,
'Twas not the morn-blush widening into day,
But evening, coloured by the dying sun
While darkness is quick hastening:—I will tell
My state as though 'twere none of mine—despair
Cannot come near me—thus it is with me.
Souls alter not, and mine must progress still;
And this I knew not when I flung away
My youth's chief aims. I ne'er supposed the loss
Of what few I retained; for no resource
Awaits me—now behold the change of all.
I cannot chain my soul, it will not rest
In its clay prison; this most narrow sphere—
It has strange powers, and feelings, and desires,
Which I cannot account for, nor explain,
But which I stifle not, being bound to trust
All feelings equally—to hear all sides:
Yet I cannot indulge them, and they live,
Referring to some state or life unknown. . . .

My selfishness is satiated not,
It wears me like a flame; my hunger for
All pleasure, howso'er minute, is pain;
I envy—how I envy him whose mind
Turns with its energies to some one end!
To elevate a sect, or a pursuit,

However mean—so my still baffled hopes
Seek out abstractions; I would have but one
Delight on earth, so it were wholly mine;
One rapture all my soul could fill—and this
Wild feeling places me in dream afar,
In some wide country, where the eye can see
No end to the far hills and dales bestrewn
With shining towers and dwellings. I grow mad
Well-nigh, to know not one abode but holds
Some pleasure—for my soul could grasp them all,
But must remain with this vile form. I look
With hope to age at last, which quenching much,
May let me concentrate the sparks it spares.

This restlessness of passion meets in me
A craving after knowledge: the sole proof
Of a commanding will is in that power
Repressed; for I beheld it in its dawn,
That sleepless harpy, with its budding wings,
And I considered whether I should yield
All hopes and fears, to live alone with it,
Finding a recompence in its wild eyes;
And when I found that I should perish so,
I bade its wild eyes close from me for ever;—
And I am left alone with my delights,—
So it lies in me a chained thing—still ready
To serve me, if I loose its slightest bond—
I cannot but be proud of my bright slave.

And thus I know this earth is not my sphere,
For I cannot so narrow me, but that
I still exceed it; in their elements
My love would pass my reason—but since here
Love must receive its object from this earth,
While reason will be chainless, the few truths
Caught from its wanderings have sufficed to quell
All love below;—then what must be that love
Which, with the object it demands, would quell
Reason, tho' it soared with the seraphim?
No—what I feel may pass all human love,
Yet fall far short of what my love should be;
And yet I seem more warped in this than aught
For here myself stands out more hideously.

I can forget myself in friendship, fame,
Or liberty, or love of mighty souls.

     .   .   .   .

But I begin to know what thing hate is—
To sicken, and to quiver, and grow white,
And I myself have furnished its first prey.
All my sad weaknesses, this wavering will,
This selfishness, this still decaying frame . . .
But I must never grieve while I can pass
Far from such thoughts—as now—Andromeda!
And she is with me—years roll, I shall change,
But change can touch her not—so beautiful
With her dark eyes, earnest and still, and hair
Lifted and spread by the salt-sweeping breeze;
And one red-beam, all the storm leaves in heaven,
Resting upon her eyes and face and hair,
As she awaits the snake on the wet beach,
By the dark rock, and the white wave just breaking
At her feet; quite naked and alone,—a thing
You doubt not, nor fear for, secure that God
Will come in thunder from the stars to save her.
Let it pass—I will call another change.
I will be gifted with a wond'rous soul,
Yet sunk by error to men's sympathy,
And in the wane of life; yet only so
As to call up their fears, and there shall come
A time requiring youth's best energies;
And straight I fling age, sorrow, sickness off,
And I rise triumphing over my decay.

     .   .   .   .

And thus it is that I supply the chasm
'Twixt what I am and all that I would be.
But then to know nothing—to hope for nothing—
To seize on life's dull joys from a strange fear,
Lest, losing them, all's lost, and nought remains.

     .   .   .   .

There's some vile juggle with my reason here—
I feel I but explain to my own loss
These impulses—they live no less the same.
Liberty! what though I despair—my blood
Rose not at a slave's name proudlier than now,
And sympathy obscured by sophistries.

Why have not I sought refuge in myself,
But for the woes I saw and could not stay—
And love!—do I not love thee, my Pauline?

    .   .   .   .

I cherish prejudice, lest I be left
Utterly loveless—witness this belief
In poets, tho' sad change has come there too;
No more I leave myself to follow them:
Unconsciously I measure me by them.
Let me forget it; and I cherish most
My love of England—how her name—a word
Of her's in a strange tongue makes my heart beat! . . .

    .   .   .   .

Pauline, I could do any thing—not now—
All's fever—but when calm shall come again—
I am prepared—I have made life my own—
I would not be content with all the change
One frame should feel—but I have gone in thought
Thro' all conjuncture—I have lived all life
When it is most alive—where strangest fate
New shapes it past surmise—the tales of men
Bit by some curse—or in the grasp of doom
Half-visible and still increasing round,
Or crowning their wide being's general aim. . . .

These are wild fancies, but I feel, sweet friend,
As one breathing his weakness to the ear
Of pitying angel—dear as a winter flower;
A slight flower growing alone, and offering
Its frail cup of three leaves to the cold sun,
Yet joyous and confiding, like the triumph
Of a child—and why am I not worthy thee?

    .   .   .   .

I can live all the life of plants, and gaze
Drowsily on the bees that flit and play,
Or bare my breast for sunbeams which will kill,
Or open in the night of sounds, to look
For the dim stars; I can mount with the bird,
Leaping airily his pyramid of leaves
And twisted boughs of some tall mountain tree,
Or rise cheerfully springing to the heavens—

Or like a fish breathe in the morning air
In the misty sun-warm water—or with flowers
And trees can smile in light at the sinking sun,
Just as the storm comes—as a girl would look
On a departing lover—most serene.

Pauline, come with me—see how I could build
A home for us, out of the world; in thought—
I am inspired—come with me, Pauline!

Night, and one single ridge of narrow path
Between the sullen river and the woods
Waving and muttering—for the moonless night
Has shaped them into images of life,
Like the upraising of the giant-ghosts,
Looking on earth to know how their sons fare.
Thou art so close by me, the roughest swell
Of wind in the tree-tops hides not the panting
Of thy soft breasts; no—we will pass to morning—
Morning—the rocks, and vallies, and old woods.
How the sun brightens in the mist, and here,—
Half in the air, like creatures of the place,
Trusting the element—living on high boughs
That swing in the wind—look at the golden spray,
Flung from the foam-sheet of the cataract,
Amid the broken rocks—shall we stay here
With the wild hawks?—no, ere the hot noon come
Dive we down—safe;—see this our new retreat
Walled in with a sloped mound of matted shrubs,
Dark, tangled, old and green—still sloping down
To a small pool whose waters lie asleep
Amid the trailing boughs turned water plants
And tall trees over-arch to keep us in,
Breaking the sunbeams into emerald shafts,
And in the dreamy water one small group
Of two or three strange trees are got together,
Wondering at all around—as strange beasts herd
Together far from their own land—all wildness—
No turf nor moss, for boughs and plants pave all,
And tongues of bank go shelving in the waters,
Where the pale-throated snake reclines his head,
And old grey stones lie making eddies there;
The wild mice cross them dry-shod—deeper in—

Shut thy soft eyes—now look—still deeper in:
This is the very heart of the woods—all round,
Mountain-like, heaped above us; yet even here
One pond of water gleams—far off the river
Sweeps like a sea, barred out from land; but one—
One thin clear sheet has over-leaped and wound
Into this silent depth, which gained, it lies
Still, as but let by sufferance; the trees bend
O'er it as wild men watch a sleeping girl,
And thro' their roots long creeping plants stretch out
Their twined hair, steeped and sparkling; farther on,
Tall rushes and thick flag-knots have combined
To narrow it; so, at length, a silver thread
It winds, all noiselessly, thro' the deep wood,
Till thro' a cleft way, thro' the moss and stone,
It joins its parent-river with a shout.
Up for the glowing day—leave the old woods:
See, they part, like a ruined arch, the sky!
Nothing but sky appears, so close the root
And grass of the hill-top level with the air—
Blue sunny air, where a great cloud floats, laden
With light, like a dead whale that white birds pick,
Floating away in the sun in some north sea.
Air, air—fresh life-blood—thin and searching air—
The clear, dear breath of God that loveth us:
Where small birds reel and winds take their delight.
Water is beautiful, but not like air.
See, where the solid azure waters lie,
Made as of thickened air, and down below,
The fern-ranks, like a forest spread themselves,
As tho' each pore could feel the element;
Where the quick glancing serpent winds his way—
Float with me there, Pauline, but not like air.
Down the hill—stop—a clump of trees, see, set
On a heap of rocks, which look o'er the far plains,
And envious climbing shrubs would mount to rest,
And peer from their spread boughs. There they wave,
　　　looking
At the muleteers, who whistle as they go
To the merry chime of their morning bells, and all
The little smoking cots, and fields, and banks,
And copses, bright in the sun; my spirit wanders.
Hedge-rows for me—still, living, hedge-rows, where

The bushes close, and clasp above, and keep
Thought in—I am concentrated—I feel;—
But my soul saddens when it looks beyond;
I cannot be immortal, nor taste all.
O God! where does this tend—these struggling aims![1]
What would I have? what is this " sleep," which seems
To bound all? can there be a " waking " point
Of crowning life? The soul would never rule—
It would be first in all things—it would have
Its utmost pleasure filled—but that complete
Commanding for commanding sickens it.

The last point that I can trace is, rest beneath
Some better essence than itself—in weakness;
This is " myself "—not what I think should be,
And what is that I hunger for but God?

My God, my God! let me for once look on thee
As tho' nought else existed: we alone.

And as creation crumbles, my soul's spark
Expands till I can say, " Even from myself
" I need thee, and I feel thee, and I love thee;
" I do not plead my rapture in thy works

[1] Je crains bien que mon pauvre ami ne soit pas toujours parfaitement compris dans ce qui reste à lire de cet étrange fragment—mais il est moins propre que tout autre à éclaircir ce qui de sa nature ne peut jamais être que songe et confusion. D'ailleurs je ne sais trop si en cherchant à mieux co-ordonner certaines parties l'on ne courrait pas le risque de nuire au seul mérite auquel une production si singulière peut prétendre—celui de donner une idée assez précise du genre qu'elle n'a fait que ébaucher.—Ce début sans prétention, ce remuement des passions qui va d'abord en accroissant et puis s'appaise par degrés, ces élans de l'âme, ce retour soudain sur soi-même, et par dessus tout, la tournure d'esprit toute particulière de mon ami rendent les changemens presque impossibles. Les raisons qu'il fait valoir ailleurs, et d'autres encore plus puissantes, ont fait trouver grâce à mes yeux pour cet écrit qu'autrement je lui eusse conseillé de jeter au feu.—Je n'en crois pas moins au grand principe de toute composition—à ce principe de Shakespeare, de Raffaelle, de Beethoven, d'où il suit que la concentration des idées est dûe bien plus à leur conception, qu'à leur mise en execution . . . j'ai tout lieu de craindre que la première de ces qualités ne soit encore étrangère à mon ami—et je doute fort qu'un redoublement de travail lui fasse acquérir la seconde. Le mieux serait de brûler ceci; mais que faire?

Je crois que dans ce qui suit il fait allusion à un certain examen qu'il fit autrefois de l'âme ou plutôt de son âme, pour découvrir la suite des objets auxquels il lui serait possible d'atteindre, et dont chacun une fois obtenu devait former une espèce de plateau d'où l'on pouvait apercevoir d'autres buts, d'autres projets, d'autres jouissances qui, à leur tour, devaient être surmontés. Il en résultait que l'oubli et le sommeil devaient tout terminer. Cette idée que je ne saisis pas parfaitement lui est peutêtre aussi intelligible qu'à moi.

PAULINE.

" For love of thee—or that I feel as one
" Who cannot die—but there is that in me
" Which turns to thee, which loves, or which should love."

Why have I girt myself with this hell-dress?
Why have I laboured to put out my life?
Is it not in my nature to adore,
And e'en for all my reason do I not
Feel him, and thank him, and pray to him?—*Now*.
Can I forego the trust that he loves me?
Do I not feel a love which only ONE . . .
O thou pale form, so dimly seen, deep-eyed,
I have denied thee calmly—do I not
Pant when I read of thy consummate deeds,
And burn to see thy calm pure truths out-flash
The brightest gleams of earth's philosophy?
Do I not shake to hear aught question thee? . . .

If I am erring save me, madden me,
Take from me powers, and pleasures—let me die
Ages, so I see thee: I am knit round
As with a charm, by sin and lust and pride,
Yet tho' my wandering dreams have seen all shapes
Of strange delight, oft have I stood by thee—
Have I been keeping lonely watch with thee,
In the damp night by weeping Olivet,
Or leaning on thy bosom, proudly less—
Or dying with thee on the lonely cross—
Or witnessing thy bursting from the tomb!

A mortal, sin's familiar friend doth here
Avow that he will give all earth's reward,
But to believe and humbly teach the faith,
In suffering, and poverty, and shame,
Only believing he is not unloved. . . .

And now, my Pauline, I am thine for ever!
I feel the spirit which has buoyed me up
Deserting me: and old shades gathering on;
Yet while its last light waits, I would say much,
And chiefly, I am glad that I have said
That love which I have ever felt for thee,
But seldom told; our hearts so beat together,

That speech is mockery, but when dark hours come:
And I feel sad; and thou, sweet, deem'st it strange;
A sorrow moves me, thou canst not remove.
Look on this lay I dedicate to thee,
Which thro' thee I began, and which I end,
Collecting the last gleams to strive to tell
That I am thine, and more than ever now—
That I am sinking fast—yet tho' I sink
No less I feel that thou hast brought me bliss,
And that I still may hope to win it back.
Thou know'st, dear friend, I could not think all calm,
For wild dreams followed me, and bore me off,
And all was indistinct. Ere one was caught
Another glanced: so dazzled by my wealth,
Knowing not which to leave nor which to choose,
For all my thoughts so floated, nought was fixed—
And then thou said'st a perfect bard was one
Who shadowed out the stages of all life,
And so thou badest me tell this my first stage:—
'Tis done: and even now I feel all dim the shift
Of thought. These are my last thoughts; I discern
Faintly immortal life, and truth, and good.
And why thou must be mine is, that e'en now,
In the dim hush of night—that I have done—
With fears and sad forebodings: I look thro'
And say, " E'en at the last I have her still,
" With her delicious eyes as clear as heaven,
" When rain in a quick shower has beat down mist,
" And clouds float white in the sun like broods of swans."
How the blood lies upon her cheek, all spread
As thinned by kisses; only in her lips
It wells and pulses like a living thing,
And her neck looks, like marble misted o'er
With love-breath, a dear thing to kiss and love.
Standing beneath me—looking out to me,
As I might kill her and be loved for it.

Love me—love me, Pauline, love nought but me;
Leave me not. All these words are wild and weak,
Believe them not, Pauline. I stooped so low
But to behold thee purer by my side,
To show thou art my breath—my life—a last
Resource—an extreme want: never believe

Aught better could so look to thee, nor seek
Again the world of good thoughts left for me.
There were bright troops of undiscovered suns.
Each equal in their radiant course. There were
Clusters of far fair isles, which ocean kept
For his own joy, and his waves broke on them
Without a choice. And there was a dim crowd
Of visions, each a part of the dim whole.
And a star left his peers and came with peace
Upon a storm, and all eyes pined for him,
And one isle harboured a sea-beaten ship,
And the crew wandered in its bowers, and plucked
Its fruits, and gave up all their hopes for home.
And one dream came to a pale poet's sleep,
And he said, " I am singled out by God,
" No sin must touch me." I am very weak,
But what I would express is,—Leave me not,
Still sit by me—with beating breast, and hair
Loosened—watching earnest by my side,
Turning my books, or kissing me when I
Look up—like summer wind. Be still to me
A key to music's mystery, when mind fails,
A reason, a solution and a clue,
You see I have thrown off my prescribed rules:
I hope in myself—and hope, and pant, and love—
You'll find me better—know me more than when
You loved me as I was. Smile not; I have
Much yet to gladden you—to dawn on you.

No more of the past—I'll look within no more—
I have too trusted to my own wild wants—
Too trusted to myself—to intuition.
Draining the wine alone in the still night,
And seeing how—as gathering films arose,
As by an inspiration life seemed bare
And grinning in its vanity, and ends
Hard to be dreamed of, stared at me as fixed,
And others suddenly became all foul,
As a fair witch turned an old hag at night.
No more of this—we will go hand in hand,
I will go with thee, even as a child,
Looking no further than thy sweet commands.
And thou hast chosen where this life shall be—

The land which gave me thee shall be our home,
Where nature lies all wild amid her lakes
And snow-swathed mountains, and vast pines all girt
With ropes of snow—where nature lies all bare,
Suffering none to view her but a race
Most stinted and deformed—like the mute dwarfs
Which wait upon a naked Indian queen.
And there (the time being when the heavens are thick
With storms) I'll sit with thee while thou dost sing
Thy native songs, gay as a desert bird
Who crieth as he flies for perfect joy,
Or telling me old stories of dead knights,
Or I will read old lays to thee—how she,
The fair pale sister, went to her chill grave
With power to love, and to be loved, and live.
Or we will go together, like twin gods
Of the infernal world, with scented lamp
Over the dead—to call and to awake—
Over the unshaped images which lie
Within my mind's cave—only leaving all
That tells of the past doubts. So when spring comes,
And sunshine comes again like an old smile,
And the fresh waters, and awakened birds,
And budding woods await us—I shall be
Prepared, and we will go and think again,
And all old loves shall come to us—but changed
As some sweet thought which harsh words veiled before;
Feeling God loves us, and that all that errs,
Is a strange dream which death will dissipate;
And then when I am firm we'll seek again
My own land, and again I will approach
My old designs, and calmly look on all
The works of my past weakness, as one views
Some scene where danger met him long before
Ah! that such pleasant life should be but dreamed!

But whate'er come of it—and tho' it fade,
And tho' ere the cold morning all be gone
As it will be;—tho' music wait for me,
And fair eyes and bright wine, laughing like sin,
Which steals back softly on a soul half saved;
And I be first to deny all, and despise
This verse, and these intents which seem so fair:

Still this is all my own, this moment's pride,
No less I make an end in perfect joy.
E'en in my brightest time, a lurking fear
Possessed me. I well knew my weak resolves,
I felt the witchery that makes mind sleep
Over its treasures—as one half afraid
To make his riches definite—but now
These feelings shall not utterly be lost,
I shall not know again that nameless care,
Lest leaving all undone in youth, some new
And undreamed end reveal itself too late:
For this song shall remain to tell for ever,
That when I lost all hope of such a change
Suddenly Beauty rose on me again.
No less I make an end in perfect joy,
For I, having thus again been visited,
Shall doubt not many another bliss awaits,
And tho' this weak soul sink, and darkness come,
Some little word shall light it up again,
And I shall see all clearer and love better;
I shall again go o'er the tracts of thought,
As one who has a right; and I shall live
With poets—calmer—purer still each time,
And beauteous shapes will come to me again,
And unknown secrets will be trusted me,
Which were not mine when wavering—but now
I shall be priest and lover, as of old.

Sun-treader, I believe in God, and truth,
And love; and as one just escaped from death
Would bind himself in bands of friends to feel
He lives indeed—so, I would lean on thee;
Thou must be ever with me—most in gloom
When such shall come—but chiefly when I die,
For I seem dying, as one going in the dark
To fight a giant—and live thou for ever,
And be to all what thou hast been to me—
All in whom this wakes pleasant thoughts of me,
Know my last state is happy—free from doubt,
Or touch of fear. Love me and wish me well!

RICHMOND,
October 22, 1832.

PARACELSUS

Inscribed to AMÉDÉE DE RIPERT-MONCLAR by his affectionate Friend R.B. (London: *March* 15, 1835.)

PERSONS

Aureolus Paracelsus
Festus and Michal, his friends
Aprile, an Italian Poet

I. PARACELSUS ASPIRES

Scene.—*Würzburg—a garden in the environs.* 1512

Festus, Paracelsus, Michal

Par. Come close to me, dear friends; still closer; thus!
Close to the heart which, though long time roll by
Ere it again beat quicker, pressed to yours,
As now it beats—perchance a long, long time—
At least henceforth your memories shall make
Quiet and fragrant as befits their home.
Nor shall my memory want a home in yours—
Alas, that it requires too well such free
Forgiving love as shall embalm it there!
For if you would remember me aright—
As I was born to be—you must forget
All fitful, strange, and moody waywardness
Which e'er confused my better spirit, to dwell
Only on moments such as these, dear friends!
—My heart no truer, but my words and ways
More true to it: as Michal, some months hence,
Will say "this autumn was a pleasant time,"
For some few sunny days; and overlook
Its bleak wind, hankering after pining leaves.
Autumn would fain be sunny—I would look
Liker my nature's truth; and both are frail,
And both beloved for all their frailty!
Mich.   Aureole!
Par. Drop by drop!—she is weeping like a child!

29

Not so! I am content—more than content—
Nay, Autumn wins you best by this its mute
Appeal to sympathy for its decay!
Look up, sweet Michal, nor esteem the less
Your stained and drooping vines their grapes bow down,
Nor blame those creaking trees bent with their fruit,
That apple-tree with a rare after-birth
Of peeping blooms sprinkled its wealth among!
Then for the winds—what wind that ever raved
Shall vex that ash that overlooks you both,
So proud it wears its berries? Ah! at length,
The old smile meet for her, the lady of this
Sequestered nest! This kingdom, limited
Alone by one old populous green wall,
Tenanted by the ever-busy flies,
Grey crickets, and shy lizards, and quick spiders,
Each family of the silver-threaded moss—
Which, look through, near, this way, and it appears
A stubble-field, or a cane-brake—a marsh
Of bulrush whitening in the sun: laugh now!
Fancy the crickets, each one in his house,
Looking out, wondering at the world—or best,
Yon painted snail, with his gay shell of dew,
Travelling to see the glossy balls high up
Hung by the caterpillar, like gold lamps!
    Mich. In truth we have lived carelessly and well!
    Par. And shall, my perfect pair—each, trust me, born
For the other; nay, your very hair, when mixed,
Is of one hue. For where save in this nook
Shall you two walk, when I am far away,
And wish me prosperous fortune? Stay! . . . Whene'er
That plant shall wave its tangles lightly and softly,
As a queen's languid and imperial arm
Which scatters crowns among her lovers, you
Shall be reminded to predict to me
Some great success! Ah, see! the sun sinks broad
Behind St. Saviour's: wholly gone, at last!
    Fest. Now, Aureole, stay those wandering eyes awhile!
You are ours to-night at least; and while you spoke
Of Michal and her tears, the thought came back
That none could leave what he so seemed to love:
But that last look destroys my dream—that look!
As if, where'er you gazed, there stood a star!

How far was Würzburg, with its church and spire,
And garden-walls, and all things they contain,
From that look's far alighting?
    Par.   I but spoke
And looked alike from simple joy, to see
The beings I love best, shut in so well
From all rude chances like to be my lot,
That, when afar, my weary spirit,—disposed
To lose awhile its care in soothing thoughts
Of them, their pleasant features, looks, and words,—
Need never hesitate, nor apprehend
Encroaching trouble may have reached them too,
Nor have recourse to Fancy's busy aid
To fashion even a wish in their behalf
Beyond what they possess already here;
But, unobstructed, may at once forget
Itself in them, assured how well they are.
Beside, this Festus knows, he thinks me one
Whom quiet and its charms attract in vain,
One scarce aware of all the joys I quit
Too fill'd with airy hopes to make account
Of soft delights which free hearts garner up:
Whereas, behold how much our sense of all
That's beauteous proves alike! When Festus learns
That every common pleasure of the world
Affects me as himself; that I have just
As varied appetites for joy derived
From common things; a stake in life, in short,
Like his; a stake which rash pursuit of aims
That life affords not, would as soon destroy;—
He may convince himself, that, this in view,
I shall act well advised: and last, because,
Though heaven and earth, and all things, were at stake,
Sweet Michal must not weep, our parting eve!
    Fest.   True: and the even is deepening, and we sit
As little anxious to begin our talk
As though to-morrow I could open it
As we paced arm in arm the cheerful town
At sun-dawn; and continue it by fits
(Old Tritheim busied with his class the while)
In that dim chamber where the noon-streaks peer
Half frightened by the awful tomes around;
And here at home unbosom all the rest

From even-blush to midnight; but, to-morrow! . . .
Have I full leave to tell my inmost mind?
We two were brothers, and henceforth the world
Will rise between us:—all my freest mind?
'Tis the last night, dear Aureole!

    Par.   Oh, say on!
Devise some test of love—some arduous feat
To be performed for you—say on! If night
Be spent the while, the better! Recall how oft
My wondrous plans, and dreams, and hopes, and fears,
Have—never wearied you . . . oh, no! . . . as I
Recall, and never vividly as now,
Your true affection, born when Einsiedeln
And its green hills were all the world to us,
And still increasing to this night, which ends
My further stay at Würzburg . . . Oh, one day
You shall be very proud! Say on, dear friends!

    Fest. In truth? 'Tis for my proper peace, indeed,
Rather than yours; for vain all projects seem
To stay your course: I said my latest hope
Is fading even now. A story tells
Of some far embassy despatched to buy
The favour of an eastern king, and how
The gifts they offered proved but dazzling dust
Shed from the ore-beds native to his clime:
Just so, the value of repose and love,
I meant should tempt you, better far than I
You seem to comprehend—and yet desist
No whit from projects where repose nor love
Have part.

    Par.   Once more? Alas! as I forbode!

    Fest. A solitary briar the bank puts forth
To save our swan's nest floating out to sea.

    Par. Dear Festus, hear me. What is it you wish?
That I should lay aside my heart's pursuit,
Abandon the sole ends for which I live,
Reject God's great commission—and so die!
You bid me listen for your true love's sake:
Yet how has grown that love? Even in a long
And patient cherishing of the selfsame spirit
It now would quell; as though a mother hoped
To stay the lusty manhood of the child
Once weak upon her knees. I was not born

Informed and fearless from the first, but shrank
From aught which marked me out apart from men:
I would have lived their life, and died their death,
Lost in their ranks, eluding destiny:
But you first guided me through doubt and fear,
Taught me to know mankind and know myself;
And now that I am strong and full of hope,
That, from my soul, I can reject all aims
Save those your earnest words made plain to me:
Now, that I touch the brink of my design,
When I would have a triumph in their eyes,
A glad cheer in their voices—Michal weeps,
And Festus ponders gravely!

    Fest.   When you deign
To hear my purpose . . .

    Par.   Hear it?   I can say
Beforehand all this evening's conference!
'Tis this way, Michal, that he uses: first,
Or he declares, or I, the leading points
Of our best scheme of life, what is man's end,
And what God's will—no two faiths e'er agreed
As his with mine: next, each of us allows
Faith should be acted on as best we may:
Accordingly, I venture to submit
A plan, in lack of better, for pursuing
The path which God's will seems to authorize:
Well—he discerns much good in it, avows
This motive worthy, that hope plausible,
A danger here, to be avoided—there,
An oversight to be repaired: at last
Our two minds go together—all the good
Approved by him, I gladly recognize;
All he counts bad, I thankfully discard;
And nought forbids my looking up at last
For some stray comfort in his cautious brow—
When, lo! I learn that, spite of all, there lurks
Some innate and inexplicable germ
Of failure in my schemes; so that at last
It all amounts to this—the sovereign proof
That we devote ourselves to God, is seen
In living just as though there were no God:
A life which, prompted by the sad and blind
Lusts of the world, Festus abhors the most—

But which these tenets sanctify at once;
Though to less subtle wits it seems the same,
Consider it how they may.
> *Mich.*　　　　　　　　Is it so, Festus?
He speaks so calmly and kindly—is it so?
> *Par.*　Reject those glorious visions of God's love
And man's design; laugh loud that God should send
Vast longings to direct us; say how soon
Power satiates these, or lust, or gold; I know
The world's cry well, and how to answer it!
But this ambiguous warfare . . .
> *Fest.*　　　　　　　. . . Wearies so
That you will grant no last leave to your friend
To urge it?—for his sake, not yours? I wish
To send my soul in good hopes after you;
Never to sorrow that uncertain words,
Erringly apprehended—a new creed,
Ill understood—begot rash trust in you,
And shared in your undoing.
> *Par.*　　　　　　　Choose your side:
Hold or renounce: but meanwhile blame me not
Because I dare to act on your own views,
Nor shrink when they point onward, nor espy
A peril where they most ensure success.
> *Fest.*　Prove that to me—but that! Prove you abide
Within their warrant, nor presumptuous boast
God's labour laid on you; prove, all you covet
A mortal may expect; and, most of all,
Prove the strange course you now affect, will lead
To its attainment—and I bid you speed,
Nay, count the minutes till you venture forth!
You smile; but I had gathered from slow thought—
Much musing on the fortunes of my friend—
Matter I deemed could not be urged in vain:
But it all leaves me at my need: in shreds
And fragments I must venture what remains.
> *Mich.*　Ask at once, Festus, wherefore he should scorn . . .
> *Fest.*　Stay, Michal: Aureole, I speak guardedly
And gravely, knowing well, whate'er your error,
This is no ill-considered choice of yours—
No sudden fancy of an ardent boy.
Not from your own confiding words alone
Am I aware your passionate heart long since

Gave birth to, nourished, and at length matures
This scheme.   I will not speak of Einsiedeln,
Where I was born your elder by some years
Only to watch you fully from the first:
In all beside, our mutual tasks were fixed
Even then—'twas mine to have you in my view
As you had your own soul and those intents
Which filled it when, to crown your dearest wish,
With a tumultuous heart, you left with me
Our childhood's home to join the favoured few
Whom, here at Würzburg, Tritheim deigns to teach
A portion of his lore: and not the best
Of those so favoured, whom you now despise,
Came earnest as you came; resolved, like you,
To grasp all, and retain all, and deserve
By patient toil a wide renown like his.
And this new ardour which supplants the old,
I watched, too; 'twas significant and strange,
In one matched to his soul's content at length
With rivals in the search for Wisdom's prize,
To see the sudden pause, the total change;
From contest, the transition to repose—
From pressing onward as his fellows pressed,
To a blank idleness; yet most unlike
The dull stagnation of a soul, content,
Once foiled, to leave betimes a thriveless quest.
That careless bearing, free from all pretence
Even of contempt for what it ceased to seek—
Smiling humility, praising much, yet waiving
What it professed to praise—though not so well
Maintained but that rare outbreaks, fierce as brief,
Revealed the hidden scorn, as quickly curbed—
That ostentatious show of past defeat,
That ready acquiescence in contempt,
I deemed no other than the letting go
His shivered sword, of one about to spring
Upon his foe's throat; but it was not thus:
Not that way looked your brooding purpose then.
For after-signs disclosed, what you confirmed,
That you prepared to task to the uttermost
Your strength, in furtherance of a certain aim,
Which—while it bore the name your rivals gave
Their own most puny efforts—was so vast

In scope that it included their best flights,
Combined them, and desired to gain one prize
In place of many,—the secret of the world,
Of man, and man's true purpose, path, and fate:
—That you, not nursing as a mere vague dream
This purpose, with the sages of the Past,
Have struck upon a way to this, if all
You trust be true, which following, heart and soul,
You, if a man may, dare aspire to KNOW:
And that this aim shall differ from a host
Of aims alike in character and kind,
Mostly in this,—to seek its own reward
In itself only, not an alien end
To blend therewith; no hope, nor fear, nor joy,
Nor woe, to elsewhere move you, but this pure
Devotion to sustain you or betray:
Thus you aspire.

   Par.   You shall not state it thus:
I should not differ from the dreamy crew
You speak of. I profess no other share
In the selection of my lot, than this,
A ready answer to the will of God
Who summons me to be his organ: all
Whose innate strength supports them shall succeed
No better than your sages.

   Fest.   Such the aim, then,
God sets before you; and 'tis doubtless need
That he appoint no less the way of praise
Than the desire to praise; for, though I hold
With you, the setting forth such praise to be
The natural end and service of a man,
And think such praise is best attained when man
Attains the general welfare of his kind—
Yet, this, the end, is not the instrument.
Presume not to serve God apart from such
Appointed channel as He wills shall gather
Imperfect tributes—for that sole obedience
Valued, perchance. He seeks not that his altars
Blaze—careless how, so that they do but blaze.
Suppose this, then; that God selected you
To KNOW (heed well your answers, for my faith
Shall meet implicitly what they affirm)
I cannot think you dare annex to such

Selection aught beyond a steadfast will,
An intense hope, nor let your gifts create
Scorn or neglect of ordinary means
Conducive to success—make destiny
Dispense with man's endeavour. Now dare you search
Your inmost heart, and candidly avow
Whether you have not rather wild desire
For this distinction, than security
Of its existence; whether you discern
The path to the fulfilment of your purpose
Clear as that purpose—and again, that purpose
Clear as your yearning to be singled out
For its pursuer. Dare you answer this?
   Par. (After a pause.) No, I have nought to fear! Who will
     may know
The secret'st workings of my soul. What though
It be so?—if indeed the strong desire
Eclipse the aim in me?—if splendour break
Upon the outset of my path alone,
And duskest shade succeed? What fairer seal
Shall I require to my authentic mission
Than this fierce energy—this instinct striving
Because its nature is to strive?—enticed
By the security of no broad course,
With no success forever in its eyes!
How know I else such glorious fate my own,
But in the restless irresistible force
That works within me? Is it for human will
To institute such impulses?—still less,
To disregard their promptings? What should I
Do, kept among you all; your loves, your cares,
Your life—all to be mine? Be sure that God
Ne'er dooms to waste the strength he deigns impart!
Ask the gier-eagle why she stoops at once
Into the vast and unexplored abyss,
What full-grown power informs her from the first,
Why she not marvels, strenuously beating
The silent boundless regions of the sky!
Be sure they sleep not whom God needs! Nor fear
Their holding light his charge, when every hour
That finds that charge delayed, is a new death.
This for the faith in which I trust; and hence
I can abjure so well the idle arts

These pedants strive to learn and teach; Black Arts,
Great Works, the Secret and Sublime, forsooth—
Let others prize: too intimate a tie
Connects me with our God! A sullen fiend
To do my bidding, fallen and hateful sprites
To help me—what are these, at best, beside
God helping, God directing everywhere,
So that the earth shall yield her secrets up,
And every object shall be charged to strike,
Teach, gratify, her master God appoints?
And I am young, my Festus, happy and free!
I can devote myself; I have a life
To give; I, singled out for this, the One!
Think, think; the wide east, where old Wisdom sprung;
The bright south, where she dwelt; the hopeful north,
All are passed o'er—it lights on me! 'Tis time
New hopes should animate the world, new light
Should dawn from new revealings to a race
Weighed down so long, forgotten so long; so shall
The heaven reserved for us, at last receive
Creatures whom no unwonted splendours blind,
But ardent to confront the unclouded blaze
Whose beams not seldom blest their pilgrimage,
Not seldom glorified their life below.
    Fest. My words have their old fate and make faint stand
Against your glowing periods. Call this, truth—
Why not pursue it in a fast retreat,
Some one of Learning's many palaces,
After approved example; seeking there
Calm converse with the great dead, soul to soul,
Who laid up treasure with the like intent?
—So lift yourself into their airy place,
And fill out full their unfulfilled careers,
Unravelling the knots their baffled skill
Pronounced inextricable, true!—but left
Far less confused? A fresh eye, a fresh hand,
Might do much at their vigour's waning-point;
Succeeding with new-breathed and earnest force,
As at old games a runner snatched the torch
From runner still: this way success might be.
But you have coupled with your enterprise,
An arbitrary self-repugnant scheme
'Of seeking it in strange and untried paths.

What books are in the desert? writes the sea
The secret of her yearning in vast caves
Where yours will fall the first of human feet?
Has Wisdom sate there and recorded aught
You press to read? Why turn aside from her
To visit, where her vesture never glanced,
Now—solitudes consigned to barrenness
By God's decree, which who shall dare impugn?
Now—ruins where she paused but would not stay,
Old ravaged cities that, renouncing her,
She called an endless curse on, so it came—
Or, worst of all, now—men you visit, men,
Ignoblest troops that never heard her voice,
Or hate it, men without one gift from Rome
Or Athens,—these shall Aureole's teachers be!
Rejecting past example, practice, precept,
Aidless 'mid these he thinks to stand alone:
Thick like a glory round the Stagyrite
Your rivals throng, the sages: here stand you!
Whate'er you may protest, knowledge is not
Paramount in your love; or for her sake
You would collect all help from every source—
Rival or helper, friend, foe, all would merge
In the broad class of those who showed her haunts,
And those who showed them not.

Par. What shall I say?
Festus, from childhood I have been possessed
By a fire—by a true fire, or faint or fierce,
As from without some master, so it seemed,
Repressed or urged its current: this but ill
Expresses what I would convey—but rather
I will believe an angel ruled me thus,
Than that my soul's own workings, own high nature,
So became manifest. I knew not then
What whispered in the evening, and spoke out
At midnight. If some mortal, born too soon,
Were laid away in some great trance—the ages
Coming and going all the while—till dawned
His true time's advent, and could then record
The words they spoke who kept watch by his bed,—
Then I might tell more of the breath so light
Upon my eyelids, and the fingers warm
Among my hair. Youth is confused; yet never

So dull was I but, when that spirit passed,
I turned to him, scarce consciously, as turns
A water-snake when fairies cross his sleep.
And having this within me and about me
While Einsiedeln, its mountains, lakes, and woods
Confined me—what oppressive joy was mine
When life grew plain, and I first viewed the thronged,
The ever-moving concourse of mankind!
Believe that ere I joined them—ere I knew
The purpose of the pageant, or the place
Consigned to me within its ranks—while yet
Wonder was freshest and delight most pure—
'Twas then that least supportable appeared
A station with the brightest of the crowd,
A portion with the proudest of them all!
And from the tumult in my breast, this only
Could I collect—that I must thenceforth die,
Or elevate myself far, far above
The gorgeous spectacle. I seemed to long
At once to trample on—yet save mankind—
To make some unexampled sacrifice
In their behalf—to wring some wondrous good
From heaven or earth for them—to perish, winning
Eternal weal in the act: as who should dare
Pluck out the angry thunder from its cloud,
That, all its gathered flame discharged on him,
No storm might threaten summer's azure sleep:
Yet never to be mixed with men so much
As to have part even in my own work—share
In my own largess. Once the feat achieved,
I would withdraw from their officious praise,
Would gently put aside their profuse thanks:
Like some knight traversing a wilderness,
Who, on his way, may chance to free a tribe
Of desert-people from their dragon-foe;
When all the swarthy race press round to kiss
His feet, and choose him for their king, and yield
Their poor tents, pitched among the sand-hills, for
His realm; and he points, smiling, to his scarf,
Heavy with riveled gold, his burgonet,
Gay set with twinkling stones—and to the east,
Where these must be displayed!

   Fest.   Good: let us hear

No more about your nature, " which first shrank
" From all that marked you out apart from men! "
  Par. I touch on that: these words but analyse
That first mad impulse—'twas as brief as fond;
For as I gazed again upon the show,
I soon distinguished here and there a shape
Palm-wreathed and radiant, forehead and full eye.
Well pleased was I their state should thus at once
Interpret my own thoughts:—" Behold the clue
" To all," I rashly said, " and what I pine
" To do, these have accomplished: we are peers!
" They know, and therefore rule: I, too, will know! "
You were beside me, Festus, as you say;
You saw me plunge in their pursuits whom Fame
Is lavish to attest the lords of mind;
Not pausing to make sure the prize in view
Would satiate my cravings when obtained—
But since they strove I strove. Then came a slow
And strangling failure. We aspired alike,
Yet not the meanest plodder Tritheim schools
But faced me, all-sufficient, all-content,
Or staggered only at his own strong wits;
While I was restless, nothing satisfied,
Distrustful, most perplexed. I would slur over
That struggle; suffice it, that I loathed myself
As weak compared with them, yet felt somehow
A mighty power was brooding, taking shape
Within me: and this lasted till one night
When, as I sate revolving it and more,
A still voice from without said—" See'st thou not,
" Desponding child, whence came defeat and loss?
" Even from thy strength. Consider: hast thou gazed
" Presumptuously on Wisdom's countenance,
" No veil between; and can thy hands which falter
" Unguided by thy brain the mighty sight
" Continues to absorb, pursue their task
" On earth like these around thee—what their sense
" Which radiance ne'er distracted, clear descries?
" If thou wouldst share their fortune, choose their life.
" Unfed by splendour. Let each task present
" Its petty good to thee. Waste not thy gifts
" In profitless waiting for the gods' descent,
" But have some idol of thine own to dress

" With their array. Know, not for knowing's sake,
" But to become a star to men for ever.
" Know, for the gain it gets, the praise it brings,
" The wonder it inspires, the love it breeds.
" Look one step onward, and secure that step."
And I smiled as one never smiles but once;
Then first discovering my own aim's extent,
Which sought to comprehend the works of God,
And God himself, and all God's intercourse
With the human mind; I understood, no less,
My fellow's studies, whose true worth I saw,
But smiled not, well aware who stood by me.
And softer came the voice—" There is a way—
" 'Tis hard for flesh to tread therein, imbued
" With frailty—hopeless, if indulgence first
" Have ripened inborn germs of sin to strength:
" Wilt thou adventure for my sake and man's,
" Apart from all reward? " And last it breathed—
" Be happy, my good soldier; I am by thee,
" Be sure, even to the end! "—I answered not,
Knowing Him. As He spoke, I was endued
With comprehension and a steadfast will;
And when He ceased, my brow was sealed His own.
If there took place no special change in me,
How comes it all things wore a different hue
Thenceforward?—pregnant with vast consequence—
Teeming with grand results—loaded with fate;
So that when quailing at the mighty range
Of secret truths which yearn for birth, I haste
To contemplate undazzled some one truth,
Its bearings and effects alone—at once
What was a speck expands into a star,
Asking a life to pass exploring thus,
Till I near craze. I go to prove my soul!
I see my way as birds their trackless way—
I shall arrive! what time, what circuit first,
I ask not: but unless God send his hail
Or blinding fire-balls, sleet, or stifling snow,
In some time—his good time—I shall arrive:
He guides me and the bird. In his good time.
    Mich. Vex him no further, Festus; it is so!
    Fest. Just thus you help me ever. This would hold
Were it the trackless air, and not a path

Inviting you, distinct with footprints yet
Of many a mighty spirit gone that way.
You may have purer views than theirs, perhaps,
But they were famous in their day—the proofs
Remain. At least accept the light they lend.

   Par. Their light! the sum of all is briefly this:
They laboured, and grew famous; and the fruits
Are best seen in a dark and groaning earth,
Given over to a blind and endless strife
With evils, which of all your Gods abates?
No; I reject and spurn them utterly,
And all they teach. Shall I still sit beside
Their dry wells, with a white lip and filmed eye,
While in the distance heaven is blue above
Mountains where sleep the unsunned tarns?

   Fest.   And yet
As strong delusions have prevailed ere now:
Men have set out as gallantly to seek
Their ruin; I have heard of such—yourself
Avow all hitherto have failed and fallen.

   Mich. Nay, Festus, when but as the pilgrims faint
Through the drear way, do you expect to see
Their city dawn afar amid the clouds?

   Par. Ay, sounds it not like some old well-known tale?
For me, I estimate their works and them
So rightly, that at times I almost dream
I too have spent a life the sages' way,
And tread once more familiar paths. Perchance
I perished in an arrogant self-reliance
An age ago; and in that act, a prayer
For one more chance went up so earnest, so
Instinct with better light let in by Death,
That life was blotted out—not so completely
But scattered wrecks enough of it remain,
Dim memories; as now, when seems once more
The goal in sight again: all which, indeed,
Is foolish, and only means—the flesh I wear,
The earth I tread, are not more clear to me
Than my belief, explained to you or no.

   Fest. And who am I to challenge and dispute
That clear belief? I put away all fear.

   Mich. Then Aureole is God's commissary! he shall
Be great and grand—and all for us!

Par.   No, sweet!
Not great and grand. If I can serve mankind
'Tis well—but there our intercourse must end:
I never will be served by those I serve.

    Fest.   Look well to this; here is a plague-spot, here,
Disguise it how you may! 'Tis true, you utter
This scorn while by your side and loving us;
'Tis but a spot as yet; but it will break
Into a hideous blotch if overlooked.
How can that course be safe which from the first
Produces carelessness to human love?
It seems you have abjured the helps which men
Who overpass their kind, as you would do,
Have humbly sought—I dare not thoroughly probe
This matter, lest I learn too much: let be,
That popular praise would little instigate
Your efforts, nor particular approval
Reward you; put reward aside; alone
You shall go forth upon your arduous task,
None shall assist you, none partake your toil,
None share your triumph—still you must retain
Some one to cast your glory on, to share
Your rapture with. Were I elect like you,
I would encircle me with love, and raise
A rampart of my fellows; it should seem
Impossible for me to fail, so watched
By gentle friends who made my cause their own;
They should ward off Fate's envy—the great gift,
Extravagant when claimed by me alone,
Being so a gift to them as well as me.
If danger daunted me or ease seduced,
How calmly their sad eyes should gaze reproach!

    Mich.   O Aureole, can I sing when all alone,
Without first calling, in my fancy, both
To listen by my side—even I! And you?
Do you not feel this?—say that you feel this!

    Par.   I feel 'tis pleasant that my aims, at length
Allowed their weight, should be supposed to need
A further strengthening in these goodly helps!
My course allures for its own sake—its sole
Intrinsic worth; and ne'er shall boat of mine
Adventure forth for gold and apes at once.
Your sages say, " if human, therefore weak: "

If weak, more need to give myself entire
To my pursuit; and by its side, all else . . .
No matter! I deny myself but little
In waiving all assistance save its own—
Would there were some real sacrifice to make!
Your friends the sages threw their joys away,
While I must be content with keeping mine.

    Fest. But do not cut yourself from human weal?
You cannot thrive—a man that dares affect
To spend his life in service to his kind,
For no reward of theirs, nor bound to them
By any tie: nor do so, Aureole! No—
There are strange punishments for such. Give up
(Although no visible good flow thence) some part
Of the glory to another; hiding thus,
Even from yourself, that all is for yourself.
Say, say almost to God—" I have done all
" For her—not for myself! "

    Par.   And who, but lately,
Was to rejoice in my success like you?
Whom should I love but both of you?

    Fest.   I know not:
But know this, you, that 'tis no wish of mine
You should abjure the lofty claims you make;
Although I can no longer seek, indeed,
To overlook the truth, that there will be
A monstrous spectacle upon the earth,
Beneath the pleasant sun, among the trees:
—A being knowing not what love is. Hear me!
You are endowed with faculties which bear
Annexed to them as 'twere a dispensation
To summon meaner spirits to do their will,
And gather round them at their need; inspiring
Such with a love themselves can never feel—
Passionless 'mid their passionate votaries.
I know not if you joy in this or no,
Or ever dream that common men can live
On objects you prize lightly, but which make
Their heart's sole treasure: the affections seem
Beauteous at most to you, which we must taste
Or die: and this strange quality accords,
I know not how, with you; sits well upon
That luminous brow, though in another it scowls

An eating brand—a shame. I dare not judge you:
The rules of right and wrong thus set aside,
There's no alternative—I own you one
Of higher order, under other laws
Than bind us; therefore, curb not one bold glance!
'Tis best aspire. Once mingled with us all . . .

    Mich. Stay with us, Aureole! cast those hopes away,
And stay with us! An angel warns me, too,
Man should be humble; you are very proud:
And God, dethroned, has doleful plagues for such!
He warns me not to dread a quick repulse,
Nor slow defeat, but a complete success!
You will find all you seek, and perish so!

    Par. (*After a pause.*) Are these the barren first fruits of
      my life?
Is love like this the natural lot of all?
How many years of pain might one such hour
O'erbalance? Dearest Michal, dearest Festus,
What shall I say, if not that I desire
To merit this your love; and will, dear friends,
In swerving nothing from my first resolves.
See, the great moon! and ere the mottled owls
Were wide awake, I was to go. It seems
You acquiesce at last in all save this—
If I am like to compass what I seek
By the untried career I chuse; and then,
If that career, making but small account
Of much of life's delight, will yet retain
Sufficient to sustain my soul—for thus
I understand these fond fears just expressed.
And first; the lore you praise and I neglect,
The labours and the precepts of old time,
I have not slightly disesteemed. But, friends,
Truth is within ourselves; it takes no rise
From outward things, whate'er you may believe
There is an inmost centre in us all,
Where truth abides in fulness; and around
Wall upon wall, the gross flesh hems it in,
This perfect, clear perception—which is truth;
A baffling and perverting carnal mesh
Blinds it, and makes all error: and, " *to know* "
Rather consists in opening out a way
Whence the imprisoned splendour may escape,

Than in effecting entry for a light
Supposed to be without. Watch narrowly
The demonstration of a truth, its birth,
And you trace back the effluence to its spring
And source within us, where broods radiance vast,
To be elicited ray by ray, as chance
Shall favour: chance—for hitherto, your sage
Even as he knows not how those beams are born,
As little knows he what unlocks their fount;
And men have oft grown old among their books
To die, case-hardened in their ignorance,
Whose careless youth had promised what long years
Of unremitted labour ne'er performed:
While, contrary, it has chanced some idle day,
That autumn loiterers just as fancy-free
As the midges in the sun, have oft given vent
To truth—produced mysteriously as cape
Of cloud grown out of the invisible air.
Hence, may not truth be lodged alike in all,
The lowest as the highest? some slight film
The interposing bar which binds it up,
And makes the idiot, just as makes the sage
Some film removed, the happy outlet whence
Truth issues proudly? See this soul of ours!
How it strives weakly in the child, is loosed
In manhood, clogged by sickness, back compelled
By age and waste, set free at last by death:
Why is it, flesh enthralls it or enthrones?
What is this flesh we have to penetrate?
Oh, not alone when life flows still do truth
And power emerge, but also when strange chance
Ruffles its current; in unused conjuncture,
When sickness breaks the body, hunger, watching,
Excess, or languor—oftenest death's approach—
Peril, deep joy, or woe. One man shall crawl
Through life, surrounded with all stirring things,
Unmoved—and he goes mad; and from the wreck
Of what he was, by his wild talk alone,
You first collect how great a spirit he hid.
Therefore, set free the soul alike in all,
Discovering the true laws by which the flesh
Bars in the spirit! We may not be doomed
To cope with seraphs, but at least the rest

Shall cope with us. Make no more giants, God!
But elevate the race at once! We ask
To put forth just our strength, our human strength,
All starting fairly, all equipped alike,
Gifted alike, all eagle-eyed, true-hearted—
See if we cannot beat thy angels yet!
Such is my task. I go to gather this
The sacred knowledge, here and there dispersed
About the world, long lost or never found.
And why should I be sad, or lorn of hope?
Why ever make man's good distinct from God's?
Or, finding they are one, why dare mistrust?
Who shall succeed if not one pledged like me?
Mine is no mad attempt to build a world
Apart from His, like those who set themselves
To find the nature of the spirit they bore,
And, taught betimes that all their gorgeous dreams
Were only born to vanish in this life,
Refused to fit them to this narrow sphere,
But chose to figure forth another world
And other frames meet for their vast desires,—
Still, all a dream! Thus was life scorned; but life
Shall yet be crowned: twine amaranth! I am priest!
And all for yielding with a lively spirit
A poor existence—parting with a youth
Like theirs who squander every energy
Convertible to good, on painted toys,
Breath-bubbles, gilded dust! And though I spurn
All adventitious aims, from empty praise
To love's award, yet whoso deems such helps
Important, and concerns himself for me,
May know even these will follow with the rest—
As in the steady rolling Mayne, asleep
Yonder, is mixed its mass of schistous ore.
My own affections, laid to rest awhile,
Will waken purified, subdued alone
By all I have achieved; till then—till then . . .
Ah! the time-wiling loitering of a page
Through bower and over lawn, till eve shall bring
The stately lady's presence whom he loves—
The broken sleep of the fisher whose rough coat
Enwraps the queenly pearl—these are faint types!
See how they look on me—I triumph now!

But one thing, Festus, Michal!—I have told
All I shall e'er disclose to mortal: say—
Do you believe I shall accomplish this?
    Fest. I do believe!
    Mich.   I ever did believe!
    Par. Those words shall never fade from out my brain!
This earnest of the end shall never fade!
Are there not, Festus, are there not, dear Michal,
Two points in the adventure of the diver:
One—when, a beggar, he prepares to plunge?
One—when, a prince, he rises with his pearl?
Festus, I plunge!
    Fest.   I wait you when you rise!

II. PARACELSUS ATTAINS

SCENE. *Constantinople.—" The House of the Greek-conjuror."*
1521

PARACELSUS

Over the waters in the vapourous west
The sun goes down as in a sphere of gold
Behind the outstretched city, which between,
With all that length of domes and minarets,
Athwart the splendour, black and crooked runs
Like a Turk verse along a scimetar.
There lie, thou saddest writing, and awhile
Relieve my aching sight. 'Tis done at last!
Strange—and the juggles of a sallow cheat
Could win me to this act! 'Tis as yon cloud
Should voyage unwreck'd o'er many a mountain-top
And break upon a molehill. I have dared
Come to a pause with knowledge; scan for once
The heights already reach'd, without regard
To the extent above; fairly compute
What I have clearly gained; for once excluding
My future which should finish and fulfil
All half-gains, and conjectures, and mere hopes—
And this, because a fortune-teller bids
His credulous enquirers write thus much,
Their previous life's attainment, in his book,

Before his promised secret, as he vaunts,
Make that life perfect: here, accordingly,
'Mid the uncouth recordings of such dupes,
—Scrawled in like fashion, lie my life's results!
These few blurred characters suffice to note
A stranger wandered long through many lands,
And reaped the fruit he coveted in a few
Discoveries, as appended here and there,
The fragmentary produce of much toil,
In a dim heap, fact and surmise together
Confusedly massed, as when acquired; himself
Too bent on gaining more to calmly stay
And scrutinize the little which he gained:
Slipt in the blank space 'twixt an idiot's gibber
And a mad lover's ditty—lies the whole!

And yet those blottings chronicle a life—
A whole life,—mine! No thought to turn to act,
No problem for the fancy, but a life
Spent and decided, wasted past recall,
Or worthy beyond peer. Stay, turn the page
And take its chance,—thus: what, concerning " life "
Does this remembrancer set down?—" We say
" ' Time fleets, youth fades, life is an empty dream.'
" 'Tis the mere echo of time; and he whose heart
" Beat first beneath a human heart, whose speech
" Was copied from a human tongue, can never
" Recall when he was living yet knew not this.
" Nevertheless long seasons come and go,
" Till some one hour's experience shows what nought,
" He deemed, could clearer show; and ever after
" An altered brow, and eye, and gait, and speech
" Attest that now he knows the adage true
" ' Time fleets, youth fades, life is an empty dream.' "

Ay, my brave chronicler, and this same time
As well as any: let my hour speak now!

Now! I can go no farther; well or ill—
'Tis done. I must desist and take my chance;
I cannot keep on the stretch; 'tis no back-shrinking—
For let the least assurance dawn, some end
To my toil seem possible, and I proceed

At any price, by any sacrifice:
Else, here I pause: the old Greek's prophecy
Is like to turn out true—" I shall not quit
" His chamber till I know what I desire!"
Was it the light wind sung it, o'er the sea?

An end, a rest! strange how the notion, once
Admitted, gains strength every moment! Rest!
Where kept that thought so long? this throbbing brow
To cease—this beating heart to cease—its crowd
Of gnawing thoughts to cease!—To dare let down
My strung, so high-strung brain—to dare unnerve
My harassed o'ertasked frame—to know my place,
—My portion, my reward, my failure even,
Assigned, made sure for ever!—To lose myself
Among the common creatures of the world—
To draw some gain from having been a man—
Neither to hope nor fear—to live at length!
Oh, were it but in failure, to have rest!
What, sunk insensibly so deep? Has all
Been undergone for this? Was this the prayer
My labour qualified me to present
With no fear of refusal? Had I gone
Carelessly through my task, and so judged fit
To moderate my hopes; nay, were it now
My sole concern to exculpate myself
And lessen punishment,—I could not chuse
An humbler mood to wait for the decree!
No, no, there needs not this; no, after all,
At worst I have performed my share of the task:
The rest is God's concern—mine, merely this,
To know that I have obstinately held
By my own work. The mortal whose brave foot
Has trod, unscathed, the temple-courts so far
That he descries at length the shrine of shrines,
Must let no sneering of the demons' eyes,
Whose wrath he met unquailing, follow sly
And fasten on him, fairly past their power,
If where he stands he dares but stay; no, no—
He must not stagger, faint and fall at last,
—Knowing a charm to baffle them; behold,
He bares his front—a mortal ventures thus
Serene amid the echoes, beams, and glooms!

If he be priest henceforth, or if he wake
The god of the place to ban and blast him there,—
Both well! What's failure or success to me?
I have subdued my life to the one end
Ordained life; there alone I cannot doubt,
That only way I may be satisfied.
Yes, well have I subdued my life! beyond
The obligation of my strictest vows,
The contemplation of my wildest bond,
Which gave, in truth, my nature freely up,
In what it should be, more than what it was—
Consenting that whatever passions slept,
Whatever impulses lay unmatured,
Should wither in the germ,—but scarce foreseeing
That the soil, doomed thus to perpetual waste,
Would seem one day, remembered in its youth
Beside the parched sand-tract which now it is,
Already strewn with faint blooms, viewless then.
I ne'er engaged to root up loves so frail
I felt them not; yet now, 'tis very plain
Some soft spots had their birth in me at first—
If not love, say, like love: there was a time
When yet this wolfish hunger after knowledge
Set not remorselessly love's claims aside;
This heart was human once, or why recall
Einsiedeln, now, and Würzburg, which the Mayne
Forsakes her course to fold as with an arm?

And Festus—my poor Festus, with his praise,
And counsel, and grave fears—where is he now?
Or the sweet maiden, long ago his bride?
I surely loved them—that last night, at least,
When we . . . gone! gone! the better: I am saved
The sad review of an ambitious youth,
Choked by vile lusts, unnoticed in their birth.
But let grow up and wind around a will
Till action was destroyed. No, I have gone
Purging my path successively of aught
Wearing the distant likeness of such lusts.
I have made life consist of one idea:
Ere that was master—up till that was born
I bear a memory of a pleasant life
Whose small events I treasure; till one morn

I ran o'er the seven little grassy fields,
Startling the flocks of nameless birds, to tell
Poor Festus, leaping all the while for joy,
To leave all trouble for futurity,
Since I had just determined to become
The greatest and most glorious man on earth.
And since that morn all life has been forgot;
All is one day—one only step between
The outset and the end: one tyrant aim,
Absorbing all, fills up the interval—
One vast unbroken chain of thought, kept up
Through a career or friendly or opposed
To its existence: life, death, light and shade
The shows of the world, were bare receptacles
Or indices of truth to be wrung thence,
Not instruments of sorrow or delight:
For some one truth would dimly beacon me
From mountains rough with pines, and flit and wink
O'er dazzling wastes of frozen snow, and tremble
Into assured light in some branching mine,
Where ripens, swathed in fire, the liquid gold—
And all the beauty, all the wonder fell
On either side the truth, as its mere robe;
Men saw the robe—I saw the august form.
So far, then, I have voyaged with success,
So much is good, then, in this working sea
Which parts me from that happy strip of land—
But o'er that happy strip a sun shone, too!
And fainter gleams it as the waves grow rough,
And still more faint as the sea widens; last
I sicken on a dead gulph, streaked with light
From its own putrifying depths alone!
Then—God was pledged to take me by the hand;
Now—any miserable juggler bends
My pride to him. All seems alike at length:
Who knows which are the wise and which the fools?
God may take pleasure in confounding pride
By hiding secrets with the scorned and base—
He who stoops lowest may find most—in short,
I am here; and all seems natural; I start not;
And never having glanced behind to know
If I had kept my primal light from wane,
Am thus insensibly grown—what I am!

Oh, bitter; very bitter!
                    And more bitter,
To fear a deeper curse, an inner ruin—
Plague beneath plague—the last turning the first
To light beside its darkness. Better weep
My youth and its brave hopes, all dead and gone
In tears which burn! Would I were sure to win
Some startling secret in their stead!—a tincture
Of force to flush old age with youth, or breed
Gold, or imprison moonbeams till they change
To opal shafts!—only that, hurling it
Indignant back, I might convince myself
My aims remained as ever supreme and pure!
Even now, why not desire, for mankind's sake,
That if I fail, some fault may be the cause,—
That, though I sink, another may succeed?
O God, the despicable heart of us!
Shut out this hideous mockery from my heart!

'Twas politic in you, Aureole, to reject
Single rewards, and ask them in the lump;
At all events, once launched, to hold straight on:
For now 'tis all or nothing. Mighty profit
Your gains will bring if they stop short of such
Full consummation! As a man, you had
A certain share of strength, and that is gone
Already in the getting these you boast.
Do not they seem to laugh, as who should say—
" Great master, we are here indeed; dragged forth
" To light; this hast thou done; be glad! now, seek
" The strength to use which thou hast spent in getting! "

And yet 'tis surely much, 'tis very much,
Thus to have emptied youth of all its gifts,
To feed a fire meant to hold out till morn
Arrive with inexhaustible light; and lo,
I have heaped up my last, and day dawns not!
While I am left with grey hair, faded hands,
And furrowed brow. Ha, have I, after all,
Mistaken the wild nursling of my breast?
Knowledge it seemed, and Power, and Recompense!
Was she who glided through my room of nights,—
Who laid my head on her soft knees, and smoothed

The damp locks,—whose sly soothings just began
When my sick spirit craved repose awhile—
God! was I fighting Sleep off for Death's sake?
God! Thou art Mind! Unto the Master-Mind
Mind should be precious. Spare my mind alone!
All else I will endure: if, as I stand
Here, with my gains, thy thunder smite me down,
I bow me; 'tis thy will, thy righteous will;
I o'erpass life's restrictions, and I die:
And if no trace of my career remain,
Save a thin corpse at pleasure of the wind
In these bright chambers, level with the air,
See thou to it! But if my spirit fail,
My once proud spirit forsake me at the last,
Hast thou done well by me? So do not thou!
Crush not my mind, dear God, though I be crushed!
Hold me before the frequence of thy seraphs,
And say—" I crushed him, lest he should disturb
" My law. Men must not know their strength: behold,
" Weak and alone, how near he raised himself!"

But if delusions trouble me—and Thou,
Not seldom felt with rapture in thy help
Throughout my toil and wanderings, dost intend
To work man's welfare through my weak endeavour—
To crown my mortal forehead with a beam
From thine own blinding crown—to smile, and guide
This puny hand, and let the work so framed
Be styled my work,—hear me! I covet not
An influx of new power, an angel's soul:
It were no marvel then—but I have reached
Thus far, a man; let me conclude, a man!
Give but one hour of my first energy,
Of that invincible faith—one only hour!
That I may cover with an eagle-glance
The truths I have, and spy some certain way
To mould them, and completing them, possess!

Yet God is good: I started sure of that,
And why dispute it now? I'll not believe
But some undoubted warning long ere this
Had reached me: stars would write his will in heaven,
As once when a labarum was not deemed

Too much for the old founder of these walls.
Then, if my life has not been natural,
It has been monstrous: yet, till late, my course
So ardently engrossed me, that delight,
A pausing and reflecting joy, 'tis plain,
Though such were meant to follow as its fruit,
Could find no place in it. True, I am worn;
But who clothes summer, who is Life itself?
God, that created all things, can renew!
And then, though after life to please me now
Must have no likeness to the past, what hinders
Reward from springing out of toil, as changed
As bursts the flower from earth, and root, and stalk?
What use were punishment, unless some sin
Be first detected? let me know that first!
(*Aprile, from within*)

I hear a voice, perchance I heard
Long ago, but all too low,
So that scarce a thought was stirred
If really spoke the voice or no:
I heard it in my youth, when first
The waters of my life outburst:
But now their stream ebbs faint, I hear
The voice, still low, but fatal-clear—
As if all Poets, that God meant
Should save the world, and therefore lent
Great gifts to, but who, proud, refused
To do his work, or lightly used
Those gifts, or failed through weak endeavour,
And mourn, cast off by him forever,—
As if these leaned in airy ring
To call me; this the song they sing.

    " Lost, lost! yet come,
      With our wan troupe make thy home:
      Come, come! for we
      Will not breathe, so much as breathe
      Reproach to thee!
      Knowing what thou sink'st beneath:
      So we sank in those old years,
      Who did bid thee, come! thou last
      Who, a living man, hast life o'erpast,

And all together we, thy peers,
Will pardon ask for thee, the last
Whose trial is done, whose lot is cast
With those who watch, but work no more—
Who gaze on life, but live no more:
And yet we trusted thou shouldst speak
God's message which our lips, too weak,
Refused to utter,—shouldst redeem
Our fault: such trust, and all, a dream!
So we chose thee a bright birth-place
Where the richness ran to flowers—
Couldst not sing one song for grace?
Nor make one blossom man's and ours?
Must one more recreant to his race
Die with unexerted powers
And join us, leaving as he found
The world, he was to loosen, bound?
Anguish! ever and for ever;
Still beginning, ending never!
Yet, lost and last one, come!
How couldst understand, alas,
What our pale ghosts strove to say,
As their shades did glance and pass
Before thee, night and day?
Thou wert blind, as we were dumb;
Once more, therefore, come, O come!
How shall we better arm the spirit
Who next shall thy post of life inherit—
How guard him from thy ruin?
Tell us of thy sad undoing
Here, where we sit, ever pursuing
Our weary task, ever renewing
Sharp sorrow, far from God who gave
Our powers, and man they could not save!"

APRILE enters.

A spirit better armed, succeeding me?
Ha, ha! our king that wouldst be, here at last?
Art thou the Poet who shall save the world?
Thy hand to mine. Stay, fix thine eyes on mine.
Thou wouldst be king? Still fix thine eyes on mine!
    Par.   Ha, ha! why crouchest not? Am I not king?
So torture is not wholly unavailing!

Have my fierce spasms compelled thee from thy lair?
Art thou the Sage I only seemed to be,
Myself of after-time, my very self
With sight a little clearer, strength more firm,
Who robs me of my prize and takes my place
For just a fault, a weakness, a neglect?
I scarcely trusted God with the surmise
That such might come, and thou didst hear the while!

    Apr.   Thine eyes are lustreless to mine; my hair
Is soft, nay silken soft: to talk with thee
Flushes my cheek, and thou art ashy-pale,
True, thou hast laboured, hast withstood her lips,
The siren's! Yes, 'tis like thou hast attained!
Tell me, dear master, wherefore now thou comest?
I thought thy solemn songs would have their meed
In after-time; that I should hear the earth
Exult in thee, and echo with thy praise,
While I was laid forgotten in my grave.

    Par.   Not so! I know thee, I am not thy dupe!
Thou art ordained to follow in my track,
Even as thou sayest, succeeding to my place,
Reaping my sowing—as I scorned to reap
The harvest sown by sages passed away.
Thou art the sober searcher, cautious striver,
As if, except through me, thou had searched or striven!
Ay! tell the world! Degrade me, after all.
To an aspirant after fame, not truth—
To all but envy of thy fate, be sure!

    Apr.   Nay, sing them to me; I shall envy not:
Thou shalt be king! Sing thou, and I will stand
Beside, and call deep silence for thy songs,
And worship thee, as I had ne'er been meant
To fill thy throne—but none shall ever know!
Sing to me: for already thy wild eyes
Unlock my heart-springs, as some crystal-shaft
Reveals by some chance blaze its parent fount
After long time—so thou reveal'st my soul!
All will flash forth at last, with thee to hear!

    Par.   (His secret! my successor's secret—fool!)
I am he that aspired to KNOW—and thou?

    Apr.   I would LOVE infinitely, and be loved!

    Par.   Poor slave! I am thy king indeed.

    Apr.   Thou deem'st

That—born a spirit, dowered even as thou,
Born for thy fate—because I could not curb
My yearnings to possess at once the full
Enjoyment; yet neglected all the means
Of realising even the frailest joy;
Gathering no fragments to appease my want,
Yet nursing up that want till thus I die—
Thou deem'st I cannot trace thy safe, sure march,
O'er perils that o'erwhelm me, triumphing,
Neglecting nought below for aught above,
Despising nothing and ensuring all—
Nor that I could (my time to come again)
Lead thus my spirit securely as thine own:
Listen, and thou shalt see I know thee well.
I would love infinitely . . . Ah, lost! lost!
  O ye who armed me at such cost.
  Your faces shall I bear to see
  With your gifts even yet on me?—
 Par. (Ah, 'tis some moonstruck creature after all!
Such fond fools as are like to haunt this den:
They spread contagion, doubtless: yet he seemed
To echo one foreboding of my heart
So truly, that . . . no matter! Now he stands
With eve's last sunbeam staying on his hair
Which turns to it, as if they were akin:
And those clear smiling eyes of saddest blue
Nearly set free, so far they rise above
The painful fruitless striving of that brow
And enforced knowledge of those lips, firm set
In slow despondency's eternal sigh!
Has he, too, missed life's end, and learned the cause?)
Be calm, I charge thee, by thy fealty!
Tell me what thou wouldst be, and what I am.
 Apr. I would love infinitely, and be loved.
First: I would carve in stone, or cast in brass,
The forms of earth. No ancient hunter, raised
Up to the gods by his renown; no nymph
Supposed the sweet soul of a woodland tree,
Or sapphirine spirit of a twilight star,
Should be too hard for me; no shepherd-king,
Regal with his white locks; no youth who stands
Silent and very calm amid the throng,
His right hand ever hid beneath his robe

Until the tyrant pass; no law-giver;
No swan-soft woman, rubbed with lucid oils,
Given by a god for love of her—too hard!
Each passion sprung from man, conceived by man,
Would I express and clothe it in its right form,
Or blend with others struggling in one form,
Or show repressed by an ungainly form.
For, if you marvelled at some mighty spirit
With a fit frame to execute his will—
Ay, even unconsciously to work his will—
You should be moved no less beside some strong,
Rare spirit, fettered to a stubborn body,
Endeavouring to subdue it, and inform it
With its own splendour! All this I would do,
And I would say, this done, " God's sprites being made,
" He grants to each a sphere to be its world,
" Appointed with the various objects needed
" To satisfy its spiritual desires;
" So, I create a world for these my shapes
" Fit to sustain their beauty and their strength!"
And, at their word, I would contrive and paint
Woods, valleys, rocks, and plains, dells, sands, and wastes,
Lakes which, when morn breaks on their quivering bed,
Blaze like a wyvern flying round the sun;
And ocean-isles so small, the dog-fish tracking
A dead whale, who should find them, would swim thrice
Around them, and fare onward—all to hold
The offspring of my brain. Nor these alone—
Bronze labyrinths, palace, pyramid, and crypt,
Baths, galleries, courts, temples, and terraces,
Marts, theatres, and wharfs—all filled with men!
Men everywhere! And this performed in turn,
When those who looked on, pined to hear the hopes,
And fears, and hates, and loves which moved the crowd,—
I would throw down the pencil as the chisel,
And I would speak: no thought which ever stirred
A human breast should be untold; no passions,
No soft emotions, from the turbulent stir
Within a heart fed with desires like mine—
To the last comfort, shutting the tired lids
Of him who sleeps the sultry noon away
Beneath the tent-tree by the way-side well;
And this in language as the need should be,

Now poured at once forth in a burning flow,
Now piled up in a grand array of words.
This done, to perfect and consummate all,
Even as a luminous haze links star to star,
I would supply all chasms with music, breathing
Mysterious notions of the soul, no way
To be defined save in strange melodies.
Last, having thus revealed all I could love,
And having received all love bestowed on it,
I would die: so preserving through my course
God full on me, as I was full on men:
And He would grant my prayer—" I have gone through
" All loveliness of life; make more for me,
" If not for men—or take me to thyself,
" Eternal, infinite Love!"

                        If thou hast ne'er
Conceived this mighty aim, this full desire,
Thou hast not passed my trial, and thou art
No king of mine.
    Par.   Ah me!
    Apr.   But thou art here!
Thou didst not gaze like me upon that end
Till thine own powers for compassing the bliss
Were blind with glory; nor grow mad to grasp
At once the prize long patient toil should claim;
Nor spurn all granted short of that. And I
Would do as thou, a second time: nay, listen—
Knowing ourselves, our world, our task so great,
Our time so brief,—'tis clear if we refuse
The means so limited, the tools so rude
To execute our purpose, life will fleet,
And we shall fade, and leave our task undone.
Rather, grow wise in time: what though our work
Be fashioned in despite of their ill-service,
Be crippled every way? 'Twere little praise
Did full resources wait on our good will
At every turn. Let all be as it is.
Some say the earth is even so contrived
That tree, and flower, a vesture gay, conceal
A bare and skeleton framework: had we means
That answered to our mind! But now I seem
Wrecked on a savage isle: how rear thereon
My palace? Branching palms the props shall be,

Fruit glossy mingling; gems are for the east;
Who heeds them? I can waive them. Serpent's scales,
Birds' feathers, downy furs, and fishes' skins
Must help me; and a little here and there
Is all I can aspire to: still my art
Shall show its birth was in a gentler clime.
" Had I green jars of malachite, this way
" I'd range them: where those sea-shells glisten above,
" Cressets should hang, by right: this way we set
" The purple carpets, as these mats are laid,
" Woven of mere fern and rush and blossoming flag."
Or if, by fortune, some completer grace
Be spared to me, some fragment, some slight sample
Of my own land's completer workmanship,
Some trifle little heeded there, but here
The place's one perfection—with what joy
Would I enshrine the relic—cheerfully
Foregoing all the marvels out of reach!
Could I retain one strain of all the psalm
Of the angels—one word of the fiat of God—
To let my followers know what such things are!
I would adventure nobly for their sakes:
When nights were still, and still, the moaning sea,
And far away I could descry the land
Whence I departed, whither I return,
I would dispart the waves, and stand once more
At home, and load my bark, and hasten back,
And fling my gains before them, rich or poor—
" Friends," I would say, " I went far, far for them,
" Past the high rocks the haunt of doves, the mounds
" Of red earth from whose sides strange trees grow out,
" Past tracks of milk-white minute blinding sand,
" Till, by a mighty moon, I tremblingly
" Gathered these magic herbs, berry and bud,
" In haste—not pausing to reject the weeds,
" But happy plucking them at any price.
" To me, who have seen them bloom in their own soil,
" They are scarce lovely: plait and wear them, you!
" And guess, from what they are, the springs that fed—
" The stars that sparkled o'er them, night by night,
" The snakes that travelled far to sip their dew! "
Thus for my higher loves; and thus even weakness
Would win me honour. But not these alone

Should claim my care; for common life, its wants
And ways, would I set forth in beauteous hues:
The lowest hind should not possess a hope,
A fear, but I'd be by him, saying better
Than he his own heart's language.   I would live
For ever in the thoughts I thus explored,
As a discoverer's memory is attached
To all he finds: they should be mine henceforth,
Imbued with me, though free to all before;
For clay, once cast into my soul's rich mine
Should come up crusted o'er with gems: nor this
Would need a meaner spirit, than the first:
Nay, 'twould be but the selfsame spirit, clothed
In humbler guise, but still the selfsame spirit—
As one spring wind unbinds the mountain snow,
And comforts violets in their hermitage.
But master, poet, who hast done all this,
How didst thou 'scape the ruin I have met?
Didst thou, when nerving thee to this attempt,
Ne'er range thy mind's extent, as some wide hall,
Dazzled by shapes that filled its length with light,
Shapes clustered there to rule thee, not obey—
That will not wait thy summons, will not rise
Singly, nor when thy practised eye and hand
Can well transfer their loveliness, but crowd
By thee for ever, bright to thy despair?
Didst thou ne'er gaze on each by turns, and ne'er
Resolve to single out *one*, though the rest
Should vanish, and to give that one, entire
In beauty, to the world; forgetting, so,
Its peers, whose number baffles mortal power?
And, this determined, wert thou ne'er seduced
By memories, and regrets, and passionate love,
To glance once more farewell? and did their eyes
Fasten thee, brighter and more bright, until
Thou couldst but stagger back unto their feet,
And laugh that man's applause or welfare once
Could tempt thee to forsake them? Or when years
Had passed, and still their love possessed thee wholly;
When from without some murmur startled thee
Of darkling mortals, famished for one ray
Of thy so-hoarded luxury of light,
Didst thou ne'er strive even yet to break those spells,

And prove thou couldst recover and fulfil
Thy early mission, long ago renounced,
And, to that end, select some shape once more?
And did not mist-like influences, thick films,
Faint memories of the rest, that charmed so long
Thine eyes, float fast, confuse thee, bear thee off,
As whirling snowdrifts blind a man who treads
A mountain ridge, with guiding spear, through storm?
Say, though I fell, I had excuse to fall;
Say, I was tempted sorely: say but this,
Dear lord, Aprile's lord!

Par.   Clasp me not thus,
Aprile! . . . That the truth should reach me thus!
We are weak dust. Nay, clasp not, or I faint!

Apr. My king! and envious thoughts could outrage thee!
Lo, I forget my ruin, and rejoice
In thy success, as thou! Let our God's praise
Go bravely through the world at last! What care
Through me or thee? I feel thy breath . . . why, tears?
Tears in the darkness—and from thee to me?

Par. Love me henceforth, Aprile, while I learn
To love; and, merciful God, forgive us both!
We wake at length from weary dreams; but both
Have slept in fairy-land: though dark and drear
Appears the world before us, we no less
Wake with our wrists and ancles jewelled still.
I, too, have sought to KNOW as thou to LOVE—
Excluding love as thou refusedst knowledge.
Still thou hast beauty and I, power. We wake:
What penance canst devise for both of us?

Apr. I hear thee faintly . . . the thick darkness! Even
Thine eyes are hid. 'Tis as I knew: I speak,
And now I die. But I have seen thy face!
O, poet, think of me, and sing of me!
But to have seen thee, and to die so soon!

Par. Die not, Aprile: we must never part.
Are we not halves of one dissevered world,
Whom this strange chance unites once more? Part? never!
Till thou, the lover, know; and I, the knower,
Love—until both are saved. Aprile, hear!
We will accept our gains, and use them—now!
God, he will die upon my breast! Aprile!

Apr. To speak but once, and die! yet by his side.

Hush! hush!

               Ha! go you ever girt about
With phantoms, powers? I have created such,
But these seem real as I!

    Par.   Whom can you see
Through the accursed darkness?

    Apr.   Stay; I know,
I know them; who should know them well as I?—
White brows, lit up with glory; poets all!

    Par. Let him but live, and I have my reward!

    Apr. Yes; I see now—God is the PERFECT POET,
Who in creation acts his own conceptions,
Shall man refuse to be ought less than God?
Man's weakness is his glory—for the strength
Which raises him to heaven and near God's self,
Came spite of it: God's strength his glory is,
For thence came with our weakness sympathy
Which brought God down to earth, a man like us.
Had you but told me this at first! . . . Hush! hush!

    Par. Live! for my sake, because of my great sin,
To help my brain, oppressed by these wild words
And their deep import. Live! 'tis not too late:
I have a quiet home for us, and friends.
Michal shall smile on you . . . Hear you? Lean thus,
And breathe my breath: I shall not lose one word
Of all your speech—no little world, Aprile!

    Apr. No, no. . . . Crown me? I am not one of you!
'Tis he, the king, you seek. I am not one . . .

    Par. Give me thy spirit, at least! Let me love, too!

I have attained and now I may depart.

III. PARACELSUS

SCENE.—*A chamber in the house of Paracelsus at Basil.* 1526

PARACELSUS, FESTUS

    Par. Heap logs, and let the blaze laugh out!

    Fest.   True, true!
'Tis very fit that all, time, chance, and change
Have wrought since last we sate thus, face to face,
And soul to soul—all cares, far-looking fears,

Vague apprehensions, all vain fancies bred
By your long absence, should be cast away,
Forgotten in this glad unhoped renewal
Of our affections.

    Par.   Oh, omit not aught
Which witnesses your own and Michal's love!
I bade you not spare that! Forget alone
The honours and the glories, and the rest,
You seemed disposed to tell profusely out.

    Fest. Nay, even your honours, in a sense, I waive:
The wondrous Paracelsus—Life's dispenser,
Fate's commissary, idol of the schools,
And Courts, shall be no more than Aureole still—
Still Aureole and my friend, as when we parted
Some twenty years ago, and I restrained
As I best could the promptings of my spirit,
Which secretly advanced you, from the first,
To the pre-eminent rank which, since your own
Adventurous ardour, nobly triumphing,
Has won for you.

    Par.   Yes, yes; and Michal's face
Still wears that quiet and peculiar light,
Like the dim circlet floating round a pearl?

    Fest. Just so.

    Par.   And yet her calm sweet countenance,
Though saintly, was not sad; for she would sing
Alone . . . Does she still sing alone, bird-like,
Not dreaming you are near? Her carols dropt
In flakes through that old leafy bower built under
The sunny wall at Würzburg, from her lattice
Among the trees above, while I, unseen,
Sate conning some rare scroll from Tritheim's shelves,
Much wondering notes so simple could divert
My mind from study. Those were happy days!
Respect all such as sing when all alone.

    Fest. Scarcely alone—her children, you may guess,
Are wild beside her . . .

    Par.   Ah, those children quite
Unsettle the pure picture in my mind:
A girl—she was so perfect, so distinct . . .
No change, no change! Not but this added grace
May blend and harmonise with its compeers,
And Michal may become her motherhood;

But 'tis a change—and I detest all change,
And most a change in aught I loved long since!
So, Michal . . . you have said she thinks of me?
   Fest. O very proud will Michal be of you!
Imagine how we sate, long winter-nights,
Scheming and wondering—shaping your presumed
Adventures, or devising their reward;
Shutting out fear with all the strength of hope.
Though it was strange how, even when most secure
In our domestic peace, a certain dim
And flitting shade could sadden all; it seemed
A restlessness of heart, a silent yearning,
A sense of something wanting, incomplete—
Not to be put in words, perhaps avoided
By mute consent—but, said or unsaid, felt
To point to one so loved and so long lost.
And then the hopes rose and shut out the fears—
How you would laugh should I recount them now!
I still predicted your return at last,
With gifts beyond the greatest vaunt of all,
All Tritheim's wondrous troop; did one of which
Attain renown by any chance, I smiled—
As well aware of who would prove his peer.
Michal was sure some woman, long ere this,
As beautiful as you were sage, had loved . . .
   Par. Far-seeing, truly, to discern so much
In the fantastic projects and day-dreams
Of a raw, restless boy!
   Fest.   Say, one whose sunrise
Well warranted our faith in this full noon!
Can I forget the anxious voice which said,
" Festus, have thoughts like these e'er shaped themselves
" In other brains than mine—have their possessors
" Existed in like circumstance—were they weak
" As I—or ever constant from the first,
" Despising youth's allurements, and rejecting
" As spider-films the shackles I endure?
" Is there hope for me? "—and I answered grave
As an acknowledged elder, calmer, wiser,
More gifted mortal. O you must remember,
For all your glorious . . .
   Par.   Glorious? ay, this hair,
These hands—nay, touch them, they are mine! Recall

With all the said recallings, times when thus
To lay them by your own ne'er turned you pale,
As now. Most glorious, are they not?
   Fest.   Why . . . why . . .
Something must be subtracted from success
So wide, no doubt. He would be scrupulous, truly,
Who should object such drawbacks. Still, still, Aureole,
You are changed—very changed! 'Twere losing nothing
To look well to it: you must not be stolen
From the enjoyment of your well-won meed.
   Par. My friend! you seek my pleasure, past a doubt:
By talking, not of me, but of yourself,
You will best gain your point.
   Fest.   Have I not said
All touching Michal and my children? Sure
You know, by this, full well how Aennchen looks
Gravely, while one disparts her thick brown hair;
And Aureole's glee when some stray gannet builds
Amid the birch-trees by the lake. Small hope
Have I that he will honour, the wild imp,
His namesake! Sigh not! 'tis too much to ask
That all we love should reach the same proud fate.
But you are very kind to humour me
By showing interest in my quiet life;
You, who of old could never tame yourself
To tranquil pleasures, must at heart despise . . .
   Par. Festus, strange secrets are let out by Death,
Who blabs so oft the follies of this world:
And I am Death's familiar, as you know.
I helped a man to die, some few weeks since,
Warped even from his go-cart to one end—
The living on princes' smiles, reflected from
A mighty herd of favourites. No mean trick
He left untried; and truly well nigh wormed
All traces of God's finger out of him.
Then died, grown old; and just an hour before—
Having lain long with blank and soulless eyes—
He sate up suddenly, and with natural voice
Said, that in spite of thick air and closed doors
God told him it was June; and he knew well,
Without such telling, hare-bells grew in June;
And all that kings could ever give or take
Would not be precious as those blooms to him.

Just so, allowing I am passing wise,
It seems to me much worthier argument
Why pansies, eyes that laugh, bear beauty's prize
From violets, eyes that dream—(your Michal's choice)—
Than all fools find to wonder at in me,
Or in my fortunes: and be very sure
I say this from no prurient restlessness—
No self-complacency—itching to turn,
Vary, and view its pleasure from all points,
And, in this matter, willing other men
Should argue and demonstrate to itself
The realness of the very joy it tastes.
What joy is better than the news of friends
Whose memories were a solace to me oft,
As mountain-baths to wild fowls in their flight?
Yes, ofter than you wasted thought on me
If you were sage, and rightly valued bliss!
But there's no taming nor repressing hearts:
God knows I need such!—So you heard me speak?
   Fest. Speak? when?
   Par.   When but this morning at my class?
There was noise and crowd enough. I saw you not.
Surely you know I am engaged to fill
The chair here?—that 'tis part of my proud fate
To lecture to as many thick-sculled youths
As please, each day, to throng the theatre,
To my great reputation, and no small
Danger of Basil's benches, long unused
To crack beneath such honour?
   Fest.   I was there;
I mingled with the throng: shall I avow
I had small care to listen?—too intent
On gathering from the murmurs of the crowd
A full corroboration of my hopes!
What can I learn about your powers? but they
Know, care for nought beyond your actual state—
Your actual value; and yet worship you!
Those various natures whom you sway as one!
But ere I go, be sure I shall attend . . .
   Par. Stop, o' God's name: the thing's by no means yet
Past remedy! Shall I read this morning's work
—At least in substance? Nought so worth the gaining
As an apt scholar! Thus then, with all due

Precision and emphasis—(you, besides, are clearly
Guiltless of understanding a whit more
The subject than your stool—allowed to be
A notable advantage) . . .

    Fest.   Surely, Aureole,
You laugh at me!

    Par.   I laugh? Ha, ha! thank heaven,
I charge you, if't be so! for I forget
Much—and what laughter should be like! No less,
However, I forego that luxury,
Since it alarms the friend who brings it back.
True, laughter like my own must echo strange
To thinking men; a smile were better far—
So make me smile! If the exulting look
You wore but now be smiling, 'tis so long
Since I have smiled! Alas, such smiles are born
Alone of hearts like yours, or shepherds old
Of ancient time, whose eyes, calm as their flocks.
Saw in the stars mere garnishry of heaven,
In earth a stage for altars, nothing more.
Never change, Festus: I say, never change!

    Fest.   My God, if he be wretched after all!

    Par.   When last we parted, Festus, you declared,
—Or did your Michal's soft lips whisper words
I have preserved? She told me she believed
I should succeed (meaning, that in the search
I then engaged in, I should meet success),
And yet be wretched: now, she augured false.

    Fest.   Thank heaven! but you spoke strangely! could I
          venture
To think bare apprehension lest your friend,
Dazzled by your resplendent course, might find
Henceforth less sweetness in his own, awakes
Such earnest mood in you? Fear not, dear friend,
That I shall leave you, inwardly repining
Your lot was not my own!

    Par.   And this, for ever!
For ever! gull who may, they will be blind!
They will not look nor think—'tis nothing new
In them; but surely he is not of them!
My Festus, do you know, I reckoned, you—
Though all beside were sand-blind—you, my friend,
Would look at me, once close, with piercing eye,

Untroubled by the false glare that confounds
A weaker vision; would remain serene,
Though singular, amid a gaping throng.
I feared you, or had come, sure, long ere this,
To Einsiedeln. Well, error has no end,
And Rhasis is a sage, and Basil boasts
A tribe of wits, and I am wise and blest
Past all dispute! 'Tis vain to fret at it.
I have vowed long since that my worshippers
Shall owe to their own deep sagacity
All further information, good or bad:
And little risk my reputation runs,
Unless perchance the glance now searching me
Be fixed much longer—for it seems to spell,
Dimly, the characters a simpler man
Might read distinct enough. Old eastern books
Say, the fallen prince of morning some short space
Remained unchanged in feature—nay, his brow
Seemed hued with triumph: every spirit then
Praising; *his* heart on flame the while:—a tale!
Well, Festus, what discover you, I pray?
    Fest. Some foul deed sullies then a life which else
Were raised supreme?
    Par.   Good: I do well—most well!
Why strive to make men hear, feel, fret themselves
With what 'tis past their power to comprehend?
I would not strive now: only, having nursed
The faint surmise that one yet walked the earth,
One, at least, not the utter fool of show,
Not absolutely formed to be the dupe
Of shallow plausibilities alone;
One who, in youth found wise enough to choose
The happiness his riper years approve,
Was yet so anxious for another's sake,
That, ere his friend could rush upon a course
Mad, ruinous, the converse of his own,
His gentler spirit essayed, prejudged for him
The perilous path, foresaw its destiny,
And warned the weak one in such tender words,
Such accents—his whole heart in every tone—
That oft their memory comforted that friend
When rather it should have increased despair:
—Having believed, I say, that this one man

Could never lose the wisdom from the first
His portion—how should I refuse to grieve
At even my gain if it attest his loss,
At triumph which so signally disturbs
Our old relation, proving me more wise?
Therefore, once more reminding him how well
He prophesied, I note the single flaw
That spoils his prophet's title: in plain words
You were deceived, and thus were you deceived—
I have not been successful, and yet am
Most wretched: there—'tis said at last; but give
No credit, lest you force me to concede
That common sense yet lives upon the earth.

    Fest.   You surely do not mean to banter me?
    Par.   You know, or (if you have been wise enough
To cleanse your memory of such matters) knew,
As far as words of mine could make it clear,
That 'twas my purpose to find joy or grief
Solely in the fulfilment of my plan,
Or plot, or whatsoe'er it was; rejoicing
Alone as it proceeded prosperously,
Sorrowing alone when any chance retarded
Its progress. That was in those Würzburg days!
Not to prolong a theme I thoroughly hate,
I have pursued this plan with all my strength;
And having failed therein most signally,
Cannot object to ruin, utter and drear
As all-excelling would have been the prize
Had fortune favoured me. I scarce do right
To vex your frank good spirit, late rejoiced
By my supposed prosperity, I know,
And, were I lucky in a glut of friends,
Would well agree to let your error live,
Nay, strengthen it with fables of success:
But mine is no condition to refuse
The transient solace of so rare a chance,
My solitary luxury, my Festus—
Accordingly I venture to put off
The wearisome vest of falsehood galling me,
Secure when he is by. I lay me bare,
Prone at his mercy—but he is my friend!
Not that he needs retain his aspect grave;
That answers not my purpose; for 'tis like,

Some sunny morning—Basil being drained
Of its wise population, every corner
Of the amphitheatre crammed with learned clerks,
Here Œcolampadius, looking worlds of wit,
Here Castellanus, as profound as he,
Munsterus here, Frobenius there,—all squeezed,
And staring, and expectant,—then, I say,
'Tis like that the poor zany of the show,
Your friend, will choose to put his trappings off
Before them, bid adieu to cap and bells
And motley with a grace but seldom judged
Expedient in such cases:—the grim smile
That will go round! It is not therefore best
To venture a rehearsal like the present
In a small way? Where are the signs I seek,
The first-fruits and fair sample of the scorn
Due to all quacks? Why, this will never do!

    Fest.   These are foul vapours, Aureole; nought beside!
The effect of watching, study, weariness.
Were there a spark of truth in the confusion
Of these wild words, you would not outrage thus
Your youth's companion. I shall ne'er regard
These wanderings, bred of faintness and much study.
You would not trust a trouble thus to me,
To Michal's friend.

    Par.   I have said it, dearest Festus!
The manner is ungracious, probably;
More may be told in broken sobs, one day,
And scalding tears, ere long: but I thought best
To keep that off as long as possible.
Do you wonder still?

    Fest.   No; it must oft fall out
That one whose labour perfects any work,
Shall rise from it with eyes so worn, that he
Of all men least can measure the extent
Of what he has accomplished. He alone,
Who, nothing tasked, is nothing weary too,
Can clearly scan the little he effects:
But we, the bystanders, untouched by toil,
Estimate each aright.

    Par.   This worthy Festus
Is one of them, at last! 'Tis so with all!
First, they set down all progress as a dream,

And next, when he, whose quick discomfiture
Was counted on, accomplishes some few
And doubtful steps in his career,—behold,
They look for every inch of ground to vanish
Beneath his tread, so sure they judge success!

Fest. Few doubtful steps? when death retires before
Your presence—when the noblest of mankind,
Broken in body, or subdued in mind,
May through your skill renew their vigour, raise
The shattered frame to pristine stateliness?
When men in racking pain may purchase dreams
Of what delights them most—swooning at once
Into a sea of bliss, or rapt along
As in a flying sphere of turbulent light?
When we may look to you as one ordained
To free the flesh from fell disease, as frees
Our Luther's burning tongue the fettered soul?
When . . .

Par. Rather, when and where, friend, did you get
This notable news?

Fest. Even from the common voice;
From those whose envy, daring not dispute
The wonders it decries, attributes them
To magic and such folly.

Par. Folly? Why not
To magic, pray? You find a comfort doubtless
In holding, God ne'er troubles him about
Us or our doings: once we were judged worth
The devil's tempting . . . I offend: forgive me,
And rest content. Your prophecy on the whole
Was fair enough as prophesyings go;
At fault a little in detail, but quite
Precise enough in the main; accordingly
I pay due homage: you guessed long ago
(The prophet!) I should fail—and I have failed.

Fest. You mean to tell me, then, the hopes which fed
Your youth have not been realised as yet?
Some obstacle has barred them hitherto?
Or that their innate . . .

Par. As I said but now,
You have a very decent prophet's fame,
So you but shun details here. Little matters
'Whether those hopes were mad,—the aims they sought,

Safe and secure from all ambitious fools;
Or whether my weak wits are overcome
By what a better spirit would scorn: I fail.
And now methinks 'twere best to change a theme,
I am a sad fool to have stumbled on.
I say confusedly what comes uppermost;
But there are times when patience proves at fault,
As now; this morning's strange encounter—you
Beside me once again! you, whom I guessed
Alive, since hitherto (with Luther's leave)
No friend have I among the saints at rest,
To judge by any good their prayers effect—
I knew you would have helped me!—So would He,
My strange competitor in enterprise,
Bound for the same end by another path,
Arrived, or ill or well, before the time,
At our disastrous journey's doubtful close—
How goes it with Aprile? Ah, your heaven
Receives not into its beatitudes
Mere martyrs for the world's sake; heaven shuts fast:
The poor mad poet is howling by this time!
Since you are my sole friend then, here or there,
I could not quite repress the varied feelings
This meeting wakens; they have had their vent,
And now forget them. Do the rear-mice still
Hang like a fret-work on the gate (or what
In my time was a gate) fronting the road
From Einsiedeln to Lachen?

    Fest.   Trifle not!
Answer me—for my sake alone. You smiled
Just now, when I supposed some deed, unworthy
Yourself might blot the else so bright result;
Yet if your motives have continued pure,
Your earnest will unfaltering, if you still
Remain unchanged, and if, in spite of this,
You have experienced a defeat that proves
Your aims for ever unattainable—
I say not, you would cheerfully resign
The contest—mortal hearts are not so fashioned—
But sure you would resign it ne'ertheless.
You sought not fame, nor gain, nor even love;
No end distinct from knowledge,—I repeat
Your very words: once satisfied that knowledge

D 41

Is a mere dream, you would announce as much,
Yourself the first. But how is the event?
You are defeated—and I find you here!
   Par. As though " here " did not signify defeat!
I spoke not of my little labours here—
But of the break-down of my general aims:
That you, aware of their extent and scope,
Should look on these sage lecturings, approved
By beardless boys, and bearded dotards,—these
As a fit consummation of such aims,
Is worthy notice! A professorship
At Basil! Since you see so much in it,
And think my life was reasonably drained
Of life's delights to render me a match
For duties arduous as such post demands,—
Far be it from me to deny my power
To fill the petty circle lotted out
From infinite space, or justify the host
Of honours thence accruing: so, take notice.
This jewel dangling from my neck preserves
The features of a prince, my skill restored
To plague his people some few years to come:
And all through a pure whim. He had eased the earth
For me, but that the droll despair which seized
The vermin of his household, tickled me.
I came to see: here, drivelled the physician,
Whose most infallible nostrum was at fault;
There quaked the astrologer, whose horoscope
Had promised him interminable years;
Here a monk fumbled at the sick man's mouth
With some undoubted relic—a sudary
Of the Virgin; while some other dozen knaves
Of the same brotherhood (he loved them ever)
Were actively preparing 'neath his nose
Such a suffumigation as, once fired,
Had stunk the patient dead ere he could groan.
I cursed the doctor, and upset the brother;
Brushed past the conjuror; vowed that the first gust
Of stench from the ingredients just alight
Would raise a cross-grained devil in my sword,
Not easily laid; and ere an hour, the prince
Slept as he never slept since prince he was.
A day—and I was posting for my life,

Placarded through the town as one whose spite
Had near availed to stop the blessed effects
Of the doctor's nostrum, which, well seconded
By the sudary, and most by the costly smoke—
Not leaving out the strenuous prayers sent up
Hard by, in the abbey—raised the prince to life;
To the great reputation of the seer,
Who, confident, expected all along
The glad event—the doctor's recompense—
Much largess from his highness to the monks—
And the vast solace of his loving people,
Whose general satisfaction to increase,
The prince was pleased no longer to defer
The burning of some dozen heretics,
Remanded 'till God's mercy should be shown
Touching his sickness, as a prudent pledge
To make it surer: last of all were joined
Ample directions to all loyal folk
To swell the complement, by seizing me
Who—doubtless some rank sorcerer—had endeavoured
To thwart these pious offices, obstruct
The prince's cure, and frustrate Heaven, by help
Of certain devils dwelling in his sword.
By luck, the prince in his first fit of thanks
Had forced this bauble on me as an earnest
Of further favours.   This one case may serve
To give sufficient taste of many such,
So let them pass: those shelves support a pile
Of patents, licenses, diplomas, titles,
From Germany, France, Spain, and Italy:
They authorise some honour: ne'ertheless,
I set more store by this Erasmus sent;
He trusts me; our Frobenius is his friend,
And him " I raised " (nay, read it) " from the dead " . . .
I weary you, I see; I merely sought
To show, there's no great wonder after all
That while I fill the class room, and attract
A crowd to Basil, I get leave to stay;
And therefore need not scruple to accept
The utmost they can offer—if I please:
For 'tis but right the world should be prepared
To treat with favour e'en fantastic wants
Of one like me, used up in serving her.

Just as the mortal, whom the Gods in part
Devoured, received in place of his lost limb
Some virtue or other—cured disease, I think;
You mind the fables we have read together.

    Fest.   You do not think I comprehend a word:
The time was, Aureole, you were apt enough
To clothe the airiest thoughts in specious breath:
But surely you must feel how vague and strange
These speeches sound.

    Par.   Well, then: you know my hopes;
I am assured, at length, those hopes were vain;
That truth is just as far from me as ever;
That I have thrown my life away; that sorrow
On that account is vain, and further effort
To mend and patch what's marred beyond repairing,
As useless: and all this was taught to me
By the convincing, good old-fashioned method
Of force—by sheer compulsion. Is that plain?

    Fest.   Dear Aureole! you confess my fears were just?
God wills not . . .

    Par.   Now, 'tis this I most admire—
The constant talk men of your stamp keep up
Of God's will, as they style it; one would swear
Man had but merely to uplift his eye
To see the will in question charactered
On the heaven's vault. 'Tis hardly wise to moot
Such topics: doubts are many and faith is weak.
I know as much of any will of God's,
As knows some dumb and tortured brute what Man,
His stern lord, wills from the perplexing blows
That plague him every way, and there, of course,
Where least he suffers, longest he remains—
My case; and for such reasons I plod on,
Subdued, but not convinced. I know as little
Why I deserve to fail, as why I hoped
Better things in my youth. I simply know
I am no master here, but trained and beaten
Into the path I tread; and here I stay,
Until some further intimation reach me,
Like an obedient drudge: though I prefer
To view the whole thing as a task imposed,
Which, whether dull or pleasant, must be done—
Yet, I deny not, there is made provision

Of joys which tastes less jaded might affect;
Nay, some which please me too, for all my pride—
Pleasures that once were pains: the iron ring
Festering about a slave's neck grows at length
Part of the flesh it eats, I hate no more
A host of petty, vile delights, undreamed of,
Or spurned, before; such now supply the place
Of my dead aims: as in the autumn woods
Where tall trees used to flourish, from their roots
Springs up a fungous brood, sickly and pale,
Chill mushrooms, coloured like a corpse's cheek.
   Fest. If I interpret well what words I seize,
It troubles me but little that your aims,
Vast in their dawning, and most likely grown
Extravagantly since, have baffled you.
Perchance I am glad; you merit greater praise;
Because they are too glorious to be gained,
You do not blindly cling to them and die;
You fell, but have not sullenly refused
To rise, because an angel worsted you
In wrestling, though the world holds not your peer,
And though too harsh and sudden is the change
To yield content as yet—still, you pursue
The ungracious path as though 'twere rosy-strewn.
'Tis well: and your reward, or soon or late,
Will come from Him whom no man serves in vain.
   Par. Ah, very fine! For my part, I conceive
The very pausing from all further toil,
Which you find heinous, would be as a seal
To the sincerity of all my deeds.
To be consistent I should die at once;
I calculated on no after-life;
Yet (how crept in, how fostered, I know not)
Here am I with as passionate regret
For youth, and health, and love so vainly lost,
As if their preservation had been first
And foremost in my thoughts; and this strange fact
Humbled me wondrously, and had due force
In rendering me the more disposed to follow
A certain counsel, a mysterious warning—
You will not understand—but 'twas a man
With aims not mine, but yet pursued like mine,
With the same fervor and no more success,

Who perished in my sight; but summoned me
As I would shun the ghastly fate I saw,
To serve my race at once; to wait no longer
'Till God should interfere in my behalf,
And let the next world's knowledge dawn on this;
But to distrust myself, put pride away,
And give my gains, imperfect as they were,
To men. I have not leisure to explain
How since, a strange succession of events
Has raised me to the station you behold,
Wherein I seem to turn to most account
The mere wreck of the past,—perhaps receive
Some feeble glimmering token that God views
And may approve my penance: therefore here
You find me—doing most good or least harm:
And if folks wonder much and profit little
'Tis not my fault; only, I shall rejoice
When my part in the farce is shuffled through,
And the curtain falls; I must hold out till then.
    Fest. 'Till when, dear Aureole?
    Par.   'Till I'm fairly thrust
From my proud eminence. Fortune is fickle
And even professors fall: should that arrive,
I see no sin in ceding to my bent.
You little fancy what rude shocks apprize us
We sin: God's intimations rather fail
In clearness than in energy: 'twere well
Did they but indicate the course to take
Like that to be forsaken. I would fain
Be spared a further sample! Here I stand,
And here I stay, be sure, till forced to flit.
    Fest. Remain but firm on that head; long ere then
All I expect will come to pass, I trust:
The cloud that wraps you will have disappeared.
Meantime, I see small chance of such event:
They praise you here as one whose lore, divulged
Already, eclipses all the past can show,
But whose achievements, marvellous as they be,
Are faint anticipations of a glory
About to be revealed. When Basil's crowds
Dismiss their teacher, I shall be content
That he depart.
    Par.   This favour at their hands

I look for earlier than your view of things
Would warrant. Of the crowd you saw to-day
Remove the full half sheer amazement draws,
The novelty, nought else; and next, the tribe
Whose innate blockish dullness just perceives
That unless miracles (as seem my works)
Be wrought in their behalf, their chance is slight
To puzzle the devil; next, the numerous set
Who bitterly hate established schools, so help
The teacher that oppugns them, and o'erthrows,
Till having planted his own doctrine, he
May reckon on their rancour in his turn.
Take, too, the sprinkling of sagacious knaves
Whose cunning runs not counter to the vogue,
But seeks, by flattery and nursing craft,
To force my system to a premature
Short-lived development . . . Why swell the list?
Each has his end to serve, and his best way
Of serving it: remove all these, remains
A scantling—a poor dozen at the best—
That really come to learn for learning's sake;
Worthy to look for sympathy and service,
And likely to draw profit from my pains.
    Fest. 'Tis no encouraging picture: still these few
Redeem their fellows. Once implant the germ,
Its growth, if slow, is sure.
    Par.   God grant it so!
I would make some amends: but if I fail,
The luckless rogues have this excuse to urge,
That much is in my method and my manner,
My uncouth habits, my impatient spirit,
Which hinders of reception and result
My doctrine: much to say, small skill to speak!
Those old aims suffered not a looking-off,
Though for an instant; therefore, only when
I thus renounced them and resolved to reap
Some present fruit—to teach mankind some truth
So dearly purchased—only then I found
Such teaching was an art requiring cares
And qualities peculiar to itself;
That to possess was one thing—to display,
Another. Had renown been in my thoughts,
Or popular praise, I had soon discovered it!

One grows but little apt to learn these things.
   Fest. If it be so, which nowise I believe,
There needs no waiting fuller dispensation
To leave a labour to so little use:
Why not throw up the irksome charge at once?
   Par. A task, a task! . . .
                   But wherefore hide from you
The whole extent of degradation, once
Engaged in the confession? Spite of all
My fine talk of obedience, and repugnance,
Docility, and what not, 'tis yet to learn
If when the old task really is performed,
And my will free once more, to choose a new,
I shall do aught but slightly modify
The nature of the hated one I quit.
In plain words, I am spoiled: my life still tends
As first it tended. I am broken and trained
To my old habits; they are part of me.
I know, and none so well, my darling ends
Are proved impossible: no less, no less
Even now what humours me, fond fool, as when
Their faint ghosts sit with me, and flatter me,
And send me back content to my dull round?
How can I change this soul?—this apparatus
Constructed solely for their purposes,
So well adapted to their every want,
To search out and discover, prove and perfect;
This intricate machine, whose most minute,
Least obvious motions have their charm to me
Though to none else—an aptitude I seize,
An object I perceive, a use, a meaning,
A property, a fitness, I explain,
And I alone:—how can I change my soul?
And this wronged body, worthless save when tasked
Under that soul's dominion—used to care
For its bright master's cares, and quite subdue
Its proper cravings—not to ail, nor pine,
So the soul prosper—whither drag this poor,
Tried, patient body? God! how I essayed,
To live like that mad poet, for awhile,
To catch Aprile's spirit, as I hoped,
And love alone! and how I felt too warped
And twisted and deformed! what should I do,

Even tho' released from drudgery, but return
Faint, as you see, and halting, blind and sore,
To my old life—and die as I begun!
I cannot feed on beauty, for the sake
Of beauty only; nor can drink in balm
From lovely objects for their loveliness;
My nature cannot lose her first intent;
I still must hoard, and heap, and class all truths
With one ulterior purpose: I must know!
Would God translate me to his throne, believe
That I should only listen to his words
To further my own aims! For other men,
Beauty is prodigally strewn around,
And I were happy could I quench as they
This mad and thriveless longing, be content
With beauty for itself alone: alas!
I have addressed a frock of heavy mail,
Yet may not join the troop of sacred knights;
And now the forest-creatures fly from me,
The grass-banks cool, the sunbeams warm no more!
Best follow, dreaming that ere night arrives
I shall o'ertake the company, and ride
Glittering as they!
    Fest.   I think I apprehend
What you would say: if you, in truth, design
To enter once more on the life thus left,
Seek not to hide that all this consciousness
Of failure is assumed.
    Par.   My friend, my friend,
I speak, you listen; I explain, perhaps
You understand: there our communion ends.
Have you learnt nothing from to-day's discourse?
When we would thoroughly know the sick man's state
We feel awhile the fluttering pulse, press soft
The hot brow, look upon the languid eye,
And thence divine the rest. Must I lay bare
My heart, hideous and beating, or tear up
My vitals for your gaze, ere you will deem
Enough made known? You! who are you, forsooth?
That is the crowning operation claimed
By the arch-demonstrator—heaven the hall,
And earth the audience. Let Aprile and you
Secure good places—'twill be worth your while.

Fest. Are you mad, Aureole? What can I have said
To call for this? I judged from your own words.

Par. Oh, true! A fevered wretch describes the ape
That mocks him from the bed-foot, and you turn
All gravely thither at once; or he recounts
The perilous journey he has late performed,
And you are puzzled much how that could be!
You find me here, half stupid and half mad:
It makes no part of my delight to search
Into these things, much less to undergo
Another's scrutiny; but so it chances
That I am led to trust my state to you:
And the event is, you combine, contrast,
And ponder on my foolish words, as though
They thoroughly conveyed all hidden here—
Here, loathsome with despair, and hate, and rage!
Is there no fear, no shrinking, or no shame?
Will you guess nothing? will you spare me nothing?
Must I go deeper? Aye or no?

 Fest.   Dear friend . . .

 Par. True: I am brutal—'tis a part of it;
The plague's sign—you are not a lazar-haunter,
How should you know? Well then, you think it strange
I should profess to have failed utterly,
And yet propose an ultimate return
To courses void of hope: and this, because
You know not what temptation is, nor how
'Tis like to ply men in the sickliest part.
You are to understand, that we who make
Sport for the gods, are hunted to the end:
There is not one sharp volley shot at us,
Which if we manage to escape with life,
Though touched and hurt, we straight may slacken pace
And gather by the way-side herbs and roots
To staunch our wounds, secure from further harm—
No; we are chased to life's extremest verge.
It will be well indeed if I return,
A harmless busy fool, to my old ways!
I would forget hints of another fate,
Significant enough, which silent hours
Have lately scared me with.

 Fest.   Another! and what?

 Par. After all, Festus, you say well: I stand

A man yet—I need never humble me.
I would have been—something, I know not what:
But though I cannot soar, I do not crawl:
There are worse portions than this one of mine;
You say well!
    Fest.   Ah! . . .
    Par.   And deeper degradation!
If the mean stimulants of vulgar praise,
And vanity, should become the chosen food
Of a sunk mind; should stifle even the wish
To find its early aspirations true;
Should teach it to breathe falsehood like life-breath—
An atmosphere of craft, and trick, and lies;
Should make it proud to emulate or surpass
Base natures in the practices which woke
Its most indignant loathing once . . . No, no!
Utter damnation is reserved for Hell!
I had immortal feelings—such shall never
Be wholly quenched—no, no!
                    My friend, you wear
A melancholy face, and truth to speak,
There's little cheer in all this dismal work;
But 'twas not my desire to set abroach
Such memories and forebodings. I foresaw
Where they would drive; 'twere better you detailed
News of Lucerne or Zurich; or I described
Great Egypt's flaring sky, or Spain's cork-groves.
    Fest. I have thought now: yes, this mood will pass away.
I know you, and the lofty spirit you bear,
And easily ravel out a clue to all.
These are the trials meet for such as you,
Nor must you hope exemption: to be mortal
Is to be plied with trials manifold.
Look round! The obstacles which kept the rest
Of men from your ambition, you have spurned;
Their fears, their doubts, the chains that bind them best,
Were flax before your resolute soul, which nought
Avails to awe, save these delusions, bred
From its own strength, its selfsame strength, disguised—
Mocking itself. Be brave, dear Aureole! Since
The rabbit has his shade to frighten him,
The fawn his rustling bough, mortals their cares,
And higher natures yet their power to laugh

At these entangling fantasies, as you
At trammels of a weaker intellect.
Measure your mind's height by the shade it casts!
I know you.
  Par.   And I know you, dearest Festus!
And how you love unworthily; and how
All admiration renders blind.
  Fest.   You hold
That admiration blinds?
  Par.   Aye, and alas!
  Fest. Nought blinds you less than admiration will.
Whether it be that all love renders wise
In its degree; from love which blends with love—
Heart answering heart—to love which spends itself
In silent mad idolatry of some
Pre-eminent mortal, some great soul of souls,
Which ne'er will know how well it is adored:—
I say, such love is never blind; but rather
Alive to every the minutest spot
Which mars its object, and which hate (supposed
So vigilant and searching) dreams not of:
Love broods on such: what then? When first perceived
Is there no sweet strife to forget, to change,
To overflush those blemishes with all
The glow of general goodness they disturb?
—To make those very defects an endless source
Of new affection grown from hopes and fears?
And, when all fails, is there no gallant stand
Made even for much proved weak? no shrinking-back
Lest, rising even as its idol sinks,
It nearly reach the sacred place, and stand
Almost a rival of that idol? Trust me,
If there be fiends who seek to work our hurt,
To ruin and drag down earth's mightiest spirits,
Even at God's foot, 'twill be from such as love,
Their zeal will gather most to serve their cause;
At least from those who hate, who most essay
By contumely and scorn to blot the light
Which will have entrance even to their hearts;
For thence will our Defender tear the veil
And show within each heart, as in a shrine,
The giant image of Perfection, grown
In hate's despite, whose calumnies were spawned

In the untroubled presence of its eyes!
True admiration blinds not; nor am I
So blind: I call your sin exceptional;
It springs from one whose life has passed the bounds
Prescribed to life. Compound that fault with God!
I speak of men; to common men like me
The weakness you confess endears you more—
Like the far traces of decay in suns:
I bid you have good cheer!
    Par.   *Præclarè! Optimè!*
Think of a quiet mountain-cloistered priest
Instructing Paracelsus! yet, 'tis so.
Come, I will show you where my merit lies.
'Tis in the advance of individual minds
That the slow crowd should ground their expectation
Eventually to follow—as the sea
Waits ages in its bed, 'till some one wave
Out of the multitude aspires, extends
The empire of the whole, some feet perhaps,
Over the strip of sand which would confine
Its fellows so long time: thenceforth the rest,
Even to the meanest, hurry in at once,
And so much is clear gained. I shall be glad
If all my labours, failing of aught else,
Suffice to make such inroad, and procure
A wider range for thought: nay, they do this;
For, whatsoe'er my notions of true knowledge
And a legitimate success may be,
I am not blind to my undoubted rank
When classed with others: I precede my age:
And whoso wills, is very free to mount
These labours as a platform, whence their own
May have a prosperous outset: but, alas!
My followers—they are noisy as you heard,
But for intelligence—the best of them
So clumsily wield the weapons I supply
And they extol, that I begin to doubt
Whether their own rude clubs and pebble-stones
Would not do better service than my arms
Thus vilely swayed—if error will not fall
Sooner before the old awkward batterings
Than my more subtle warfare, not half learned.
    Fest. I would supply that art, then, and withhold

Its arms until you have taught their mystery.
   Par.   Content you, 'tis my wish; I have recourse
To the simplest training. Day by day I seek
To wake the mood, the spirit which alone
Can make those arms of any use to men.
Of course, they are for swaggering forth at once
Graced with Ulysses' club, Achilles' shield—
Flash on us, all in armour, thou Achilles!
Make our hearts dance to thy resounding step!
A proper sight to scare the crows away!
   Fest.   Pity you choose not, then, some other method
Of coming at your point. The marvellous art
At length established in the world bids fair
To remedy all hindrances like these:
Trust to Frobenius' press the precious lore
Obscured by uncouth manner, or unfit
For raw beginners; let his types secure
A deathless monument to after-times;
Meanwhile wait confidently and enjoy
The ultimate effect: sooner or later,
You shall be all-revealed.
   Par.   The old dull question
In a new form; no more. Thus: I possess
Two sorts of knowledge; one,—vast, shadowy,
Hints of the unbounded aim I once pursued:
The other consists of many secrets, learned
While bent on nobler prize,—perhaps a few
First principles which may conduct to much:
These last I offer to my followers here.
Now bid me chronicle the first of these,
My ancient study, and in effect you bid me
Revert to the wild courses just abjured:
I must go find them scattered through the world.
Then, for the principles, they are so simple
(Being chiefly of the overturning sort),
That one time is as proper to propound them
As any other—to-morrow at my class,
Or half a century hence embalmed in print:
For if mankind intend to learn at all,
They must begin by giving faith to them,
And acting on them; and I do not see
But that my lectures serve indifferent well:
No doubt these dogmas fall not to the earth,

For all their novelty and rugged setting.
I think my class will not forget the day
I let them know the gods of Israel,
Aëtius, Oribasius, Galen, Rhasis,
Serapion, Avicenna, Averröes,—
Were blocks!
    Fest.   And that reminds me, I heard something
About your waywardness: you burned their books,
It seems, instead of answering those sages.
    Par. And who said that?
    Fest.   Some I met yesternight
With Œcolampadius. As you know, the purpose
Of this short stay at Basil was to learn
His pleasure touching certain missives sent
For our Zuinglius and himself. 'Twas he
Apprized me that the famous teacher here
Was my old friend.
    Par.   Ah, I forgot; you went . . .
    Fest. From Zurich with advices for the ear
Of Luther, now at Wittemburg—(you know,
I make no doubt, the differences of late
With Carolostadius)—and returning sought
Basil and . . .
    Par.   I remember. Here's a case, now,
Will teach you why I answer not, but burn
The books you mention: pray, does Luther dream
His arguments convince by their own force
The crowds that own his doctrine? No, indeed:
His plain denial of established points
Ages had sanctified and men supposed
Could never be oppugned while earth was under
And heaven above them—points which chance, or time
Affected not—did more than the array
Of argument which followed. Boldly deny!
There is much breath-stopping, hair-stiffening
Awhile; then, amazed glances, mute awaiting
The thunderbolt which does not come; and next,
Reproachful wonder and enquiry: those
Who else had never stirred, are able now
To find the rest out for themselves—perhaps
To outstrip him who set the whole at work,
—As never will my wise class its instructor.
And you saw Luther?

Fest.   'Tis a wondrous soul!
Par.   True: the so-heavy chain which galled mankind
Is shattered, and the noblest of us all
Must bow to the deliverer—nay, the worker
Of our own projects—we who long before
Had burst its trammels, but forgot the crowd,
We should have taught, still groaned beneath the load:
This he has done and nobly. Speed that may!
Whatever be my chance or my despair,
What benefits mankind must glad me too:
And men seem made, though not as I believed,
For something better than the times produce:
Witness these gangs of peasants your new lights
From Suabia have possessed, whom Munzer leads,
And whom the duke, the landgrave, and the elector
Will calm in blood! Well, well—'tis not my world!
     Fest.   Hark!
     Par.   'Tis the melancholy wind astir
Within the trees: the embers too are grey,
Morn must be near.
     Fest.   Best ope the casement: see,
The night, late strewn with clouds and flying stars,
Is blank and motionless: how peaceful sleep
The tree-tops all together! Like an asp,
The wind slips whispering from bough to bough.
     Par.   Ay; you would gaze on a wind-shaken tree
By the hour, nor count time lost.
     Fest.   So you shall gaze:
Those happy times will come again . . .
     Par.   Gone! gone!
Those pleasant times! Does not the moaning wind
Seem to bewail that we have gained such gains
And bartered sleep for them?
     Fest.   It is our trust
That there is yet another world to mend
All error and mischance.
     Par.   Another world!
And why this world, this common world, to be
A make-shift, a mere foil, how fair soever,
To some fine life to come? Man must be fed
With angel's food, forsooth; and some few traces
Of a diviner nature which look out
Through his corporeal baseness, warrant him

In a supreme contempt for all provision
For his inferior tastes—some straggling marks
Which constitute his essence, just as truly
As here and there a gem would constitute
The rock, their barren bed, a diamond.
But were it so—were man all mind—he gains
A station little enviable. From God
Down to the lowest spirit ministrant,
Intelligence exists which casts our mind
Into immeasurable shade. No, no:
Love, hope, fear, faith—these make humanity;
These are its signs, and note, and character;
And these I have lost!—gone, shut from me for ever,
Like a dead friend, safe from unkindness more!
See morn at length. The heavy darkness seems
Diluted; grey and clear without the stars;
The shrubs bestir and rouse themselves, as if
Some snake that weighed them down all night, let go
His hold; and from the east, fuller and fuller
Day, like a mighty river, is flowing in;
But clouded, wintry, desolate, and cold:
Yet see how that broad, prickly, star-shaped plant,
Half down in the crevice, spreads its woolly leaves,
All thick and glistening with diamond dew.
And you depart for Einsiedeln this day:
And we have spent all night in talk like this!
If you would have me better for your love,
Revert no more to these sad themes.

   Fest.   One favour,
And I have done. I leave you, deeply moved;
Unwilling to have fared so well, the while
My friend has changed so sorely: if this mood
Shall pass away—if light once more arise
Where all is darkness now—if you see fit
To hope, and trust again, and strive again;
You will remember—not our love alone—
But that my faith in God's desire for man
To trust on his support, (as I must think
You trusted,) is obscured and dim through you;
For you are thus, and this is no reward.
Will you not call me to your side, dear friend?

IV. PARACELSUS ASPIRES

Scene.—*A House at Colmar, in Alsatia.* 1528

PARACELSUS, FESTUS

Par. (*To John Oporinus, his secretary.*) *Sic itur ad astra !*
    Dear Von Visenburg
Is scandalised, and poor Torinus paralysed,
And every honest soul that Basil holds
Aghast; and yet we live, as one may say,
Just as though Liechtenfels had never set
So true a value on his sorry carcass,
And learned Pütter had not frowned us dumb.
We live; and shall as surely start to-morrow
For Nuremburg, as we drink speedy scathe
To Basil in this mantling wine, suffused
With a delicate blush—no fainter tinge is born
I' th' shut heart of a bud: pledge me, good John—
" Basil; a hot plague ravage it, with Pütter
" To stop the plague!" Even so? Do you too share
Their panic—the reptiles? Ha, ha! faint through *them,*
Desist for *them !*—while means enough exist
To bow the stoutest braggart of the tribe
Once more in crouching silence—means to breed
A stupid wonder in each fool again,
Now big with admiration at the skill
Which stript a vain pretender of his plumes;
And, that done, means to brand each slavish brow
So deeply, surely, ineffaceably,
That thenceforth flattery shall not pucker it
Out of the furrow of that hideous stamp
Which shows the next they fawn on, what they are,
This Basil with its magnates one and all,
Whom I curse soul and limb. And now dispatch,
Dispatch my trusty John; and what remains
To do, whate'er arrangements for our trip
Are yet to be completed, see you hasten
This night; we'll weather the storm at least: to-morrow
For Nuremburg! Now leave us; this grave clerk
Has divers weighty matters for my ear, (*Oporinus goes out*)
And spare my lungs. At last, my gallant Festus,

I am rid of this arch-knave that follows me
As a gaunt crow a gasping sheep; at last
May give a loose to my delight. How kind,
How very kind, my first, best, only friend!
Why this looks like fidelity. Embrace me:
Not a hair silvered yet! Right: you shall live
Till I am worth your love; you shall be proud,
And I—but let time show. Did you not wonder?
I sent to you because our compact weighed
Upon my conscience—(you recal the night
At Basil, which the gods confound)—because
Once more I aspire! I call you to my side;
You come. You thought my message strange?
    Fest.   So strange
That I must hope, indeed, your messenger
Has mingled his own fancies with the words
Purporting to be yours.
    Par.   He said no more,
'Tis probable, than the precious folks I leave
Said fifty-fold more roughly. Well-a-day,
'Tis true; poor Paracelsus is exposed
At last; a most egregious quack he proves,
And those he overreached must spit their hate
On one who, utterly beneath contempt,
Could yet deceive their topping wits. You heard
Bare truth; and at my bidding you come here
To speed me on my enterprise, as once
Your lavish wishes sped me, my own friend?
    Fest. What is your purpose, Aureole?
    Par.   Oh, for purpose,
There is no lack of precedents in a case
Like mine; at least, if not precisely mine,
The case of men cast off by those they sought
To benefit . . .
    Fest.   They really cast you off?
I only heard a vague tale of some priest,
Cured by your skill, who wrangled at your claim,
Knowing his life's worth best; and how the judge
The matter was referred to, saw no cause
To interfere, nor you to hide your full
Contempt of him; nor he, again, to smother
His wrath thereat, which raised so fierce a flame
That Basil soon was made no place for you.

Par.　The affair of Liechtenfels? the shallowest cause,
The last and silliest outrage—mere pretence!
I knew it, I foretold it from the first,
How soon the stupid wonder you mistook
For genuine loyalty—a cheering promise
Of better things to come—would pall and pass;
And every word comes true.　Saul is among
The prophets!　Just so long as I was pleased
To play off the mere marvels of my art—
Fantastic gambols leading to no end—
I got huge praise; but one can ne'er keep down
Our foolish nature's weakness: there they flocked,
Poor devils, jostling, swearing, and perspiring,
Till the walls rang again; and all for me!
I had a kindness for them, which was right;
But then I stopped not till I tacked to that
A trust in them and a respect—a sort
Of sympathy for them: I must needs begin
To teach them, not amaze them; " to impart
" The spirit which should instigate the search
" Of truth: " just what you bade me! I spoke out.
Forthwith a mighty squadron, in disgust,
Filed off—" the sifted chaff of the sack," I said,
Redoubling my endeavours to secure
The rest; when lo! one man had stayed thus long
Only to ascertain if I supported
This tenet of his, or that; another loved
To hear impartially before he judged,
And having heard, now judged; this bland disciple
Passed for my dupe, but all along, it seems,
Spied error where his neighbours marvelled most:
That fiery doctor who had hailed me friend,
Did it because my bye-paths, once proved wrong
And beaconed properly, would commend again
The good old ways our sires jogged safely o'er,
Though not their squeamish sons; the other worthy
Discovered divers verses of St. John,
Which, read successively, refreshed the soul,
But, muttered backwards, cured the gout, the stone,
The cholic, and what not:—*quid multa ?*　The end
Was a clear class-room, with a quiet leer
From grave folk, and a sour reproachful glance
From those in chief, who, cap in hand, installed

The new professor scarce a year before;
And a vast flourish about patient merit
Obscured awhile by flashy tricks, but sure
Sooner or later to emerge in splendour—
Of which the example was some luckless wight
Whom my arrival had discomfited,
But now, it seems, the general voice recalled
To fill my chair, and so efface the stain
Basil had long incurred. I sought no better—
Nought but a quiet dismissal from my post;
While from my heart I wished them better suited,
And better served. Good night to Basil, then!
But fast as I proposed to rid the tribe
Of my obnoxious back, I could not spare them
The pleasure of a parting kick.
    Fest.   You smile:
Despise them as they merit!
    Par.   If I smile,
'Tis with as very contempt as ever turned
Flesh into stone: this courteous recompense;
This grateful . . . Festus, were your nature fit
To be defiled, your eyes the eyes to ache
At gangrened blotches, eating poisonous blains,
The ulcered barky scurf of leprosy
Which finds—a man, and leaves—a hideous thing
That cannot but be mended by hell fire,
—I say that, could you see as I could show,
I would lay bare to you these human hearts
Which God cursed long ago, and devils make since
Their pet nest and their never-tiring home.
O, sages have discovered we are born
For various ends—to love, to know: has ever
One stumbled, in his search, on any signs
Of a nature in him formed to hate? To hate?
If that be our true object which evokes
Our powers in fullest strength, be sure 'tis hate!
    Fest.   But I have yet to learn your purpose, Aureole!
    Par.   What purpose were the fittest now for me?
Decide! To sink beneath such ponderous shame—
To shrink up like a crushed snail—undergo
In silence and desist from further toil,
And so subside into a monument
Of one their censure blasted; or to bow

Cheerfully as submissively—to lower
My old pretensions even as Basil dictates—
To drop into the rank her wits assign me,
And live as they prescribe, and make that use
Of my poor knowledge which their rules allow—
Proud to be patted now and then, and careful
To practise the true posture for receiving
The amplest benefit from their hoofs' appliance,
When they shall condescend to tutor me.
Then one may feel resentment like a flame,
Prompting to deck false systems in Truth's garb,
And tangle and entwine mankind with error,
And give them darkness for a dower, and falsehood
For a possession: or one may mope away
Into a shade through thinking; or else drowse
Into a dreamless sleep, and so die off:
But I, but I—now Festus shall divine!
—Am merely setting out in life once more,
Embracing my old aims!   What thinks he now?
    Fest.   Your aims? the aims?—to know? and where is
        found
The early trust . . .
    Par.   Nay, not so fast; I say,
The aims—not the old means.   You know what made me
A laughing-stock; I was a fool; you know
The when and the how: hardly those means again!
Not but they had their beauty—who should know
Their passing beauty, if not I?   But still
They were dreams, so let them vanish: yet in beauty,
If that may be.   Stay—thus they pass in song!

    (*He sings.*)
        Heap cassia, sandal-buds, and stripes
            Of labdanum, and aloe-balls
        Smeared with dull nard an Indian wipes
            From out her hair: (such balsam falls
            Down sea-side mountain pedestals,
        From summits where tired winds are fain,
        Spent with the vast and howling main,
        To treasure half their island-gain.)

        And strew faint sweetness from some old
            Egyptian's fine worm-eaten shroud,

Which breaks to dust when once unrolled;
   And shred dim perfume, like a cloud
   From chamber long to quiet vowed,
With mothed and dropping arras hung,
Mouldering the lute and books among
Of queen, long dead, who lived there young.

Mine, every word!—and on such pile shall die
My lovely fancies, with fair perished things,
Themselves fair and forgotten; yes, forgotten,
Or why abjure them? So I made this rhyme
That fitting dignity might be preserved:
No little proud was I; though the list of drugs
Smacks of my old vocation, and the verse
Halts like the best of Luther's psalms!
   Fest.   But, Aureole,
Talk not thus wildly and madly. I am here—
Did you know all, indeed! I have travelled far
To learn your wishes. Be yourself again!
For in this mood I recognize you less
Than in the horrible despondency
I witnessed last. You may account this, joy;
But rather let me gaze on that despair
Than hear these incoherent words, and see
This flushed cheek and intensely-sparkling eye!
   Par. Why, man, I was light-hearted in my prime,
I am light-hearted now; what would you have?
Aprile was a poet, I make songs—
'Tis the very augury of success I want!
Why should I not be joyous now as then?
   Fest. Joyous! and how? and what remains for joy?
You have declared the ends (which I am sick
Of naming) are impracticable.
   Par.   Aye,
Pursued as I pursued them—the arch-fool!
Listen: my plan will please you not, 'tis like;
But you are little versed in the world's ways.
This is my plan—(first drinking its good luck)—
I will accept all helps; all I despised
So rashly at the outset, equally
With early impulses, late years have quenched:
I have tried each way singly—now for both!
All helps—no one sort shall exclude the rest.

I seek to KNOW and to ENJOY at once,
Not one without the other as before.
Suppose my labour should seem God's own cause
Once more, as first I dreamed, it shall not balk me
Of the meanest, earthliest, sensualest delight
That may be snatched; for every joy is gain,
And why spurn gain, however small? My soul
Can die then, nor be taunted " what was gained?"
Nor, on the other hand, if pleasure meets me
As though I had not spurned her hitherto,
Shall she o'ercloud my spirit's rapt communion
With the tumultuous past, the teeming future,
Glorious with visions of a full success!

    Fest. Success!

    Par. And wherefore not? Why not prefer
Results obtained in my best state of being,
To those derived alone from seasons dark
As the thoughts they bred? When I was best—my youth
Unwasted—seemed success not surest too?
It is the nature of darkness to obscure.
I am a wanderer: I remember well
One journey, how I feared the track was missed,
So long the city I desired to reach
Lay hid; when suddenly its spires afar
Flashed through the circling clouds; conceive my joy!
Too soon the vapours closed o'er it again,
But I had seen the city, and one such glance
No darkness could obscure: nor shall the present,
A few dull hours, a passing shame or two,
Destroy the vivid memories of the past.
I will fight the battle out!—a little tired,
Perhaps—but still an able combatant.
You look at my grey hair and furrowed brow?
But I can turn even weakness to account:
Of many tricks I know, 'tis not the least
To push the ruins of my frame, whereon
The fire of vigour trembles scarce alive,
Into a heap, and send the flame aloft!
What should I do with age? so sickness lends
An aid; it being, I fear, the source of all
We boast of: mind is nothing but disease,
And natural health is ignorance.

    Fest. I see

But one good symptom in this notable plan:
I feared your sudden journey had in view
To wreak immediate vengeance on your foes;
'Tis not so: I am glad.
 Par.   And if I pleased
To spit on them, to trample them, what then?
'Tis sorry warfare truly, but the fools
Provoke it: I had spared their self-conceit,
But if they must provoke me—cannot suffer
Forbearance on my part—if I may keep
No quality in the shade, must needs put forth
Power to match power, my strength against their strength,
And teach them their own game with their own arms—
Why be it so, and let them take their chance!
I am above them like a God—in vain
To hide the fact—what idle scruples, then,
Were those that ever bade me soften it,
Communicate it gently to the world,
Instead of proving my supremacy,
Taking my natural station o'er their heads,
Then owning all the glory was a man's,
And in my elevation man's would be!
But live and learn, though life's short; learning, hard!
Still, one thing I have learned—not to despair:
And therefore, though the wreck of my past self,
I fear, dear Pütter, that your lecture-room
Must wait awhile for its best ornament,
The penitent empiric, who set up
For somebody, but soon was taught his place—
Now, but too happy to be let confess
His error, snuff the candles, and illustrate
(*Fiat experientia corpore vili*)
Your medicine's soundness in his person. Wait,
Good Pütter!
 Fest.   He who sneers thus, is a God!
 Par. Ay, ay, laugh at me! I am very glad
You are not gulled by all this swaggering; you
Can see the root of the matter!—how I strive
To put a good face on the overthrow
I have experienced, and to bury and hide
My degradation in its length and breadth;
How the mean motives I would make you think
Just mingle as is due with nobler aims,

The appetites I modestly allow
May influence me—as I am mortal still—
Do goad me, drive me on, and fast supplant
My youth's desires: you are no stupid dupe;
You find me out! Yes, I had sent for you
To palm these childish lies upon you, Festus!
Laugh—you shall laugh at me!
  Fest.   The past, then, Aureole,
Proves nothing? Is our interchange of love
Yet to begin? Have I to swear I mean
No flattery in this speech or that? For you,
Whate'er you say, there is no degradation,
These low thoughts are no inmates of your mind;
Or wherefore this disorder? You are vexed
As much by the intrusion of base views,
Familiar to your adversaries, as they
Were troubled should your qualities alight
Amid their murky souls: not otherwise,
A stray wolf which the winter forces down
From our bleak hills, suffices to affright
A village in the vales—while foresters
Sleep calm though all night long the famished troops
Snuff round and scratch against their crazy huts:
These evil thoughts are monsters, and will flee.
  Par. May you be happy, Festus, my own friend!
  Fest. Nay, further; the delights you fain would think
The superseders of your nobler aims,
Though ordinary and harmless stimulants,
Will ne'er content you . . .
  Par.   Hush! I once despised them,
But that soon passes: we are high at first
In our demands, nor will abate a jot
Of toil's strict value; but time passes o'er,
And humbler spirits accept what we refuse;
In short, when some such comfort is doled out
As these delights, we cannot long retain
The bitter contempt which urges us at first
To hurl it back, but hug it to our breast
And thankfully retire. This life of mine
Must be lived out, and a grave thoroughly earned:
I am just fit for that and nought beside.
I told you once, I cannot now Enjoy,
Unless I deem my knowledge gains through joy;

Nor can I Know, but straight warm tears reveal
My need of linking also joy to knowledge:
So on I drive—enjoying all I can,
And knowing all I can. I speak, of course,
Confusedly; this will better explain—feel here!
Quick beating, is it not?—a fire of the heart
To work off someway, this as well as any!
So, Festus sees me fairly launched; his calm
Compassionate look might have disturbed me once,
But now, far from rejecting, I invite
What bids me press the closer, lay myself
Open before him, and be soothed with pity;
And hope, if he command hope; and believe
As he directs me—satiating myself
With his enduring love: and Festus quits me
To give place to some credulous disciple
Who holds that God is wise, but Paracelsus
Has his peculiar merits. I suck in
That homage, chuckle o'er that admiration,
And then dismiss the fool; for night is come,
And I betake myself to study again,
Till patient searchings after hidden lore
Half wring some bright truth from its prison; my frame
Trembles, my forehead's veins swell out, my hair
Tingles for triumph! Slow and sure the morn
Shall break on my pent room, and dwindling lamp,
And furnace dead, and scattered earths and ores,
When, with a failing heart and throbbing brow,
I must review my captured truth, sum up
Its value, trace what ends to what begins,
Its present power with its eventual bearings,
Latent affinities, the views it opens,
And its full length in perfecting my scheme;
I view it sternly circumscribed, cast down
From the high place my fond hopes yielded it,
Proved worthless—which, in getting, yet had cost
Another wrench to this fast-falling frame;
Then, quick, the cup to quaff, that chases sorrow!
I lapse back into youth, and take again
Mere hopes of bliss for proofs that bliss will be,
—My fluttering pulse, for evidence that God
Means good to me, will make my cause his own;
See! I have cast off this remorseless care

Which clogged a spirit born to soar so free,
And my dim chamber has become a tent,
Festus is sitting by me, and his Michal . . .
Why do you start?   I say, she listening here,
(For yonder's Würzburg through the orchard-boughs)
Motions as though such ardent words should find
No echo in a maiden's quiet soul,
But her pure bosom heaves, her eyes fill fast
With tears, her sweet lips tremble all the while!
Ha, ha!
    Fest.   It seems, then, you expect to reap
No unreal joy from this your present course,
But rather . . .
    Par.   Death! To die! I owe that much
To what, at least, I was. I should be sad
To live contented after such a fall—
To thrive and fatten after such reverse!
The whole plan is a makeshift, but will last
My time.
    Fest.   And you have never mused and said,
" I had a noble purpose, and full strength
" To compass it; but I have stopped half-way,
" And wrongly give the first-fruits of my toil
" To objects little worthy of the gift:
" Why linger round them still? why clench my fault?
" Why seek for consolation in defeat—
" In vain endeavours to derive a beauty
" From ugliness? Why seek to make the most
" Of what no power can change, nor strive instead
" With mighty effort to redeem the past,
" And, gathering up the treasures thus cast down,
" To hold a steadfast course till I arrive
" At their fit destination, and my own? "
You have never pondered thus?
    Par.   Have I, you ask?
Often at midnight, when most fancies come,
Would some such airy project visit me:
But ever at the end . . .   or will you hear
The same thing in a tale, a parable?
It cannot prove more tedious; listen then!
You and I, wandering over the world wide,
Chance to set foot upon a desert coast:
Just as we cry, " No human voice before

Broke the inveterate silence of these rocks!"
—Their querulous echo startles us; we turn:
What ravaged structure still looks o'er the sea?
Some characters remain, too! While we read,
The sharp, salt wind, impatient for the last
Of even this record, wistfully comes and goes,
Or sings what we recover, mocking it.
This is the record; and my voice, the wind's.

(*He sings.*)
    Over the sea our galleys went,
With cleaving prows in order brave,
To a speeding wind and a bounding wave—
    A gallant armament:
Each bark built out of a forest-tree,
    Left leafy and rough as first it grew,
And nailed all over the gaping sides,
    Within and without, with black-bull hides,
Seethed in fat and suppled in flame,
To bear the playful billows' game;
So each good ship was rude to see,
Rude and bare to the outward view,
    But each upbore a stately tent;
Where cedar-pales in scented row
Kept out the flakes of the dancing brine:
And an awning drooped the mast below.
In fold on fold of the purple fine,
That neither noon-tide, nor star-shine,
Nor moonlight cold which maketh mad,
    Might pierce the regal tenement.
When the sun dawned, oh, gay and glad
We set the sail and plied the oar;
But when the night-wind blew like breath
For joy of one day's voyage more,
We sang together on the wide sea,
Like men at peace on a peaceful shore;
Each sail was loosed to the wind so free,
Each helm made sure by the twilight star,
And in a sleep as calm as death,
We, the strangers from afar,
    Lay stretched along, each weary crew
In a circle round its wondrous tent,
Whence gleamed soft light and curled rich scent,

And with light and perfume, music too:
So the stars wheeled round, and the darkness past,
And at morn we started beside the mast,
And still each ship was sailing fast!

One morn, the land appeared!—a speck
Dim trembling betwixt sea and sky—
Avoid it, cried our pilot, check
   The shout, restrain the longing eye!
But the heaving sea was black behind
For many a night and many a day,
And land, though but a rock, drew nigh;
So we broke the cedar pales away,
Let the purple awning flap in the wind,
And a statue bright was on every deck!
We shouted, every man of us,
And steered right into the harbour thus,
With pomp and pœan glorious.

An hundred shapes of lucid stone!
   All day we built a shrine for each—
A shrine of rock for every one—
Nor paused we till in the westering sun
   We sate together on the beach
To sing, because our task was done;
When lo! what shouts and merry songs!
What laughter all the distance stirs!
What raft comes loaded with its throngs
Of gentle islanders?
" The isles are just at hand," they cried;
   " Like cloudlets faint at even sleeping,
" Our temple-gates are opened wide,
   " Our olive-groves thick shade are keeping
" For the lucid shapes you bring "—they cried.
Oh, then we woke with sudden start
From our deep dream; we knew, too late,
How bare the rock, how desolate,
To which we had flung our precious freight:
   Yet we called out—" Depart!
" Our gifts, once given, must here abide:
   " Our work is done; we have no heart
" To mar our work, though vain "—we cried.

Fest. In truth?

Par.　　　　　　Nay, wait: all this in tracings faint
May still be read on that deserted rock,
On rugged stones, strewn here and there, but piled
In order once; then follows—mark what follows—
" The sad rhyme of the men who proudly clung
" To their first fault, and withered in their pride! "

Fest. Come back, then, Aureole; as you fear God, come!
This is foul sin; come back: renounce the past,
Forswear the future; look for joy no more,
But wait death's summons amid holy sights,
And trust me for the event—peace, if not joy!
Return with me to Einsiedeln, dear Aureole.

Par. No way, no way: it would not turn to good.
A spotless child sleeps on the flowering moss—
'Tis well for him; but when a sinful man,
Envying such slumber, may desire to put
His guilt away, shall he return at once
To rest by lying there? Our sires knew well
(Spite of the grave discoveries of their sons)
The fitting course for such; dark cells, dim lamps,
A stone floor one may writhe on like a worm;
No mossy pillow, blue with violets!

Fest. I see no symptom of these absolute
And tyrannous passions. You are calmer now,
This verse-making can purge you well enough,
Without the terrible penance you describe.
You love me still: the lusts you fear, will never
Outrage your friend. To Einsiedeln, once more!
Say but the word!

Par.　　　　　　No, no; those lusts forbid:
They crouch, I know, cowering with half-shut eye
Beside you; 'tis their nature. Thrust yourself
Between them and their prey; let some fool style me
Or king or quack, it matters not, and try
Your wisdom then, at urging their retreat!
No, no; learn better and look deeper, Festus!
If you knew how a devil sneers within me
While you are talking now of this, now that,
As though we differed scarcely save in trifles!

Fest. Do we so differ? True, change must proceed,
Whether for good or ill; keep from me, which!
God made you and knows what you may become—

Do not confide all secrets: I was born
To hope, and you . . .
    Par.   To trust: you know the fruits!
    Fest. Listen: I do believe, what you call trust
Was self-reliance at the best: for, see!
So long as God would kindly pioneer
A path for you, and screen you from the world,
Procure you full exemption from man's lot,
Man's common hopes and fears, on the mere pretext
Of your engagement in his service—yield you
A limitless license, make you God, in fact,
And turn your slave—you were content to say
Most courtly praises! What is it, at last,
But selfishness without example? None
Could trace God's will so plain as you, while yours
Remained implied in it; but now you fail,
And we, who prate about that will, are fools!
In short, God's service is established here
As he determines fit, and not your way,
And this you cannot brook! Such discontent
Is weak. Renounce all creatureship at once!
Affirm an absolute right to have and use
Your energies; as though the rivers should say—
" We rush to the ocean; what have we to do
" With feeding streamlets, lingering in the marshes,
" Sleeping in lazy pools? " Set up that plea,
That will be bold at least!
    Par.   Perhaps, perhaps!
Your only serviceable spirits are those
The east produces:—lo, the master nods,
And they raise terraces, spread garden-grounds
In one night's space; and, this done, straight begin
Another century's sleep, to the great praise
Of him that framed them wise and beautiful,
Till a lamp's rubbing, or some chance akin,
Wake them again. I am of different mould.
I would have soothed my lord, and slaved for him,
And done him service past my narrow bond,
And thus I get rewarded for my pains!
Beside, 'tis vain to talk of forwarding
God's glory otherwise; this is alone
The sphere of its increase, as far as men
Increase it; why, then, look beyond this sphere?

We are his glory; and if we be glorious,
Is not the thing achieved?

   Fest.   Shall one like me
Judge hearts like yours? Though years have changed you
   much,
And you have left your first love, and retain
Its empty shade to veil your crooked ways,
Yet I still hold that you have honoured God;
And who shall call your course without reward?
For, wherefore this repining at defeat,
Had triumph ne'er inured you to high hopes?
I urge you to forsake the life you curse,
And what success attends me?—simply talk
Of passion, weakness, and remorse; in short,
Any thing but the naked truth: you choose
This so-despised career, and rather praise
Than take my happiness, or other men's.
Once more, return!

   Par.   And soon. Oporinus
Has pilfered half my secrets by this time:
And we depart by day-break. I am weary,
I know not how; not even the wine-cup soothes
My brain to-night . . .
Do you not thoroughly despise me, Festus?
No flattery! One like you, needs not be told
We live and breathe deceiving and deceived.
Do you not scorn me from your heart of hearts?
Me and my cant—my petty subterfuges—
My rhymes, and all this frothy shower of words—
My glozing, self-deceit—my outward crust
Of lies, which wrap, as tetter, morphew, furfair
Wrap the sound flesh?—so, see you flatter not!
Why, even God flatters! but my friend, at least,
Is true. I would depart, secure henceforth
Against all further insult, hate, and wrong
From puny foes: my one friend's scorn shall brand me—
No fear of sinking deeper!

   Fest.   No, dear Aureole!
No, no; I came to counsel faithfully:
There are old rules, made long ere we were born,
By which I judge you. I, so fallible,
So infinitely low beside your spirit
Mighty, majestic!—even I can see

E ⁴¹

You own some higher law than ours which call
Sin, what is no sin—weakness, what is strength;
But I have only these, such as they are,
To guide me; and I blame you where they blame,
Only so long as blaming promises
To win peace for your soul; the more, that sorrow
Has fallen on me of late, and they have helped me
So that I faint not under my distress.
But wherefore should I scruple to avow
In spite of all, as brother judging brother,
Your fate to me is most inexplicable:
And should you perish without recompense
And satisfaction yet—too hastily
I have relied on love: you may have sinned,
But you have loved. As a mere human matter—
As I would have God deal with fragile men
In the end—I say that you will triumph yet!

   Par.   Have you felt sorrow, Festus?—'tis because
You love me. Sorrow, and sweet Michal yours!
Well thought on; never let her know this last
Dull winding-up of all: these miscreants dared
Insult me—me she loved; so grieve her not.

   Fest.   Your ill success can little grieve her now.

   Par.   Michal is dead! pray Christ we do not craze!

   Fest.   Aureole, dear Aureole, look not on me thus!
Fool, fool! this is the heart grown sorrow-proof—
I cannot bear those eyes.

   Par.   Nay, really dead?

   Fest.   'Tis scarce a month . . .

   Par.   Stone dead!—then you have laid her
Among the flowers ere this. Now, do you know,
I can reveal a secret which shall comfort
Even you. I have no julep, as men think,
To cheat the grave; but a far better secret.
Know then, you did not ill to trust your love
To the cold earth: I have thought much of it:
For I believe we do not wholly die.

   Fest.   Aureole . . .

   Par.   Nay, do not laugh; there is a reason
For what I say: I think the soul can never
Taste death. I am, just now, as you may see,
Very unfit to put so strange a thought
In an intelligible dress of words;

But take it as my trust, she is not dead.
   Fest. But not on this account alone? you surely,
—Aureole, you have believed this all along?
   Par. And Michal sleeps among the roots and dews,
While I am moved at Basil, and full of schemes
For Nuremberg, and hoping and despairing,
As though it mattered how the farce plays out,
So it be quickly played. Away, away!
Have your will, rabble! while we fight the prize,
Troop you in safety to the snug back-seats,
And leave a clear arena for the brave
About to perish for your sport!—Behold!

V. PARACELSUS ATTAINS

Scene.—*A cell in the Hospital of St. Sebastian, at
Salzburg.* 1541

Festus, Paracelsus

   Fest. No change! The weary night is well nigh spent,
The lamp burns low, and through the casement-bars
Grey morning glimmers feebly—yet no change!
Another night, and still no sigh has stirred
That fallen discoloured mouth, no pang relit
Those fixed eyes, quenched by the decaying body,
Like torch-flame choked in dust: while all beside
Was breaking, to the last they held out bright,
As a strong-hold where life intrenched itself;
But they are dead now—very blind and dead.
He will drowse into death without a groan!

My Aureole—my forgotten, ruined Aureole!
The days are gone, are gone! How grand thou wert:
And now not one of those who struck thee down—
Poor, glorious spirit—concerns him even to stay
And satisfy himself his little hand
Could turn God's image to a livid thing.
Another night, and yet no change! 'Tis much
That I should sit by him, and bathe his brow,
And chafe his hands—'tis much; but he will sure
Know me, and look on me, and speak to me

Once more—but only once! His hollow cheek
Looked all night long as though a creeping laugh
At his own state were just about to break
From the dying man: my brain swam, my throat swelled,
And yet I could not turn away. In truth,
They told me how, when first brought here, he seemed
Resolved to live—to lose no faculty;
Thus striving to keep up his shattered strength,
Until they bore him to this stifling cell:
When straight his features fell—an hour made white
The flushed face and relaxed the quivering limb;
Only the eye remained intense awhile,
As though it recognised the tomb-like place;
And then he lay as here he lies.

       Ay, here!
Here is earth's noblest, nobly garlanded—
Her bravest champion, with his well-won meed—
Her best achievement, her sublime amends
For countless generations, fleeting fast
And followed by no trace;—the creature-god
She instances when angels would dispute
The title of her brood to rank with them—
Angels, this is our angel!—those bright forms
We clothe with purple, crown and call to thrones,
Are human, but not his: those are but men
Whom other men press round and kneel before—
Those palaces are dwelt in by mankind;
Higher provision is for him you seek
Amid our pomps and glories: see it here!
Behold earth's paragon! Now, raise thee, clay!

God! Thou art Love! I build my faith on that!
Even as I watch beside thy tortured child,
Unconscious whose hot tears fall fast by him,
So doth thy right hand guide us through the world
Wherein we stumble. God! what shall we say?
How has he sinned? How else should he have done?
Surely he sought thy praise—thy praise, for all
He might be busied by the task so much
As to forget awhile its proper end.
Dost thou well, Lord? Thou canst not but prefer
That I should range myself upon his side—
How could he stop at every step to set

Thy glory forth? Hadst Thou but granted him
Success, thy honour would have crowned success,
A halo round a star. Or, say he erred,—
Save him, dear God; it will be like thee: bathe him
In light and life! Thou art not made like us;
We should be wroth in such a case; but Thou
Forgivest—so, forgive these passionate thoughts,
Which come unsought, and will not pass away!
I know thee, who hast kept my path, and made
Light for me in the darkness—tempering sorrow
So that it reached me like a solemn joy;
It were too strange that I should doubt thy love:
But what am I?   Thou madest him, and knowest
How he was fashioned. I could never err
That way: the quiet place beside thy feet,
Reserved for me, was ever in my thoughts;
But he—Thou shouldst have favoured him as well!

Ah! he wakes! Aureole, I am here—'tis Festus!
I cast away all wishes save one wish—
Let him but know me—only speak to me!
He mutters—louder and louder; any other
Than I, with brain less laden, could collect
What he pours forth. Dear Aureole, do but look!
Is it talking or singing this he utters fast?
Misery, that he should fix me with his eye—
Quick talking to some other all the while!
If he would husband this wild vehemence,
Which frustrates its intent!—I heard, I know
I heard my name amid those rapid words:
O he will know me yet; Could I divert
This current—lead it somehow gently back
Into the channels of the past!—His eye,
Brighter than ever! It must recognise!

Let me speak to him in another's name.
I am Erasmus: I am here to pray
That Paracelsus use his skill for me.
The schools of Paris and of Padua send
These questions for your learning to resolve.
We are your students, noble master: leave
This wretched cell; what business have you here?
Our class awaits you; come to us once more.

(O agony! the utmost I can do
Touches him not; how else arrest his ear?)
I am commissioned . . . I shall craze like him—
Better be mute, and see what God shall send.
      Par. Stay, stay with me!
      Fest.   I will; I am come here
To stay with you—Festus, you loved of old;
Festus, you know, you must know!
      Par.   Festus! Where's
Aprile, then? Has he not chaunted softly
The melodies I heard all night? I could not
Get to him for a cold hand on my breast,
But I made out his music well enough,
O, well enough! If they have filled him full
With magical music, as they freight a star
With light, and have remitted all his sin,
They will forgive me too, I too shall know!
      Fest. Festus, your Festus!
      Par.   Ask him if Aprile
Knows as he Loves—if I shall Love and Know?
I try; but that cold hand, like lead—so cold!
      Fest. My hand, see!
      Par.   Ah, the curse, Aprile, Aprile!
We get so near—so very, very near!
'Tis an old tale: Jove strikes the Titans down
Not when they set about their mountain-piling,
But when another rock would crown their work!
And Phaeton—doubtless his first radiant plunge
Astonished mortals; though the gods were calm,
And Jove prepared his thunder: all old tales!
      Fest. And what are these to you?
      Par.   Ay, fiends must laugh
So cruelly, so well; most like I never
Could tread a single pleasure under foot,
But they were grinning by my side, were chuckling
To see me toil, and drop away by flakes!
Hell-spawn! I am glad, most glad, that thus I fail!
You that hate men and all who wish their good—
Your cunning has o'ershot its aim. One year,
One month, perhaps, and I had served your turn!
You should have curbed your spite awhile. But now,
Who will believe 'twas you that held me back?
Listen: there's shame, and hissing, and contempt,

And none but laughs who names me—none but spits
Measureless scorn upon me—me alone,
The quack, the cheat, the liar,—all on me!
And thus your famous plan to sink mankind
In silence and despair, by teaching them
One of their race had probed the inmost truth,
Had done all man could do, yet failed no less—
Your wise plan proves abortive.   Men despair?
Ha, ha! why they are hooting the empiric,
The ignorant and incapable fool who rushed
Madly upon a work beyond his wits;
Nor doubt they but the simplest of themselves
Could bring the matter to triumphant issue!
So pick and choose among them all, Accursed!
Try now, persuade some other to slave for you,
To ruin body and soul to work your ends:
No, no; I am the first and last, I think!
   Fest.   Dear friend; who are accursed? who has done . . .
   Par.   What have I done? Fiends dare ask that? or you,
Brave men?   Oh, you can chime in boldly, backed
By the others!   What had you to do, sage peers?
Here stand my rivals, truly—Arab, Jew,
Greek, join dead hands against me: all I ask
Is, that the world enrol my name with theirs,
And even this poor privilege, it seems,
They range themselves, prepared to disallow!
Only observe: why fiends may learn from them!
How they talk calmly of my throes—my fierce
Aspirings, terrible watchings—each one claiming
Its price of blood and brain; how they dissect
And sneeringly disparage the few truths
Got at a life's cost; they too hanging the while
About my neck, their lies misleading me,
And their dead names brow-beating me! Grey crew,
Yet steeped in fresh malevolence from hell,
Is there a reason for your hate?   My truths
Have shaken a little the palm about each head?
Just think, Aprile, all these leering dotards
Were bent on nothing less than being crowned
As we!   That yellow blear-eyed wretch in chief,
To whom the rest cringe low with feigned respect—
Galen, of Pergamos and hell; nay speak
The tale, old man!   We met there face to face:

I said the crown should fall from thee: once more
We meet as in that ghastly vestibule:
Look to my brow! Have I redeemed my pledge?
   Fest. Peace, peace; ah, see!
   Par.   Oh, emptiness of fame!
Oh Persic Zoroaster, lord of stars!
—Who said these old renowns, dead long ago,
Could make me overlook the living world
To gaze through gloom at where they stood, indeed,
But stand no longer? What a warm light life
After the shade! In truth, my delicate witch,
My serpent-queen, you did but well to hide
The juggles I had else detected. Fire
May well run harmless o'er a breast like yours!
The cave was not so darkened by the smoke
But that your white limbs dazzled me: Oh, white,
And panting as they twinkled, wildly dancing!
I cared not for your passionate gestures then,
But now I have forgotten the charm of charms,
The foolish knowledge which I came to seek,
While I remember that quaint dance; and thus
I am come back, not for those mummeries,
But to love you, and to kiss your little feet,
Soft as an ermine's winter coat!
   Fest.   A sense
Will struggle through these thronging words at last,
As in the angry and tumultuous west
A soft star trembles through the drifting clouds.
These are the strivings of a spirit which hates
So sad a vault should coop it, and calls up
The past to stand between it and its fate:
Were he at Einsiedeln—or Michal here!
   Par. Cruel! I see her now—I kneel—I shriek—
I clasp her vesture—but she fades, still fades;
And she is gone; sweet human love is gone!
'Tis only when they spring to heaven that angels
Reveal themselves to you; they sit all day
Beside you, and lie down at night by you.
Who care not for their presence—muse or sleep—
And all at once they leave you and you know them!
We are so fooled, so cheated! Why, even now
I am not too secure against foul play:
The shadows deepen, and the walls contract—

No doubt some treachery is going on!
'Tis very dusk. Where are we put, Aprile?
Have they left us in the lurch? This murky, loathsome
Death-trap—this slaughter-house—is not the hall
In the golden city! Keep by me, Aprile!
There is a hand groping amid the blackness
To catch us. Have the spider-fingers got you,
Poet? Hold on me for your life; if once
They pull you!—Hold!
                           'Tis but a dream—no more.
I have you still—the sun comes out again;
Let us be happy—all will yet go well!
Let us confer: is it not like, Aprile,
That spite of trouble, this ordeal passed,
The value of my labours ascertained,
Just as some stream foams long among the rocks
But after glideth glassy to the sea,
So, full content shall henceforth be my lot?
What think you, poet? Louder! Your clear voice
Vibrates too like a harp-string. Do you ask
How could I still remain on earth, should God
Grant me the great approval which I seek?
I, you, and God can comprehend each other,
But men would murmur, and with cause enough;
For when they saw me, stainless of all sin,
Preserved and sanctified by inward light,
They would complain that comfort, shut from them,
I drank thus unespied; that they live on,
Nor taste the quiet of a constant joy,
For ache, and care, and doubt, and weariness,
While I am calm; help being vouchsafed to me,
And hid from them!—'Twere best consider that!
You reason well, Aprile; but at least
Let me know this, and die! Is this too much?
I will learn this, if God so please, and die!

If thou shalt please, dear God, if thou shalt please!
We are so weak, we know our motives least
In their confused beginning: if at first
I sought . . . But wherefore bare my heart to thee?
I know thy mercy; and already thoughts
Flock fast about my soul to comfort it,
And intimate I cannot wholly fail,

For love and praise would clasp me willingly
Could I resolve to seek them: Thou art good,
And I should be content; yet—yet first show
I have done wrong in daring! Rather give
The supernatural consciousness of strength
That fed my youth—one only hour of that
With thee to help—O what should bar me then!

Lost, lost! Thus things are ordered here! God's creatures,
And yet he takes no pride in us!—none, none!
Truly there needs another life to come!
If this be all—(I must tell Festus that)
And other life await us not—for one,
I say 'tis a poor cheat, a stupid bungle,
A wretched failure. I, for one, protest
Against it—and I hurl it back with scorn!

Well, onward though alone: small time remains,
And much to do: I must have fruit, must reap
Some profit from my toils. I doubt my body
Will hardly serve me through: while I have laboured
It has decayed; and now that I demand
Its best assistance, it will crumble fast:
A sad thought—a sad fate! How very full
Of wormwood 'tis, that just at altar-service,
The rapt hymn rising with the rolling smoke,
When glory dawns, and all is at the best—
The sacred fire may flicker, and grow faint,
And die, for want of a wood-piler's help!
Thus fades the flagging body, and the soul
Is pulled down in the overthrow: well, well—
Let men catch every word—let them lose nought
Of what I say; something may yet be done.

They are ruins! Trust me who am one of you!
All ruins—glorious once, but lonely now.
It makes my heart sick to behold you crouch
Beside your desolate fane; the arches dim,
The crumbling columns grand against the moon:
Could I but rear them up once more—but that
May never be, so leave them! Trust me, friends,
Why should you linger here when I have built
A far resplendent temple, all your own?

Trust me, they are but ruins! See, Aprile,
Men will not heed! Yet were I not prepared
With better refuge for them, tongue of mine
Should ne'er reveal how blank their dwelling is;
I would sit down in silence with the rest.

Ha, what? you spit at me, you grin and shriek
Contempt into my ear—my ear which drank
God's accents once? you curse me? Why men, men,
I am not formed for it! Those hideous eyes
Follow me sleeping, waking, praying God,
And will not let me even die: spare, spare me,
Sinning or no, forget that, only spare me
That horrible scorn; you thought I could support it,
But now you see what silly fragile creature
Cowers thus. I am not good nor bad enough,
Not Christ, nor Cain, yet even Cain was saved
From hate like this: let me but totter back,
Perhaps I shall elude those jeers which creep
Into my very brain, and shut these scorched
Eyelids, and keep those mocking faces out.

Listen, Aprile! I am very calm:
Be not deceived, there is no passion here,
Where the blood leaps like an imprisoned thing.
I am calm; I will exterminate the race!
Enough of that: 'tis said and it shall be.
And now be merry—safe and sound am I,
Who broke through their best ranks to get at you;
And such a havoc, such a route, Aprile!
    Fest. Have you no thought, no memory for me,
Aureole? I am so wretched—my pure Michal
Is gone, and you alone are left to me,
And even you forget me: take my hand—
Lean on me, thus. Do you not know me, Aureole?
    Par. Festus, my own friend, you are come at last?
As you say, 'tis an awful enterprize—
But you believe I shall go through with it:
'Tis like you, and I thank you; thank him for me,
Dear Michal! See how bright St. Saviour's spire
Flames in the sunset; all its figures quaint
Gay in the glancing light: you might conceive them
A troop of yellow-vested, white-haired Jews,

Bound for their own land where redemption dawns!

Fest. Not that blest time—not our youth's time, dear
   God!

Par. Ha—stay! true, I forgot—all is done since!
And he is come to judge me: how he speaks,
How calm, how well! yes, it is true, all true;
All quackery; all deceit! myself can laugh
The first at it, if you desire: but still
You know the obstacles which taught me tricks
So foreign to my nature—envy, and hate—
Blind opposition—brutal prejudice—
Bald ignorance—what wonder if I sunk
To humour men the way they most approved?
My cheats were never palmed on such as you,
Dear Festus! I will kneel if you require me,
Impart the meagre knowledge I possess,
Explain its bounded nature, and avow
My insufficiency—whate'er you will:
I give the fight up! let there be an end.
A privacy, an obscure nook for me.
I want to be forgotten even by God!
But if that cannot be, dear Festus, lay me,
When I shall die, within some narrow grave,
Not by itself—for that would be too proud—
But where such graves are thickest; let it look
Nowise distinguished from the hillocks round,
So that the peasant at his brother's bed
May tread upon my own and know it not;
And we shall all be equal at the last,
Or classed according to life's natural ranks,
Fathers, sons, brothers, friends—not rich, nor wise,
Nor gifted: lay me thus, then say " He lived
" Too much advanced before his brother men:
" They kept him still in front; 'twas for their good.
" But yet a dangerous station. It were strange
" That he should tell God he had never ranked
" With men: so, here at least he is a man! "

Fest. That God shall take thee to his breast, dear Spirit,
Unto his breast, be sure! and here on earth
Shall splendour sit upon thy name for ever!
Sun! all the heaven is glad for thee: what care
If lower mountains light their snowy phares
At thine effulgence, yet acknowledge not

The source of day? Men look up to the sun:
For after-ages shall retrack thy beams,
And put aside the crowd of busy ones,
And worship thee alone—the master-mind,
The thinker, the explorer, the creator!
Then, who should sneer at the convulsive throes
With which thy deeds were born, would scorn as well
The winding sheet of subterraneous fire
Which, pent and writhing, sends no less at last
Huge islands up amid the simmering sea!
Behold thy might in me! thou hast infused
Thy soul in mine; and I am grand as thou,
Seeing I comprehend thee—I so simple,
Thou so august! I recognise thee first;
I saw thee rise, I watched thee early and late,
And though no glance reveal thou dost accept
My homage—thus no less I proffer it,
And bid thee enter gloriously thy rest!
 Par. Festus!
 Fest.   I am for noble Aureole, God!
I am upon his side, come weal or woe!
His portion shall be mine! He has done well!
I would have sinned, had I been strong enough,
As he has sinned! Reward him or I waive
Reward! If thou canst find no place for him,
He shall be king elsewhere, and I will be
His slave for ever! There are two of us!
 Par. Dear Festus!
 Fest.   Here, dear Aureole! ever by you!
 Par. Nay, speak on, or I dream again. Speak on!
Some story, any thing—only your voice.
I shall dream else. Speak on! ay, leaning so!
  Fest. Softly the Mayne river glideth;
  Close by where my love abideth;
  Sleep's no softer: it proceeds
  On through lawns, on through meads,
  On and on, whate'er befall,
  Meandering and musical,
  Though the niggard pasture's edge
  Bears not on its shaven ledge
  Aught but weeds and waving grasses
  To view the river as it passes,
  Save here and there a scanty patch

Of primroses, too faint to catch
A weary bee . . .
   Par. More, more; say on!
   Fest.   The river pushes
Its gentle way through strangling rushes,
Where the glossy king-fisher
Flutters when noon-heats are near,
Glad the shelving banks to shun,
Red and steaming in the sun,
Where the shrew-mouse with pale throat
Burrows, and the speckled stoat,
Where the quick sand-pipers flit
In and out the marl and grit
That seems to breed them, brown as they.
Nought disturbs the river's way,
Save some lazy stork that springs,
Trailing it with legs and wings,
Whom the shy fox from the hill
Rouses, creep he ne'er so still.
   Par. My heart! they loose my heart, those simple words;
Its darkness passes, which nought else could touch;
Like some dark snake that force may not expel,
Which glideth out to music sweet and low.
What were you doing when your voice broke through
A chaos of ugly images? You, indeed!
Are you alone here?
   Fest.   All alone: you know me?
This cell?
   Par.   An unexceptionable vault—
Good brick and stone—the bats kept out, the rats
Kept in—a snug nook: how should I mistake it?
   Fest. But wherefore am I here?
   Par.   Ah! well remembered:
Why, for a purpose—for a purpose, Festus!
'Tis like me: here I trifle while time fleets,
And this occasion, lost, will ne'er return!
You are here to be instructed. I will tell
God's message; but I have so much to say,
I fear to leave half out: all is confused
No doubt; but doubtless you will learn in time.
He would not else have brought you here: no doubt
I shall see clearer soon.
   Fest.   Tell me but this—

You are not in despair?

 Par.   I? and for what?

 Fest. Alas, alas! he knows not, as I feared!

 Par. What is it you would ask me with that earnest,
Dear, searching face?

 Fest.   How feel you, Aureole?

 Par.   Well!
Well: 'tis a strange thing. I am dying, Festus,
And now that fast the storm of life subsides,
I first perceive how great the whirl has been:
I was calm then, who am so dizzy now—
Calm in the thick of the tempest, but no less
A partner of its motion, and mixed up
With its career. The hurricane is spent
And the good boat speeds through the brightening weather;
But is it earth or sea that heaves below?
For the gulf rolls like a meadow, overstrewn
With ravaged boughs and remnants of the shore;
And now some islet, loosened from the land,
Swims past with all its trees, sailing to ocean;
And now the air is full of up-torn canes,
Light strippings from the fan-trees, tamarisks
Unrooted, with their birds still clinging to them,
All high in the wind. Even so my varied life
Drifts by me. I am young, old, happy, sad,
Hoping, desponding, acting, taking rest,
And all at once: that is, those past conditions
Float back at once on me. If I select
Some special epoch from the crowd, 'tis but
To will, and straight the rest dissolve away,
And only that particular state is present,
With all its long-forgotten circumstance,
Distinct and vivid as at first—myself
A careless looker-on, and nothing more!
Indifferent and amused, but nothing more!
And this is death: I understand it all.
New being waits me; new perceptions must
Be born in me before I plunge therein;
Which last is Death's affair; and while I speak,
Minute by minute he is filling me
With power; and while my foot is on the threshold
Of boundless life—the doors unopened yet,
All preparations not complete within—

I turn new knowledge upon old events,
And the effect is . . . But I must not tell;
It is not lawful. Your own turn will come
One day. Wait, Festus! You will die like me!

    Fest. 'Tis of that past life that I burn to hear !

    Par. You wonder it engages me just now?
In truth, I wonder too. What's life to me?
Where'er I look is fire, where'er I listen
Music, and where I tend bliss overmore.
Yet how can I refrain? 'Tis a refined
Delight to view those chances,—one last view.
I am so near the perils I escape,
That I must play with them and turn them over,
To feel how fully they are past and gone.
Still it is like some further cause exists
For this peculiar mood—some hidden purpose;
Did I not tell you something of it, Festus?
I had it fast, but it has somehow slipt
Away from me; it will return anon.

    Fest. (Indeed his cheek seems young again, his voice
Complete with its old tones: that little laugh
Concluding every phrase, with up-turned eye,
As though one stooped above his head, to whom
He looked for confirmation and applause,—
Where was it gone so long, being kept so well?
Then, the fore-finger pointing as he speaks,
Like one who traces in an open book
The matter he declares; 'tis many a year
Since I remarked it last: and this in him,
But now a ghastly wreck!)

                      And can it be,
Dear Aureole, you have then found out at last
That worldly things are utter vanity?
That man is made for weakness, and should wait
In patient ignorance till God appoint . . .

    Par. Ha, the purpose; the true purpose: that is it!
How could I fail to apprehend! You here,
I thus! But no more trifling; I see all,
I know all: my last mission shall be done
If strength suffice. No trifling! Stay; this posture
Hardly befits one thus about to speak:
I will arise.

    Fest.   Nay, Aureole, are you wild?

You cannot leave your couch.

Par.   No help; no help;
Not even your hand.   So! there, I stand once more!
Speak from a couch?   I never lectured thus.
My gown—the scarlet, lined with fur; now put
The chain about my neck; my signet-ring
Is still upon my hand, I think—even so;
Last, my good sword; ha, trusty Azoth, leapest
Beneath thy master's grasp for the last time?
This couch shall be my throne: I bid these walls
Be consecrate; this wretched cell become
A shrine; for here God speaks to men through me!
Now, Festus, I am ready to begin.

Fest. I am dumb with wonder.

Par.   Listen, therefore, Festus!
There will be time enough, but none to spare,
I must content myself with telling only
The most important points.   You doubtless feel
That I am happy, Festus; very happy.

Fest. 'Tis no delusion which uplifts him thus!
Then you are pardoned, Aureole, all your sin?

Par. Ay, pardoned! yet why pardoned?

Fest.   'Tis God's praise
That man is bound to seek, and you . . .

Par.   Have lived!
We have to live alone to set forth well
God's praise. 'Tis true, I sinned much, as I thought,
And in effect need mercy, for I strove
To do that very thing; but, do your best
Or worst, praise rises, and will rise for ever.
Pardon from Him, because of praise denied—
Who calls me to Himself to exalt Himself?
We might laugh as I laugh!

Fest.   Then all comes
To the same thing. 'Tis fruitless for mankind
To fret themselves with what concerns them not;
They are no use that way: they should lie down
Content as God has made them, nor go mad
In thriveless cares to better what is ill.

Par. No, no; mistake me not; let me not work
More harm than I have done! This is my case:
If I go joyous back to God, yet bring
No offering, if I render up my soul

Without the fruits it was ordained to bear,
If I appear the better to love God
For sin, as one who has no claim on him,—
Be not deceived; it may be surely thus
With me, while higher prizes still await
The mortal persevering to the end.
For I too have been something, though too soon
I left the instincts of that happy time!

    Fest.   What happy time? For God's sake, for man's sake,
What time was happy? All I hope to know
That answer will decide. What happy time?

    Par.   When, but the time I vowed my help to man?

    Fest.   Great God, thy judgments are inscrutable!

    Par.   Yes, it was in me; I was born for it—
I, Paracelsus: it was mine by right.
Doubtless a searching and impetuous soul
Might learn from its own motions that some task
Like this awaited it about the world;
Might seek somewhere in this blank life of ours
For fit delights to stay its longings vast;
And, grappling Nature, so prevail on her
To fill the creature full she dared to frame
Hungry for joy; and, bravely tyrannous,
Grow in demand, still craving more and more,
And make each joy conceded prove a pledge
Of other joy to follow—bating nought
Of its desires, still seizing fresh pretence
To turn the knowledge and the rapture wrung
As an extreme, last boon, from Destiny,
Into occasion for new covetings,
New strifes, new triumphs:—doubtless a strong soul
Alone, unaided might attain to this,
So glorious is our nature, so august
Man's inborn uninstructed impulses,
His naked spirit so majestical!
But this was born in me; I was made so;
Thus much time saved: the feverish appetites,
The tumult of unproved desires, the unaimed
Uncertain yearnings, aspirations blind,
Distrust, mistake, and all that ends in tears
Were saved me; thus I entered on my course!
You may be sure I was not all exempt
From human trouble; just so much of doubt

As bade me plant a surer foot upon
The sun-road—kept my eye unruined mid
The fierce and flashing splendour—set my heart
Trembling so much as warned me I stood there
On sufferance—not to idly gaze, but cast
Light on a darkling race; save for that doubt,
I stood at first where all aspire at last
To stand; the secret of the world was mine.
I knew, I felt, (perception unexpressed,
Uncomprehended by our narrow thought,
But somehow felt and known in every shift
And change in spirit,—nay, in every pore
Of the body, even,)—what God is, what we are,
What life is—how God tastes an infinite joy
In infinite ways—one everlasting bliss,
From whom all being emanates, all power
Proceeds; in whom is life for evermore,
Yet whom existence in its lowest form
Includes; where dwells enjoyment there is He!
With still a flying point of bliss remote,
A happiness in store afar, a sphere
Of distant glory in full view; thus climbs
Pleasure its heights for ever and for ever!
The centre-fire heaves underneath the earth,
And the earth changes like a human face;
The molten ore bursts up among the rocks,
Winds into the stone's heart, outbranches bright
In hidden mines, spots barren river-beds,
Crumbles into fine sand where sunbeams bask—
God joys therein! The wroth sea's waves are edged
With foam, white as the bitten lip of Hate,
When in the solitary, waste, strange groups
Of young volcanos come up, cyclops-like,
Staring together with their eyes on flame;—
God tastes a pleasure in their uncouth pride!
Then all is still: earth is a wintry clod;
But spring-wind, like a dancing psaltress, passes
Over its breast to waken it; rare verdure
Buds tenderly upon rough banks, between
The withered tree-roots and the cracks of frost,
Like a smile striving with a wrinkled face;
The grass grows bright, the boughs are swoln with blooms,
Like chrysalids impatient for the air;

The shining dorrs are busy; beetles run
Along the furrows, ants make their ado;
Above, birds fly in merry flocks—the lark
Soars up and up, shivering for very joy;
Afar the ocean sleeps; white fishing-gulls
Flit where the strand is purple with its tribe
Of nested limpets; savage creatures seek
Their loves in wood and plain; and God renews
His ancient rapture! Thus he dwells in all,
From life's minute beginnings, up at last
To man—the consummation of this scheme
Of being, the completion of this sphere
Of life: whose attributes had here and there
Been scattered o'er the visible world before,
Asking to be combined—dim fragments meant
To be united in some wondrous whole—
Imperfect qualities throughout creation,
Suggesting some one creature yet to make—
Some point where all those scattered rays should meet
Convergent in the faculties of man.
Power; neither put forth blindly, nor controlled
Calmly by perfect knowledge; to be used
At risk, inspired or checked by hope and fear:
Knowledge; not intuition, but the slow
Uncertain fruit of an enhancing toil,
Strengthened by love: love; not serenely pure,
But strong from weakness, like a chance-sown plant
Which, cast on stubborn soil, puts forth changed buds,
And softer stains, unknown in happier climes;
Love which endures, and doubts, and is oppressed,
And cherished, suffering much, and much sustained,
A blind, oft-failing, yet believing love,
A half-enlightened, often-chequered trust:—
Hints and previsions of which faculties,
Are strewn confusedly everywhere about
The inferior natures; and all lead up higher,
All shape out dimly the superior race,
The heir of hopes too fair to turn out false,
And Man appears at last: so far the seal
Is put on life; one stage of being complete,
One scheme wound up; and from the grand result
A supplementary reflux of light,
Illustrates all the inferior grades, explains

Each back step in the circle. Not alone
For their possessor dawn those qualities,
But the new glory mixes with the heaven
And earth: Man, once descried, imprints for ever
His presence on all lifeless things; the winds
Are henceforth voices, in a wail or shout,
A querulous mutter, or a quick gay laugh—
Never a senseless gust now man is born!
The herded pines commune, and have deep thoughts,
A secret they assemble to discuss,
When the sun drops behind their trunks which glare
Like grates of hell: the peerless cup afloat
Of the lake-lily is an urn, some nymph
Swims bearing high above her head: no bird
Whistles unseen, but through the gaps above
That let light in upon the gloomy woods,
A shape peeps from the breezy forest-top,
Arch with small puckered mouth and mocking eye:
The morn has enterprise,—deep quiet droops
With evening; triumph takes the sun-set hour,
Voluptuous transport ripens with the corn
Beneath a warm moon like a happy face:
—And this to fill us with regard for man,
With apprehension for his passing worth,
Desire to work his proper nature out,
And ascertain his rank and final place;
For these things tend still upward—progress is
The law of life—man's self is not yet Man!
Nor shall I deem his object served, his end
Attained, his genuine strength put fairly forth,
While only here and there a star dispels
The darkness, here and there a towering mind
O'erlooks its prostrate fellows: when the host
Is out at once to the despair of night,
When all mankind alike is perfected,
Equal in full-blown powers—then, not till then,
I say, begins man's general infancy!
For wherefore make account of feverish starts
Of restless members of a dormant whole—
Impatient nerves which quiver while the body
Slumbers as in a grave? O, long ago
The brow was twitched, the tremulous lids astir,
The peaceful mouth disturbed; half-uttered speech

Ruffled the lip, and then the teeth were set,
The breath drawn sharp, the strong right-hand clenched
    stronger,
As it would pluck a lion by the jaw;
The glorious creature laughed out even in sleep!
But when full roused, each giant-limb awake,
Each sinew strung, the great heart pulsing fast,
He shall start up, and stand on his own earth,
And so begin his long triumphant march,
And date his being thence,—thus wholly roused,
What he achieves shall be set down to him!
When all the race is perfected alike
As Man, that is: all tended to mankind,
And, man produced, all has its end thus far;
But in completed man begins anew
A tendency to God.   Prognostics told
Man's near approach; so in man's self arise
August anticipations, symbols, types
Of a dim splendour ever on before,
In that eternal circle run by life:
For men begin to pass their nature's bound,
And find new hopes and cares which fast supplant
Their proper joys and griefs; and outgrow all
The narrow creeds of right and wrong, which fade
Before the unmeasured thirst for good; while peace
Rises within them ever more and more.
Such men are even now upon the earth,
Serene amid the half-formed creatures round,
Who should be saved by them and joined with them.
Such was my task, and I was born to it—
Free, as I said but now, from much that chains
Spirits, high-dowered, but limited and vexed
By a divided and delusive aim.
A shadow mocking a reality
Whose truth avails not wholly to disperse
The flitting mimic called up by itself,
And so remains perplexed and nigh put out
By its fantastic fellow's wavering gleam.
I, from the first, was never cheated so;
I never fashioned out a fancied good
Distinct from man's; a service to be done,
A glory to be ministered unto,
With powers put forth at man's expense, withdrawn

From labouring in his behalf; a strength
Denied that might avail him! I cared not
Lest his success ran counter to success
Elsewhere: for God is glorified in man,
And to man's glory, vowed I soul and limb.
Yet, constituted thus, and thus endowed,
I failed: I gazed on power till I grew blind—
On power; I could not take my eyes from that—
That only, I thought, should be preserved, increased
At any risk, displayed, struck out at once—
The sign, and note, and character of man.
I saw no use in the past: only a scene
Of degradation, imbecility—
The record of disgraces best forgotten,
A sullen page in human chronicles
Fit to erase: I saw no cause why man
Should not be all-sufficient even now;
Or why his annals should be forced to tell
That once the tide of light, about to break
Upon the world, was sealed within its spring;
I would have had one day, one moment's space,
Change man's condition, push each slumbering claim
To mastery o'er the elemental world
At once to full maturity, then roll
Oblivion o'er the tools, and hide from man,
What night had ushered morn. Not so, dear child
Of after-days, wilt thou reject the Past,
Big with deep warnings of the proper tenure
By which thou hast the earth: the Present for thee
Shall have distinct and trembling beauty, seen
Beside that Past's own shade, whence, in relief,
Its brightness shall stand out: nor on thee yet
Shall burst the Future, as successive zones
Of several wonder open on some spirit
Flying secure and glad from heaven to heaven;
But thou shalt painfully attain to joy,
While hope, and fear, and love, shall keep thee man!
All this was hid from me: as one by one
My dreams grew dim, my wide aims circumscribed,
As actual good within my reach decreased,
While obstacles sprung up this way and that,
To keep me from effecting half the sum,
Small as it proved; as objects, mean within

The primal aggregate, seemed, even the least,
Itself a match for my concentred strength—
What wonder if I saw no way to shun
Despair?   The power I sought for man, seemed God's!
In this conjuncture, as I prayed to die,
A strange adventure made me know, One Sin
Had spotted my career from its uprise;
I saw Aprile—my Aprile there!
And as the poor melodious wretch disburthened
His heart, and moaned his weakness in my ear,
I learned my own deep error; love's undoing
Taught me the worth of love in man's estate,
And what proportion love should hold with power
In his right constitution; love preceding
Power, and with much power, always much more love;
Love still too straitened in its present means,
And earnest for new powers to set it free.
I learned this, and supposed the whole was learned:
And thus, when men received with stupid wonder
My first revealings, would have worshipped me,
And I despised and loathed their proffered praise—
When, with awakened eyes, they took revenge
For past credulity in casting shame
On my real knowledge, and I hated them—
It was not strange I saw no good in man,
To overbalance all the wear and waste
Of faculties, displayed in vain, but born
To prosper in some better sphere: and why?
In my own heart love had not been made wise
To trace love's faint beginnings in mankind,
To know even hate is but a mask of love's,
To see a good in evil, and a hope
In ill-success; to sympathize, be proud
Of their half-reasons, faint aspirings, dim
Struggles for truth, their poorest fallacies,
Their prejudice, and fears, and cares, and doubts;
Which all touch upon nobleness, despite
Their error, all tend upwardly though weak,
Like plants in mines which never saw the sun,
But dream of him, and guess where he may be,
And do their best to climb and get to him.
All this I knew not, and I failed.   Let men
Regard me, and the poet dead long ago

Who once loved rashly; and shape forth a third,
And better tempered spirit, warned by both:
As from the over-radiant star too mad
To drink the light-springs, beamless thence itself—
And the dark orb which borders the abyss,
Ingulfed in icy night,—might have its course
A temperate and equidistant world.
Meanwhile, I have done well, though not all well.
As yet men cannot do without contempt—
'Tis for their good, and therefore fit awhile
That they reject the weak, and scorn the false,
Rather than praise the strong and true, in me.
But after, they will know me! If I stoop
Into a dark tremendous sea of cloud,
It is but for a time; I press God's lamp
Close to my breast—its splendour, soon or late,
Will pierce the gloom: I shall emerge one day!
You understand me? I have said enough?
    Fest. Now die, dear Aureole!
    Par.   Festus, let my hand—
This hand, lie in your own—my own true friend!
Aprile! Hand in hand with you, Aprile!

    Fest. And this was Paracelsus!

STRAFFORD:

AN HISTORICAL TRAGEDY

Dedicated, in all Affectionate Admiration, to
WILLIAM C. MACREADY, ESQ.
by his Most Grateful and Devoted Friend, R.B.
(*April* 23, 1837.)

PREFACE

I HAD for some time been engaged in a Poem of a very different nature, when induced to make the present attempt; and am not without apprehension that my eagerness to freshen a jaded mind by diverting it to the healthy natures of a grand epoch, may have operated unfavourably on the represented play, which is one of Action in Character rather than Character in Action. To remedy this, in some degree, considerable curtailment will be necessary, and, in a few instances, the supplying details not required, I suppose, by the mere reader. While a trifling success would much gratify, failure will not wholly discourage me from another effort: experience is to come, and earnest endeavours may yet remove many disadvantages.

The portraits are, I think, faithful; and I am exceedingly fortunate in being able, in proof of this, to refer to the subtle and eloquent exposition of the characters of Eliot and Strafford, in the Lives of Eminent British Statesmen now in the course of publication in Lardner's Cyclopædia, by a writer whom I am proud to call my friend; and whose biographies of Hampden, Pym, and Vane, will, I am sure, fitly illustrate the present year—the Second Centenary of the Trial concerning Ship-Money. My Carlisle, however, is purely imaginary: I at first sketched her singular likeness roughly in, as suggested by Matthew and the memoir-writers—but it was too artificial, and the substituted outline is exclusively from Voiture and Waller.

The Italian boat-song in the last scene is from Redi's *Bacco*, long since naturalized in the joyous and delicate version of Leigh Hunt.

DRAMATIS PERSONÆ

(Theatre-Royal Covent Garden, May 1, 1837)

CHARLES THE FIRST	Mr. DALE.
Earl of HOLLAND	HUCKEL.
Lord SAVILE	TILBURY.
Sir HENRY VANE	THOMPSON.
WENTWORTH, Viscount WENTWORTH, Earl of STRAFFORD	MACREADY.
JOHN PYM	VANDENHOFF.
JOHN HAMPDEN	HARRIS.
The younger VANE	J. WEBSTER.
DENZIL HOLLIS	G. BENNET.
BENJAMIN RUDYARD	PRITCHARD.
NATHANIEL FIENNES	WORREL.
Earl of LOUDON	BENDER.
MAXWELL, *Usher of the Black Rod* . .	RANSFORD.
BALFOUR, *Constable of the Tower* . . .	COLLETT.
A Puritan	WEBSTER.
Queen HENRIETTA	Miss VINCENT.
LUCY PERCY, Countess of CARLISLE . .	HELEN FAUCIT.

Presbyterians, Scots Commissioners, Adherents of Strafford, Secretaries, Officers of the Court, etc. Two of Strafford's Children.

STRAFFORD

ACT I

SCENE I.—*A House near Whitehall.*

HAMPDEN, HOLLIS, *the* younger VANE, RUDYARD, FIENNES, *and many of the Presbyterian Party*, LOUDON *and other Scots Commissioners : some seated, some standing beside a table strewn over with papers, etc.*

Vane.   I say, if he be here . . .
Rud.   And he is here!
Hol.   For England's sake let every man be still
Nor speak of him, so much as say his name,
Till Pym rejoin us!   Rudyard—Vane—remember
One rash conclusion may decide our course
And with it England's fate—think—England's fate!
Hampden, for England's sake they should be still!
Vane.   You say so, Hollis?   well, I must be still!
It is indeed too bitter that one man—
Any one man . . .
Rud.   You are his brother, Hollis!
Hamp.   Shame on you, Rudyard! time to tell him that,
When he forgets the Mother of us all.
Rud.   Do I forget her? . . .
Hamp.   —You talk idle hate
Against her foe: is that so strange a thing?
Is hating Wentworth all the help she needs?
A Puritan.   The Philistine strode, cursing as he went:
But David—five smooth pebbles from the brook
Within his scrip . . .
Rud.   —Be you as still as David!
Fien.   Here's Rudyard not ashamed to wag a tongue
Stiff with ten years disuse of Parliaments;
Why, when the last sate, Wentworth sate with us!
Rud.   Let's hope for news of them now he returns:
—But I'll abide Pym's coming.
Vane.   Now by Heaven

135

They may be cool that can, silent that can,
Some have a gift that way: Wentworth is here—
Here—and the King's safe closeted with him
Ere this! and when I think on all that's past
Since that man left us—how his single arm
Roll'd back the good of England, roll'd it back
And set the woeful Past up in its place . . .

    A Puritan.   Exalting Dagon where the Ark should be!

    Vane. . . . How that man has made firm the fickle King
—Hampden, I will speak out—in aught he feared
To venture on before; taught Tyranny
Her dismal trade, the use of all her tools,
To ply the scourge yet screw the gag so close
That strangled agony bleeds mute to death:
—How he turns Ireland to a private stage
For training infant villanies, new ways
Of wringing treasure out of tears and gore,
Unheard oppressions nourished in the dark
To try how much Man's nature can endure
—If he dies under it, what harm? if not . . .

    Fien.   Why, one more trick is added to the rest
Worth a King's knowing—

    Rud.   —And what Ireland bears
England may learn to bear.

    Vane.   . . . How all this while
That man has set himself to one dear task,
The bringing Charles to relish more and more
Power . . .

    Rud.   Power without law . . .

    Fien.   Power and blood too . . .

    Vane. . . . Can I be still?

    Hamp.   For that you should be still.

    Vane.   Oh, Hampden, then and now! The year he left us
The People by its Parliament could wrest
The Bill of Rights from the reluctant King:
And now,—he'll find in an obscure small room
A stealthy gathering of great-hearted men
That take up England's cause: England is—here!

    Hamp.   And who despairs of England?

    Rud.   That do I
If Wentworth is to rule her. I am sick
To think her wretched masters, Hamilton,
The muckworm Cottington, the maniac Laud,

May yet be longed for back again.   I say
I do despair.
    Vane.   And, Rudyard, I'll say this—
And, (*turning to the rest*) all true men say after me! not loud—
But solemnly, and as you'd say a prayer:
This Charles, who treads our England under foot,
Has just so much—it may be fear or craft—
As bids him pause at each fresh outrage; friends,
He needs some sterner hand to grasp his own,
Some voice to ask, " Why shrink?—am I not by? "
—A man that England loved for serving her,
Found in his heart to say, " I know where best
The iron heel shall bruise her, for she leans
Upon me when you trample."   Witness, you!
But inasmuch as life is hard to take
From England . . .
    Many Voices.   Go on, Vane!   'Tis well said, Vane!
    Vane.   . . . Who has not so forgotten Runnymead. . . .
    Voices.   'Tis well and bravely spoken, Vane!   Go on!
    Vane.   . . . There are some little signs of late she knows
The ground no place for her! no place for her!
When the King beckons—and beside him stands
The same bad man once more, with the same smile,
And the same savage gesture!   Now let England
Make proof of us.
    Voices.   Strike him—the Renegade—
Haman—Ahithophel—
    Hamp. (*To the Scots.*) Gentlemen of the North,
It was not thus the night your claims were urged,
And we pronounced the League and Covenant
Of Scotland to be England's cause as well!
Vane, there, sate motionless the whole night through.
    Vane.   Hampden . . .
    Fien.   Stay Vane!
    Lou.   Be patient, gallant Vane!
    Vane.   Mind how you counsel patience, Loudon! you
Have still a Parliament, and a brave League
To back it; you are free in Scotland still—
While we are brothers (as these hands are knit
So let our hearts be!)—hope's for England yet!
But know you why this Wentworth comes? to quench
This faintest hope? that he brings war with him?
Know you this Wentworth?   What he dares?

Lou.   Dear Vane,
We know—'tis nothing new . . .
     Vane.   And what's new, then,
In calling for his life?   Why Pym himself . . .
You must have heard—ere Wentworth left our cause
He would see Pym first; there were many more
Strong on the People's side and friends of his,—
Eliot that's dead, Rudyard and Hampden here,
But Wentworth cared not for them; only, Pym
He would see—Pym and he were sworn, they say,
To live and die together—so they met
At Greenwich: Wentworth, you are sure, was long,
Specious enough, the devil's argument
Lost nothing in his lips; he'd have Pym own
A Patriot could not do a purer thing
Than follow in his track; they two combined
Could put down England.   Well, Pym heard him out—
One glance—you know Pym's eye—one word was all:
" You leave us, Wentworth: while your head is on
" I'll not leave you."
     Hamp.   Has Pym left Wentworth, then?
Has England lost him?   Will you let him speak,
Or put your crude surmises in his mouth?
Away with this! (*To the rest.*) Will you have Pym or Vane?
     Voices.   Wait Pym's arrival! Pym shall speak!
     Hamp.   Meanwhile
Let Loudon read the Parliament's report
From Edinburgh: our last hope, as Vane says,
Is in the stand it makes.   Loudon!
     Vane. (*As* LOUDON *is about to read*)—No—no—
Silent I can be: not indifferent!
     Hamp.   Then each keep silence, praying God a space
That he will not cast England quite away
In this her visitation! (*All assume a posture of reverence.*)
     A Puritan.   Seven years long
The Midianite drove Israel into dens
And caves.
                    Till God sent forth a mighty man,

                    (PYM *enters.*)

Even Gideon! (*All start up.*)
     Pym.   Wentworth's come: he has not reached
Whitehall: they've hurried up a Council there

To lose no time and find him work enough.
Where's Loudon?   Your Scots' Parliament . . .
   Lou.   Is firm:
We were about to read reports . . .
   Pym.   The King
Has just dissolved your Parliament.
   Lou. and other of the Scots.   Great God!
An oath-breaker!   Stand by us England then!
   Pym.   The King's too sanguine; doubtless Wentworth's
     here;
But still some little form might be kept up.
   Hol. Now speak, Vane!   Rudyard, you had much to say!
   Hamp. The rumour's false, then . . .
   Pym.   Ay, the Court gives out
His own concerns have brought him back: I know
'Tis Charles recalls him: he's to supersede
The tribe of Cottingtons and Hamiltons
Whose part is played: there's talk enough, by this,—
Merciful talk, the King thinks: time is now
To turn the record's last and bloody leaf
That, chronicling a Nation's great despair,
Tells they were long rebellious, and their Lord
Indulgent, till, all kind expedients tried,
He drew the sword on them, and reigned in peace.
Laud's laying his religion on the Scots
Was the last gentle entry:—the new page
Shall run, the King thinks, " Wentworth thrust it down
At the sword's point."
   A Puritan.   I'll do your bidding, Pym,—
England's and yours . . . one blow!
   Pym.   A glorious thing—
We all say, friends, it is a glorious thing
To right that England!   Heaven grows dark above,—
Let's snatch one moment ere the thunder fall
To say how well the English spirit comes out
Beneath it! all have done their best, indeed,
From lion Eliot, that grand Englishman,
To the least here: and who, the least one here,
When She is saved (and her redemption dawns
Dimly, most dimly, but it dawns—it dawns)—
Who'd give at any price his hope away
Of being named along with the Great Men?
One would not . . . no, one would not give that up!

Hamp.   And one name shall be dearer than all names:
When children, yet unborn, are taught that name
After their fathers',—taught one matchless man . . .

Pym. . . . Saved England?

                    What if Wentworth's should be still
That name?

Rud. and others.   We have just said it, Pym! His death
    Saves her!

Fien.   We said that! There's no way beside!

A Puritan. I'll do your bidding, Pym! They struck
    down Joab
And purged the land.

Vane.   No villanous striking-down!

Rud.   No—a calm vengeance: let the whole land rise
And shout for it. No Feltons!

Pym.   Rudyard, no.
England rejects all Feltons; most of all
Since Wentworth . . .

                    Hampden, say the praise again
That England will award me . . . But I'll think
You know me, all of you. Then, I believe,
—Spite of the past,—Wentworth rejoins you, friends!

Rud. and others. Wentworth! apostate . . .

Vane.   Wentworth, double-dyed
A traitor! Is it Pym, indeed . . .

Pym.   . . . Who says
Vane never knew that Wentworth—loved that Wentworth—
Felt glad to stroll with him, arm lock'd in arm,
Along the streets to see the People pass
And read in every island-countenance
Fresh argument for God against the King,—
Never sate down . . . say, in the very house
Where Eliot's brow grew broad with noble thoughts
(You've joined us, Hampden, Hollis, you as well,)
And then left talking over Gracchus' death . . .

Vane. . . . To frame, we know it, Pym, the choicest clause
In the Petition of Rights: which Wentworth framed
A month before he took at the King's hand
His Northern Presidency, which that Bill
Denounced . . .

Rud.   And infamy along with it!

A Puritan. For whoso putteth his right-hand to the
    plough

And turneth back . . .

Pym.   Never more, never more
Walked we together! Most alone I went;
I have had friends—all here are fast my friends—
But I shall never quite forget that friend!
(*After a pause*) And yet it could not but be real in him!
You Vane, you Rudyard, have no right to trust
That Wentworth . . . O will no one hope with me?
—Vane—think you Wentworth will shed English blood
Like water?

A Puritan.   Ireland is Aceldama!

Pym.   Will he turn Scotland to a hunting ground
To please the King, now that he knows the King?
The People or the King? The People, Hampden,
Or the King . . . and that King—Charles! Will no one
    hope?

Hamp.   Pym, we do know you: you'll not set your heart
On any baseless thing: but say one deed
Of Wentworth's, since he left us . . . (*Shouting without.*)

Vane.   Pym, he comes
And they shout for him!—Wentworth!—he's with Charles—
The king embracing him—now—as we speak . . .
And he, to be his match in courtesies,
Taking the whole war's risk upon himself!—
Now—while you tell us here how changed he is—
Do you hear, Pym? The People shout for him!

Fien.   We'll not go back, now! Hollis has no brother—
Vane has no father . . .

Vane.   Pym should have no friend!
Stand you firm, Pym! Eliot's gone, Wentworth's lost,
We have but you, and stand you very firm!
Truth is eternal, come below what will,
But . . . I know not . . . if you should fail . . .
O God! O God!

Pym. (*apart and in thought*).   And yet if 'tis a dream, no
    more,
That Wentworth chose their side, and brought the King
To love it as though Laud had loved it first,
And the Queen after—that he led their cause
Calm to success and kept it spotless through,
So that our very eyes could look upon
The travail of our soul, and close content
That violence, which something mars even Right

That sanctions it, had taken off no grace
From its serene regard. Only a dream!

 Hamp. Proceed to England's work: who reads the list?

 A Voice. " Ship-money is refused or fiercely paid
In every county, save the northern ones
Where Wentworth's influence " . . . (*Renewed shouting.*)

 Vane (*passionately striking the table*). I, in England's
  name
Declare her work, this way, at end! till now—
Up to this moment—peaceful strife was well!
We English had free leave to think: till now,
We had a shadow of a Parliament:
'Twas well: but all is changed: they threaten us:
They'll try brute-force for law—here—in our land!

 Many Voices. True hearts with Vane! The old true hearts
with Vane!

 Vane. Till we crush Wentworth for her, there's no act
Serves England!

 Voices.   Vane for England!

 Pym (*as he passes slowly before them*). Pym should be
Something to England! I seek Wentworth, friends!

Scene II.—*Whitehall.*

Enter CARLISLE *and* WENTWORTH.

 Went. And the King?

 Car.   Dear Wentworth, lean on me; sit then;
I'll tell you all; this horrible fatigue
Will kill you.

 Went.   No; or—Lucy, just your arm;
I'll not sit till I've cleared this up with him:
After that, rest. The King?

 Car.   Confides in you.

 Went. Why? why now?
      —They have kind throats, the people!
Shout for me . . . they!—poor fellows.

 Car.   Did they shout?
—We took all measures to keep off the crowd—
Did they shout for you?

 Went.   Wherefore should they not?
Does the King take such measures for himself?

Beside, there's such a dearth of malcontents,
You say?

  Car.   I said but few dared carp at you . . .

  Went. At me? at us, Carlisle! The King and I!
He's surely not disposed to let me bear
Away the fame from him of these late deeds
In Ireland? I am yet his instrument
Be it for well or ill?

                  He trusts me then?

  Car. The King, dear Wentworth, purposes, I know,
To grant you, in the face of all the Court . . .

  Went. All the Court! Evermore the Court about us!
Savile and Holland, Hamilton and Vane
About us,—then the King will grant me . . . Lady,
Will the King leave these,—leave all these—and say
"Tell me your whole mind, Wentworth!"

  Car.   But you said
You would be calm.

  Went.   Lucy, and I am calm!
How else shall I do all I come to do,
—Broken, as you may see, body and mind—
How shall I serve the King? time wastes meanwhile,
You have not told me half . . . His footstep! No.
—But now, before I meet him,—(I am calm)—
Why does the King distrust me?

  Car.   He does not
Distrust you.

  Went.   Lucy, you can help me . . . you
Have even seemed to care for me: help me!
Is it the Queen?

  Car.   No—not the Queen—the party
That poisons the Queen's ear,—Savile—and Holland . . .

  Went. I know—I know—and Vane, too, he's one too?
Go on—and he's made Secretary—Well?
—Or leave them out and go straight to the charge!
The charge!

  Car.   O there's no charge—no precise charge—
Only they sneer, make light of . . . one may say
Nibble at what you do.

  Went.   I know: but Lucy,
Go on, dear Lucy—Oh I need you so!
I reckoned on you from the first!—Go on!
. . . Was sure could I once see this gentle girl

When I arrived, she'd throw an hour away
To help her weary friend. . . .
 Car.   You thought of me,
Dear Wentworth?
 Went.   . . . But go on! The People here . . .
 Car. They do not think your Irish Government
Of that surpassing value . . .
 Went.   The one thing
Of value! The one service that the crown
May count on! All that keeps these very things
In power, to vex me . . . not that they do vex me,
Only it might vex some to hear that service
Decried—the sole support that's left the King!
 Car. So the Archbishop says.
 Went.   Ah? well, perhaps
The only hand held up in its defence
May be old Laud's!
     These Hollands, then, these Saviles
Nibble? They nibble?—that's the very word!
 Car. Your profit in the Customs, Bristol says, . . .
 Went. Enough! 'tis too unworthy,—I am not
So patient as I thought!
      What's Pym about?
 Car. Pym?
 Went.   Pym and the People.
 Car.   Oh, the Faction!
Extinct—of no account—there'll never be
Another Parliament.
 Went.   Tell Savile that!
You may know—(ay, you do—the creatures here
Never forget!) that in my earliest life
I was not . . . not what I am now! The King
May take my word on points concerning Pym
Before Lord Savile's, Lucy, or if not,
Girl, they shall ruin their vile selves, not me,
These Vanes and Hollands—I'll not be their tool—
Pym would receive me yet!
      —But then the King!—
I'll bear it all. The King—where is he, Girl?
 Car. He is apprised that you are here: be calm!
 Went. And why not meet me now? Ere now? You said
He sent for me . . . he longed for me!
 Car.   Because . . .

He is now . . . I think a Council's sitting now
About this Scots affair . . .
    Went.   A Council sits?
They have not taken a decided course
Without me in this matter?
    Car.   I should say . . .
    Went. The War? They cannot have agreed to that?
Not the Scots' War?—without consulting me—
Me—that am here to show how rash it is,
How easy to dispense with?
                   —Ah, you too
Against me! well,—the King may find me here.
(*As* CARLISLE *is going.*)—Forget it, Lucy: cares make
    peevish: mine
Weigh me (but 'tis a secret) to my grave.
    Car. For life or death I am your own, dear friend!
(*Aside.*) I could not tell him . . . sick too! . . . And the
    King
Shall love him! Wentworth here, who can withstand
His look?—And he did really think of me?
O 'twas well done to spare him all the pain!   (*Exit.*)
    Went. Heartless! . . . but all are heartless here.
                           Go now,
Forsake the people!
           —I did not forsake
The People: they shall know it . . . when the King
Will trust me!—who trusts all beside at once
While I . . . have not spoke Vane and Savile fair,
And am not trusted: have but saved the Throne:
Have not picked up the Queen's glove prettily,
And am not trusted!
           But he'll see me now:
And Weston's dead—and the Queen's English now—
More English—oh, one earnest word will brush
These reptiles from . . . (*footsteps within.*)
               The step I know so well!
'Tis Charles!—But now—to tell him . . . no—to ask him
What's in me to distrust:—or, best begin
By proving that this frightful Scots affair
Is just what I foretold: I'll say, " my liege " . . .
And I feel sick, now! and the time is come—
And one false step no way to be repaired . . .
You were revenged, Pym, could you look on me!

(PYM *enters*.)

Went. I little thought of you just then.
Pym.   No? I
Think always of you, Wentworth.
        Went. (*Aside.*)   The old voice!
I wait the King, sir.
        Pym.   True—you look so pale:
A council sits within; when that breaks up
He'll see you.
        Went.   Sir, I thank you.
        Pym.   Oh, thank Laud!
You know when Laud once gets on Church affairs
The case is desperate: he'll not be long
To-day: He only means to prove, to-day,
We English all are mad to have a hand
In butchering the Scots for serving God
After their fathers' fashion: only that.
        Went. Sir, keep your jests for those who relish them!
(*Aside.*) Does *he* enjoy their confidence? (*To* P.) 'Tis kind
To tell me what the Council does.
        Pym.   You grudge
That I should know it had resolved on war
Before you came? no need—you shall have all
The credit, trust me.
        Went.   Have they, Pym . . . not dared—
They have not dared . . . that is—I know you not—
Farewell—the times are changed.
        Pym.   —Since we two met
At Greenwich? Yes—poor patriots though we be,
You shall see something here, some slight return
For your exploits in Ireland! Changed indeed,
Could our friend Eliot look from out his grave!
Ah, Wentworth, one thing for acquaintance-sake;
Just to decide a question; have you, now,
Really felt well since you forsook us?
        Went.   Pym—
You're insolent!
        Pym.   Oh, you misapprehend!
Don't think I mean the advantage is with me:
I was about to say that, for my part,
I've never quite held up my head since then,—
Been quite myself since then: for first, you see,

I lost all credit after that event
With those who recollect how sure I was
Wentworth would outdo Eliot on our side.
    Went. By Heaven . . .
    Pym. Forgive me: Savile, Vane, and Holland
Eschew plain-speaking: 'tis a trick I have.
    Went. How, when, where,—Savile, Vane and Holland
        speak,—
Plainly or otherwise,—would have my scorn,
My perfect scorn, Sir . . .
    Pym.   . . . Did not my poor thoughts
Claim somewhat?
    Went.   Keep your thoughts! believe the King
Mistrusts me for their speaking, all these Vanes
And Saviles! make your mind up, all of you,
That I am discontented with the King!
    Pym. Why, you may be—I should be, that I know,
Were I like you.
    Went.   Like me?
    Pym.   I care not much
For titles; our friend Eliot died no Lord,
Hampden's no Lord, and Savile is a Lord:
But you care, since you sold your soul for one.
I can't think, therefore, Charles did well to laugh
When you twice prayed so humbly for an Earldom.
    Went. Pym . . .
    Pym. And your letters were the movingest!
Console yourself: I've borne him prayers just now
From Scotland not to be opprest by Laud—
And moving in their way: he'll pay, be sure,
As much attention as to those you sent.
    Went. False! a lie, Sir!
                . . . Who told you, Pym?
                        —But then
The King did very well . . . nay, I was glad
When it was shewn me why;—I first refused it!
. . . Pym, you were once my friend—don't speak to me!
    Pym. Oh, Wentworth, ancient brother of my soul,
That all should come to this!
    Went.   Leave me!
    Pym.   My friend,
Why should I leave you?
    Went.   To tell Rudyard this,

And Hampden this! . . .

   Pym.   Whose faces once were bright
At my approach . . . now sad with doubt and fear,
Because I hope in you—Wentworth—in you
Who never mean to ruin England—you
Who shake, with God's great help, this frightful dream
Away, now, in this Palace, where it crept
Upon you first, and are yourself—your good
And noble self—our Leader—our dear Chief—
Hampden's own friend—

                    This is the proudest day!
Come Wentworth! Do not even see the King!
The rough old room will seem itself again!
We'll both go in together—you've not seen
Hampden so long—come—and there's Vane—I know
You'll love young Vane! This is the proudest day!

(The KING *enters.* WENTWORTH *lets fall* PYM'S *hand.)*

   Cha. Arrived, my Lord?—This Gentleman, we know,
Was your old friend:

             (To PYM.) The Scots shall be informed
What we determine for their happiness.   *(Exit* PYM.)
You have made haste, my Lord.

   Went.   Sire . . . I am come . . .

   Cha. To aid us with your counsel: this Scots' League
And Covenant spreads too far, and we have proofs
That they intrigue with France: the Faction, too . . .

   Went. (Kneels.) Sire, trust me! but for this once, trust
     me, Sire!

   Cha. What can you mean?

   Went.   That you should trust me! now!
Oh—not for my sake! but 'tis sad, so sad
That for distrusting me, you suffer—you
Whom I would die to serve: Sire, do you think
That I would die to serve you?

   Cha.   But rise, Wentworth!

   Went. What shall convince you? What does Savile do
To . . . Ah, one can't tear out one's heart—one's heart—
And show it, how sincere a thing it is!

   Cha. Have not I trusted you?

   Went.   Say aught but that!
It is my comfort, mark you: all will be
So different when you trust me . . . as you shall!

It has not been your fault,—I was away,
Maligned—away—and how were you to know?
I am here, now—you mean to trust me, now—
All will go on so well!

   Cha.   Be sure I will—
I've heard that I should trust you: as you came
Even Carlisle was telling me . . .

   Went.   No,—hear nothing—
Be told nothing about me! you're not told
Your right-hand serves you, or your children love you!

   Cha.   You love me . . . only rise!

   Went.   I can speak now.
I have no right to hide the truth. 'Tis I
Can save you; only I. Sire, what is done!

   Cha.   Since Laud's assured . . . the minutes are within . . .
Loath as I am to spill my subjects' blood . . .

   Went.   That is, he'll have a war: what's done is done!

   Cha. They have intrigued with France; that's clear to Laud.

   Went.   Has Laud suggested any way to meet
The war's expence?

   Cha.   He'd not decide on that
Until you joined us.

   Went.   Most considerate!
You're certain they intrigue with France, these Scots?
(*Aside.*) The People would be with us!

   Cha.   Very sure.

   Went.   (The People for us . . . were the People for us!)
Sire, a great thought comes to reward your trust!
Summon a parliament! in Ireland first,
And then in England.

   Cha.   Madness!

   Went. (*Aside.*)   That puts off
The war—gives time to learn their grievances—
To talk with Pym—(*To* CHARLES). I know the faction as
They style it, . . .

   Cha.   . . . Tutors Scotland!

   Went.   All their plans
Suppose no parliament: in calling one
You take them by surprise. Produce the proofs
Of Scotland's treason; bid them help you, then!
Even Pym will not refuse!

   Cha.   You would begin
With Ireland?

Went.   Take no care for that: that's sure
To prosper.
 Cha.   You shall rule me: you were best
Return at once: but take this ere you go! (*Giving a paper.*)
Now, do I trust you? You're an Earl: my Friend
Of Friends: yes, Strafford, while . . . You hear me not!
 Went. Say it all o'er again—but once again—
The first was for the music—once again!
 Cha. Strafford, my brave friend, there were wild reports—
Vain rumours . . . Henceforth touching Strafford is
To touch the apple of my sight: why gaze
So earnestly?
 Went.   I am grown young again,
And foolish! . . . what was it we spoke of?
 Cha.   Ireland,
The Parliament,—
 Went.   I may go when I will?
—Now?
 Cha. Are you tired so soon of me?
 Went.   My King . . .
But you will not so very much dislike
A Parliament? I'd serve you any way!
 Cha. You said just now this was the only way.
 Went. Sire, I will serve you!
 Cha.   Strafford, spare yourself—
You are so sick, they tell me, . . .
 Went.   'Tis my soul
That's well and happy, now!
       This Parliament—
We'll summon it, the English one—I'll care
For everything: You shall not need them much!
 Cha. If they prove restive . . .
 Went.   I shall be with you!
 Cha. Ere they assemble?
 Went.   I will come, or else
Deposit this infirm humanity
I' the dust! My whole heart stays with you, my King!

(*As* STRAFFORD *goes out, the* QUEEN *enters.*)

 Cha. That man must love me!
 Queen.   Is it over then?
Why he looks yellower than ever! well,
At least we shall not hear eternally

Of his vast services: he's paid at last.

    Cha.   Not done with: he engages to surpass
All yet performed in Ireland.

    Queen.   I had thought
Nothing beyond was ever to be done.
The War, Charles—will he raise supplies enough?

    Cha.   We've hit on an expedient; he . . . that is
I have advised . . . we have decided on
The calling—in Ireland—of a Parliament.

    Queen.   O truly! You agree to that? Is this
The first fruit of his counsel? But I guessed
As much.

    Cha.   This is too idle, Henrietta!
I should know best: He will strain every nerve,
And once a precedent established . . .

    Queen.   Notice
How sure he is of a long term of favours!
He'll see the next, and the next after that;
No end to Parliaments!

    Cha.   Well, it is done:
He talks it smoothly, doubtless: if, indeed,
The Commons here . . .

    Queen.   Here! you will summon them
Here? Would I were in France again to see
A King!

    Cha.   But Henrietta . . .

    Queen.   O the Scots
Do well to spurn your rule!

    Cha.   But, listen, Sweet . . .

    Queen.   Let Strafford listen—you confide in him!

    Cha.   I do not, Love—I do not so confide . . .
The Parliament shall never trouble us
. . . Nay, hear me! I have schemes—such schemes—we'll buy
The leaders off: without that, Strafford's counsel
Had ne'er prevailed on me. Perhaps I call it
To have excuse for breaking it—for ever—
And whose will then the blame be? See you not?
Come, Dearest!—look! the little fairy, now,
That cannot reach my shoulder! Dearest, come!

                                (Exeunt.)

END OF THE FIRST ACT

ACT II

SCENE I.—(As in Act I. Scene I.)

The same Party enters confusedly ; among the first, the younger
VANE *and* RUDYARD.

Rud.   Twelve subsidies!
Vane.   O Rudyard, do not laugh
At least!
Rud.   True: Strafford called the Parliament—
'Tis he should laugh!
   A Puritan (entering).—Out of the serpent's root
Comes forth a cockatrice.
   Fien. (entering).   —A stinging one,
If that's the Parliament: twelve subsidies!
A stinging one! but, brother, where's your word
For Strafford's other nest-egg—the Scots' War?
   The Puritan.   His fruit shall be a fiery flying serpent.
   Fien.   Shall be? It chips the shell, man; peeps abroad:
Twelve subsidies!—
                          Why, how now Vane?
   Rud.   Hush, Fiennes!
   Fien.   Ah? . . . but he was not more a dupe than I,
Or you, or any here the day that Pym
Returned with the good news. Look up, dear Vane!
We all believed that Strafford meant us well
In summoning the Parliament . . .

(HAMPDEN *enters.*)

   Vane (starting up).   Now, Hampden,
Clear me! I would have leave to sleep again!
I'd look the People in the face again!
Clear me from having, from the first, hoped, dreamed
Better of Strafford! Fool!
   Hamp.   You'll grow one day
A steadfast light to England, Vane!
   Rud.   Ay, Fiennes,
Strafford revived our Parliaments: before,
War was but talked of; there's an army, now:
Still, we've a Parliament. Poor Ireland bears
Another wrench (she dies the hardest death!)

Why . . . speak of it in Parliament! and, lo,
'Tis spoken!—and console yourselves.

Fien.   The jest!
We clamoured, I suppose, thus long, to win
The privilege of laying on ourselves
A sorer burthen than the King dares lay!

Rud.   Mark now: we meet at length: complaints pour in
From every county: all the land cries out
On loans and levies, curses ship-money,
Calls vengeance on the Star-chamber: we lend
An ear: " ay, lend them all the ears you have,"
Puts in the King; " my subjects, as you find,
" Are fretful, and conceive great things of you:
" Just listen to them, friends: you'll sanction me
" The measures they most wince at, make them yours
" Instead of mine, I know: and, to begin,
" They say my levies pinch them,—raise me straight
" Twelve subsidies ! "

Fien. and others.   All England cannot furnish
Twelve subsidies !

Hol.   But Strafford, just returned
From Ireland . . . what has he to do with that?
How could he speak his mind? He left before
The Parliament assembled: Rudyard, friends,
He could not speak his mind! and Pym, who knows
Strafford . . .

Rud.   Would I were sure we know ourselves!
What is for good, what, bad—who friend, who foe!

Hol.   Do you count Parliaments no gain?

Rud.   A gain?
While the King's creatures overbalance us?
—There's going on, beside, among ourselves
A quiet, slow, but most effectual course
Of buying over, sapping, . . .

A Puritan.   . . . . Leavening
The lump till all is leaven.

A Voice.   Glanville's gone.

Rud.   I'll put a case; had not the Court declared
That no sum short of just twelve subsidies
Will be accepted by the King—our House
Would have consented to that wretched offer
To let us buy off Ship-money?

Hol.   Most like,

If . . . say six subsidies, will buy it off,
The House . . .
   Rud.   . . . Will grant them! Hampden, do you
     hear?
Oh, I congratulate you that the King
Has gained his point at last . . . our own assent
To that detested tax! all's over then!
There's no more taking refuge in this room
And saying, " Let the King do what he will,
" We, England, are no party to our shame,—
" Our day will come!" Congratulate with me!

(PYM *enters.*)

   Vane.   Pym, Strafford called this Parliament, 'tis like—
But we'll not have our Parliaments like those
In Ireland, Pym!
   Rud.   Let him stand forth, that Strafford!
One doubtful act hides far too many sins;
It can be stretched no more—and, to my mind,
Begins to drop from those it covers.
   Other Voices.   Pym,
Let him avow himself! No fitter time!
We wait thus long for you!
   Rud.   Perhaps, too long!
Since nothing but the madness of the Court
In thus unmasking its designs at once
Had saved us from betraying England. Stay—
This Parliament is Strafford's: let us vote
Our list of grievances too black by far
To suffer talk of subsidies: or best—
That Ship-money's disposed of long ago
By England; any vote that's broad enough:
And then let Strafford, for the love of it,
Support his Parliament!
   Vane.   And vote as well
No war's to be with Scotland! Hear you, Pym?
We'll vote, no War! No part nor lot in it
For England!
   Many Voices.   Vote, no War! Stop the new levies!
No Bishop's War! At once! When next we meet!
   Pym.   Much more when next we meet!
                    —Friends, which of you
Since first the course of Strafford was in doubt

Has fallen the most away in soul from me?

Vane. I sate apart, even now, under God's eye,
Pondering the words that should denounce you, Pym,
In presence of us all, as one at league
With England's enemy!

Pym. You are a good
And gallant spirit, Henry! Take my hand
And say you pardon me for all the pain
Till now! Strafford is wholly ours.

Many Voices. 'Tis sure?

Pym. Most sure—for Charles dissolves the Parliament
While I speak here! . . . (*Great emotion in the assembly.*)
. . . And I must speak, friends, now!
Strafford is ours! The King detects the change,
Casts Strafford off for ever, and resumes
His ancient path: no Parliament for us—
No Strafford for the King!

Come all of you
To bid the King farewell, predict success
To his Scots expedition, and receive
Strafford, our comrade now! The next will be
Indeed a Parliament!

Vane. Forgive me, Pym!

Voices. This looks like truth—Strafford can have, indeed,
No choice!

Pym. Friends, follow me! he's with the King:
Come Hampden, and come Rudyard, and come Vane—
This is no sullen day for England, Vane!
Strafford shall tell you!

Voices. To Whitehall then! Come!
(*Exuent omnes.*)

SCENE II.—*Whitehall.*

CHARLES *seated*, STRAFFORD *standing beside a table
covered with maps, etc.*

Cha. Strafford . . .

Straf. Is it a dream? my papers, here—
Thus—as I left them—all the plans you found
So happy—(look! The track you pressed my hand
For pointing out!)—and in this very room
Over these very plans, you tell me, Sire,
With the same face, too,—tell me just one thing

That ruins them! How's this? what may this mean?
Sire, who has done this?

   Cha.   Strafford, none but I!
You bade me put the rest away—indeed
You are alone!

   Straf.   Alone—and like to be!
No fear, when some unworthy scheme's grown ripe,
Of those who hatched it leaving you to loose
The mischief on the world! Laud hatches war,
Falls to his prayers, and leaves the rest to me—
And I'm alone!

   Cha.   At least, you knew as much
When first you undertook the war.

   Straf.   My liege,
Is this the way? I said, since Laud would lap
A little blood, 'twere best to hurry o'er
The loathsome business—not to be whole months
At slaughter—one blow—only one—then, peace—
Save for the dreams! I said, to please you both
I'd lead an Irish Army to the West,
While in the South the English . . . but you look
As though you had not told me fifty times
'Twas a brave plan! My Army is all raised—
I am prepared to join it . . .

   Cha.   Hear me, Strafford!

   Straf. . . . When, for some little thing, my whole design
Is set aside—(where is the wretched paper?)
I am to lead—(ay, here it is)—to lead
This English Army: why? Northumberland
That I appointed, chooses to be sick—
Is frightened: and, meanwhile, who answers for
The Irish Parliament? or Army, either?
Is this my plan? I say, is this my plan?

   Cha.   You are disrespectful, Sir!

   Straf.   Do not believe—
My liege, do not believe it! I am yours—
Yours ever—'tis too late to think about—
To the death, yours! Elsewhere, this untoward step
Shall pass for mine—the world shall think it mine—
But, here! But, here! I am so seldom here!
Seldom with you, my King! I—soon to rush
Alone—upon a Giant—in the dark!

   Cha.   My Strafford!

Straf. (*Seats himself at the table ; examines papers awhile ; then, breaking off*)
   ... " Seize the passes of the Tyne " ...
But don't you see—see all I say is true?
My plan was sure to prosper,—so, no cause
To ask the Parliament for help; whereas
We need them—frightfully ...
  Cha.   Need this Parliament?
  Straf. —Now, for God's sake, mind—not one error more!
We can afford no error—we draw, now,
Upon our last resource—this Parliament
Must help us!
  Cha.   I've undone you, Strafford!
  Straf.   Nay—
Nay—don't despond—Sire—'tis not come to that!
I have not hurt you? Sire—what have I said
To hurt you? I'll unsay it! Don't despond!
Sire, do you turn from me?
  Cha.   My friend of friends!
  Straf. (*After a pause*). We'll make a shift! Leave me
    the Parliament!
They help us ne'er so little but I'll make
A vast deal out of it. We'll speak them fair:
They're sitting: that's one great thing: that half gives
Their sanction to us: that's much: don't despond!
Why, let them keep their money, at the worst!
The reputation of the People's help
Is all we want: we'll make shift yet!
  Cha.   Dear Strafford
  Straf. But meantime, let the sum be ne'er so small
They offer, we'll accept it: any sum—
For the look of it: the least grant tells the Scots
The Parliament is ours ... their staunch ally
Is ours: that told, there's scarce a blow to strike!
What will the grant be? What does Glanville think?
  Cha. Alas ...
  Straf.   My liege?
  Cha.   Strafford ...
  Straf.   But answer me!
Have they ... O surely not refused us all?
All the twelve subsidies? We never looked
For all of them! How many do they give?
  Cha. You have not heard ...

Straf.   (What has he done?)—Heard what?
But speak at once, Sire—this grows terrible!

                   (*The King continuing silent.*)
You have dissolved them!—I'll not leave this man.
   Cha.   'Twas Vane—his ill-judged vehemence that . . .
   Straf.   Vane?
   Cha.   He told them, as they were about to vote
The half, that nothing short of all the twelve
Would serve our turn, or be accepted.
   Straf.   Vane!
Vane! and you promised me that very Vane . . .
O God, to have it gone, quite gone from me
The one last hope—I that despair, *my* hope—
That I should reach his heart one day, and cure
All bitterness one day, be proud again
And young again, care for the sunshine too,
And never think of Eliot any more,—
God, and to toil for this, go far for this,
Get nearer, and still nearer, reach this heart—
And find Vane there!

         (*Suddenly taking up a paper, and continuing with a
           forced calmness.*)
                 Northumberland is sick:
Well then, I take the Army: Wilmot leads
The Horse, and he with Conway must secure
The passes of the Tyne: Ormond supplies
My place in Ireland. Here, we'll try the City:
If they refuse a loan . . . debase the coin
And seize the bullion! we've no other choice.
Herbert . . .
(*Flinging down the paper.*) And this while I am here! with
     you!
And there are hosts such, hosts like Vane! I go,—
And, I once gone, they'll close around you, Sire,
When the least pique, pettiest mistrust, is sure
To ruin me—and you along with me!
Do you see that? And you along with me!
—Sire, you'll not ever listen to these men,
And I away, fighting your battle? Sire,
If they—if She—charge me—no matter what
You say, " At any time when he returns
" His head is mine." Don't stop me there! You know
My head is yours . . . only, don't stop me there!

Cha. Too shameful, Strafford! You advised the war,
And . . .
Straf. I! I! that was never spoken with
Till it was entered on! That loathe the war!
That say it is the maddest, wickedest . . .
Do you know, Charles, I think, within my heart,
That you would say I did advise the war;
And if, thro' your own weakness, falsehood, Charles,
These Scots, with God to help them, drive me back . . .
You will not step between the raging People
And me, to say . . .
                    I knew you! from the first
I knew you! Never was so cold a heart!
Remember that I said it—that I never
Believed you for a moment!
                         —And, you loved me?
You thought your perfidy profoundly hid
Because I could not share your whisperings
With Vane? With Savile? But your hideous heart—
I had your heart to see, Charles! Oh, to have
A heart of stone—of smooth, cold, frightful stone!
Ay, call them! Shall I call for you? The Scots
Goaded to madness? Or the English—Pym—
Shall I call Pym, your subject? Oh, you think
I'll leave them in the dark about it all?
They shall not know you? Hampden, Pym shall not . . .

(*Enter* PYM, HAMPDEN, VANE, *etc.*)

(*Dropping on his knee.*) Thus favoured with your gracious
        countenance
What shall a rebel League avail against
Your servant, utterly and ever yours?
(*To the rest*) So, Gentlemen, the King's not even left
The privilege of bidding me farewell
Who haste to save the People—that you style
Your People—from the mercies of the Scots
And France their friend?
(*To* CHARLES)   Pym's grave grey eyes are fixed
Upon you, Sire!
(*To the rest*)   Your pleasure, Gentlemen?
Hamp. The King dissolved us—'tis the King we seek
And not Lord Strafford.
Straf.   . . . Strafford, guilty too

Of counselling the measure: (*To* CHARLES) (Hush . . . you
　　know . . .
You have forgotten . . . Sire, I counselled it!)
—(*Aloud*)　A heinous matter, truly!　But the King
Will yet see cause to thank me for a course
Which now, perchance . . . (Sire, tell them so!) . . . he
　　blames.
Well, choose some fitter time to make your charge—
I shall be with the Scots—you understand?—
Then yelp at me!
　　　　　　　　　　　Meanwhile, your Majesty
Binds me, by this fresh token of your trust . . .

> (*Under the pretence of an earnest farewell,* STRAFFORD *conducts*
> CHARLES *to the door, in such a manner as to hide his agita-*
> *tion from the rest:* VANE *and others gazing at them: as*
> *the King disappears, they turn as by one impulse to*
> PYM, *who has not changed his original posture of*
> *surprise.*)

Hamp.　Leave we this arrogant strong wicked man!
Vane and others.　Dear Pym!　Come out of this unworthy
　　place
To our old room again!　Come, dearest Pym!
　　　　　　(STRAFFORD *just about to follow the King, looks back.*)
Pym. (*To* STRAFFORD)　Keep tryst! the old appointment's
　　made anew:
Forget not we shall meet again!
　　Straf.　　　　　　　　　Be it so!
And if an Army follows me?
　　Vane.　　　　　　　　His friends
Will entertain your Army!
　　Pym.　　　　　　　　I'll not say
You have misreckoned, Strafford: time will . . .
　　　　　　　　　　　　　　　　　　　Perish
Body and spirit!　Fool to feign a doubt—
Pretend the scrupulous and nice reserve
Of one whose prowess is to do the feat.
What share have I in it?　Shall I affect
To see no dismal sign above your head
When God suspends his ruinous thunder there?
Strafford is doomed!　Touch him no one of you!
　　　　　　　　　　　　(*Exeunt* PYM, HAMPDEN, *etc.*)
　　Straf.　Pym, we shall meet again!

(*Enter* CARLISLE.)

                              You here, girl?
Car.   Hush—
I know it all—hush, dearest Strafford!
  Straf.   Ah?
Well. I shall make a sorry soldier, Lucy!
All Knights begin their enterprise, you know,
Under the best of auspices; 'tis morn—
The Lady girds his sword upon the Youth—
(He's always very young)—the trumpets sound—
Cups pledge him, and . . . and . . . the King blesses him —
You need not turn a page of the Romance
To learn the Dreadful Giant's fate! Indeed
We've the fair Lady here; but she apart,—
A poor man, never having handled lance,
And rather old, weary, and far from sure
His Squires are not the Giant's friends: well—well—
Let us go forth!
  Car.   Go forth?
  Straf.   What matters it?
We shall die gloriously—as the book says.
  Car. To Scotland? not to Scotland?
  Straf.   Am I sick
Like your good brother, brave Northumberland?
Beside the walls seem falling on me!
  Car.   Strafford,
The wind that saps these walls can undermine
Your camp in Scotland, too! Whence creeps the wind?
Have you no eyes except for Pym? Look here!
A breed of silken creatures lurk and thrive
In your contempt: you'll vanquish Pym? Friend, Vane
Can vanquish you! And Vane you think to fly?—
Rush on the Scots! Do nobly! Vane's slight sneer
Shall test success—adjust the praise—suggest
The faint result: Vane's sneer shall reach you there!
—You do not listen!
  Straf.   Oh . . . I give that up—
There's fate in it—I give all here quite up.
Care not what Vane does or what Holland does
Against me! 'Tis so idle to withstand them—
In no case tell me what they do!
  Car.   But Strafford . . .

Straf. I want a little strife, beside—real strife:
This petty, palace-warfare does me harm:
I shall feel better, fairly out of it.

Car. Why do you smile?

Straf. I got to fear them, girl!
I could have torn his throat at first, that Vane,
As he leered at me on his stealthy way
To the Queen's closet, Lucy—but of late
I often found it in my heart to say
" Vane—don't traduce me to her ! "

Car. But the King . . .

Straf. The King stood there, 'tis not so long ago,
—There, and the whisper, Lucy, " Be my friend
" Of friends ! "—My King ! I would have . . .

Car. . . . Died for him ?

Straf. . . . Sworn him true, Lucy : I will die for him.

Car. (*Aside.*) What can he mean ? You'd say he loved
him still !
(*To* STRAFFORD.) But go not, Strafford ! . . . But you must
renounce
This project on the Scots ! Die ! wherefore die ?
Charles never loved you !

Straf. And he will not, now :
He's not of those who care the more for you
That you're unfortunate.

Car. Then wherefore die ?
For such a master ?

Straf. You that told me first
How good he was—when I must leave true friends
To find a truer friend !—that drew me here
From Ireland,—" I had but to show myself
" And Charles would spurn Vane, Savile, and the rest "—
You, girl, to ask me that ?

Car. (*Aside.*) If he have set
His heart abidingly on Charles !
(*To* STRAFFORD.) Dear friend,
I shall not see you any more !

Straf. Yes, girl—
There's one man here that I shall meet !

Car. (*Aside.*) The King !—
What way to save him from the King ?
My soul . . .
That lent from its own store the charmed disguise

That clothes the King . . . he shall behold my soul!
(*To* STRAFFORD.)   Strafford . . . (I shall speak best if you'll
 not gaze
Upon me.) . . . You would perish, too! So sure! . . .
Could you but know what 'tis to bear, my Strafford,
One Image stamped within you, turning blank
The else imperial brilliance of your mind,—
A weakness, but most precious,—like a flaw
I' the diamond which would shape forth some sweet face
Yet to create, and meanwhile treasured there
Lest Nature lose her gracious thought for ever!
 Straf.   When could it be? . . . no! . . . yet . . . was it
  the day
We waited in the anteroom, till Holland
Should leave the presence-chamber?
 Car.   What?
 Straf.   —That
Described to you my love for Charles?
 Car. (*Aside.*) Ah, no—
One must not lure him from a love like that!
Oh, let him love the King and die! 'Tis past . . .
I shall not serve him worse for that one brief
And passionate hope . . . silent for ever now!
(*To* STRAFFORD.) And you are really bound for Scotland then?
I wish you well: you must be very sure
Of the King's faith, for Pym and all his crew
Will not be idle—setting Vane aside!
 Straf.   If Pym is busy,—you may write of Pym.
 Car.   What need when there's your king to take your part?
He may endure Vane's counsel; but for Pym—
Think you he'll suffer Pym to . . .
 Straf.   Girl, your hair
Is glossier than the Queen's!
 Car.   Is that to ask
A curl of me?
 Straf. Scotland·—the weary way!
 Car.   Stay, let me fasten it.
       —A rival's, Strafford?
 Straf. (*Showing the George.*) He hung it there: twine
  yours around it, girl!
 Car.   No—no—another time—I trifle so!
And there's a masque on foot: farewell: the Court
Is dull: do something to enliven us

In Scotland; we expect it at your hands.
   Straf. I shall not fall in Scotland.
   Car.   Prosper—if
You'll think of me sometimes!
   Straf.   How think of him
And not of you? of you—the lingering streak
(A golden one) in my good fortune's eve?
   Car. Strafford . . .
               Well, when the eve has its last streak
The night has its first star!   (*Exit.*)
   Straf.   That voice of hers . . .
You'd think she had a heart sometimes! His voice
Is soft too.
         Only God can save him now.
Be Thou about his bed, about his path! . . .
His path! Where's England's path? Diverging wide,
And not to join again the track my foot
Must follow—whither? All that forlorn way—
Among the tombs! Far—far—till . . . What, they do
Then join again, these paths? For, huge in the dusk,
There's—Pym to face!
              Why then I have a Foe
To close with, and a fight to fight at last
That's worth my soul! What—do they beard the King—
And shall the King want Strafford at his need—
My King—at his great need? Am I not here?

    . . . Not in the common blessed market-place
Pressed on by the rough artisans, so proud
To catch a glance from Wentworth! They'll lie down
Hungry and say "Why, it must end some day—
"Is he not watching for our sake?"
                    —Not there!
But in Whitehall—the whited sepulchre—
The . . .
       (*At the Window, and looking on London.*)
      Curse nothing to-night! Only one name
They'll curse in all those streets to-night! Whose fault?
Did I make kings—set up, the first, a man
To represent the multitude, receive
All love in right of them—supplanting them
Until you love the man and not the king——
The man with the mild voice and mournful eyes

That send me forth . . .
     To breast the bloody sea
That sweeps before me—with one star to guide—
Night has its first supreme forsaken star!

           (Exit.)

END OF THE SECOND ACT

ACT III

SCENE I.—*Opposite Westminster Hall.*

SIR HENRY VANE, Lord SAVILE, Lord HOLLAND, *and
others of the Court.*

Vane. The Commons thrust you out?
 Savile.   And what kept you
From sharing their civility?
 Vane.   Kept me?
Fresh news from Scotland, sir! worse than the last
If that may be! all's up with Strafford there!
Nothing's to bar the mad Scots marching hither
The next fine morning! That detained me, sir!
Well now, before they thrust you out, go on,
Their speaker . . . did the fellow Lenthall say
All we set down for him?
 Hol.   Not a word missed!
Ere he began, we entered, Savile, I
And Bristol and some more, in hopes to breed
A wholesome awe in the new Parliament—
But such a gang of graceless ruffians, Vane!
They glared at us . . .
 Vane.   So many?
 Savile.   Not a bench
Without its complement of burly knaves—
Your son, there, Vane, among them—Hampden leant
Upon his shoulder—think of that!
 Vane.   I'd think
On Lenthall's speech, if I could get at it . . .
He said, I hope, how grateful they should be
For this unlooked-for summons from the King?
 Hol. Just as we drilled him . . .

Vane. That the Scots will march
On London?

Hol. All, and made so much of it
A dozen subsidies at least seemed sure
To follow, when . . .

Vane. Well?

Hol. 'Tis a strange thing now!
I've a vague memory of a sort of sound—
A voice—a kind of vast, unnatural voice—
Pym, Sir, was speaking! Savile, help me out,—
What was it all?

Sav. Something about "a matter" . . .
No . . . "a work for England."

Bristol. "England's great revenge"
He talked of.

Sav. How should I be used to Pym
More than yourselves?

Hol. However that may be,
'Twas something with which we had nought to do,
For we were "strangers" and 'twas "England's work"—
(All this while looking us straight in the face)
In other words, our presence might be spared:
So, in the twinkling of an eye, before
I settled to my mind what ugly brute
Was likest Pym just then, they yelled us out,
Locked the doors after us, and here are we!

Vane. Old Eliot's method . . .

Sav. Ah, now, Vane, a truce
To Eliot and his times, and the great Duke,
And how to manage Parliaments! 'Twas you
Advised the Queen to summon this—why Strafford
To do him justice would not hear of it!

Vane. Say, rather, you have done the best of turns
To Strafford—he's at York—we all know why!
I would you had not set the Scots on Strafford
Till he had put down Pym for us, my lord!

Sav. I? did I alter Strafford's plans? did I . . .

(Enter a Messenger.)

Mes. The Queen, my lords . . . she sends me . . .
follow me
At once . . . 'tis very urgent . . . she would have
Your counsel . . . something perilous and strange

Occasions her command.
    Sav.   We follow, friend!
Now Vane . . . your Parliament will plague us all!
    Vane.   No Strafford here beside!
    Sav.   If you dare hint
I had a hand in his betrayal, Sir . . .
    Hol.   Nay find a fitter time for quarrels—Pym
Will overmatch the best of you; and, think,
The Queen!
    Vane.   Come on then (*as they go out.*) . . . understand,
      I loathe
Strafford as much as any—but he serves
So well to keep off Pym—to screen us all!
I would we had reserved him yet awhile!   (*Exeunt.*)

SCENE II.—*Whitehall.*

The QUEEN *and* CARLISLE.

    Queen.   It cannot be!
    Car.   It is so.
    Queen.   Why the House
Have hardly met!
    Car.   They met for that.
    Queen.   No—no—
Meet to impeach Lord Strafford! 'Tis a jest!
    Car.   A bitter one.
    Queen.   Consider! 'Tis the House
We summoned so reluctantly—which nothing
But the disastrous issue of the war
Persuaded us to summon; they'll wreak all
Their spite on us, no doubt; but the old way
Is to begin by talk of grievances!
They have their grievances to busy them!
    Car.   Pym has begun his speech.
    Queen.   Where's Vane? . . . That is
Pym will impeach Lord Strafford if he leaves
His Presidency—he's at York, you know,
Since the Scots beat him—why should he leave York?
    Car.   Because the King sends for him.
    Queen.   Ah . . . but if
The King did send for him, he let him know
We had been forced to call a Parliament—

A step which Strafford, now I come to think,
Was vehement against . . .

    Car.   The policy
Escaped him of first striking Parliaments
To earth, then setting them upon their feet
And giving them a sword: but this is idle!
—Did the King send for Strafford?

                                   He will come.

    Queen.   And what am I to do?

    Car.   What do! Fail, Madam!
Be ruined for his sake! what matters how
So it but stand on record that you made
An effort—only one?

    Queen.   The King's away
At Theobald's.

    Car.   Send for him at once—he must
Dissolve the House.

    Queen.   Wait till Vane finds the truth
Of the report—then . . .

    Car.   . . . it will matter little
What the King does. Strafford that serves you all—
That's fighting for you now!

               (*Enter* Sir H. VANE.)

    Vane.   The Commons, Madam,
Are sitting with closed doors—a huge debate—
No lack of noise—but nothing, I should guess,
Concerning Strafford: Pym has certainly
Not spoken yet.

    Queen. (*To* CARLISLE.) You hear?

    Car.   I do not hear
That the King's sent for!

    Vane.   Savile will be able
To tell you more.

               (*Enter* HOLLAND.)

    Queen.   The last news, Holland?

    Hol.   Pym
Is raving like a fiend! The whole House means
To follow him together to Whitehall
And force the King to give up Strafford.

    Queen.   Strafford?

    Hol. If they content themselves with Strafford! Laud

Is talked of, Cottington and Windebank too,
Pym has not left out one of them . . . I would
You heard Pym raving!
 Queen.   Vane, find out the King!
Tell the King, Vane, the People follow Pym
To brave us at Whitehall!

      (*Enter* SAVILE.)

 Sav.   Not to Whitehall—
'Tis to the Lords they go—they'll seek redress
On Strafford from his peers—the legal way,
They call it . . .
 Queen.   (Wait, Vane!)
 Sav.   . . . But the adage gives
Long life to threatened men! Strafford can save
Himself so readily: at York, remember,
In his own county, what has he to fear?
The Commons only mean to frighten him
From leaving York.
 Queen.   Surely he will not come!
Carlisle, he will not come!
 Car.   Once more, the King
Has sent for Strafford—He will come.
 Vane.   O doubtless;
And bring destruction with him; that's his way.
What but his coming spoilt all Conway's plan?
The King must take his counsel, choose his friends,
Be wholly ruled by him! What's the result?
The North that was to rise—Ireland to help—
What came of it? In my poor mind a fright
Is no prodigious punishment.
 Car.   A fright?
Pym will fail worse than Strafford if he thinks
To frighten him. (*To the* QUEEN.) You will not save him,
  then?
 Sav. When something like a charge is made, the King
Will best know how to save him: and 'tis clear
That, while he suffers nothing by the matter,
The King will reap advantage: this in question,
No dinning you with ship-money complaints!
 Queen. (*To* CARLISLE.) If we dissolve them, who will pay
  the army?
Protect us from the insolent Scots?

Car.   In truth
I know not, Madam: Strafford's fate concerns
Me little: you desired to learn what course
Would save him: I obey you.
Vane.   Notice, too,
There can't be fairer ground for taking full
Revenge—(Strafford's revengeful)—than he'll have
Against this very Pym.
Queen.   Why, he shall claim
Vengeance on Pym!
Vane.   And Strafford, who is he
To 'scape unscathed amid the accidents
That harass all beside? I, for my part,
Should look for something of discomfiture
Had the King trusted me so thoroughly
And been so paid for it.
Hol.   He'll keep at York:
All will blow over: he'll return no worse—
Humbled a little—thankful for a place
Under as good a man—Oh, we'll dispense
With seeing Strafford for a month or two!

(Enter STRAFFORD.)

Queen. You here!
Straf.   The King sends for me, Madam.
Queen.   Sir . . .
The King . . .
Straf. An urgent matter that imports the King . . .
(*To* CARLISLE.) Why, Lucy, what's in agitation now
That all this muttering and shrugging, see,
Begins at me? They do not speak!
Car.   Oh welcome!
. . . And we are proud of you . . . all very proud
To have you with us, Strafford . . . you were brave
At Durham . . . You did well there . . . Had you not
Been stayed you might have . . . we said, even now,
Our last, last hope's in you!
Vane. (*To* CARLISLE.) The Queen would speak
                          A word with you!
Straf. (*To* VANE.) Will one of you vouchsafe
To signify my presence to the King?
Sav. An urgent matter?
Straf.   None that touches you,

Lord Savile!   Say it were some treacherous,
Sly, pitiful intriguing with the Scots—
You would go free, at least!   (*Aside.*)   They half divine
My purpose!   (*To the* QUEEN.)   Madam, shall I see the
    King?
The service I would render much concerns
His welfare.
    Queen.   But his Majesty, my lord,
May not be here, may . . .
    Straf.   Its importance, then,
Must plead excuse for this withdrawal, Madam—
And for the grief it gives Lord Savile here.
    Queen. (*Who has been conversing with* VANE *and* HOLLAND.)
      The King will see you, Sir.
(*To* CARLISLE.)   Mark me: Pym's worst
Is done by now—he has impeached the Earl,
Or found the Earl too strong for him, by now;
Let us not seem instructed!   We should work
No good to Strafford, but deform ourselves
With shame in the world's eye!   (*To* STRAFFORD.)   His
    Majesty
Has much to say with you.
    Straf. (*Aside.*)   Time fleeting too!
(*To* CARLISLE.)   No means of getting them away, Carlisle?
What does she whisper?   Does she know my purpose?
What does she think of it?   Get them away!
    Queen. (*To* CARLISLE.)   He comes to baffle Pym—he
    thinks the danger
Far off—tell him no word of it—a time
For help will come—we'll not be wanting, then!
Keep him in play, Carlisle—you, self-possessed
And calm!   (*To* STRAFFORD.)   To spare your Lordship some
    delay
I will myself acquaint the King.   (*To* CARLISLE.)   Beware!
          (*Exeunt* QUEEN, VANE, HOLLAND *and* SAVILE.)
    Straf.   She knows it?
    Car.   Tell me, Strafford . . .
    Straf.   Afterward!
The moment's the great moment of all time!
She knows my purpose?
    Car.   Thoroughly—just now
She bade me hide it from you.
    Straf.   Quick, dear girl . . .

The whole grand scheme?

Car. (*Aside.*) Ah, he would learn if they
Connive at Pym's procedure! Could they but
Have once apprized the King! But there's no time
For falsehood, now. (*To* STRAFFORD.) Strafford, the whole
is known.

Straf. Known and approved?

Car. Hardly discountenanced.

Straf. And the king—say the king consents as well!

Car. The king's not yet informed, but will not dare
To interpose.

Straf. What need to wait him, then?
He'll sanction it! I stayed, girl, tell him, long!
It vexed me to the soul—this waiting here—
You know him—there's no counting on the king!
Tell him I waited long!

Car. (*Aside.*) What can he mean?
Rejoice at the king's hollowness?

Straf. I knew
They would be glad of it,—all over once,
I knew they would be glad . . . but he'd contrive,
The Queen and he, to mar, by helping it,
An angel's making!

Car. (*Aside.*) Is he mad? (*To* STRAFFORD.) Dear
Strafford,
You were not wont to look so happy.

Straf. Girl,
I tried obedience thoroughly: I took
The king's wild plan . . . of course, ere I could reach
My army—Conway ruined it: I drew
The wrecks together, raised all heaven and earth,
And would have fought the Scots—the King at once
Made truce with them; then, Lucy, then, dear girl,
God put it in my mind to love, serve, die
For Charles—but never to obey him more!
While he endured their insolence at Ripon
I fell on them at Durham.

. . . But you'll tell
The king I waited? All the anteroom
Is filled with my adherents.

Car. Strafford—Strafford,
What daring act is this you hint?

Straf. No—no!

'Tis here—not daring if you knew!—all here!

> (*Drawing papers from his breast.*)

Full proof—see—ample proof—does the Queen know
I have such damning proof? Bedford and Essex,
Broke, Warwick, Savile (did you notice Savile?
The simper that I spoilt?) Say, Mandeville—
Sold to the Scots, body and soul, by Pym!

 Car. Great heaven!

 Straf.   From Savile and his lords, to Pym—
I crush them, girl—Pym shall not ward the blow
Nor Savile crawl aside from it! The Court
And the Cabal—I crush them!

 Car.   And you go . . .
Strafford,—and now you go? . . .

 Straf.   About no work
In the back-ground, I promise you! I go
Straight to the House of Lords to claim these men.
Mainwaring!

 Car. Stay—stay, Strafford!

 Straf.   She'll return—
The Queen—some little project of her own—
No time to lose—the King takes fright perhaps—

 Car. Pym's strong, remember!

 Straf.   Very strong—as fits
The Faction's Head . . . with no offence to Hampden.
Vane, Rudyard and my loving Hollis—one
And all they lodge within the Tower to-night
In just equality. Bryan! Mainwaring!

> (*Many of his Adherents enter.*)

The Peers debate just now (a lucky chance)
On the Scots war—my visit's opportune:
When all is over, Bryan, you'll proceed
To Ireland: these dispatches, mark me, Bryan,
Are for the Deputy, and these for Ormond—
We'll want the Army here—my Army, raised
At such a cost, that should have done such good,
And was inactive all the time! no matter—
We'll find a use for it. Willis . . . no—You!
You, friend, make haste to York—bear this, at once . . .
Or,—better stay for form's sake—see yourself
The news you carry. You remain with me
To execute the Parliament's command,

Mainwaring—help to seize the lesser knaves:
Take care there's no escaping at backdoors!
To not have one escape—mind me—not one!
I seem revengeful, Lucy? Did you know
What these men dare!

   Car.   It is so much they dare!

   Straf. I proved that long ago; my turn is now!
Keep sharp watch, Goring, on the citizens;
Observe who harbours any of the brood
That scramble off: be sure they smart for it!
Our coffers are but lean.

                  And you, girl, too,
Shall have your task—deliver this to Laud—
Laud will not be the slowest in my praise!
" Thorough " he'll say!

             —Foolish, to be so glad!
This sort of life is vivid, after all!
'Tis worth while, Lucy, having foes like mine
For the dear bliss of crushing them! To-day
Is worth the living for!

   Car.   That reddening brow!
You seem . . .

   Straf.   Well—do I not? I would be well—
I could not but be well on such a day!
And, this day ended, 'tis of slight import
How long the ravaged frame subjects the soul
In Strafford!

   Car.   Noble Strafford!

   Straf.   No farewell!
I'll see you, girl, to-morrow—the first thing!
—If she should come to stay me!

   Car.   Go—'tis nothing—
Only my heart that swells—it has been thus
Ere now—go, Strafford!

   Straf.   To-night, then, let it be!
I must see Him . . . I'll see you after Him . . .
I'll tell you how Pym looked. Follow me, friends!
You, gentlemen, shall see a sight this hour
To talk of all your lives. Close after me!
" My friend of friends! "   (*Exeunt* STRAFFORD, *etc.*)

   Car.   The King—ever the King!
No thought of one beside, whose little word
Unveils the King to him—one word from me—

Which yet I do not breathe!

                              Ah, have I spared
Strafford a pang, and shall I seek reward
Beyond that memory? Surely, too, some way
He is the better for my love . . . No, no,
He would not look so joyous—I'll believe
His very eye would never sparkle thus,
Had I not prayed for him this long, long while!

                                        (*Exit.*)

SCENE III.—*The Antechamber of the House of Lords.*

*Many of the Presbyterian Party. The Adherents
of* STRAFFORD, *etc.*

A Group of PRESBYTERIANS.—1. I tell you he struck
    Maxwell—Maxwell sought
To stay the Earl: he struck him and passed on.

    2. Fear as you may, keep a good countenance
Before these ruffians!

    3.   Strafford here the first—
With the great army at his back!

    4.   No doubt!
I would Pym had made hàste . . . that's Bryan, hush—
The fellow pointing.

    STRAFFORD'S *Followers.*—1. Mark these worthies, now!

    2. A goodly gathering! " Where the carcass is
There shall the eagles " . . . what's the rest?

    3.   For eagles
Say crows.

    A PRESBYTERIAN. Stand back, Sirs!

    One of STRAFFORD'S *Followers.* Are we in Geneva?

    A PRESBYTERIAN. No—nor in Ireland, we have leave to
    breathe.

    One of STRAFFORD'S *Followers.* Really? Behold how
    grand a thing it is
To serve " King Pym "! There's someone at Whitehall
That lives obscure, but Pym lives . . .

    The PRESBYTERIAN.   Nearer!

    A Follower of STRAFFORD.   Higher
We look to see him! [*To his Companions.*] I'm to have St.
    John

In charge; was he among the knaves just now
That followed Pym within there?
    Another.   The gaunt man
Talking with Rudyard. Did the Earl expect
Pym at his heels so fast? I like it not.

                          (*Enter* MAXWELL.)
    Another. Why, man, they rush into the net. Here's
    Maxwell—
Ha, Maxwell?—How the brethren flock around
The fellow! Do you feel the Earl's hand yet
Upon your shoulder, Maxwell?
    Max.   Gentlemen,
Stand back! a great thing passes here.
    A Follower of STRAFFORD. (*To another.*) The Earl
Is at his work! [*To* M.] Say, Maxwell, what great thing!
Speak out! [*To a* Presbyterian.] Friends, I've a kindness for
    you! Friends,
I've seen you with St. John . . . O stockishness!
Wear such a ruff, and never call to mind
St. John's head in a charger?
                        What—the plague—
Not laugh?
    Another. Say, Maxwell, what it is!
    Another.   Hush—wait—
The jest will be to wait—
    First.   And who's to bear
These quiet hypocrites? You'd swear they came . . .
Came . . . just as we come!
    (*A Puritan enters hastily and without observing* STRAFFORD'S
        Followers.)
    The PURITAN.   How goes on the work?
Has Pym . . .
    A Follower of STRAFFORD. The secret's out at last—Aha.
The carrion's scented! Welcome, crow the first!
Gorge merrily you with the blinking eye!
" King Pym has fallen! "
    The PURITAN.   Pym?
    A STRAFFORD.   Pym!
    A PRESBYTERIAN.   Only Pym?
    Many of STRAFFORD'S *Followers.* No, brother—not Pym
    only—Vane as well—
Rudyard as well—Hampden—Saint John as well—
    A PRESBYTERIAN. My mind misgives . . . can it be true?

Another. Lost! Lost!

A STRAFFORD. Say we true, Maxwell?

The PURITAN. Pride before destruction,
A haughty spirit goeth before a fall.

Many of STRAFFORD'S *Followers.* Ah now! The very thing!
    A word in season!
A golden apple in a silver picture
To greet Pym as he passes!

(*The folding-doors at the back begin to open, noise and light
    issuing.*)

Max. Stand back, all!

Many of the PRESBYTERIANS. I'll die with Pym! And I!

STRAFFORD'S *Followers.* Now for the text—
He comes! Quick!

The PURITAN. (*With uplifted arms.*) How hath the
    Oppressor ceased!
The Lord hath broken the staff of the wicked:
The sceptre of the Rulers—he who smote
The People in wrath with a continual stroke—
That ruled the nations in his anger . . . He
Is persecuted and none hindereth!

(*At the beginning of this speech, the doors open, and
    STRAFFORD in the greatest disorder, and amid cries
    from within of " Void the House," staggers out. When
    he reaches the front of the Stage, silence.*)

Straf. Impeach me! Pym! I never struck, I think,
The felon on that calm insulting mouth
When it proclaimed—Pym's mouth proclaimed me . . . God!
Was it a word, only a word that held
The outrageous blood back on my heart . . . which beats!
Which beats! Some one word . . . " Traitor," did he say
Bending that eye, brimful of bitter fire,
Upon me?

Max. (*Advancing.*) In the Commons' name, their servant
Demands Lord Strafford's sword.

Straf. What did you say?

Max. The Commons bid me ask your Lordship's sword.

Straf. (*Suddenly recovering, and looking round, draws it,
    and turns to his followers.*) Let us go forth—follow me,
    gentlemen—
Draw your swords too—cut any down that bar us!
On the King's service! Maxwell, clear the way!

(*The* PRESBYTERIANS *prepare to dispute his passage.*)

Straf. Ha—true! . . . That is, you mistake me, utterly—
I will stay—the King himself shall see me—here—
Here—I will stay, Mainwaring!—First of all,
(*To* MAXWELL) Your tablets, fellow! (*He writes on them.*)
(*To* MAINWARING.) Give that to the King!)
Yes, Maxwell, for the next half-hour, I will . . .
I will remain your prisoner, I will!
Nay, you shall take my sword!

(MAXWELL *advances to take it.*)
No—no—not that!
Their blood, perhaps, may wipe out all thus far—
And up to that—not that! Why, friend, you see
When the King lays his head beneath my foot
It will not pay for that! Go, all of you!

Max. I grieve, my lord, to disobey: none stir.

Straf. This gentle Maxwell!—Do not touch him, Bryan!
(*To the* PRESBYTERIANS.) Whichever cur of you will carry
this
I'll save him from the fate of all the rest—
I'll have him made a Peer—I'll . . . none will go?
None? (*Cries from within of* "STRAFFORD.")
(*To his* FOLLOWERS.) Slingsby, I've loved you at least—my
friend,
Stab me! I have not time to tell you why . . .
You then, dear Bryan! You Mainwaring, then!
. . . Ah, that's because I spoke so hastily
At Allerton—the King had vexed me . . .
(*To the* PRESBYTERIANS.) You
Miscreants—you then—that I'll exterminate!
—Not even you? If I live over it
The King is sure to have your heads—you know
I'm not afraid of that—you understand
That if I chose to wait—made up my mind
To live this minute—he would do me right!
But what if I can't live this minute through?
If nothing can repay that minute? Pym
With his pursuing smile—Pym to be there!

(*Louder cries of* "STRAFFORD.")
The King! I troubled him—stood in the way
Of his negotiations—was the one
Great obstacle to peace—the Enemy
Of Scotland—and he sent for me—from York—
My safety guaranteed—having prepared

A Parliament! I see! And at Whitehall
The Queen was whispering with Vane . . . I see
The trap! I curse the King! I wish Pym well!
Wish all his brave friends well! Say, all along
Strafford was with them—all along, at heart,
I hated Charles and wish them well! And say
    (tearing off the George and dashing it down)
That as I tread this gew-gaw under foot,
I cast his memory from me! One stroke, now!
   (His own adherents disarm him. Renewed cries of
    " STRAFFORD.")
I'll not go . . . they shall drag me by the hair!
(Changing suddenly to calm.) England! I see her arm in this!
 I yield.
Why—'tis the fairest triumph! Why desire
To cheat them? I would never stoop to that—
Be mean enough for that! Let all have end!
Don't repine, Slingsby . . . have they not a right?
They claim me—hearken—lead me to them, Bryan!
No—I myself should offer up myself.
Pray you now . . . Pym awaits me . . . pray you now!
 (Putting aside those who attempt to support him, STRAFFORD
  reaches the door—they open wide. HAMPDEN, *etc., and*
  a crowd discovered ; and at the bar, PYM *standing apart.*
  As STRAFFORD *kneels the scene shuts.)*

END OF THE THIRD ACT.

ACT IV

SCENE I.—*Whitehall.*

The KING, *the* QUEEN, HOLLIS, CARLISLE. (VANE, HOLLAND,
  SAVILE, *in the background.)*

 Car. Answer them, Hollis, for his sake!—One word!
 Cha. (*To* HOLLIS.) You stand, silent and cold, as though
  I were
Deceiving you—my friend, my playfellow
Of other times! What wonder after all?
Just so I dreamed my People loved me!

Hol.   Sire,
It is yourself that you deceive, not me!
You'll quit me comforted—your mind made up
That since you've talked thus much and grieved thus much,
All you can do for Strafford has been done.
    Queen. If you kill Strafford . . . come, we grant you leave,
Suppose . . .
    Hol.   I may withdraw, Sire?
    Car.   Hear them out!
'Tis the last chance for Strafford! Hear them out!
    Hol. " If we kill Strafford "—on the eighteenth day
Of Strafford's trial—*We !*
    Cha.   Pym, my good Hollis—
Pym, I should say!
    Hol.   Ah, true—Sire, pardon me!
You witness our proceedings every day,
But the screened gallery, I might have guessed,
Admits of such a partial glimpse at us—
Pym takes up all the room, shuts out the view!
Still, on my honour, Sire, the rest of the place
Is not unoccupied: The Commons sit
—That's England; Ireland sends, and Scotland too,
Their representatives: the Peers that judge
Are easily distinguished; one remarks
The People here and there . . . but the close curtain
Must hide so much!
    Queen.   Acquaint your insolent crew,
This day the curtain shall be dashed aside!
It served a purpose!
    Hol.   Think! This very day?
Ere Strafford rises to defend himself?
    Cha. I will defend him, Sir; sanction the past–
This day—it ever was my purpose! Rage
At me, not Strafford! Oh I shall be paid
By Strafford's look!
    Car. (*To* Hollis.) Nobly! Oh will he not
Do nobly?
    Hol.   Sire, you will do honestly;
And, for that look, I too would be a king!
    Cha. (*After a pause.*) Only, to do this now—just when they seek
To make me out a tyrant—one that's deaf

To subjects' prayers,—shall I oppose them now?
It seems their will the Trial should proceed . . .
'Tis palpably their will!

Hol. You'll lose your throne:
But it were no bright moment save for that!
Strafford, your prime support, the sole roof-tree
That props this quaking House of Privilege,
(Floods come, winds beat, and see—the treacherous sand!)
Doubtless if the mere putting forth an arm
Could save him, you'd save Strafford!

Cha. And they mean
Calmly to consummate this wrong! No hope?
This ineffaceable wrong! No pity then?

Hol. No plague in store for perfidy?—Farewell!
You summoned me . . . (*To* CARLISLE.) You, Lady, bade
me come
To save the Earl! I came, thank God for it,
To learn how far such perfidy can go!
. . . You dare to talk with me of saving him
Who have just ruined Strafford!

Cha. I?

Hol. See, now!
Eighteen days long he throws, one after one,
Our charges back: a blind moth-eaten law!
—He'll break from us at last! And whom to thank?
The Mouse that gnawed the Lion's net for him
Got a good friend,—but he, the other Mouse,
That looked on while the Lion freed himself—
Fared he so well, does any fable say?

Cha. What can you mean?

Hol. Pym never could have proved
Strafford's design of bringing up the troops
To force this kingdom to obedience: Vane—
Your servant, Vane . . .

Queen. Well, Sir?

Hol. . . . Has proved it.

Cha. Vane?

Hol. This day! Did Vane deliver up or no
Those notes which, furnished by his son to Pym,
Have sealed . . .

Cha. Speak Vane! As I shall live, I know
Nothing that Vane has done! What treason next?
I wash my hands of it! Vane, speak the truth!

—Ask Vane himself!

Hol.   I will not speak to Vane
Who speak to Pym and Hampden every day!

  Queen. Speak to Vane's master then! Why should he wish
For Strafford's death?

Hol.   Why? Strafford cannot turn
As you sit there—bid you come forth and say
If every hateful act were not set down
In his commission?—Whether you contrived
Or no that all the violence should seem
His work, the gentle ways—your own, as if
He counteracted your kind impulses
While . . . but you know what he could say! And then
Would he produce, mark you, a certain charge
To set your own express commands aside,
If need were, and be blameless! He'd say, then . . .

  Cha. Hold!

Hol.   . . . Say who bade him break the Parliament,—
Find out some pretext to set up sword-law . . .

  Queen. Retire, Sir!

Cha.   Vane—once more—what Vane dares do
I know not . . . he is rash . . . a fool . . . I know
Nothing of Vane!

Hol.   Well—I believe you; Sire,
Believe me, in return, that . . .
(*Turning to* CARLISLE.)   Gentle Lady,
The few words I would say the stones might hear
Sooner than these . . . I'll say them all to you,
You, with the heart! The question, trust me, takes
Another shape, to-day; 'tis not if Charles
Or England shall succumb,—but which shall pay
The forfeit, Strafford or his Master: Sire,
You loved me once . . . think on my warning now!
                              (*Exit.*)

  Cha. On you and on your warning both!—Carlisle!
That paper!

  Queen.   But consider!

Cha.   Give it me!
There—signed—will that content you?—Do not speak!
You have betrayed me, Vane!—See, any day
(According to the tenour of that paper)
He bids your brother bring the Army up,

Strafford shall head it and take full revenge!
Seek Strafford! Let him have it, look, before
He rises to defend himself!

    Queen.   In truth?
Clever of Hollis, now, to work a change
Like this! You were reluctant . . .

    Cha.   Say, Carlisle,
Your brother Percy brings the Army up—
Falls on the Parliament——(I'll think of you,
My Hollis)—say we plotted long . . . 'tis *mine.*
The scheme is mine, remember! Say I cursed
Vane's folly in your hearing! If that man
Does rise to do us shame, the fault shall lie
With you, Carlisle!

    Car.   Nay, fear not me! but still
That's a bright moment, Sire, you throw away . . .
Oh, draw the veil and save him!

    Queen.   Go, Carlisle!

    Car. (*Aside and going.*) I shall see Strafford—speak to
    him: my heart
Must never beat so, then!

                   And if I tell
The truth? What's gained by falsehood? There they stand
Whose trade it is—whose life it is! How vain
To gild such rottenness! Strafford shall know,
Thoroughly know them!

    The Queen. (*As she leaves the* KING, *etc.*) Trust to me!
    [*To* CARLISLE.] Carlisle,
You seem inclined, alone of all the Court,
To serve poor Strafford: this bold plan of yours
Merits much praise, and yet . . .

    Car.   Time presses, Madam.

    Queen. Yet . . . may it not be something premature?
Strafford defends himself to-day—reserves
Some wondrous effort . . . one may well suppose—
He'll say some overwhelming fact, Carlisle!

    Car. Aye, Hollis hints as much.

    Cha.   Why linger then?
Haste with the scheme—my scheme—I shall be there
To watch his look! Tell him I watch his look!

    Queen. Stay, we'll precede you!

    Car.   At your pleasure.

    Cha.   Say . . .

Say . . . Vane is hardly ever at Whitehall!
I shall be there, remember!
   Car.   Doubt me not!
   Cha.   On our return, Carlisle, we wait you here!
   Car.   I'll bring his answer; Sire, I follow you.

                            (Exeunt K., etc.)

Ah . . . but he would be very sad to find
The King so faithless, and I take away
All that he cares to live for: let it go—
'Tis the King's scheme!
                My Strafford, I can save . . .
Nay, I *have* saved you—yet am scarce content,
Because my poor name will not cross your mind . . .
Strafford, how much I am unworthy you!

                                (Exit.)

Scene II.—*A Passage adjoining Westminster Hall.*

Many groups of Spectators *of the Trial (which is visible from the back of the Stage)*—Officers *of the Court, etc.*

   1st Spec.   More crowd than ever! . . . Not know Hampden, man?
That's he—by Pym—Pym that is speaking now!
No, truly—if you look so high you'll see
Little enough of either!
   2nd Spec.   Hush . . . Pym's arm
Points like a prophet's rod.
   3rd Spec.   Ay—ay—we've heard
Some pretty speaking . . . yet the Earl escapes!
   4th Spec.   I fear it: just a foolish word or two
About his children . . . and they see, forsooth,
Not England's Foe in Strafford—but the Man
Who, sick, half-blind . . .
   2nd Spec.   What's that Pym's saying now
That makes the curtains flutter . . . look! A hand
Clutches them . . . Ah! The King's hand!
   5th Spec.   I had thought
Pym was not near so tall! What said he, friend?
   2nd Spec.   " Nor is this way a novel way of blood " . . .
And the Earl turns as if to . . . look! look!
   Many Spectators.   Heaven—

What ails him . . . no—he rallies . . . see—goes on
And Strafford smiles.   Strange!

(*Enter a* PURITAN.)

The Puritan.   Haselrig!
Many Spectators.   Friend?   Friend?
The Puritan.   Lost—utterly lost . . . just when we looked
for Pym
To make a stand against the ill effects
Of the Earl's speech!   Is Haselrig without?
Pym's message is to him!   (*Exit.*)
   3rd Spec.   Now, said I true?
Will the Earl leave them yet at fault or no?
   1st Spec.   Never believe it, man!   These notes of Vane's
Ruin the Earl.
   5th Spec.   A brave end . . . not a whit
Less firm, less . . . Pym all over!   Then, the Trial
Is closed . . . no . . . Strafford means to speak again!
   An Officer.   Stand back, there!
   5th Spec.   Why the Earl is coming hither!
Before the court breaks up!   His brother, look,—
You'd say he deprecated some fierce act
In Strafford's mind just now!
   An Officer.   Stand back, I say!
   2nd Spec.   Who's the veiled woman that he talks with?
   Many Spectators.   Hush—
The Earl! the Earl!

      [*Enter* STRAFFORD, SLINGSBY *and other Secretaries,*
            HOLLIS, CARLISLE, MAXWELL, BALFOUR, *etc.*
            STRAFFORD *converses with* CARLISLE.]

   Hol.   So near the end!   Be patient—
Return!
   Straf.   [*To his Secretaries.*]   Here—anywhere—or—'tis
freshest here . . .
(To spend one's April here—the blossom-month!)
Set it down here!   [*They arrange a table, papers, etc.*]
                    What, Pym to quail, to sink
Because I glance at him, yet . . .
                    Well, to end—
What's to be answered, Slingsby?   Let us end.
(*To* CARLISLE.)   Girl, I refuse his offer; whatsoe'er
It be!   Too late!   Tell me no word of him!

(*To* HOLLIS.) 'Tis something, Hollis, I assure you that
To stand, sick as you are, some eighteen days
Fighting for life and fame against a pack
Of very curs, that lie thro' thick and thin,
Eat flesh and bread by wholesale, and can't say
" Strafford " if it would take my life!

 Car.   Be kind
This once!   Glance at the paper . . . if you will
But glance at it. . . .

 Straf.   Already at my heels!
Pym's faulting bloodhounds scent the track again!
Peace, girl!   Now, Slingsby!

 (*Messengers from Lane and other of* STRAFFORD'S *Counsel
within the Hall are coming and going during the Scene.*)

 Straf. (*Setting himself to write and dictate.*) I shall beat you,
  Hollis!
Do you know that?   In spite of all your tricks—
In spite of Pym!   Your Pym that shrank from me!
Eliot would have contrived it otherwise!
(*To a Messenger.*) In truth?   This slip, tell Lane, contains as
  much
As I can call to mind about the matter.
(*To* HOLLIS.)   Eliot would have disdained . . .
(*Calling after the Messenger.*) And Radcliffe, say—
The only person who could answer Pym—
Is safe in prison, just for that!
(*Continuing to* HOLLIS.)   Well—Well—
It had not been recorded in that case,
I baffled you!
(*To* CARLISLE.)   Nay, girl, why look so grieved?
All's gained without the King!   You saw Pym quail?
. . . What shall I do when they acquit me, think you,
But tranquilly resume my task as though
Nothing had intervened since I proposed
To call that traitor to account!   Such tricks,
Trust me, shall not be played a second time—
Even against old Laud, with his grey hair . . .
Your good work, Hollis!—And to make amends
You, Lucy, shall be there when I impeach
Pym and his fellows!

 Hol.   Wherefore not protest
Against our whole proceeding long ago?

Why feel indignant now? Why stand this while
Enduring patiently . . .
   Straf. (*To* CARLISLE). Girl, I'll tell you—
You—and not Pym . . . you, the slight graceful girl
Tall for a flowering lily—and not Charles . . .
Why I stood patient! I was fool enough
To see the will of England in Pym's will—
To dream that I had wronged her—and to wait
Her judgment,—when, behold, in place of it . . .
(*To a Messenger who whispers.*) Tell Lane to answer no such
    question! Law . . .
I grapple with their law! I'm here to try
My actions by their standard, not my own!
Their Law allowed that levy . . . what's the rest
To Pym, or Lane, or any but myself?
   Car. Then cast not thus your only chance away—
The King's so weak . . . secure this chance! 'Twas Vane
—Vane, recollect, who furnished Pym the notes . . .
   Straf. Fit . . . very fit . . . those precious notes of
    Vane,
To close the trial worthily! I feared
Some spice of nobleness might linger yet
To spoil the character of all the past!
It pleased me . . . and (*rising passionately*) I will go back
    and say
As much—to them—to England! Follow me!
I have a word to say! There! my defence
Is done!
(*To* CARLISLE.) Stay . . . why be proud? Why care to own
My gladness—my surprise? . . . no—not surprise!
Oh, why insist upon the little pride
Of doing all myself and sparing him
The pain? Girl, say the triumph is my King's!
When Pym grew pale, and trembled, and sank down—
His image was before me . . . could I fail?
Girl, care not for the past—so indistinct—
Obscure—there's nothing to forgive in it
'Tis so forgotten! From this day begins
A new life, founded on a new belief
In Charles . . .
   Hol.   Pym comes . . . tell Pym it is unfair!
Appeal to Pym! Hampden—and Vane! see, Strafford!
Say how unfair . . .

Straf.   To Pym?   I would say nothing!
I would not look upon Pym's face again!
   Car.   Stay . . . let me have to think I pressed your hand!
                                        [*Exeunt* STRAFFORD, *etc.*]

(*Enter* HAMPDEN *and* VANE.)

   Vane.   O Hampden, save that great misguided man!
Plead Strafford's cause with Pym—I have remarked
He moved no muscle when we all spoke loud
Against him . . . you had but to breathe—he turned
Those kind, large eyes upon you—kind to all
But Strafford . . . whom I murder!

[*Enter* PYM (*conversing with the Solicitor-General* ST. JOHN),
   the Managers of the Trial, FIENNES, RUDYARD, *etc.*]

   Rud.   Horrible!
Till now all hearts were with you. . . .   I withdraw
For one!   Too horrible!   Oh we mistake
Your purpose, Pym . . . you cannot snatch away
The last spar from the drowning man!
   Fien.   He talks
With St. John of it—see how quietly!
(*To other* PRESBYTERIANS.)   You'll join us?   Mind, we own
   he merits death—
But this new course is monstrous!   Vane, take heart!
This Bill of his attainder shall not have
One true man's hand to it.
   Vane.   But hear me, Pym!
Confront your Bill—your own Bill . . . what is it?
You cannot catch the Earl on any charge . . .
No man will say the Law has hold of him
On any charge . . . and therefore you resolve
To take the general sense on his desert,—
As though no law existed, and we met
To found one!—You refer to every man
To speak his thoughts upon this hideous mass
Of half-borne-out assertions—dubious hints
Hereafter to be cleared—distortions—aye,
And wild inventions.   Every man is saved
The task of fixing any single charge
On Strafford: he has but to see in him
The Enemy of England . . .
   Pym.   A right scruple!

I have heard some called England's Enemy
With less consideration.

   Vane.   Pity me!
Me—brought so low—who hoped to do so much
For England—her true Servant—Pym, your friend . . .
Indeed you made me think I was your friend!
But I have murdered Strafford . . . I have been
The instrument of this! who shall remove
That memory from me?

   Pym.   I absolve you, Vane!
Take you no care for aught that you have done!

   Vane.   Dear Hampden, not this Bill! Reject this Bill!
He staggers thro' the ordeal . . . let him go!
Strew no fresh fire before him! Plead for us!
With Pym . . . what God is he, to have no heart
Like ours, yet make us love him?

   Rud.   Hampden, plead
For us! When Strafford spoke your eyes were thick
With tears . . . save him, dear Hampden!

   Hamp.   England speaks
Louder than Strafford! Who are we, to play
The generous pardoner at her expense—
Magnanimously waive advantages—
And if he conquer us . . . applaud his skill?

   Vane.   (*To* Pym.) He was your friend!

   Pym.   I have heard that before.

   Fien.   But England trusts you . . .

   Hamp.   Shame be his, who turns
The opportunity of serving her
She trusts him with, to his own mean account—
Who would look nobly frank at her expense!

   Fien.   I never thought it could have come to this!

   Pym.   (*Turning from* St. John.) But I have made myself
       familiar, Fiennes,
With that one thought—have walked, and sat, and slept,
That thought before me! I have done such things,
Being the chosen man that should destroy
This Strafford! You have taken up that thought
To play with—for a gentle stimulant—
To give a dignity to idler life
By the dim prospect of this deed to come . . .
But ever with the softening, sure belief,
That all would come some strange way right at last!

Fien. Had we made out some weightier charge . . .
Pym.   You say
That these are petty charges! Can we come
To the real charge at all? There he is safe!
In tyranny's stronghold! Apostasy
Is not a crime—Treachery not a crime!
The cheek burns, the blood tingles, when you name
Their names, but where's the power to take revenge
Upon them? We must make occasion serve:
The Oversight, pay for the Giant Sin
That mocks us!
    Rud.   But this unexampled course—
This Bill . . .
    Pym.   By this, we roll the clouds away
Of Precedent and Custom, and at once
Bid the great light which God has set in all,
The conscience of each bosom, shine upon
The guilt of Strafford: each shall lay his hand
Upon his breast, and say if this one man
Deserve to die, or no, by those he sought
First to undo.
    Fien.   You, Vane—you answer him!
    Vane. Pym, you see farthest . . . I can only see
Strafford . . . I'd not pass over that pale corse
For all beyond!
    Rud. and others. Pym, you would look so great!
Forgive him! He would join us! now he finds
How false the King has been! The pardon, too,
Should be your own! Yourself should bear to Strafford
The pardon of the Commons!
    Pym. (*Starting.*)   Meet him? Strafford?
Have we to meet once more, then? Be it so!
And yet—the prophecy seemed half fulfilled
When, at the trial, as he gazed—my youth—
Our friendship—all old thoughts came back at once
And left me, for a time . . .
    Vane. (*Aside to* RUDYARD). Moved, is he not?
    Pym. To-morrow we discuss the points of law
With Lane . . . to-morrow!
    Vane.   Time enough, dear Pym!
See, he relents! I knew he would relent!
    Pym. The next day, Haselrig, *you* introduce
The Bill of his Attainder. (*After a pause.*) Pray for me!

SCENE III.—*Whitehall.*

The KING.

Cha. Strafford, you are a Prince! Not to reward you
—Nothing does that—but only for a whim!
My noble servant!—To defend himself
Thus irresistibly . . . withholding aught
That seemed to implicate us!

We have done
Less gallantly by Strafford! Well, the future
Must recompense the past.

She tarries long!
I understand you, Strafford, now!

The scheme—
Carlisle's mad scheme—he'll sanction it, I fear,
For love of me! 'Twas too precipitate:
Before the Army's fairly on its march,
He'll be at large: no matter . . .

Well, Carlisle?

(*Enter* PYM.)

Pym. Fear me not, Sire . . . my mission is to save,
This time!
Cha. To break thus on me!—Unannounced . . .
Pym. It is of Strafford I would speak.
Cha. No more
Of Strafford! I have heard too much from you!
Pym. I spoke, Sire, for the People: will you hear
A word upon my own account?
Cha. Of Strafford?
(*Aside.*) So, turns the tide already? Have we tamed
The insolent brawler?—Strafford's brave defence
Is swift in its effect! (*To* PYM.) Lord Strafford, Sir,
Has spoken for himself!
Pym. Sufficiently.
I would apprize you of the novel course
The people take: the Trial fails, . . .
Cha. Yes—yes—
We are aware, Sir: for your part in it
Means shall be found to thank you.
Pym. Pray you, read
This schedule! (*as the* KING *reads it*) I would learn from your
own mouth

—(It is a matter much concerning me)—
Whether, if two Estates of England shall concede
The death of Strafford, on the grounds set forth
Within that parchment, you, Sire, can resolve
To grant your full consent to it. That Bill
Is framed by me: if you determine, Sire,
That England's manifested will shall guide
Your judgment, ere another week that will
Shall manifest itself. If not,—I cast
Aside the measure.

    Cha.   . . . You can hinder, then,
The introduction of that Bill?

    Pym.   I can.

    Cha. He is my friend, Sir: I have wronged him: mark
    you,
Had I not wronged him—this might be!—You think
Because you hate the Earl . . . (turn not away—
We know you hate him)—no one else could love
Strafford . . . but he has saved me—many times—
Think what he has endured . . . proud too . . . you feel
What he endured!—And, do you know one strange,
One frightful thing? We all have used that man
As though he had been ours . . . with not a source
Of happy thoughts except in us . . . and yet
Strafford has children, and a home as well,
Just as if we had never been! . . . Ah Sir,
You are moved—you—a solitary man
Wed to your cause—to England if you will!

    Pym. Yes . . . think, my soul . . . to England! Draw
    not back!

    Cha. Prevent that Bill, Sir . . . Oh, your course
Was fair till now! Why, in the end, 'tis I should sign
The warrant for his death! You have said much
That I shall ponder on; I never meant
Strafford should serve me any more: I take
The Commons' counsel: but this Bill is yours—
Not worthy of its leader . . . care not, Sir,
For that, however! I will quite forget
You named it to me! You are satisfied?

    Pym. Listen to me, Sire! Eliot laid his hand,
Wasted and white, upon my forehead once;
Wentworth . . . he's gone now; . . . has talked on, whole
    nights,

And I beside him; Hampden loves me; Sire,
How can I breathe and not wish England well—
And her King well?

   Cha.   I thank you, Sir! You leave
That King his servant! Thanks, Sir!

   Pym.   Let me speak
—Who may not speak again! whose spirit yearns
For a cool night after this weary day!
—Who would not have my heart turn sicker yet
In a new task, more fatal, more august,
More full of England's utter weal or woe . . .
I thought, Sire, could I find myself with you—
After this Trial—alone—as man to man—
I might say something—warn you—pray you—save you—
Mark me, King Charles, save——you!
But God must do it. Yet I warn you, Sire—
(With Strafford's faded eyes yet full on me)
As you would have no deeper question moved
—" How long the Many shall endure the One " . . .
Assure me, Sire, if England shall assent
To Strafford's death, you will not interfere!
Or——

   Cha.   God forsakes me! I am in a net . . .
I cannot move! Let all be as you say!

(Enter CARLISLE.)

   Car.   He loves you—looking beautiful with joy
Because you sent me! he would spare you all
The pain! he never dreamed you would forsake
Your servant in the evil day—nay, see
Your scheme returned! That generous heart of his!
He needs it not—or, needing it, disdains
A course that might endanger you—you, Sire,
Whom Strafford from his inmost soul . . .
(*Seeing* PYM.)   No fear—
No fear for Strafford! all that's true and brave
On your own side shall help us! we are now
Stronger than ever!

                Ha—what, Sire, is this?
All is not well! What parchment have you there?

(CHARLES drops it, and exit.)

   Pym.   Sire, much is saved us both: farewell!
   Car.   Stay—stay—

This cursed measure—you'll not dare—you mean
To frighten Charles! This Bill—look—

(*As* Pym *reads it.*)
Why, your lip
Whitens—you could not read one line to me
Your voice would falter so! It shakes you now—
And will you dare . . .

Pym.   No recreant yet to her!
The great word went from England to my soul,
And I arose! The end is very near!   (*Exit.*)

Car. I save him! All have shrunk from him beside—
'Tis only I am left! Heaven will make strong
The hand as the true heart! Then let me die!

(*Exit.*)

END OF THE FOURTH ACT

ACT V.

Scene I.—*Whitehall.*

Hollis, Carlisle.

Hol. Tell the King, then! Come in with me!
Car.   Not so!
He must not hear, 'till it succeeds!
Hol.   Vain! Vain!
No dream was half so vain—you'll rescue Strafford
And outwit Pym! I cannot tell you . . . girl,
The block pursues me—all the hideous show . . .
To-day . . . is it to-day? And all the while
He's sure of the King's pardon . . . think I have
To tell this man he is to die!
The King
May rend his hair, for me! I'll not see Strafford!
Car. Only, if I succeed, remember——Charles
Has saved him! He would hardly value life
Unless his gift.
My staunch friends wait! Go in—
You must go in to Charles!
Hol.   And all beside
Left Strafford long ago—the King has signed

The warrant for his death . . . the Queen was sick
Of the eternal subject! For the Court,—
The Trial was amusing in its way
Only too much of it . . . the Earl withdrew
In time! But you—fragile—alone—so young!
Amid rude mercenaries—you devised
A plan to save him! Even tho' it fails
What shall reward you?

   Car.   I may go, you think,
To France with him? And you reward me, friend!
Who lived with Strafford even from his youth
Before he set his heart on state-affairs
And they bent down that noble brow of his—
I have learned somewhat of his latter life
And all the future I shall know—but, Hollis,
I ought to make his youth my own as well!
Tell me——when he is saved!

   Hol.   My gentle girl,
He should know all—should love you—but 'tis vain!

   Car. No—no—too late now! Let him love the King!
'Tis the King's scheme! I have your word—remember!—
We'll keep the old delusion up! But, hush!
Hush! Each of us has work to do, beside!
Go to the King! I hope—Hollis—I hope!
Say nothing of my scheme! Hush, while we speak
Think where He is! Now for my gallant friends!   (*Exit.*)

   Hol. Where He is! Calling wildly upon Charles—
Guessing his fate—pacing the prison floor . . .
Let the King tell him! I'll not look on Strafford!

                                         (*Exit.*)

                    Scene II.—*The Tower.*

    Strafford *sitting with his Children.*   *They sing.*

                O bell' andare
                Per barca in mare,
                Verso la sera
                Di Primavera !

William. (The boat's in the broad moonlight all this while)

                Verso la sera
                Di Primavera.

And the boat shoots from underneath the moon

Into the shadowy distance—only still
You hear the dripping oar,

       Verso la sera . . .

And faint—and fainter—and then all's quite gone,
Music and light and all, like a lost star.
    Anne. But you should sleep, father: you were to sleep!
    Straf. I do sleep, dearest; or if not—you know
There's such a thing as . . .
    Wil.   You're too tired to sleep?
    Straf. It will come by and bye and all day long,
In that old quiet house I told you of:
We'll sleep safe there.
    Anne.   Why not in Ireland?
    Straf.   Ah!
Too many dreams!—That song's for Venice, William:
You know how Venice looks upon the map . . .
Isles that the mainland hardly can let go?
    Wil. You've been to Venice, father?
    Straf.   I was young then.
    Wil. A city with no King; that's why I like
Even a song that comes from Venice!
    Straf.   William!
    Wil. Oh, I know why! Anne, do you love the King?
But I'll see Venice for myself one day.
    Straf. See many lands, boy—England last of all,—
That way you'll love her best.
    Wil.   Why do men say
You sought to ruin her, then!
    Straf.   Ah . . . they say that.
    Wil. Why?
    Straf.   I suppose they must have words to say,
As you to sing.
    Anne.   But they make songs beside:
Last night I heard one, in the street beneath,
That named you . . . Oh, the names!
    Wil.   Don't mind her, father!
They soon left off when I called out to them!
    Straf. We shall so soon be out of it, my boy!
'Tis not worth while: who heeds a foolish song?
    Wil. Why, not the King!
    Straf.   Well: it has been the fate
Of better men, and yet . . . why not feel sure

That Time, who in the twilight comes to mend
All the fantastic Day's caprice—consign
Unto the ground once more the ignoble term,
And raise the Genius on his orb again—
That Time will do me right?
  Anne.   (Shall we sing, William?
He does not look thus when we sing.)
  Straf.   For Ireland,—
Something is done . . . too little, but enough
To show what might have been:—
  Wil.   (I have no heart
To sing now! Anne, how very sad he looks!
Oh I so hate the King for all he says!)
  Straf. Forsook them! What, the common songs will run
That I forsook the People? Nothing more?
. . . Aye, Fame, the scribe, will pause awhile, no doubt,
Turning a deaf ear to her thousand slaves
Noisy to be enrolled,—will register
All curious glosses, subtle notices,
Ingenious clearings-up one fain would see
Beside that plain inscription of The Name—
The Patriot Pym, or the Apostate Strafford!
   (*The Children resume their song timidly, but break off.*)

    Enter HOLLIS *and an* Attendant.

  Straf. No . . . Hollis? in good time!—Who is he?
  Hol.   One
That must be present.
  Straf.   Ah—I understand——
They will not let me see poor Laud alone!
How politic! They'd use me by degrees
To solitude: and just as you came in
I was solicitous what life to lead
When Strafford's " not so much as Constable
" In the King's service." Is there any means
To keep one's self awake? What would you do
After this bustle, Hollis, in my place?
  Hol. Strafford . . .
  Straf.   Observe, not but that Pym and you
Will find me news enough—news I shall hear
Under a quince tree by a fish-pond side
At Wentworth. Or, a better project now—
What if when all is over, and the Saints

Reign, and the Senate goes on swimmingly,—
What if I venture up, some day, unseen—
To saunter through the Town—notice how Pym,
The Tribune, likes Whitehall—drop quietly
Into a tavern—hear a point discussed—
As, whether Strafford's name were John or Richard—
And be myself appealed to . . . I, who shall
Myself have near forgotten!
    Hol.   I would speak . . .
    Straf.   Then you shall speak,—not now: I want, just now,
To hear the sound of my own tongue.   This place
Is full of ghosts!
    Hol.   Will you not hear me, Strafford?
    Straf.   Oh, readily! . . . Only, one droll thing more,—
The minister! Who will advise the King,
And yet have health—children, for aught I know!
—My patient pair of traitors! Ah . . . but, William—
Does not his cheek grow thin?
    Wil.   'Tis you look thin,
Father!
    Straf.   A scamper o'er the breezy wolds
Sets all to-rights!
    Hol.   You cannot sure forget
A prison-roof is o'er you, Strafford?
    Straf.   No,
Why, no. I would not touch on that, the first.
I left you that. Well, Hollis?
                    . . . . Say at once
The King could find no time to set me free!
A mask at Theobald's?
    Hol.   Hush . . . no such affair
Detains him.
    Straf.   True: what needs so great a matter?
The Queen's lip may be sore!—Well: when he pleases,—
Only, I want the air: it vexes one
To be pent up so long!
    Hol.   The King . . . I bear
His message, Strafford . . . pray you, let me speak!
    Straf.   Go, William! Anne, try o'er your song again!
                      (*The Children retire.*)
They shall be loyal, friend, at all events.
I know your message: you have nothing new
To tell me: from the first I guessed as much.

I know, instead of coming here at once—
Leading me forth before them by the hand,—
I know the King will leave the door ajar
As though I were escaping . . . let me fly
While the mob gapes upon some show prepared
On the other side of the river!

   Hol. (*To his Companion.*)   Tell him all;
I knew my throat would thicken thus . . . Speak, you!

   Straf. 'Tis all one—I forgive him. Let me have
The order of release!

             . . . I've heard, as well,
Of certain poor manœuvrings to avoid
The granting pardon at his proper risk;
First, he must prattle somewhat to the Lords—
Must talk a trifle with the Commons first—
Be grieved I should abuse his confidence,
And far from blaming them, and . . .

                 . . . Where's the order?

   Hol. Spare me!

   Straf.   Why . . . he'd not have me steal away?
—With an old doublet and a steeple hat
Like Prynne's? Be smuggled into France, perhaps?
Hollis, 'tis for my children! 'Twas for them
I e'er consented to stand day by day
And give those Puritans the best of words—
Be patient—speak when called upon—observe
Their rules,—and not give all of them the lie!

   Hol. No — Strafford . . . no escape . . . no . . .
    dearest Strafford!

   Straf. What's in that boy of mine that he should be
Son to a prison-breaker? I shall stay
And he'll stay with me. Charles should know as much—
He too has children!

(*Turning to* HOLLIS's *Companion.*) Ah, you feel for me!
No need to hide that face! Though it have looked
Upon me from the judgment-seat . . . I know
Strangely, that somewhere it has looked on me . . .
Still there is One who does not come—there's One
That shut out Heaven from me . . .

   Hol.   Think on it then!
On Heaven . . . and calmly . . . as one . . . as one to die!

   Straf. Die? True, friend, all must die, and all must need
Forgiveness: I forgive him from my soul.

Hol. Be constant, now . . . be grand and brave . . . be
   now
Just as when . . . Oh, I cannot stay for words . . .
'Tis a world's wonder . . . but . . . but . . . you must
   die!
   Straf. Sir, if your errand is to set me free
This heartless jest will . . .
                       Hollis—you turn white,
And your lip shivers!—What if . . .
                              Oh, we'll end,
We'll end this! See this paper—warm . . . feel . . . warm
With lying next my heart! Whose hand is there?
Whose promise? Read! Read loud! For God to hear!
" Strafford shall take no hurt " . . . read it, I say!
" In person, honour, nor estate." . . .
   Hol.   The King . . .
   Straf. I could unking him by a breath! You sit
Where Loudon sate . . . Loudon, who came to tell
The certain end, and offer me Pym's pardon
If I'd forsake the King—and I stood firm
On my King's faith! The King who lived . . .
   Hol.   To sign
The warrant for your death.
   Straf.   " Put not your trust
" In Princes, neither in the sons of men,
" In whom is no salvation! " On that King—
Upon his head . . .
   Cha. O Hollis, he will curse me!
   Hol. The scaffold is prepared—they wait for you—
He has consented . . .
   Cha.   No, no—stay first—Strafford!
You would not see me perish at your foot . . .
It was wrung from me! Only curse me not!
The Queen had cruel eyes! And Vane declared . . .
And I believed I could have rescued you . . .
Strafford—they threaten me! and . . . well, speak now,
And let me die!—
   Hol. (*To* STRAFFORD.) As you hope grace from God,
Be merciful to this most wretched man!
VOICES FROM WITHIN.

Verso la sera
Di Primavera.

Straf. (*After a pause.*)   You'll be good to those children,
  Sire?   I know
You'll not believe her even should the Queen
Think they take after one they never saw!
I had intended that my son should live
A stranger to these matters . . . but you are
So utterly deprived of friends! He too
Must serve you—will you not be good to him?
Stay—Sire—stay—do not promise—do not swear!
And, Hollis—do the best you can for me!
I've not a soul to trust to: Wandesford's dead—
And you've got Radcliffe safe—and Laud is here . . .
I've had small time of late for my affairs—
But I'll trust any of you . . . Pym himself—
No one could hurt them: there's an infant, too—
. . . These tedious cares! Your Majesty could spare them—
But 'tis so awkward—dying in a hurry!
. . . Nay—Pardon me, my King! I had forgotten
Your education, trials, and temptations
And weakness . . . I have said a peevish word—
But, mind I bless you at the last!   You know
'Tis between you and me . . . What has the world
To do with it? Farewell!
    Cha. (*At the door.*)   Balfour! Balfour!
. . . What, die? Strafford to die? This Strafford here?
Balfour! . . . Nay Strafford, do not speak . . . Balfour!

Enter BALFOUR.

The Parliament . . . go to them—I grant all
Demands!   Their sittings shall be permanent—
Tell them to keep their money if they will . . .
I'll come to them for every coat I wear
And every crust I eat, only I choose
To pardon Strafford—Strafford—my brave friend!
    Bal. (*Aside.*) Is he mad, Hollis?
    Cha.   Strafford, now, to die!
. . . But the Queen . . . ah, the Queen!—make haste,
    Balfour!
—You never heard the people howl for blood,
Beside!
    Bal.   Your Majesty may hear them now
The walls can hardly keep their murmurs out
Please you retire!

Cha.   Take all the troops, Balfour!

Bal. There are some hundred thousand of the crowd.

Cha. Come with me, Strafford! You'll not fear them,
  friend!

Straf. Balfour, say nothing to the world of this!
I charge you, as a dying man, forget
You gazed upon this agony of one . . .
Of one . . . or if . . . why you may say, Balfour,
The King was sorry—very—'tis no shame!
Yes, you may say he even wept, Balfour,—
And that I walked the lighter to the block
Because of it. I shall walk lightly, Sire!
—For I shall save you . . . save you at the last!
Earth fades, Heaven dawns on me . . . I shall wake next
Before God's throne: the moment's close at hand
When Man the first, last time, has leave to lay
His whole heart bare before its maker—leave
To clear up the long error of a life
And choose one happiness for evermore.
With all mortality about me, Charles,
The sudden wreck—the dregs—the violent death . . .
I'll pray for you! Thro' all the Angel-song
Shall penetrate one weak and quivering prayer—
I'll say how good you are . . . inwardly good
And pure . . . (*The* King *falls :* Hollis *raises him.*)
                   Be witness, he could not prevent
My death! I'll go—ere he awakes—go now!
All must be ready—did you say, Balfour,
The crowd began to murmur?—They'll be kept
Too late for sermon at St. Antholin's!
Now—but tread softly—children are at play
In the next room—Ah, just my children—Hollis!
—Or . . . no—support the King! (*A door is unbarred.*)
                    Hark . . . they are here!
Stay, Hollis!—Go, Balfour! I'll follow . . .

CARLISLE (*entering with many Attendants*).

Car.   Me!
Follow me, Strafford, and be saved! . . . The King?
(*To the* King.) Well—as you ordered . . . They are ranged
  without . . .
The convoy . . . (*Seeing the* King's *state.*)
(*To* STRAFFORD.) You know all then! Why, I thought

It looked so well that Charles should save you—Charles
Alone . . . 'tis shame that you should owe it me—
Me . . . no, not shame! Strafford, you'll not feel shame
At being saved by me?

   Hol.   All true! Oh Strafford,
She saves you! all her deed . . . this girl's own deed
—And is the boat in readiness? . . . You, friend,
Are Billingsley, no doubt! Speak to her, Strafford!
See how she trembles . . . waiting for your voice!
The world's to learn its bravest story yet!

   Car. Talk afterward! Long nights in France enough
To sit beneath the vines and talk of home!

   Straf. You love me, girl! Ah, Strafford can be
    loved
As well as Vane! I could escape, then?

   Car.   Haste . . .
Advance the torches, Bryan!

   Straf.   I will die!
They call me proud . . . but England had no right
When she encountered me—her strength to mine—
To find the chosen foe a craven! Girl,
I fought her to the utterance—I fell—
I am hers now . . . and I will die! Beside
The lookers-on! Eliot is all about
This place with his most uncomplaining brow!

   Car. Strafford!

   Straf.   I think if you could know how much
I love you, you would be repaid, my girl!

   Car. Then, for my sake!

   Straf.   Even for your sweet sake . . .
I stay.

   Hol. For *their* sake!

   Straf.   I bequeath a stain.
Leave me! Girl, humour me and let me die!

   Hol. No way to draw him hence—Carlisle—no way?

   Car. (*Suddenly to* CHARLES.) Bid him escape . . . wake,
    King! Bid him escape!

   Straf. (*Looks earnestly at him.*) Yes, I will go! Die, and
    forsake the King?
I'll not draw back from the last service.

   Car. Strafford!

   Straf.   And, after all, what is disgrace to me?
Let us come, girl! . . . That it should end this way

Lead then . . . but I feel strangely . . . it was not
To end this way!

 Car.   Lean—lean on me!

 Straf.   My King!

Oh, had he trusted me—his Friend of friends—
Had he but trusted me!

 Car.   Leave not the King—

I can support him, Hollis!

 Straf. (*Starting as they approach the door at the back.*)

          Not this way;

This gate . . . I dreamed of it . . . this very gate!

 Car. It opens on the river—our good boat

Is moored below—our friends are there!

 Straf.   The same!

Only with something ominous and dark,
Fatal, inevitable . . .

 Cha.   Strafford! Strafford!

 Straf. Not by this gate . . . I feel it will be there.

I dreamed of it I tell you . . . touch it not!

 Car. To save the King,—Strafford, to save the King!

  (*As* STRAFFORD *opens the door,* PYM *is discovered with*
  HAMPDEN, VANE, *etc.* STRAFFORD *falls back to the*
  front of the stage : PYM *follows slowly and confronts*
  him.)

 Pym. Have I done well? Speak, England! Whose great
  sake

I still have laboured for, with disregard
To my own heart,—for whom my youth was made
Barren, my future dark, to offer up
Her sacrifice—this man, this Wentworth here—
That walked in youth with me—loved me it may be,
And whom, for his forsaking England's cause,
I hunted by all means (trusting that she
Would sanctify all means) even to the grave
That yawns for him. And saying this, I feel
No bitter pang than first I felt, the hour
I swore that Wentworth might leave us,—but I
Would never leave him: I do leave him now!
I render up my charge (be witness, God!)
To England who imposed it! I have done
Her bidding—poorly, wrongly,—it may be
With ill effects—for I am but a man . . .

Still, I have done my best, my very best,
Not faltering for a moment! I have done!

(After a pause.)

And that said, I will say . . . yes, I will say
I never loved but this man—David not
More Jonathan! Even thus, I love him now:
And look for my chief portion in that world
Where great hearts led astray are turned again,
(Soon it may be . . . and . . . yes . . . it will be soon:
My mission over, I shall not live long!)—
. . . Aye here I know I talk—and I will talk
Of England—and her great reward—as all
I look for there; but in my inmost heart
Believe I think of stealing quite away
To walk once more with Wentworth—with my friend
Purged from all error, gloriously renewed,
And Eliot shall not blame us! Then indeed . . .
(This is no meeting, Wentworth! Tears rise up
Too hot . . . A thin mist—is it blood?—enwraps
The face I loved so!) Then, shall the meeting be!
Then—then—then—I may kiss that hand, I know!
   Straf. (*Walks calmly up to* Pym *and offers his hand.*) I
have loved England too; we'll meet then, Pym!
As well to die! Youth is the time—our youth,
To think and to decide on a great course:
Age with its action follows; but 'tis dreary
To have to alter one's whole life in age—
The time past, the strength gone! as well die now.
When we meet, Pym, I'd be set right—not now!
I'd die as I have lived . . . too late to change!
Best die. Then if there's any fault, it will
Be smothered up: much best! You'll be too busy
With your hereafter, you will have achieved
Too many triumphs to be always dwelling
Upon my downfall, Pym? Poor little Laud
May dream his dream out of a perfect Church
In some blind corner? And there's no one left . . .

(He glances on the King.)

I trust the King now wholly to you, Pym!
And yet . . . I know not! what if with this weakness . . .
And I shall not be there . . . And he'll betray
His friends—if he has any . . . And he's false . . .
And loves the Queen, and . . .

Oh, my fate is nothing—
Nothing! But not that awful head . . . not that!

Pym, save the King! Pym, save him! Stay—you shall . . .
For you love England! I, that am dying, think
What I must see . . . 'tis here . . . all here! My God!
Let me but gasp out, in one word of fire,
How Thou wilt plague him, satiating Hell!
What? England that you love—our land—become
A green and putrefying charnel, left
Our children . . . some of us have children, Pym—
Some who, without that, still must ever wear
A darkened brow, an over-serious look,
And never properly be young . . .

No word!
You will not say a word—to me—to Him!

(*Turning to* CHARLES.)

Speak to him . . . as you spoke to me . . . that day!
Nay, I will let you pray to him, my King—
Pray to him! He will kiss your feet, I know!
What if I curse you? Send a strong Curse forth
Clothed from my heart, lapped round with horror, till
She's fit, with her white face, to walk the world
Scaring kind natures from your cause and you—
Then sit down with you, at the board-head,
The gathering for prayer . . .

  Vane.   O speak, Pym! Speak!
  Straf. . . . Creep up, and quietly follow each one home—
You—you—you—be a nestling Care for each
To sleep with, hardly moaning in his dreams . . .
She gnaws so quietly . . . until he starts—
Gets off with half a heart eaten away . . .
Oh you shall 'scape with less, if she's my child!
  Vane. (*To* PYM.) We never thought of this . . . surely
   not dreamed
Of this . . . it never can . . . could come to this!
  Pym. (*After a pause.*) If England should declare her will
   to me . . .
  Straf. No—not for England, now—not for Heaven,
   now . . .
See, Pym—for me! My sake! I kneel to you!
There . . . I will thank you for the death . . . my friend,
This is the meeting . . . you will send me proud

To my chill grave! Dear Pym—I'll love you well!
Save him for me, and let me love you well!
   Pym. England—I am thine own! Dost thou exact
That service? I obey thee to the end!
   Straf. (*As he totters out.*) O God, I shall die first—I shall
    die first!

(Curtain falls.)

THE END

SORDELLO

To J. Milsand, of Dijon.

Dear Friend,—Let the next poem be introduced by your
name, therefore remembered along with one of the deepest
of my affections, and so repay all trouble it ever cost me.
I wrote it twenty-five years ago for only a few, counting
even in these on somewhat more care about its subject than
they really had. My own faults of expression were many;
but with care for a man or book such would be surmounted,
and without it what avails the faultlessness of either? I
blame nobody, least of all myself, who did my best then and
since; for I lately gave time and pains to turn my work into
what the many might,—instead of what the few must,—
like: but after all, I imagined another thing at first, and
therefore leave as I find it. The historical decoration was
purposely of no more importance than a background requires;
and my stress lay on the incidents in the development of a
soul: little else is worth study. I, at least, always thought
so—you, with many known and unknown to me, think so—
others may one day think so; and whether my attempt
remain for them or not, I trust, though away and past it,
to continue ever yours,

R. B.

London: June 9, 1863.

SORDELLO

BOOK THE FIRST

WHO will, may hear Sordello's story told:
His story? Who believes me shall behold
The man, pursue his fortunes to the end
Like me; for as the friendless people's friend
Spied from his hill-top once, despite the din
And dust of multitudes, Pentapolin
Named o' the Naked Arm, I single out
Sordello, compassed murkily about
With ravage of six long sad hundred years:
Only believe me. Ye believe?
                                        Appears
Verona . . . Never, I should warn you first,
Of my own choice had this, if not the worst
Yet not the best expedient, served to tell
A story I could body forth so well
By making speak, myself kept out of view,
The very man as he was wont to do,
And leaving you to say the rest for him:
Since, though I might be proud to see the dim
Abysmal Past divide its hateful surge,
Letting of all men this one man emerge
Because it pleased me, yet, that moment past,
I should delight in watching first to last
His progress as you watch it, not a whit
More in the secret than yourselves who sit
Fresh-chapleted to listen: but it seems
Your setters-forth of unexampled themes,
Makers of quite new men, producing them
Had best chalk broadly on each vesture's hem
The wearer's quality, or take his stand
Motley on back and pointing-pole in hand
Beside them; so for once I face ye, friends,
Summoned together from the world's four ends,
Dropped down from Heaven or cast up from Hell,

living without

To hear the story I propose to tell.
Confess now, poets know the dragnet's trick,
Catching the dead if Fate denies the quick
And shaming her; 'tis not for Fate to choose
Silence or song because she can refuse
Real eyes to glisten more, real hearts to ache
Less oft, real brows turn smoother for our sake:
I have experienced something of her spite;
But there's a realm wherein she has no right
And I have many lovers: say but few
Friends Fate accords me? Here they are; now view
The host I muster! Many a lighted face
Foul with no vestige of the grave's disgrace;
What else should tempt them back to taste our air
Except to see how their successors fare?
My audience: and they sit, each ghostly man
Striving to look as living as he can,
Brother by breathing brother; thou art set,
Clear-witted critic, by . . . but I'll not fret
A wondrous soul of them, nor move Death's spleen
Who loves not to unlock them. Friends! I mean
The living in good earnest—ye elect
Chiefly for love—suppose not I reject
Judicious praise, who contrary shall peep
Some fit occasion forth, for fear ye sleep,
To glean your bland approvals. Then, appear,
Verona! stay—thou, spirit, come not near
Now—nor this time desert thy cloudy place
To scare me, thus employed, with that pure face!
I need not fear this audience, I make free
With them, but then this is no place for thee!
The thunder-phrase of the Athenian, grown
Up out of memories of Marathon,
Would echo like his own sword's griding screech
Braying a Persian shield,—the silver speech
Of Sidney's self, the starry paladin,
Turn intense as a trumpet sounding in
The knights to tilt—wert thou to hear! What heart
Have I to play my puppets, bear my part
Before these worthies?

            Lo, the Past is hurled
In twain: upthrust, out-staggering on the world,
Subsiding into shape, a darkness rears

Its outline, kindles at the core, appears
Verona.   'Tis six hundred years and more
Since an event. The Second Friedrich wore
The purple, and the Third Honorius filled
The holy chair. That autumn eve was stilled:
At last remains of sunset dimly burned
O'er the far forests like a torch-flame turned
By the wind back upon its bearer's hand
In one long flare of crimson; as a brand
The woods beneath lay black. A single eye
From all Verona cared for the soft sky:
But, gathering in its ancient market-place,
Talked group with restless group; and not a face
But wrath made livid, for among them were
Death's staunch purveyors, such as have in care
To feast him. Fear had long since taken root
In every breast, and now these crushed its fruit,
The ripe hate, like a wine: to note the way
It worked while each grew drunk! men grave and grey
Stood, with shut eyelids, rocking to and fro,
Letting the silent luxury trickle slow
About the hollows where a heart should be;
But the young gulped with a delirious glee
Some foretaste of their first debauch in blood
At the fierce news: for, be it understood,
Envoys apprised Verona that her prince
Count Richard of Saint Boniface, joined since
A year with Azzo, Este's Lord, to thrust
Taurello Salinguerra, prime in trust
With Ecelin Romano, from his seat
Ferrara,—over zealous in the feat
And stumbling on a peril unaware,
Was captive, " trammelled in his proper snare,"
They phrase it, " taken by his own intrigue: "
Immediate succour, from the Lombard League
Of fifteen cities that affect the Pope,
For Azzo therefore and his fellow—hope
Of the Guelf cause, a glory overcast!
Men's faces, late agape, are now aghast:
Prone is the purple pavice; Este makes
Mirth for the Devil when he undertakes
To pay the Ecelin; as if it cost
Merely your pushing-by to gain a post

Like his! The patron tells ye, once for all,
There be sound reasons that preferment fall
On our beloved . . .
              Duke o' the Rood, why not?
Shouted an Estian, grudge ye such a lot?
The hill-cat boasts some cunning of her own,
Some stealthy trick to better beasts unknown
That quick with prey enough her hunger blunts
And feeds her fat while gaunt the lion hunts.
Taurello, quoth an envoy, as in wane
Dwelt at Ferrara. Like an osprey fain
To fly but forced the earth his couch to make
Far inland till his friend the tempest wake,
Wait he the Kaiser's coming; and as yet
That fast friend sleeps, and he too sleeps; but let
Only the billow freshen, and he snuffs
The aroused hurricane ere it enroughs
The sea it means to cross because of him:
Sinketh the breeze? His hope-sick eye grows dim;
Creep closer on the creature! Every day
Strengthens the Pontiff; Ecelin, they say,
Dozes at Oliero, with dry lips
Telling upon his perished finger-tips
How many ancestors are to depose
Ere he be Satan's Viceroy when the doze
Deposits him in hell; so Guelfs rebuilt
Their houses; not a drop of blood was spilt
When Cino Bocchimpane chanced to meet
Buccio Virtù; God's wafer, and the street
Is narrow! Tutti Santi, think, a-swarm
With Ghibellins, and yet he took no harm.
This could not last. Off Salinguerra went
To Padua, Podestà, with pure intent,
Said he, my presence, judged the single bar
To permanent tranquillity, may jar
No longer—so! his back is fairly turned?
The pair of goodly palaces are burned,
The gardens ravaged, and your Guelf is drunk
A week with joy; the next, his laughter sunk
In sobs of blood, for he found, some strange way,
Old Salinguerra back again; I say,
Old Salinguerra in the town once more
Uprooting, overturning, flame before,

Blood fetlock-high beneath him; Azzo fled;
Who scaped the carnage followed; then the dead
Were pushed aside fiom Salinguerra's throne,
He ruled once more Ferrara, all alone,
Till Azzo, stunned awhile, revived, would pounce
Coupled with Boniface, like lynx and ounce,
On the gorged bird. The burghers ground their teeth
To see troop after troop encamp beneath
I' the standing corn thick o'er the scanty patch
It took so many patient months to snatch
Out of the marsh; while just within their walls
Men fed on men. Astute Taurello calls
A parley: let the Count wind up the war!
Richard, light-hearted as a plunging star,
Agrees to enter for the kindest ends
Ferrara, flanked with fifty chosen friends,
No horse-boy more for fear your timid sort
Should fly Ferrara at the bare report.
Quietly through the town they rode, jog-jog;
Ten, twenty, thirty . . . curse the catalogue
Of burnt Guelf houses! Strange Taurello shows
Not the least sign of life—whereat arose
A general growl: How? With his victors by?
I and my Veronese? My troops and I?
Receive us, was your word? so jogged they on,
Nor laughed their host too openly: once gone
Into the trap . . .
                    Six hundred years ago!
Such the time's aspect and peculiar woe
(Yourselves may spell it yet in chronicles,
Albeit the worm, our busy brother, drills
His sprawling path through letters anciently
Made fine and large to suit some abbot's eye)
When the new Hohenstauffen dropped the mask,
Flung John of Brienne's favour from his casque,
Forswore crusading, had no mind to leave
Saint Peter's proxy leisure to retrieve
Losses to Otho and to Barbaross,
Or make the Alps less easy to recross;
And thus confirming Pope Honorius' fear,
Was excommunicate that very year.
The triple-bearded Teuton come to life!
Groaned the Great League; and, arming for the strife,

Wide Lombardy, on tiptoe to begin,
Took up, as it was Guelf or Ghibellin,
Its cry; what cry?
           The Emperor to come!
His crowd of feudatories, all and some
That leapt down with a crash of swords, spears, shields,
One fighter on his fellow, to our fields,
Scattered anon, took station here and there,
And carried it, till now, with little care—
Cannot but cry for him; how else rebut
Us longer? Cliffs an earthquake suffered jut
In the mid-sea, each domineering crest
Nothing save such another throe can wrest
From out (conceive) a certain chokeweed grown
Since o'er the waters, twine and tangle thrown
Too thick, too fast accumulating round,
Too sure to over-riot and confound
Ere long each brilliant islet with itself
Unless a second shock save shoal and shelf,
Whirling the sea-drift wide: alas, the bruised
And sullen wreck! Sunlight to be diffused
For that! Sunlight, 'neath which, a scum at first,
The million fibres of our chokeweed nurst
Dispread themselves, mantling the troubled main,
And, shattered by those rocks, took hold again
So kindly blazed it—that same blaze to brood
O'er every cluster of the multitude
Still hazarding new clasps, ties, filaments,
An emulous exchange of pulses, vents
Of nature into nature; till some growth
Unfancied yet exuberantly clothe
A surface solid now, continuous, one:
The Pope, for us the People, who begun
The People, carries on the People thus,
To keep that Kaiser off and dwell with us!
See you?
           Or say, Two Principles that live
Each fitly by its Representative:
Hill-cat . . . who called him so, our gracefullest
Adventurer? the ambiguous stranger-guest
Of Lombardy (sleek but that ruffling fur,
Those talons to their sheath!) whose velvet purr
Soothes jealous neighbours when a Saxon scout

... Arpo or Yoland, is it? one without
A country or a name, presumes to couch
Beside their noblest; until men avouch
That of all Houses in the Trivisan
Conrad descries no fitter, rear or van,
Than Ecelo! They laughed as they enrolled
That name at Milan on the page of gold
For Godego, Ramon, Marostica,
Cartiglion, Bassano, Loria,
And every sheep-cote on the Suabian's fief!
No laughter when his son, the Lombard Chief
Forsooth, as Barbarossa's path was bent
To Italy along the Vale of Trent,
Welcomed him at Roncaglia! Sadness now—
The hamlets nested on the Tyrol's brow,
The Asolan and Euganean hills,
The Rhetian and the Julian, sadness fills
Them all that Ecelin vouchsafes to stay
Among and care about them; day by day
Choosing this pinnacle, the other spot,
A castle building to defend a cot,
A cot built for the castle to defend,
Nothing but castles, castles, nor an end
To boasts how mountain ridge may join with ridge
By sunken gallery and soaring bridge—
He takes, in brief, a figure that beseems
The griesliest nightmare of the Church's dreams,
A Signory firm-rooted, unestranged
From its old interests, and nowise changed
By its new neighbourhood; perchance the vaunt
Of Otho, " my own Este shall supplant
Your Este," come to pass. The sire led in
A son as cruel; and this Ecelin
Had sons, in turn, and daughters sly and tall,
And curling and compliant; but for all
Romano (so they style him) thrives; that neck
Of his so pinched and white, that hungry cheek
Prove 'tis some fiend, not him, men's flesh is meant
To feed: whereas Romano's instrument,
Famous Taurello Salinguerra, sole
I' the world, a tree whose boughs are slipt the bole
Successively, why should not he shed blood
To further a design? Men understood

Living was pleasant to him as he wore
His careless surcoat, glanced some missive o'er,
Propped on his truncheon in the public way.
Ecelin lifts two writhen hands to pray
At Oliero's convent now: so, place
For Azzo, Lion of the . . . why disgrace
A worthiness conspicuous near and far
(Atti at Rome while free and consular,
Este at Padua to repulse the Hun)
By trumpeting the Church's princely son
Styled Patron of Rovigo's Polesine,
Ancona's March, Ferrara's . . . ask, in fine,
Your chronicles, commenced when some old monk
Found it intolerable to be sunk
(Vexed to the quick by his revolting cell)
Quite out of summer while alive and well:
Ended when by his mat the Prior stood,
Mid busy promptings of the brotherhood,
Striving to coax from his decrepit brains
The reason Father Porphyry took pains
To blot those ten lines out which used to stand
First on their charter drawn by Hildebrand.
   The same night wears. Verona's rule of yore
Was vested in a certain Twenty-four;
And while within his palace these debate
Concerning Richard and Ferrara's fate,
Glide we by clapping doors, with sudden glare
Of cressets vented on the dark, nor care
For aught that's seen or heard until we shut
The smother in, the lights, all noises but
The carroch's booming; safe at last! Why strange
Such a recess should lurk behind a range
Of banquet-rooms? Your finger—thus—you push
A spring, and the wall opens, would you rush
Upon the banqueters, select your prey,
Waiting the slaughter-weapons in the way
Strewing this very bench; with sharpened ear
A preconcerted signal to appear;
Or if you simply crouch with beating heart
Bearing in some voluptuous pageant part
To startle them. Nor mutes nor masquers now;
Nor any . . . does that one man sleep whose brow
The dying lamp-flame sinks and rises o'er?

What woman stood beside him? not the more
Is he unfastened from the earnest eyes
Because that arras fell between! Her wise
And lulling words are yet about the room,
Her presence wholly poured upon the gloom
Down even to her vesture's creeping stir:
And so reclines he, saturate with her,
Until an outcry from the square beneath
Pierces the charm: he springs up, glad to breathe
Above the cunning element, and shakes
The stupor off as (look you) morning breaks
On the gay dress, and, near concealed by it,
The lean frame like a half-burnt taper, lit
Erst at some marriage-feast, then laid away
Till the Armenian bridegroom's dying-day,
In his wool wedding-robe; for he—for he—
" Gate-vein of this heart's blood of Lombardy "
(If I should falter now)—for he is Thine!
Sordello, thy forerunner, Florentine!
A herald-star I know thou didst absorb
Relentless into the consummate orb
That scared it from its right to roll along
A sempiternal path with dance and song
Fulfilling its allotted period
Serenest of the progeny of God
Who yet resigns it not; his darling stoops
With no quenched lights, desponds with no blank troops
Of disenfranchised brilliances, for, blent
Utterly with thee, its shy element
Like thine upburneth prosperous and clear:
Still, what if I approach the august sphere
Named now with only one name, disentwine
That under current soft and argentine
From its fierce mate in the majestic mass
Leavened as the sea whose fire was mix. with glass
In John's transcendent vision, launch once more
That lustre? Dante, pacer of the shore
Where glutted Hell disgorgeth filthiest gloom,
Unbitten by its whirring sulphur-spume—
Or whence the grieved and obscure waters slope
Into a darkness quieted by hope—
Plucker of amaranths grown beneath God's eye
In gracious twilights where his Chosen lie,

I would do this! If I should falter now—
  In Mantua-territory half is slough
Half pine-tree forest; maples, scarlet-oaks
Breed o'er the river-beds; even Mincio chokes
With sand the summer through; but 'tis morass
In winter up to Mantua walls. There was
(Some thirty years before this evening's coil)
One spot reclaimed from the surrounding spoil,
Goito; just a castle built amid
A few low mountains; firs and larches hid
Their main defiles and rings of vineyard bound
The rest: some captured creature in a pound,
Whose artless wonder quite precludes distress
Secure beside in its own loveliness,
So peered with airy head, below, above,
The castle at its toils the lapwings love
To glean among at grape-time. Pass within:
A maze of corridors contrived for sin,
Dusk winding-stairs, dim galleries got past,
You gain the inmost chambers, gain at last
A maple-panelled room: that haze which seems
Floating about the panel, if there gleams
A sunbeam over it will turn to gold
And in light-graven characters unfold
The Arab's wisdom everywhere; what shade
Marred them a moment, those slim pillars made,
Cut like a company of palms to prop
The roof, each kissing top entwined with top,
Leaning together; in the carver's mind
Some knot of bacchanals, flushed cheek combined
With straining forehead, shoulders purpled, hair
Diffused between, who in a goat-skin bear
A vintage; graceful sister-palms: but quick
To the main wonder now. A vault, see; thick
Black shade about the ceiling, though fine slits
Across the buttress suffer light by fits
Upon a marvel in the midst: nay, stoop—
A dullish grey-streaked cumbrous font, a group
Round it, each side of it, where'er one sees,
Upholds it—shrinking Caryatides
Of just-tinged marble like Eve's lilied flesh
Beneath her Maker's finger when the fresh
First pulse of life shot brightening the snow:

The font's edge burthens every shoulder, so
They muse upon the ground, eyelids half closed,
Some, with meek arms behind their backs disposed,
Some, crossed above their bosoms, some, to veil
Their eyes, some, propping chin and cheek so pale,
Some, hanging slack an utter helpless length
Dead as a buried vestal whose whole strength
Goes when the grate above shuts heavily;
So dwell these noiseless girls, patient to see,
Like priestesses because of sin impure
Penanced for ever, who resigned endure,
Having that once drunk sweetness to the dregs;
And every eve Sordello's visit begs
Pardon for them: constant as eve he came
To sit beside each in her turn, the same
As one of them, a certain space: and awe
Made a great indistinctness till he saw
Sunset slant cheerful through the buttress chinks,
Gold seven times globed; surely our maiden shrinks
And a smile stirs her as if one faint grain
Her load were lightened, one shade less the stain
Obscured her forehead, yet one more bead slipt
From off the rosary whereby the crypt
Keeps count of the contritions of its charge?
Then with a step more light, a heart more large,
He may depart, leave her and every one
To linger out the penance in mute stone.
Ah, but Sordello? 'Tis the tale I mean
To tell you. In this castle may be seen,
On the hill tops, or underneath the vines,
Or southward by the mound of firs and pines
That shuts out Mantua, still in loneliness,
A slender boy in a loose page's dress,
Sordello: do but look on him awhile
Watching ('tis autumn) with an earnest smile
The noisy flock of thievish birds at work
Among the yellowing vineyards; see him lurk
('Tis winter with its sullenest of storms)
Beside that arras-length of broidered forms.
On tiptoe, lifting in both hands a light
Which makes yon warrior's visage flutter bright
—Ecelo, dismal father of the brood,
And Ecelin, close to the girl he wooed

—Auria, and their Child, with all his wives
From Agnes to the Tuscan that survives,
Lady of the castle, Adelaide: his face
—Look, now he turns away! Yourselves shall trace
(The delicate nostril swerving wide and fine,
A sharp and restless lip, so well combine
With that calm brow) a soul fit to receive
Delight at every sense; you can believe
Sordello foremost in the regal class
Nature has broadly severed from her mass
Of men and framed for pleasure as she frames
Some happy lands that have luxurious names
For loose fertility; a footfall there
Suffices to upturn to the warm air
Half-germinating spices, mere decay
Produces richer life, and day by day
New pollen on the lily-petal grows,
And still more labyrinthine buds the rose.
You recognise at once the finer dress
Of flesh that amply lets in loveliness
At eye and ear, while round the rest is furled
(As though she would not trust them with her world)
A veil that shows a sky not near so blue,
And lets but half the sun look fervid through;
How can such love like souls on each full-fraught
Discovery brooding, blind at first to aught
Beyond its beauty; till exceeding love
Becomes an aching weight, and, to remove
A curse that haunts such natures—to preclude
Their finding out themselves can work no good
To what they love nor make it very blest
By their endeavour, they are fain invest
The lifeless thing with life from their own soul
Availing it to purpose, to control,
To dwell distinct and have peculiar joy
And separate interests that may employ
That beauty fitly, for its proper sake;
Nor rest they here: fresh births of beauty wake
Fresh homage; every grade of love is past,
With every mode of loveliness; then cast
Inferior idols off their borrowed crown
Before a coming glory: up and down
Runs arrowy fire, while earthly forms combine

To throb the secret forth; a touch divine—
And the scaled eyeball owns the mystic rod:
Visibly through his garden walketh God.
    So fare they—Now revert: one character
Denotes them through the progress and the stir;
A need to blend with each external charm,
Bury themselves, the whole heart wide and warm,
In something not themselves; they would belong
To what they worship—stronger and more strong
Thus prodigally fed—that gathers shape
And feature, soon imprisons past escape
The votary framed to love and to submit
Nor ask, as passionate he kneels to it,
Whence grew the idol's empery. So runs
A legend; Light had birth ere moons and suns,
Flowing through space a river and alone,
Till chaos burst and blank the spheres were strown
Hither and thither, foundering and blind,
When into each of them rushed Light—to find
Itself no place, foiled of its radiant chance.
Let such forego their just inheritance,
For there's a class that eagerly looks, too,
On beauty, but, unlike the gentler crew,
Proclaims each new revealment born a twin
With a distinctest consciousness within
Referring still the quality, now first
Revealed, to their own soul; its instinct nursed
In silence, now remembered better, shown
More thoroughly, but not the less their own;
A dream come true; the special exercise
Of any special function that implies
The being fair or good or wise or strong,
Dormant within their nature all along—
Whose fault? So homage other souls direct
Without, turns inward; how should this deject
Thee, soul? they murmur: wherefore strength be quelled
Because, its trivial accidents withheld,
Organs are missed that clog the world, inert,
Wanting a will, to quicken and exert,
Like thine—existence cannot satiate
Cannot surprise: laugh thou at envious fate,
Who from earth's simplest combination stampt
|With individuality—uncrampt

By living its faint elemental life,
Dost soar to heaven's complexest essence, rife
With grandeurs, unaffronted to the last,
Equal to being all.

              In truth?   Thou hast
Life, then—wilt challenge life for us: thy race
Is vindicated so, obtains its place
In thy ascent, the first of us; whom we
May follow, to the meanest, finally,
With our more bounded wills?

                    Ah, but to find
A certain mood enervate such a mind,
Counsel it slumber in the solitude
Thus reached nor, stooping, task for mankind's good
Its nature just as life and time accord
(Too narrow an arena to reward
Emprize—the world's occasion worthless since
Not absolutely fitted to evince
Its mastery) or if yet worse befall,
And a desire possess it to put all
That nature forth, forcing our straightened sphere
Contain it; to display completely here
The mastery another life should learn,
Thrusting in time eternity's concern,
So that Sordello. . . . Fool, who spied the mark
Of leprosy upon him, violent dark
Already as he loiters?   Born just now—
With the new century—beside the glow
And efflorescence out of barbarism;
Witness a Greek or two from the abysm
That stray through Florence-town with studious air,
Calming the chisel of that Pisan pair . . .
If Nicolo should carve a Christus yet!
While at Sienna is Guidone set,
Forehead on hand; a painful birth must be
Matured ere San Eufemio's sacristy
Or transept gather fruits of one great gaze
At the noon-sun: look you!   An orange haze—
The same blue stripe round that—and, i' the midst,
Thy spectral whiteness, mother-maid, who didst
Pursue the dizzy painter!

                  Woe then worth
Any officious babble letting forth

The leprosy confirmed and ruinous
To spirit lodged in a contracted house!
Go back to the beginning rather; blend
It gently with Sordello's life; the end
Is piteous, you shall see, but much between
Pleasant enough; meantime some pyx to screen
The full-grown pest, some lid to shut upon
The goblin! As they found at Babylon,
(Colleagues mad Lucius and sage Antonine)
Sacking the city, by Apollo's shrine
Its pride, in rummaging the rarities,
A cabinet; be sure who made the prize
Opened it greedily; and out there curled
Just such another plague, for half the world
Was stung. Crawl in then, hag, and crouch asquat,
Keeping that blotchy bosom thick in spot
Until your time is ripe! The coffer-lid
Is fastened and the coffer safely hid
Under the Loxian's choicest gifts of gold.
Who will may hear Sordello's story told,
And how he never could remember when
He dwelt not at Goito; calmly then
About this secret lodge of Adelaide's
Glided his youth away: beyond the glades
On the fir-forest's border, and the rim
Of the low range of mountain, was for him
No other world: but that appeared his own
To wander through at pleasure and alone.
The castle too seemed empty; far and wide
Might he disport; unless the northern side
Lay under a mysterious interdict—
Slight, just enough remembered to restrict
His roaming to the corridors, the vault
Where those font-bearers expiate their fault,
The maple-chamber, and the little nooks
And nests and breezy parapet that looks
Over the woods to Mantua; there he strolled.
Some foreign women-servants, very old,
Tended and crept about him—all his clue
To the world's business and embroiled ado
Distant a dozen hill-tops at the most.
And first a simple sense of life engrossed
Sordello in his drowsy Paradise;

The day's adventures for the day suffice—
Its constant tribute of perceptions strange
With sleep and stir in healthy interchange
Suffice, and leave him for the next at ease
Like the great palmer-worm that strips the trees,
Eats the life out of every luscious plant,
And when September finds them sere or scant
Puts forth two wondrous winglets, alters quite,
And hies him after unforeseen delight;
So fed Sordello, not a shard disheathed;
As ever round each new discovery wreathed
Luxuriantly the fancies infantine
His admiration, bent on making fine
Its novel friend at any risk, would fling
In gay profusion forth: a ficklest king
Confessed those minions! Eager to dispense
So much from his own stock of thought and sense
As might enable each to stand alone
And serve him for a fellow; with his own
Joining the qualities that just before
Had graced some older favourite: so they wore
A fluctuating halo, yesterday
Set flicker and to-morrow filched away;
Those upland objects each of separate name,
Each with an aspect never twice the same,
Waxing and waning as the new-born host
Of fancies, like a single night's hoar-frost,
Gave to familiar things a face grotesque;
Only, preserving through the mad burlesque
A grave regard: conceive; the orpine patch
Blossoming earliest on the log-house-thatch
The day those archers wound along the vines—
Related to the Chief that left their lines
To climb with clinking step the northern stair
Up to the solitary chambers where
Sordello never came. Thus thrall reached thrall;
He o'er-festooning every interval
As the adventurous spider, making light
Of distance, shoots her threads from depth to height,
From barbican to battlement; so flung
Fantasies forth and in their centre swung
Our architect: the breezy morning fresh
Above, and merry; all his waving mesh

Laughing with lucid dew-drops rainbow-edged.
This world of ours by tacit pact is pledged
To laying such a spangled fabric low
Whether by gradual brush or gallant blow:
But its abundant will was balked here: doubt
Rose tardily in one so fenced about
From most that nurtures judgment, care and pain:
Judgment, that dull expedient we are fain,
Less favoured, to adopt betimes and force
Stead us, diverted from our natural course
Of joys; contrive some yet amid the dearth,
Vary and render them, it may be, worth
Most we forego: suppose Sordello hence
Selfish enough, without a moral sense
However feeble; what informed the boy
Others desired a portion in his joy?
Or say a ruthful chance broke woof and warp—
A heron's nest beat down by March winds sharp,
A fawn breathless beneath the precipice,
A bird with unsoiled breast and filmless eyes
Warm in the brake—could these undo the trance
Lapping Sordello? Not a circumstance
That makes for you, friend Naddo! Eat fern-seed
And peer beside us and report indeed
If (your word) Genius dawned with throes and stings
And the whole fiery catalogue, while springs,
Summers, and winters quietly came and went,
Putting at length that period to content
By right the world should have imposed: bereft
Of its good offices, Sordello, left
To study his companions, managed rip
Their fringe off, learn the true relationship,
Core with its crust, their natures with his own;
Amid his wild-wood sights he lived alone:
As if the poppy felt with him! Though he
Partook the poppy's red effrontery
Till Autumn spoils their fleering quite with rain,
And, turbanless, a coarse brown rattling crane
Protrudes: that's gone! yet why renounce, for that,
His disenchanted tributaries—flat
Perhaps, but scarce so utterly forlorn
Their simple presence may not well be borne
Whose parley was a transport once: recall

The poppy's gifts, it flaunts you, after all,
A poppy: why distrust the evidence
Of each soon satisfied and healthy sense?
The new-born Judgment answered: little boots
Beholding other creatures' attributes
And having none: or say that it sufficed,
Yet, could one but possess, oneself, (enticed
Judgment) some special office! Nought beside
Serves you? Well then, be somehow justified
For this ignoble wish to circumscribe
And concentrate, rather than swell, the tribe
Of actual pleasures: what now from without
Effects it?—proves, despite a lurking doubt,
Mere sympathy sufficient, trouble spared;
—He tasted joys by proxy, clearly fared
The better for them; thus much craved his soul.
Alas, from the beginning Love is whole
And true; if sure of nought beside, most sure
Of its own truth at least; nor may endure
A crowd to see its face, that cannot know
How hot the pulses throb its heart below;
While its own helplessness and utter want
Of means to worthily be ministrant
To what it worships, do but fan the more
Its flame, exalt the idol far before
Itself as it would have it ever be;
Souls like Sordello, on the contrary,
Coerced and put to shame, retaining Will,
Care little, take mysterious comforts still,
But look forth tremblingly to ascertain
If others judge their claims not urged in vain
—Will say for them their stifled thoughts aloud;
So they must ever live before a crowd:
Vanity, Naddo tells you.

                              Whence contrive
A crowd, now? These brave women just alive,
That archer-troop? Forth glided—not alone
Each painted warrior, every girl of stone,
—Nor Adelaide bent double o'er a scroll,
One maiden at her knees, that eve his soul
Shook as he stumbled through the arras'd glooms
On them, for, 'mid quaint robes and weird perfumes,
Started the meagre Tuscan up (her eyes

The maiden's also, bluer with surprise)
—But the entire out-world: whatever scraps
And snatches, song and story, dreams perhaps,
Conceited the world's offices, and he
Transferred to the first comer, flower or tree,
Nor counted a befitting heritage
Each, of its own right, singly to engage
Some Man, no other: such availed to stand
Alone: strength, wisdom, grace on every hand
Soon disengaged themselves; and he discerned
A sort of human life: at least, was turned
A stream of life-like figures through his brain
—Lord, Liegeman, Valvassor and Suzerain,
Ere he could choose, surrounded him; a stuff
To work his pleasure on; there, sure enough,
But as for gazing, what shall fix that gaze?
Are they to amply testify the ways
He who convoked them sends his soul along
With the cloud's thunder or a dove's brood-song?
While they live each its life, boast each its own
Peculiar dower of bliss, stand each alone
In some one point where something dearest loved
Is easiest gained—far worthier to be proved
Than aught he envies in the forest-wights!
No simple and self-evident delights,
But mixed desires of unimagined range,
Contrasts or combinations, new and strange,
Irksome perhaps, yet plainly recognised
By this, the sudden company—loves prized
By those who are to prize his own amount
Of loves. Once care because such make account,
Allow a foreign recognition stamp
The current value, and your crowd shall vamp
You counterfeits enough; and so their print
Be on the piece, 'tis gold, attests the mint
And good, pronounce they whom my new appeal
Is made to: if their casual print conceal—
This arbitrary good of theirs o'ergloss
What I have lived without, nor felt my loss—
Qualities strange, ungainly, wearisome,
—What matter? so must speech expand the dumb
Part sigh, part smile with which Sordello, late
No foolish woodland-sights could satiate,

Betakes himself to study hungrily
Just what the puppets his crude fantasy
Supposes notablest, popes, kings, priests, knights,
May please to promulgate for appetites;
Accepting all their artificial joys
Not as he views them, but as he employs
Each shape to estimate the other's stock
Of attributes, that on a marshalled flock
Of authorised enjoyments he may spend
Himself, be Men, now, as he used to blend
With tree and flower—nay more entirely, else
'Twere mockery: for instance, how excels
My life that Chieftain's? (who apprised the youth
Ecelin, here, becomes this month in truth,
Imperial Vicar?) Turns he in his tent
Remissly? Be it so—my head is bent
Deliciously amid my girls to sleep:
What if he stalks the Trentine-pass? Yon steep
I climbed an hour ago with little toil—
We are alike there: but can I, too, foil
The Guelfs' paid stabber, carelessly afford
St. Mark's a spectacle, the sleight o' the sword
Baffling their project in a moment? Here
No rescue! Poppy he is none, but peer
To Ecelin, assuredly: his hand,
Fashioned no otherwise, should wield a brand
With Ecelin's success—try, now! He soon
Was satisfied, returned as to the moon
From earth; left each abortive boy's-attempt
For feats, from failure happily exempt,
In fancy at his beck. One day I will
Accomplish it! Are they not older still
—Not grown up men and women? 'Tis besides
Only a dream; and though I must abide
With dreams now, I may find a thorough vent
For all myself, acquire an instrument
For acting what these people act; my soul
Hunting a body out; obtain its whole
Desire some day! How else express chagrin
And resignation, show the hope steal in
With which he let sink from an aching wrist
The rough-hewn ash-bow, and a gold shaft hiss'd
Into the Syrian air, struck Malek down

Superbly! Crosses to the breach! God's Town
Was gained Him back! Why bend rough ash-bows more?
  So lives he: if not careless as before,
Comforted: for one may anticipate,
Rehearse the future; be prepared when fate
Shall have prepared in turn real men whose names
Startle, real places of enormous fames,
Estes abroad and Ecelins at home
To worship him, Mantuas, Veronas, Rome
To witness it. Who grudges time so spent!
Rather test qualities to heart's content—
Summon them, thrice selected, near and far—
Compress the starriest into one star
So grasp the whole at once! The pageant's thinned
Accordingly; from rank to rank, like wind
His spirit passed to winnow and divide;
Back fell the simpler phantasms; every side
The strong clave to the wise; with either classed
The beauteous; so, till two or three amassed
Mankind's beseemingnesses, and reduced
Themselves eventually, graces loosed,
And lavished strengths, to heighten up One Shape
Whose potency no creature should escape:
Can it be Friedrich of the bowmen's talk?
Surely that grape-juice, bubbling at the stalk,
Is some grey scorching Saracenic wine
The Kaiser quaffs with the Miramoline—
Those swarthy hazel-clusters, seamed and chapped,
Or filberts russet-sheathed and velvet-capped,
Are dates plucked from the bough John Brienne sent
To keep in mind his sluggish armament
Of Canaan . . . Friedrich's, all the pomp and fierce
Demeanour! But harsh sounds and sights transpierce
So rarely the serene cloud where he dwells
Whose looks enjoin, whose lightest words are spells
Upon the obdurate; that arm indeed
Has thunder for its slave; but where's the need
Of thunder if the stricken multitude
Hearkens, arrested in its angriest mood,
While songs go up exulting, then dispread,
Dispart, disperse, lingering overhead
Like an escape of angels? 'Tis the tune,
'Nor much unlike the words the women croon

Smilingly, colourless and faint designed
Each as a worn-out queen's face some remind
Of her extreme youth's love-tales. Eglamor
Made that! Half minstrel and half emperor,
Who but ill objects vexed him? Such he slew.
The kinder sort were easy to subdue
By those ambrosial glances, dulcet tones;
And these a gracious hand advanced to thrones
Beneath him. Wherefore twist and torture this,
Striving to name afresh the antique bliss,
Instead of saying, neither less nor more,
He had discovered, as our world before,
Apollo? That shall be the name; nor bid
Me rag by rag expose how patchwork hid
The man—what thefts of every clime and day
Contributed to purfle the array
He climbs with (June's at deep) some close ravine
'Mid clatter of its million pebbles sheen,
Over which singing soft the runnel slipt
Elate with rains: into whose streamlet dipt
He foot, yet trod, you thought, with unwet sock—
Though really on the stubs of living rock
Ages ago it crenneled; vines for roof,
Lindens for wall; before him, aye aloof,
Flittered in the cool some azure damsel-fly,
Child of the simmering quiet, there to die:
Emerging whence, Apollo still, he spied
Mighty descents of forest; multiplied
Tuft on tuft, here, the frolic myrtle-trees;
There gendered the grave maple-stocks at ease;
And, proud of its observer, strait the wood
Tried old surprises on him; black it stood
A sudden barrier ('twas a cloud passed o'er)
So dead and dense the tiniest brute no more
Must pass; yet presently (the cloud despatched)
Each clump, forsooth, was glistering detached
A shrub, oak-boles shrunk into ilex-stems!
Yet could not he denounce the stratagems
He saw thro', till, hours thence, aloft would hang
White summer-lightnings; as it sank and sprang
In measure, that whole palpitating breast
Of Heaven, 'twas Apollo nature prest
At eve to worship.

                 Time stole: by degrees
The Pythons perished off; his votaries
Sunk to respectful distance; songs redeem
Their pains, but briefer; their dismissals seem
Emphatic; only girls are very slow
To disappear: his Delians! Some that glow
O' the instant, more with earlier loves to wrench
Away, reserves to quell, disdains to quench;
Alike in one material circumstance—
All soon or late adore Apollo! Glance
The bevy through, divine Apollo's choice,
A Daphne! We secure Count Richard's voice
In Este's counsels, one for Este's ends
As our Taurello, say his faded friends,
By granting him our Palma! The sole child,
They mean, of Agnes Este who beguiled
Ecelin, years before this Adelaide
Wedded and turned him wicked; but the maid
Rejects his suit, those sleepy women boast.
She, scorning all beside, deserves the most
Sordello: so conspicuous in his world
Of dreams sate Palma. How the tresses curled
Into a sumptuous swell of gold and wound
About her like a glory, even the ground
Was bright as with shed sunbeams; (breathe not, breathe
Not)—poised, see, one leg doubled underneath,
Its small foot buried in the dimpling snow,
Rests, but the other, listlessly below,
O'er the couch-side swings feeling for cool air,
The vein-streaks swoln a richer violet where
The languid blood lies heavily; and calm
On her slight prop, each flat and outspread palm,
As but suspended in the act to rise
By consciousness of beauty, whence her eyes
Turn with so frank a triumph, for she meets
Apollo's gaze in the pine-glooms.
                           Time fleets
That's worst! Because the pre-appointed age
Approaches. Fate is tardy with the stage
She all but promised. Lean he grows and pale,
Though restlessly at rest. Hardly avail
Fancies to soothe him. Time steals, yet alone
He tarries here! The earnest smile is gone.

How long this might continue matters not:
For ever, possibly; since to the spot
None come: for lingering Taurello quits
Mantua at last, and light our lady flits
Back to her place disburthened of a care.
Strange—to be constant here if he is there!
Is it distrust? Oh, never! for they both
Goad Ecelin alike—Romano's growth
So daily manifest that Azzo's dumb
And Richard wavers . . . let but Friedrich come!
—Find matter for the minstrelsy's report
Lured from the Isle and its young Kaiser's court
To sing us a Messina morning up;
Who, double rillets of a drinking cup,
Sparkle along to ease the land of drouth,
Northward to Provence that, and thus far south
The other: what a method to apprise
Neighbours of births, espousals, obsequies!
Which in their very tongue the Troubadour
Records; and his performance makes a tour,
For Trouveres bear the miracle about,
Explain its cunning to the vulgar rout,
Until the Formidable House is famed
Over the country—as Taurello aimed
Who introduced, although the rest adopt,
The novelty. Their games her absence stopped
Begin afresh now Adelaide, recluse
No longer, in the light of day pursues
Her plans at Mantua—whence an accident
That breaking on Sordello's mixed content
Opened, like any flash that cures the blind,
The veritable business of mankind.

BOOK THE SECOND

THE woods were long austere with snow: at last
Pink leaflets budded on the beech, and fast
Larches, scattered through pine-tree solitudes,
Brightened, " as in the slumbrous heart o' the woods
Our buried year, a witch, grew young again
To placid incantations, and that stain

About were from her caldron, green smoke blent
With those black pines "—so Eglamor gave vent
To a chance fancy: whence a just rebuke
From his companion; brother Naddo shook
The solemnest of brows: Beware, he said,
Of setting up conceits in Nature's stead!
Forth wandered our Sordello. Nought so sure
As that to-day's adventure will secure
Palma, the forest-lady—only pass
O'er yon damp mound and its exhausted grass,
Under that brake where sundawn feeds the stalks
Of withered fern with gold, into those walks
Of pine and take her! Buoyantly he went.
Again his stooping forehead was besprent
With dew-drops from the skirting ferns. Then wide
Opened the great morass, shot every side
With flashing water through and through; a-shine,
Thick steaming, all alive. Whose shape divine
Quivered i' the farthest rainbow-vapour, glanced
Athwart the flying herons? He advanced,
But warily; though Mincio leaped no more,
Each foot-fall burst up in the marish-floor
A diamond jet: and if you stooped to pick
Rose-lichen, or molest the leeches quick,
And circling blood-worms, minnow, newt or loach,
A sudden pond would silently encroach
This way and that. On Palma passed. The verge
Of a new wood was gained. She will emerge
Flushed, now, and panting; crowds to see; will own
She loves him—Boniface to hear, to groan,
To leave his suit! One screen of pine-trees still
Opposes: but—the startling spectacle—
Mantua, this time! Under the walls—a crowd
Indeed—real men and women—gay and loud
Round a pavilion. How he stood!
                                    In truth
No prophecy had come to pass: his youth
In its prime now—and where was homage poured
Upon Sordello?—born to be adored,
And suddenly discovered weak, scarce made
To cope with any, cast into the shade
By this and this. Yet something seemed to prick
And tingle in his blood; a sleight—a trick—

And much would be explained. It went for naught—
The best of their endowments were ill bought
With his identity: nay, the conceit
This present roving leads to Palma's feet
Was not so vain . . . list! The word, Palma? Steal
Aside, and die, Sordello; this is real,
And this—abjure!

        What next? The curtains, see,
Dividing! She is there; and presently
He will be there—the proper You, at length—
In your own cherished dress of grace and strength:
Most like the very Boniface . . .

                  Not so.
It was a showy man advanced; but though
A glad cry welcomed him, then every sound
Sank and the crowd disposed themselves around,
—This is not he, Sordello felt; while " Place
For the best Troubadour of Boniface,"
Hollaed the Jongleurs, " Eglamor whose lay
Concludes his patron's Court of Love to-day."
Obsequious Naddo strung his master's lute
With the new lute-string, Elys, named to suit
The song. He stealthily at watch, the while,
Biting his lip to keep down a great smile
Of pride: then up he struck. Sordello's brain
Swam; for he knew a sometime deed again;
So could supply each foolish gap and chasm
The minstrel left in his enthusiasm,
Mistaking its true version—was the tale
Not of Apollo? Only, what avail
Luring her down, that Elys an he pleased,
If the man dares no further? Has he ceased?
And, lo, the people's frank applause half done,
Sordello was beside him, had begun
(Spite of indignant twitchings from his friend
The Trouvere) the true lay with the true end,
Taking the other's names and time and place
For his. On flew the song, a giddy race,
After the flying story; word made leap
Out word; rhyme—rhyme; the lay could barely keep
Pace with the action visibly rushing past:
Both ended. Back fell Naddo more aghast
Than your Egyptian from the harassed bull

That wheels abrupt and, bellowing, fronts full
His plague, who spies a scarab 'neath his tongue,
And finds 'twas Apis' flank his hasty prong
Insulted. But the people—but the cries,
And crowding round, and proffering the prize!
(For he had gained some prize)—He seemed to shrink
Into a sleepy cloud, just at whose brink
One sight withheld him; there sat Adelaide,
Silent; but at her knees the very maid
Of the North Chamber, her red lips as rich,
The same pure fleecy hair; one curl of which,
Golden and great, quite touched his cheek as o'er
She leant, speaking some six words and no more;
He answered something, anything; and she
Unbound a scarf and laid it heavily
Upon him, her neck's warmth and all; again
Moved the arrested magic; in his brain
Noises grew, and a light that turned to glare,
And greater glare, until the intense flare
Engulfed him, shut the whole scene from his sense,
And when he woke 'twas many a furlong thence,
At home: the sun shining his ruddy wont;
The customary birds'-chirp; but his front
Was crowned—was crowned! Her scented scarf around
His neck! Whose gorgeous vesture heaps the ground?
A prize? He turned, and peeringly on him
Brooded the women faces, kind and dim,
Ready to talk. The Jongleurs in a troup
Had brought him back, Naddo and Squarcialupe
And Tagliafer; how strange! a childhood spent
Assuming, well for him, so brave a bent!
Since Eglamor, they heard, was dead with spite,
And Palma chose him for her minstrel.

                                        Light
Sordello rose—to think, now; hitherto
He had perceived. Sure a discovery grew
Out of it all! Best live from first to last
The transport o'er again. A week he passed
Sucking the sweet out of each circumstance,
From the bard's outbreak to the luscious trance
Bounding his own achievement. Strange! A man
Recounted that adventure, and began
Imperfectly; his own task was to fill

The frame-work up, sing well what he sang ill,
Supply the necessary points, set loose
As many incidents of little use
—More imbecile the other, not to see
Their relative importance clear as he!
But for a special pleasure in the act
Of singing—had he ever turned, in fact,
From Elys, to sing Elys?—from each fit
Of rapture, to contrive a song of it?
True, this snatch or the other seemed to wind
Into a treasure, helped himself to find
A beauty in himself; for, see, he soared
By means of that mere snatch to many a hoard
Of fancies; as some falling cone bears oft
The eye, along the fir-tree-spire, aloft
To a dove's nest. Then how divine the cause
Such a performance should exact applause
From men if they have fancies too? Can Fate
Decree they find a beauty separate
In the poor snatch itself . . . our Elys, there,
(" Her head that's sharp and perfect like a pear,
So close and smooth are laid the few fine locks
Coloured like honey oozed from topmost rocks
Sun-blanched the livelong summer ")—if they heard
Just those two rhymes, assented at my word,
And loved them as I love them who have run
These fingers through those fine locks, let the sun
Into the white cool skin . . . nay, thus I clutch
Those locks!—I needs must be a God to such.
Or if some few, above themselves, and yet
Beneath me, like their Eglamor, have set
An impress on our gift? So men believe
And worship what they know not, nor receive
Delight from. Have they fancies—slow, perchance,
Not at their beck, which indistinctly glance
Until by song each floating part be linked
To each, and all grow palpable, distinct?
He pondered this.

            Meanwhile sounds low and drear
Stole on him, and a noise of footsteps, near
And nearer, and the underwood was pushed
Aside, the larches grazed, the dead leaves crushed
At the approach of men. The wind seemed laid;

Only, the trees shrunk slightly and a shade
Came o'er the sky although 'twas midday yet:
You saw each half-shut downcast violet
Flutter—a Roman bride, when they dispart
Her unbound tresses with the Sabine dart,
Holding that famous rape in memory still,
Felt creep into her curls the iron chill,
And looked thus, Eglamor would say—indeed
'Tis Eglamor, no other, these precede
Home hither in the woods. 'Twere surely sweet
Far from the scene of one's forlorn defeat
To sleep! thought Naddo, who in person led
Jongleurs and Trouveres, chanting at their head,
A scanty company; for, sooth to say,
Our beaten Troubadour had seen his day:
Old worshippers were something shamed, old friends
Nigh weary; still the death proposed amends:
Let us but get them safely through my song
And home again, quoth Naddo.
                                                  All along,
This man (they rest the bier upon the sand)
---This calm corpse with the loose flowers in its hand,
Eglamor, lived Sordello's opposite:
For him indeed was Naddo's notion right
And Verse a temple-worship vague and vast,
A ceremony that withdrew the last
Opposing bolt, looped back the lingering veil
Which hid the holy place—should one so frail
Stand there without such effort? or repine
That much was blank, uncertain at the shrine
He knelt before, till, soothed by many a rite,
The Power responded, and some sound or sight
Grew up, his own forever! to be fixed
In rhyme, the beautiful, forever; mixed
With his own life, unloosed when he should please
Having it safe at hand, ready to ease
All pain, remove all trouble; every time
He loosed that fancy from its bonds of rhyme,
Like Perseus when he loosed his naked love
Faltering; so distinct and far above
Himself, these fancies! He, no genius rare,
Transfiguring in fire or wave or air
At will, but a poor gnome that, cloistered up,

In some rock-chamber with his agate cup,
His topaz rod, his seed-pearl, in these few
And their arrangement finds enough to do
For his best art. Then, how he loved that art!
The calling marking him a man apart
From men—one not to care, take counsel for
Cold hearts, comfortless faces (Eglamor
Was neediest of his tribe) since verse, the gift,
Was his, and men, the whole of them, must shift
Without it, e'en content themselves with wealth
And pomp and power, snatching a life by stealth.
So Eglamor was not without his pride!
The sorriest bat which cowers through noontide
While other birds are jocund, has one time
When moon and stars are blinded, and the prime
Of earth is its to claim, nor find a peer;
And Eglamor was noblest poet here,
He knew, among the April woods he cast
Conceits upon in plenty as he past,
That Naddo might suppose him not to think
Entirely on the coming triumph; wink
At the one weakness! 'Twas a fervid child
That song of his—no brother of the guild
Had e'er conceived its like. The rest you know;
The exaltation and the overthrow;
Our poet lost his purpose, lost his rank,
His life—to that it came. Yet envy sank
Within him, as he heard Sordello out,
And, for the first time, shouted—tried to shout
Like others, not from any zeal to show
Pleasure that way: the common sort did so,
And what was Eglamor? who, bending down
The same, placed his beneath Sordello's crown,
Printed a kiss on his successor's hand,
Left one great tear on it, then joined his band
—In time; for some were watching at the door—
Who knows what envy may effect? Give o'er,
Nor charm his lips, nor craze him! (here one spied
And disengaged the withered crown)—Beside
His crown! How prompt and clear those verses rung
To answer yours! nay sing them. And he sung
Them calmly. Home he went; friends used to wait
His coming, anxious to congratulate,

But, to a man, so quickly runs report,
Could do no less than leave him, and escort
His rival. That eve, then, bred many a thought
What must his future life be: was he brought
So low, who was so lofty this spring morn?
At length he said, Best sleep now with my scorn,
And by to-morrow I devise some plain
Expedient! So he slept, nor woke again.
They found as much, those friends, when they returned
O'erflowing with the marvels they had learned
About Sordello's paradise, his roves
Among the hills and valleys, plains and groves,
Wherein, no doubt, this lay was roughly cast,
Polished by slow degrees, completed last
To Eglamor's discomfiture and death.

Such form the chanters now, and, out of breath,
They lay the beaten man in his abode,
Naddo reciting that same luckless ode,
Doleful to hear: Sordello could explore
By means of it, however, one step more
In joy; and, mastering the round at length,
Learnt how to live in weakness as in strength,
When from his covert forth he stood, addressed
Eglamor, bade the tender ferns invest,
Primeval pines o'ercanopy his couch,
And, most of all, his fame—(shall I avouch
Eglamor heard it, dead though he might look,
And laughed as from his brow Sordello took
The crown, and laid it on his breast, and said,
It was a crown, now, fit for poet's head?)
—Continue. Nor the prayer quite fruitless fell;
A plant they have yielding a three-leaved bell
Which whitens at the heart ere noon, and ails
Till evening; evening gives it to her gales
To clear away with such forgotten things
As are an eyesore to the morn: this brings
Him to their mind, and bears his very name.

So much for Eglamor. My own month came;
'Twas a sunrise of blossoming and May.
Beneath a flowering laurel thicket lay
Sordello; each new sprinkle of white stars
That smell fainter of wine than Massic jars
Dug up at Baiæ, when the south wind shed

The ripest, made him happier; filleted
And robed the same, only a lute beside
Lay on the turf. Before him far and wide
The country stretched: Goito slept behind
—The castle and its covert which confined
Him with his hopes and fears; so fain of old
To leave the story of his birth untold.
At intervals, 'spite the fantastic glow
Of his Apollo-life, a certain low
And wretched whisper winding through the bliss
Admonished, no such fortune could be his,
And was quite false and sure to fade one day:
The closelier drew he round him his array
Of brilliance to expel the truth. But when
A reason for his difference from men
Surprised him at the grave, he took no rest
While aught of that old life, superbly drest
Down to its meanest incident, remained
A mystery—alas, they soon explained
Away Apollo! and the tale amounts
To this: when at Vicenza both her Counts
Banished the Vivaresi kith and kin,
Those Maltraversi hung on Ecelin,
Reviling as he followed; he for spite
Must fire their quarter, though that self-same night
Among the flames young Ecelin was born
Of Adelaide, there too, and barely torn
From the roused populace hard on the rear
By a poor archer when his chieftain's fear
Was high; into the thick Elcorte leapt,
Saved her, and died; no creature left except
His child to thank. And when the full escape
Was known—how men impaled from chine to nape
Unlucky Prata, all to pieces spurned
Bishop Pistore's concubines, and burned
Taurello's entire household, flesh and fell,
Missing the sweeter prey—such courage well
Might claim reward. The orphan, ever since,
Sordello, had been nurtured by his prince
Within a blind retreat where Adelaide
(For, once this notable discovery made,
The past at every point was understood)
Can harbour easily when times are rude,

When Este schemes for Palma—would retrieve
That pledge, when Mantua is not fit to leave
Longer unguarded with a vigilant eye,
Taurello bides there so ambiguously
(He who can have no motive now to moil
For his own fortunes since their utter spoil)
As it were worth while yet (goes the report)
To disengage himself from us. In short,
Apollo vanished; a mean youth, just named
His lady's minstrel, was to be proclaimed
—How shall I phrase it? Monarch of the World.
But on the morning that array was furled
For ever, and in place of one a slave
To longings, wild, indeed, but longings save
In dreams as wild, suppressed—one daring not
Assume the mastery such dreams allot,
Until a magical equipment, strength,
Grace, wisdom, decked him too,—he chose at length
(Content with unproved wits and failing frame)
In virtue of his simple Will, to claim
That mastery, no less—to do his best
With means so limited, and let the rest
Go by,—the seal was set: never again
Sordello could in his own sight remain
One of the many, one with hopes and cares
And interests nowise distinct from theirs,
Only peculiar in a thriveless store
Of fancies, which were fancies and no more;
Never again for him and for the crowd
A common law was challenged and allowed
If calmly reasoned of, howe'er denied
By a mad impulse nothing justified
Short of Apollo's presence: the divorce
Is clear: why needs Sordello square his course
By any known example? Men no more
Compete with him than tree and flower before;
Himself, inactive, yet is greater far
Than such as act, each stooping to his star,
Acquiring thence his function; he has gained
The same result with meaner mortals trained
To strength or beauty, moulded to express
Each the idea that rules him; since no less
He comprehends that function but can still

Embrace the others, take of Might his fill
With Richard as of Grace with Palma, mix
Their qualities, or for a moment fix
On one, abiding free meantime, uncramped
By any partial organ, never stamped
Strong, so to Strength turning all energies—
Wise, and restricted to becoming Wise—
That is, he loves not, nor possesses One
Idea that, star-like over, lures him on
To its exclusive purpose. Fortunate
This flesh of mine ne'er strove to emulate
A soul so various—took no casual mould
Of the first fancy and contracted, cold,
Lay clogged forever thence, averse to change
As that. Whereas it left her free to range,
Remains itself a blank, cast into shade,
Encumbers little, if it cannot aid.
So, range, my soul! Who by self-consciousness
The last drop of all beauty dost express—
The grace of seeing grace, a quintessence
For thee: while for the world, that can dispense
Wonder on men, themselves that wonder—make
A shift to love at second hand and take
Those for its idols who but idolize,
Themselves,—that loves the soul as strong, as wise,
Whose love is Strength, is Wisdom,—such shall bow
Surely in unexampled worship now,
Discerning me!—
                    (Dear monarch, I beseech,
Notice how lamentably wide a breach
Is here! discovering this, discover too
What our poor world has possibly to do
With it! As pigmy natures as you please—
So much the better for you; take your ease;
Look on, and laugh; style yourself God alone;
Strangle some day with a cross olive-stone;
All that is right enough: but why want us
To know that you yourself know thus and thus?
Nay finish—)
                    —Bow to me conceiving all
Man's life, who sees its blisses, great and small,
Afar—not tasting any: no machine
To exercise my utmost will is mine,

Therefore mere consciousness for me! Perceive
What I could do, a mastery believe,
Asserted and established to the throng
By their selected evidence of Song
Which now shall prove whate'er they are, or seek
To be, I am—who take no pains to speak,
Change no old standards of perfection, vex
With no strange forms created to perplex,
But mean perform their bidding and no more,
At their own satiating-point give o'er,
And each shall love in me the love that leads
His soul to its perfection. Song, not Deeds,
(For we get tired) was chosen. Fate would brook
Mankind no other organ; He would look
For not another channel to dispense
His own volition and receive their sense
Of its existing, but would be content,
Obstructed else, with merely verse for vent—
Nor should, for instance, Strength an outlet seek
And striving be admired, nor Grace bespeak
Wonder, displayed in gracious attitudes,
Nor Wisdom, poured forth, change unseemly moods;
But he would give and take on Song's one point;
Like some huge throbbing-stone that, poised a-joint,
Sounds to affect on its basaltic bed
Must sue in just one accent: tempests shed
Thunder, and raves the landstorm: only let
That key by any little noise be set—
The far benighted hunter's halloo pitch
On that, the hungry curlew chance to scritch
Or serpent hiss it, rustling through the rift,
However loud, however low—all lift
The groaning monster, stricken to the heart.
Lo ye, the world's concernment, for its part,
And this, for his, will hardly interfere!
Its businesses in blood and blaze this year
—But wile the hour away—a pastime slight
Till he shall step upon the platform: right!
And now thus much is settled, cast in rough,
Proved feasible, be counselled! thought enough,
Slumber, Sordello! any day will serve:
Were it a less digested plan! how swerve
To-morrow? Meanwhile eat these sun-dried grapes

And watch the soaring hawk there! Life escapes
Merrily thus.
     He thoroughly read o'er
His truchman Naddo's missive six times more,
Praying him visit Mantua and supply
A famished world.
       The evening star was high
When he reached Mantua, but his fame arrived
Before him: friends applauded, foes connived,
And Naddo looked an angel, and the rest
Angels, and all these angels would be blest
Supremely by a song—the thrice renowned
Goito manufacture. Then he found
(Casting about to satisfy the crowd)
That happy vehicle, so late allowed,
A sore annoyance; 'twas the song's effect
He cared for, scarce the song itself: reflect!
In the past life what might be singing's use?
Just to delight his Delians, whose profuse
Praise, not the toilsome process which procured
That praise, enticed Apollo: dreams abjured,
No over-leaping means for ends—take both
For granted or take neither! I am loth
To say the rhymes at last were Eglamor's;
But Naddo, chuckling, bade competitors
Go pine; the Master certes meant to waste
No effort, cautiously had probed the taste
He'd please anon: true bard, in short, disturb
His title if they could; nor spur nor curb,
Fancy nor reason, wanting in him; whence
The staple of his verses, common sense:
He built on Man's broad nature—gift of gifts
That power to build! The world contented shifts
With counterfeits enough, a dreary sort
Of warriors, statesmen, ere it can extort
Its poet-soul—that's, after all, a freak
(The having eyes to see and tongue to speak)
With our herd's stupid sterling happiness
So plainly incompatible that—yes—
Yes—should a son of his improve the breed
And turn out poet he were cursed indeed.
Well, there's Goito to retire upon
If the worst happen; best go stoutly on

Now! thought Sordello.
                     Ay, and goes on yet!
You pother with your glossaries to get
A notion of the Troubadour's intent—
His Rondels, Tenzons, Virlai or Sirvent—
Much as you study arras how to twirl
His Angelot, plaything of page and girl,
Once; but you surely reach, at last,—or, no!
Never quite reach what struck the people so,
As from the welter of their time he drew
Its elements successively to view,
Followed all actions backward on their course
And catching up, unmingled at the source,
Such a Strength, such a Weakness, added then
A touch or two, and turned them into Men.
Virtue took form, nor Vice refused a shape;
Here Heaven opened, there was Hell agape,
As Saint this simpered past in sanctity,
Sinner the other flared portentous by
A greedy People: then why stop, surprised
At his success? The scheme was realised
Too suddenly in one respect: a crowd
Praising, eyes quick to see, and lips as loud
To speak, delicious homage to receive,
Bianca's breath to feel upon his sleeve
Who said, " But Anafest—why asks he less
Than Lucio, in your verses? how confess
It seemed too much but yestereve!" The youth
Who bade him earnestly " avow the truth,
You love Bianca, surely, from your song;
I knew I was unworthy!" soft or strong,
In poured such tributes ere he had arranged
Ethereal ways to take them, sorted, changed,
Digested: courted thus at unawares,
In spite of his pretensions and his cares
He caught himself shamefully hankering
After your obvious petty joys that spring
From real life, fain relinquish pedestal
And condescend with pleasures—one and all
To be renounced, no doubt; for thus to chain
Himself to single joys and so refrain
From tasting their quintessence, frustrates, sure,
His prime design; each joy must he abjure

Even for love of it.

              He laughed: what sage
But perishes if from his magic page
He look because, at the first line, a proof
'Twas heard salutes him from the cavern roof?
On! Give thyself, excluding aught beside,
To the day's task; compel thy slave provide
Its utmost at the soonest; turn the leaf
Thoroughly conned; these lays of thine, in brief—
Cannot men bear, now, somewhat better?—fly
A pitch beyond this unreal pageantry
Of essences? the period sure has ceased
For such: present us with ourselves, at least,
Not portions of ourselves, mere loves and hates
Made flesh: wait not!

              Awhile the poet waits
However. The first trial was enough:
He left imagining, to try the stuff
That held the imaged thing and, let it writhe
Never so fiercely, scarce allowed a tithe
To reach the light—his Language. How he sought
The cause, conceived a cure, and slow re-wrought
That Language, welding words into the crude
Mass from the new speech round him, till a rude
Armour was hammered out, in time to be
Approved beyond the Roman panoply
Melted to make it, boots not. This obtained
With some ado, no obstacle remained
To using it; accordingly he took
An action with its actors, quite forsook
Himself to live in each, returned anon
With the result—a creature, and by one
And one proceeded leisurely equip
Its limbs in harness of his workmanship.
Accomplished! Listen, Mantuans! Fond essay!
Piece after piece that armour broke away
Because perceptions whole, like that he sought
To clothe, reject so pure a work of thought
As language: Thought may take Perception's place
But hardly co-exist in any case,
Being its mere presentment—of the Whole
By Parts, the Simultaneous and the Sole
By the Successive and the Many. Lacks

The crowd perceptions? painfully it tacks
Together thoughts Sordello, needing such,
Has rent perception into: it's to clutch
And reconstruct—his office to diffuse,
Destroy: as difficult obtain a Muse
In short, as be Apollo. For the rest,
E'en if some wondrous vehicle exprest
The whole dream, what impertinence in me
So to express it, who myself can be
The dream! nor, on the other hand, are those
I sing to over-likely to suppose
A higher than the highest I present
Now, and they praise already: be content
Both parties, rather: they with the old verse,
And I with the old praise—far go, fare worse!
A few adhering rivets loosed, upsprings
The angel, sparkles off his mail, and rings
Whirled from each delicatest limb it warps,
As might Apollo from the sudden corpse
Of Hyacinth have cast his luckless quoits.
He set to celebrating the exploits
Of Montfort o'er the Mountaineers.

                        Then came
The world's revenge: their pleasure now his aim
Merely—what was it? Not to play the fool
So much as learn our lesson in your school,
Replied the world; he found that every time
He gained applause by any given rhyme
His auditory recognised no jot
As he intended, and mistaking not
Him for his meanest hero, ne'er was dunce
Sufficient to believe him—All at once.
His Will . . . conceive it caring for his Will!
—Mantuans, the main of them, admiring still
How a mere singer, ugly, stunted, weak,
Had Montfort at completely (so to speak)
His fingers' ends; while past the praise-tide swept
To Montfort, either's share distinctly kept,
The true meed for true merit—His abates
Into a sort he most repudiates,
And on them angrily he turns. Who were
The Mantuans, after all, that he should care
About their recognition, ay or no?

In spite of the convention months ago,
(Why blink the truth) was not he forced to help
This same ungrateful audience, every whelp
Of Naddo's litter, make them pass for peers
With the bright band of those Goito years,
As erst he toiled for flower or tree? Why there
Sate Palma! Adelaide's funereal hair
Ennobled the next corner. Ay, he strewed
A fairy dust upon that multitude
Although he feigned to take them by themselves;
His giants dignified those puny elves,
Sublimed their faint applause. In short he found
Himself still footing a delusive round,
Remote as ever from the self-display
He meant to compass, hampered every way
By what he hoped assistance. Wherefore then
Continue, make believe to find in men
A use he found not?

                           Weeks, months, years went by;
And, lo, Sordello vanished utterly,
Sundered in twain; each spectral part at strife
With each; one jarred against another life;
The Poet thwarting hopelessly the Man
Who, fooled no longer, free in fancy ran
Here, there; let slip no opportunities
Forsooth, as pitiful beside the prize
To drop on him some no-time and acquit
His constant faith (the Poet-half's to wit)
That waiving any compromise between
No joy and all joy kept the hunger keen
Beyond most methods—of incurring scoff
From the Man-portion not to be put off
With self-reflectings by the Poet's scheme
Though ne'er so bright; which sauntered forth in dream,
Dress'd any how, nor waited mystic frames,
Immeasurable gifts, astounding claims,
But just his sorry self; who yet might be
Sorrier for aught he in reality
Achieved, so pinioned that the Poet-part,
Fondling, in turn of fancy, Verse; the Art
Developing his soul a thousand ways;
Potent, by its assistance, to amaze
The multitude with majesties, convince

Each sort of nature that same nature's prince
Accosted it: language, the makeshift, grew
Into a bravest of expedients, too;
Apollo, seemed it now, perverse had thrown
Quiver and bow away, the lyre alone
Sufficed: while, out of dream, his day's work went
To tune a crazy tenzon or sirvent—
So hampered him the Man-part, thrust to judge
Between the bard and the bard's audience, grudge
A minute's toil that missed its due reward!
But the complete Sordello, Man and Bard,
John's cloud-girt angel, this foot on the land,
That on the sea, with open in his hand
A bitter-sweetling of a book—was gone.

   And if internal struggles to be one,
That frittered him incessantly piece-meal,
Referred, ne'er so obliquely, to the real
Mantuans! intruding ever with some call
To action while he pondered, once for all,
Which looked the easier effort—to pursue
This course, still leap o'er paltry joys, yearn through
The present ill-appreciated stage
Of self-revealment and compel the age
Know him: or else, forswearing bard-craft, wake
From out his lethargy and nobly shake
Off timid habits of denial, mix
With men, enjoy like men: ere he could fix
On aught, in rushed the Mantuans; much they cared
For his perplexity! Thus unprepared,
The obvious if not only shelter lay
In deeds the dull conventions of his day
Prescribed the like of him: why not be glad
'Tis settled Palma's minstrel, good or bad,
Submits to this and that established rule?
Let Vidal change or any other fool
His murrey-coloured robe for philamot
And crop his hair; so skin-deep, is it not,
Such vigour? Then, a sorrow to the heart,
His talk! Whatever topics they might start
Had to be groped for in his consciousness
Strait, and as strait delivered them by guess:
Only obliged to ask himself, " What was,"
A speedy answer followed, but, alas,

One of God's large ones, tardy to condense
Itself into a period: answers whence
A tangle of conclusions must be stripp'd
At any risk ere, trim to pattern clipp'd,
They matched rare specimens the Mantua flock
Regaled him with, each talker from his stock
Of sorted o'er opinions, every stage,
Juicy in youth, or desiccate with age,
Fruits like the fig-tree's, rathe-ripe, rotten-rich,
Sweet-sour, all tastes to take: a practice which
He too had not impossibly attained,
Once either of those fancy-flights restrained;
For, at conjecture how the words appear
To others, playing there what passes here,
And occupied abroad by what he spurned
At home, 'twas slipt the occasion he returned
To seize: he'd strike that lyre adroitly—speech,
Would but a twenty cubic plectre reach;
A clever hand, consummate instrument,
Were both brought close! each excellency went
For nothing else. The question Naddo asked
Had just a life-time moderately tasked
To answer, Naddo's fashion; more disgust
And more; why move his soul, since move it must
At minute's notice or as good it failed
To move at all? The end was, he retailed
Some ready-made opinion, put to use
This quip, that maxim, ventured reproduce
Gestures and tones, at any folly caught
Serving to finish with, nor too much sought
If false or true 'twas spoken; praise and blame
Of what he said grew pretty well the same
—Meantime awards to meantime acts: his soul,
Unequal to the compassing a Whole,
Saw in a tenth part less and less to strive
About. And as for Men in turn . . . contrive
Who could to take eternal interest
In them, so hate the worst, so love the best!
Though in pursuance of his passive plan
He hailed, decried the proper way.

                                   As man
So figured he; and how as Poet? Verse
Came only not to a stand-still. The worse,

That this poor piece of daily work to do
Was not sink Under any rivals; who
Loudly and long enough, without these qualms,
Tuned, from Bocafoli's stark-naked psalms,
To Plara's sonnets spoilt by toying with,
As knops that stud some almug to the pith
Prickèd for gum, wry thence, and crinklèd worse
Than pursed-up eyelids of a river-horse
Sunning himself o' the slime when whirrs the breeze.
Ha, ha! Of course he might compete with these
But—but—

        Observe a pompion-twine afloat;
Pluck me one cup from off the castle-moat—
Along with cup you raise leaf, stalk and root,
The entire surface of the pool to boot.
So could I pluck a cup, put in one song
A single sight, did not my hand, too strong,
Twitch in the least the root-strings of the whole.
How should externals satisfy my soul?
Why that's precise the error Squarcialupe
(Hazarded Naddo) finds; the man can't stoop
To sing us out, quoth he, a mere romance;
He'd fain do better than the best, enhance
The subjects' rarity, work problems out
Therewith: now you're a bard, a bard past doubt,
And no philosopher; why introduce
Crotchets like these? fine, surely, but no use
In poetry—which still must be, to strike,
Based upon common sense; there's nothing like
Appealing to our nature! what beside
Was your first poetry? No tricks were tried
In that, no hollow thrills, affected throes!
The man, said we, tells his own joys and woes—
We'll trust him. Would you have your songs endure?
Build on the human heart!—Why to be sure
Yours is one sort of heart—but I mean theirs,
Ours, every one's, the healthy heart one cares
To build on! Central peace, mother of strength,
That's father of . . . nay, go yourself that length,
Ask those calm-hearted doers what they do
When they have got their calm! Nay, is it true
Fire rankles at the heart of every globe?
Perhaps! But these are matters one may probe

Too deeply for poetic purposes:
Rather select a theory that . . . yes
Laugh! what does that prove? . . . stations you midway
And saves some little o'er-refining. Nay,
That's rank injustice done me! I restrict
The poet? Don't I hold the poet picked
Out of a host of warriors, statesmen—did
I tell you? Very like! as well you hid
That sense of power you have! True bards believe
Us able to achieve what they achieve—
That is, just nothing—in one point abide
Profounder simpletons than all beside:
Oh ay! The knowledge that you are a bard
Must constitute your prime, nay sole, reward!
So prattled Naddo, busiest of the tribe
Of genius-haunters—how shall I describe
What grubs or nips, or rubs, or rips—your louse
For love, your flea for hate, magnanimous,
Malignant, Pappacoda, Tagliafer,
Picking a sustenance from wear and tear
By implements it sedulous employs
To undertake, lay down, mete out, o'er-toise
Sordello? fifty creepers to elude
At once! They settled stanchly; shame ensued:
Behold the monarch of mankind succumb
To the last fool who turned him round his thumb,
As Naddo styled it! 'Twas not worth oppose
The matter of a moment, gainsay those
He aimed at getting rid of; better think
Their thoughts and speak their speech, secure to slink
Back expeditiously to his safe place,
And chew the cud—what he and what his race
Were really, each of them. Yet even this
Conformity was partial. He would miss
Some point, brought into contact with them ere
Assured in what small segment of the sphere
Of his existence they attended him;
Whence blunders, falsehoods rectify—a grim
List—slur it over! How? If dreams were tried,
His will swayed sicklily from side to side
Not merely neutralized his waking act
But tended e'en in fancy to distract
The intermediate will, the choice of means:

He lost the art of dreaming: Mantua scenes
Supplied a baron, say, he sung before,
Handsomely reckless, full to running o'er
Of gallantries; abjure the soul, content
With body, therefore! Scarcely had he bent
Himself in dream thus low when matter fast
Cried out, he found, for spirit to contrast
And task it duly; by advances slight,
The simple stuff becoming composite,
Count Lori grew Apollo—best recall
His fancy! Then would some rough peasant-Paul
Like those old Ecelin confers with, glance
His gay apparel o'er; that countenance
Gathered his shattered fancy into one,
And, body clean abolished, soul alone
Sufficed the grey Paulician: by and by
To balance the ethereality
Passions were needed; foiled he sank again.
    Meanwhile the world rejoiced ('tis time explain)
Because a sudden sickness set it free
From Adelaide. Missing the motherbee
Her mountain hive Romano swarmed; at once
A rustle-forth of daughters and of sons
Blackened the valley. I am sick too, old,
Half crazed I think; what good's the Kaiser's gold
To such an one? God help me! for I catch
My children's greedy sparkling eyes at watch—
He bears that double breastplate on, they say,
So many minutes less than yesterday!
Besides Monk Hilary is on his knees
Now, sworn to kneel and pray till God shall please
Exact a punishment for many things
You know and some you never knew; which brings
To memory, Azzo's sister Beatrix
And Richard's Giglia are my Alberic's
And Ecelin's betrothed; the Count himself
Must get my Palma: Ghibellin and Guelf
Mean to embrace each other. So began
Romano's missive to his fighting-man
Taurello on the Tuscan's death, away
With Friedrich sworn to sail from Naples' bay
Next month for Syria. Never thunder-clap
Out of Vesuvius' mount like this mishap

Startled him. That accursed Vicenza! I
Absent, and she selects this time to die!
Ho, fellows, for Vicenza! Half a score
Of horses ridden dead he stood before
Romano in his reeking spurs: too late—
Boniface urged me, Este could not wait,
The chieftain stammered; let me die in peace—
Forget me! Was it I e'er craved increase
Of rule? Do you and Friedrich plot your worst
Against the Father: as you found me first
So leave me now. Forgive me! Palma, sure,
Is at Goito still. Retain that lure—
Only be pacified!

              The country rung
With such a piece of news: on every tongue
How Ecelin's great servant, congeed off,
Had done a long day's service, so might doff
The green and yellow to recover breath
At Mantua, whither, since Retrude's death,
(The girlish slip of a Sicilian bride
From Otho's House he carried to reside
At Mantua till the Ferrarese should pile
A structure worthy her imperial style,
The gardens raise, their tenantry enshrine
She never lived to see) although his line
Was ancient in her archives and she took
A pride in him, that city, nor forsook
Her child though he forsook himself and spent
A prowess on Romano surely meant
For his own purposes—he ne'er resorts
If wholly satisfied (to trust reports)
With Ecelin. So forward in a trice
Were shows to greet him. Take a friend's advice,
Quoth Naddo to Sordello, nor be rash
Because your rivals (nothing can abash
Some folks) demur that we pronounced you best
To sound the great man's welcome; 'tis a test
Remember; Strojavacca looks asquint,
The rough fat sloven; and there's plenty hint
Your pinions have received of late a shock—
Out-soar them, cobswan of the silver flock!
Sing well! A signal wonder song's no whit
Facilitated.

Fast the minutes flit;
Another day, Sordello finds, will bring
The soldier, and he cannot choose but sing;
So quits, a last shift, Mantua—slow, alone:
Out of that aching brain, a very stone,
Song must be struck. What occupies that front?
Just how he was more awkward than his wont
The night before, when Naddo, who had seen
Taurello on his progress, praised the mien
For dignity no crosses could affect—
Such was a joy, and might not he detect
A satisfaction if established joys
Were proved imposture? Poetry annoys
Its utmost: wherefore fret? Verses may come
Or keep away! And thus he wandered, dumb
Till evening, when he paused, thoroughly spent,
On a blind hill-top; down the gorge he went,
Yielding himself up as to an embrace;
The moon came out; like features of a face
A querulous fraternity of pines,
Sad blackthorn clumps, leafless and grovelling vines
Also came out, made gradually up
The picture; 'twas Goito's mountain-cup
And castle. He had dropped through one defile
He never dared explore, the Chief erewhile
Had vanished by. Back rushed the dream, enwrapt
Him wholly. 'Twas Apollo now they lapped
Those mountains, not a pettish minstrel meant
To wear his soul away in discontent
Brooding on fortune's malice; heart and brain
Swelled; he expanded to himself again
As that thin seedling spice-tree starved and frail
Pushing between cat's head or ibis' tail
Crusted into the porphyry pavement smooth
—Suffered remain just as it sprung to soothe
The Soldan's pining daughter, never yet
Well in the chilly green-glazed minaret—
When rooted up the sunny day she died
And flung into the common court beside
Its parent tree. Come home, Sordello! Soon
Was he low muttering beneath the moon
Of sorrow saved, of quiet evermore,
How from his purposes maintained before

Only resulted wailing and hot tears.
Ah, the slim castle! dwindled of late years,
But more mysterious; gone to ruin—trails
Of vine thro' every loop-hole. Nought avails
The night as, torch in hand, he must explore
The maple chamber—did I say its floor
Was made of intersecting cedar beams?
Worn now with gaps so large there blew cold streams
Of air quite from the dungeon; lay your ear
Close and 'tis like, one after one, you hear
In the blind darkness water-drops. The nests
And nooks retain their long ranged vesture-chests
Empty and smelling of the iris-root
The Tuscan grated o'er them to recruit
Her wasted wits. Palma was gone that day,
Said the remaining women. Last, he lay
Beside the Carian group reserved and still.
    The Body, the Machine for Acting Will
Had been at the commencement proved unfit;
That for Reflecting, Demonstrating it,
Mankind—no fitter: was the Will Itself
In fault?
                His forehead pressed the moonlit shelf
Beside the youngest marble maid awhile;
Then, raising it, he thought, with a long smile,
I shall be king again! as he withdrew
The envied scarf; into the font he threw
His crown.
                Next day, no poet! Wherefore? asked
Taurello, when the dance of Jongleurs masked
As devils ended; don't a song come next?
The master of the pageant looked perplext
Till Naddo's whisper came to his relief:
His Highness knew what poets were: in brief,
Had not the tetchy race prescriptive right
To peevishness, caprice? or, call it spite,
One must receive their nature in its length
And breadth, expect the weakness with the strength!
So phrasing, till, his stock of phrases spent,
The easy-natured soldier smiled assent,
Settled his portly person, smoothed his chin,
And nodded that the bull-chase might begin.

BOOK THE THIRD

AND the font took them: let our laurels lie!
Braid moonfern now with mystic trifoly
Because once more Goito gets, once more,
Sordello to itself! A dream is o'er
And the suspended life begins anew;
Quiet those throbbing temples, then, subdue
That cheek's distortion! Nature's strict embrace,
Putting aside the past, shall soon efface
Its print as well—factitious humours grown
Over the true—loves, hatreds not his own—
And turn him pure as some forgotten vest
Woven of painted byssus, silkiest
Tufting the Tyrrhene whelk's pearl-sheeted lip,
Left welter where a trireme let it slip
I' the sea and vexed a Satrap; so the stain
O' the world forsakes Sordello with its pain,
Its pleasure: how the tinct loosening escapes
Cloud after cloud! Mantua's familiar shapes
Die, fair and foul die, fading as they flit,
Men, women, and the pathos and the wit,
Wise speech and foolish, deeds to smile or sigh
For, good, bad, seemly or ignoble, die:
The last face glances through the eglantines,
The last voice murmurs 'twixt the blossomed vines
This May of the Machine supplied by Thought
To compass Self-perception idly sought
By forcing half himself—an insane pulse
Of a God's blood on clay it could convulse
Never transmute—on human sights and sounds
To watch the other half with; irksome bounds
It ebbs from to its source, a fountain sealed
Forever. Better sure be unrevealed
Than part-revealed: Sordello well or ill
Is finished with: what further use of Will?
—Point in the prime idea not realised,
An oversight, inordinately prized
No less, and pampered with enough of each
Delight to prove the whole above its reach.
To need become all natures yet retain
The law of one's own nature—to remain

Oneself, yet yearn . . . aha, that chesnut, think,
To yearn for this first larch-bloom crisp and pink,
With those pale fragrant tears where zephyrs staunch
March wounds along the fretted pine-tree branch!
Will and the means to show it, great and small
Material, spiritual, abjure them all
Save any so distinct as to be left
Amuse, not tempt become: and, thus bereft,
Say just as I am fashioned would I be!
Nor, Moon, is it Apollo now but me
Thou visitest to comfort and befriend;
Swim thou into my heart and there an end
Since I possess thee! nay thus shut mine eyes
And know, quite know, by that heart's fall and rise
If thou dost bury thee in clouds and when
Out-standest: wherefore practise upon Men
To make that plainer to myself?

Slide here

Over a sweet and solitary year
Wasted: or simply notice change in him—
How eyes, bright with exploring once, grew dim
And satiate with receiving.   Some distress
Occasioned, too, a sort of consciousness
Under the imbecility; nought kept
That down: he slept, but was aware he slept
And frustrate so: as who brainsick made pact
Erst with the overhanging cataract
To deafen him, yet may distinguish now
His own blood's measured clicking at his brow.
  To finish.   One declining Autumn day—
Few birds about the heaven chill and grey,
No wind that cared trouble the tacit woods—
He sauntered home complacently, their moods
According, his and Nature's.   Every spark
Of Mantua life was trodden out; so dark
The embers that the Troubadour who sung
Hundreds of songs forgot, its trick the tongue,
Its craft the brain, how either brought to pass
Singing so e'er; that faculty might class
With any of Apollo's now.   The year
Began to find its early promise sere
As well.   Thus beauty vanishes!   Your stone
Outlasts your flesh.   Nature's and his youth gone,

They left the world to you and wished you joy.
When stopping his benevolent employ
A presage shuddered through the welkin; harsh
The earth's remonstrance followed. 'Twas the marsh
Gone of a sudden. Mincio in its place
Laughed a broad water in next morning's face
And, where the mists broke up immense and white
I' the steady wind, burnt like a spilth of light
Out of the crashing of a myriad stars.
And here was Nature, bound by the same bars
Of fate with him!
           No: youth once gone is gone:
Deeds let escape are never to be done:
Leaf-fall and grass-spring for the year, but us—
Oh forfeit I unalterably thus
My chance? nor two lives wait me, this to spend
Learning save that? Nature has leisure mend
Mistake, occasion, knows she, will recur—
Landslip or seabreach how affects it her
With her magnificent resources? I
Must perish once and perish utterly!
Not any strollings now at even-close
Down the field-path, Sordello, by thorn-rows
Alive with lamp-flies, swimming spots of fire
And dew, outlining the black cypress's spire
She waits you at, Elys, who heard you first
Woo her the snow-month—ah, but ere she durst
Answer 'twas April! Linden-flower-time-long
Her eyes were on the ground; 'tis July, strong
Now; and because white dust-clouds overwhelm
The woodside, here or by the village elm
That holds the moon she meets you, somewhat pale,
But letting you lift up her coarse flax veil
And whisper (the damp little hand in yours)
Of love—heart's love—your heart's love that endures
Till death. Tush! No mad mixing with the rout
Of haggard ribalds wandering about
The hot torchlit wine-scented island-house
Where Friedrich holds his wickedest carouse
Parading to the gay Palermitans,
Soft Messinese, dusk Saracenic clans
From Nuocera, those tall grave dazzling Norse,
Clear-cheeked, lank-haired, toothed whiter than the morse,

Queens of the caves of jet stalactites
He sent his barks to fetch through icy seas,
The blind night seas without a saving-star,
And here in snowy birdskin robes they are,
Sordello, here, mollitious alcoves gilt
Superb as Byzant-domes that devils built
—Ah, Byzant, there again! no chance to go
Ever like august pleasant Dandolo,
Worshipping hearts about him for a wall,
Conducted, blind eyes, hundred years and all,
Through vanquished Byzant to have noted him
What pillar, marble massive, sardius slim,
'Twere fittest we transport to Venice' Square—
Flattered and promised life to touch them there
Soon, by his fervid sons of senators!
No more lives, deaths, loves, hatreds, peaces, wars—
Ah, fragments of a Whole ordained to be!
Points in the life I waited! what are ye
But roundels of a ladder which appeared
Awhile the very platform it was reared
To lift me on—that Happiness I find
Proofs of my faith in, even in the blind
Instinct which bade forego you all unless
Ye led me past yourselves? Ay, Happiness
Awaited me; the way life should be used
Was to acquire, and deeds like you conduced
To teach it by a self-revealment (deemed
That very use too long). Whatever seemed
Progress to that was Pleasure; aught that stayed
My reaching it—No Pleasure. I have laid
The roundels down; I climb not; still aloft
The platform stretches! Blisses strong and soft
I dared not entertain elude me; yet
Never of what they promised could I get
A glimpse till now! The common sort, the crowd,
Exist, perceive; with Being are endowed,
However slight, distinct from what they See,
However bounded: Happiness must be
To feed the first by gleanings from the last,
Attain its qualities, and slow or fast
Become what one beholds; such peace-in-strife
By transmutation is the Use of Life,
The Alien turning Native to the soul

Or body—which instructs me; I am whole
There and demand a Palma; had the world
Been from my soul to a like distance hurled
'Twere Happiness to make it one with me—
Whereas I must, ere I begin to Be,
Include a world, in flesh, I comprehend
In spirit now; and this done, what's to blend
With? Nought is Alien here—my Will
Owns it already; yet can turn it still
Less Native, since my Means to correspond
With Will are so unworthy 'twas my bond
To tread the very ones that tantalise
Me now into a grave, never to rise—
I die then! Will the rest agree to die?
Next Age or no? Shall its Sordello try
Clue after clue and catch at last the clue
I miss, that's underneath my finger too,
Twice, thrice a day, perhaps,—some yearning traced
Deeper, some petty consequence embraced
Closer! Why fled I Mantua then? Complained
So much my Will was fettered, yet remained
Content within a tether half the range
I could assign it?—able to exchange
My ignorance, I felt, for knowledge, and
Idle because I could thus understand—
Could e'en have penetrated to its core
Our mortal mystery, and yet forbore,
Preferred elaborating in the dark
My casual stuff, by any wretched spark
Born of my predecessors, tho' one stroke
Of mine had brought the flame forth! Mantua's yoke,
My minstrel's-trade, was to behold mankind,
And my own matter—just to bring my mind
Behold, just extricate, for my acquist,
Each object suffered stifle in the mist
Convention, hazard, blindness could impose
In their relation to myself.
                                        He rose.
The level wind carried above the firs
Clouds, the irrevocable travellers,
Onward.
              Pushed thus into a drowsy copse,
Arms twine about my neck, each eyelid drops

Under a humid finger; while there fleets
Outside the screen a pageant time repeats
Never again! To be deposed—immured
Clandestinely—still petted, still assured
To govern were fatiguing work—the Sight
Fleeting meanwhile! 'Tis noontide—wreak ere night
Somehow one's will upon it rather! Slake
This thirst somehow, the poorest impress take
That serves! A blasted bud displays you, torn,
Faint rudiments of the full flower unborn;
But who divines what petal coats o'erclasp
Of the bulb dormant in the Mummy's grasp
Taurello sent . . .

     Taurello? Palma sent
Your Trouvere, (Naddo interposing leant
Over the lost bard's shoulder) and believe
You cannot more reluctantly conceive
Than I pronounce her message: we depart
Together: what avail a poet's heart
Verona and her gauds? five blades of grass
Suffice him. News? Why, where your marish was,
On its mud-banks smoke rises after smoke
I' the valley like a spout of hell new broke.
Oh, the world's tidings! little thanks, I guess,
For them. The father of our Patroness
Playing Taurello an astounding trick
Parts between Ecelin and Alberic
His wealth and goes into a convent: both
Wed Guelfs: the Count and Palma plighted troth
A week since at Verona: and she wants
You doubtless to contrive the marriage-chants
Ere Richard storms Ferrara. Your response
To Palma? Wherefore jest? Depart at once?
A good resolve! In truth I hardly hoped
So prompt an acquiescence. Have you groped
Out wisdom in the wilds here?—Thoughts may be
Over-poetical for poetry?
Pearl-white you minstrels liken Palma's neck,
And yet what spoils an orient like some speck
Of genuine white turning its own white grey?
You take me? Curse the cicales!

      One more day—
One eve—appears Verona! Many a group,

(You mind) instructed of the osprey's swoop
On lynx and ounce, was gathering—Christendom
Sure to receive, whate'er it might be, from
The evening's purpose cheer or detriment
Since Friedrich only waited some event
Like this of Ghibellins establishing
Themselves within Ferrara, ere, as King
Of Lombardy, he'd glad descend there, wage
Old warfare with the Pontiff, disengage
His barons from the burghers, and restore
The rule of Charlemagne broken of yore
By Hildebrand. That eve-long each by each
Sordello sate and Palma: little speech
At first in that dim closet, face with face
Despite the tumult in the market-place
Exchanging quick low laughters: now would gush
Word upon word to meet a sudden flush,
A look left off, a shifting lips' surmise—
But for the most part their two histories
Ran best thro' the locked fingers and linked arms.
And so the night flew on with its alarms
Till in burst one of Palma's retinue;
Now Lady, gasped he. Then arose the two
And leaned into Verona's air dead still.
A balcony lay black beneath until
Out 'mid a gush of torchfire, grey-haired men
Came on it and harangued the people: then
Sea-like that people surging to and fro
Shouted, Hale forth the Carroch—trumpets, ho,
A flourish! run it in the ancient grooves—
Back from the bell! Hammer! that whom behooves
May hear the League is up! Peal! learn who list
Verona means not be the first break tryst
To-morrow with the League.
                Enough. Now turn--
Over the Eastern cypresses: discern
You any beacon set a-glimmer?
                     Rang
The air with shouts that overpowered the clang
Of the incessant carroch even. Haste—
The Candle's at the gate-way! ere it waste
Each soldier stands beside, armed fit to march
With Tiso Sampier thro' that Eastern arch!

Ferrara's succoured, Palma!

                Once again
They sate together; some strange thing in train
To say, so difficult was Palma's place
In taking, with a coy fastidious grace
Like the bird's flutter ere it fix and feed;
But when she felt she held her friend indeed
Safe, she threw back her curls, began implant
Her lessons; telling of another want
Goito's quiet nourished than his own;
Palma—to serve, as him—be served, alone
Importing; Agnes' milk so neutralised
The blood of Ecelin. Nor be surprised
If, while Sordello nature captive led,
In dream was Palma wholly subjected
To some out-soul which dawned not though she pined
Delaying still (pursued she) heart and mind
To live: how dared I let expand the force
Within me till some out-soul whose resource
It grew for should direct it? Every law
Of life, its fitnesses and every flaw,
Must that determine whose corporeal shape
Would be no other than the prime escape
And revelation to me of a Will
Orb-like o'ershrouded and inscrutable
Above except the point I was to know,
Shone that myself, my powers, might overflow
So far, so much; as now it signified
Which earthly shape it henceforth chose to guide
Me by, whose lip selected to declare
Its oracles, what fleshly garb would wear:
—The first of intimations, whom to love;
The next, how love him. And that orb, above
The castle-covert and the mountain-close
Slow in appearing, if beneath arose
Cravings, aversions, and our green precinct
Took pride in me at unawares distinct
With this or that endowment, how represt,
At once such jetting power shrunk to the rest!
Was I to have a chance touch spoil me, leave
My spirit thence unfitted to receive
The consummating spell?—that spell so near
Moreover: waits he not the waking year?

His almond-blossoms must be honey-ripe
By this; to welcome him fresh runnels stripe
The thawed ravines; because of him the wind
Walks like a herald. I shall surely find
Him now!
      And chief that earnest April morn
Of Richard's Love-court was it time, so worn
And white her cheek, so idly her blood beat,
Sitting that morn beside the Lady's feet
And saying as she prompted; till outburst
One face from all the faces—not then first
She knew it; where in maple-chamber glooms,
Crowned with what sanguine-heart pomegranate blooms
Advanced it ever? Men's acknowledgment
Sanctioned her own: 'twas taken, Palma's bent,
She said.
      And day by day the Tuscan dumb
Sat scheming, scheming; Ecelin would come
Gaunt, scared, Cesano baffles me, he'd say:
Better I fought it out my father's way!
Strangle Ferrara in its drowning flats
And you and your Taurello yonder—what's
Romano's business there? An hour's concern
To cure the froward Chief! induced return
Much heartened from those overmeaning eyes,
Wound up to persevere, his enterprise
Marked out anew, its exigent of wit
Apportioned, she at liberty to sit
And scheme against the next emergence, I—
To covet what I deemed their sprite, made fly
Or fold the wing—to con your horoscope
For leave command those steely shafts shoot ope
Or straight assuage their blinding eagerness
To blank smooth snow: what semblance of success
To any of my plans for making you
Romano's lord? That chief—her Children too—
There Salinguerra would obstruct me sheer,
And the insuperable Tuscan here
Stayed me! But one wild eve that Lady died
In her lone chamber: only I beside:
Taurello far at Naples, and my sire
At Padua, Ecelin away in ire
With Alberic: she held me thus—a clutch

To make our spirits as our bodies touch—
And so began flinging the past up, heaps
Of uncouth treasure from their sunless sleeps
Within her soul; deeds rose along with dreams,
Fragments of many miserable schemes,
Secrets, more secrets, then—no, not the last—
'Mongst others, like a casual trick o' the past,
How . . . ay, she told me, gathering her face
That face of hers into one arch-grimace
To die with . . .

         Friend, 'tis gone! but not the fear
Of that fell laughing, heard as now I hear.
Nor faltered voice, nor seemed her heart grow weak,
When i' the midst abrupt she ceased to speak
—Dead, as to serve a purpose, mark, for in
Rushed o' the very instant Ecelin
(How summoned who divines?) looking as if
Part understood he why his mate lay stiff
Already in my arms for, Girl, how must
I manage Este in the matter thrust
Upon me, how unravel their bad coil?
Since (he declared) 'tis on your brow—a soil
Like hers there! then said in a breath he lacked
No counsel after all, had signed no pact
With devils, nor was treason here or there,
Goito or Vicenza, his affair:
He'd bury it in Adelaide's deep grave
And begin life afresh, nor either, slave
For any Friedrich's or Taurello's sake!
What booted him to meddle or to make
In Lombardy? 'Twas afterward I knew
The meaning of his promise to undo
All she had done—why marriages were made,
New friendships entered on, old followers paid
In curses for their pains, people's amaze
At height, when passing out by Gate St. Blaise
He stopped short in Vicenza, bent his head
Over a friar's neck, had vowed, he said,
Long since, nigh thirty years, because his wife
And child were saved there, to bestow his life
On God, his gettings on the Church.

               Exiled
Within Goito, still that dream beguiled

Her days and nights; 'twas found the orb she sought
To serve, those glimpses came of Fomalhaut
No other: how then serve it?—authorise
Him and Romano mingle destinies?
And straight Romano's angel stood beside
Her who had else been Boniface's bride,
For Salinguerra 'twas, the neck low bent,
The voice lightened to music as he meant
To learn not teach me how Romano waxed,
Wherefore he waned, and why if I relaxed
My grasp (think, I!) would drop a thing effete,
Frayed by itself, unequal to complete
The course, and counting every step astray
A gain so much. Romano every way
Stable, a House now—why this starting back
Into the very outset of its track?
This recent patching-principle allied
Our House with other Houses—what beside
Concerned the apparition, yon grim Knight
Who followed Conrad hither in such plight
His utmost wealth was reckoned in his steed?
For Ecelo, that prowler, was decreed
A task in the beginning hazardous
To him as ever task can be to us,
But did the weather-beaten thief despair
When first our crystal cincture of warm air,
That binds the Trivisan as its spice-belt
(Crusaders say) the tract where Jesus dwelt,
Furtive he pierced and Este was to face—
Despaired Saponian Strength of Lombard Grace?
Said he for making surer aught made sure,
Maturing what already was mature?
No; his heart prompted Ecelo, Confront
Este, inspect yourself. What's nature? Wont.
Discard three-parts your nature and adopt
The rest as an advantage! Old Strength propped
The earliest of Podestas among
The Vincentines, no less than, while there sprung
His Palace up in Padua like a threat,
Their noblest spied a Grace unnoticed yet
In Conrad's crew. Thus far the object gained,
Romano was established; has remained—
For are you not Italian, truly peer

With Este?   Azzo better soothes its[1] ear
Than Alberic? or is this lion's-crine
From over-mount (this yellow hair of mine)
So weak a graft on Agnes Este's stock?
(Thus went he on with something of a mock)
Wherefore recoil then from the very fate
Conceded you, refuse to imitate
Your model farther?   Este long since left
Being mere Este: as a blade its heft,
Este requires the Pope to further him:
And you, the Kaiser: whom your father's whim
Foregoes or, better, never shall forego
If Palma dares pursue what Ecelo
Commenced but Ecelin desists from: just
As Adelaide of Susa could intrust
Her donative (that's Piedmont to the Pope,
The Alpine-pass for him to shut or ope
'Twixt France and Italy) to the superb
Matilda's perfecting,—lest aught disturb
Our Adelaide's great counter-project for
Giving her Trentine to the Emperor
And passage here from Germany, shall you
Take it, my slender plodding talent, too—
Urged me Taurello with his half-smile.

He

As Patron of the scattered family
Conveyed me to his Mantua, kept in bruit
Azzo's alliances and Richard's suit
Until, the Kaiser excommunicate,
Nothing remains, Taurello said, but wait
Some rash procedure: Palma was the link,
As Agnes' child, between us, and they shrink
From losing Palma: judge if we advance
Your father's method your inheritance!
The day she was betrothed to Boniface
At Padua by Taurello's self, took place
The outrage of the Ferrarese: again,
That day she sought Verona with the train
Agreed for, by Taurello's policy
Convicting Richard of the fault, since she
Was present to annul or to confirm,
Richard, whose patience had outstayed its term,
Quitted Verona for the siege.

And now
What glory may engird Sordello's brow
For this?   A month since Oliero sunk
All Ecelin that was into a Monk;
But how could Salinguerra so forget
His liege of thirty summers as grudge yet
One effort to recover him?   He sent
Forthwith the tidings of the Town's event
To Oliero, adding, he, despite
The recent folly, recognised his right
To order such proceedings: should he wring
Its uttermost advantage out, or fling
This chance away?   If not him, who was Head
Now of the House?   Through me that missive sped;
My father's answer will by me return.
Behold!   For him, he writes, no more concern
With strife than for his children with the plots
Of Friedrich.   Old engagements out he blots
For aye: Taurello shall no more subserve,
Nor Ecelin impose.   Lest this unnerve
Him therefore at this juncture, slack his grip
Of Richard, suffer the occasion slip,
I, in his sons' default (who, mating with
Este, forsake Romano as the frith
Its mainsea for the firmland that makes head
Against) I stand, Romano; in their stead
Assume the station they desert, and give
Still, as the Kaiser's Representative,
Taurello licence he demands.   Midnight—
Morning—by noon to-morrow, making light
Of the League's issue, we, in some gay weed
Like yours disguised together, may precede
The arbitrators to Ferrara; reach
Him, let Taurello's noble accents teach
The rest! then say if I have misconceived
Your destiny, too readily believed
The Kaiser's cause your own!
                              And Palma's fled.
Though no affirmative disturbs the head
A dying lamp-flame sinks and rises o'er
Like the alighted planet Pollux wore,
Until, morn breaking, he resolves to be
Gate-vein of this heart's blood of Lombardy,

Soul to their body—have their aggregate
Of souls and bodies, and so conquer fate
Though he should live, a centre of disgust
Even, apart, core of the outward crust
He vivifies, assimilates.   For thus
Bring I Sordello to the rapturous
Exclaim at the crowd's cry, because one round
Of life was quite accomplished and he found
Not only that a soul, howe'er its might,
Is insufficient to its own delight,
Both in corporeal organs and in skill
By means of such to body forth its Will—
And, after, insufficient to apprise
Men of that Will, oblige them recognise
The Hid by the Revealed—but that, the last
Nor lightest of the struggles overpast,
His Will, bade abdicate, which would not void
The throne, might sit there, suffer he enjoyed
The same a varied and divine array
Incapable of homage the first way
Nor fit to render incidentally
Tribute connived at, taken by the by,
In joys: and if thus warranted rescind
The ignominious exile of mankind
Whose proper service, ascertained intact
As yet (by Him to be themselves made act,
Not watch Sordello acting each of them)
Was to secure—if the true diadem
Seemed imminent while our Sordello drank
The wisdom of that golden Palma, thank
Verona's Lady in her Citadel
Founded by Gaulish Brennus legends tell—
And truly when she left him the sun reared
A head like the first clamberer's that peered
A-top the Capitol, his face on flame
With triumph, triumphing till Manlius came.
Nor slight too much my rhymes—" that spring, dispread,
Dispart, disperse, lingering overhead
Like an escape of angels?" Rather say
My transcendental platan! mounting gay
(An archimage so courts a novice-queen)
With tremulous silvered trunk, whence branches sheen
Laugh out, thick foliaged next, a-shiver soon

With coloured buds, then glowing like the moon
One mild flame, last a pause, a burst, and all
Her ivory limbs are smothered by a fall,
Bloom-flinders and fruit-sparkles and leaf-dust,
Ending the weird work prosecuted just
For her amusement; he decrepit, stark,
Dozes; her uncontrolled delight may mark
Apart—
      Yet not so, surely never so!
Only as good my soul were suffered go
O'er the lagune: forth fare thee, put aside
Entrance thy synod, as a God may glide
Out of the world he fills and leave it mute
A myriad ages as we men compute,
Returning into it without a break
I' the consciousness! They sleep, and I awake
O'er the lagune.
          Sordello said once, note
In just such songs as Eglamor, say, wrote
With heart and soul and strength, for he believed
Himself achieving all to be achieved
By singer—in such songs you find alone
Completeness, judge the song and singer One
And either's purpose answered, his in it
Or its in him: while from true works (to wit
Sordello's dream-performances that will
Be never more than dream) escapes there still
Some proof the singer's proper life's beneath
The life his song exhibits, this a sheath
To that; a passion and a knowledge far
Transcending these, majestic as they are,
Smoulder; his lay was but an episode
In the bard's life. Which evidence you owed
To some slight weariness, a looking-off
Or start-away, the childish skit or scoff
In " Charlemagne," for instance, dreamed divine
In every point except one restive line
(Those daughters!)—what significance may lurk
In that? My life commenced before that work,
Continues after it, as on I fare
With no more stopping possibly, no care
To jot down (says the bard) the why and how
And where and when of life, as I do now:

But shall I cease to live for that? Alas
For you! who sigh, when shall it come to pass
We read that story, when will he compress
The future years, his whole life's business,
Into another lay which that one flout,
Howe'er inopportune it be, lets out
Engrosses him already while professed
To meditate with us eternal rest?
Strike sail! slip cable! here the galley's moored
For once, the awning's stretched, the poles assured
Noontide above; except the wave's crisp dash,
Or buzz of colibri, or tortoise' splash,
The margin's silent; out with every spoil
Made in our tracking, coil by mighty coil,
This serpent of a river to his head
I' the midst! Admire each treasure as we spread
The turf to help us tell our history
Aright: give ear then, gentles, and descry
The groves of giant rushes how they grew
Like demon's endlong tresses we sailed through,
How mountains yawned, forests to give us vent
Opened, each doleful side, yet on we went
Till . . . may that beetle (shake your cap) attest
The springing of a land-wind from the West!
Wherefore? Ah, yes, you frolic it to-day:
To-morrow, and the pageant's moved away
Down to the poorest tent-pole: we and you
Part company: no other may pursue
Eastward your voyage, be informed what fate
Intends, if triumph or decline await
The tempter of the everlasting steppe.
    I sung this on an empty palace-step
At Venice: why should I break off, nor sit
Longer upon my step, exhaust the fit
England gave birth to? Who's adorable
Enough reclaim a —— no Sordello's Will
Alack!—be queen to me? That Bassanese
Busied among her smoking fruit-boats? These
Perhaps from our delicious Asolo
Who twinkle, pigeons o'er the portico
Not prettier, bind late lilies into sheaves
To deck the bridge-side chapel, dropping leaves
Soiled by their own loose gold-meal? Ah, beneath

The cool arch stoops she, brownest-cheek! Her wreath
Endures a month—a half-month—if I make
A queen of her, continue for her sake
Sordello's story? Nay, that Paduan girl
Splashes with barer legs where a live whirl
In the dead black Giudecca proves sea-weed
Drifting has sucked down three, four, all indeed
Save one pale-red striped, pale-blue turbaned post
For gondolas.
　　　　　　　You sad dishevelled ghost
That pluck at me and point, are you advised
I breathe? Let stay those girls (e'en her disguised
—Jewels in the locks that love no crownet like
Their native field-buds and the green wheat spike,
So fair!—Who left this end of June's turmoil,
Shook off, as might a lily its gold soil,
Pomp, save a foolish gem or two, and free
Came join the peasants o'er the kissing sea.)
Look they too happy, too tricked out? Confess
You have so niggard stock of happiness
To share that, do one's uttermost, dear wretch,
One labours ineffectually stretch
It o'er you so that mother, children, both
May equitably flaunt the sumpter-cloth!
No: tear the robe yet farther: be content
With seeing some few score pre-eminent
Through shreds of it, acknowledged happy wights,
Engrossing what should furnish all, by rights—
(At home we dizen scholars, chiefs and kings,
But in this magic weather hardly clings
The old garb gracefully: Venice, a type
Of Life, 'twixt blue and blue extends, a stripe,
As Life, the somewhat, hangs 'twixt nought and nought:
'Tis Venice, and 'tis Life—as good you sought
To spare me the Piazza's slippery stone,
Or stay me thrid her cross canals alone,
As hinder Life what seems the single good
Sole purpose, one thing to be understood
Of Life)—best, be they Peasants, be they Queens,
Take them, I say, made happy any means,
Parade them for the common credit, vouch
A luckless residue we send to crouch
In corners out of sight was just as framed

For happiness, its portion might have claimed
And so, could we concede that portion stalked
Fastuous as any—such my project, baulked
Already; hardly venture I adjust
A lappet when I find you! To mistrust
Me! nor unreasonably. You, no doubt,
Have the true knack of tiring suitors out
With those thin lips on tremble, lashless eyes
Inveterately tear-shot—there, be wise
Mistress of mine, there, there, as if I meant
You insult! Shall your friend (not slave) be shent
For speaking home? Beside care-bit erased
Broken-up beauties ever took my taste
Supremely, and I love you more, far more
Than her I looked should foot Life's temple-floor—
Years ago, leagues at distance, when and where
A whisper came, Seek others, since thy care
Is found, a life's provision; if a race
Should be thy mistress, and into one face
The many faces crowd? Ah, had I, judge,
Or no, your secret? Rough apparel—grudge
All ornaments save tag or tassel worn
To hint we are not thoroughly forlorn—
Slouch bonnet, unloop mantle, careless go
Alone (that's saddest but it must be so)
Through Venice, sing now and now glance aside,
Aught desultory or undignified,
And, ravishingest lady, will you pass
Or not each formidable group, the mass
Before the Basilike (that feast gone by,
God's day, the great June Corpus Domini)
And wistfully foregoing proper men,
Come timid up to me for alms? And then
The luxury to hesitate, feign do
Some unexampled grace, when whom but you
Dare I bestow your own upon? And hear
Me out before you say it is to sneer
I call you ravishing, for I regret
Little that she, whose early foot was set
Forth as she'd plant it on a pedestal,
Now i' the silent city, seems to fall
Towards me—no wreath, only a lip's unrest
To quiet, surcharged eyelids to be pressed

Dry of their tears upon my bosom: strange
Such sad chance should produce in thee such change,
My love! warped men, souls, bodies! yet God spoke
Of right-hand foot and eye—selects our yoke
Sordello! as your poetship may find:
So sleep upon my shoulder, child, nor mind
Their foolish talk; we'll manage reinstate
The matter; ask moreover, when they prate
Of evil men past hope, don't each contrive
Despite the evil you abuse to live?
Keeping, each losel, thro' a maze of lies,
His own conceit of truth? to which he hies
By obscure tortuous windings, if you will,
But to himself not inaccessible;
He sees it, and his lies are for the crowd
We cannot see; some fancied right allowed
His vilest wrong, empowered the fellow clutch
One pleasure from the multitude of such
Denied him: then assert, all men appear
To think all better than themselves, by here
Trusting a crowd they wrong; but really, say,
All men think all men stupider than they,
Since save themselves no other comprehends
The complicated scheme to make amends
—Evil, the scheme by which, thro' Ignorance
Good labours to exist. A slight advance
Merely to find the sickness you die through
And nought beside: but if one can't eschew
One's portion in the common lot, at least
One can avoid an ignorance increased
Tenfold by dealing out hint after hint
How nought is like dispensing without stint
The water of life—so easy to dispense
Beside, when one has probed the centre whence
Commotion's born—could tell you of it all
—Meantime, just meditate my madrigal
O' the mugwort that conceals a dewdrop safe!
What, dullard? we and you in smothery chafe
Babes, baldheads, stumbled thus far into Zin
The Horrid, getting neither out nor in,
A hungry sun above us, sands among
Our throats, each dromedary lolls a tongue,
Each camel churns a sick and frothy chap,

And you, 'twixt tales of Potiphar's mishap
And sonnets on the earliest ass that spoke,
Remark you wonder any one needs choak
With founts about! Potsherd him, Gibeonites.
While awkwardly enough your Moses smites
The rock though he forego his Promised Land,
Thereby, have Satan claim his carcass, and
Dance, forsooth, Metaphysic Poet . . . ah
Mark ye the dim first oozings? Meribah!
And quaffing at the fount my courage gained
Recall—not that I prompt ye—who explained . . .
Presumptuous! interrupts one. You not I
'Tis Brother, marvel at and magnify
Mine office; office, quotha? can we get
To the beginning of the office yet?
What do we here? simply experiment
Each on the other's power and its intent
When elsewhere tasked, if this of mine were trucked
For thine to either's profit,—watch construct,
In short, an engine: with a finished one
What it can do is all, nought how 'tis done;
But this of ours yet in probation, dusk
A kernel of strange wheelwork thro' its husk
Grows into shape by quarters and by halves;
Remark this tooth's spring, wonder what that valve's
Fall bodes, presume each faculty's device,
Make out each other more or less precise—
The scope of the whole engine's to be proved—
We die: which means to say the whole's removed,
Dismounted wheel by wheel that complex gin,
To be set up anew elsewhere, begin
A task indeed but with a clearer clime
Than the murk lodgment of our building-time:
And then, I grant you, it behoves forget
How 'tis done—all that must amuse us yet
So long: and while thou turnest on thy heel
Pray that I be not busy slitting steel
Or shredding brass upon a virgin shore
Under a cluster of fresh stars, before
I name a tithe the wheels I trust to do!
So occupied, then, are we: hitherto,
At present, and a weary while to come,
The office of ourselves nor blind nor dumb

And seeing somewhat of man's state, has been,
The worst of us, to say they so have seen;
The better, what it was they saw; the best,
Impart the gift of seeing to the rest:
So that I glance, says such an one, around,
And there's no face but I can read profound
Disclosures in; this stands for hope, that—fear,
And for a speech, a deed in proof, look here!
Stoop, else the strings of blossom, where the nuts
O'erarch, will blind thee! said I not? she shuts
Both eyes this time, so close the hazels meet!
Thus, prisoned in the Piombi, I repeat
Events one rove occasioned, o'er and o'er,
Putting 'twixt me and madness evermore
Thy sweet shape, Elys; therefore stoop—
　　　　　　　　　　　　　　　That's truth!
(Applaud you) the incarcerated youth
Would say that!
　　　　　　　Youth? Plara the bard? set down
That Plara spent his youth in a grim town
Whose cramped ill-featured streets huddled about
The minster for protection, never out
Of its black belfry's shadow or bells' roar:
Brighter the sun illumed the suburbs, more
Ugly and absolute that shade's reproof
For any chance escape of joy some roof
Taller than they allowed the rest detect
Before the sole permitted laugh (suspect
Who could, 'twas meant for laughter, that ploughed cheek's
Repulsive gleam!) when the sun stopped both peaks
Of the cleft belfry like a fiery wedge,
Then sunk, a huge flame on its socket's edge,
Whose leavings on the grey grass oriel-pane,
Were ghastly some few minutes more: no rain—
The Minster minded that! in heaps the dust
Lay every where: that town, the Minster's trust,
Held Plara; who, its denizen, bade hail
In twice twelve sonnets, Naddo Tempe's vale.
　Exact the town, the minster and the street!
　As all mirth triumphs, sadness means defeat:
Lust triumphs and is gay, Love's triumphed o'er
And sad: but Lucio's sad: I said before
Love's sad, not Lucio; one who loves may be

As gay his love has leave to hope, as he
Downcast that lusts' desire escapes the springe:
'Tis of the mood itself I speak, what tinge
Determines it, else colourless, or mirth,
Or melancholy, as from Heaven or Earth.

Ay, that's the variation's gist! Indeed?
Thus far advanced in safety then, proceed!
And having seen too what I saw, be bold
Enough encounter what I do behold
(That's sure) but you must take on trust! Attack
The use and purpose of such sights! Alack,
Not so unwisely hastes the crowd dispense
On Salinguerras praise in preference
To the Sordellos: men of action these!
Who seeing just as little as you please
Yet turn that little to account; engage
With, do not gaze at; carry on a stage
The work o' the world, not merely make report
The work existed ere their time—In short,
When at some future no-time a brave band
Sees, using what it sees, then shake my hand
In heaven, my brother! Meanwhile where's the hurt
To keep the Makers-see on the alert
At whose defection mortals stare aghast
As though Heaven's bounteous windows were slammed fast
Incontinent? whereas all you beneath
Should scowl at, curse them, bruise lips, break their teeth
Who ply the pullies for neglecting you:
And therefore have I moulded, made anew
A Man, delivered to be turned and tried,
Be angry with or pleased at. On your side
Have ye times, places, actors of your own?
Try them upon Sordello once full-grown,
And then—ah then! If Hercules first parched
His foot in Egypt only to be marched
A sacrifice for Jove with pomp to suit,
What chance have I? The demigod was mute
Till at the altar, where time out of mind
Such guests became oblations, chaplets twined
His forehead long enough, and he began
Slaying the slayers, nor escaped a man—
Take not affront, my gentle audience! whom
No Hercules shall make his hecatomb

Believe, none from his brows your chaplet rend—
That's your kind suffrage, yours, nay, yours, my friend
Whose great verse blares unintermittent on
Like any trumpeter at Marathon,
He'll testify who when Platæas grew scant
Put up with Ætna for a stimulant!
And well too, I acknowledged, as it loomed
Over the Midland sea that morn, presumed
All day, demolished by the blazing West
At eve, while towards it tilting cloudlets prest
Like Persian ships for Salamis.   Friend, wear
A crest proud as desert while I declare
Had I a flawless ruby fit to wring
A tear its colour from that painted king
To lose, I would, for that one smile which went
To my heart, fling it in the sea content
Wearing your verse in place, an amulet
Sovereign against low-thoughtedness and fret!
My English Eyebright, if you are not glad
That, as I stopped my task awhile, the sad
Dishevelled form wherein I put mankind
To come at times and keep my pact in mind
Renewed me,—hear no crickets in the hedge
Nor let a glowworm spot the river's edge
At home, and may the summer showers gush
Without a warning from the missel thrush!
For, Eyebright, what I sing's the fate of such
As find our common nature (overmuch
Despised because restricted and unfit
To bear the burthen they impose on it)
Cling when they would discard it; craving strength
To leap from the allotted world, at length
'Tis left—they floundering without a term
Each a God's germ, but doomed remain a germ
In unexpanded infancy, assure
Yourself, nor misconceive my portraiture
Nor undervalue its adornments quaint!
What seems a fiend perchance may prove a saint:
Ponder a story ancient pens transmit,
Then say if you condemn me or acquit.
John the Beloved, banished Antioch
For Patmos, bade collectively his flock
Farewell but set apart the closing eve

To comfort some his exile most would grieve
He knew: a touching spectacle, that house
In motion to receive him! Xanthus' spouse
You missed, made panther's meat a month since; but
Xanthus himself (for 'twas his nephew shut
'Twixt boards and sawn asunder) Polycarp,
Soft Charicle next year no wheel could warp
To swear by Cæsar's fortune, with the rest
Were ranged; thro' whom the grey disciple prest
Busily blessing right and left, just stopt
To pat one infant's curls the hangman cropt
Soon after, reached the portal; on its hinge
The door turns and he enters—what deep twinge
Ruins the smiling mouth, those wide eyes fix
Whereon? How like some spectral candlestick's
Branch the disciple's arms! Dead swooned he, woke
Anon, heaved sigh, made shift to gasp heart-broke
Get thee behind me Satan! have I toiled
To no more purpose? is the gospel foiled
Here too, and o'er my son's, my Xanthus' hearth,
Portrayed with sooty garb and features swarth—
Ah Xanthus, am I to thy roof beguiled
To see the—the—the Devil domiciled?
Whereto sobbed Xanthus, Father, 'tis yourself
Installed, a limning which our utmost pelf
Went to procure against to-morrow's loss,
And that's no twy-prong but a pastoral cross
You're painted with! The puckered brows unfold—
And you shall hear Sordello's story told.

BOOK THE FOURTH

MEANTIME Ferrara lay in rueful case;
The lady-city, for whose sole embrace
Her pair of suitors struggled, felt their arms
A brawny mischief to the fragile charms
Each tugged for—one discovering to twist
Her tresses twice or thrice about his wrist
Secured a point of vantage—one, how best
He'd parry that by planting in her breast

His elbow-spike—both parties too intent
For noticing, howe'er the battle went,
Its conqueror would have a corpse to kiss.
May Boniface be duly damned for this!
Howled some old Ghibellin as up he turned,
From the wet heap of rubbish where they burned
His house, a little skull with dazzling teeth:
A boon, sweet Christ—let Salinguerra seethe
In hell for ever, Christ, and let myself
Be there to laugh at him! moaned some young Guelf
Stumbling upon a shrivelled hand nailed fast
To the charred lintel of the doorway last
His father stood within to bid him speed.
The thoroughfares were overrun with weed
—Docks, quitchgrass, loathly mallows no man plants.
　　The stranger none of its inhabitants
Crept out of doors to taste fresh air again,
And ask the purpose of a sumptuous train
Admitted on a morning; every town
Of the East League was come by envoy down
To treat for Richard's ransom: here you saw
The Vicentine, here snowy oxen draw
The Paduan carroch, its vermilion cross
On its white field: a tip-toe o'er the fosse
Looked Legate Montelungo wistfully
After the flock of steeples he might spy
In Este's time, gone (doubts he) long ago
To mend the ramparts—sure the laggards know
The Pope's as good as here! They paced the streets
More soberly. At last, Taurello greets
The League, announced a pursuivant, will match
Its courtesy, and labours to despatch
At earliest Tito, Friedrich's Pretor, sent
On pressing matters from his post at Trent
With Mainard Count of Tyrol,—simply waits
Their going to receive the delegates.
Tito! Our delegates exchanged a glance,
And, keeping the main way, admired askance
The lazy engines of outlandish birth
Couched like a king each on its bank of earth—
Arbalist, manganel and catapult;
While stationed by, as waiting a result,
Lean silent gangs of mercenaries ceased

Working to watch the strangers—this, at least,
Were better spared; he scarce presumes gainsay
The League's decision! Get our friend away
And profit for the future: how else teach
Azzo 'tis not so safe within claw's reach
Till Salinguerra's final gasp be blown?
Those mere convulsive scratches find the bone
—Who bade him bloody the spent osprey's nare?
    The carrochs halted in the public square.
Pennons of every blazon once a-flaunt,
Men prattled, freelier that the crested gaunt
White ostrich with a horse-shoe in her beak
Was missing; whosoever chose might speak
Ecelin boldly out: so, Ecelin
Needed his wife to swallow half the sin
And sickens by himself: the devil's whelp
He styles his son dwindles away, no help
From conserves, your fine triple-curded froth
Of virgin's blood, your Venice viper-broth—
Eh? Jubilate! Tush! no little word
You utter here that's not distinctly heard
At Oliero: he was absent sick
When we besieged Bassano—who i' the thick
O' the work perceived the progress Azzo made
Like Ecelin? through his witch Adelaide
Who managed it so well that night by night
At their bed-foot stood up a soldier-sprite
First fresh, pale by-and-by without a wound,
And when he came with eyes filmed as in swound
They knew the place was taken—Ominous
Your Ghibellins should get what cautelous
Old Redbeard sought from Azzo's sire to wrench
Vainly; St. George contrived his town a trench
O' the marshes, an impermeable bar:
Young Ecelin is meant the tutelar
Of Padua rather; veins embrace upon
His hand like Brenta and Bacchiglion . . .
What now? The founts! God's bread, touch not a plank!
A crawling hell of carrion—every tank
Choke-full! found out just now to Cino's cost—
The same who gave Taurello's side for lost,
And, making no account of fortune's freaks,
Refused to budge from Padua then, but sneaks

Back now with Concorezzi—'faith! they drag
Their carroch to San Vital, plant the flag
On his own Palace so adroitly razed
He knew it not; a sort of Guelf folk gazed
And laughed apart; Cino disliked their air—
Must pluck up spirit, show he does not care—
Seats himself on the tank's edge—will begin
To hum, *za za, Cavaler Ecelin*—
A silence; he gets warmer, clinks to chime,
Now both feet plough the ground, deeper each time,
At last, *za za*, and up with a fierce kick
Comes his own mother's face caught by the thick
Grey hair about his spur!

               Which means, they lift
The covering Taurello made a shift
To stretch upon the truth; as well avoid
Further disclosures; leave them thus employed.
Our dropping Autumn morning clears apace,
And poor Ferrara puts a softened face
On her misfortunes, save one spot—this tall
Huge foursquare line of red brick garden-wall
Bastioned within by trees of every sort
On three sides, slender, spreading, long and short,
(Each grew as it contrived, the poplar ramped,
The fig-tree reared itself,) but stark and cramped,
Made fools of; whence upon the very edge,
Running 'twixt trunk and trunk to smooth one ledge
Of shade, are shrubs inserted, warp and woof,
Which smother up that variance. Scale the roof
Of solid tops and o'er the slope you slide
Down to a grassy space level and wide,
Here and there dotted with a tree, but trees
Of rarer leaf, each foreigner at ease,
Set by itself; and in the centre spreads,
Born upon three uneasy leopards' heads,
A laver, broad and shallow, one bright spirt
Of water bubbles in: the walls begirt
With trees leave off on either hand: pursue
Your path along a wondrous avenue
Those walls abut on, heaped of gleamy stone,
With aloes leering everywhere, grey-grown
From many a Moorish summer; how they wind
Out of the fissures! likelier to bind

The building than those rusted cramps which drop
Already in the eating sunshine. Stop
Yon fleeting shapes above there! Ah, the pride
Or else despair of the whole country-side—
A range of statues, swarming o'er with wasps,
God, goddess, woman, man, your Greek rough-rasps
In crumbling Naples marble! meant to look
Like those Messina marbles Constance took
Delight in, or Taurello's self conveyed
To Mantua for his mistress, Adelaide,
A certain font with caryatides
Since cloistered at Goito; only, these
Are up and doing, not abashed, a troop
Able to right themselves—who see you, stoop
O' the instant after you their arms! unplucked
By this or that you pass, for they conduct
To terrace raised on terrace, and, between,
Creatures of brighter mould and braver mien
Than any yet, the choicest of the Isle
No doubt; here, left a sullen breathing-while,
Up-gathered on himself the Fighter stood
For his last fight, and, wiping treacherous blood
Out of the eyelids just held ope beneath
Those shading fingers in their iron sheath,
Steadied his strengths amid the buzz and stir
Of a dusk hideous amphitheatre
At the announcement of his over-match
To wind the day's diversion up, despatch
Their pertinacious friend: while, limbs one heap,
The Slave, no breath in her round mouth, watched leap
Dart after dart forth as her hero's car
Clove dizzily the solid of the war
—Let coil about his knees for pride in him.
We reach the farthest terrace and the grim
San Pietro Palace stops us.

                  Such the state
Of Salinguerra's plan to emulate
Sicilian marvels that his girlish wife
Retrude still might lead her ancient life
In her new home—whereat enlarged so much
Neighbours upon the novel princely touch
He took who here imprisons Boniface.
Here must the Envoys come to sue for grace;

And here, emerging from the labyrinth
Below, two minstrels pause beside the plinth
Of the door-pillar.
            One had really left
Verona for the cornfields (a poor theft
From the morass) where Este's camp was made,
The Envoys' march, the Legate's cavalcade—
Looked cursorily o'er, but scarce as when,
Eager for cause to stand aloof from men
At every point save the fantastic tie
Acknowledged in his boyish sophistry,
He made account of such. A crowd; he meant
To task the whole of it; each part's intent
Concerned him therefore, and the more he pried
The less became Sordello satisfied
With his own figure at the moment. Sought
He respite from his task? descried he aught
Novel in the anticipated sight
Of all those livers upon all delight?
A phalanx as of myriad points combined
Whereby he still had imaged that mankind
His youth was passed in dreams of rivalling,
His age—in plans to show at least the thing
So dreamed, but now he hastened to impress
With his own will, effect a happiness
From theirs, supply a body to his soul
Thence, and become eventually whole
With them as he had hoped to be without—
Made these the mankind he was mad about?
Because a few of them were notable
Must all be figured worthy note? As well
Expect to find Taurello's triple line
Of trees a single and prodigious pine.
Real pines rose here and there, but, close among,
Thrust into and mixed up with pines, a throng
Of shrubs you saw, a nameless common sort
O'erpast in dreams, left out of the report,
Fast hurried into corners, or at best
Admitted to be fancied like the rest.
Reckon that morning's proper chiefs; how few!
And yet the people grew, the people grew,
Grew ever, as with many there indeed,
More left behind and most who should succeed

Simply in virtue of their faces, eyes,
Petty enjoyments and huge miseries,
Were veritably mingled with, made great
Those chiefs: no overlooking Mainard's state
Nor Concorezzi's station, but instead
Of stopping there, each dwindled to be head
Of infinite and absent Tyrolese
Or Paduans; startling too the more that these
Seemed passive and disposed of, uncared for,
Yet doubtless on the whole (quoth Eglamor)
Smiling—for if a wealthy man decays
And out of store of such must wear all days
One tattered suit alike in sun and shade,
'Tis commonly some tarnished fine brocade
Fit for a feast-night's flourish and no more;
Nor otherwise poor Misery from her store
Of looks is fain upgather, keep unfurled
For common wear as she goes through the world
The faint remainder of some worn-out smile
Meant for a feast-night's service merely. While
Crowd upon crowd rose on Sordello thus,—
Crowds no way interfering to discuss
Much less dispute life's joys with one employed
In envying them, or, if they enjoyed,
There lingered somewhat indefinable
In every look and tone, the mirth as well
As woe, that fixed at once his estimate
Of the result, their good or bad estate,—
Old memories flocked but with a new effect:
And the new body, ere he could suspect,
Cohered, mankind and he were really fused,
The new self seemed impatient to be used
By him, but utterly another way
Than that anticipated: strange to say,
They were too much below him, more in thrall
Than he, the adjunct than the principal.
What booted scattered brilliances? the mind
Of any number he might hope to bind
And stamp with his own thought, howe'er august,
If all the rest should grovel in the dust?
No: first a mighty equilibrium sure
To be established, privilege procure
For them himself had long possessed! he felt

An error, an exceeding error melt—
While he was occupied with Mantuan chants
Behoved him think of men and of their wants
Such as he now distinguished every side,
As his own want that might be satisfied,
And, after that, of wondrous qualities
Of his own soul demanding exercise,
And like demand it longer: nor a claim
On their part, nor was virtue in the aim
At serving them on his, but, past retrieve,
He in their toils felt with them, nor could leave,
Wonder that in the eagerness to rule,
Impress his will upon them, he the fool
Had never entertained the obvious thought
This last of his arrangements would be fraught
With good to them as well, and he should be
Rejoiced thereat; and if, as formerly,
He sighed the merry time of life must fleet,
'Twas deeplier now, for could the crowds repeat
Their poor experiences? His hand that shook
Was twice to be deplored. The Legate, look!
With eyes, like fresh-blown thrush-eggs on a thread,
Faint-blue and loosely floating in his head,
Large tongue, moist open mouth; and this long while
That owner of the idiotic smile
Serves them! He fortunately saw in time
His fault however, and the office prime
Includes the secondary—best accept
Both offices; Taurello its adept
Could teach him the preparatory one,
And how to do what he had fancied done
Long previously, ere take the greater task.
How render then these people happy? ask
The people's friends: for there must be one good,
One way to it—the Cause! he understood
The meaning now of Palma; else why are
The great ado, the trouble wide and far,
These Guelfs and Ghibellins, the Lombard's hope
Or its despair! 'twixt Emperor or Pope
The confused shifting sort of Eden tale—
Of hardihood recurring still to fail—
That foreign interloping fiend, this free
And native overbrooding Deity—

Yet a dire fascination o'er the palms
His presence ruined troubling through calms
Of Paradise—or, on the other hand,
The Pontiff, as your Kaisers understand,
That, snake-like, cursed of God to love the ground,
With lulling eye breaks in the noon profound
Some saving tree—who but the Kaiser drest
As the dislodging angel of the pest
Then? yet that pest bedropt, flat head, full fold,
With coruscating dower of dyes; behold
The secret, so to speak, and master-spring
Of the whole contest! which of them shall bring
Men good—perchance the most good—ay, it may
Be that; the question is which knows the way.

 And hereupon Count Mainard strutted past
Out of San Pietro; never looked the last
Of archers, slingers; and our friend began
To recollect strange modes of serving man—
Arbalist, catapult, brake, manganel,
And more: this way of theirs may, who can tell,
Need perfecting, said he: all's better solved
At once: Taurello 'twas the task devolved
On late—confront Taurello!
                                              And at last
They did confront him. Scarcely an hour past
When forth Sordello came, older by years
Than at his entry. Unexampled fears
Oppressed him, and he staggered off, blind, mute
And deaf, like some fresh-mutilated brute,
Into Ferrara—not the empty town
That morning witnessed: he went up and down
Streets whence the veil was stripped shred after shred,
So that in place of huddling with their dead
Indoors to answer Salinguerra's ends,
Its folk may shift to crawl and sit like friends
With any one. A woman gave him choice
Of her two daughters, the infantile voice
Or dimpled knee, for half a chain his throat
Was clasped with; but an archer knew the coat—
Its blue cross and eight lilies, bade beware
One dogging him in concert with the pair
Though thrumming on the sleeve that hid his knife.
Night set in early, autumn dews fell rife,

And fires were kindled while the Leaguers' mass
Began at every carroch—he must pass
Between that kneeling people: presently
The carroch of Verona caught his eye
With purple trappings; silently he bent
Over its fire, when voices violent
Began, Affirm not whom the youth was like
That, striking from the porch, I did not strike
Again; I too have chesnut hair; my kin
Hate Azzo and stand up for Ecelin;
Here, minstrel, drive bad thoughts away; sing; take
My glove for guerdon! and for that man's sake
He turned: A song of Eglamor's! scarce named,
When, Our Sordello's, rather! all exclaimed;
Is not Sordello famousest for rhyme?
He had been happy to deny, this time;
Profess as heretofore the aching head,
The failing heart; suspect that in his stead
Some true Apollo had the charge of them,
Was champion to reward or to condemn
So his intolerable risk might shift
Or share itself; but Naddo's precious gift
Of gifts returned, be certain! at the close—
I made that, said he to a youth who rose
As if to hear: 'twas Palma through the band
Conducted him in silence by the hand.

Back now for Salinguerra. Tito of Trent
Gave place, remember, to the pair; who went
In turn at Montelungo's visit—one
After the other are they come and gone,
A drear vast presence-chamber roughly set
In order for this morning's use; you met
The grim black twy-necked eagle, coarsely blacked
With ochre on the naked walls, nor lacked
There green and yellow tokens either side;
But the new symbol Tito brought had tried
The Legate's patience—nay, if Palma knew
What Salinguerra almost meant to do
Until the sight of her restored his lip
A certain half-smile three months' chieftainship
Had banished? Afterward the Legate found
No change in him, nor asked what badge he wound
And unwound carelessly! Now sate the Chief

Silent as when our couple left whose brief
Encounter wrought so opportune effect
In thoughts he summoned not, nor would reject—
Though time if ever, 'twas to pause now—fix
On any sort of ending: wiles and tricks
Exhausted, judge! his charge, the crazy town,
Just managed to be hindered crashing down—
His last sound troops ranged—care observed to post
His last of the maimed soldiers innermost—
So much was plain enough, but somehow struck
Him not before: and now with this strange luck
Of Tito's news, rewarding his address
So well, what thought he of? How the success
With Friedrich's rescript there would either hush
Ecelin's fiercest scruple up, or flush
Young Ecelin's white cheek, or, last, exempt
Himself from telling what there was to tempt?
No: that this minstrel was Romano's last
Servant—himself the first! Could he contrast
The whole! that minstrel's thirty autumns spent
In doing nought, his notablest event
This morning's journey hither, as we told—
Who yet was lean, outworn and really old,
A stammering awkward youth (scarce dared he raise
His eye before that magisterial gaze)
—And Salinguerra with his fears and hopes
Of sixty years, his Emperors and Popes,
Cares and contrivances, yet you would say
A youth 'twas nonchalantly looked away
Through the embrasure northward o'er the sick
Expostulating trees—so agile, quick
And graceful turned the head on the broad chest
Encased in pliant steel, his constant vest,
Whence split the sun off in a spray of fire
Across the room; and, loosened of its tire
Of steel, that head let see the comely brown
Large massive locks discoloured as a crown
Encircled them, so frayed the basnet where
A sharp white line divided clean the hair;
Glossy above, glossy below, it swept
Curling and fine about a brow thus kept
Calm, laid coat upon coat, marble and sound:
This was the mystic mark the Tuscan found,

Mused of, turned over books about. Square-faced,
No lion more; two vivid eyes, enchased
In hollows filled with many a shade and streak
Settling from the bold nose and bearded cheek;
Nor might the half-smile reach them that deformed
A lip supremely perfect else—unwarmed,
Unwidened, less or more; indifferent
Whether on trees or men his thoughts were bent—
Thoughts rarely, after all, in trim and train
As now: a period was fulfilled again;
Such in a series made his life, compressed
In each, one story serving for the rest—
Therefore he smiled. Beyond stretched garden-grounds
Where late the adversary, breaking bounds,
Procured him an occasion That above,
That eagle, testified he could improve
Effectually; the Kaiser's symbol lay
Beside his rescript, a new badge by way
Of baldric; while another thing that marred
Alike emprize, achievement and reward,
Ecelin's missive was conspicuous too.
  What a past life those flying thoughts pursue!
As his no name in Mantua half so old;
But at Ferrara, where his sires enrolled
It latterly, the Adelardi spared
Few means to rival them: both factions shared
Ferrara, so that, counted out, 'twould yield
A product very like the city's shield,
Half black and white, or Ghibellin and Guelf,
As after Salinguerra styled himself
And Este who, till Marchesalla died
—Last of the Adelardi, never tried
His fortune there; but Marchesalla's child
Transmits (can Blacks and Whites be reconciled
And young Taurello wed Linguetta) wealth
And sway to a sole grasp: each treats by stealth
Already: when the Guelfs, the Ravennese
Arrive, assault the Pietro quarter, seize
Linguetta, and are gone! Our first dismay
Abated somewhat, hurries down to lay
The after indignation Boniface,
No meaner spokesman: Learn the full disgrace
Averted ere you blame us, wont to rate

Your Salinguerra, and sole potentate
That might have been, 'mongst Este's valvassors—
Ay, Azzo's—who, not privy to, abhors
Our step—but we were zealous. Azzo's then
To do with! Straight a meeting of old men:
The Lombard Eagle of the azure sphere
With Italy to build in, builds he here?
This deemed—the other owned upon advice—
A third reflected on the matter twice—
In fine, young Salinguerra's staunchest friends
Talked of the townsmen making him amends,
Gave him a goshawk, and affirmed there was
Rare sport, one morning, over the morass
A mile or so. He sauntered through the plain,
Was restless, fell to thinking, turned again
In time for Azzo's entry with the bride;
Count Boniface rode smirking at his side:
There's half Ferrara with her, whispers flew,
And all Ancona! If the stripling knew!
  Anon the stripling was in Sicily
Where Heinrich ruled in right of Constance; he
Was gracious nor his guest incapable;
Each understood the other. So it fell,
One Spring, when Azzo, thoroughly at ease,
Had near forgotten what precise degrees
He crept by into such a downy seat,
Over the Count trudged in a special heat
To bid him of God's love dislodge from each
Of Salinguerra's Palaces; a breach
Might yawn else not so readily to shut,
For who was just arrived at Mantua but
The youngster, sword to thigh, tuft upon chin,
With tokens for Celano, Ecelin,
Pistore and the like! Next news: no whit
Do any of Ferrara's domes befit
His wife of Heinrich's very blood: a band
Of foreigners assemble, understand
Garden-constructing, level and surround,
Build up and bury in. A last news crowned
The consternation: since his infant's birth
He only waits they end his wondrous girth
Of trees that link San Pietro with Tomà
To visit us. When, as its Podestà

Regaled him at Vicenza, Este, there
With Boniface beforehand, each aware
Of plots in progress, gave alarm, expelled
A party which abetted him, but yelled
Too hastily. The burning and the flight,
And how Taurello, occupied that night
With Ecelin, lost his wife and son, were told;
—Not how he bore the blow, retained his hold,
Got friends safe through, left enemies the worst
O' the fray, and hardly seemed to care at first—
But afterward you heard not constantly
Of Salinguerra's House so sure to be!
Though Azzo simply gained by the event
A shifting of his plagues—this one content
To fall behind the other and estrange,
You will not say, his nature, but so change
That in Romano sought he wife and child,
And for Romano's sake was reconciled
To losing individual life, deep sunk,
A very pollard mortised in a trunk
Which Arabs out of wantonness contrive
Shall dwindle that the alien stock may thrive
Till forth that vine-palm feathers to the root
And red drops moisten them its arid fruit.
Once set on Adelaide, the subtle mate
And wholly at his beck, to emulate
The Church's valiant women deed for deed,
To paragon her namesake, win the meed
Of its Matilda,—and they overbore
The rest of Lombardy—not as before
By an instinctive truculence, but patched
The Kaiser's strategy until it matched
The Pontiff's, sought old ends by novel means;
Only, Romano Salinguerra screens.
Heinrich was somewhat of the tardiest
To comprehend, nor Philip acquiesced
At once in the arrangement; reasoned, plied
His friend with offers of another bride,
A statelier function—fruitlessly; 'tis plain
Taurello's somehow one to let remain
Obscure; and Otho, free to judge of both,
—Ecelin the unready, harsh and loth,
And this more plausible and facile wight

With every point a-sparkle—chose the right,
Admiring how his predecessors harped
On the wrong man: thus, quoth he, wits are warped
By outsides! Carelessly, withal, his life
Suffered its many turns of peace and strife
In many lands—you hardly could surprise
A man who shamed Sordello (recognise)
In this as much beside, that, unconcerned
What qualities are natural or earned,
With no ideal of graces, as they came
He took them, singularly well the same—
Speaking a dozen languages because
Your Greek eludes you, leave the least of flaws
In contracts, while, through Arab lore, deter
Who may the Tuscan, once Jove trined for her,
From Friedrich's path! Friedrich, whose pilgrimage
The same man puts aside, whom he'll engage
To leave next year John Brienne in the lurch,
And see Bassano for Saint Francis' church
—Profound on Guido the Bolognian's piece
That, if you lend him credit, rivals Greece—
Angels, with aureoles like golden quoits
Pitched home, applauding Ecelin's exploits
In Painimrie. He strung the angelot;
Made rhymes thereto; for prowess, clove he not
Tiso, last siege, from crest to crupper? why
Detail you thus a varied mastery
But that Taurello, ever on the watch
For men, to read their hearts and thereby catch
Their capabilities and purposes,
Displayed himself so far as displayed these:
While our Sordello only cared to know
About men as a means for him to show
Himself, and men were much or little worth
According as they kept in or drew forth
That self; the other's choicest instruments
Surmised him shallow. Meantime malcontents
Dropped off, town after town grew wiser; how
Change the world's face? said people; as 'tis now
It has been, will be ever: very fine
Subjecting things profane to things divine
In talk: this contumacy will fatigue
The vigilance of Este and the League,

Observe! accordingly, their basement sapped,
Azzo and Boniface were soon entrapped
By Ponte Alto, and in one month's space
Slept at Verona: either left a brace
Of sons—so three years after, either's pair
Lost Guglielm and Aldobrand its heir:
Azzo remained and Richard—all the stay
Of Este and St. Boniface, at bay
As 'twere; when either Ecelin grew old
Or his brain altered—not the proper mould
For new appliances—his old palm stock
Endured no influx of strange strengths: he'd rock
As in a drunkenness, or chuckle low
As proud of the completeness of his woe,
Then weep—real tears! Now make some mad onslaught
On Este, heedless of the lesson taught
So painfully—now cringe, sue peace, but peace
At price of all advantage; therefore cease
The fortunes of Romano! Up at last
Rose Este and Romano sank as fast.
And men remarked this sort of peace and war
Commenced while Salinguerra was afar:
And every friend besought him, but in vain,
To wait his old adherent, call again
Taurello: not he—who had daughters, sons,
Could plot himself, nor needed any one's
Advice. 'Twas Adelaide's remaining staunch
Prevented his destruction root and branch
Forthwith; Goito green above her, gay
He made alliances, gave lands away
To whom it pleased accept them, and withdrew
For ever from the world. Taurello, who
Was summoned to the convent, then refused
A word,—however patient, thus abused,
At Este's mercy through his imbecile
Ally, was fain dismiss the foolish smile,
And a few movements of the happier sort
Changed matters, put himself in men's report
As heretofore; he had to fight, beside,
And that became him ever. So in pride
And flushing of this kind of second youth
He dealt a good-will blow: Este in truth
Was prone—and you remembered, somewhat late,

A laughing old outrageous stifled hate
He bore that Este—how it would outbreak
At times spite of disguise, like an earthquake
In sunny weather—as that noted day
When with his hundred friends he offered slay
Azzo before the Kaiser's face: and how
On Azzo's calm refusal to allow
A liegeman's challenge straight he too was calmed:
His hate, no doubt, would bear to lie embalmed,
Bricked up, the moody Pharaoh, to survive
All intermediate crumblings, be alive
At earth's catastrophe—'twas Este's crash
Not Azzo's he demanded, so no rash
Procedure! Este's true antagonist
Rose out of Ecelin: all voices whist,
Each glance was sharpened, wit predicted. He
'Twas leaned in the embrasure presently,
Amused with his own efforts, now, to trace
With his steel-sheathed forefinger Friedrich's face
I' the dust: and as the trees waved sere, his smile
Deepened, and words expressed its thought erewhile.

Ay, fairly housed at last, my old compeer?
That we should stick together all the year
I kept Verona!—How old Boniface,
Old Azzo caught us in its market-place,
He by that pillar, I this pillar, each
In mid swing, more than fury of his speech,
Egging our rabble on to disavow
Allegiance to the Marquis—Bacchus, how
They caught us! Ecelin must turn their drudge;
Nor, if released, will Salinguerra grudge
Paying arrears of tribute due long since—
Bacchus! My man could promise then, nor wince,
The bones-and-muscles! sound of wind and limb,
Spoke he the set excuse I framed for him;
And now he sits me, slavering and mute,
Intent on chafing each starved purple foot
Benumbed past aching with the altar slab—
Will no vein throb there when some monk shall blab
Spitefully to the circle of bald scalps
" Friedrich's affirmed to be our side the Alps "
—Eh, brother Lactance, brother Anaclet?
Sworn to abjure the world and the world's fret,

God's own now? drop the dormitory bar,
Enfold the scanty grey serge scapular
Twice o'er the cowl to muffle memories out—
So! but the midnight whisper turns a shout,
Eyes wink, mouths open, pulses circulate
In the stone walls: the past, the world you hate
Is with you, ambush, open field—or see
The surging flame—they fire Vicenza—glee!
Follow, let Pilio and Bernardi chafe—
Bring up the Mantuans—through San Biagio—safe
Ah, the mad people waken? Ah, they writhe
And reach you? if they block the gate—no tithe
Can pass—keep back you Bassanese! the edge,
Use the edge—sheer, thrust, hew, melt down the wedge,
Let out the black of those black upturned eyes!
Hell—are they sprinkling fire too? the blood fries
And hisses on your brass gloves as they tear
Those upturned faces choking with despair.
Brave! Slidder through the reeking gate—how now!
You six had charge of her? And then the vow
Comes, and the foam spirts, hair's plucked, till one shriek
(I hear it) and you fling—you cannot speak—
Your gold-flowered basnet to a man who haled
The Adelaide he dared scarce view unveiled
This morn, naked across the fire: how crown
The archer that exhausted lays you down
Your infant, smiling at the flame, and dies?
While one, while mine . . .

                  Bacchus! I think there lies
More than one corpse there (and he paced the room)
—Another cinder somewhere—'twas my doom
Beside, my doom: if Adelaide is dead
I am the same, this Azzo lives instead
Of that to me, and we pull any how
Este into a heap—the matter's now
At the true juncture slipping us so oft;
Ay, Heinrich died and Otho, please you, doffed
His crown at such a juncture: let but hold
Our Friedrich's purpose, let this chain enfold
The neck of . . . who but this same Ecelin?
That must recoil when the best days begin—
Recoil? that's nought; if the recoiler leaves
His name for me to fight with, no one grieves!

But he must interfere, forsooth, unlock
His cloister to become my stumbling-block
Just as of old! Ay, ay, there 'tis again—
The land's inevitable Head—explain
The reverences that subject us! Count
These Ecelins now! not to say as fount,
Originating power of thought, from twelve
That drop i' the trenches they joined hands to delve
Six shall surpass him, but . . . why, men must twine
Somehow with something! Ecelin's a fine
Clear name! 'Twere simpler, doubtless, twine with me
At once: our cloistered friend's capacity
Was of a sort! I had to share myself
In fifty portions, like an o'ertasked elf
That's forced illume in fifty points the vast
Rare vapour he's environed by: at last
My strengths, though sorely frittered, e'en converge
And crown—no, Bacchus, they have yet to urge
The man be crowned!
                        That aloe, an he durst,
Would climb! just such a bloated sprawler first
I noted in Messina's castle court
The day I came, and Heinrich asked in sport
If I would pledge my faith to win him back
His right in Lombardy; for, once bid pack
Marauders, he continued, in my stead
You rule, Taurello! and upon this head
Laid the silk glove of Constance—I see her
Too, mantled head to foot in miniver,
Retrude following!
                        I am absolved
From further toil: the empery devolved
On me, 'twas Tito's word: and think, to lay
For once my plan, pursue my plan my way,
Prompt nobody, and render an account
Taurello to Taurello! nay, I mount
To Friedrich—he conceives the post I kept,
Who did true service, able or inept,
Who's worthy guerdon, Ecelin or I:
Me guerdoned, counsel follows; would he vie
With the Pope really? Azzo, Boniface
Compose a right-arm Hohenstauffen's race
Must break ere govern Lombardy; I point

How easy 'twere to twist once out of joint,
The socket from the bone; my Azzo's stare
Meanwhile! for I, this idle strap to wear,
Shall—fret myself abundantly, what end
To serve? There's left me twenty years to spend
—How better than my old way? Had I one
Who laboured overthrow my work—a son
Hatching with Azzo superb treachery,
To root my pines up and then poison me,
Suppose—'twere worth while frustrate that! Beside
Another life's ordained me: the world's tide
Rolls, and what hope of parting from the press
Of waves, a single wave through weariness
That's gently led aside, laid upon shore?
My life must be lived out in foam and roar,
No question. Fifty years the province held
Taurello; troubles raised, and troubles quelled,
He in the midst—who leaves this quaint stone place,
Those trees a year or two, then, not a trace
Of him! How obtain hold, fetter men's tongues
Like that Sordello with his foolish songs—
To which, despite our bustle, he is linked?
—Flowers one may teaze, that never seem extinct;
Ay, that patch, surely, green as ever, where
I set Her Moorish lentisk, by the stair,
To overawe the aloes—and we trod
Those flowers, how call you such? into the sod;
A stately foreigner—and worlds of pain
To make it thrive, arrest rough winds—all vain!
It would decline—these would not be destroyed—
And now, where is it—where can you avoid
The flowers? I frighten children twenty years
Longer!—which way, too, Ecelin appears
To thwart me, for his son's besotted youth
Gives promise of the proper tiger-tooth,
They prattle, at Vicenza! Fate, fate, fate,
My fine Taurello! go you, promulgate
Friedrich's decree, and here's shall aggrandise
Young Ecelin—our Prefect's badge! a prize
Too precious, certainly.
                              How now? Compete
With my old comrade? shuffle from their seat
His children? Paltry dealing! don't I know

Ecelin? now, I think, and years ago!
What's changed—the weakness? did not I compound
For that, and undertake preserve him sound
Despite it? Say Taurello's hankering
After the boy's preferment—this play-thing
To carry, Bacchus! And he laughed.

                        Remark
Why schemes wherein cold-blooded men embark
Prosper, when your enthusiastic sort
Fail: for these last are ever stopping short—
(Much to be done—so little they can do!)
The careless tribe see nothing to pursue
Should they desist; meanwhile their scheme succeeds.

   Thoughts were caprices in the course of deeds
Methodic with Taurello; so he turned,
Enough amused by fancies fairly earned
Of Este's horror-struck submitted neck,
And Boniface completely at his beck,
To his own petty but immediate doubt
If he could pacify the League without
Conceding Richard; just to this was brought
That interval of vain discursive thought!
As, shall I say, some Ethiop, past pursuit
Of all enslavers, dips a shackled foot,
Burnt to the blood, into the drowsy black
Enormous water current, his sole track
To his own tribe again, where he is King;
And laughs because he guesses, numbering
The yellower poison-wattles on the pouch
Of the first lizard wrested from its couch
Under the slime (whose skin, the while, he strips
To cure his nostril with, and festered lips,
And eyeballs bloodshot through the desert blast)
That he has reached its boundary, at last
May breathe;—thinks o'er enchantments of the South
Sovereign to plague his enemies, their mouth
And nails, and hair; but, these enchantments tried
In fancy, puts them soberly aside
For truth, cool projects, a return with friends,
The likelihood of winning wild amends
Ere long; thinks that, takes comfort silently,
And from the river's brink his wrongs and he
Hugging revenge close to their hearts, are soon

L 41

Off striding for the Mountains of the Moon.
  Midnight: the watcher nodded on his spear,
Since clouds dispersing left a passage clear,
If any meagre and discoloured moon
Should venture forth; and such was peering soon
Above the harassed city—her close lanes
Closer, not half so tapering her fanes,
As though she shrunk into herself to keep
What little life was saved more safely. Heap
By heap the watch-fires mouldered, and beside
The blackest spoke Sordello and replied
Palma with none to listen. 'Tis your Cause—
What makes a Ghibellin? There should be laws—
(Remember how my youth escaped! I trust
To you for manhood, Palma; tell me just
As any child)—laws secretly at work
Explaining this. Assure me good may lurk
Under the bad; my multitude has part
In your designs, their welfare is at heart
With Salinguerra, to their interest
Refer the deeds he dwelt on—so divest
Our conference of much that scared me: why
Affect that heartless tone to Tito? I
Esteemed myself, yes, in my inmost mind
This morn, a recreant to that wide mankind
O'erlooked till now: why boast my spirit's force,
—That force denied its object? why divorce
These, then admire my spirit's flight the same,
As though it bore a burden, which could tame
No pinion, from dead void to living space?
—That orb consigned to chaos and disgrace,
Why vaunt complacently my frantic dance,
Making a feat's facilities enhance
The marvel? But I front Taurello, one
Of happier fate, and what I should have done
He does; the multitude aye paramount
With him, its making progress may account
For his abiding still: when . . . but you heard
His talk with Tito—the excuse preferred
For burning those five hostages—and broached
By way of blind, as you and I approached,
I do believe.
            She spoke: then he, My thought

Plainer expressed! All Friedrich's profit—nought
Of these meantime, of conquests to achieve
For them, of wretchednesses to relieve
While profiting that Friedrich. Azzo, too,
Supports a cause: what is it? Guelfs pursue
Their ends by means like yours, or better?

         When
The Guelfs were shown alike, men ranged with men,
And deed with deed, blaze, blood, with blood and blaze,
Morn broke: once more, Sordello, meet its gaze
Proudly—the people's charge against thee fails
In every point, while either party quails!
These are the busy ones—be silent thou!
Two parties take the world up, and allow
No third, yet have one principle, subsist
By the same method; whoso shall enlist
With either, ranks with man's inveterate foes.
So there is one less quarrel to compose
'Twixt us: the Guelf's, the Ghibellin's to curse—
I have done nothing, but both sides do worse
Than nothing; nay to me, forgotten, reft
Of insight, lapped by trees and flowers, was left
The notion of a service—ha? What lured
Me here, what mighty aim was I assured
Moved Salinguerra? if a Cause remained
Intact, distinct from these, and fate ordained,
For all the past, that Cause for me?

           One pressed
Before them here, a watcher, to suggest
The subject for a ballad: he must know
The tale of the dead worthy, long ago
Consul of Rome—that's long ago for us,
Minstrels and bowmen, idly squabbling thus
In the world's corners—but too late, no doubt,
For the brave time he sought to bring about
—Not know Crescentius Nomentanus? Then
He cast about for terms to tell him, when
Sordello disavowed it, how they used
Whenever their Superior introduced
A novice to the Brotherhood—(for I
Was just a brown-sleeve brother, merrily
Appointed too, quoth he, till Innocent
Bade me relinquish, to my small content,

My wife or my brown sleeves) out some one spoke
Ere nocturns of Crescentius, to revoke
The edict issued after his demise
That blotted memory, and effigies,
All out except a floating power, a name
Including, tending to produce the same
Great act. Rome, dead, forgotten, lived at least
Within that man, though to a vulgar priest
And a vile stranger, fit to be a slave
Of Rome's, Pope John, King Otho, fortune gave
The rule there: but Crescentius, haply drest
In white, called Roman Consul for a jest,
Taking the people at their word, forth stept
As upon Brutus' heel, nor ever kept
Us waiting; stept he forth and from his brain
Gave Rome out on its ancient place again,
Ay, bade proceed with Brutus' Rome kings styled
Themselves the citizens of, and, beguiled
Thereby, were fain select the lustrous gem
Out of a lapfull, spoil their diadem
—The Senate's cypher was so hard to scratch!
He flashes like a phanal, men too catch
The flame, and Rome's accomplished; when returned
Otho and John the Consul's step had spurned,
With Hugo Lord of Este, to redress
The wrongs of each. Crescentius in the stress
Of adverse fortune bent. They crucified
Their Consul in the Forum and abide
Such slaves at Rome e'er since, that I—(for I
Was once a brown-sleeve brother, merrily
Appointed)—I had option to keep wife
Or keep brown sleeves, and managed in the strife
Lose both. A song of Rome!

                    And Rome, indeed,
Robed at Goito in fantastic weed,
The Mother-City of his Mantuan days,
Looked an established point of light whence rays
Traversed the world; and all the clustered homes
Beside of men were bent on being Romes
In their degree; the question was how each
Should most resemble Rome, clean out of reach
Herself; nor struggled either principle
To change what it aspired possess—Rome, still

For Friedrich or Honorius.

               Rome's the Cause!
The Rome of the old Pandects, our new laws—
The Capitol turned Castle Angelo
And structures that inordinately glow
Corrected by the Theatre forlorn
As a black mundane shell, its world late born
—Verona, that's beside it. These combined,
We typify the scheme to put mankind
Once more in full possession of their rights
By his sole agency. On me it lights
To build up Rome again—me, first and last:
For such a Future was endured the Past!
And thus in the grey twilight forth he sprung
To give his thought consistency among
The People's self, and let their truth avail
Finish the dream grown from the archer's tale.

BOOK THE FIFTH

Is it the same Sordello in the dusk
As at the dawn? merely a perished husk
Now, that arose a power like to build
Up Rome again? The proud conception chilled
So soon? Ay, watch that latest dream of thine
—A Rome indebted to no Palatine,
Drop arch by arch, Sordello! Art possest
Of thy wish now—rewarded for thy quest
To-day among Ferrara's squalid sons—
Are this and this and this the shining ones
Meet for the Shining City? Sooth to say
Our favoured tenantry pursue their way
After a fashion! This companion slips
On the smooth causey, t'other blinkard trips
At his mooned sandal. Leave to lead the brawls
Here i' the atria? No, friend. He that sprawls
On aught but a stibadium suffers . . . goose,
Puttest our lustral vase to such an use?
Oh, huddle up the day's disasters—march
Ye runagates, and drop thou, arch by arch,
Rome!

Yet before they quite disband—a whim—
Study a shelter, now, for him, and him,
Nay, even him, to house them! any cave
Suffices—throw out earth. A loophole? Brave!
They ask to feel the sun shine, see the grass
Grow, hear the larks sing? Dead art thou, alas,
And I am dead! But here's our son excels
At hurdle-weaving any Scythian, fells
Oak and devises rafters, dreams and shapes
That dream into a door-post, just escapes
The mystery of hinges. Lie we both
Perdue another age. The goodly growth
Of brick and stone! Our building-pelt was rough,
But that descendant's garb suits well enough
A portico-contriver. Speed the years—
What's time to us? and lo, a city rears
Itself! nay, enter—what's the grave to us?
So, our forlorn acquaintance carry thus
A head! successively sewer, forum, cirque—
Last age that aqueduct was counted work,
And now they tire the artificer upon
Blank alabaster, black obsidion,
—Careful Jove's face be duly fulgurant,
And mother Venus' kiss-creased nipples pant
Back into pristine pulpiness, ere fixed
Above the baths. What difference betwixt
This Rome and ours? Resemblance what between
The scurvy dumb-show and the pageant sheen—
These Romans and our rabble? Rest thy wit
And listen: step by step,—a workman fit
With each, nor too fit,—to one's task, one's time,—
No leaping o'er the petty to the prime,
When just the substituting osier lithe
For bulrushes, and after, wood for withe
To further loam and roughcast work a stage,
Exacts an architect, exacts an age,—
Nor tables of the Mauritanian tree
For men whose maple-log's their luxury,—
And Rome's accomplished! Better (say you) merge
At once all workmen in the demiurge,
All epochs in a life-time, and all tasks
In one: undoubtedly the city basks
I' the day—while those you'd feast there want the knack

Of keeping fresh-chalked gowns from speck and brack,
Distinguish not your peacock from your swan,
Or Mareotic juice from Cœcuban,
Nay sneer . . . enough! 'twas happy to conceive
Rome on a sudden, nor shall fate bereave
Us of that credit: for the rest, her spite
Is an old story—serves us very right
For adding yet another to the dull
List of devices—things proved beautiful
Could they be done, Sordello cannot do.
    He sate upon the terrace, plucked and threw
The powdery aloe-cusps away, saw shift
Rome's walls, and drop arch after arch, and drift
Mist-like afar those pillars of all stripe,
Mounds of all majesty. Thou archetype,
Last of my dreams and loveliest, depart!
    And then a low voice wound into his heart:
Sordello (lower than a Pythoness
Conceding to a Lydian King's distress
The cause of his long error—one mistake
Of her past oracle) Sordello, wake!
Where is the vanity? Why count you, one
The first step with the last step? What is gone
Except that aëry magnificence—
That last step you took first? an evidence
You were . . . no matter. Let those glances fall!
This basis, this beginning step of all,
Which proves you one of us, is this gone too?
Pity to disconcert one versed as you
In fate's ill-nature, but its full extent
Eludes Sordello, even: the veil's rent,
Read the black writing—that collective man
Outstrips the individual! Who began
The greatnesses you know?—ay, your own art
Shall serve us: put the poet's mimes apart—
Close with the poet—closer—what? a dim
Too plain form separates itself from him?
Alcamo's song enmeshes the lulled Isle,
Woven into the echoes left erewhile
Of Nina's, one soft web of song: no more
Turning his name, flower-like o'er and o'er!
An elder poet in the younger's place—
Take Nina's strength—but lose Alcamo's grace?

Each neutralizes each then! gaze your fill;
Search further and the past presents you still
New Ninas, new Alcamos, time's mid-night
Concluding,—better say its evenlight
Of yesterday. You, now, in this respect
Of benefiting people (to reject
The favour of your fearful ignorance
A thousand phantasms eager to advance,
Refer you but to those within your reach)
Were you the first who got, to use plain speech,
The Multitude to be materialized?
That loose eternal unrest—who devised
An apparition i' the midst? the rout
Who checked, the breathless ring who formed about
That sudden flower? Get round at any risk
The gold-rough pointel, silver-blazing disk
O' the lily! Swords across it! Reign thy reign
And serve thy frolic service, Charlemagne!
—The very child of over-joyousness,
Unfeeling thence, strong therefore: Strength by stress
Of Strength comes of a forehead confident,
Two widened eyes expecting heart's content,
A calm as out of just-quelled noise, nor swerves
The ample cheek for doubt, in gracious curves
Abutting on the upthrust nether lip—
He wills, how should he doubt then? Ages slip—
Was it Sordello pried into the work
So far accomplished, and discovering lurk
A company amid the other clans,
Only distinct in priests for castellans
And popes for suzerains (their rule confessed
Its rule, their interest its interest,
Living for sake of living—there an end,
Wrapt in itself, no energy to spend
In making adversaries or allies);
Dived he into its capabilities
And dared create out of that sect a soul
Should turn the multitude, already whole,
To some account? Speak plainer! Is't so sure
God's church lives by a King's investiture?
Look to last step: a staggering—a shock—
What's sand shall be demolished, but the rock
Endures—a column of black fiery dust

Blots heaven—woe, woe, 'tis prematurely thrust
Aside, that step!—the air clears—nought's erased
Of the true outline?   Thus much is firm based—
The other was a scaffold: see you stand
Buttressed upon his mattock Hildebrand
Of the huge brain-mask welded ply o'er ply
As in a forge; it buries either eye
White and extinct, that stupid brow; teeth clenched,
The neck's tight-corded, too, the chin deep-trenched,
As if a cloud enveloped him while fought
Under it all, grim prizers, thought with thought
At dead-lock, agonising he, until
The victor thought leap radiant up, and Will,
The slave with folded arms and drooping lids
They fought for, lean forth flame-like as it bids.
—A root, the crippled mandrake of the earth,
Thwarted and dwarfed and blasted in its birth,
Be certain; fruit of suffering's excess,
Whence feeling, therefore stronger: still by stress
Of strength, work Knowledge! Full three hundred years
For men to wear away in smiles and tears
Between the two that nearly seem to touch,
Observe you: quit one workman and we clutch
Another, letting both their trains go by—
The actors—out of either's policy,
Heinrich, on this hand, Otho, Barbaross,
May carry the Imperial crowns across,
Aix' Iron, Milan's Silver, and Rome's Gold—
As Alexander, Innocent uphold
On that the Papal keys—but, link on link,
Why is it neither chain betrays a chink?
How coalesce the small and great? Alack,
For one thrust forward, fifty such fall back!
The couple there alone help Gregory?
Hark—from the hermit Peter's thin sad cry
At Claremont, yonder to the serf that says
Friedrich's no liege of his while he delays
Getting the Pope's curse off him! The Crusade—
Or trick of breeding strength by other aid
Than strength, is safe: hark—from the wild harangue
Of Vimmercato, to the carroch's clang
Yonder! The League—or trick of turning strength
Against pernicious strength, is safe at length:

Yet hark—from Mantuan Albert's making cease
The fierce ones, to Saint Francis preaching peace
Yonder! God's Truce—or trick to supersede
The use of strength at all, is safe. Indeed
We trench upon the future! Who shall found
Next step, next age—trail plenteous o'er the ground
Vine-like, produced by joy and sorrow, whence
Unfeeling and yet feeling, strongest thence:
Knowledge by stress of Knowledge is it? No—
E'en were Sordello ready to forego
His work for this, 'twere overleaping work
Some one must do before, howe'er it irk:
No end's in sight yet of that second road:
Who means to help must still support the load
Hildebrand lifted—why hast Thou, he groaned,
Imposed, my God, a thing thy Paul had moaned,
Thy Moses failed beneath, on me? and yet
That grandest of the tasks God ever set
On man left much to do: a mighty wrench—
The scaffold falls—but half the pillars blench
Merely, start back again—perchance have been
Taken for buttresses: crash every screen,
Hammer the tenons better, and engage
A gang about your work, for the next age
Or two, of Knowledge, part by Strength and part
By Knowledge! then—Ay, then perchance may start
Sordello on his race—but who'll divulge
Time's secrets? lo, a step's awry, a bulge
To be corrected by a step we thought
Got over long ago—till that is wrought,
No progress! and that scaffold in its turn
Becomes, its service o'er, a thing to spurn.
Meanwhile, your some half-dozen years of life
Longer, dispose you to forego the strife—
Who takes exception? 'Tis Ferrara, mind,
Before us, and Goito's left behind:
As you then were, as half yourself, desist!
—The warrior-part of you may, an it list,
Finding real faulchions difficult to poise,
Fling them afar and taste the cream of joys
By wielding one in fancy,—what is bard
Of you, may spurn the vehicle that marred
Elys so much, and in mere fancy glut

His sense on her free beauties—we have but
To please ourselves for law, and you could please
What then appeared yourself by dreaming these
Rather than doing these: now, fancy's trade
Is ended, mind, nor one half may evade
The other half: our friends are half of you:
Out of a thousand helps, just one or two
Can be accomplished presently—but flinch
From these (as from the faulchion raised an inch,
Elys described a couplet) and make proof
Of fancy,—and while one half lolls aloof
O' the grass, completing Rome to the tip-top—
See if, for that, the other half will stop
A tear, begin a smile: that rabble's woes,
Ludicrous in their patience as they chose
To sit about their town and quietly
Be slaughtered,—the poor reckless soldiery,
With their ignoble rhymes on Richard, how
Polt-foot, sang they, was in a pitfall now,
Cheering each other from the engine-mounts,—
That crippled sprawling idiot who recounts
How, lopt of limbs, he lay, stupid as stone,
Till the pains crept from out him one by one,
And wriggles round the archers on his head
To earn a morsel of their chesnut bread,—
And Cino, always in the self-same place
Weeping; beside that other wretch's case
Eyepits to ear one gangrene since he plied
The engine in his coat of raw sheep's hide
A double watch in the noon sun; and see
Lucchino, beauty, with the favours free,
Trim hacqueton, and sprucely scented hair,
Campaigning it for the first time—cut there
In two already, boy enough to crawl
For latter orpine round the Southern wall,
Tomà, where Richard's kept, because that whore
Marfisa the fool never saw before
Sickened for flowers this wearisomest siege!
Then Tiso's wife—men liked their pretty liege,
Cared for her least of whims once, Berta, wed
A twelvemonth gone, and, now poor Tiso's dead,
Delivering herself of his first child
On that chance heap of wet filth, reconciled

To fifty gazers. (Here a wind below
Made moody music augural of woe
From the pine barrier)—What if, now the scene
Draws to a shutting, if yourself have been
—You, plucking purples in Goito's moss
Like edges of a trabea (not to cross
Your consul-feeling) or dry aloe-shafts
Here at Ferrara—He whom fortune wafts
This very age her best inheritance
Of opportunities? Yet we advance
Upon the last! Since talking is your trade,
There's Salinguerra left you to persuade,
And then—

       No—no—which latest chance secure!
Leapt up and cried Sordello: this made sure
The Past is yet redeemable whose work
Was—help the Guelfs, and I, howe'er it irk,
Thus help! He shook the foolish aloe-haulm
Out of his doublet, paused, proceeded calm
To the appointed presence. The large head
Turned on its socket; And your spokesman, said
The large voice, is Elcorte's happy sprout?
Few such (so finishing a speech no doubt
Addressed to Palma, silent at his side)
Our sober councils have diversified:
Elcorte's son!—but forward as you may,
Our lady's minstrel with so much to say!
The hesitating sunset floated back,
Rosily traversed in a single track
The chamber, from the lattice o'er the girth
Of pines to the huge eagle blacked in earth
Opposite, outlined sudden, spur to crest,
That solid Salinguerra, and caressed
Palma's contour; 'twas Day looped back Night's pall;
Sordello had a chance left spite of all.

And much he made of the convincing speech
He meant should compensate the Past and reach
Through his youth's daybreak of unprofit, quite
To his noon's labour, so proceed till night
At leisure! The contrivances to bind
Taurello body with the Cause and mind,
—Was the consummate rhetoric just that?
Yet most Sordello's argument dropped flat

Through his accustomed fault of breaking yoke,
Disjoining him who felt from him who spoke:
Was 't not a touching incident—so prompt
A rendering the world its just accompt
Once proved its debtor? Who'd suppose before
This proof that he, Goito's God of yore,
At duty's instance could demean himself
So memorably, dwindle to a Guelf?
Be sure, in such delicious flattery steeped,
His inmost self at the out-portion peeped
Thus occupied; then stole a glance at those
Appealed to, curious if her colour rose
Or his lip moved, while he discreetly urged
The need of Lombardy's becoming purged
At soonest of her barons; the poor part
Abandoned thus missing the blood at heart,
Spirit in brain, unseasonably off
Elsewhere! But, though his speech was worthy scoff,
Good-humoured Salinguerra, famed for tact
That way, who, careless of his phrase, ne'er lacked
The right phrase, and harangued Honorius dumb
At his accession, looked as all fell plumb
To purpose and himself took interest
In every point his new instructor pressed
—Left playing with the rescript's white wax seal
To scrutinize Sordello head to heel:
Then means he . . yes, assent sure? Well? Alas,
He said no more than, So it comes to pass
That poesy, sooner than politics,
Makes fade young hair: to think his speech could fix
Taurello!
              Then a flash; he knew the truth:
So fantasies shall break and fritter youth
That he has long ago lost earnestness,
Lost will to work, lost power to express
Even the need of working! Ere the grave
No more occasions now, though he should crave
One such in right of superhuman toil
To do what was undone, repair his spoil,
Alter the Past—nought brings again the chance!
Not that he was to die: he saw askance
Protract the ignominious years beyond
To dream in—time to hope and time despond,

Remember and forget, be sad, rejoice
As saved a trouble, suited to his choice,
—One way or other idle life out, drop
No few smooth verses by the way—for prop
A thyrsus these sad people should, the same,
Pick up, set store by, and, so far from blame,
Plant o'er his hearse convinced his better part
Survived him. Rather tear men out the heart
Of the truth! Sordello muttered, and renewed
His propositions for the Multitude.

But Salinguerra who, the last attack,
Threw himself in his ruffling corslet back
To hear the better, smilingly resumed
Some task; beneath the carroch's warning boomed;
He must decide with Tito; courteously
He turned then, even seeming to agree
With his admonisher—" Assist the Pope,
Extend his domination, fill the scope
Of the Church based on All, by All, for All—
Change Secular to Evangelical "—
Echoing his very sentence: all seemed lost,
When sudden he looked, laughingly almost,
To Palma: This opinion of your friend's
For instance, would it answer Palma's ends?
Best, were it not, turn Guelf, submit our Strength
(Here he drew out his baldric to its length)
To the Pope's Knowledge—letting Richard slip,
Wide to the walls throw ope your gates, equip
Azzo with . . . but no matter! Who'll subscribe
To a trite censure of the minstrel tribe
Henceforward? or pronounce, as Heinrich used,
" Spear-heads for battle, burr-heads for the joust "
—When Constance, for his couplets, would promote
Alcamo from a parti-coloured coat
To holding her lord's stirrup in the wars.
Not that I see where couplet-making jars
With common sense: at Mantua we had borne
This chanted, easier than their most forlorn
Of bull-fights,—that's indisputable!
                                        Brave!
Whom vanity nigh slew, contempt shall save!
All's at an end: a Troubadour suppose
Mankind's to class him with their friends or foes?

A puny uncouth ailing vassal think
The world and him in some especial link?
Abrupt the visionary tether's burst—
What's to reward or what to be amerced
If a poor drudge, solicitous to dream
Deservingly, gets tangled by his theme
So far as to conceit his knack or gift
Or whatsoe'er it be of verse might lift
The globe, a lever like the hand and head
Of—Men of Action, as the Jongleurs said,
—The Great Men, in the people's dialect?
    And not a moment did this scorn affect
Sordello: scorn the poet? They, for once,
Asking " what was," obtained a full response.
Bid Naddo think at Mantua, he had but
To look into his promptuary, put
His hand on a set thought in a set speech:
And was Sordello fitted thus for each
Conjuncture? No wise; since within his soul
Perception brooded unexpressed and whole:
A healthy spirit like a healthy frame
Craves aliment in plenty and, the same,
Changes, assimilates its aliment:
Perceived Sordello, on a truth intent?
Next day no formularies more you saw
Than figs or olives in a sated maw
—'Tis Knowledge, whither such perceptions tend,
They lose themselves in that, means to an end,
The Many Old producing some One New,
A Last unlike the First. If lies are true,
The Caliph Haroun's man of brass receives
A meal, ay, millet grains and lettuce leaves
Together in his stomach rattle loose—
You find them perfect next day to produce
But ne'er expect the man, on strength of that,
Can roll an iron camel-collar flat
Like Haroun's self! I tell you, what was stored
Parcel by parcel through his life, outpoured
That eve, was, for that age, a novel thing:
And round those three the People formed a ring,
Suspended their own vengeance, chose await
The issue of this strife to reinstate
Them in the right of taking it—in fact

He must be proved their lord ere they exact
Amends for that lord's defalcation. Last,
A reason why the phrases flowed so fast
Was in his quite forgetting for the time
Himself in his amazement that his rhyme
Disguised the royalty so much: he there—
They full face to him—and yet unaware
Who was the King and who . . . But if I lay
On thine my spirit and compel obey
His lord—Taurello? Impotent to build
Another Rome, but hardly so unskilled
In what such builder should have been as brook
One shame beyond the charge that he forsook
His function! Set me free that shame I bend
A brow before, suppose new years to spend,
Allow each chance, nor fruitlessly, recur—
Measure thee with the Minstrel, then, demur
At any crown he claims! That I must cede
As 'tis my right to my especial meed—
Confess you fitter help the world than I
Ordained its champion from eternity,
Is much: but to behold you scorn the post
I quit in your behalf—as aught's to boast
Unless you help the world! And while he rung
The changes on this theme, the roof up-sprung,
The sad walls of the presence-chamber died
Into the distance, or, embowering vied
With far-away Goito's vine-frontier;
And crowds of faces (only keeping clear
The rose-light in the midst, his vantage-ground
To fight their battle from) deep clustered round
Sordello, with good wishes no mere breath,
Kind prayers for him no vapour, since, come death,
Come life, he was fresh-sinewed every joint,
Each bone new-marrowed as whom Gods anoint
Though mortal to their rescue: now let sprawl
The snaky volumes hither, Typhon's all
For Hercules to trample—good report
From Salinguerra's only to extort?
So was I (closed he his inculcating
A poet must be earth's essential king)
So was I, royal so, and if I fail
'Tis not the royalty ye witness quail

But one deposed who, caring not exert
Its proper essence, trifled malapert
With accidents instead—good things assigned
The herald of a better thing behind—
And, worthy through display of these, put forth
Never the inmost all-surpassing worth
That constitutes him King precisely since
As yet no other creature may evince
Its like: the power he took most pride to test,
Whereby all forms of life had been professed
At pleasure, forms already on the earth,
Was but a means to power whose novel birth
Should, in its novelty, be kingship's proof—
Now, whether he came near or kept aloof,
Those forms unalterable first to last
Proved him her copy, not the protoplast
Of Nature: what would come of being free
By action to exhibit tree for tree,
Bird, beast for beast and bird, or prove earth bore
A veritable man or woman more?
Means to an end, such proofs; and what the end?
Your essence, whatsoe'er it be, extend—
Never contract! Already you include
The multitude; now let the multitude
Include yourself, and the result is new;
Themselves before, the multitude turn you;
This were to live and move and have (in them)
Your being, and secure a diadem
That's to transmit (because no cycle yearns
Beyond itself, but on itself returns)
When the full sphere in wane, the world o'erlaid
Long since with you, shall have in turn obeyed
Some orb still prouder, some displayer, still
More potent than the last, of human Will,
And some new King depose the old. Of such
Am I—whom pride of this elates too much?
Safe, rather say, mid troops of peers again;
I, with my words, hailed brother of the train
Once deeds sufficed: for, let the world roll back,
Who fails, through deeds diverse so e'er, re-track
My purpose still, my task? A teeming crust—
Air, flame, earth, wave at conflict—see! Needs must
Emerge some Calm embodied these refer

(Saturn—no yellow-bearded Jupiter!)
The brawl to; some existence like a pact
And protest against Chaos, some first fact
I' the faint of Time . . . my deep of life, I know,
Is unavailing e'en to poorly show
(For here the Chief immeasurably yawned)
Deeds in their due gradation till Song dawned—
The fullest effluence of the finest mind
All in degree, no way diverse in kind
From those about us, minds which, more or less,
Lofty or low, in moving seek impress
Themselves on somewhat; but one mind has climbed
Step after step, by just ascent sublimed:
Thought is the soul of act, and stage by stage,
Is soul from body still to disengage
As tending to a freedom which rejects
Such help and incorporeally affects
The world, producing deeds but not by deeds,
Swaying, in others, frames itself exceeds,
Assigning them the simpler tasks it used
As patiently perform till Song produced
Acts, by thoughts only, for the mind: divest
Mind of e'en Thought, and, lo, God's unexpressed
Will dawns above us. But so much to win
Ere that! A lesser round of steps within
The last. About me, faces! and they flock,
The earnest faces. What shall I unlock
By song? behold me prompt, whate'er it be,
To minister: how much can mortals see
Of Life? No more? I covet the first task
And marshal you Life's elemental Masque
Of men, on evil or on good lay stress,
This light, this shade make prominent, suppress
All ordinary hues that softening blend
Such natures with the level: apprehend
Which evil is, which good, if I allot
Your Hell, the Purgatory, Heaven ye wot,
To those you doubt concerning: I enwomb
Some wretched Friedrich with his red-hot tomb,
Some dubious spirit, Lombard Agilulph
With the black chastening river I engulph;
Some unapproached Matilda I enshrine
With languors of the planet of decline—

These fail to recognise, to arbitrate
Between henceforth, to rightly estimate
Thus marshalled in the Masque! Myself, the while,
As one of you, am witness, shrink or smile
At my own showing! Next age—what's to do?
The men and women stationed hitherto
Will I unstation, good and bad, conduct
Each nature to its farthest or obstruct
At soonest in the world: Light, thwarted, breaks
A limpid purity to rainbow flakes,
Or Shadow, helped, freezes to gloom: behold
How such, with fit assistance to unfold,
Or obstacles to crush them, disengage
Their forms, love, hate, hope, fear, peace make, war wage,
In presence of you all! Myself implied
Superior now, as, by the platform's side,
Bidding them do and suffer to content
The world . . . no—that I wait not—circumvent
A few it has contented, and to these
Offer unveil the last of mysteries
I boast! Man's life shall have yet freer play:
Once more I cast external things away
And Natures, varied now, so decompose
That . . . but enough! Why fancy how I rose,
Or rather you advanced since evermore
Yourselves effect what I was fain before
Effect, what I supplied yourselves suggest,
What I leave bare yourselves can now invest?
How we attained to talk as brothers talk,
In half-words, call things by half-names, no balk
From discontinuing old aids—To-day
Takes in account the work of Yesterday—
Has not the world a Past now, its adept
Consults ere he dispense with or accept
New aids? a single touch more may enhance,
A touch less turn to insignificance
Those structures' symmetry the Past has strewed
Your world with, once so bare: leave the mere rude
Explicit details, 'tis but brother's speech
We need, speech where an accent's change gives each
The other's soul—no speech to understand
By former audience—need was then expand,
Expatiate—hardly were they brothers! true—

Nor I lament my less remove from you,
Nor reconstruct what stands already: ends
Accomplished turn to means: my art intends
New structure from the ancient: as they changed
The spoils of every clime at Venice, ranged
The horned and snouted Lybian God, upright
As in his desert, by some simple bright
Clay cinerary pitcher—Thebes as Rome,
Athens as Byzant rifled, till their Dome
From Earth's reputed consummations razed
A seal the all-transmuting Triad blazed
Above. Ah, whose that fortune? ne'ertheless
E'en he must stoop contented to express
No tithe of what's to say—the vehicle
Never sufficient—but his work is still
For faces like the faces that select
The single service I am bound effect
Nor murmur, bid me, still as poet, bow
Taurello to the Guelf cause, disallow
The Kaiser's coming—which with heart, soul, strength,
I labour for, this eve, who feel at length
My past career's outrageous vanity
And would (as vain amends) die, even die
Now I first estimate the boon of life,
So death might bow Taurello—sure this strife
Is the last strife—the People my support.
  My poor Sordello! what may we extort
By this, I wonder? Palma's lighted eyes
Turned to Taurello who, as past surprise,
Began, You love him—what you'd say at large
If I say briefly? First your father's charge
To me, his friend, peruse: I guessed indeed
You were no stranger to the course decreed
Us both: I leave his children to the saints:
As for a certain project, he acquaints
The Pope with that, and offers him the best
Of your possessions to permit the rest
Go peaceably—to Ecelin, a stripe
Of soil the cursed Vicentines will gripe,
—To Alberic, a patch the Trevisan
Clutches already; extricate who can
Treville, Villarazzi, Puissolo,
Cartiglione, Loria—all go,

And with them go my hopes! 'Tis lost, then! Lost
This eve, our crisis, and some pains it cost
Procuring; thirty years—as good I'd spent
Like our admonisher! But each his bent
Pursues—no question, one might live absurd
Oneself this while, by deed as he by word,
Persisting to obtrude an influence where
'Tis made account of much as . . . nay, you fare
With twice the fortune, youngster—I submit,
Happy to parallel my waste of wit
With the renowned Sordello's—you decide
A course for me—Romano may abide
Romano,—Bacchus! Who'd suppose the dearth
Of Ecelins and Alberics on earth?
Say there's a thing in prospect, must disgrace
Betide competitors? An obscure place
Suits me—there wants youth, bustle, one to stalk
And attitudinize—some fight, more talk,
Most flaunting badges—'twere not hard make clear
Since Friedrich's very purposes lie here
—Here—pity they are like to lie! For me,
Whose station's fixed unceremoniously
Long since, small use contesting; I am but
The liegeman, you are born the lieges—shut
That gentle mouth now!—or resume your kin
In your sweet self; Palma were Ecelin
For me and welcome! Could that neck endure
This bauble for a cumbrous garniture
You should . . . or might one bear it for you? Stay—
I have not been so flattered many a day
As by your pale friend—Bacchus! The least help
Would lick the hind's fawn to a lion's whelp—
His neck is broad enough—a ready tongue
Beside—too writhled—but, the main thing, young—
I could . . . why look ye!

                         And the badge was thrown
Across Sordello's neck: this badge alone
Makes you Romano's Head—the Lombard's Curb
Turns on your neck which would, on mine, disturb
My pauldron, said Taurello. A mad act,
Nor dreamed about a moment since—in fact
Not when his sportive arm rose for the nonce—
But he had dallied overmuch, this once,

With power: the thing was done, and he, aware
The thing was done, proceeded to declare
(So like a nature made to serve, excel
In serving, only feel by service well)
That he should make him all he said and more:
As good a scheme as any: what's to pore
At in my face? he asked—ponder instead
This piece of news; you are Romano's Head—
One cannot slacken pace so near the goal,
Suffer my Azzo to escape heart-whole
This time! For you there's Palma to espouse—
For me, one crowning trouble ere I house
Like my compeer.
                        On which ensued a strange
And solemn visitation—mighty change
O'er every one of them—each looked on each—
Up in the midst a truth grew, without speech.
And when the giddiness sank and the haze
Subsided, they were sitting, no amaze,
Sordello with the baldric on, his sire
Silent though his proportions seemed aspire
Momently; and, interpreting the thrill
Nigh at its ebb, Palma you found was still
Relating somewhat Adelaide confessed
A year ago, while dying on her breast,
Of a contrivance that Vicenza night,
Her Ecelin had birth: their convoy's flight,
Cut off a moment, coiled inside the flame
That wallowed like a dragon at his game
The toppling city through—San Biagio rocks!
And wounded lies in her delicious locks
Retrude, the frail mother, on her face,
None of her wasted, just in one embrace
Covering her child: when, as they lifted her,
Cleaving the tumult, mighty, mightier
And mightiest Taurello's cry outbroke,
Leapt like a tongue of fire that cleaves the smoke,
Midmost to cheer his Mantuans onward—drown
His colleague's clamour, Ecelin's up, down
The disarray: failed Adelaide see then
Who was the natural Chief, the Man of Men?
Outstripping time her Ecelin burst swathe,
Stood up with haggard eyes beyond the scathe

From wandering after his heritage
Lost once and lost for aye—what could engage
That deprecating glance? A new Shape leant
On a familiar Shape—gloatingly bent
O'er his discomfiture; 'mid wreaths it wore,
Still one outflamed the rest—her child's before
'Twas Salinguerra's for his child: scorn, hate,
Rage, startled her from Ecelin—too late!
A moment's work, and rival's foot had spurned
Never that brow to earth! Ere sense returned—
The act conceived, adventured, and complete,
They stole away towards an obscure retreat
Mother and child—Retrude's self not slain
(Nor even here Taurello moved) though pain
Was fled; and what assured them most 'twas fled,
All pain, was, if you raised the pale hushed head
'Twould turn this way and that, waver awhile,
And only settle into its old smile
(Graceful as the disquieted water-flag
Steadying itself, remarked they, in the quag
On either side their path) when suffered look
Downward: they marched: no sign of life once shook
The company's close litter of crossed spears
Till, as they reached Goito, a few tears
Slipt in the sunset from her long black lash,
And she was gone. So far the action rash—
No crime. They laid Retrude in the font
Taurello's very gift, her child was wont
To sit beneath—constant as eve he came
To sit by its attendant girls the same
As one of them. For Palma, she would blend
With this magnific spirit to the end
That ruled her first—but scarcely had she dared
To disobey the Adelaide who scared
Her into vowing never to disclose
A secret to her husband which so froze
His blood at half recital she contrived
To hide from him Taurello's infant lived
Lest, by revealing that, himself should mar
Romano's fortunes: and, a crime so far,
Palma received that action: she was told
Of Salinguerra's nature, and his cold
Calm acquiescence in his lot! But free

Impart the secret to Romano, she
Engaged to repossess Sordello of
His heritage, and hers, and that way doff
The mask, but after years, long years!—while now
Was not Romano's sign-mark on that brow?

  Across Taurello's heart his arms were locked:
And 'twas, when speak he did, as if he mocked
The minstrel, who had not to move, he said,
Nor stir—should Fate defraud him of a shred
Of this son's infancy? much less of youth
(Laughingly all this) which to aid, in truth,
Himself, reserved on purpose, had not grown
Old, not too old—'twas better keep alone
Till now, and never idly meet till now:
—Then, in the same breath, told Sordello how
The intimations of this eve's event
Were futile—Friedrich means advance to Trent,
Thence to Verona, then to Rome—there stop—
Tumble the Church down, institute a-top
The Alps a Prefecture of Lombardy:
—That's now—no prophesying what may be
Anon, beneath a monarch of the clime,
Native of Gesi, passing his youth's prime
At Naples. Tito bids my choice decide
On whom . . .

                    Embrace him, madman! Palma cried
Who through the laugh saw sweatdrops burst apace
And his lips' blanching: he did not embrace
Sordello, but he laid Sordello's hand
On his own eyes, mouth, forehead.

                                    Understand,
This while Sordello was becoming flushed
Out of his whiteness; thoughts rushed, fancies rushed;
He pressed his hand upon his head and signed
Both should forbear him. Nay, the best's behind!
Taurello laughed—not quite with the same laugh:
The truth is, thus you scatter, ay, like chaff
The Guelfs a despicable monk recoils
From—nor expect a fickle Kaiser spoils
Our triumph!—Friedrich? Think you I intend
Friedrich shall reap the fruits of blood I spend
And brain I waste? Think you the people clap
Their hands at my out-hewing this wild gap

For any Friedrich to fill up? 'Tis mine—
That's yours: I tell you towards some such design
Have I worked blindly, yes, and idly, yes,
And for another, yes—but worked no less
With instinct at my heart: I else had swerved,
While now—look round! My cunning has preserved
Samminiato—that's a central place
Secures us Florence, boy, in Pisa's case
By land as she by sea; with Pisa ours,
And Florence, and Pistoia, one devours
The land at leisure! Gloriously dispersed—
Brescia, observe, Milan, Piacenza first
That flanked us (ah, you know not!) in the March;
On these we pile, as keystone of our arch,
Romagna and Bologna, whose first span
Covered the Trentine and the Valsugan;
Sofia's Egna by Bolgiano's sure . . .
So he proceeded. Half of all this pure
Delusion, doubtless, nor the rest too true,
But what was undone he felt sure to do
As ring by ring he wrung off, flung away
The pauldron-rings to give his sword-arm play—
Need of the sword now! That would soon adjust
Aught wrong at present; to the sword intrust
Sordello's whiteness, undersize: 'twas plain
He hardly rendered right to his own brain—
Like a brave hound men educate to pride
Himself on speed or scent nor aught beside,
As though he could not, gift by gift, match men
Palma had listened patiently: but when
'Twas time expostulate, attempt withdraw
Taurello from his child, she, without awe
Took off his iron arms from, one by one,
Sordello's shrinking shoulders and, that done,
Made him avert his visage and relieve
Sordello (you might see his corslet heave
The while) who, loose, rose—tried to speak—then sank:
They left him in the chamber—all was blank.

   And even reeling down the castle-stair
Taurello kept up, as though unaware
Palma was guide to him, the old device
—Something of Milan—how we muster thrice
The Torriani's strength there—all along

Our own Visconti cowed them—thus the song
Continued even while she bade him stoop,
Thrid somehow, by some glimpse of arrow-loop,
The turnings to the gallery below,
Where he stopped short as Palma let him go.
When he had sate in silence long enough
Splintering the stone bench, braving a rebuff
She stopt the truncheon; only to commence
One of Sordello's poems, a pretence
For speaking, some poor rhyme of Elys' hair
And head that's sharp and perfect like a pear,
So smooth and close are laid the few fine locks
Stained like pale honey oozed from topmost rocks
Sun-blanched the livelong Summer—from his worst
Performance, the Goito, as his first:
And that at end, conceiving from the brow
And open mouth no silence would serve now,
Went on to say the whole world loved that man
And, for that matter, thought his face, tho' wan,
Eclipsed the Count's—he sucking in each phrase
As if an angel spoke: the foolish praise
Ended, he drew her on his mailed knees, made
Her face a frame-work with his hands, a shade,
A crown, an aureole—there must she remain
(Her little mouth compressed with smiling pain
As in his gloves she felt her tresses twitch)
To get the best look at, in fittest niche
Dispose his saint; that done, he kissed her brow—
Lauded her father for his treason now,
He told her, only how could one suspect
The wit in him? whose clansman, recollect,
Was ever Salinguerra—she, the same,
Romano and his lady—so might claim
To know all, as she should—and thus begun
Schemes with a vengeance, schemes on schemes, not one
Fit to be told that foolish boy, he said,
But only let Sordello Palma wed,
—Then!
              'Twas a dim long narrow place at best:
Midway a sole grate showed the fiery West
As shows its corpse the world's end some split tomb—
A gloom, a rift of fire, another gloom
Faced Palma—but at length Taurello set

Her free; the grating held one ragged jet
Of fierce gold fire: he lifted her within
The hollow underneath—how else begin
Fate's second marvellous cycle, else renew
The ages than with Palma plain in view?
Then paced the passage, hands clenched, head erect,
Pursuing his discourse; a grand unchecked
Monotony made out from his quick talk
And the recurring noises of his walk;
—Somewhat too much like the o'ercharged assent
Of two resolved friends in one danger blent,
Who hearten each the other against heart—
Boasting there's nought to care for, when, apart
The boaster, all's to care for: he, beside
Some shape not visible, in power and pride
Approached, out of the dark, ginglingly near,
Nearer, passed close in the broad light, his ear
Crimson, eyeballs suffused, temples full-fraught,
Just a snatch of the rapid speech you caught,
And on he strode into the opposite dark
Till presently the harsh heel's turn, a spark
I' the stone, and whirl of some loose embossed thong
That crashed against the angle aye so long
After the last, punctual to an amount
Of mailed great paces you could not but count,
Prepared you for the pacing back again:
And by the snatches might you ascertain
That, Friedrich's Prefecture surmounted, left
By this alone in Italy, they cleft
Asunder, crushed together, at command
Of none, were free to break up Hildebrand,
Rebuild, he and Sordello, Charlemagne—
But garnished, Strength with Knowledge, if we deign
Accept that compromise and stoop to give
Rome law, the Cæsars' Representative.
—Enough that the illimitable flood
Of triumphs after triumphs, understood
In its faint reflux (you shall hear) sufficed
Young Ecelin for appanage, enticed
Him still, these long since quiet in their graves,
He found 'twas looked for that a long life's braves
Should somehow be made good—so, weak and worn,
Must stagger up at Milan, one grey morn

Of the To-Come, to fight his latest fight.
And Salinguerra's prophecy at height—
He voluble with a raised arm and stiff,
A blaring voice, a blazing eye, as if
He had our very Italy to keep
Or cast away, or gather in a heap
To garrison the better—ay, his word
Was, "run the cucumber into a gourd,
Drive Trent upon Apulia "—at their pitch
Who spied the continents and islands which
Grew sickles, mulberry leaflets in the map—
(Strange that three such confessions so should hap
To Palma Dante spoke with in the clear
Amorous silence of the Swooning-sphere.
Cunizza, as he called her! Never ask
Of Palma more! She sate, knowing her task
Was done, the labour of it—for success
Concerned not Palma, passion's votaress)
Triumph at height, I say, Sordello crowned—
Above the passage suddenly a sound
Stops speech, stops walk: back shrinks Taurello, bids
With large involuntary asking lids
Palma interpret. 'Tis his own foot-stamp—
Your hand! His summons! Nay, this idle damp
Befits not. Out they two reeled dizzily:
" Visconti's strong at Milan," resumed he
In the old somewhat insignificant way
(Was Palma wont years afterward to say)
As though the spirit's flight sustained thus far
Dropped at that very instant. Gone they are—
Palma, Taurello; Eglamor anon,
Ecelin, Alberic . . . ah, Naddo's gone!
—Labours this moonrise what the Master meant:
" Is Squarcialupo speckled?—purulent
I'd say, but when was Providence put out?
He carries somehow handily about
His spite nor fouls himself! " Goito's vines
Stand like a cheat detected—stark rough lines
The moon breaks through, a grey mean scale against
The vault where, this eve's Maiden, thou remains't
Like some fresh martyr, eyes fixed—who can tell?
As Heaven, now all's at end, did not so well
Spite of the faith and victory, to leave

Its virgin quite to death in the lone eve:
While the persisting hermit-bee . . . ha! wait
No longer—these in compass, forward fate!

BOOK THE SIXTH

THE thought of Eglamor's least like a thought,
And yet a false one, was, Man shrinks to nought
If matched with symbols of immensity—
Must quail, forsooth, before a quiet sky
Or sea, too little for their quietude:
And, truly, somewhat in Sordello's mood
Confirmed its speciousness while evening sank
Down the near terrace to the further bank,
And only one spot left out of the night
Glimmered upon the river opposite—
A breadth of watery heaven like a bay,
A sky-line space of water, ray for ray
And star for star, one richness where they mixed
As this and that wing of an angel, fixed,
Tumultuary splendors folded in
To die: nor turned he till Ferrara's din
(Say, the monotonous speech from a man's lip
Who lets some first and eager purpose slip
In a new fancy's birth; the speech keeps on
Though elsewhere its informing soul be gone)
Aroused him—surely offered succour; fate
Paused with this eve; ere she precipitate
Herself . . . put off strange after-thoughts awhile,
That voice, those large hands, that portentous smile . . .
What help to pierce the Future as the Past
Lay in the plaining city?
                              And at last
The main discovery and prime concern,
All that just now imported him to learn,
His truth, like yonder slow moon to complete
Heaven, rose again, and naked at his feet
Lighted his old life's every shift and change,
Effort with counter-effort; nor the range
Of each looked wrong except wherein it checked

Some other—which of these could he suspect
Prying into them by the sudden blaze?
The real way seemed made up of all the ways—
Mood after mood of the one mind in him;
Tokens of the existence, bright or dim,
Of a transcendent all-embracing sense
Demanding only outward influence,
A soul, in Palma's phrase, above his soul,
Power to uplift his power, such moon's control,
Over the sea-depths, and their mass had swept
Onward from the beginning and still kept
Its course; but years and years the sky above
Held none, and so, untasked of any love,
His sensitiveness idled, now amort,
Alive now, and to sullenness or sport
Given wholly up, disposed itself anew
At every passing instigation, grew
And dwindled at caprice, in foam-showers spilt,
Wedge-like insisting, quivered now a gilt
Shield in the sunshine, now a blinding race
Of whitest ripples o'er the reef—found place
For myriad charms; not gathered up and, hurled
Right from its heart, encompassing the world.
So had Sordello been, by consequence,
Without a function: others made pretence
To strengths not half his own, yet had some core
Within, submitted to some moon, before
It still, superior still whate'er its force,
Were able therefore to fulfil a course
Nor missed Life's crown, authentic attribute—
To each who lives must be a certain fruit
Of having lived in his degree, a stage
Earlier or later in men's pilgrimage,
To stop at; and to which those spirits tend
Who, still discovering beauty without end,
Amass the scintillations for one star
—Something unlike them, self-sustained, afar,
And meanwhile nurse the dream of being blest
By winning it to notice and invest
Their souls with alien glory some one day
Whene'er the nucleus, gathering shape alway,
Round to the perfect circle—soon or late
According as themselves are formed to wait;

Whether 'tis human beauty will suffice
—The yellow hair and the luxurious eyes,
Or human intellect seem best, or each
Combine in some ideal form past reach
On earth, or else some shade of these, some aim,
Some love, hate even, take their place the same
That may be served—all this they do not lose,
Waiting for death to live, nor idly choose
What Hell shall be—a progress thus pursued
Through all existence, still above the food
That's offered them, still towering beyond
The widened range in virtue of their bond
Of sovereignty: not that a Palma's Love
A Salinguerra's Hate would equal prove
To swaying all Sordello: wherefore doubt,
Love meet for such a Strength, some Moon's without
To match his Sea?—fear, Good so manifest,
Only the Best breaks faith?—but that the Best
Somehow eludes us ever, still might be
And is not: crave you gems? where's penury
Of their material round us? pliant earth,
The plastic flame—what balks the Mage his birth
—Jacynth in balls, or lodestone by the block?
Flinders enrich the strand and veins the rock—
No more! Ask creatures? Life in tempest, Thought
Clothes the keen hill-top, mid-day woods are fraught
With fervors . . . ah, these forms are well enough—
But we had hoped, encouraged by the stuff
Profuse at Nature's pleasure, Men beyond
These Men! and thus, perchance, are over-fond
In arguing, from Good the Best, from force
Divided—force combined, an ocean's course
From this our sea whose mere intestine pants
Had seemed at times sufficient to our wants.
—External Power? If none be adequate
And he have been ordained (a prouder fate)
A law to his own sphere? the need remove
All incompleteness, be that law that love?
Nay, really such be others' laws, though veiled
In mercy to each vision that had failed
If unassisted by its Want, for lure,
Embodied? stronger vision could endure
The simple want—no bauble for a truth!

The People were himself; and by the ruth
At their condition was he less impelled
Alter the discrepancy he beheld
Than if, from the sound Whole, a sickly Part
Subtracted were transformed, decked out with art,
Then palmed on him as alien woe—the Guelf
To succour, proud that he forsook himself?
No: All's himself—all service, therefore, rates
Alike, nor serving one part, immolates
The rest: but all in time! That lance of yours
Makes havoc soon with Malek and his Moors,
That buckler's lined with many a Giant's beard
Ere long, Porphyrio, be the lance but reared,
The buckler wielded handsomely as now;
But view your escort, bear in mind your vow,
Count the pale tracts of sand to pass ere that,
And, if you hope we struggle through this flat,
Put lance and buckler up—next half-month lacks
A sturdy exercise of mace or axe
To cleave this dismal brake of prickly-pear
That bristling holds Cydippe by the hair,
Lames barefoot Agathon.

                Oh, People, urge
Your claims!—for thus he ventured to the verge
Push a vain mummery which perchance distrust
Of his fast-slipping resolution thrust
No less: accordingly the Crowd—as yet
He had inconsciously contrived forget
To dwell upon the points . . . one might assuage
The signal horrors sooner than engage
With a dim vulgar vast unobvious grief
Not to be fancied off, obtain relief
In brilliant fits, cured by a happy quirk,
But by dim vulgar vast unobvious work
To correspond—however, forth they stood:
And now content thy stronger vision, brood
On thy bare want: the grave stript turf by turf,
Study the corpse-face thro' the taint-worms' scurf!

  Down sank the People's Then; uprose their Now.
These sad ones render service to! And how
Piteously little must that service prove
—Had surely proved in any case! for move
Each other obstacle away, let youth

Had been aware it had surprised a Truth
'Twere service to impart—can Truth be seized,
Settled forthwith, and of the captive eased
Its captor look around, since this alit
So happily, no gesture luring it,
The earnest of a flock to follow? Vain,
Most vain! a life's to spend ere this he chain,
To the poor crowd's complacence; ere the crowd
Pronounce it captured he descries a cloud
Its kin of twice the plumage—he, in turn,
If he shall live as many lives, may learn
Secure—not otherwise. Then Mantua called
Back to his mind how certain bards were thralled
—Buds blasted, but of breaths more like perfumes
Than Naddo's staring nosegay's carrion blooms
Could boast—some rose that burnt heart out in sweets,
A spendthrift in the Spring, no Summer greets—
Some Dularete, drunk with truths and wine,
Grown bestial dreaming how become divine.
Yet to surmount this obstacle, commence
With the commencement, merits crowning! Hence
Must Truth be casual Truth, elicited
In sparks so mean, at intervals dispread
So rarely, that 'tis like at no one time
Of the world's story has not Truth, the prime
Of Truth, the very Truth which loosed had hurled
Its course aright, been really in the world
Content the while with some mean spark by dint
Of some chance-blow, the solitary hint
Of buried fire, which, rip its breast, would stream
Sky-ward!
   Sordello's miserable gleam
Was looked for at the moment: he would dash
This badge to earth and all it brought, abash
Taurello thus, perhaps persuade him wrest
The Kaiser from his purpose; would attest
His constancy in any case. Before
He dashes it, however, think once more!
For, was that little truly service? Ay—
I' the end, no doubt; but meantime? Plain you spy
Its ultimate Effect, but many flaws
Of vision blur each intervening Cause;
Were the day's fraction clear as the life's sum

Of service, Now as filled as the To-come
With evidence of good—nor too minute
A share to vie with evil! How dispute
The Guelfs were fitliest maintain in rule?
That made the life's work: not so easy school
Your day's work—say, on natures circumstanced
So variously, which yet, as each advanced
Or might impede that Guelf rule, it behoved
You, for the Then's sake, hate what Now you loved,
Love what you hated; nor if one man bore
Brand upon temples while his fellow wore
The aureole, would it task us to decide—
But portioned duly out, the Future vied
Never with the unparcelled Present! Smite
Or spare so much on warrant all so slight?
The Present's complete sympathies to break,
Aversions bear with, for a Future's sake
So feeble? Tito ruined through one speck,
The Legate saved by his sole lightish fleck?
This were work, true—but work performed at cost
Of other work—aught gained here, elsewhere lost—
For a new segment spoil an orb half-done—
Rise with the People one step, and sink . . . one?
Would it were one step—less than the whole face—
Of things our novel duty bids erase!
Harms are to vanquish; what? the Prophet saith,
The Minstrel singeth vainly then? Old faith,
Old courage, born of the surrounding harms,
Were not, from highest to the lowest, charms?
Oh, flame persists, but is not glare as staunch?
Where the salt marshes stagnate, crystals branch—
Blood dries to crimson—Evil's beautified
In every shape! But Beauty thrust aside
You banish Evil: wherefore? After all
Is Evil our result less natural
Than Good? For overlook the Season's strife
With tree and flower—the hideous animal life,
Of which who seeks shall find a grinning taunt
For his solution, must endure the vaunt
Of Nature's angel, as a child that knows
Himself befooled, unable to propose
Aught better than the fooling—and but care
For Men, the varied People then and there,

Of which 'tis easy saying Good and Ill
Claim him alike! Whence rose the claim but still
From Ill, the fruit of Ill—what else could knit
Him theirs but Sorrow? Any free from it
Were also free from him! A happiness
Could be distinguished in this morning's press
Of miseries—the fool's who passed a gibe
On one, said he, so wedded to his tribe
He carries green and yellow tokens in
His very face that he's a Ghibellin—
Much hold on him that fool obtained! Nay mount
Yet higher; and upon Men's own account
Must Evil stay: for what is Joy? To heave
Up one obstruction more, and common leave
What was peculiar—by this act destroy
Itself; a partial death is every joy;
The sensible escape, enfranchisement
Of a sphere's essence: once the vexed—content,
The cramped—at large, the growing circle—round,
All's to begin again—some novel bound
To break, some new enlargement's to entreat,
The sphere though larger is not more complete.
Now for Mankind's experience: who alone
Might style the unobstructed world his own?
Whom palled Goito with its perfect things?
Sordello's self; whereas for Mankind springs
Salvation—hindrances are interposed
For them, not all Life's view at once disclosed
To creatures sudden on its summit left
With Heaven above and yet of wings bereft—
But lower laid, as at the mountain's foot
Where, range on range, the girdling forests shoot
Between the prospect and the throngs who scale
Earnestly ever, piercing veil by veil,
Confirmed with each discovery; in their soul
The Whole they seek by Parts—but, found that Whole,
Could they revert? Oh, testify! The space
Of time we judge so meagre to embrace
The Parts, were more than plenty, once attained
The Whole, to quite exhaust it: for nought's gained
But leave to look—not leave to do: Beneath
Soon sates the looker—look Above, then! Death
Tempts ere a tithe of Life be tasted. Live

First, and die soon enough, Sordello! Give
Body and spirit the bare right they claim
To pasture thee on a voluptuous shame
That thou, a pageant-city's denizen,
Art neither vilely lodged midst Lombard men—
Canst force joy out of sorrow, seem to truck
Thine attributes away for sordid muck,
Yet manage from that very muck educe
Gold; then subject, nor scruple, to thy cruce
The world's discardings; think, if ingots pay
Such pains, the clods that yielded them are clay
To all save thee, and clay remain though quenched
Thy purging-fire; who's robbed then? Would I wrenched
An ample treasure forth!—As 'tis, why crave
A share that ruins me and will not save
Yourselves?—imperiously command I quit
The course that makes my joy nor will remit
Your woe? Would all arrive at joy? Reverse
The order (time instructs you) nor coerce
Each unit till, some predetermined mode,
The total be emancipate; our road
Is one, our times of travel many; thwart
No enterprising soul's precocious start
Before the general march; if slow or fast
All straggle up to the same point at last,
Why grudge my having gained a month ago
The brakes at balm-shed, asphodels in blow,
While you were landlocked? Speed your Then, but how
This badge would suffer me improve my Now!

His time of action for, against, or with
Our world (I labour to extract the pith
Of this and more) grew up, that even-tide,
Gigantic with its power of joy beside
The world's eternity of impotence
To profit though at all his joy's expense.
Make nothing of that time because so brief?
Rather make more—instead of joy take grief
Before its novelty have time subside;
No time for the late savour—leave untried
Virtue, the creaming honey wine, quick squeeze
Vice like a biting spirit from the lees
Of life—together let wrath, hatred, lust,
All tyrannies in every shade be thrust

Upon this Now, which time may reason out
As mischiefs, far from benefits, no doubt—
But long ere then Sordello will have slipt
Away—you teach him at Goito's crypt
There's a blank issue to that fiery thrill!
Stirring, the Few cope with the Many, still:
So much of dust as, quiet, makes a mass
Unable to produce three tufts of grass,
Shall, troubled by the whirlwind, render void
The whole calm glebe's endeavour: be employed
And e'en though somewhat smarts the Crowd for this,
Contributes each his pang to make up bliss,
'Tis but one pang—one blood-drop to the bowl
Which brimful tempts the sluggish asp uncowl
So quick, stains ruddily the dull red cape,
And, kindling orbs dull as the unripe grape
Before, avails forthwith to disentrance
The mischief—soon to lead a mystic dance
Among you! Nay, who sits alone in Rome?
Have those great hands indeed hewn out a home
For me—compelled to live? Oh Life, life-breath,
Life-blood,—ere sleep be travail, life ere death!
This life to feed my soul, direct, oblique,
But always feeding! Hindrances? They pique—
Helps? such . . . but wherefore say my soul o'ertops
All height—than every depth profounder drops?
Enough that I can live, and would live! Wait
For some transcendent life reserved by Fate
To follow this? Oh, never! Fate I trust
The same my soul to; for, as who flings dust
Perchance—so facile was the deed, she chequed
The void with these materials to affect
That soul diversely—these consigned anew
To nought by death, why marvel if she threw
A second and superber spectacle
Before it? What may serve for sun—what still
Wander a moon above me—what else wind
About me like the pleasures left behind?
And how shall some new flesh that is not flesh
Cling to me? what's new laughter—soothes the fresh
Sleep like sleep? Fate's exhaustless for my sake
In brave resource, but whether bids she slake
My thirst at this first rivulet or count

No draught worth lip save from the rocky fount
Above i' the clouds, while here she's provident
Of (taste) loquacious pearl the soft tree-tent
Guards, with its face of reate and sedge, nor fail
The silver globules and gold-sparkling grail
At bottom—Oh, 'twere too absurd to slight
For the hereafter the to-day's delight!
Quench thirst at this, then seek next well-spring—wear
Home-lilies ere strange lotus in my hair!
Here is the Crowd, whom I with freest heart
Offer to serve, contented for my part
To give this life up once for all, but grant
I really serve; if otherwise, why want
Aught further of me? Life they cannot chuse
But set aside—wherefore should I refuse
The gift? I take it—I, for one, engage
Never to falter through the pilgrimage—
Or end it howling that the stock or stone
Were enviable, truly: I, for one,
Will praise the world you style mere anteroom
To the true palace—but shall I assume
—My foot the courtly gait, my tongue the trope,
My eye the glance, before the doors fly ope
One moment? What—with guarders row on row,
Gay swarms of varletry that come and go,
Pages to dice with, waiting-girls unlace
The plackets of, pert claimants help displace,
Heart-heavy suitors get a rank for; laugh
At yon sleek parasite, break his own staff
Cross Beetle-brows the Usher's shoulder; why—
Admitted to the presence by and bye,
Should thought of these recurring make me grieve
Among new sights I reach, old sights I leave?
—Cool citrine-crystals, fierce pyropus-stone—
Bare floor-work too!—But did I let alone
That black-eyed peasant in the vestibule
Once and for ever?—Floor-work? No such fool!
Rather, were Heaven to forestall Earth, I'd say
Must I be blessed or you? Then my own way
Bless me—a firmer arm, a fleeter foot,
I'll thank you, but to no mad wings transmute
These limbs of mine—our greensward is too soft;
Nor camp I on the thunder-cloud aloft—

We feel the bliss distinctlier having thus
Engines subservient, not mixed up with us—
Better move palpably through Heaven—nor, freed
Of flesh forsooth, from space to space proceed
'Mid flying synods of worlds—but in Heaven's marge
Show Titan still, recumbent o'er his targe
Solid with stars—the Centaur at his game
Made tremulously out in hoary flame!
   Life! Yet the very cup whose extreme dull
Dregs, even, I would quaff, was dashed, at full,
Aside so oft; the death I fly, revealed
So oft a better life this life concealed
And which sage, champion, martyr, thro' each path
Have hunted fearlessly—the horrid bath,
The crippling-irons and the fiery chair:
—'Twas well for them; let me become aware
As they, and I relinquish Life, too! Let
Life's secret but disclose itself! Forget
Vain ordinances, I have one appeal—
I feel, am what I feel, know what I feel
—So much is Truth to me—What Is then? Since
One object viewed diversely may evince
Beauty and ugliness—this way attract,
That way repel, why gloze upon the fact?
Why must a single of the sides be right?
Who bids choose this and leave its opposite:
No abstract Right for me—in youth endued
With Right still present, still to be pursued,
Thro' all the interchange of circles, rife
Each with its proper law and mode of life,
Each to be dwelt at ease in: thus to sway
Regally with the Kaiser, or obey
Implicit with his Serf of fluttering heart,
Or, like a sudden thought of God's, to start
Up in the presence, then go forth and shout
That some should pick the unstrung jewels out—
Were well!
          And, as in moments when the Past
Gave partially enfranchisement, he cast
Himself quite thro' mere secondary states
Of his soul's essence, little loves and hates,
Into the mid vague yearnings overlaid
By these; as who should pierce hill, plain, grove, glade,

And so into the very nucleus probe
That first determined there exist a Globe:
And as that's easiest half the globe dissolved,
So seemed Sordello's closing-truth evolved
In his flesh-half's break-up—the sudden swell
Of his expanding soul showed Ill and Well,
Sorrow and Joy, Beauty and Ugliness,
Virtue and Vice, the Larger and the Less,
All qualities, in fine, recorded here,
Might be but Modes of Time and this one Sphere,
Urgent on these but not of force to bind
As Time—Eternity, as Matter—Mind,
If Mind, Eternity shall choose assert
Their attributes within a Life: thus girt
With circumstance, next change beholds them cinct
Quite otherwise—with Good and Ill distinct,
Joys, sorrows, tending to a like result—
Contrived to render easy, difficult,
This or the other course of . . . what new bond
In place of flesh may stop their flight beyond
Its new sphere, as that course does harm or good
To its arrangements. Once this understood,
As suddenly he felt himself alone,
Quite out of Time and this World, all was known.
What made the secret of the past despair?
(Most imminent when he seemed most aware
Of greatness in the Past—naught turned him mad
Like craving to expand the power he had,
Not a new power to be expanded)—just
This made it; Soul on Matter being thrust,
'Tis Joy when so much Soul is wreaked in Time
On Matter,—let the Soul attempt sublime
Matter beyond its scheme and so prevent
Or more or less that deed's accomplishment,
And Sorrow follows: Sorrow to avoid—
Let the Employer match the thing Employed,
Fit to the finite his infinity,
And thus proceed for ever, in degree
Changed but in kind the same, still limited
To the appointed circumstance and dead
To all beyond: a sphere is but a sphere—
Small, Great, are merely terms we bandy here—
Since to the spirit's absoluteness all

Are like: now of the present sphere we call
Life, are conditions—take but this among
Many; the Body was to be so long
Youthful, no longer—but, since no control
Tied to that Body's purposes his Soul,
It chose to understand the Body's trade
More than the Body's self—had fain conveyed
Its boundless, to the body's bounded lot—
So, the soul permanent, the body not,—
Scarce the one minute for enjoying here,
The soul must needs instruct its weak compeer,
Run o'er its capabilities and wring
A joy thence it holds worth experiencing—
Which, far from half discovered even,—lo,
The minute's gone, the body's power's let go
Apportioned to that joy's acquirement! Broke,
Say, morning o'er the earth and all it woke—
From the volcano's vapour-flag to hoist
Black o'er the spread of sea, to the low moist
Dale's silken barley-spikes sullied with rain,
Swayed earthwards, heavily to rise again—
(The Small a sphere as perfect as the Great
To the Soul's absoluteness)—meditate
On such an Autumn-morning's cluster-chord
And the whole music it was framed afford,
And, the chord's might discovered, what should pluck
One string, the finger, was found palsy-struck.
And then what marvel if the Spirit, shown
A saddest sight—the Body lost alone
Thro' its officious proffered help, deprived
Of this and that enjoyment Fate contrived,
Virtue, Good, Beauty, each allowed slip hence,—
Vain-gloriously were fain, for recompense,
To stem the ruin even yet, protract
The Body's term, supply the power it lacked
From its infinity, compel it learn
These qualities were only Time's concern,
That Body may, with its assistance, barred—
Advance the same, vanquished—obtain reward,
Reap joy where sorrow was intended grow,
Of Wrong made Right and turn Ill Good below—
And the result is, the poor Body soon
Sinks under what was meant a wondrous boon,

Leaving its bright accomplice all aghast.
　So much was plain then, proper in the Past;
To be complete for, satisfy the whole
Series of spheres—Eternity, his soul
Exceeded, so was incomplete for, each
One sphere—our Time.　But does our knowledge reach
No farther?　Is the cloud of hindrance broke
But by the failing of the fleshly yoke,
Its loves and hates, as now when they let soar
The spirit, self-sufficient as before,
Tho' but the single space that shall elapse
'Twixt its enthralment in new bonds perhaps?
Must Life be ever but escaped, which should
Have been enjoyed?　nay, might have been and would,
Once ordered rightly, and a Soul's no whit
More than the Body's purpose under it
(A breadth of watery heaven like a bay,
A sky-like space of water, ray for ray
And star for star, one richness where they mixed
As this and that wing of an angel, fixed,
Tumultuary splendours folded in
To die) and which thus, far from first begin
Exciting discontent, but surest quelled
The Body if aspiring it rebelled.
But how so order Life?　Still brutalise
The soul, the sad world's method—muffled eyes
To all that was before, shall after be
This sphere—and every other quality
Save some sole and immutable Great and Good
And Beauteous whither fate has loosed its hood
To follow?　Never may some soul see All
—The Great before and after and the Small
Now, yet be saved by this the simplest lore,
And take the single course prescribed before,
As the king-bird with ages on his plumes
Travels to die in his ancestral glooms?
But where descry the Love that shall select
That course?　Here is a Soul whom to affect
Nature has plied with all her means—from trees
And flowers—e'en to the Multitude . . . and these
Decides he save or no?　One word to end!
　Ah my Sordello, I this once befriend
And speak for you.　A Power above him still

Which, utterly incomprehensible,
Is out of rivalry, which thus he can
Love, tho' unloving all conceived by Man—
What need! And of—none the minutest duct
To that out-Nature, nought that would instruct
And so let rivalry begin to live—
But of a Power its representative
Who, being for authority the same,
Communication different, should claim
A course the first chose and this last revealed—
This Human clear, as that Divine concealed—
The utter need!

           What has Sordello found?
Or can his spirit go the mighty round
At length, end where our souls begun? as says
Old fable, the two doves were sent two ways
About the world—where in the midst they met
Tho' on a shifting waste of sand, men set
Jove's temple? Quick, what has Sordello found?
For they approach—approach—that foot's rebound . . .
Palma? No, Salinguerra tho' in mail;
They mount, have reached the threshold, dash the veil
Aside—and you divine who sat there dead
Under his foot the badge; still, Palma said,
A triumph lingering in the wide eyes
Wider than some spent swimmer's if he spies
Help from above in his extreme despair
And, head far back on shoulder thrust, turns there
With short and passionate cry; as Palma prest
In one great kiss her lips upon his breast
It beat. By this the hermit-bee has stopped
His day's toil at Goito—the new cropped
Dead vine-leaf answers, now 'tis eve, he bit,
Twirled so, and filed all day—the mansion's fit—
God counselled for; as easy guess the word
That passed betwixt them and become the third
To the soft small unfrighted bee, as tax
Him with one fault—so one remembrance racks
Of the stone maidens and the font of stone
He, creeping thro' the crevice, leaves alone—
Alas, my friend—Alas Sordello! whom
Anon we laid within that cold font-tomb—
And yet again alas!

                                        And now is't worth
Our while bring back to mind, much less set forth
How Salinguerra extricates himself
Without Sordello?   Ghibellin and Guelf
May fight their fiercest?   If Count Richard sulked
In durance or the Marquis paid his mulct,
Who cares, Sordello gone?   The upshot, sure,
Was peace; our chief made some frank overture
That prospered; compliment fell thick and fast
On its disposer, and Taurello passed
With foe and friend for an outstripping soul
Nine days at least: then, fairly reached the goal,
He, by one effort, blotted the great hope
Out of his mind, no further tried to cope
With Este that mad evening's style, but sent
Away the Legate and the League, content
No blame at least the brothers had incurred,
—Despatched a message to the Monk he heard
Patiently first to last, scarce shivered at,
Then curled his limbs up on his wolfskin mat
And ne'er spoke more,—informed the Ferrarese
He but retained their rules so long as these
Lingered in pupilage—and last, no mode
Apparent else of keeping safe the road
From Germany direct to Lombardy
For Friedrich, none, that is, to guarantee
The faith and promptitude of who should next
Obtain Sofia's dowry, sore perplexed—
(Sofia being youngest of the tribe
Of daughters Ecelin was wont to bribe
The envious magnates with—nor since he sent
Enrico Egna this fair child had Trent
Once failed the Kaiser's purposes—we lost
Egna last year, and who takes Egna's post—
Opens the Lombard gate if Friedrich knock?)
Himself espoused the Lady of the Rock
In pure necessity, and so destroyed
His slender last of chances, quite made void
Old prophecy, and spite of all the schemes
Overt and covert, youth's deeds, age's dreams,
Was sucked into Romano: and so hushed
He up this evening's work, that when 'twas brushed
Somehow against by a blind chronicle

Which, chronicling whatever woe befell
Ferrara, scented this the obscure woe
And " Salinguerra's sole son Giacomo
Deceased, fatuous and doting, ere his Sire,"
The townsfolk rubbed their eyes, could but admire
Which of Sofia's five he meant. The chaps
Of his dead hope were tardy to collapse,
Obliterated not the beautiful
Distinctive features at a crash—scarce dull
Next year, as Azzo, Boniface withdrew
Each to his stronghold; then (securely too
Ecelin at Campese slept—close by
Who likes may see him in Solagna lie
With cushioned head and gloved hand to denote
The Cavalier he was)—then his heart smote
Young Ecelin, conceive! Long since adult,
And, save Vicenza's business, what result
In blood and blaze? so hard 'twas intercept
Sordello till Sordello's option! Stept
Its lord on Lombardy—for in the nick
Of time when he at last and Alberic
Closed with Taurello, came precisely news
That in Verona half the souls refuse
Allegiance to the Marquis and the Count—
Have cast them from a throne they bid him mount,
Their Podestà, thro' his ancestral worth:
Ecelin flew there, and the town henceforth
Was wholly his—Taurello sinking back
From temporary station to a track
That suited: news received of this acquist,
Friedrich did come to Lombardy—who missed
Taurello? Yet another year—they took
Vicenza, left the Marquis scarce a nook
For refuge, and, when hundreds two or three
After conspired to call themselves " the Free,"
Opposing Alberic, these Bassanese,
(Without Sordello!)—Ecelin at ease
Slaughtered them so observably that oft
A little Salinguerra looked with soft
Blue eyes up, asked his sire the proper age
To get appointed his proud uncle's page:
More years passed, and that sire was dwindled down
To a mere showy turbulent soldier, grown

Better through age, his parts still in repute,
Subtle—how else?—but hardly so astute
As his contemporaneous friends professed—
Undoubtedly a brawler—for the rest,
Known by each neighbour, so allowed for, let
Keep his incorrigible ways, nor fret
Men who had missed their boyhood's bugbear—trap
The ostrich, suffer our bald osprey flap
A battered pinion—was the word.   In fine,
One flap too much and Venice's marine
Was meddled with; no overlooking that!
We captured him in his Ferrara, fat
And florid at a banquet, more by fraud
Than force, to speak the truth—there's slender laud
Ascribed you for assisting eighty years
To pull his death on such a man—fate shears
The life-cord prompt enough whose last fine threads
You fritter: so, presiding his board-head,
A great smile your assurance all went well
With Friedrich (as if he were like to tell!)
In rushed (a plan contrived before) our friends,
Made some pretence at fighting, just amends
For the shame done his eighty years—apart
The principle, none found it in his heart
To be much angry with Taurello—gained
Our galleys with the prize, and what remained
But carry him to Venice for a show?
—Set him, as 'twere, down gently—free to go
His gait, inspect our square, pretend observe
The swallows soaring their eternal curve
'Twixt Theodore and Mark, if citizens
Gathered importunately, fives and tens,
To point their children the Magnifico,
All but a monarch once in firm-land, go
His gait among us now—it took, indeed,
Fully this Ecelin to supersede
That man, remarked the seniors.   Singular
Sordello's inability to bar
Rivals the stage, that evening, mainly brought
About by his strange disbelief that aught
Was to be done, should fairly thrust the Twain
Under Taurello's tutelage, that, brain
And heart and hand, he forthwith in one rod

Indissolubly bound to baffle God
Who loves the world—should thus allow the thin
Grey wizened dwarfish devil Ecelin,
And massy-muscled big-boned Alberic
(Mere man, alas) to put his problem quick
To demonstration—prove wherever's will
To do, there's plenty to be done, or ill
Or good: anointed, then, to rend and rip—
Kings of the gag and flesh-hook, screw and whip,
They plagued the world: a touch of Hildebrand
(So far from obsolete!) made Lombards band
Together, cross their coats as for Christ's cause,
And saving Milan win the world's applause.
Ecelin perished: and I think grass grew
Never so pleasant as in Valley Rù
By San Zenon where Alberic in turn
Saw his exasperated captors burn
Seven children with their mother, and, regaled
So far, tied on to a wild horse, was trailed
To death through raunce and bramble-bush: I take
God's part and testify that mid the brake
Wild o'er his castle on Zenone's knoll
You hear its one tower left, a belfry, toll—
Cherups the contumacious grasshopper,
Rustles the lizard and the cushats chirre
Above the ravage: there, at deep of day
A week since, heard I the old Canon say
He saw with his own eyes a barrow burst
And Alberic's huge skeleton unhearsed
Five years ago, no more: he added, June's
A month for carding off our first cocoons
The silkworms fabricate—a double news,
Nor he nor I could tell the worthier.   Choose!
    And Naddo gone, all's gone; not Eglamor!
Believe I knew the face I waited for,
A guest my spirit of the golden courts:
Oh strange to see how, despite ill-reports,
Disuse, some wear of years, that face retained
Its joyous look of love! Suns waxed and waned,
And still my spirit held an upward flight,
Spiral on spiral, gyres of life and light
More and more gorgeous—ever that face there
The last admitted! crossed, too, with some care

As perfect triumph were not sure for all,
But on a few enduring damp must fall,
A transient struggle, haply a painful sense
Of the inferior nature's clinging—whence
Slight starting tears easily wiped away,
Fine jealousies soon stifled in the play
Of irrepressible admiration—not
Aspiring, all considered, to their lot
Who ever, just as they prepare ascend
Spiral on spiral, wish thee well, impend
Thy frank delight at their exclusive track,
That upturned fervid face and hair put back!
    Is there no more to say? He of the rhymes—
Many a tale of this retreat betimes
Was born: Sordello die at once for men?
The Chroniclers of Mantua tired their pen
Relating how a Prince Visconti saved
Mantua and elsewhere notably behaved—
Who thus by fortune's ordering events
Passed with posterity to all intents
For just the God he never could become:
As Knight, Bard, Gallant, men were never dumb
In praise of him: while what he should have been,
Could be, and was not,—the one step too mean
For him to take, we suffer at this day
Because of; Ecelin had pushed away
Its chance ere Dante could arrive to take
That step Sordello spurned, for the world's sake!
He did much—but Sordello's step was gone.
Thus had Sordello ta'en that step alone,
Apollo had been compassed—'twas a fit
He wished should go to him, not he to it
—As one content to merely be supposed
Singing or fighting elsewhere, while he dozed
Really at home—and who was chiefly glad
To have achieved the few real deeds he had
Because that way assured they were not worth
Doing, so spared from doing them henceforth—
A tree that covets fruitage and yet tastes
Never itself, itself—had he embraced
Our cause then, Men had plucked Hesperian fruit
And, praising that, just thrown him in to boot
All he was anxious to appear but scarce

Solicitous to be: a sorry farce
Such life is after all—cannot I say
He lived for some one better thing? this way—
Lo, on a heathy brown and nameless hill
By sparkling Asolo, in mist and chill,
Morning just up, higher and higher runs
A child barefoot and rosy—See! the sun's
On the square castle's inner-court's green wall
—Like the chine of some fossil animal
Half turned to earth and flowers; and thro' the haze
(Save where some slender patches of grey maize,
Are to be overleaped) that boy has crost
The whole hill-side of dew and powder-frost
Matting the balm and mountain camomile:
Up and up goes he, singing all the while
Some unintelligible words to beat
The lark, God's poet, swooning at his feet
So worsted is he at the few fine locks
Stained like pale honey oozed from topmost rocks
Sunblanched the livelong summer.—All that's left
Of the Goito lay! And thus bereft,
Sleep and forget, Sordello . . . in effect
He sleeps, the feverish poet—I suspect
Not utterly companionless; but, friends,
Wake up; the ghost's gone, and the story ends
I'd fain hope, sweetly—seeing, peri or ghoul,
That spirits are conjectured fair or foul,
Evil or good, judicious authors think,
According as they vanish in a stink
Or in a perfume: friends be frank; ye snuff
Civet, I warrant: really? Like enough—
Merely the savour's rareness—any nose
May ravage with impunity a rose—
Rifle a musk-pod and 'twill ache like yours:
I'd tell you that same pungency ensures
An after-gust—but that were overbold:
Who would has heard Sordello's story told.

THE END

PIPPA PASSES

A DRAMA

I Dedicate my Best Intentions, in this Poem, Most
Admiringly to the Author of "Ion,"—
Most Affectionately to
MR. SERJEANT TALFOURD.

LONDON: 1841.

R.B.

New Year's Day at Asolo in the Trevisan.—*A large,
mean, airy chamber. A girl, Pippa, from the silk-mills,
springing out of bed.*

Day!
Faster and more fast,
O'er night's brim, day boils at last;
Boils, pure gold, o'er the cloud-cup's brim
Where spurting and supprest it lay—
For not a froth-flake touched the rim
Of yonder gap in the solid gray
Of the eastern cloud, an hour away;
But forth one wavelet, then another, curled,
Till the whole sunrise, not to be supprest,
Rose, reddened, and its seething breast
Flickered in bounds, grew gold, then overflowed the world.

Oh, Day, if I squander a wavelet of thee,
A mite of my twelve hours' treasure,
The least of thy gazes or glances,
(Be they grants thou art bound to, or gifts above measure)
One of thy choices, or one of thy chances,
(Be they tasks God imposed thee, or freaks at thy pleasure)
—My Day, if I squander such labour or leisure,
Then shame fall on Asolo, mischief on me!

Thy long blue solemn hours serenely flowing,
Whence earth, we feel, gets steady help and good—
Thy fitful sunshine minutes, coming, going,

348

In which, earth turns from work in gamesome mood—
All shall be mine! But thou must treat me not
As the prosperous are treated, those who live
At hand here, and enjoy the higher lot,
In readiness to take what thou wilt give,
And free to let alone what thou refusest;
For, Day, my holiday, if thou ill-usest
Me, who am only Pippa—old-year's sorrow,
Cast off last night, will come again to-morrow—
Whereas, if thou prove gentle, I shall borrow
Sufficient strength of thee for new-year's sorrow.
All other men and women that this earth
Belongs to, who all days alike possess,
Make general plenty cure particular dearth,
Get more joy, one way, if another, less:
Thou art my single day, God lends to leaven
What were all earth else, with a feel of heaven;
Sole light that helps me through the year, thy sun's!
Try, now! Take Asolo's Four Happiest Ones—
And let thy morning rain on that superb
Great haughty Ottima; can rain disturb
Her Sebald's homage? All the while thy rain
Beats fiercest on her shrub-house window-pane,
He will but press the closer, breathe more warm
Against her cheek; how should she mind the storm?
And, morning past, if mid-day shed a gloom
O'er Jules and Phene,—what care bride and groom
Save for their dear selves? 'Tis their marriage-day;
And while they leave church, and go home their way
Hand clasping hand,—within each breast would be
Sunbeams and pleasant weather spite of thee!
Then, for another trial, obscure thy eve
With mist,—will Luigi and his mother grieve,—
The Lady and her child, unmatched, forsooth,
She in her age, as Luigi in his youth,
For true content? The cheerful town, warm, close,
And safe, the sooner that thou art morose
Receives them! And yet once again, outbreak
In storm at night on Monsignor, they make
Such stir about,—whom they expect from Rome
To visit Asolo, his brothers' home,
And say here masses proper to release
A soul from pain,—what storm dares hurt his peace?

Calm would he pray, with his own thoughts to ward
Thy thunder off, nor want the angels' guard!
But Pippa—just one such mischance would spoil
Her day that lightens the next twelvemonth's toil
At wearisome silk-winding, coil on coil!
And here I let time slip for nought!
Aha,—you foolhardy sunbeam—caught
With a single splash from my ewer!
You that would mock the best pursuer,
Was my basin over-deep?
One splash of water ruins you asleep,
And up, up, fleet your brilliant bits
Wheeling and counterwheeling,
Reeling, broken beyond healing—
Now grow together on the ceiling!
That will task your wits!
Whoever quenched fire first, hoped to see
Morsel after morsel flee
As merrily, as giddily . . .
Meantime, what lights my sunbeam on,
Where settles by degrees the radiant cripple?
Oh, is it surely blown, my martagon?
New-blown and ruddy as St. Agnes' nipple,
Plump as the flesh-bunch on some Turk bird's poll!
Be sure if corals, branching 'neath the ripple
Of ocean, bud there,—fairies watch unroll
Such turban-flowers; I say, such lamps disperse
Thick red flame through that dusk green universe!
    I am queen of thee, floweret;
      And each fleshy blossom
    Preserve I not—(safer
      Than leaves that embower it,
      Or shells that embosom)
    —From weevil and chafer?
    Laugh through my pane, then; solicit the bee;
    Gibe him, be sure; and, in midst of thy glee,
    Love thy queen, worship me!

—Worship whom else? For am I not, this day,
Whate'er I please? What shall I please to-day?
My morning, noon, eve, night—how spend my day?
To-morrow I must be Pippa who winds silk,
The whole year round, to earn just bread and milk:

But, this one day, I have leave to go,
And play out my fancy's fullest games;
I may fancy all day—and it shall be so—
That I taste of the pleasures, am called by the names
Of the Happiest Four in our Asolo!

See! Up the Hill-side yonder, through the morning,
Some one shall love me, as the world calls love:
I am no less than Ottima, take warning!
The gardens, and the great stone house above,
And other house for shrubs, all glass in front,
Are mine; where Sebald steals, as he is wont,
To court me, while old Luca yet reposes;
And therefore, till the shrub-house door encloses,
I . . . what, now?—give abundant cause for prate
About me—Ottima, I mean—of late,
Too bold, too confident she'll still face down
The spitefullest of talkers in our town—
How we talk in the little town below!
But love, love, love—there's better love, I know!
This foolish love was only day's first offer;
I choose my next love to defy the scoffer:
For do not our Bride and Bridegroom sally
Out of Possagno church at noon?
Their house looks over Orcana valley—
Why should I not be the bride as soon
As Ottima? For I saw, beside,
Arrive last night that little bride—
Saw, if you call it seeing her, one flash
Of the pale, snow-pure cheek and black bright tresses,
Blacker than all except the black eyelash;
I wonder she contrives those lids no dresses!
—So strict was she, the veil
Should cover close her pale
Pure cheeks—a bride to look at and scarce touch,
Scarce touch, remember, Jules!—for are not such
Used to be tended, flower-like, every feature,
As if one's breath would fray the lily of a creature?
A soft and easy life these ladies lead!
Whiteness in us were wonderful indeed—
    Oh, save that brow its virgin dimness,
    Keep that foot its lady primness,
    Let those ancles never swerve

From their exquisite reserve,
Yet have to trip along the streets like me,
All but naked to the knee!
How will she ever grant her Jules a bliss
So startling as her real first infant kiss?
Oh, no—not envy, this!

—Not envy, sure!—for if you gave me
Leave to take or to refuse,
In earnest, do you think I'd choose
That sort of new love to enslave me?
Mine should have lapped me round from the beginning:
As little fear of losing it as winning!
Lovers grow cold, men learn to hate their wives,
And only parents' love can last our lives:
At eve the son and mother, gentle pair,
Commune inside our Turret; what prevents
My being Luigi? while that mossy lair
Of lizards through the winter-time, is stirred
With each to each imparting sweet intents
For this new-year, as brooding bird to bird—
(For I observe of late, the evening walk
Of Luigi and his mother, always ends
Inside our ruined turret, where they talk,
Calmer than lovers, yet more kind than friends)
Let me be cared about, kept out of harm,
And schemed for, safe in love as with a charm;
Let me be Luigi! . . . If I only knew
What was my mother's face—my father, too!
Nay, if you come to that, best love of all
Is God's; then why not have God's love befall
Myself as, in the Palace by the Dome,
Monsignor?—who to-night will bless the home
Of his dead brother; and God will bless in turn
That heart which beats, those eyes which mildly burn
With love for all men: I, to-night at least,
Would be that holy and beloved priest!

Now wait!—even I already seem to share
In God's love: what does New-year's hymn declare?
What other meaning do these verses bear?

All service ranks the same with God :
If now, as formerly He trod

Paradise, His presence fills
Our earth, each only as God wills
Can work—God's puppets, best and worst,
Are we ; there is no last nor first.

Say not a " small event ? " Why " small ? "
Costs it more pain than this, ye call
A " great event," should come to pass,
Than that ? Untwine me from the mass
Of deeds which make up life, one deed
Power shall fall short in, or exceed !

And more of it, and more of it!—oh, yes—
I will pass by, and see their happiness,
And envy none—being just as great, no doubt,
Useful to men, and dear to God, as they!
A pretty thing to care about
So mightily, this single holiday!
  But let the sun shine! Wherefore repine?
  —With thee to lead me, O Day of mine,
  Down the grass-path grey with dew,
  Under the pine-wood, blind with boughs,
  Where the swallow never flew
  As yet, nor cicale dared carouse—
  Dared carouse!   *[She enters the street.*

I.—MORNING. *Up the Hill-side, inside the Shrub-house.*
LUCA'S *Wife,* OTTIMA, *and her Paramour, the German*
SEBALD.

Seb. (*sings.*) *Let the watching lids wink !*
     Day's a-blaze with eyes, think—
     Deep into the night, drink !
Otti. Night? Such may be your Rhine-land nights,
   perhaps;
But this blood-red beam through the shutter's chink,
—We call such light, the morning's: let us see!
Mind how you grope your way, though! How these tall
Naked geraniums straggle! Push the lattice—
Behind that frame!—Nay, do I bid you?—Sebald,
It shakes the dust down on me! Why, of course
The slide-bolt catches.—Well, are you content,

Or must I find you something else to spoil?
Kiss and be friends, my Sebald! Is it full morning?
Oh, don't speak then!

   Seb.   Ay, thus it used to be!
Ever your house was, I remember, shut
Till mid-day—I observed that, as I strolled
On mornings thro' the vale here: country girls
Were noisy, washing garments in the brook—
Hinds drove the slow white oxen up the hills—
But no, your house was mute, would ope no eye—
And wisely—you were plotting one thing there,
Nature, another outside: I looked up—
Rough white wood shutters, rusty iron bars,
Silent as death, blind in a flood of light;
Oh, I remember!—and the peasants laughed
And said, "The old man sleeps with the young wife!"
This house was his, this chair, this window—his!

   Otti.   Ah, the clear morning! I can see St. Mark's:
That black streak is the belfry. Stop: Vicenza
Should lie . . . There's Padua, plain enough, that blue!
Look o'er my shoulder—follow my finger—

   Seb.   Morning?
It seems to me a night with a sun added:
Where's dew? where's freshness? That bruised plant, I bruised
In getting thro' the lattice yestereve,
Droops as it did. See, here's my elbow's mark
In the dust on the sill.

   Otti.   Oh, shut the lattice, pray!

   Seb.   Let me lean out. I cannot scent blood here,
Foul as the morn may be—

                     There, shut the world out!
How do you feel now, Ottima? There—curse
The world, and all outside! Let us throw off
This mask: how do you bear yourself? Let's out
With all of it!

   Otti.   Best never speak of it.

   Seb.   Best speak again and yet again of it,
Till words cease to be more than words. "His blood,"
For instance—let those two words mean "His blood"
And nothing more. Notice—I'll say them now,
"His blood."

   Otti.   Assuredly if I repented

The deed—
 Seb.   Repent? who should repent, or why?
What puts that in your head? Did I once say
That I repented?
 Otti.   No—I said the deed—
 Seb. " The deed," and " the event "—just now it was
" Our passion's fruit "—the devil take such cant!
Say, once and always, Luca was a wittol,
I am his cut-throat, you are—
 Otti.   Here is the wine—
I brought it when we left the house above—
And glasses too—wine of both sorts. Black? white, then?
 Seb. But am not I his cut-throat? What are you?
 Otti. There, trudges on his business from the Duomo
Benet the Capuchin, with his brown hood
And bare feet—always in one place at church,
Close under the stone wall by the south entry;
I used to take him for a brown cold piece
Of the wall's self, as out of it he rose
To let me pass—at first, I say, I used—
Now—so has that dumb figure, fastened on me—
I rather should account the plastered wall
A piece of him, so chilly does it strike.
This, Sebald?
 Seb.   No—the white wine—the white wine!
Well, Ottima, I promised no new year
Should rise on us the ancient shameful way,
Nor does it rise: pour on! To your black eyes!
Do you remember last damned New Year's day?
 Otti. You brought those foreign prints. We looked at
    them
Over the wine and fruit. I had to scheme
To get him from the fire. Nothing but saying
His own set wants the proof-mark, roused him up
To hunt them out.
 Seb.   'Faith, he is not alive
To fondle you before my face!
 Otti.   Do you
Fondle me, then! who means to take your life
For that, my Sebald?
 Seb.   Hark you, Ottima,
One thing's to guard against. We'll not make much
One of the other—that is, not make more

Parade of warmth, childish officious coil,
Than yesterday—as if, sweet, I supposed
Proof upon proof was needed now, now first,
To show I love you—yes, still love you—love you
In spite of Luca and what's come to him
—Sure sign we had him ever in our thoughts,
White sneering old reproachful face and all!
We'll even quarrel, love, at times, as if
We still could lose each other—were not tied
By this—conceive you?
   Otti.   Love—
   Seb.   Not tied so sure—
Because tho' I was wrought upon—have struck
His insolence back into him—am I
So surely yours?—therefore, forever yours?
   Otti. Love, to be wise, (one counsel pays another)
Should we have—months ago—when first we loved,
For instance that May morning we two stole
Under the green ascent of sycamores—
If we had come upon a thing like that
Suddenly—
   Seb.   "A thing" . . there again—" a thing!"
   Otti. Then, Venus' body, had we come upon
My husband Luca Gaddi's murdered corpse
Within there, at his couch-foot, covered close—
Would you have pored upon it?   Why persist
In poring now upon it?   For 'tis here—
As much as there in the deserted house—
You cannot rid your eyes of it: for me,
Now he is dead I hate him worse—I hate—
Dare you stay here?   I would go back and hold
His two dead hands, and say, I hate you worse
Luca, than—
   Seb.   Off, off; take your hands off mine!
'Tis the hot evening—off! oh, morning, is it?
   Otti. There's one thing must be done—you know what
           thing.
Come in and help to carry.   We may sleep
Anywhere in the whole wide house to-night.
   Seb. What would come, think you, if we let him lie
Just as he is?   Let him lie there until
The angels take him: he is turned by this
Off from his face, beside, as you will see.

Otti. This dusty pane might serve for looking-glass.
Three, four—four grey hairs! Is it so you said
A plait of hair should wave across my neck?
No—this way!

Seb.   Ottima, I would give your neck,
Each splendid shoulder, both those breasts of yours,
That this were undone! Killing?—Kill the world
So Luca lives again!—Ay, lives to sputter
His fulsome dotage on you—yes, and feign
Surprise that I returned at eve to sup,
When all the morning I was loitering here—
Bid me dispatch my business and begone.
I would—

Otti.   See!

Seb.   No, I'll finish! Do you think
I fear to speak the bare truth once for all?
All we have talked of is, at bottom, fine
To suffer—there's recompense in guilt;
One must be venturous and fortunate—
What is one young for, else? In age we'll sigh
O'er the wild, reckless, wicked days flown over;
Still we have lived! The vice was in its place.
But to have eaten Luca's bread, have worn
His clothes, have felt his money swell my purse—
Do lovers in romances sin that way?
Why, I was starving when I used to call
And teach you music—starving while you plucked me
These flowers to smell!

Otti.   My poor lost friend!

Seb.   He gave me
Life—nothing less: what if he did reproach
My perfidy, and threaten, and do more—
Had he no right? What was to wonder at?
He sate by us at table quietly—
Why must you lean across till our cheeks touch'd?
Could he do less than make pretence to strike me?
'Tis not for the crime's sake—I'd commit ten crimes
Greater, to have this crime wiped out—undone!
And you—O, how feel you? feel you for me?

Otti. Well, then—I love you better now than ever—
And best (look at me while I speak to you)—
Best for the crime—nor do I grieve, in truth
This mask, this simulated ignorance,

This affectation of simplicity,
Falls off our crime; this naked crime of ours
May not, now, be looked over—look it down, then!
Great? let it be great—but the joys it brought,
Pay they or no its price? Come—they or it!
Speak not! The past, would you give up the past
Such as it is, pleasure and crime together?
Give up that noon I owned my love for you—
The garden's silence—even the single bee
Persisting in his toil, suddenly stopt
And where he hid you only could surmise
By some campanula's chalice set a-swing
As he clung there—" Yes, I love you!"

    Seb.   And I drew
Back; put far back your face with both my hands
Lest you should grow too full of me—your face
So seemed athirst for my whole soul and body!

    Otti.   And when I ventured to receive you here,
Made you steal hither in the mornings—

    Seb.   When
I used to look up 'neath the shrub-house here,
Till the red fire on its glazed windows spread
To a yellow haze?

    Otti.   Ah—my sign was, the sun
Inflamed the sere side of yon chestnut tree
Nipt by the first frost.

    Seb.   You would always laugh
At my wet boots—I had to stride thro' grass
Over my ancles.

    Otti.   Then our crowning night—

    Seb.   The July night?

    Otti.   The day of it too, Sebald!
When the heaven's pillars seemed o'erbowed with heat,
Its black-blue canopy seemed let descend
Close on us both, to weigh down each to each,
And smother up all life except our life.
So lay we till the storm came.

    Seb.   How it came!

    Otti.   Buried in woods we lay, you recollect;
Swift ran the searching tempest overhead;
And ever and anon some bright white shaft
Burnt thro' the pine-tree roof—here burnt and there,
As if God's messenger thro' the close wood screen

Plunged and replunged his weapon at a venture,
Feeling for guilty thee and me: then broke
The thunder like a whole sea overhead—
   Seb. Yes!
   Otti. —While I stretched myself upon you, hands
To hands, my mouth to your hot mouth, and shook
All my locks loose, and covered you with them—
You, Sebald, the same you—
   Seb. Slower, Ottima—
   Otti. And as we lay—
   Seb. Less vehemently! Love me—
Forgive me—take not words—mere words—to heart—
Your breath is worse than wine! Breathe slow, speak
    slow—
Do not lean on me—
   Otti. Sebald, as we lay,
Rising and falling only with our pants,
Who said, " Let death come now—'tis right to die!
Right to be punished—nought completes such bliss
But woe! " Who said that?
   Seb. How did we ever rise?
Was't that we slept ? Why did it end?
   Otti.   I felt you,
Fresh tapering to a point the ruffled ends
Of my loose locks 'twixt both your humid lips—
(My hair is fallen now—knot it again!)
   Seb. I kiss you now, dear Ottima, now, and now!
This way? Will you forgive me—be once more
My great Queen?
   Otti.   Bind it thrice about my brow;
Crown me your queen, your spirit's arbitress,
Magnificent in sin. Say that!
   Seb.   I crown you
My great white queen, my spirit's arbitress,
Magnificent—

       (*From without is heard the voice of* PIPPA, *singing—*

               The year's at the spring,
               And day's at the morn ;
               Morning's at seven ;
               The hill-side's dew-pearled :
               The lark's on the wing ;
               The snail's on the thorn ;

God's in his heaven—
All's right with the world !

(PIPPA *passes.*)

Seb. God's in his heaven! Do you hear that? Who spoke?
You, you spoke!
   Otti.   Oh—that little ragged girl!
She must have rested on the step—we give them
But this one holiday the whole year round.
Did you ever see our silk-mills—their inside?
There are ten silk-mills now belong to you.
She stoops to pick my double heartsease . . . Sh!
She does not hear—you call out louder!
   Seb.   Leave me!
Go, get your clothes on—dress those shoulders!
   Otti.   Sebald?
   Seb. Wipe off that paint. I hate you!
   Otti.   Miserable!
   Seb. My God! and she is emptied of it now!
Outright now!—how miraculously gone
All of the grace—had she not strange grace once?
Why, the blank cheek hangs listless as it likes,
No purpose holds the features up together,
Only the cloven brow and puckered chin
Stay in their places—and the very hair,
That seemed to have a sort of life in it,
Drops, a dead web!
   Otti.   Speak to me—speak not of me!
   Seb. —That round great full-orbed face, where not an angle
Broke the delicious indolence—all broken!
   Otti. To me—not of me!—ungrateful, perjured cheat—
A coward, too—but ingrate's worse than all!
Beggar—my slave—a fawning, cringing lie!
Leave me!—betray me!—I can see your drift—
A lie that walks, and eats, and drinks!
   Seb.   My God!
Those morbid, olive, faultless shoulder-blades—
I should have known there was no blood beneath!
   Otti. You hate me, then? You hate me, then?
   Seb.   To think
She would succeed in her absurd attempt,
And fascinate by sinning; and show herself
Superior—Guilt from its excess, superior

To Innocence. That little peasant's voice
Has righted all again. Though I be lost,
I know which is the better, never fear,
Of vice or virtue, purity or lust,
Nature, or trick—I see what I have done,
Entirely now! Oh, I am proud to feel
Such torments—let the world take credit thence—
I, having done my deed, pay too its price!
I hate, hate—curse you! God's in his heaven!
   Otti.   —Me!
Me! no, no, Sebald—not yourself—kill me!
Mine is the whole crime—do but kill me—then
Yourself—then—presently—first hear me speak—
I always meant to kill myself—wait, you!
Lean on my breast—not as a breast; don't love me
The more because you lean on me, my own
Heart's Sebald! There—there—both deaths presently!
   Seb. My brain is drowned now—quite drowned: all
     I feel
Is . . . is at swift-recurring intervals,
A hurrying-down within me, as of waters
Loosened to smother up some ghastly pit—
There they go—whirls from a black, fiery sea!
   Otti. Not to me, God—to him be merciful!

Talk by the way, while Pippa *is passing from the Hillside to
Orcana. Foreign Students of Painting and Sculpture, from
Venice, assembled opposite the House of* Jules, *a young
French Statuary.*

1st *Student.* Attention! my own post is beneath this
window, but the pomegranate clump yonder will hide three
or four of you with a little squeezing, and Schramm and his
pipe must lie flat in the balcony. Four, five—who's a de-
faulter? We want everybody, for Jules must not be suffered
to hurt his bride when the jest's found out.

2nd *Stud.* All here! Only our poet's away—never having
much meant to be present, moonstrike him! The airs of that
fellow, that Giovacchino! He was in violent love with himself,
and had a fair prospect of thriving in his suit, so unmolested
was it,—when suddenly a woman falls in love with him, too;
and out of pure jealousy he takes himself off to Trieste,
immortal poem and all—whereto is this prophetical epitaph
appended already, as Bluphocks assures me—" *Here a mam-*

moth-poem lies,—Fouled to death by butterflies." His own fault, the simpleton! Instead of cramp couplets, each like a knife in your entrails, he should write, says Bluphocks, both classically and intelligibly.—*Æsculapius, an Epic. Catalogue of the drugs: Hebe's plaister—One strip Cools your lip. Phœbus' emulsion—One bottle Clears your throttle. Mercury's bolus—One box Cures . . .*

3d Stud. Subside, my fine fellow! If the marriage was over by ten o'clock, Jules will certainly be here in a minute with his bride.

2d Stud. Good!—Only, so should the poet's muse have been universally acceptable, says Bluphocks, *et canibus nostris . . .* and Delia not better known to our literary dogs than the boy—Giovacchino!

1st Stud. To the point, now. Where's Gottlieb, the newcomer? Oh,—listen, Gottlieb, to what has called down this piece of friendly vengeance on Jules, of which we now assemble to witness the winding-up. We are all agreed, all in a tale, observe, when Jules shall burst out on us in a fury by and bye: I am spokesman—the verses that are to undeceive Jules bear my name of Lutwyche—but each professes himself alike insulted by this strutting stone-squarer, who came singly from Paris to Munich, and thence with a crowd of us to Venice and Possagno here, but proceeds in a day or two alone again—oh, alone, indubitably!—to Rome and Florence. He, forsooth, take up his portion with these dissolute, brutalised, heartless bunglers!—So he was heard to call us all: now is Schramm brutalised, I should like to know? Am I heartless?

Gott. Why, somewhat heartless; for, suppose Jules a coxcomb as much as you choose, still, for this mere coxcombry, you will have brushed off—what do folks style it?—the bloom of his life. Is it too late to alter? These love-letters, now, you call his . . I can't laugh at them.

4th Stud. Because you never read the sham letters of our inditing which drew forth these.

Gott. His discovery of the truth will be frightful.

4th Stud. That's the joke. But you should have joined us at the beginning: there's no doubt he loves the girl—loves a model he might hire by the hour!

Gott. See here! "He has been accustomed," he writes, "to have Canova's women about him, in stone, and the world's women beside him in flesh; these being as much below, as those, above—his soul's aspiration: but now he is to have the real." . . . There you laugh again! I say, you wipe off the very dew of his youth.

1st Stud. Schramm! (Take the pipe out of his mouth, somebody)—will Jules lose the bloom of his youth?

Schramm. Nothing worth keeping is ever lost in this world: look at a blossom—it drops presently, having done its service and lasted its time; but fruits succeed, and where would be the blossom's place could it continue? As well affirm that your eye is no longer in your body, because its earliest favourite, whatever it may have first loved to look on, is dead and done with—as that any affection is lost to the soul when its first object, whatever happened first to satisfy it, is superseded in due course. Keep but ever looking, whether with the body's eye or the mind's, and you will soon find something to look on! Has a man done wondering at women?—There follow men, dead and alive, to wonder at. Has he done wondering at men?—There's God to wonder at: and the faculty of wonder may be, at the same time, old and tired enough with respect to its first object, and yet young and fresh sufficiently, so far as concerns its novel one. Thus . . .

1st Stud. Put Schramm's pipe into his mouth again! There, you see! Well, this—Jules . . . a wretched fribble—oh, I watched his disportings at Possagna, the other day! Canova's gallery—you know: there he marches first resolvedly past great works by the dozen without vouchsafing an eye: all at once he stops full at the *Psiche-fanciulla*—cannot pass that old acquaintance without a nod of encouragement—" In your new place, beauty? Then behave yourself as well here as at Munich—I see you!" Next he posts himself deliberately before the unfinished *Pietà* for half an hour without moving, till up he starts of a sudden, and thrusts his very nose into—I say, into—the group; by which gesture you are informed that precisely the sole point he had not fully mastered in Canova's practice was a certain method of using the drill in the articulation of the knee-joint—and that, likewise, has he mastered at length! Good bye, therefore, to poor Canova—whose gallery no longer need detain his successor Jules, the predestinated novel thinker in marble!

5th Stud. Tell him about the women—go on to the women.

1st Stud. Why, on that matter he could never be supercilious enough. How should we be other (he said) than the poor devils you see, with those debasing habits we cherish? He was not to wallow in that mire, at least: he would wait, and love only at the proper time, and meanwhile put up with the *Psiche-fanciulla*. Now I happened to hear of a young Greek—real Greek—girl at Malamocco; a true Islander, do you see, with Alciphron's " hair like sea-moss "—Schramm knows!—white and quiet as an apparition, and fourteen years old at farthest,—a daughter of Natalia, so she swears —that hag Natalia, who helps us to models at three *lire* an hour. We selected this girl for the heroine of our jest. So, first, Jules received a scented letter—somebody had seen his Tydeus at the academy, and my picture was nothing to it— a profound admirer bade him persevere—would make herself known to him ere long—(Paolina, my little friend of the *Fenice*, transcribes divinely). And in due time, the mysterious correspondent gave certain hints of her peculiar charms— the pale cheeks, the black hair—whatever, in short, had struck us in our Malamocco model: we retained her name, too—Phene, which is by interpretation, sea eagle. Now, think of Jules finding himself distinguished from the herd of us by such a creature! In his very first answer he proposed marrying his monitress: and fancy us over these letters, two, three times a day, to receive and dispatch! I concocted the main of it: relations were in the way—secrecy must be observed— in fine, would he wed her on trust, and only speak to her when they were indissolubly united? St—st—Here they come!

6th Stud. Both of them! Heaven's love, speak softly! speak within yourselves!

5th Stud. Look at the bridegroom! Half his hair in storm, and half in calm,—patted down over the left temple,—like a frothy cup one blows on to cool it! and the same old blouse that he murders the marble in!

2d Stud. Not a rich vest like yours, Hannibal Scratchy!— rich, that your face may the better set it off!

6th Stud. And the bride! Yes, sure enough, our Phene! Should you have known her in her clothes? How magnificently pale!

Gott. She does not also take it for earnest, I hope?

1st Stud. Oh, Natalia's concern, that is! We settle with Natalia.

6th Stud. She does not speak—has evidently let out no word. The only thing is, will she equally remember the rest

of her lesson, and repeat correctly all those verses which are
to break the secret to Jules?

Gott. How he gazes on her! Pity—pity!

1st *Stud.* They go in—now, silence! You three,—not
nearer the window, mind, than that pomegranate—just
where the little girl, who a few minutes ago passed us singing,
is seated!

II.—*Noon. Over Orcana. The House of* JULES, *who crosses
its threshold with* PHENE—*she is silent, on which* JULES
begins—

Do not die, Phene—I am yours now—you
Are mine now—let fate reach me how she likes,
If you'll not die—so, never die! Sit here—
My work-room's single seat: I over-lean
This length of hair and lustrous front—they turn
Like an entire flower upward—eyes—lips—last
Your chin—no, last your throat turns—'tis their scent
Pulls down my face upon you! Nay, look ever
This one way till I change, grow you—I could
Change into you, beloved!
                You by me,
And I by you—this is your hand in mine—
And side by side we sit: all's true. Thank God!
I have spoken—speak, you!
                —O, my life to come!
My Tydeus must be carved, that's there in clay;
Yet how be carved, with you about the chamber?
Where must I place you? When I think that once
This room-full of rough block-work seemed my heaven
Without you! Shall I ever work again—
Get fairly into my old ways again—
Bid each conception stand while, trait by trait,
My hand transfers its lineaments to stone?
Will my mere fancies live near you, my truth—
The live truth—passing and repassing me—
Sitting beside me?
            Now speak!
                Only, first,
See, all your letters! Was't not well contrived?
Their hiding-place is Psyche's robe; she keeps
Your letters next her skin: which drops out foremost?

Ah,—this that swam down like a first moonbeam
Into my world!
              Again those eyes complete
Their melancholy survey, sweet and slow,
Of all my room holds; to return and rest
On me, with pity, yet some wonder too—
As if God bade some spirit plague a world,
And this were the one moment of surprise
And sorrow while she took her station, pausing
O'er what she sees, finds good, and must destroy!
What gaze you at? Those? Books, I told you of;
Let your first word to me rejoice them, too:
This minion, a Coluthus, writ in red
Bistre and azure by Bessarion's scribe—
Read this line . . no, shame—Homer's be the Greek
First breathed me from the lips of my Greek girl!
My Odyssey in coarse black vivid type
With faded yellow blossoms 'twixt page and page,
To mark great places with due gratitude;
" He said, and on Antinous directed
" A bitter shaft " . . . a flower blots out the rest!
Again upon your search? My statues, then!
—Ah, do not mind that—better that will look
When cast in bronze—an Almaign Kaiser, that,
Swart-green and gold, with truncheon based on hip.
This, rather, turn to! What, unrecognised?
I thought you would have seen that here you sit
As I imagined you,—Hippolyta,
Naked upon her bright Numidian horse!
Recall you this, then? " Carve in bold relief "—
So you commanded—" carve, against I come,
" A Greek, in Athens, as our fashion was,
" Feasting, bay-filleted and thunder-free,
" Who rises 'neath the lifted myrtle-branch :
" ' Praise those who slew Hipparchus,' cry the guests,
" ' While o'er thy head the singer's myrtle waves
" ' As erst above our champions' : stand up, all ! ' "
See, I have laboured to express your thought!
Quite round, a cluster of mere hands and arms,
(Thrust in all senses, all ways, from all sides,
Only consenting at the branches' end
They strain toward) serves for frame to a sole face—
The Praiser's—in the centre—who with eyes

Sightless, so bend they back to light inside
His brain where visionary forms throng up,
Sings, minding not that palpitating arch
Of hands and arms, nor the quick drip of wine
From the drenched leaves o'erhead, nor crowns cast off,
Violet and parsley crowns to trample on—
Sings, pausing as the patron-ghosts approve,
Devoutly their unconquerable hymn!
But you must say a " well " to that—say, " well! "
Because you gaze—am I fantastic, sweet?
Gaze like my very life's stuff, marble—marbly
Even to the silence! why before I found
The real flesh Phene, I inured myself
To see, throughout all nature, varied stuff
For better nature's birth by means of art:
With me, each substance tended to one form
Of beauty—to the human Archetype—
On every side occurred suggestive germs
Of that—the tree, the flower—or take the fruit—
Some rosy shape, continuing the peach,
Curved beewise o'er its bough; as rosy limbs,
Depending, nestled in the leaves—and just
From a cleft rose-peach the whole Dryad sprang!
But of the stuffs one can be master of,
How I divined their capabilities!
From the soft-rinded smoothening facile chalk
That yields your outline to the air's embrace,
Half-softened by a halo's pearly gloom;
Down to the crisp imperious steel, so sure
To cut its one confided thought clean out
Of all the world: but marble!—'neath my tools
More pliable than jelly—as it were
Some clear primordial creature dug from depths
In the Earth's heart, where itself breeds itself,
And whence all baser substance may be worked;
Refine it off to air, you may—condense it
Down to the diamond;—is not metal there,
When o'er the sudden specks my chisel trips?
—Not flesh—as flake off flake I scale, approach,
Lay bare those blueish veins of blood asleep?
Lurks flame in no strange windings where, surprised
By the swift implement sent home at once,
Flushes and glowings radiate and hover

About its track?—

                 Phene? what—why is this?
That whitening cheek, those still-dilating eyes!
Ah, you will die—I knew that you would die!

PHENE *begins, on his having long remained silent.*

Now the end's coming—to be sure, it must
Have ended sometime! Tush—why need I speak
Their foolish speech? I cannot bring to mind
One half of it, besides; and do not care
For old Natalia now, nor any of them.
Oh, you—what are you?—if I do not try
To say the words Natalia made me learn,
To please your friends,—it is to keep myself
Where your voice lifted me, by letting it
Proceed—but can it? Even you, perhaps,
Cannot take up, now you have once let fall,
The music's life, and me along with that—
No, or you would! We'll stay, then, as we are
—Above the world.

              You creature with the eyes!
If I could look for ever up to them,
As now you let me,—I believe, all sin,
All memory of wrong done or suffering borne,
Would drop down, low and lower, to the earth
Whence all that's low comes, and there touch and stay
—Never to overtake the rest of me,
All that, unspotted, reaches up to you,
Drawn by those eyes! What rises is myself,
Not so the shame and suffering; but they sink,
Are left, I rise above them—Keep me so
Above the world!

              But you sink, for your eyes
Are altering—altered! Stay—" I love you, love you " ...
I could prevent it if I understood
More of your words to me—was't in the tone
Or the words, your power?

                 Or stay—I will repeat
Their speech, if that contents you! Only, change
No more, and I shall find it presently
—Far back here, in the brain yourself filled up.
Natalia threatened me that harm would follow

Unless I spoke their lesson to the end,
But harm to me, I thought she meant, not you.
Your friends,—Natalia said they were your friends
And meant you well,—because I doubted it,
Observing (what was very strange to see)
On every face, so different in all else,
The same smile girls like us are used to bear,
But never men, men cannot stoop so low;
Yet your friends, speaking of you, used that smile,
That hateful smirk of boundless self-conceit
Which seems to take possession of this world
And make of God their tame confederate,
Purveyor to their appetites . . . you know!
But no—Natalia said they were your friends,
And they assented while they smiled the more,
And all came round me,—that thin Englishman
With light, lank hair seemed leader of the rest;
He held a paper—" What we want," said he,
Ending some explanation to his friends—
" Is something slow, involved and mystical,
" To hold Jules long in doubt, yet take his taste
" And lure him on, so that, at innermost
" Where he seeks sweetness' soul, he may find—this!
" —As in the apple's core, the noisome fly:
" For insects on the rind are seen at once,
" And brushed aside as soon, but this is found
" Only when on the lips or loathing tongue."
And so he read what I have got by heart—
I'll speak it,—" Do not die, love! I am yours " . . .
Stop—is not that, or like that, part of words
Yourself began by speaking? Strange to lose
What costs much pains to learn! Is this more right?

I am a painter who cannot paint ;
In my life, a devil rather than saint,
In my brain, as poor a creature too—
No end to all I cannot do !
Yet do one thing at least I can—
Love a man, or hate a man
Supremely : thus my love began.
Through the Valley of Love I went,
In its lovingest spot to abide,
And just on the verge where I pitched my tent,
I found Hate dwelling beside.

(Let the Bridegroom ask what the painter meant,
Of his Bride, of the peerless Bride !)
And further, I traversed Hate's grove,
In its hatefullest nook to dwell ;
But lo, where I flung myself prone, couched Love
Where the deepest shadow fell.
(The meaning—those black bride's-eyes above,
Not the painter's lip should tell !)

" And here," said he, " Jules probably will ask,
" *You have black eyes, love,—you are, sure enough,*
" *My peerless bride,—so do you tell, indeed,*
" *What needs some explanation—what means this ?* "
—And I am to go on, without a word—
So I grew wiser in Love and Hate,
From simple, that I was of late.
For once, when I loved, I would enlace
Breast, eyelids, hands, feet, form and face
Of her I loved, in one embrace—
As if by mere love I could love immensely !
And when I hated, I would plunge
My sword, and wipe with the first lunge
My foe's whole life out, like a sponge—
As if by mere hate I could hate intensely !
But now I am wiser, know better the fashion
How passion seeks aid from its opposite passion,
And if I see cause to love more, or hate more
Than ever man loved, ever hated, before—
And seek in the Valley of Love,
The spot, or the spot in Hate's Grove,
Where my soul may the sureliest reach
The essence, nought less, of each,
The Hate of all Hates, or the Love
Of all Loves, in its Valley or Grove,—
I find them the very warders
Each of the other's borders.
I love most, when Love is disguised
In Hate ; and when Hate is surprised
In Love, then I hate most : ask
How Love smiles through Hate's iron casque,
Hate grins through Love's rose-braided mask,—
And how, having hated thee,
I sought long and painfully

To wound thee, and not prick
The skin, but pierce to the quick—
Ask this, my Jules, and be answered straight
By thy bride—how the painter Lutwyche can hate !

JULES *interposes.*

Lutwyche—who else? But all of them, no doubt,
Hated me: they at Venice—presently
Their turn, however ! You I shall not meet:
If I dreamed, saying this would wake me !
                                        Keep
What's here, this gold—we cannot meet again.
Consider—and the money was but meant
For two years' travel, which is over now,
All chance, or hope, or care, or need of it !
This—and what comes from selling these, my casts,
And books, and medals, except . . . let them go
Together, so the produce keeps you safe
Out of Natalia's clutches !—If by chance
(For all's chance here) I should survive the gang
At Venice, root out all fifteen of them,
We might meet somewhere, since the world is wide—

(*From without is heard the voice of* PIPPA, *singing—*

Give her but a least excuse to love me !
When—where—
How—can this arm establish her above me,
If fortune fixed her as my lady there,
There already, to eternally reprove me ?
(" Hist "—said Kate the queen ;
But " Oh—" cried the maiden, binding her tresses,
" 'Tis only a page that carols unseen
" Crumbling your hounds their messes ! ")

Is she wronged ?—To the rescue of her honour,
My heart !
Is she poor ?—What cost it to be styled a donour ?
Merely an earth's to cleave, a sea's to part !
But that fortune should have thrust all this upon her !
(" Nay, list,"—bade Kate the queen ;
And still cried the maiden, binding her tresses,
" 'Tis only a page that carols unseen
" Fitting your hawks their jesses ! ")   (PIPPA *passes.*)

JULES *resumes.*

What name was that the little girl sang forth?
Kate? The Cornaro, doubtless, who renounced
The crown of Cyprus to be lady here
At Asolo, where still the peasants keep
Her memory; and songs tell how many a page
Pined for the grace of one so far above
His power of doing good to, as a queen—
" She never could be wronged, be poor," he sighed,
" For him to help her!"
               Yes, a bitter thing
To see our lady above all need of us;
Yet so we look ere we will love; not I,
But the world looks so. If whoever loves
Must be, in some sort, god or worshipper,
The blessing or the blest one, queen or page,
Why should we always choose the page's part?
Here is a woman with utter need of me,—
I find myself queen here, it seems!
                  How strange!
Look at the woman here with the new soul,
Like my own Psyche's,—fresh upon her lips
Alit, the visionary butterfly,
Waiting my word to enter and make bright,
Or flutter off and leave all blank as first.
This body had no soul before, but slept
Or stirred, was beauteous or ungainly, free
From taint or foul with stain, as outward things
Fastened their image on its passiveness:
Now, it will wake, feel, live—or die again!
Shall to produce form out of unshaped stuff
Be art—and, further, to evoke a soul
From form, be nothing? This new soul is mine!

Now, to kill Lutwyche, what would that do?—save
A wretched dauber, men will hoot to death
Without me, from their laughter!—Oh, to hear
God's voice plain as I heard it first, before
They broke in with that laughter! I heard them
Henceforth, not God!
              To Ancona—Greece—some isle!
I wanted silence only—there is clay
Every where. One may do whate'er one likes

In Art—the only thing is, to make sure
That one does like it—which takes pains to know.
    Scatter all this, my Phene—this mad dream!
Who—what is Lutwyche—what Natalia's friends,
What the whole world except our love—my own,
Own Phene? But I told you, did I not,
Ere night we travel for your land—some isle
With the sea's silence on it? Stand aside—
I do but break these paltry models up
To begin art afresh. Shall I meet Lutwyche,
And save him from my statue's meeting him?
Some unsuspected isle in the far seas!
Like a god going thro' his world there stands
One mountain for a moment in the dusk,
Whole brotherhoods of cedars on its brow—
And you are ever by me while I gaze
—Are in my arms as now—as now—as now!
Some unsuspected isle in the far seas!
Some unsuspected isle in far off seas!

Talk by the way, while PIPPA *is passing from Orcana to the
Turret. Two or three of the Austrian Police loitering with*
BLUPHOCKS, *an English vagabond, just in view of the Turret.*

Bluphocks.[1] So, that is your Pippa, the little girl who
passed us singing? Well, your Bishop's Intendant's money
shall be honestly earned:—now, don't make me that sour
face because I bring the Bishop's name into the business—
we know he can have nothing to do with such horrors—we
know that he is a saint and all that a Bishop should be, who
is a great man besides. *Oh! were but every worm a maggot,
Every fly a grig, Every bough a christmas faggot, Every tune
a jig!* In fact, I have abjured all religions; but the last I
inclined to, was the Armenian—for I have travelled, do you
see, and at Koenigsberg, Prussia Improper (so styled because
there's a sort of bleak hungry sun there,) you might remark
over a venerable house-porch, a certain Chaldee inscription;
and brief as it is, a mere glance at it used absolutely to change
the mood of every bearded passenger. In they turned, one
and all; the young and lightsome, with no irreverent pause,
the aged and decrepit, with a sensible alacrity,—'twas the
Grand Rabbi's abode, in short. Struck with curiosity, I lost

[1] " He maketh his sun to rise on the evil and on the good, and
sendeth rain on the just and on the unjust."

notime inlearning Syriac—(theseare vowels,youdogs,—follow
my stick's end in the mud—*Celarent, Darii, Ferio !*) and one
morning presented myself spelling-book in hand, a, b, c,—
I picked it out letter by letter, and what was the purport of
this miraculous posy? Some cherished legend of the past
you'll say—" *How Moses hocus-pocust Egypt's land with fly
and locust,*"—or, " *How to Jonah sounded harshish, Get thee
up and go to Tarshish,*"—or, " *How the angel meeting Balaam,
Straight his ass returned a salaam ;* "—in no wise!— " *Shacka-
brach—Boach—somebody or other—Isaac, Re-cei-ver, Pur-
cha-ser and Ex-chan-ger of—Stolen goods !* " So talk to me
of the religion of a bishop! I have renounced all bishops save
Bishop Beveridge—mean to live so—and die—*As some Greek
dog-sage, dead and merry, Hellward bound in Charon's wherry
—With food for both worlds, under and upper, Lupine-seed and
Hecate's supper, and never an obolos* . . . (Though thanks to
you, or this Intendant thro' you, or this Bishop through his
Intendant—I possess a burning pocket-full of *zwanzigers*) . .
To pay the Stygian ferry !

1st Pol. There is the girl, then; go and deserve them
the moment you have pointed out to us Signor Luigi and
his mother. (*To the rest*) I have been noticing a house yonder,
this long while—not a shutter unclosed since morning!

2d Pol. Old Luca Gaddi's, that owns the silk-mills here:
he dozes by the hour—wakes up, sighs deeply, says he should
like to be Prince Metternich, and then dozes again, after
having bidden young Sebald, the foreigner, set his wife to
playing draughts: never molest such a household, they
mean well.

Blup. Only, cannot you tell me something of this little
Pippa, I must have to do with?—one could make something
of that name. Pippa—that is, short for Felippa—rhyming
to—*Panerge consults Hertrippa—Believ'st thou,King Agrippa?*
Something might be done with that name.

2d Pol. Put into rhyme that your head and a ripe musk-
melon would not be dear at half a *zwanziger !* Leave this
fooling, and look out—the afternoon's over or nearly so.

3d Pol. Where in this passport of Signor Luigi does our
principal instruct you to watch him so narrowly? There?
what's there beside a simple signature? (That English fool's
busy watching.)

2d Pol. Flourish all round—" put all possible obstacles in
his way; " oblong dot at the end—" Detain him till further

advices reach you;" scratch at bottom—"send him back
on pretence of some informality in the above;" ink-spurt on
right-hand side, (which is the case here)—"Arrest him at
once," why and wherefore, I don't concern myself, but my
instructions amount to this: if Signor Luigi leaves home
to-night for Vienna, well and good—the passport deposed
with us for our *visa* is really for his own use, they have mis-
informed the Office, and he means well; but let him stay over
to-night—there has been the pretence we suspect—the
accounts of his corresponding and holding intelligence with
the Carbonari are correct—we arrest him at once—to-morrow
comes Venice—and presently, Spielberg. Bluphocks makes
the signal sure enough! That is he, entering the turret with
his mother, no doubt.

III.—*Evening. Inside the Turret.* Luigi *and his Mother
entering.*

Mother. If there blew wind, you'd hear a long sigh, easing
The utmost heaviness of music's heart.
    Luigi. Here in the archway?
    Mother.   Oh, no, no—in farther,
Where the echo is made—on the ridge.
    Luigi.   Here surely, then.
How plain the tap of my heel as I leaped up!
Hark—"*Lucius Junius!*" The very ghost of a voice,
Whose body is caught and kept by . . . what are those?
Mere withered wall-flowers, waving overhead?
They seem an elvish group with thin bleached hair
Who lean out of their topmost fortress—looking
And listening, mountain men, to what we say,
Hands under chin of each grave earthy face:
Up and show faces all of you!—"*All of you!*"
That's the king's dwarf with the scarlet comb; now hark—
Come down and meet your fate! Hark—"*Meet your fate!*"
    Mother. Let him not meet it, my Luigi—do not
Go to his City! putting crime aside,
Half of these ills of Italy are feigned—
Your Pellicos and writers for effect,
Write for effect.
    Luigi.   Hush! say A. writes, and B.
    Mother. These A.'s and B.'s write for effect, I say.

Then, evil is in its nature loud, while good
Is silent—you hear each petty injury—
None of his daily virtues; he is old,
Quiet, and kind, and densely stupid—why
Do A. and B. not kill him themselves?

   Luigi.   They teach
Others to kill him—me—and, if I fail,
Others to succeed; now, if A. tried and failed
I could not teach that: mine's the lesser task.
Mother, they visit night by night . . .

   Mother.   —You, Luigi?
Ah, will you let me tell you what you are?

   Luigi. Why not? Oh, the one thing you fear to hint,
You may assure yourself I say and say
Ever to myself; at times—nay, even as now
We sit, I think my mind is touched—suspect
All is not sound: but is not knowing that,
What constitutes one sane or otherwise?
I know I am thus—so all is right again!
I laugh at myself as through the town I walk,
And see men merry as if no Italy
Were suffering; then I ponder—" I am rich,
" Young, healthy; why should this fact trouble me,
" More than it troubles these? " But it does trouble me!
No—trouble's a bad word—for as I walk
There's springing and melody and giddiness,
And old quaint terms and passages of my youth—
Dreams long forgotten, little in themselves—
Return to me—whatever may amuse me,
And earth seems in a truce with me, and heaven
Accords with me, all things suspend their strife,
The very cicalas laugh " There goes he, and there!
" Feast him, the time is short—he is on his way
" For the world's sake—feast him this once, our friend! "
And in return for all this, I can trip
Cheerfully up the scaffold-steps: I go
This evening, mother!

   Mother.   But mistrust yourself—
Mistrust the judgment you pronounce on him.

   Luigi. Oh, there I feel—am sure that I am right!

   Mother. Mistrust your judgment, then, of the mere means
Of this wild enterprise: say you are right,—
How should one in your state e'er bring to pass

What would require a cool head, a cold heart,
And a calm hand? You never will escape.
   Luigi.   Escape—to even wish that, would spoil all!
The dying is best part of it. Too much
Have I enjoyed these fifteen years of mine,
To leave myself excuse for longer life—
Was not life pressed down, running o'er with joy,
That I might finish with it ere my fellows
Who, sparelier feasted, make a longer stay?
I was put at the board-head, helped to all
At first; I rise up happy and content.
God must be glad one loves his world so much—
I can give news of earth to all the dead
Who ask me:—last year's sunsets, and great stars
That had a right to come first and see ebb
The crimson wave that drifts the sun away—
Those crescent moons with notched and burning rims
That strengthened into sharp fire, and there stood,
Impatient of the azure—and that day
In March, a double rainbow stopped the storm—
May's warm, slow, yellow moonlit summer nights—
Gone are they, but I have them in my soul!
   Mother.   (He will not go!)
   Luigi.   You smile at me! 'Tis true.—
Voluptuousness, grotesqueness, ghastliness,
Environ my devotedness as quaintly
As round about some antique altar wreathe
The rose festoons, goats' horns, and oxen's skulls.
   Mother.   See now: you reach the city—you must cross
His threshold—how?
   Luigi.   Oh, that's if we conspired!
Then would come pains in plenty, as you guess—
But guess not how the qualities required
For such an office—qualities I have—
Would little stead me otherwise employed,
Yet prove of rarest merit here—here only.
Every one knows for what his excellence
Will serve, but no one ever will consider
For what his worst defect might serve; and yet
Have you not seen me range our coppice yonder
In search of a distorted ash?—it happens
The wry spoilt branch's a natural perfect bow!
Fancy the thrice-sage, thrice-precautioned man

Arriving at the palace on my errand!
No, no—I have a handsome dress packed up—
White satin here, to set off my black hair—
In I shall march—for you may watch your life out
Behind thick walls—make friends there to betray you;
More than one man spoils everything.   March straight—
Only, no clumsy knife to fumble for—
Take the great gate, and walk (not saunter) on
Thro' guards and guards——I have rehearsed it all
Inside the Turret here a hundred times—
Don't ask the way of whom you meet, observe,
But where they cluster thickliest is the door
Of doors; they'll let you pass—they'll never blab
Each to the other, he knows not the favourite,
Whence he is bound and what's his business now—
Walk in—straight up to him—you have no knife—
Be prompt, how should he scream?   Then, out with you!
Italy, Italy, my Italy!
You're free, you're free!   Oh mother, I could dream
They got about me—Andrea from his exile,
Pier from his dungeon, Gaultier from his grave!
　　Mother.   Well, you shall go.   Yet seems this patriotism
The easiest virtue for a selfish man
To acquire!   He loves himself—and next, the world—
If he must love beyond,—but nought between:
As a short-sighted man sees nought midway
His body and the sun above.   But you
Are my adored Luigi—ever obedient
To my least wish, and running o'er with love—
I could not call you cruel or unkind!
Once more, your ground for killing him!—then go!
　　Luigi.   Now do you ask me, or make sport of me?
How first the Austrians got these provinces—
(If that is all, I'll satisfy you soon)
. . . Never by conquest but by cunning, for
That treaty whereby . . .
　　Mother.　　　　　　　Well?
　　Luigi.　　　　　　　　　　(Sure he's arrived,
The tell-tale cuckoo—spring's his confidant,
And he lets out her April purposes!)
Or . . better go at once to modern times—
He has . . they have . . in fact, I understand
But can't re-state the matter; that's my boast;

Others could reason it out to you, and prove
Things they have made me feel.
   Mother.   Why go to-night?
Morn's for adventure. Jupiter is now
A morning star. I cannot hear you, Luigi!
   Luigi. "I am the bright and morning-star," God saith—
And, " to such an one I give the morning-star!"
The gift of the morning-star—have I God's gift
Of the morning-star?
   Mother.   Chiara will love to see
That Jupiter an evening-star next June.
   Luigi. True, mother. Well, for those who live through
      June!
Great noontides, thunder storms, all glaring pomps
Which triumph at the heels of sovereign June
Leading his glorious revel thro' our world.
Yes, Chiara will be here—
   Mother.   In June—remember,
Yourself appointed that month for her coming—
   Luigi. Was that low noise the echo?
   Mother.   The night-wind.
She must be grown—with her blue eyes upturned
As if life were one long and sweet surprise:
In June she comes.
   Luigi.   We were to see together
The Titian at Treviso—there, again!

   (*From without is heard the voice of* PIPPA, *singing*—

> *A king lived long ago,*
> *In the morning of the world,*
> *When earth was nigher heaven than now :*
> *And the king's locks curled*
> *Disparting o'er a forehead full*
> *As the milk-white space 'twixt horn and horn*
> *Of some sacrificial bull—*
> *Only calm as a babe new-born :*
> *For he was got to a sleepy mood,*
> *So safe from all decrepitude,*
> *From age with its bane, so sure gone by,*
> *(The Gods so loved him while he dreamed,)*
> *That, having lived thus long, there seemed*
> *No need the king should ever die.*

Luigi. No need that sort of king should ever die!

> [*From without.*] *Among the rocks his city was :*
> *Before his palace, in the sun,*
> *He sate to see his people pass,*
> *And judge them every one*
> *From its threshold of smooth stone.*
> *They haled him many a valley-thief*
> *Caught in the sheep-pens—robber-chief,*
> *Swarthy and shameless—beggar-cheat—*
> *Spy-prowler—or rough pirate found*
> *On the sea-sand left aground ;*
> *And sometimes clung about his feet,*
> *With bleeding lip and burning cheek,*
> *A woman, bitterest wrong to speak*
> *Of one with sullen thickset brows :*
> *And sometimes from the prison-house*
> *The angry priests a pale wretch brought,*
> *Who through some chink had pushed and pressed,*
> *On knees and elbows, belly and breast,*
> *Worm-like into the temple,—caught*
> *At last there by the very God*
> *Who ever in the darkness strode*
> *Backward and forward, keeping watch*
> *O'er his brazen bowls, such rogues to catch !*
> *And these, all and every one,*
> *The king judged, sitting in the sun.*

Luigi. That king should still judge sitting in the sun!

> [*From without.*] *His councillors, on left and right,*
> *Looked anxious up,—but no surprise*
> *Disturbed the king's old smiling eyes,*
> *Where the very blue had turned to white.*
> *'Tis said a Python scared one day*
> *The breathless city, till he came,*
> *With forky tongue and eyes on flame,*
> *Where the old king sate to judge alway ;*
> *But when he saw the sweepy hair,*
> *Girt with a crown of berries rare*
> *Which the God will hardly give to wear*
> *To the maiden who singeth, dancing bare*
> *In the altar-smoke by the pine-torch lights,*

> *At his wondrous forest rites,—*
> *Beholding this, he did not dare,*
> *Approach that threshold in the sun,*
> *Assault the old king smiling there.*
> *Such grace had kings when the world begun!*

(PIPPA *passes.*)

Luigi. And such grace have they, now that the world ends!
The Python in the city, on the throne,
And brave men, God would crown for slaying him,
Lurk in bye-corners lest they fall his prey.
Are crowns yet to be won, in this late trial,
Which weakness makes me hesitate to reach?
'Tis God's voice calls, how could I stay? Farewell!

Talk by the way, while PIPPA *is passing from the Turret to
the Bishop's brother's House, close to the Duomo S. Maria.
Poor* Girls *sitting on the steps.*

1st Girl. There goes a swallow to Venice—the stout sea-
farer!
Seeing those birds fly, makes one wish for wings.
Let us all wish; you, wish first!

2d Girl.   I? This sunset
To finish.

3d Girl. That old . . . somebody I know,
Greyer and older than my grandfather,
To give me the same treat he gave last week—
Feeding me on his knee with fig-peckers,
Lampreys, and red Breganze-wine, and mumbling
The while some folly about how well I fare,
To be let eat my supper quietly—
Since had he not himself been late this morning
Detained at—never mind where,—had he not . . .
" Eh, baggage, had I not!"—

2d Girl.   How she can lie!

3d Girl. Look there—by the nails—

2d Girl.   What makes your fingers red?

3d Girl. Dipping them into wine to write bad words with,
On the bright table—how he laughed!

1st Girl.   My turn:
Spring's come and summer's coming: I would wear
A long loose gown—down to the feet and hands—
With plaits here, close about the throat, all day:
And all night lie, the cool long nights, in bed—

And have new milk to drink—apples to eat,
Deuzans and junetings, leather-coats . . . ah, I should
    say,
This is away in the fields—miles!

    3d Girl.   Say at once
You'd be at home—she'd always be at home!
Now comes the story of the farm among
The cherry orchards, and how April snowed
White blossoms on her as she ran: why, fool,
They've rubbed out the chalk-mark of how tall you were,
Twisted your starling's neck, broken his cage,
Made a dunghill of your garden—

    1st Girl.   They, destroy
My garden since I left them? well—perhaps!
I would have done so—so I hope they have!
A fig-tree curled out of our cottage wall—
They called it mine, I have forgotten why,
It must have been there long ere I was born;
Cric—cric—I think I hear the wasps o'erhead
Pricking the papers strung to flutter there
And keep off birds in fruit-time—coarse long papers,
And the wasps eat them, prick them through and through.

    3d Girl.   How her mouth twitches! Where was I?—before
She broke in with her wishes and long gowns
And wasps—would I be such a fool!—Oh, here!
This is my way—I answer every one
Who asks me why I make so much of him—
(If you say, you love him—straight " he'll not be gulled ")
" He that seduced me when I was a girl
Thus high—had eyes like yours, or hair like yours,
Brown, red, white,"—as the case may be—that pleases!
(See how that beetle burnishes in the path—
There sparkles he along the dust! and, there—
Your journey to that maize-tuft's spoilt at least!)

    1st Girl.   When I was young, they said if you killed one
Of those sunshiny beetles, that his friend
Up there, would shine no more that day nor next.

    2d Girl.   When you were young? Nor are you young,
    that's true!
How your plump arms, that were, have dropped away!
Why, I can span them! Cecco beats you still?
No matter, so you keep your curious hair.
I wish they'd find a way to dye our hair

Your colour—any lighter tint, indeed,
Than black—the men say they are sick of black,
Black eyes, black hair!

4th Girl. Sick of yours, like enough!
Do you pretend you ever tasted lampreys
And ortolans? Giovita, of the palace,
Engaged (but there's no trusting him) to slice me
Polenta with a knife that has cut up
An ortolan.

2d Girl. Why, there! is not that, Pippa
We are to talk to, under the window,—quick,—
Where the lights are?

1st Girl. No—or she would sing;
—For the Intendant said . . .

3d Girl. Oh, you sing first—
Then, if she listens and comes close . . . I'll tell you,
Sing that song the young English noble made,
Who took you for the purest of the pure,
And meant to leave the world for you—what fun!

2d Girl [*Sings.*]

> You'll love me yet!—and I can tarry
> Your love's protracted growing:
> June reared that bunch of flowers you carry
> From seeds of April's sowing.
>
> I plant a heartfull now—some seed
> At least is sure to strike
> And yield—what you'll not pluck indeed,
> Not love, but, may be, like!
>
> You'll look at least on love's remains,
> A grave's one violet:
> Your look?—that pays a thousand pains.
> What's death?—You'll love me yet!

3d Girl. [*To* PIPPA *who approaches.*] Oh, you may come closer—we shall not eat you! Why, you seem the very person that the great rich handsome Englishman has fallen so violently in love with! I'll tell you all about it.

IV.—*Night. The Palace by the Duomo.* MONSIGNOR, *dismissing his* Attendants.

Mon. Thanks, friends, many thanks. I chiefly desire life now, that I may recompense every one of you. Most I know something of already. What, a repast prepared?

Benedicto benedicatur . . . ugh . . . ugh! Where was I?
Oh, as you were remarking, Ugo, the weather is mild, very
unlike winter-weather,—but I am a Sicilian, you know, and
shiver in your Julys here: To be sure, when 'twas full summer
at Messina, as we priests used to cross in procession the great
square on Assumption Day, you might see our thickest yellow
tapers twist suddenly in two, each like a falling star, or sink
down on themselves in a gore of wax. But go, my friends,
but go! [*To the* Intendant] Not you, Ugo! [*The others leave
the apartment*] I have long wanted to converse with you,
Ugo!

Inten.   Uguccio—

Mon. . . 'guccio Stefani, man! of Ascoli, Fermo, and
Fossombruno;—what I do need instructing about, are these
accounts of your administration of my poor brother's affairs.
Ugh! I shall never get through a third part of your accounts:
take some of these dainties before we attempt it, however:
are you bashful to that degree? For me, a crust and water
suffice.

Inten.   Do you choose this especial night to question me?

Mon.   This night, Ugo.   You have managed my late
brother's affairs since the death of our elder brother—fourteen
years and a month, all but three days. On the 3rd of December,
I find him . . .

Inten.   If you have so intimate an acquaintance with your
brother's affairs, you will be tender of turning so far back—
they will hardly bear looking into, so far back.

Mon.   Ay, ay, ugh, ugh,—nothing but disappointments
here below! I remark a considerable payment made to
yourself on this 3rd of December. Talk of disappointments!
There was a young fellow here, Jules, a foreign sculptor, I did
my utmost to advance, that the church might be a gainer
by us both: he was going on hopefully enough, and of a
sudden he notifies to me some marvellous change that has
happened in his notions of art; here's his letter,—" He
never had a clearly conceived Ideal within his brain till to-day.
Yet since his hand could manage a chisel, he has practised
expressing other men's Ideals—and, in the very perfection
he has attained to, he foresees an ultimate failure—his unconscious hand will pursue its prescribed course of old years, and
will reproduce with a fatal expertness the ancient types, let
the novel one appear never so palpably to his spirit: there is
but one method of escape—confiding the virgin type to as

chaste a hand, he will turn painter instead of sculptor, and paint, not carve, its characteristics,"—strike out, I dare say, a school like Correggio: how think you Ugo?

Inten. Is Correggio a painter?

Mon. Foolish Jules! and yet, after all, why foolish? He may—probably will, fail egregiously; but if there should arise a new painter, will it not be in some such way by a poet, now, or a musician, (spirits who have conceived and perfected an Ideal through some other channel) transferring it to this, and escaping our conventional roads by pure ignorance of them; eh, Ugo? If you have no appetite, talk at least, Ugo!

Inten. Sir, I can submit no longer to this course of yours: first, you select the group of which I formed one,—next you thin it gradually,—always retaining me with your smile,— and so do you proceed till you have fairly got me alone with you between four stone walls: and now then? Let this farce, this chatter end now—what is it you want with me?

Mon. Ugo . . .

Inten. From the instant you arrived, I felt your smile on me as you questioned me about this and the other article in those papers—why your brother should have given me this villa, that *podere*,—and your nod at the end meant,—what?

Mon. Possibly that I wished for no loud talk here: if once you set me coughing, Ugo!—

Inten. I have your brother's hand and seal to all I possess: now ask me what for! what service I did him—ask me!

Mon. I had better not—I should rip up old disgraces —let out my poor brother's weaknesses. By the way, Maffeo of Forli, (which, I forgot to observe, is your true name) was the interdict ever taken off you, for robbing that church at Cesena?

Inten. No, nor needs be—for when I murdered your brother's friend, Pasquale, for him . . .

Mon. Ah, he employed you in that business, did he? Well, I must let you keep, as you say, this villa and that *podere*, for fear the world should find out my relations were of so indifferent a stamp! Maffeo, my family is the oldest in Messina, and century after century have my progenitors gone on polluting themselves with every wickedness under Heaven: my own father . . . rest his soul!—I have, I know, a chapel to support that it may rest: my dear two dead brothers were,—what you know tolerably well; I, the youngest, might have rivalled them in vice, if not in wealth, but from my boyhood I came out from among them, and so am not the partaker of their plagues. My glory springs from another source; or if from this, by contrast only,—for I, the bishop, am the brother of your employers, Ugo. I hope to repair some of their wrong, however; so far as my brother's ill-gotten treasure reverts to me, I can stop the consequences of his crime; and not one *soldo* shall escape me. Maffeo, the sword we quiet men spurn away, you shrewd knaves pick up and commit murders with; what opportunities the virtuous forego, the villainous seize. Because, to pleasure myself, apart from other considerations, my food would be millet-cake, my dress sack-cloth, and my couch straw,—am I therefore to let you, the off-scouring of the earth, seduce the poor and ignorant, by appropriating a pomp these will be sure to think lessens the abominations so unaccountably and exclusively associated with it? Must I let villas and *poderes* go to you, a murderer and thief, that you may beget by means of them other murderers and thieves? No . . . if my cough would but allow me to speak!

Inten. What am I to expect? You are going to punish me?

Mon. Must punish you, Maffeo. I cannot afford to cast away a chance. I have whole centuries of sin to redeem, and only a month or two of life to do it in! How should I dare to say . . .

Inten. "Forgive us our trespasses"—

Mon. My friend, it is because I avow myself a very worm, sinful beyond measure, that I reject a line of conduct you would applaud, perhaps: shall I proceed, as it were, a-pardoning?—I?—who have no symptom of reason to assume that aught less than my strenuousest efforts will keep myself out of mortal sin, much less, keep others out. No—I do trespass, but will not double that by allowing you to trespass

Inten. And suppose the villas are not your brother's to give, nor yours to take? Oh, you are hasty enough just now!

Mon. 1, 2—No. 3!—ay, can you read the substance of a letter, No. 3, I have received from Rome? It is precisely on the ground there mentioned, of the suspicion I have that a certain child of my late elder brother, who would have succeeded to his estates, was murdered in infancy by you, Maffeo, at the instigation of my late brother—that the Pontiff enjoins on me not merely the bringing that Maffeo to condign punishment, but the taking all pains, as guardian of that infant's heritage for the Church, to recover it parcel by parcel, howsoever, whensoever, and wheresoever. While you are now gnawing those fingers, the police are engaged in sealing up your papers, Maffeo, and the mere raising my voice brings my people from the next room to dispose of yourself. But I want you to confess quietly, and save me raising my voice. Why, man, do I not know the old story? The heir between the succeeding heir, and that heir's ruffianly instrument, and their complot's effect, and the life of fear and bribes, and ominous smiling silence? Did you throttle or stab my brother's infant? Come, now!

Inten. So old a story, and tell it no better? When did such an instrument ever produce such an effect? Either the child smiles in his face, or, most likely, he is not fool enough to put himself in the employer's power so thoroughly—the child is always ready to produce—as you say—howsoever, wheresoever, and whensoever.

Mon. Liar!

Inten. Strike me? Ah, so might a father chastise! I shall sleep soundly to-night at least, though the gallows await me to-morrow; for what a life did I lead! Carlo of Cesena reminds me of his connivance, every time I pay his annuity (which happens commonly thrice a year). If I remonstrate, he will confess all to the good bishop—you!

Mon. I see thro' the trick, caitiff! I would you spoke truth for once; all shall be sifted, however—seven times sifted.

Inten. And how my absurd riches encumbered me! I dared not lay claim to above half my possessions. Let me but once embosom myself, glorify Heaven, and die!

Sir, you are no brutal, dastardly idiot like your brother I frightened to death—let us understand one another. Sir, I will make away with her for you—the girl—here close at hand; not the stupid obvious kind of killing; do not speak—know nothing of her or me! I see her every day—saw her this morning: of course there is to be no killing; but at Rome the courtesans perish off every three years, and I can entice her thither—have, indeed, begun operations already. There's a certain lusty, blue-eyed, florid-complexioned, English knave I and the Police employ occasionally.—You assent, I perceive—no, that's not it—assent I do not say—but you will let me convert my present havings and holdings into cash, and give me time to cross the Alps? 'Tis but a little black-

eyed, pretty singing Felippa, gay silk-winding girl. I have
kept her out of harm's way up to this present; for I always
intended to make your life a plague to you with her! 'Tis as
well settled once and for ever: some women I have procured
will pass Bluphocks, my handsome scoundrel, off for somebody; and once Pippa entangled!—you conceive? Through
her singing? Is it a bargain?

(From without is heard the voice of PIPPA, *singing—*

> *Over-head the tree-tops meet—*
> *Flowers and grass spring 'neath one's feet—*
> *There was nought above me, and nought below,*
> *My childhood had not learned to know !*
> *For, what are the voices of birds*
> *—Ay, and of beasts,—but words—our words,*
> *Only so much more sweet ?*
> *The knowledge of that with my life begun !*
> *But I had so near made out the sun,*
> *And counted your stars, the Seven and One,*
> *Like the fingers of my hand :*
> *Nay, I could all but understand*
> *Wherefore through heaven the white moon ranges ;*
> *And just when out of her soft fifty changes*
> *No unfamiliar face might overlook me—*
> *Suddenly God took me !*   (PIPPA *passes.*)

Mon. [*Springing up.*] My people—one and all—all—
within there! Gag this villain—tie him hand and foot! He
dares—I know not half he dares—but remove him—quick!
Miserere mei, Domine ! quick, I say!

PIPPA'S *Chamber again. She enters it.*

The bee with his comb,
The mouse at her dray,
The grub in its tomb,
Wile winter away;
But the fire-fly and hedge-shrew and lob-worm, I pray,
How fare they?
Ha, ha, best thanks for your counsel, my Zanze—
" Feast upon lampreys, quaff the Breganze "—
The summer of life's so easy to spend,
And care for to-morrow so soon put away !
But winter hastens at summer's end,

And fire-fly, hedge-shrew, lob-worm, pray,
How fare they?
No bidding me then to . . . what did she say?
" Pare your nails pearlwise, get your small feet shoes
" More like . . . (what said she?)—and less like canoes—"
How pert that girl was!—would I be those pert
Impudent staring women! it had done me,
However, surely no such mighty hurt
To learn his name who passed that jest upon me:
No foreigner, that I can recollect,
Came, as she says, a month since, to inspect
Our silk-mills—none with blue eyes and thick rings
Of English-coloured hair, at all events.
Well—if old Luca keeps his good intents,
We shall do better: see what next year brings.
I may buy shoes, my Zanze, not appear
More destitute than you, perhaps, next year!
Bluph . . . something! I had caught the uncouth name
But for Monsignor's people's sudden clatter
Above us—bound to spoil such idle chatter
As ours; it were, indeed, a serious matter
If silly talk like ours should put to shame
The pious man, the man devoid of blame,
The . . . ah, but—ah, but, all the same,
No mere mortal has a right
To carry that exalted air;
Best people are not angels quite—
While—not the worst of people's doings scare
The devils; so there's that proud look to spare!
Which is mere counsel to myself, mind! for
I have just been the holy Monsignor!
And I was you too, Luigi's gentle mother,
And you too, Luigi!—how that Luigi started
Out of the Turret—doubtlessly departed
On some good errand or another,
For he past just now in a traveller's trim,
And the sullen company that prowled
About his path, I noticed, scowled
As if they had lost a prey in him.
And I was Jules the sculptor's bride,
And I was Ottima beside,
And now what am I?—tired of fooling!
Day for folly, night for schooling!

New year's day is over and spent,
Ill or well, I must be content!
Even my lily's asleep, I vow:
Wake up—here's a friend I've pluckt you!
See—call this flower a heart's-ease now!
And something rare, let me instruct you,
Is this—with petals triply swollen,
Three times spotted, thrice the pollen,
While the leaves and parts that witness
The old proportions and their fitness
Here remain, unchanged unmoved now—
So call this pampered thing improved now!
Suppose there's a king of the flowers
And a girl-show held in his bowers—
" Look ye, buds, this growth of ours,"
Says he, " Zanze from the Brenta,
I have made her gorge polenta
Till both cheeks are near as bouncing
As her . . . name there's no pronouncing!
See this heightened colour too—
For she swilled Breganze wine
Till her nose turned deep carmine—
'Twas but white when wild she grew!
And only by this Zanze's eyes
Of which we could not change the size,
The magnitude of what's achieved
Otherwise, may be perceived! "
Oh what a drear, dark close to my poor day!
How could that red sun drop in that black cloud!
Ah, Pippa, morning's rule is moved away,
Dispensed with, never more to be allowed,
Day's turn is over—now arrives the night's—
Oh, Lark, be day's apostle
To mavis, merle and throstle,
Bid them their betters jostle
From day and its delights!
But at night, brother Howlet, far over the woods,
Toll the world to thy chantry—
Sing to the bats' sleek sisterhoods
Full complines with gallantry—
Then, owls and bats, cowls and twats,
Monks and nuns, in a cloister's moods,
Adjourn to the oak-stump pantry!

[After she has begun to undress herself.
Now, one thing I should like really to know:
How near I ever might approach all these
I only fancied being, this long day—
—Approach, I mean, so as to touch them—so
As to . . . in some way . . . move them—if you please,
Do good or evil to them some slight way.
For instance, if I wind
Silk to-morrow, my silk may bind   *[Sitting on the bedside.*
And broider Ottima's cloak's hem—
Ah, me and my important part with them,
This morning's hymn half promised when I rose!
True in some sense or other, I suppose,
Though I passed by them all, and felt no sign.
                                   [As she lies down.
God bless me! I can pray no more to-night.
No doubt, some way or other, hymns say right.
All service is the same with God—
With God, whose puppets, best and worst,
Are we : there is no last nor first.—   *[She sleeps.*

KING VICTOR AND KING CHARLES[1]

A TRAGEDY

PERSONS

VICTOR AMADEUS, First King of Sardinia.
CHARLES EMMANUEL, his Son, Prince of Piedmont.
POLYXENA, Wife of Charles.
D'ORMEA, Minister.

SCENE.—*The Council Chamber of Rivoli Palace, near Turin, communicating with a Hall at the back, an Apartment to the left and another to the right of the stage.*

TIME, 1730-1

FIRST YEAR, 1730

KING VICTOR. PART I

CHARLES, POLYXENA.

Cha. You think so? Well, I do not.
Pol. My beloved,
All must clear up—we shall be happy yet:
This cannot last for ever . . oh, may change
To-day, or any day!
Cha. —May change? Ah yes—
May change!
Pol. Endure it, then.
Cha. No doubt, a life

[1] So far as I know, this Tragedy is the first artistical consequence of what Voltaire termed " a terrible event without consequences; " and although it professes to be historical, I have taken more pains to arrive at the history than most readers would thank me for particularising: since acquainted, as I will hope them to be, with the chief circumstances of Victor's remarkable European career—nor quite ignorant of the sad and surprising facts I am about to reproduce (a tolerable account of which is to be found, for instance, in Abbé Roman's *Récit*, or even the fifth of Lord Orrery's Letters from Italy)—I cannot expect them to be versed, nor desirous of becoming so, in all the details of the memoirs, correspondence, and relations of the time. From these only may be obtained a knowledge of the fiery and audacious

Like this drags on, now better and now worse;
My father may . . . may take to loving me;
And he may take, too, D'Ormea closer yet
To counsel him;—may even cast off her
—That bad Sebastian: but he also may
. . Or, no, Polyxena, my only friend,
He may not force you from me?

Pol.　　　　　　　　　Now, force me
From you!—me, close by you as if there gloomed
No D'Ormeas, no Sebastians on our path—
At Rivoli or Turin, still at hand,
Arch-Counseller, prime confidant . . . force me!

　Cha.　Because I felt as sure, as I feel sure
We clasp hands now, of being happy once.
Young was I, quite neglected, nor concerned
By the world's business that engrossed so much
My father and my brother: if I peered
From out my privacy,—amid the crash
And blaze of nations, domineered those two;
'Twas war, peace—France our foe, now—England, friend—
In love with Spain—at feud with Austria!—Well—
I wondered—laughed a moment's laugh for pride
In the chivalrous couple—then let drop
My curtain—" I am out of it," I said—
When . . .

　　Pol.　　　　You have told me, Charles.
　　Cha.　　　　　　　　　　Polyxena—
When suddenly,—a warm March day, just that!
Just so much sunshine as the cottager's child
Basks in delighted, while the cottager
Takes off his bonnet, as he ceases work,
To catch the more of it—and it must fall
Heavily on my brother . . . had you seen
Philip—the lion-featured!—not like me!

　Pol.　I know—

temper, unscrupulous selfishness, profound dissimulation, and singular
fertility in resources, of Victor—the extreme and painful sensibility,
prolonged immaturity of powers, earnest good purpose and vacillating
will of Charles—the noble and right woman's manliness of his wife
—and the ill-considered rascality and subsequent better-advised
rectitude of D'Ormea. When I say, therefore, that I cannot but
believe my statement (combining as it does what appears correct in
Voltaire and plausible in Condorcet) more true to person and thing
than any it has hitherto been my fortune to meet with, no doubt my
word will be taken, and my evidence spared as readily.

LONDON: 1842.　　　　　　　　　　　　　　　R. B.

Cha.   And Philip's mouth yet fast to mine,
His dead cheek on my cheek, his arm still round
My neck,—they bade me rise " for I was heir
To the Duke," they said, " the right hand of the Duke;"
Till then he was my father, not the Duke!
So . . let me finish . . the whole intricate
World's business their dead boy was born to, I
Must conquer,—ay, the brilliant thing he was,
I, of a sudden, must be: my faults, my follies,
—All bitter truths were told me, all at once
To end the sooner. What I simply styled
Their overlooking me, had been contempt.
How should the Duke employ himself, forsooth,
With such an one while lordly Philip rode
By him their Turin through? But he was punished
And must put up with—me! 'Twas sad enough
To learn my future portion and submit—
And then the wear and worry, blame on blame!
—For, spring-sounds in my ears, spring-smells about,
How could I but grow dizzy in their pent
Dim palace-rooms at first? My mother's look
As they discussed my insignificance—
(She and my father, and I sitting by,)—
I bore:—I knew how brave a son they missed:
Philip had gaily passed state-papers o'er,
While Charles was spelling at them painfully!
But Victor was my father spite of that.
" Duke Victor's entire life has been," I said,
" Innumerable efforts to one end;
And, on the point now of that end's success,
Our Ducal turning to a Kingly crown,
Where's time to be reminded 'tis his child
He spurns?" And so I suffered . . yet scarce suffered,
Since I had you at length!
Pol.   —To serve in place
Of monarch, minister and mistress, Charles.
Cha. But, once that crown obtained, then was't not like
Our lot would alter?—" When he rests, takes breath,
Glances around, and sees who's left to love—
Now that my mother's dead, sees I am left—
Is it not like he'd love me at the last?"
Well: Savoy turns Sardinia—the Duke's King!
Could I—precisely then—could you expect

His harshness to redouble?   These few months
Have been . . . have been . . Polyxena, do you
And God conduct me, or I lose myself!
What would he have?   What is't they want with me?
Him with this mistress and this minister,
—You see me and you hear him; judge us both!
Pronounce what I should do, Polyxena!

    Pol.   Endure, endure, beloved!   Say you not
That he's your Father?   All's so incident
To novel sway!   Beside, our life must change:
Or you'll acquire his kingcraft, or he'll find
Harshness a sorry way of teaching it.
I bear this—not that there's so much to bear—

   Cha.   You bear it?   don't I know that you, tho' bound
To silence for my sake, are perishing
Piecemeal beside me?   And how otherwise?
—When every creephole from the hideous Court
Is stopt; the Minister to dog me, here—
The Mistress posted to entrap you, there!
And thus shall we grow old in such a life—
Not careless,—never estranged,—but old: to alter
Our life, there is so much to alter!

    Pol.   Come—
Is it agreed that we forego complaints
Even at Turin, yet complain we here
At Rivoli?   'Twere wiser you announced
Our presence to the King.   What's now afoot,
I wonder?—Not that any more's to dread
Than every day's embarrassment—but guess,
For me, why train so fast succeeded train
On the high-road, each gayer still than each;
I noticed your Archbishop's pursuivant,
The sable cloak and silver cross; such pomp
Bodes . . what now, Charles?   Can you conceive?

    Cha.   Not I.

    Pol.   A matter of some moment—

    Cha.   There's our life!
Which of the group of loiterers that stared
From the lime-avenue, divines that I—
About to figure presently, he thinks,
In face of all assembled—am the one
Who knows precisely least about it?

    Pol.   Tush!

o **41**

D'Ormea's contrivance!

Cha.   Ay—how otherwise
Should the young Prince serve for the old King's foil?
—So that the simplest courtier may remark,
'Twere idle raising parties for a Prince
Content to linger D'Ormea's laughing-stock!
Something, 'tis like, about that weary business

[*Pointing to papers he has laid down, and which* POLY-
XENA *examines.*]

—Not that I comprehend three words, of course,
After all last night's study.

Pol.   The faint heart!
Why, as we rode and you rehearsed just now
Its substance . . (that's the folded speech I mean,
Concerning the Reduction of the Fiefs . .)
—What would you have?—I fancied while you spoke,
Some tones were just your father's.

Cha.   Flattery!

Pol. I fancied so:—and here lurks, sure enough,
My note upon the Spanish Claims!   You've mastered
The fief-speech thoroughly—this other, mind,
Is an opinion you deliver,—stay,
Best read it slowly over once to me;
Read—there's bare time; you read it firmly—loud
—Rather loud—looking in his face,—don't sink
Your eye once—ay, thus! " If Spain claims . . . " begin
—Just as you look at me!

Cha.   At you! Oh, truly,
You have I seen, say, marshalling your troops—
Dismissing councils—or, through doors ajar,
Head sunk on hand, devoured by slow chagrins
—Then radiant, for a crown had all at once
Seemed possible again! I can behold
Him, whose least whisper ties my spirit fast,
In this sweet brow, nought could divert me from,
Save objects like Sebastian's shameless lip,
Or, worse, the clipt grey hair and dead white face,
And dwindling eye as if it ached with guile,
Which D'Ormea wears . . .

[*As he kisses her, enter from the* KING'S *apartment*
D'ORMEA.]

                    . . I said he would divert
My kisses from your brow!

D'O. [*Aside.*] Here! So King Victor
Spoke truth for once; and who's ordained, but I,
To make that memorable? Both in call,
As he declared! Were't better gnash the teeth,
Or laugh outright now?

    Cha. [*to Pol.*]   What's his visit for?

    D'O. [*Aside.*] I question if they'll even speak to me.

    Pol. [*to Cha.*] Face D'Ormea, he'll suppose you fear him,
        else.

[*Aloud.*] The Marquis bears the King's command, no doubt.

    D'O. [*Aside.*] Precisely!—If I threatened him, perhaps?
Well, this at least is punishment enough!
Men used to promise punishment would come.

    Cha. Deliver the King's message, Marquis!

    D'O. [*Aside.*]   Ah—
So anxious for his fate? [*Aloud.*] A word, my Prince,
Before you see your father—just one word
Of counsel!

    Cha.   Oh, your counsel certainly—
Polyxena, the Marquis counsels us!
Well, sir? Be brief, however!

    D'O.   What? you know
As much as I?—preceded me, most like,
In knowledge? So! ('Tis in his eye, beside—
His voice—he knows it and his heart's on flame
Already!) You surmise why you, myself,
Del Borgo, Spava, fifty nobles more,
Are summoned thus?

    Cha.   Is the Prince used to know,
At any time, the pleasure of the King,
Before his minister?—Polyxena,
Stay here till I conclude my task—I feel
Your presence—(smile not)—thro' the walls, and take
Fresh heart. The King's within that chamber?

    D'O. [*Passing the table whereon a paper lies, exclaims, as he
      glances at it,*]   " Spain!"

    Pol. [*Aside to Cha.*] Tarry awhile: what ails the minister?

    D'O. Madam, I do not often trouble you.
The Prince loathes, and you loathe me—let that pass;
But since it touches him and you, not me,
Bid the Prince listen!

    Pol. [*to Cha.*]   Surely you will listen!
—Deceit?—Those fingers crumpling up his vest?

Cha.   Deceitful to the very fingers' ends!

D'O. [*who has approached them, overlooks the other paper*
    CHARLES *continues to hold.*]

My project for the Fiefs! As I supposed!
Sir, I must give you light upon those measures
—For this is mine, and that I spied of Spain,
Mine too!

Cha.   Release me! Do you gloze on me
Who bear in the world's face (that is, the world
You've made for me at Turin) your contempt?
—Your measures?—When was any hateful task
Not D'Ormea's imposition? Leave my robe!
What post can I bestow, what grant concede?
Or do you take me for the King?

D'O.   Not I!
Not yet for King,—not for, as yet, thank God,
One, who in . . shall I say a year—a month?
Ay!—shall be wretcheder than e'er was slave
In his Sardinia,—Europe's spectacle,
And the world's bye-word! What? The Prince aggrieved
That I've excluded him our counsels? Here

    [*Touching the paper in* CHARLES'S *hand.*

Accept a method of extorting gold
From Savoy's nobles, who must wring its worth
In silver first from tillers of the soil,
Whose hinds again have to contribute brass
To make up the amount—there's counsel, sir!
My counsel, one year old; and the fruit, this—
Savoy's become a mass of misery
And wrath, which one man has to meet—the King!
You're not the King! Another counsel, sir!
Spain entertains a project (here it lies)
Which, guessed, makes Austria offer that same King
Thus much to baffle Spain; he promises;
Then comes Spain, breathless lest she be forestalled,
Her offer follows; and he promises . . .

Cha.—Promises, sir, when he before agreed
To Austria's offer?

D'O.   That's a counsel, Prince!
But past our foresight, Spain and Austria (choosing
To make their quarrel up between themselves
Without the intervention of a friend)
Produce both treaties, and both promises . . .

Cha.   How?

D'O.   Prince, a counsel!—And the fruit of that?
Both parties covenant afresh, to fall
Together on their friend, blot out his name,
Abolish him from Europe.   So take note,
Here's Austria and here's Spain to fight against,
And what sustains the King but Savoy here,
A miserable people mad with wrongs?
You're not the King!

   Cha.   Polyxena, you said
All would clear up—all does clear up to me!

   D'O.   Clears up?   'Tis no such thing to envy, then?
You see the King's state in its length and breadth?
You blame me, now, for keeping you aloof
From counsels and the fruit of counsels?—Wait
Till I've explained this morning's business!

   Cha. [*Aside.*]   No—
Stoop to my father, yes,—to D'Ormea, no;
—The King's son, not to the King's counsellor!
I will do something,—but at least retain
The credit of my deed! [*Aloud.*] Then, D'Ormea, this
You now expressly come to tell me?

   D'O.   This
To tell!   You apprehend me?

   Cha.   Perfectly.
And further, D'Ormea, you have shown yourself,
For the first time these many weeks and months,
Disposed to do my bidding?

   D'O.   From the heart!

   Cha.   Acquaint my father, first, I wait his pleasure:
Next . . . or, I'll tell you at a fitter time.
Acquaint the King!

   D'O. [*Aside.*]   If I 'scape Victor yet!
First, to prevent this stroke at me—if not,—
Then, to avenge it! [*To* Cha.] Gracious sir, I go.   ⌊*Goes.*

   Cha.   God, I forbore!   Which more offends—that man
Or that man's master?   Is it come to this?
Have they supposed (the sharpest insult yet)
I needed e'en his intervention?   No!
No, dull am I, conceded,—but so dull,
Scarcely!   Their step decides me.

   Pol.   How decides?

   Cha.   You would be free from D'Ormea's eye and hers?

—Could fly the court with me and live content?
So—this it is for which the knights assemble!
The whispers and the closeting of late,
The savageness and insolence of old,
—For this!

   Pol.   What mean you?

   Cha.   How? you fail to catch
Their clever plot? I missed it—but could you?
These last two months of care to inculcate
How dull I am,—with D'Ormea's present visit
To prove that, being dull, I might be worse
Were I a king—as wretched as now dull—
You recognise in it no winding up
Of a long plot?

   Pol.   Why should there be a plot?

   Cha. The crown's secure now; I should shame the crown—
An old complaint; the point is, how to gain
My place for one more fit in Victor's eyes,
His mistress', the Sebastian's child.

   Pol.   In truth?

   Cha. They dare not quite dethrone Sardinia's Prince:
But they may descant on my dulness till
They sting me into even praying them
For leave to hide my head, resign my state,
And end the coil. Not see now? In a word,
They'd have me tender them myself my rights
As one incapable:—some cause for that,
Since I delayed thus long to see their drift!
I shall apprise the King he may resume
My rights this moment.

   Pol.   Pause—I dare not think
So ill of Victor.

   Cha.   Think no ill of him!

   Pol.—Nor think him, then, so shallow as to suffer
His purpose be divined thus easily.
And yet—you are the last of a great line;
There's a great heritage at stake; new days
Seemed to await this newest of the realms
Of Europe:—Charles, you must withstand this!

   Cha.   Ah—
You dare not then renounce the splendid court
For one whom all the world despises? Speak!

   Pol. My gentle husband, speak I will, and truth.

Were this as you believe, and I once sure
Your duty lay in so renouncing rule,
I could . . could?   Oh, what happiness it were—
To live, my Charles, and die alone with you!
   Cha.   I grieve I asked you.   To the Presence, then!
D'Ormea acquaints the King by this, no doubt,
He fears I am too simple for mere hints,
And that no less will serve than Victor's mouth
Teaching me in full council what I am.
—I have not breathed, I think, these many years!
   Pol.   Why—it may be!—if he desires to wed
That woman and legitimate her child—
   Cha.   You see as much?   Oh, let his will have way!
You'll not repent confiding in me, love?
There's many a brighter spot in Piedmont, far,
Than Rivoli.   I'll seek him—or, suppose
You hear first how I mean to speak my mind?
—Loudly and firmly both, this time, be sure!
I yet may see your Rhine-land—who can tell?
Once away, ever then away!   I breathe.
   Pol.   And I too breathe!
   Cha.   Come, my Polyxena!

KING VICTOR: PART II.

Enter KING VICTOR, *bearing the regalia on a cushion from his apartment.   He calls loudly.*

D'Ormea!—for patience fails me, treading thus
Among the trains that I have laid,—my knights,
Safe in the hall here—in that anteroom,
My son,—and D'Ormea, where?   Of this, one touch—
                      [Laying down the crown.
This fireball to these mute, black, cold trains—then!
Outbreak enough!
[*Contemplating it.*]   To lose all, after all!
This—glancing o'er my house for ages—shaped,
Brave meteor, like the Crown of Cyprus now—
Jerusalem, Spain, England—every change
The braver,—and when I have clutched a prize
My ancestry died wan with watching for,

To lose it!—by a slip—a fault—a trick
Learnt to advantage once, and not unlearnt
When past the use,—" just this once more " (I thought)
" Use it with Spain and Austria happily,
And then away with trick! "—An oversight
I'd have repaired thrice over, any time
These fifty years, must happen now! There's peace
At length; and I, to make the most of peace,
Ventured my project on our people here,
As needing not their help—which Europe knows,
And means, cold-blooded, to dispose herself
(Apart from plausibilities of war)
To crush the new-made King—who ne'er till now
Feared her. As Duke, I lost each foot of earth
And laughed at her: my name was left, my sword
Left, all was left! But she can take, she knows,
This crown, herself conceded . . .

　　　　　　　　　　　That's to try,
Kind Europe! My career's not closed as yet!
This boy was ever subject to my will—
Timid and tame—the fitter! D'Ormea, too—
What if the sovereign's also rid of thee
His prime of parasites?—Yet I delay!
D'Ormea!　　　[*As D'Ormea enters, the King seats himself.*
　　　　My son, the Prince—attends he?
　　D'O.
　　　　　　　　　　　　　　　　Sire,
He does attend. The crown prepared!—it seems
That you persist in your resolve.
　　Vic.　　　　　　　　Who's come?
The chancellor and the chamberlain? My knights?
　　D'O. The whole Annunziata.—If, my liege,
Your fortunes had not tottered worse than now . . .
　　Vic. Del Borgo has drawn up the schedules? mine—
My son's too? Excellent! Only, beware
Of the least blunder, or we look but fools.
First, you read the Annulment of the Oaths;
Del Borgo follows . . no, the Prince shall sign;
Then let Del Borgo read the Instrument—
On which, I enter.—
　　D'O.　　　　Sire, this may be truth;
You, sire, may do as you affect—may break
Your engine, me, to pieces: try at least
If not a spring remains worth saving! Take

My counsel as I've counselled many times!
What if the Spaniard and the Austrian threat?
There's England, Holland, Venice—which ally
Select you?

 Vic. Aha! Come, my D'Ormea,—" truth "
Was on your lip a minute since. Allies?
I've broken faith with Venice, Holland, England.
—As who knows if not you?

 D'O.   But why with me
Break faith—with one ally, your best, break faith?

 Vic. When first I stumbled on you, Marquis—('twas
At Mondovi—a little lawyer's clerk . . .)

 D'O . . . . Therefore your soul's ally!—who brought you
  through
Your quarrel with the Pope, at pains enough—
Who've simply echoed you in these affairs—
On whom you cannot, therefore, visit these
Affairs' ill fortune—whom you'll trust to guide
You safe (yes, on my soul) in these affairs!

 Vic. I was about to notice, had you not
Prevented me, that since that great town kept
With its chicane my D'Ormea's satchel stuffed,
And D'Ormea's self sufficiently recluse,
He missed a sight,—my naval armament
When I burnt Toulon. How the skiff exults
Upon the galliot's wave!—rises its height,
O'ertops it even; but the great wave bursts—
And hell-deep in the horrible profound
Buries itself the galliot:—shall the skiff
Think to escape the sea's black trough in turn?
Apply this: you have been my minister
—Next me—above me, possibly;—sad post,
Huge care, abundant lack of peace of mind;
Who would desiderate the eminence?
You gave your soul to get it—you'd yet give
Your soul to keep it, as I mean you shall,
My D'Ormea! What if the wave ebbed with me?
Whereas it cants you to another's crest—
I toss you to my son; ride out your ride!

 D'O. Ah, you so much despise me then?

 Vic.   You, D'Ormea?
Nowise : and I'll inform you why. A King
Must in his time have many ministers,

And I've been rash enough to part with mine
When I thought proper. Of the tribe, not one
(. . Or wait, did Pianezze? . . ah, just the same!)
Not one of them, ere his remonstrance reached
The length of yours, but has assured me (commonly,
Standing much as you stand,—or nearer, say,
The door to make his exit on his speech)
—I should repent of what I did: now, D'Ormea,
(Be candid—you approached it when I bade you
Prepare the schedules! But you stopped in time)
—You have not so assured me: how should I
Despise you, then?

Enter CHARLES.

   Vic. [*changing his tone.*] Are you instructed?   Do
My order, point by point! About it, sir!
   D'O. You so despise me? [*Aside.*] One last stay
        remains—
The boy's discretion there. [*to* CHARLES.]
                           For your sake, Prince,
I pleaded—wholly in your interest—
To save you from this fate!
   Cha. [*Aside.*]   Must I be told
The Prince was supplicated for—by him?
   Vic. [*to* D'O.] Apprise Del Borgo, Spava, and the rest,
Our son attends them; then return.
   D'O.   One word.
   Cha. [*Aside.*] A moment's pause and they would drive me
        hence,
I do believe!
   D'O. [*Aside.*] Let but the boy be firm!
   Vic. You disobey?
   Cha. [*to* D'O.]   You do not disobey
Me, D'Ormea? Did you promise that or no?
   D'O. Sir, I am yours—what would you? Yours am I!
   Cha. When I have said what I shall say, 'tis like
Your face will ne'er again disgust me. Go!
Through you, as through a breast of glass, I see.
And for your conduct, from my youth till now,
Take my contempt! You might have spared me much,
Secured me somewhat, nor so harmed yourself—
That's over now. Go—ne'er to come again!
   D'O. As son, the father—father as, the son!

My wits! My wits! [*Goes.*

   Vic. [*Seated.*] And you, what meant you, pray,
By speaking thus to D'Ormea?
   Cha. Let us not
Weary ourselves with D'Ormea! Those few words
Have half unsettled what I came to say.
His presence vexes to my very soul.
   Vic. One called to manage kingdoms, Charles, needs heart
To bear up under worse annoyances
Than D'Ormea seems—to me, at least.
   Cha. [*Aside.*] Ah, good!
He keeps me to the point! Then be it so.
[*Aloud.*] Last night, Sire, brought me certain papers—these—
To be reported on,—your way of late.
Is it last night's result that you demand?
   Vic. For God's sake, what has night brought forth?
     Pronounce
The .. what's your word?—result!
   Cha. Sire, that had proved
Quite worthy of your sneers, no doubt:—a few
Lame thoughts, regard for you alone could wring,
Lame as they are, from brains, like mine believe!
As 'tis, sire, I am spared both toil and sneer.
There are the papers.
   Vic. Well, sir? I suppose
You hardly burned them. Now for your result!
   Cha. I never should have done great things of course,
But .. oh, my father, had you loved me more ...
   Vic. Loved you? [*Aside.*] Has D'Ormea played me false,
     I wonder?
[*Aloud.*] Why, Charles, a king's love is diffused—yourself
May overlook, perchance, your part in it.
Our monarchy is absolutest now
In Europe, or my trouble's thrown away:
I love, my mode, that subjects each and all
May have the power of loving, all and each,
Their mode: I doubt not, many have their sons
To trifle with, talk soft to, all day long—
I have that crown, this chair, and D'Ormea, Charles!
   Cha. 'Tis well I am a subject then, not you.
   Vic. [*Aside.*] D'Ormea has told him everything.
     [*Aloud.*] Aha!
I apprehend you: when all's said, you take

Your private station to be prized beyond
My own for instance?
   Cha.   —Do and ever did
So take it: 'tis the method you pursue
That grieves . . .
   Vic.   These words! Let me express, my friend,
Your thought.   You penetrate what I supposed
A secret.   D'Ormea plies his trade betimes!
I purpose to resign my crown to you.
   Cha. To me?
   Vic.   Now—in that chamber.
   Cha.   You resign
The crown to me?
   Vic.   And time enough, Charles, sure?
Confess with me, at four-and-sixty years
A crown's a load.   I covet quiet once
Before I die, and summoned you for that.
   Cha. 'Tis I will speak: you ever hated me,
I bore it,—have insulted me, borne too—
Now you insult yourself, and I remember
What I believed you, what you really are,
And cannot bear it.   What! My life has passed
Under your eye, tormented as you know,—
Your whole sagacities, one after one,
At leisure brought to play on me—to prove me
A fool, I thought, and I submitted; now
You'd prove . . . what would you prove me?
   Vic.   This to me?
I hardly know you!
   Cha.   Know me?   Oh, indeed
You do not!   Wait till I complain next time
Of my simplicity!—for here's a sage—
Knows the world well—is not to be deceived—
And his experience, and his Macchiavels,
His D'Ormeas, teach him—what?—that I, this while,
Have envied him his crown!   He has not smiled,
I warrant,—has not eaten, drunk, nor slept,
For I was plotting with my Princess yonder!
Who knows what we might do, or might not do?
Go, now—be politic—astound the world!—
That sentry in the antechamber . . nay,
The varlet who disposed this precious trap
                              [Pointing to the crown.

That was to take me—ask them if they think
Their own sons envy them their posts!—Know me!

Vic. But you know me, it seems; so learn in brief
My pleasure. This assembly is convened . . .

Cha. Tell me, that woman put it in your head—
You were not sole contriver of the scheme,
My father!

Vic.   Now observe me, sir! I jest
Seldom—on these points, never. Here, I say,
The Knights assemble to see me concede,
And you accept, Sardinia's crown.

Cha.   Farewell!
'Twere vain to hope to change this—I can end it.
Not that I cease from being yours, when sunk
Into obscurity. I'll die for you,
But not annoy you with my presence—Sire,
Farewell! Farewell!

Enter D'ORMEA.

D'O. [*Aside.*] Ha, sure he's changed again—
Means not to fall into the cunning trap—
Then, Victor, I shall yet escape you, Victor!

Vic. [*suddenly placing the crown upon the head of* CHARLES.]
D'Ormea, your King!

[*To* CHARLES.]   My son, obey me! Charles,
Your father, clearer-sighted than yourself,
Decides it must be so. 'Faith, this looks real!
My reasons after—reason upon reason
After—but now, obey me!—Trust in me!
By this, you save Sardinia, you save me!
Why the boy swoons! [*To* D'O.] Come this side!

D'O. [*as* CHARLES *turns from him to* VICTOR.]

                                You persist?

Vic. Yes—I conceive the gesture's meaning. 'Faith,
He almost seems to hate you—how is that?
Be re-assured, my Charles! Is't over now?
Then, Marquis, tell the new King what remains
To do! A moment's work. Del Borgo reads
The act of Abdication out, you sign it,
Then I sign; after that, come back to me.

D'O. Sire, for the last time, pause!

Vic.
                        Five minutes longer
I am your sovereign, Marquis. Hesitate—

And I'll so turn those minutes to account
That . . . Ay, you recollect me!
                    [*Aside.*] Could I bring
My foolish mind to undergo the reading
That Act of Abdication!
                    [*As* CHARLES *motions* D'ORMEA *to precede him.*
                    Thanks, dear Charles!
                              [CHARLES *and* D'ORMEA *retire.*
  Vic.   A novel feature in the boy,—indeed
Just what I feared he wanted most.   Quite right,
This earnest tone—your truth, now, for effect!
It answers every purpose: with that look,
That voice,—I hear him: " I began no treaty,"
(He speaks to Spain,) " nor ever dreamed of this
" You show me; this I from my soul regret;
" But if my father signed it, bid not me
" Dishonour him—who gave me all, beside."
And, " truth," says Spain, " 'twere harsh to visit that
" Upon the Prince."   Then come the nobles trooping:
" I grieve at these exactions—I had cut
" This hand off ere impose them; but shall I
" Undo my father's deed? "—And they confer:
" Doubtless he was no party, after all;
" Give the Prince time! "—
                    Ay, give us time—but time!
Only, he must not, when the dark day comes,
Refer our friends to me and frustrate all.
We'll have no child's play, no desponding-fits,
No Charles at each cross turn entreating Victor
To take his crown again.   Guard against that!

Enter D'ORMEA.

Long live King Charles!—
                    No—Charles's counsellor!
Well, is it over, Marquis?   Did I jest?
  D'O.   " King Charles! "   What then may you be?
  Vic.   Anything!
A country gentleman that's cured of bustle,
And beats a quick retreat toward Chambery
To hunt and hawk, and leave you noisy folk
To drive your trade without him.   I'm Count Remont—
Count Tende—any little place's Count!
  D'O.   Then, Victor, Captain against Catinat,

At Staffarde, where the French beat you; and Duke
At Turin, where you beat the French; King, late,
Of Savoy, Piedmont, Montferrat, Sardinia,
—Now, " any little place's Count "—
   Vic.   Proceed!
   D'O.   Breaker of vows to God, who crowned you first;
Breaker of vows to Man, who kept you since;
Most profligate to me, who outraged God
And Man to serve you, and am made pay crimes
I was but privy to, by passing thus
To your imbecile son—who, well you know,
Must, (when the people here, and nations there,
Clamour for you, the main delinquent, slipt
From King to—Count of any little place)
—Surrender me, all left within his reach,—
I, sir, forgive you: for I see the end—
See you on your return (you will return)
To him you trust in for the moment . . .
   Vic.   How?
Trust in him? (merely a prime-minister
This D'Ormea!) How trust in him?
   D'O.   In his fear—
His love,—but pray discover for yourself
What you are weakest, trusting in!
   Vic.   Aha,
My D'Ormea, not a shrewder scheme than this
In your repertory? You know old Victor—
Vain, choleric, inconstant, rash—(I've heard
Talkers who little thought the King so close)
Felicitous, now, were't not, to provoke him
To clean forget, one minute afterward,
His solemn act—to call the nobles back
And pray them give again the very power
He has abjured!—for the dear sake of—what?
Vengeance on you! No, D'Ormea: such am I,
Counte Tende or Count anything you please,
—Only, the same that did the things you say,
And, among other things you say not, used
Your finest fibre, meanest muscle,—you
I used, and now, since you will have it so,
Leave to your fate—mere lumber in the midst,
You and your works—Why, what on earth beside
Are you made for, you sort of ministers?

D'O. —Not left, though, to my fate! Your witless son
Has more wit than to load himself with lumber:
He foils you that way, and I follow you.

    Vic.   Stay with my son—protect the weaker side!

    D'O.   Ay, be tossed to the people like a rag,
And flung by them to Spain and Austria—so
Abolishing the record of your part
In all this perfidy!

    Vic.   Prevent, beside,
My own return!

    D'O.   That's half prevented now!
'Twill go hard but you'll find a wondrous charm
In exile, to discredit me. The Alps—
Silk-mills to watch—vines asking vigilance—
Hounds open for the stag—your hawk's a-wing—
Brave days that wait the Louis of the South,
Italy's Janus!

    Vic.   So, the lawyer's clerk
Won't tell me that I shall repent!

    D'O.   You give me
Full leave to ask if you repent?

    Vic.   Whene'er,
Sufficient time's elapsed for that, you judge!

                 [*Shouts inside,* " KING CHARLES."

    D'O.   Do you repent?

    Vic. [*after a slight pause.*] . . . I've kept them waiting?
    Yes!
Come in—complete the Abdication, sir!   [*They go out.*

Enter POLYXENA.

    Pol.   A shout? The sycophants are free of Charles!
Oh, is not this like Italy? No fruit
Of his or my distempered fancy, this—
But just an ordinary fact! Beside,
Here they've set forms for such proceedings—Victor
Imprisoned his own mother—he should know,
If any, how a son's to be deprived
Of a son's right. Our duty's palpable.
Ne'er was my husband for the wily king
And the unworthy subjects—be it so!
Come you safe out of them, my Charles! Our life
Grows not the broad and dazzling life, I dreamed
Might prove your lot—for strength was shut in you

None guessed but I—strength which, untrammelled once,
Had little shamed your vaunted ancestry—
Patience and self-devotion, fortitude,
Simplicity and utter truthfulness
—All which they shout to lose!

So, now my work

Begins—to save him from regret. Save Charles
Regret?—the noble nature! He's not made
Like the Italians: 'tis a German soul.

CHARLES *enters crowned.*

Oh, where's the King's heir? Gone:—the Crown-prince?
   Gone—
Where's Savoy? Gone:—Sardinia? Gone!—But Charles
Is left! And when my Rhine-land bowers arrive,
If he looked almost handsome yester-twilight
As his grey eyes seemed widening into black
Because I praised him, then how will he look?
Farewell, you stripped and whited mulberry-trees
Bound each to each by lazy ropes of vine!
Now I'll teach you my language—I'm not forced
To speak Italian now, Charles?
[*She sees the crown.*]   What is this?
Answer me—who has done this? Answer!
  Cha.   He!
I am King now.
  Pol.   Oh worst, worst, worst of all!
Tell me—what, Victor? He has made you King?
What's he then? What's to follow this? You, King?
  Cha. Have I done wrong? Yes—for you were not by!
  Pol. Tell me from first to last.
  Cha.   Hush—a new world
Brightens before me; he is moved away
—The dark form that eclipsed it, he subsides
Into a shape supporting me like you,
And I, alone, tend upward, more and more
Tend upward: I am grown Sardinia's King.
  Pol. Now stop: was not this Victor, Duke of Savoy
At ten years old?
  Cha.   He was.
  Pol.   And the Duke spent
Since then, just four-and-fifty years in toil
To be—what?

Cha.　　　　King.

Pol.　　　　　　Then why unking himself?

Cha.　Those years are cause enough.

Pol.　　　　　　　　The only cause!

Cha.　Some new perplexities.

Pol.　　　　　　　Which you can solve,
Although he cannot?

Cha.　　　　　He assures me so.

Pol.　And this he means shall last—how long?

Cha.　　　　　　　　　How long?
Think you I fear the perils I confront?
He's praising me before the people's face—
My people!

Pol.　　　Then he's changed—grown kind, the King?
(Where can the trap be?)

Cha.　　　　　Heart and soul I pledge!
My father, could I guard the Crown you gained,
Transmit as I received it,—all good else
Would I surrender!

Pol.　　　　　Ah, it opens then
Before you—all you dreaded formerly?
You are rejoiced to be a king, my Charles?

Cha.　So much to dare? The better;—much to dread?
The better. I'll adventure tho' alone.
Triumph or die, there's Victor still to witness
Who dies or triumphs—either way, alone!

Pol.　Once I had found my share in triumph, Charles,
Or death.

Cha.　But you are I! But you I call
To take, Heaven's proxy, vows I tendered Heaven
A moment since. I will deserve the crown!

Pol.　You will. [*Aside.*] No doubt it were a glorious thing
For any people, if a heart like his
Ruled over it. I would I saw the trap!

Enter VICTOR.

'Tis he must show me.

Vic.　　　　　So the mask falls off
An old man's foolish love at last! Spare thanks—
I know you, and Polyxena I know.
Here's Charles—I am his guest now—does he bid me
Be seated? And my light-haired, blue-eyed child
Must not forget the old man far away

At Chambery, who dozes while she reigns.

  Pol.   Most grateful shall we now be, talking least
Of gratitude—indeed of anything
That hinders what yourself must have to say
To Charles.

  Cha.   Pray speak, Sire!

  Vic.   'Faith, not much to say—
Only what shows itself, once in the point
Of sight. You are now the King: you'll comprehend
Much you may oft have wondered at—the shifts,
Dissimulation, wiliness I showed.
For what's our post? Here's Savoy and here's Piedmont,
Here's Montferrat—a breadth here, a space there—
To o'er-sweep all these, what's one weapon worth?
I often think of how they fought in Greece
(Or Rome, which was it? You're the scholar, Charles!)
You made a front-thrust? But if your shield, too,
Were not adroitly planted—some shrewd knave
Reached you behind; and, him foiled, straight if thong
And handle of that shield were not cast loose,
And you enabled to outstrip the wind,
Fresh foes assailed you, either side; 'scape these,
And reach your place of refuge—e'en then, odds
If the gate opened unless breath enough
Was left in you to make its lord a speech.
Oh, you will see!

  Cha.   No: straight on shall I go,
Truth helping; win with it or die with it.

  Vic.   'Faith, Charles, you're not made Europe's fighting-
    man!
Its barrier-guarder, if you please. You hold,
Not take—consolidate, with envious French
This side, with Austrians that, these territories
I held—ay, and will hold . . . which *you* shall hold
Despite the couple! But I've surely earned
Exemption from these weary politics,
—The privilege to prattle with my son
And daughter here, tho' Europe waits the while.

  Pol.   Nay, Sire,—at Chambery, away for ever,
As soon you'll be, 'tis a farewell we bid you!
Turn these few fleeting moments to account!
'Tis just as though it were a death.

  Vic.   Indeed!

Pol. [*Aside.*] Is the trap there?

Cha.   Ay, call this parting--death!
The sacreder your memory becomes.
If I misrule Sardinia, how bring back
My father? No—that thought shall ever urge me.

Vic. I do not mean . . .

Pol. [*who watches* VICTOR *narrowly this while.*]
                              Your father does not mean
That you are ruling for your father's sake:
It is your people must concern you wholly
Instead of him. You meant this, Sire? (He drops
My hand!)

Cha.   That People is now part of me.

Vic. About the People! I took certain measures
Some short time since . . Oh, I'm aware you know
But little of my measures—these affect
The nobles—we've resumed some grants, imposed
A tax or two; prepare yourself, in short,
For clamours on that score: mark me: you yield
No jot of what's entrusted you!

Pol.   No jot
You yield!

Cha.   My father, when I took the oath,
Although my eye might stray in search of yours,
I heard it, understood it, promised God
What you require. Till from this eminence
He moves me, here I keep, nor shall concede
The meanest of my rights.

Vic. [*Aside.*]   The boy's a fool!
—Or rather, I'm a fool: for what's wrong here?
To-day the sweets of reigning—let to-morrow
Be ready with its bitters.

Enter D'ORMEA.

                           There's beside
Somewhat to press upon your notice first.

Cha. Then why delay it for an instant, Sire?
That Spanish claim, perchance? And, now you speak,
—This morning, my opinion was mature—
Which, boy-like, I was bashful in producing
To one, I ne'er am like to fear, in future!
My thought is formed upon that Spanish claim.

Vic. (Betimes, indeed.) Not now, Charles. You require

A host of papers on it—

   D'O. [*coming forward.*]   Here they are.
[*To* CHA.] I was the minister and much beside—
Of the late monarch: to say little, him
I served! on you I have, to say e'en less,
No claim. This case contains those papers: with them
I tender you my office.

   Vic. [*hastily.*]   Keep him, Charles!
There's reason for it—many reasons: you
Distrust him, nor are so far wrong there,—but
He's mixed up in the matter—he'll desire
To quit you, for occasions known to me:
Do not accept those reasons—have him stay!

   Pol. [*Aside.*] His minister thrust on us!

   Cha. [*to* D'ORMEA.]   Sir, believe,
In justice to myself, you do not need
E'en this commending: whatsoe'er might be
My feelings toward you as a private man,
They quit me in the vast and untried field
Of action. Though I shall, myself, (as late
In your own hearing I engaged to do)
Preside o'er my Sardinia, yet your help
Is necessary. Think the past forgotten,
And serve me now!

   D'O.   I did not offer you
My services—would I could serve you, Sire!
As for the Spanish matter . . .

   Vic.   But despatch
At least the dead, in my good daughter's phrase,
Before the living! Help to house me safe
Ere you and D'Ormea set the world a-gape!
Here is a paper—will you overlook
What I propose reserving for my needs?
I get as far from you as possible.
There's what I reckon my expenditure.

   Cha. [*reading.*] A miserable fifty thousand crowns!

   Vic. Oh, quite enough for country gentlemen!
Besides, the exchequer happens . . . but find out
All that, yourself!

   Cha. [*still reading.*] " Count Tende "—what means this?

   Vic. Me: you were but an infant when I burst
Through the defile of Tende upon France.
Had only my allies kept true to me!

No matter. Tende's, then, a name I take
Just as . . .
    D'O.   —The Marchioness Sebastian takes
The name of Spigno.
    Cha.   How, sir?
    Vic. [to D'ORMEA.]   Fool! All that
Was for my own detailing. [*To* CHARLES.] That anon!
    Cha. [*to* D'ORMEA.] Explain what you have said, sir!
    D'O.   I supposed
The marriage of the King to her I named,
Profoundly kept a secret these few weeks,
Was not to be one, now he's Count.
    Pol. [*Aside.*]   With us
The minister—with him the mistress!
    Cha. [*to* VICTOR.]   No—
Tell me you have not taken her—that woman
To live with, past recall!
    Vic.   And where's the crime . . .
    Pol. [*to* CHARLES.] True, sir, this is a matter past recall,
And past your cognizance. A day before,
And you had been compelled to note this—now
Why note it? The King saved his House from shame:
What the Count does, is no concern of yours.
    Cha. [*after a pause.*] The Spanish business, D'Ormea!
    Vic.   Why, my son,
I took some ill-advised . . . one's age, in fact,
Spoils everything: though I was over-reached,
A younger brain, we'll trust, may extricate
Sardinia readily. To-morrow, D'Ormea,
Inform the King!
    D'O. [*without regarding* VICTOR, *and leisurely.*] Thus stands
      the case with Spain:
When first the Infant Carlos claimed his proper
Succession to the throne of Tuscany . . .
    Vic. I tell you, that stands over! Let that rest!
There is the policy!
    Cha. [*to* D'ORMEA.] Thus much I know,
And more,—too much: the remedy?
    D'O.   Of course!
No glimpse of one—
    Vic.   No remedy at all!
It makes the remedy itself—time makes it.
    D'O. [*to* CHARLES.] But if . . .

Vic. [*still more hastily.*]   In fine, I shall take care of that—
And, with another project that I have . . .
   D'O. [*turning on him.*]   Oh, since Count Tende means to
      take again
King Victor's crown!—
   Pol. [*throwing herself at* VICTOR'S *feet.*]   E'en now retake
      it, Sire!
Oh, speak! We are your subjects both, once more!
Say it—a word effects it! You meant not,
Nor do mean now, to take it—but you must!
'Tis in you—in your nature—and the shame's
Not half the shame 'twould grow so afterward!
   Cha.   Polyxena!
   Pol.   A word recalls the Knights—
Say it!—What's promising and what's the past?
Say you are still King Victor!
   D'O.   Better say
The Count repents in brief!   [VICTOR *rises.*
   Cha.   With such a crime
I have not charged you, Sire!
   Pol.   Charles turns from me!

SECOND YEAR 1731.—KING CHARLES

PART I

Enter QUEEN POLYXENA *and* D'ORMEA—*A pause.*

   Pol.   And now, sir, what have you to say?
   D'O.   Count Tende . . .
   Pol.   Affirm not I betrayed you; you resolve
On uttering this strange intelligence
—Nay, post yourself to find me ere I reach
The capital, because you know King Charles
Tarries a day or two at Evian baths
Behind me:—but take warning,—here and thus
                    [*Seating herself in the royal seat.*
I listen, if I listen—not your friend.
Explicitly the statement, if you still
Persist to urge it on me, must proceed:
I am not made for aught else.
   D'O.   Good! Count Tende . . .

Pol. I, who mistrust you, shall acquaint King Charles,
Who even more mistrusts you.

D'O.   Does he so?

Pol. Why should he not?

D'O.   Ay, why not?   Motives, seek
You virtuous people, motives! Say, I serve
God at the devil's bidding—will that do?
I'm proud: our People have been pacified
(Really I know not how)—

Pol.   By truthfulness.

D'O. Exactly; that shows I had nought to do
With pacifying them: our foreign perils
Also exceed my means to stay: but here
'Tis otherwise, and my pride's piqued.   Count Tende
Completes a full year's absence: would you, madam,
Have the old monarch back, his mistress back,
His measures back?   I pray you, act upon
My counsel, or they will be.

Pol.   When?

D'O.   Let's think.
Home matters settled—Victor's coming now;
Let foreign matters settle—Victor's here:
Unless I stop him; as I will, this way.

Pol. [*reading the papers he presents.*]   If this should prove
     a plot 'twixt you and Victor?
You seek annoyances to give him pretext
For what you say you fear!

D'O.   Oh, possibly!
I go for nothing.   Only show King Charles
That thus Count Tende purposes return,
And style me his inviter, if you please.

Pol. Half of your tale is true; most like, the Count
Seeks to return: but why stay you with us?
To aid in such emergencies.

D'O.   Keep safe
Those papers: or, to serve me, leave no proof
I thus have counselled: when the Count returns,
And the King abdicates, 'twill stead me little
To have thus counselled.

Pol.   The King abdicate!

D'O. He's good, we knew long since—wise, we discover—
Firm, let us hope:—but I'd have gone to work
With him away.   Well!

[CHARLES *without*.]   In the Council Chamber?
D'O. All's lost!
Pol.   Oh, surely not King Charles! He's changed—
That's not this year's care-burthened voice and step:
'Tis last year's step—the Prince's voice!
D'O.   I know!

Enter CHARLES—D'ORMEA *retiring a little.*

Cha. Now wish me joy, Polyxena! Wish it me
The old way!   [*She embraces him.*
           There was too much cause for that!
But I have found myself again! What's news
At Turin? Oh, if you but felt the load
I'm free of—free! I said this year would end
Or it, or me—but I am free, thank God!
  Pol. How, Charles?
  Cha.   You do not guess? The day I found
Sardinia's hideous coil, at home, abroad,
And how my father was involved in it,—
Of course, I vowed to rest or smile no more
Until I freed his name from obloquy.
We did the people right—'twas much to gain
That point, redress our nobles' grievance, too—
But that took place here, was no crying shame:
All must be done abroad,—if I abroad
Appeased the justly-angered Powers, destroyed
The scandal, took down Victor's name at last
From a bad eminence, I then might breathe
And rest! No moment was to lose. Behold
The proud result—a Treaty, Austria, Spain
Agree to—
  D'O. [*Aside.*] I shall merely stipulate
For an experienced headsman.
  Cha.   Not a soul
Is compromised: the blotted Past's a blank:
Even D'Ormea will escape unquestioned. See!
It reached me from Vienna; I remained
At Evian to despatch the Count his news;
'Tis gone to Chambery a week ago—
And here am I: do I deserve to feel
Your warm white arms around me?
  D'O. [*coming forward.*]   He knows that?
  Cha. What, in Heaven's name, means this?

D'O.   He knows that matters
Are settled at Vienna?   Not too late!
Plainly, unless you post this very hour
Some man you trust (say, me) to Chambery,
And take precautions I'll acquaint you with,
Your father will return here.
   Cha.   Is he crazed
This D'Ormea?   Here?   For what?   As well return
To take his crown!
   D'O.   He will return for that.
   Cha. [*to* POLYXENA.]   You have not listened to this man?
   Pol.   · He spoke
About your safety—and I listened.
             [*He disengages himself from her arms.*
   Cha. [*to* D'ORMEA.]   What
Apprised you of the Count's intentions?
   D'O.   Me?
His heart, Sire; you may not be used to read
Such evidence, however; therefore read
           [*Pointing to* POLYXENA'S *papers.*
My evidence.
   Cha. [*to* POLYXENA.]   Oh, worthy this of you!
And of your speech I never have forgotten,
Tho' I professed forgetfulness; which haunts me
As if I did not know how false it was;
Which made me toil unconsciously thus long
That there might be no least occasion left
For aught of its prediction coming true!
And now, when there is left no least occasion
To instigate my father to such crime;
When I might venture to forget (I hoped)
That speech and recognise Polyxena—
Oh, worthy, to revive, and tenfold worse,
That plague now!   D'Ormea at your ear, his slanders
Still in your hand!   Silent?
   Pol.   As the wronged are.
   Cha.   And, D'Ormea, pray, since when have you presumed
To spy upon my father?   (I conceive
What that wise paper shows, and easily.)
Since when?
   D'O.   The when, and where, and how, belong
To me. 'Tis sad work, but I deal in such.
You ofttimes serve yourself—I'd serve you here:

Use makes me not so squeamish.   In a word,
Since the first hour he went to Chambery,
Of his seven servants, five have I suborned.
    Cha.   You hate my father?
    D'O.   Oh, just as you will!
                               [*Looking at* POLYXENA.
A minute since, I loved him—hate him, now!
What matters?—If you'll ponder just one thing:
Has he that Treaty?—He is setting forward
Already.   Are your guards here?
    Cha.   Well for you
They are not!   [*To* POL.]   Him I knew of old, but you—
To hear that pickthank, further his designs!   [*To* D'O.
Guards?—were they here, I'd bid them, for your trouble,
Arrest you.
    D'O.   Guards you shall not want.   I lived
The servant of your choice, not of your need.
You never greatly needed me till now
That you discard me.   This is my arrest.
Again I tender you my charge—its duty
Would bid me press you read these documents.
Here, Sire!   [*Offering his badge of office.*
    Cha. [*taking it.*]   The papers also!   Do you think
I dare not read them?
    Pol.   Read them, sir!
    Cha.   They prove,
My father, still a month within the year
Since he so solemnly consigned it me,
Means to resume his crown?   They shall prove that,
Or my best dungeon . . .
    D'O.   Even say, Chambery!
'Tis vacant, I surmise, by this.
    Cha.   You prove
Your words or pay their forfeit, sir.   Go there!
Polyxena, one chance to rend the veil
Thickening and blackening 'twixt us two!   Do say,
You'll see the falsehood of the charges proved!
Do say, at least, you wish to see them proved
False charges—my heart's love of other times!
    Pol.   Ah, Charles!
    Cha. [*to* D'ORMEA.]   Precede me, sir!
    D'O.   And I'm at length
A martyr for the truth!   No end, they say,

Of miracles. My conscious innocence!

    [*As they go out, enter—by the middle door—at which he pauses—*VICTOR.

Vic. Sure I heard voices? No! Well, I do best
To make at once for this, the heart o' the place,
The old room! Nothing changed!—So near my seat,
D'Ormea?   [*Pushing away the stool which is by the* KING'S *chair.*]

        I want that meeting over first,
I know not why. Tush, D'Ormea won't be slow
To hearten me, the supple knave! That burst
Of spite so eased him! He'll inform me . . .

                              What?
Why come I hither? All's in rough—let all
Remain rough; there's full time to draw back—nay,
There's nought to draw back from, as yet; whereas,
If reason should be, to arrest a course
Of error—reason good, to interpose
And save, as I have saved so many times,
Our House, admonish my son's giddy youth,
Relieve him of a weight that proves too much—
Now is the time,—or now, or never. 'Faith,
This kind of step is pitiful—not due
To Charles, this stealing back—hither, because
He's from his Capital! Oh, Victor! Victor!
But thus it is: the age of crafty men
Is loathsome; youth contrives to carry off
Dissimulation; we may intersperse
Extenuating passages of strength,
Ardour, vivacity, and wit—may turn
E'en guile into a voluntary grace,—
But one's old age, when graces drop away
And leave guile the pure staple of our lives—
Ah, loathsome!

           Not so—or why pause I? Turin
Is mine to have, were I so minded, for
The asking; all the Army's mine—I've witnessed
Each private fight beneath me; all the Court's
Mine too; and, best of all, my D'Ormea's still
His D'Ormea; no! There's some grace clinging yet.
Had I decided on this step, ere midnight
I'd take the crown.

            No! Just this step to rise

Exhausts me! Here am I arrived: the rest
Must be done for me. Would I could sit here
And let things right themselves, the masque unmasque
—Of the King, crownless, grey hairs and hot blood,—
The young King, crowned, but calm before his time,
They say,—the eager woman with her taunts,—
And the sad earnest wife who motions me
Away—ay, there she knelt to me! E'en yet
I can return and sleep at Chambery
A dream out. Rather shake it off at Turin,
King Victor! Is't to Turin—yes, or no?
'Tis this relentless noonday-lighted chamber,
Lighted like life, but silent as the grave,
That disconcerts me! There must be the change—
No silence last year: some one flung doors wide
(Those two great doors which scrutinise me now)
And out I went 'mid crowds of men—men talking,
Men watching if my lip fell or brow changed;
Men saw me safe forth—put me on my road:
That makes the misery of this return!
Oh, had a battle done it! Had I dropped
—Haling some battle, three entire days old,
Hither and thither by the forehead—dropped
In Spain, in Austria, best of all, in France—
Spurned on its horns or underneath its hooves,
When the spent monster goes upon its knees
To pad and pash the prostrate wretch—I, Victor,
Sole to have stood up against France—beat down
By inches, brayed to pieces finally
By some vast unimaginable charge,
A flying hell of horse and foot and guns
Over me, and all's lost, for ever lost,
There's no more Victor when the world wakes up!
Then silence, as of a raw battle-field,
Throughout the world. Then after (as whole days
After, you catch at intervals faint noise
Thro' the stiff crust of frozen blood)—there creeps
A rumour forth, so faint, no noise at all,
That a strange old man, with face outworn for wounds,
Is stumbling on from frontier town to town,
Begging a pittance that may help him find
His Turin out; what scorn and laughter follow
The coin you fling into his cap: and last,

Some bright morn, how men crowd about the midst
Of the market-place, where takes the old king breath
Ere with his crutch he strike the palace-gate
Wide ope!

       To Turin, yes or no—or no?

Re-enter CHARLES *with papers.*

  Cha. Just as I thought!   A miserable falsehood
Of hirelings discontented with their pay
And longing for enfranchisement!   A few
Testy expressions of old age that thinks
To keep alive its dignity o'er slaves
By means that suit their natures!
           [Tearing them.] Thus they shake
My faith in Victor!   *[Turning, he discovers* VICTOR.
  Vic. [*after a pause.*] Not at Evian, Charles?
What's this?   Why do you run to close the doors?
No welcome for your father?
  Cha. [*Aside.*]   Not his voice!
What would I give for one imperious tone
Of the old sort!   That's gone for ever.
  Vic.   Must
I ask once more . . .
  Cha.   No—I concede it, sir!
You are returned for . . . true, your health declined—
True, Chambery's a bleak unkindly spot;
You'd choose one fitter for your final lodge—
Veneria—or Moncaglier—ay, that's close,
And I concede it.
  Vic.   I received advices
Of the conclusion of the Spanish matter
Dated from Evian baths . . .
  Cha.   And you forbore
To visit me at Evian, satisfied
The work I had to do would fully task
The little wit I have, and that your presence
Would only disconcert me—
  Vic.   Charles?
  Cha.   —Me—set
For ever in a foreign course to yours,
And . . .
      Sir, this way of wile were good to catch,
But I have not the sleight of it.   The truth!

King Victor and King Charles 425

Though I sink under it! What brings you here?

Vic. Not hope of this reception, certainly.
From one who'd scarce assume a stranger mode
Of speech, did I return to bring about
Some awfullest calamity!

Cha. —You mean,
Did you require your crown again! Oh yes,
I should not speak otherwise! But turn not that
To jesting! Sir, the truth! Your health declines?
Is aught deficient in our equipage?
Wisely you seek myself to make complaint,
And foil the malice of the world which laughs
At petty discontents; but I shall care
That not a soul knows of this visit. Speak!

Vic. [*Aside.*] Here is the grateful, much-professing son
Who was to worship me, and for whose sake
I think to waive my plans of public good!
[*Aloud.*] Nay, Charles, if I did seek to take once more
My crown, were so disposed to plague myself—
What would be warrant for this bitterness?
I gave it—grant, I would resume it—well?

Cha. I should say simply—leaving out the why
And how—you made me swear to keep that crown:
And as you then intended . . .

Vic. Fool! What way
Could I intend or not intend? As man,
With a man's life, when I say " I intend,"
I can intend up to a certain point,
No further. I intended to preserve
The Crown of Savoy and Sardinia whole:
And if events arise demonstrating
The way I took to keep it, rather's like
To lose it . . .

Cha. Keep within your sphere and mine!
It is God's province we usurp on, else.
Here, blindfold thro' the maze of things we walk
By a slight thread of false, true, right and wrong;
All else is rambling and presumption. I
Have sworn to keep this kingdom: there's my truth.

Vic. Truth, boy, is here—within my breast; and in
Your recognition of it, truth is, too:
And in the effect of all this tortuous dealing
With falsehood, used to carry out the truth,

—In its success, this falsehood turns, again,
Truth for the world! But you are right: these themes
Are over-subtle. I should rather say
In such a case, frankly,—it fails, my scheme:
I hoped to see you bring about, yourself,
What I must bring about: I interpose
On your behalf—with my son's good in sight—
To hold what he is nearly letting go—
Confirm his title—add a grace, perhaps—
There's Sicily, for instance,—granted me
And taken back, some years since—till I give
That island with the rest, my work's half done.
For his sake, therefore, as of those he rules . . .
   Cha. Our sakes are one—and that, you could not say,
Because my answer would present itself
Forthwith;—a year has wrought an age's change:
This people's not the people now, you once
Could benefit; nor is my policy
Your policy.
   Vic. [*with an outburst.*]   I know it! You undo
All I have done—my life of toil and care!
I left you this the absolutest rule
In Europe—do you think I will sit still
And see you throw all power off to the people—
See my Sardinia, that has stood apart,
Join in the mad and democratic whirl,
Whereto I see all Europe haste full-tide?
England casts off her kings—France mimics England—
This realm I hoped was safe! Yet here I talk,
When I can save it, not by force alone,
But bidding plagues, which follow sons like you,
Fasten upon my disobedient . . .
[*Recollecting himself.*]   Surely
I could say this—if minded so—my son?
   Cha. You could not! Bitterer curses than your curse
Have I long since denounced upon myself
If I misused my power. In fear of these
I entered on those measures—will abide
By them; so, I should say, Count Tende . . .
   Vic.   No!
But no! But if, my Charles, your—more than old—
Half-foolish father urged these arguments,
And then confessed them futile, but said plainly

That he forgot his promise, found his strength
Fail him, had thought at savage Chambery
Too much of brilliant Turin, Rivoli here,
And Susa, and Veneria, and Superga—
Pined for the pleasant places he had built
When he was fortunate and young—
    Cha.   My father!
    Vic.   Stay yet—and if he said he could not die
Deprived of baubles he had put aside,
He deemed, for ever—of the Crown that binds
Your brain up, whole, sound, and impregnable,
Creating kingliness—the Sceptre, too,
Whose mere wind, should you wave it, back would beat
Invaders—and the golden Ball which throbs
As if you grasped the palpitating heart
Indeed o' the realm, to mould as you may choose!
—If I must totter up and down the streets
My sires built, where myself have introduced
And fostered laws and letters, sciences,
The civil and the military arts—
Stay, Charles—I see you letting me pretend
To live my former self once more—King Victor,
The venturous yet politic—they style me
Again, the Father of the Prince—friends wink
Good-humouredly at the delusion you
So sedulously guard from all rough truths
That else would break up the dotage!—You—
Whom now I see preventing my old shame—
I tell not, point by cruel point, my tale—
For is't not in your breast my brow is hid?
Is not your hand extended? Say you not . . .

    Enter D'ORMEA, *leading in* POLYXENA.

    Pol. [*advancing and withdrawing* CHARLES—*to* VICTOR.]
In this conjuncture, even, he would say—
(Tho' with a moistened eye and quivering lip)
The suppliant is my father—I must save
A great man from himself, nor see him fling
His well-earned fame away: there must not follow
Ruin so utter, a break-down of worth
So absolute: no enemy shall learn,
He thrust his child 'twixt danger and himself,
And, when that child somehow stood danger out,

Stole back with serpent wiles to ruin Charles
—Body, that's much,—and soul, that's more—and realm,
That's most of all! No enemy shall say . . .

   D'O. Do you repent, sir?

   Vic. [*resuming himself.*] D'Ormea? This is well!
Worthily done, King Charles, craftily done!
Judiciously you post these, to o'erhear
The little your importunate father thrusts
Himself on you to say! Ay, they'll correct
The amiable blind facility
You showed in answering his peevish suit:
What can he need to sue for? Bravely, D'Ormea,
Have you fulfilled your office: but for you,
The old Count might have drawn some few more livres
To swell his income! Had you, Lady, missed
The moment, a permission had been granted
To build afresh my ruinous old pile—
But you remembered properly the list
Of wise precautions I took when I gave
Nearly as much away—to reap the fruits
I should have looked for!

   Cha.   Thanks, sir: degrade me,
So you remain yourself. Adieu!

   Vic.   I'll not
Forget it for the future, nor presume
Next time to slight such potent mediators!
Had I first moved them both to intercede,
I might have had a chamber in Moncaglier
—Who knows?

   Cha.   Adieu!

   Vic.   You bid me this adieu
With the old spirit?

   Cha.   Adieu!

   Vic.   Charles—Charles—

   Cha.   Adieu!

                        [VICTOR *goes.*

   Cha. You were mistaken, Marquis, as you hear!
'Twas for another purpose the Count came.
The Count desires Moncaglier. Give the order!

   D'O. [*leisurely.*] Your minister has lost your confidence,
Asserting late, for his own purposes,
Count Tende would . . .

   Cha. [*flinging his badge back.*] Be still our minister!

And give a loose to your insulting joy—
It irks me more thus stifled than expressed.
Loose it!

 D'O.   There's none to loose, alas!—I see
I never am to die a martyr!

 Pol.   Charles!

 Cha. No praise, at least, Polyxena—no praise!

KING CHARLES. PART II

Night.—D'ORMEA *seated, folding papers he has been examining.*

This at the last effects it: now, King Charles
Or else King Victor—that's a balance: now
For D'Ormea the arch-culprit, either turn
O' the scale,—that's sure enough. A point to solve,
My masters—moralists—whate'er's your style!
When you discover why I push myself
Into a pitfall you'd pass safely by,
Impart to me among the rest! No matter.
Prompt are the righteous ever with their rede
To us the wicked—lesson them this once!
For safe among the wicked are you set,
Old D'Ormea. We lament life's brevity,
Yet quarter e'en the threescore years and ten,
Nor stick to call the quarter roundly " life."
D'Ormea was wicked, say, some twenty years;
A tree so long was stunted; afterward
What if it grew, continued growing, till
No fellow of the forest equalled it?
'Twas a shrub then—a shrub it still must be:
While forward saplings, at the outset checked,
In virtue of that first sprout keep their style
Amid the forest's green fraternity.
Thus I shoot up—to surely get lopped down,
And bound up for the burning. Now for it!

  Enter CHARLES *and* POLYXENA *with* Attendants.

 D'O. [*rises.*] Sire, in the due discharge of this my office—
This enforced summons of yourself from Turin,
And the disclosure I am bound to make
To-night,—there must already be, I feel,

So much that wounds . . .

Cha.   Well, sir?

D'O.   —That I, perchance,
May utter, also, what, another time,
Would irk much,—it may prove less irksome now.

Cha.   What would you utter?

D'O.   That I from my soul
Grieve at to-night's event: for you I grieve—
E'en grieve for . . .

Cha.   Tush, another time for talk!
My kingdom is in imminent danger?

D'O.   Let
The Count communicate with France—its King,
His grandson, will have Fleury's aid for this,
Though for no other war.

Cha.   First for the levies:
What forces can I muster presently?

                [D'ORMEA *delivers papers which* CHARLES *inspects.*

Cha.   Good—very good.   Montorio . . how is this?
—Equips me double the old complement
Of soldiers?

D'O.   Since his land has been relieved
From double impost, this he manages:
But under the late monarch . .

Cha.   Peace.   I know.
Count Spava has omitted mentioning
What proxy is to head these troops of his.

D'O.   Count Spava means to head his troops himself.
Something's to fight for now; " whereas," says he,
" Under the Sovereign's father " . . .

Cha.   It would seem
That all my people love me.

D'O.   Yes.

[*To* POLYXENA *while* CHARLES *continues to inspect the papers.*

                              A temper
Like Victor's may avail to keep a state;
He terrifies men and they fall not off;
Good to restrain; best, if restraint were all:
But with the silent circle round him, ends
Such sway.   Our King's begins precisely there.
For to suggest, impel, and set at work,
Is quite another function.   Men may slight,
In time of peace, the King who brought them peace:

In war,—his voice, his eyes, help more than fear.
They love you, Sire!
   Cha. [*to* Attendants.] Bring the Regalia forth.
Quit the room. And now, Marquis, answer me—
Why should the King of France invade my realm?
   D'O. Why? Did I not acquaint your Majesty
An hour ago?
   Cha.   I choose to hear again
What then I heard.
   D'O.   Because, Sire, as I said,
Your father is resolved to have the crown
At any risk; and, as I judge, calls in
These foreigners to aid him.
   Cha.   And your reason
For saying this?
   D'O. [*Aside.*] Ay, just his father's way!
[*To* Cha.] The Count wrote yesterday to your Forces' Chief,
Rhebinder,—made demand of help—
   Cha.   To try
Rhebinder—he's of alien blood: aught else?
   D'O. Receiving a refusal,—some hours after,
The Count called on Del Borga to deliver
The Act of Abdication: he refusing,
Or hesitating, rather—
   Cha.   What ensued?
   D'O. At midnight, only two hours since, at Turin
He rode in person to the citadel
With one attendant to the Soccorso gate,
And bade the governor, San Remi, open—
Admit him.
   Cha.   For a purpose I divine,
These three were faithful, then?
   D'O.   They told it me:
And I—
   Cha. Most faithful—
   D'O.   Tell it you—with this,
Moreover, of my own: if, an hour hence,
You have not interposed, the Count will be
Upon his road to France for succour.
   Cha.   Good!
You do your duty, now, to me your monarch
Fully, I warrant?—have, that is, your project
For saving both of us disgrace, past doubt?

D'O. I have my counsel,—and the only one.
A month since, I besought you to employ
Restraints which had prevented many a pang:
But now the harsher course must be pursued.
These papers, made for the emergency,
Will pain you to subscribe: this is a list
Of those suspected merely—men to watch;
This—of the few of the Count's very household,
You must, however, reluctantly, arrest;
While here's a method of remonstrance (sure
Not stronger than the case demands) to take
With the Count's self.

 Cha.   Deliver those three papers.

 Pol. [*while* CHARLES *inspects them—to* D'ORMEA.]
Your measures are not over-harsh, sir: France
Will hardly be deterred from coming hither
By these.

 D'O. What good of my proposing measures
Without a chance of their success? E'en these,
Hear what he'll say at my presenting.

 Cha. [*who has signed them.*]   There!
About the warrants! You've my signature.
What turns you pale? I do my duty by you
In acting boldly thus on your advice.

 D'O. [*reading them separately.*] Arrest the people I suspected merely?

 Cha. Did you suspect them?

 D'O.   Doubtless: but—but—Sire,
This Forquieri's governor of Turin;
And Rivarol and he have influence over
Half of the capital.—Rabella, too?
Why, Sire—

 Cha. Oh, leave the fear to me.

 D'O. [*still reading.*]   You bid me
Incarcerate the people on this list?
Sire—

 Cha. Why, you never bade arrest those men,
So close related to my father too,
On trifling grounds?

 D'O.   Oh, as for that, St. George,
President of Chambery's senators,
Is hatching treason—but—
[*Still more troubled.*] Sire, Count Cumiane

Is brother to your father's wife! What's here?
Arrest the wife herself?

 Cha.   You seem to think it
A venial crime to plot against me. Well?

 D'O. [*who has read the last paper.*] Wherefore am I thus
  ruined? Why not take
My life at once? This poor formality
Is, let me say, unworthy you! Prevent it,
You, madam! I have served you, am prepared
For all disgraces—only, let disgrace
Be plain, be proper—proper for the world
To pass its judgment on 'twixt you and me!
Take back your warrant—I will none of it.

 Cha. Here is a man to talk of fickleness!
He stakes his life upon my father's falsehood;
I bid him—

 D'O.   Not you! Were he trebly false
You do not bid me—

 Cha.   Is't not written there?
I thought so: give—I'll set it right.

 D'O.   Is it there?
Oh, yes—and plain—arrest him—now—drag here
Your father! And were all six times as plain,
Do you suppose I'd trust it?

 Cha.   Just one word!
You bring him, taken in the act of flight,
Or else your life is forfeit.

 D'O.   Ay, to Turin
I bring him? And to-morrow?

 Cha.   Here and now!
The whole thing is a lie—a hateful lie—
As I believed and as my father said.
I knew it from the first, but was compelled
To circumvent you; and the crafty D'Ormea,
That baffled Alberoni and tricked Coscia,
The miserable sower of such discord
'Twixt sire and son, is in the toils at last!
Oh, I see! you arrive—this plan of yours,
Weak as it is, torments sufficiently
A sick, old, peevish man—wrings hasty speech
And ill-considered threats from him; that's noted;
Then out you ferret papers, his amusement
In lonely hours of lassitude—examine

The day-by-day report of your paid creatures—
And back you come—all was not ripe, you find,
And, as you hope, may keep from ripening yet—
But you were in bare time! Only, 'twere best
I never saw my father—these old men
Are potent in excuses—and, meantime,
D'Ormea's the man I cannot do without.

    Pol.   Charles—

    Cha.   Ah, no question! You're for D'Ormea too!
You'd have me eat and drink, and sleep, live, die
With this lie coil'd about me, choking me!
No, no—he's caught! [*To* D'ORMEA.] You venture life, you
    say,
Upon my father's perfidy; and I
Have, on the whole, no right to disregard
The chains of testimony you thus wind
About me; though I do—do from my soul
Discredit them: still I must authorise
These measures—and I will. Perugia!

          [*Many* Officers *enter*.]   Count—
You and Solar, with all the force you have,
Are at the Marquis' orders: what he bids,
Implicitly perform! You are to bring
A traitor here; the man that's likest one
At present, fronts me; you are at his beck
For a full hour; he undertakes to show you
A fouler than himself,—but, failing that,
Return with him, and, as my father lives,
He dies this night! The clemency you've blamed
So oft, shall be revoked—rights exercised
That I've abjured.

[*To* D'ORMEA.]   Now, Sir, about the work!
To save your king and country! Take the warrant!

    D'O. [*boldly to* PERUGIA.] You hear the Sovereign's man-
    date, Count Perugia?
Obey me! As your diligence, expect
Reward! All follow to Montcaglier!

    Cha. [*in great anguish*.] D'Ormea!   [D'ORMEA *goes*.
He goes, lit up with that appalling smile!

              [*To* POLYXENA *after a pause*.
At least you understand all this?

    Pol.   These means
Of our defence—these measures of precaution?

Cha. It must be the best way. I should have else
Withered beneath his scorn.

Pol.   What would you say?

Cha. Why, you don't think I mean to keep the crown,
Polyxena?

Pol.   You then believe the story
In spite of all—That Victor's coming?

Cha.   Believe it?
I know that he is coming—feel the strength
That has upheld me leave me at his coming!
'Twas mine, and now he takes his own again.
Some kinds of strength are well enough to have;
But who's to have that strength? Let my crown go!
I meant to keep it—but I cannot—cannot!
Only, he shall not taunt me—he, the first—
See if he would not be the first to taunt me
With having left his kingdom at a word—
With letting it be conquered without stroke—
With . . . no—no—'tis no worse than when he left it.
I've just to bid him take it, and, that over,
We'll fly away—fly—for I loathe this Turin,
This Rivoli, all titles loathe, and state.
We'd best go to your country—unless God
Send I die now!

Pol.   Charles, hear me!

Cha.   —And again
Shall you be my Polyxena—you'll take me
Out of this woe! Yes, do speak—and keep speaking!
I would not let you speak just now, for fear
You'd counsel me against him: but talk, now,
As we two used to talk in blessed times:
Bid me endure all his caprices; take me
From this mad post above him!

Pol.   I believe
We are undone, but from a different cause.
All your resources, down to the least guard,
Are now at D'Ormea's beck. What if, this while,
He acts in concert with your father? We
Indeed were lost. This lonely Rivoli—
Where find a better place for them?

Cha. [*pacing the room.*]   And why
Does Victor come? To undo all that's done!
Restore the past—prevent the future! Seat

His mistress in your seat, and place in mine
. . . Oh, my own people, whom will you find there,
To ask of, to consult with, to care for,
To hold up with your hands? Whom? One that's false—
False—from the head's crown to the foot's sole, false!
The best is, that I knew it in my heart
From the beginning, and expected this,
And hated you, Polyxena, because
You saw thro' him, though I too saw thro' him,
Saw that he meant this while he crowned me, while
He prayed for me,—nay, while he kissed my brow,
I saw—
   Pol.   But if your measures take effect,
And D'Ormea's true to you?
   Cha.   Then worst of all!
I shall have loosed that callous wretch on him!
Well may the woman taunt him with his child—
I, eating here his bread, clothed in his clothes,
Seated upon his seat, give D'Ormea leave
To outrage him! We talk—perchance they tear
My father from his bed—the old hands feel
For one who is not, but who should be there—
And he finds D'Ormea! D'Ormea, too, finds him!
—The crowded chamber when the lights go out—
Closed doors—the horrid scuffle in the dark—
The accursed promptings of the minute! My guards!
To horse—and after, with me—and prevent!
   Pol. [*seizing his hand.*] King Charles! Pause here upon
      this strip of time
Allotted you out of eternity!
Crowns are from God—in his name you hold yours.
Your life's no least thing, were it fit your life
Should be abjured along with rule; but now,
Keep both! Your duty is to live and rule—
You, who would vulgarly look fine enough
In the world's eye, deserting your soul's charge,—
Ay, you would have men's praise—this Rivoli
Would be illumined: while, as 'tis, no doubt,
Something of stain will ever rest on you;
No one will rightly know why you refused
To abdicate; they'll talk of deeds you could
Have done, no doubt,—nor do I much expect
Future achievements will blot out the past,

Envelop it in haze—nor shall we two
Be happy any more; 'twill be, I feel,
Only in moments that the duty's seen
As palpably as now—the months, the years
Of painful indistinctness are to come,
While daily must we tread these palace rooms
Pregnant with memories of the past: your eye
May turn to mine and find no comfort there,
Through fancies that beset me, as yourself,
Of other courses, with far other issues,
We might have taken this great night—such bear,
As I will bear!   What matters happiness?
Duty!   There's man's one moment—this is yours!

> [*Putting the crown on his head, and the sceptre in his
> hand, she places him on his seat: a long pause and
> silence.*

Enter D'ORMEA *and* VICTOR.

  Vic.   At last I speak; but once—that once, to you!
'Tis you I ask, not these your varletry,
Who's King of us?
    Cha. [*from his seat.*]   Count Tende . . .
    Vic.   What your spies
Assert I ponder in my soul, I say—
Here to your face, amid your guards!   I choose
To take again the crown whose shadow I gave—
For still its potency surrounds the weak
White locks their felon hands have discomposed,
Or, I'll not ask who's King, but simply, who
Withholds the crown I claim?   Deliver it!
I have no friend in the wide world; nor France
Nor England cares for me: you see the sum
Of what I can avail.   Deliver it!
  Cha.   Take it, my father!
                And now say in turn,
Was it done well, my father—sure not well,
To try me thus!   I might have seen much cause
For keeping it—too easily seen cause!
But, from that moment, e'en more woefully
My life had pined away, than pine it will.
Already you have much to answer for.
My life to pine is nothing,—her sunk eyes
Were happy once!   No doubt, my people think

That I'm their King still . . . but I cannot strive!
Take it!

    Vic. [*one hand on the crown* CHARLES *offers, the other on
      his neck.*]   So few years give it quietly,
My son! It will drop from me. See you not?
A crown's unlike a sword to give away—
That, let a strong hand to a weak hand give!
But crowns should slip from palsied brows to heads
Young as this head—yet mine is weak enough,
E'en weaker than I knew. I seek for phrases
To vindicate my right. 'Tis of a piece!
All is alike gone by with me—who beat
Once D'Orleans in his lines—his very lines!
To have been Eugene's comrade, Louis' rival,
And now . . .

    Cha. [*putting the crown on him, to the rest.*]   The King
      speaks, yet none kneels, I think!

    Vic.   I am then King! As I became a King
Despite the nations—kept myself a King—
So I die King, with Kingship dying too
Around me! I have lasted Europe's time!
What wants my story of completion? Where
Must needs the damning break show! Who mistrusts
My children here—tell they of any break
'Twixt my day's sunrise and its fiery fall?
And who were by me when I died but they?
Who?—D'Ormea there!

    Cha.   What means he?

    Vic.   Ever there!
Charles—how to save your story? Mine must go!
Say—say that you refused the crown to me—
Charles, yours shall be my story! You immured
Me, say, at Rivoli. A single year
I spend without a sight of you, then die—
That will serve every purpose—tell that tale
The world!

    Cha.   Mistrust me? Help!

    Vic.   Past help, past reach!
'Tis in the heart—you cannot reach the heart:
This broke mine, that I did believe, you, Charles,
Would have denied and so disgraced me.

    Pol.   Charles
Has never ceased to be your subject, Sire!

He reigned at first through setting up yourself
As pattern: if he e'er seemed harsh to you,
'Twas from a too intense appreciation
Of your own character: he acted you—
Ne'er for an instant did I think it real,
Or look for any other than this end.
I hold him worlds the worse on that account
But so it was.

   Cha. [*to* POLYX.] I love you, now, indeed!
[*To* VICTOR.] You never knew me!

   Vic.   Hardly till this moment,
When I seem learning many other things,
Because the time for using them is past.
If 'twere to do again! That's idly wished.
Truthfulness might prove policy as good
As guile. Is this my daughter's forehead? Yes—
I've made it fitter now to be a Queen's
Than formerly—I've ploughed the deep lines there
Which keep too well a crown from slipping off!
No matter. Guile has made me King again.
Louis—'twas in King Victor's time—long since,
When Louis reign'd—and, also, Victor reign'd—
How the world talks already of us two!
God of eclipse and each discolour'd star,
Why do I linger then?

                       Ha! Where lurks he?
D'Ormea! Come nearer to your King! Now stand!
     [*Collecting his strength as* D'ORMEA *approaches.*
But you lied, D'Ormea! I do not repent.

                                  [*Dies.*

THE RETURN OF THE DRUSES

A TRAGEDY

PERSONS

The Grand-Master's Prefect.	Initiated Druses—MAANI.
The Patriarch's Nuncio.	„ „ —KARSHOOK,
The Republic's Admiral.	RAGHIB, AYOOB, and others.
LOYS DE DREUX. Knight-Novice.	Uninitiated Druses.
Initiated Druses—DJABAL.	Prefect's Guard, Nuncio's At-
„ „ —KHALIL.	tendants, Admiral's Force.
„ „ —ANAEL.	

TIME, 14—.

PLACE.—*An Islet of the Southern Sporades, colonised by Druses of Lebanon, and garrisoned by the Knights-Hospitallers of Rhodes.*

SCENE.—*A Hall in the Prefect's Palace.*

ACT I

Enter stealthily KARSHOOK, RAGHIB, AYOOB, *and other initiated* Druses, *each as he enters casting off a robe that conceals his distinctive black vest and white turban; then, as giving a loose to exultation,—*

Kar. The moon is carried off in purple fire:
Day breaks at last! Break glory, with the day,
On Djabal's dread incarnate mystery
Now ready to resume its pristine shape
Of Hakeem, as the Khalif vanished erst
In what seemed death to uninstructed eyes,
On red Mokattam's verge—our Founder's flesh,
As he resumes our Founder's function!
      Ragh.   —Death
Sweep to the Christian Prefect that enslaved
So long us sad Druse exiles o'er the sea!
      Ay. —Most joy be thine, O Mother-mount! Thy brood
Returns to thee, no outcasts as we left,

440

But thus—but thus! Behind, our Prefect's corse;
Before, a presence like the morning—thine,
Absolute Djabal late,—God Hakeem now
That day breaks!

    Kar.   Off then, with disguise at last!
As from our forms this hateful garb we strip,
Lose every tongue its glozing accent too,
Discard each limb the ignoble gesture! Cry,
'Tis the Druse Nation, warders on our mount
Of the world's secret, since the birth of time,
—No kindred slips, no offsets from thy stock,
No spawn of Christians are we, Prefect, we
Who rise . . .

    Ay.   Who shout . . .
    Ragh.   Who seize, a first-fruits, ha—
Spoil of the spoiler! Brave!

    [*They begin to tear down, and to dispute for, the decorations
       of the Hall.*

    Kar.   Hold!
    Ay.   —Mine, I say;
And mine shall it continue!

    Kar.   Just this fringe!
Take anything beside! Lo, spire on spire,
Curl serpentwise wreathed columns to the top
Of the roof, and hide themselves mysteriously
Among the twinkling lights and darks that haunt
Yon cornice! Where the huge veil, they suspend
Before the Prefect's Chamber of delight,
Floats wide, then falls again (as if its slave,
The scented air, took heart now, and anon
Lost heart, to buoy its breadths of gorgeousness
Above the gloom they droop in)—all the porch
Is jewelled o'er with frost-work charactery;
And see yon eight-point cross of white flame, winking
Hoar-silvery like some fresh-broke marble-stone:
Raze out the Rhodian's Cross there, so thou leav'st me
This single fringe!

    Ay.   Ha, wouldst thou, dog-fox? Help!
—Three hand breadths of gold fringe, my son was set
To twist, the night he died!

    Kar.   Nay, hear the knave!
And I could witness my one daughter borne,
A week since, to the Prefect's couch, yet fold

These arms, be mute, lest word of mine should mar
Our Master's work, delay the Prefect here
A day, prevent his sailing hence for Rhodes—
How know I else?—Hear me denied my right
By such a knave!

    Ragh. [*interposing.*] Each ravage for himself!
Booty enough! On, Druses! Be there found
Blood and a heap behind us: with us, Djabal
Turned Hakeem; and before us, Lebanon!
Yields the porch? Spare not! There his minions dragged
Thy daughter, Karshook, to the Prefect's couch!
Ayoob! Thy son, to soothe the Prefect's pride,
Bent o'er that task, the death-sweat on his brow,
Carving the spice-tree's heart in scroll-work there!
Onward in Djabal's name!

    [*As the tumult is at height, enter* KHALIL. *A pause and
    silence.*

    Kha.   Was it for this,
Djabal hath summoned you? Deserve you thus
A portion in to-day's event? What, here—
When most behoves your feet fall soft, your eyes
Sink low, your tongues lie still,—at Djabal's side,
Close in his very hearing, who, perchance,
Assumes e'en now God Hakeem's dreaded shape,—
Dispute you for these gauds?

    Ay.   How say'st thou, Khalil?
Doubtless our Master prompts thee! Take the fringe,
Old Karshook! I supposed it was a day . . .

    Kha. For pillage?

    Kar.   Hearken, Khalil! Never spoke
A boy so like a song-bird; we avouch thee
Prettiest of all our Master's instruments
Except thy bright twin-sister—thou and Anael
Challenge his prime regard: but we may crave
(Such nothings as we be) a portion too
Of Djabal's favor; in him we believed,
His bound ourselves, him moon by moon obeyed,
Kept silence till this daybreak—so may claim
Reward: who grudges me my claim?

    Ay.   To-day
Is not as yesterday!

    Ragh.   Stand off!

Kha.   Rebel you?
Must I, the delegate of Djabal, draw
His wrath on you, the day of our Return?
  Other Druses. Wrench from their grasp the fringe!
    Hound! must the earth
Vomit her plagues on us thro' thee?—and thee?
Plague me not, Khalil, for their fault!
  Kha.   Oh, shame!
Thus breaks to-day on you, the mystic tribe
Who, flying the approach of Osman, bore
Our faith, a merest spark, from Syria's Ridge
Its birth-place, hither! Let the sea divide
These hunters from their prey, you said, and safe
In this dim islet's virgin solitude
Tend we our faith, the spark, till happier time
Fan it to fire; till Hakeem rise again,
According to his word that, in the flesh
Which faded on Mokattam ages since,
He, at our extreme need, would interpose,
And, reinstating all in power and bliss,
Lead us himself to Lebanon once more.
Was't not thus you departed years ago,
Ere I was born?
  Druses.   'Twas even thus, years ago.
  Kha. And did you call—(according to old laws
Which bid us, lest the Sacred grow Prophane,
Assimilate ourselves in outward rites
With strangers fortune makes our lords, and live
As Christian with the Christian, Jew with Jew,
Druse only with the Druses)—did you call
Or no, to stand 'twixt you and Osman's rage,
(Mad to pursue e'en hither thro' the sea
The remnant of your tribe) a race self-vowed
To endless warfare with his hordes and him,
The White-cross Knights of the adjacent Isle?
  Kar. And why else rend we down, wrench up, raze out?
These Knights of Rhodes we thus solicited
For help, bestowed on us a fiercer pest
Than aught we fled—their Prefect; who began
His promised mere paternal governance,
By a prompt massacre of all our Sheikhs
Able to thwart the Order in its scheme
Of crushing, with our nationalities,

Each chance of our return, and taming us
Bond slaves to Rhodes for ever—all, he thinks
To end by this day's treason.

Kha.   Say I not?
You, fitted to the Order's purposes,
Your Sheikhs cut off, your very garb proscribed,
Must yet receive one degradation more;
The Knights at last throw off the mask—transfer,
As tributary now, and appanage,
This islet they are but protectors of,
To their own ever-craving lord, the Church
Which licenses all crimes that pay it thus—
You, from their Prefect, were to be consigned
Pursuant to I know not what vile pact,
To the Knights' Patriarch, ardent to outvie
His predecessor in all wickedness;
When suddenly rose Djabal in the midst,
Djabal, the man in semblance, but our God
Confessed by signs and portents.   Ye saw fire
Bicker round Djabal, heard strange music flit
Bird-like about his brow?

Druses.   We saw—we heard!
Djabal is Hakeem, the incarnate Dread,
The phantasm Khalif, King of Prodigies!

Kha.   And as he said hath not our Khalif done,
And so disposed events (from land to land
Passing invisibly) that when, this morn,
The pact of villainy complete, there comes
This Patriarch's Nuncio with this Master's Prefect
Their treason to consummate,—each will face
For a crouching handful, an uplifted nation;
For simulated Christians, confessed Druses;
And, for slaves past hope of the Mother-mount,
Freedmen returning there 'neath Venice' flag;
That Venice, which, the Hospitallers' foe,
Grants us from Candia escort home at price
Of our relinquished isle—Rhodes counts her own—
Venice, whose promised argosies should stand
Toward the harbor: is it now that you, and you,
And you, selected from the rest to bear
The burthen of the Khalif's secret, further
To-day's event, entitled by your wrongs,
And witness in the Prefect's hall his fate—

That you dare clutch these gauds? Ay, drop them!
  Kar.   True,
Most true, all this; and yet, may one dare hint,
Thou art the youngest of us?—tho' employed
Abundantly as Djabal's confidant,
Transmitter of his mandates, even now:
Much less, whene'er beside him Anael graces
The cedar throne, his Queen-bride, art thou like
To occupy its lowest step that day!
Now, Khalil, wert thou checked as thou aspirest,
Forbidden such or such an honor,—say,
Would silence serve so amply?
  Kha.   Karshook thinks
I covet honors? Well, nor idly thinks!
Honors? I have demanded of them all
The greatest!
  Kar.   I supposed so.
  Kha.   Judge yourselves!
Turn—thus: 'tis in the alcove at the back
Of yonder-columned porch, whose entrance now
The veil hides, that our Prefect holds his state:
Receives the Nuncio, when the one, from Rhodes,
The other lands from Syria; there they meet.
Now, I have sued with earnest prayers . . .
  Kar.   For what
Shall the Bride's brother vainly sue?
  Kha.   That mine—
Avenging in one blow a myriad wrongs,
—Might be the hand to slay the Prefect there!
Djabal reserves that office for himself.   [*A silence.*
Thus far, as youngest of you all, I speak
—Scarce more enlightened than yourselves: since, near
As I approach him, nearer as I trust
Soon to approach our Master, he reveals
Only the God's power, not the glory yet:
Therefore I reasoned with you: now, as servant
To Djabal, bearing his authority,
Hear me appoint your several posts! Till noon
None sees him save myself and Anael—once
The deed achieved, our Khalif, casting off
The embodied Awe's tremendous mystery,
The weakness of the flesh disguise, resumes
His proper glory, ne'er to fade again.

Enter a Druse.

The Druse.   Our Prefect lands from Rhodes!—Without a
    sign
That he suspects aught since he left our Isle;
Nor in his train a single guard beyond
The few he sailed with hence: so have we learned
From Loys . . .
    Kar.   Loys?   Is not Loys gone
For ever?
    Ayoob.   Loys, the Frank Knight, returned?
    The Druse.   Loys, the boy, stood on the leading prow
Conspicuous in his gay attire,—and leapt
Into the surf the foremost: since day-dawn
I kept watch to the Northward; take but note
Of my poor vigilance to Djabal!
    Kha.   Peace!
Thou, Karshook, with thy company, receive
The Prefect as appointed: see, all keep
The wonted shew of servitude: announce
His entry here by the accustomed peal
Of trumpets, then await the further pleasure
Of Djabal! (Loys back, whom Djabal sent
To Rhodes that we might spare the single Knight
Worth sparing!)

Enter a second Druse.

The Druse.   I espied it first!   Say I
First spied the Nuncio's galley from the South!
Saidst thou a Crossed-key's Flag would flap the mast?
It nears apace!   One galley and no more—
If Djabal chance to ask who spied the flag
Forget not, I it was!
    Kha.   Thou, Ayoob, bring
The Nuncio and his followers hither!   Break
One rule prescribed, ye wither in your blood
Die at your fault!

Enter a third Druse.

The Druse.   I shall see home, see home!
—Shall banquet in the sombre groves again!
Hail to thee, Khalil!   Venice looms afar;
The argosies of Venice, like a cloud,
Bear up from Candia in the distance!

Kha.   Joy!
Summon our people, Raghib! Bid all forth!
Tell them the long-kept secret, old and young!
Set free the captives, let the trampled raise
Their faces from the dust, because at length
The cycle is complete, God Hakeem's reign
Begins anew! Say, Venice for our guard,
Ere night we steer for Syria! Hear you, Druses?
Hear you this crowning witness to the claims
Of Djabal? Oh, I spoke of hope and fear,
Reward and punishment, because he bade
Who has the right; for me, what should I say
But, mar not those imperial lineaments,
No majesty of all that rapt regard
Vex by the least omission! Let him rise
Without a check from you!

Druses.   Let Djabal rise!

Enter LOYS.—*The* Druses *are silent.*

Loys. Who speaks of Djabal?—for I seek him, friends!
[*Aside.*] *Tu Dieu!* 'Tis as our Isle broke out in song
For joy, its Prefect-incubus drops off
To-day, and I succeed him in his rule!
But no—they cannot dream of their good fortune!
[*Aloud.*] Peace to you, Druses! I have tidings for you,
But first for Djabal: where's your tall bewitcher,
With that small Arab thin-lipped silver mouth?
    Kha. [*Aside to* KAR.] Loys, in truth! Yet Djabal cannot
      err!
    Kar. [*to* KHA.] And who takes charge of Loys? That's
      forgotten,
Despite thy wariness! Will Loys stand
And see his comrade slaughtered?
    Loys. [*Aside.*]   How they shrink
And whisper, with those rapid faces! What?
The sight of me in their oppressors' garb
Strikes terror to the simple tribe? God's shame
On those that bring our Order ill repute!
But all's at end now; better days begin
For these mild mountaineers from over-sea;
The timidest shall have in me no Prefect
To cower at thus! [*Aloud.*] I ask for Djabal—
    Kar. [*Aside.*]   Better

One lured him, ere he can suspect, inside
The corridor; 'twere easy to dispatch
A youngster. [*To* Loys.] Djabal passed some minutes since
Thro' yonder porch, and . . .
    Kha. [*Aside.*]   Hold! What, him despatch?
The only Christian of them all we charge
No tyranny upon? Who,—noblest Knight
Of all that learned from time to time their trade
Of lust and cruelty among us,—heir
To Europe's pomps, a truest child of pride,—
Yet stood between the Prefect and ourselves
From the beginning? Loys, Djabal makes
Account of, and precisely sent to Rhodes
For safety?—I take charge of him!
[*To* Loys.]   Sir Loys,—
    Loys. There, cousins! Does Sir Loys strike you dead?
    Kha. [*advancing.*] Djabal has intercourse with few or none
Till noontide: but, your pleasure?
    Loys.   " Intercourse
" With few or none? "—(Ah, Khalil, when you spoke
I saw not your smooth face! All health!—and health
To Anael! How fares Anael?)—" Intercourse
" With few or none? " Forget you, I've been friendly
With Djabal long ere you or any Druse?
—Enough of him at Rennes, I think, beneath
The Duke my father's roof! He'd tell by the hour,
With fixed white eyes beneath his swarthy brow,
Plausiblest stories . . .
    Kha.   Stories, say you?—Ah,
The quaint attire!
    Loys.   My dress for the last time!
How sad I cannot make you understand,
This ermine, o'er a shield, betokens me
Of Bretagne, ancientest of provinces
And noblest; and, what's best and oldest there,
See, Dreux', our house's blazon, which the Nuncio
Tacks to an Hospitaller's vest to-day!
    Kha. The Nuncio we await? What brings you back
From Rhodes, Sir Loys?
    Loys.   How your island tribe
Forget, the world's awake while here you drowse!
What brings me back? What should not bring me, rather?
Our Patriarch's Nuncio visits you to-day—

Is not my year's probation out?   I come
To take the knightly vows.
   Kha.   What's that you wear?
   Loys. This Rhodian cross?   The cross your Prefect wore.
You should have seen, as I saw, the full Chapter
Rise, to a man, while they transferred this cross
From that unworthy Prefect's neck to . . . (fool—
My secret will escape me!)   In a word,
My year's probation's passed, and Knight ere eve
Am I; bound, like the rest, to yield my wealth
To the common stock, to live in chastity,
(We Knights espouse alone our Order's fame)
—Change this gay weed for the black white-crossed gown,
And fight to death against the Infidel
—Not, therefore, against you, you Christians with
Such partial difference only as befits
The peacefullest of tribes!   But Khalil, prithee,
Is not the Isle brighter than wont to-day?
   Kha. Ah, the new sword!
   Loys.   See now!   You handle sword
As 'twere a camel-staff!   Pull!   That's my motto,
Annealed, " *Pro fide*," on the blade in blue.
   Kha. No curve in it?   Surely a blade should carve!
   Loys. Straight from the wrist!   Loose—it should poise
      itself!
   Kha. [*waving with irrepressible exultation the sword.*]   We
      are a nation, Loys, of old fame
Among the mountains!   Rights have we to keep
With the sword too!
[*Remembering himself.*]   But I forget—you bid me
Seek Djabal?
   Loys.   What!   A sword's sight scares you not?
(The People I will make of him and them!
Oh, let my Prefect-sway begin at once!)
Bring Djabal—say, indeed, that come he must!
   Kha. At noon seek Djabal in the Prefect's Chamber,
And find—[*Aside.*] Nay, 'tis thy cursed race's token,
Frank pride, no special insolence of thine!
[*Aloud.*] Tarry and I will do your bidding, Loys.
[*To the rest aside.*]   Now, forth you!   I proceed to Djabal
      straight.
Leave this poor boy, who knows not what he says.
Oh, will it not add joy even to thy joy,

Djabal, that I report all friends were true?

          [KHALIL *goes, followed by the* Druses.

  Loys. *Tu Dieu!* How happy I shall make these Druses!
Was't not surpassingly contrived of me
To get the long list of their wrongs by heart,
Then take the first pretence for stealing off
From these poor islanders, present myself
Sudden at Rhodes before the noble Chapter,
And (as best proof of ardour in its cause
Which ere to-night will have become, too, mine)
Acquaint it with this plague-sore in its body,
This Prefect and his villainous career?
The princely Synod! All I dared request
Was his dismissal; and they graciously
Consigned his very office to myself—
Myself may heal whate'er's diseased!

                        And good
For them, they did so! Since I never felt
How lone a lot, tho' brilliant, I embrace,
Till now that, past retrieval, it is mine—
To live thus, and thus die! Yet, as I leapt
On shore, so home a feeling greeted me
That I could half believe in Djabal's story,
He used to tempt my father with, at Rennes—
And me, too, since the story brought me here—
Of some Count Dreux and ancestor of ours
Who, sick of wandering from Bouillon's war,
Left his old name in Lebanon.

                      Long days
At least to spend in the Isle! and, my news known
An hour hence, what if Anael turns on me
The great black eyes I must forget?

                      Why, fool,
Recall them, then? My business is with Djabal,
Not Anael! Djabal tarries: if I seek him?—
The Isle is brighter than its wont to-day!

ACT II

Enter DJABAL.

Dja. That a strong man should think himself a God!
I—Hakeem? To have wandered thro' the world,
Sown falsehood, and thence reaped now scorn, now faith,
For my one chant with many a change, my tale
Of outrage, and my prayer for vengeance—this
Required, forsooth, no mere man's faculty,
Nor less than Hakeem's? The persuading Loys
To pass probation here; the getting access
By Loys to the Prefect; worst of all,
The gaining my tribe's confidence by fraud
That would disgrace the very Franks,—a few
Of Europe's secrets that subdue the flame,
The wave,—to ply a simple tribe with these,
Took Hakeem?
          And I feel this first to-day!
Does the day break, is the hour imminent
When one deed, when my whole life's deed, my deed
Must be accomplished? Hakeem? Why the God?
Shout, rather, " Djabal, Youssof's child, thought slain
" With his whole race, the Druses' Sheikhs, this Prefect
" Endeavoured to extirpate—saved, a child,
" Returns from traversing the world, a man,
" Able to take revenge, lead back the march
" To Lebanon "—so shout, and who gainsays?
But now, because delusion mixed itself
Insensibly with this career, all's changed!
Have I brought Venice to afford us convoy?
" True—but my jugglings wrought that!" " Put I heart
Into our people where no heart lurked? "—" Ah,
" What cannot an impostor do!"
                Not this!
Not do this which I do! Not bid, avaunt
Falsehood! Thou shalt not keep thy hold on me!
—Nor even get a hold on me! 'Tis now—
This day—hour—minute—'tis as here I stand
On the accursed threshold of the Prefect,
That I am found deceiving and deceived!
And now what do I do?—Hasten to the few

Deceived, ere they deceive the many—shout,
As I professed, I did believe myself!
Say, Druses, had you seen a butchery—
If Ayoob, Karshook saw——Maani there
Must tell you how I saw my father sink;
My mother's arms twine still about my neck;
I hear my brother's shriek, here's yet the scar
Of what was meant for my own death-blow—say,
If you had woke like me, grown year by year
Out of the tumult in a far-off clime,
Would it be wondrous such delusion grew?
I walked the world, asked help at every hand;
Came help or no? Not this and this? Which helps
When I returned with, found the Prefect here,
The Druses here, all here but Hakeem's self,
The Khalif of the thousand prophecies,
Reserved for such a juncture,—could I call
My mission aught but Hakeem's? Promised Hakeem
More than performs the Djabal—you absolve?
—Me, will never shame before the crowd
Yet happily ignorant?—Me, both throngs surround
The few deceived, the many unabused,
—Who, thus surrounded, slay for you and them
The Prefect, lead to Lebanon! No Khalif,
But Sheikh once more! Mere Djabal—not. . . .

Enter KHALIL *hastily.*

Kha.   —God Hakeem!
'Tis told! The whole Druse nation knows thee, Hakeem,
As we! and mothers lift on high their babes
Who seem aware, so glisten their great eyes,
Thou hast not failed us; ancient brows are proud!
Our Elders could not earlier die, it seems,
Than at thy coming! The Druse heart is thine!
Take it! my Lord and theirs, be thou adored!

Dja. [*Aside.*] Adored!—but I renounce it utterly!

Kha. Already are they instituting choirs
And dances to the Khalif, as of old
'Tis chronicled thou bad'st them.

Dja. [*Aside.*]   I abjure it!
'Tis not mine—not for me!

Kha.   Why pour they wine
Flavoured like honey and bruised mountain herbs?
Or wear those strings of sun-dried cedar-fruit?

Oh—let me tell thee—Esaad, we supposed
Doting, is carried forth, eager to see
The last sun rise on the Isle—he can see now!
The shamed Druse women never wept before:
They can look up when we reach home, they say.
Smell!—Sweet cane, saved in Lilith's breast thus long—
Sweet!—it grows wild in Lebanon.   And I
Alone do nothing for thee!   'Tis my office
Just to announce what well thou know'st—but thus
Thou bidst me.   At this selfsame moment tend
The Prefect, Nuncio, and the Admiral
Hither, by their three sea-paths—nor forget
Who were the trusty watchers!—Thou forget?
Like me, who do forget that Anael bade. . . .

   Dja. [*Aside.*] Ay, Anael, Anael—is that said at last?
Louder than all, that would be said, I knew!
What does abjuring mean, confessing mean,
To the people?   Till that woman crossed my path,
On went I, solely for my people's sake:
I saw her, and I first saw too myself,
And slackened pace: " if I should prove indeed
Hakeem—with Anael by! "

   Kha. [*Aside.*]   Ah, he is rapt!
Dare I at such a moment break on him
Even to do my sister's bidding?   Yes!
The eyes are Djabal's, and not Hakeem's yet!
Though but till I have spoken this, perchance.

   Dja. [*Aside.*] To yearn to tell her, and yet have no one
Great heart's-word that will tell her!   I could gasp
Doubtless one such word out, and die!
[*Aloud.*]   You said
That Anael . . .

   Kha.   . . . Fain would see thee, speak with thee,
Before thou change, discard this Djabal's shape
She knows, for Hakeem's shape she is to know:
Something's to say that will not from her mind:
I know not what—" Let him but come! " she said.

   Dja. [*Half-apart.*] My nation—all my Druses—how
     they?
Those I must save, and suffer thus to save,
Hold they their posts?   Wait they their Khalif too?

   Kha. All at the signal pant to flock around
That banner of a brow!

Dja. [*Aside.*]   And when they flock,
Confess them this—and after, for reward,
Be chased with howlings to her feet perchance?
—Have the poor outraged Druses, deaf and blind,
Precede me there—forestall my story, there—
Tell it in mocks and jeers—

                            I lose myself!
Who needs a Hakeem to direct him now?
I need the veriest child—why not this child?
                            [*Turning abruptly to* KHALIL.
You are a Druse too, Khalil; you were nourished
Like Anael with our mysteries: if she
Could vow, so nourished, to love only one
Who should revenge the Druses, whence proceeds
Your silence?   Wherefore made you no essay,
Who thus implicitly can execute
My bidding?   What have I done, you could not?
Who, knowing more than Anael the prostration
Of our once lofty tribe, the daily life
Of this detested . . .

                    Does he come, you say,
This Prefect?   All's in readiness?
    Kha.   The sword,
The sacred robe, the Khalif's mystic tiar,
Laid up so long, are all disposed beside
The Prefect's chamber.
    Dja.   —Why did you despair?
    Kha.   I know our Nation's state?   Too surely know,
As thou, who speak'st to prove me!   Wrongs like ours
Should wake revenge: but when I sought the wronged
And spoke,—" The Prefect stabbed your son—arise!
" Your daughter, while you starve, eats shameless bread
" In his pavilion—then, arise! "—my speech
Fell idly—'twas, " Be silent, or worse fare!
" Endure, till time's slow cycle prove complete!
" Who may'st thou be that takest on thee to thrust
" Into this peril—art thou Hakeem? "   No!
Only a mission like thy mission renders
All these obedient at a breath, subdues
Their private passions, brings their wills to one!
    Dja.   You think so?
    Kha.   Even now—when they have witnessed
Thy miracles—had I not threatened them

With Hakeem's vengeance, they would mar the whole,
And lie ere this, each with his special prize,
Safe in his dwelling, leaving our main hope
To perish! No! When these have kissed thy feet
At Lebanon, the Past purged off, the Present
Clear,—for the Future, even Hakeem's mission
May end, and I perchance, or any youth,
Can rule them thus renewed.—I talk to thee!

   Dja. And wisely. (He is Anael's brother, pure
As Anael's self.) Go say, I come to her.
Haste! I will follow you.   [KHALIL *goes.*
                    Oh, not confess
To these—the blinded multitude—confess,
Before at least the fortune of my deed
Half authorize its means! Only to her
Let me confess my fault, who in my path
Curled up like incense from a mage-king's tomb
When he would have the wayfarer descend
Thro' the earth's rift and take hid treasure up.
When should my first child's-carelessness have stopped
If not when I, whose lone youth hurried past
Letting each joy 'scape for the Druses' sake,
At length recovered in one Druse all joys?
Were her brow brighter, her eyes richer, still
Would I confess! On the gulf's verge I pause.
How could I slay the Prefect, thus and thus?
Anael, be mine to guard me, not destroy!   [*Goes.*

Enter ANAEL, *and* MAANI, *who is assisting to array her in the
            ancient dress of the Druses.*

   An. Those saffron-vestures of the tabret-girls!
Comes Djabal, think you?
   Maa.   Doubtless Djabal comes.
   An. Dost thou snow-swathe thee kinglier, Lebanon,
Than in my dreams?—Nay, all the tresses off
My forehead—look I lovely so? He says
That I am lovely.
   Maa.   Lovely! nay, that hangs
Awry.
   An. You tell me how a khandjar hangs?
The sharp side, thus, along the heart, see, marks
The maiden of our class. Are you content
For Djabal as for me?

Maa.   Content, my child.

An.   Oh, mother, tell me more of him.   He comes
Even now—tell more, fill up my soul with him!

Maa.   And did I not . . . yes, surely . . . tell you all?

An.   What will be changed in Djabal when the Change
Arrives?   Which feature?   Not his eyes!

Maa.   'Tis writ,
Our Hakeem's eyes rolled fire and clove the dark
Superbly.

An.   Not his eyes!   His voice perhaps?
Yet that's no change; for a grave current lived
—Grandly beneath the surface ever lived,
That, scattering, broke as in live silver spray
While . . . ah, the bliss . . . he would discourse to me
In that enforced, still fashion, word on word!
'Tis the old current which must swell thro' that,
For what least tone, Maani, could I lose?
'Tis surely not his voice will change!

                              —If Hakeem
Only stood by!   If Djabal, somehow, passed
Out of the radiance as from out a robe;
Possessed, but was not it!

                              He lived with you?
Well—and that morning Djabal saw me first
And heard my vow never to wed but one
Who saved my People—on that day . . . proceed!

Maa.   Once more, then: from the time of his return
In secret, changed so since he left the Isle
That I, who screened our Emir's last of sons,
This Djabal, from the Prefect's massacre
—Who bade him ne'er forget the child he was,
—Who dreamed so long the youth he might become—
I knew not in the man that child; the man
Who spoke alone of hopes to save our tribe,
How he had gone from land to land to save
Our tribe—allies were sure, nor foes to dread;
And much he mused, days, nights, alone he mused;
But never till that day when, pale and worn
As by a persevering woe, he cried
" Is there not one Druse left me? "—And I showed
The way to Khalil's and your hiding-place
From the abhorred eye of the Prefect here,
So that he saw you, heard you speak—till then,

Never did he announce—(how the moon seemed
To ope and shut, the while, above us both!)
—His mission was the mission promised us—
The cycle had revolved—all things renewing,
He was lost Hakeem clothed in flesh to lead
His children home anon, now veiled to work
Great purposes—the Druses now would change.

    An. And they have changed! And obstacles did sink,
And furtherances rose! And round his form
Played fire, and music beat her angel wings!
My people, let me more rejoice, oh, more
For you than for myself! Did I but watch
Afar the pageant, feel our Khalif pass,
One of the throng, how proud were I—tho' ne'er
Singled by Djabal's glance! But to be chosen
His own from all, the most his own of all,
To be exalted with him, side by side,
Lead the exulting Druses, meet . . . ah, how
Worthily meet the maidens who await
Ever beneath the cedars—how deserve
This honor, in their eyes? So bright are they
That saffron-vestured sound the tabrets there—
The girls who throng there in my dreams! One hour
And all is over: how shall I do aught
That may deserve next hour's exalting?—How?—
                               [Suddenly to MAANI.
Mother, I am not worthy of him! I read it
Still in his eyes! He stands as if to tell me
I am not, yet forbears! Why else revert
To one theme ever?—how mere human gifts
Suffice in myself—whose worship fades,
Whose awe goes ever off at his approach,
As now, that when he comes . . .
[As DJABEL *enters.]*   Oh, why is it
I cannot kneel to you?
    Dja.   Rather, 'tis I
Should kneel to you, my Anael!
    An.   Even so!
For never seem you—shall I speak the truth?—
Never a God to me! 'Tis the Man's hand,
Eye, voice! Oh, do you veil these to our people,
Or but to me? To them, I think, to them!
And brightness is their veil, shadow—my truth!

You mean that I should never kneel to you
—So I will kneel!

Dja. [*preventing her.*] No—no!

[*Feeling the khandjar as he raises her.*

Ha, have you chosen . . .

An.   The khandjar with our ancient garb.   But, Djabal,
Change not, be not exalted yet!   give time
That I may plan more, perfect more.   My blood
Beats—beats!

[*Aside.*]   O must I then—since Loys leaves us
Never to come again, renew in me
Those doubts so near effaced already—must
I needs confess them now to Djabal?—Own
That when I saw the stranger—heard his voice,
My faith fell, and the woeful thought flashed first
That each effect of Djabal's presence, taken
For proof of more than human attributes
In him, by me whose heart at his approach
Beat fast, whose brain while he was by swam round,
Whose soul at his departure died away,
—That every such effect might have been wrought
In others' frames, tho' not in mine, by Loys
Or any merely mortal presence?   Doubt
Is fading fast; shall I reveal it now?
How can I be rewarded presently,
With doubt unexpiated, undisclosed?

Dja. [*Aside.*] Avow the truth?   I cannot!   In what words
Avow that all she loves in me is false?
—Which yet has served that flower-like love of hers
To climb by, like the clinging gourd, and clasp
With its divinest wealth of leaf and bloom.
Could I take down the prop-work, in itself
So vile, yet interlaced and overlaid
With painted cups and fruitage—might these still
Bask in the sun, unconscious their own strength
Of matted stalk and tendril had replaced
The old support thus silently withdrawn!
But no; the beauteous fabric crushes too.
'Tis not for my sake but for Anael's sake
I leave her soul this Hakeem where it leans!
Oh, could I vanish from them—quit the Isle!
And yet,—a thought comes: here my work is done
At every point; the Druses must return—

Have convoy to their birth-place back, whoe'er
The leader be, myself or any Druse—
Venice is pledged to that: 'tis for myself,
For my own vengeance in the Prefect's death,
I stay now, not for them—to slay or spare
The Prefect, whom imports it save myself?
He cannot bar their passage from the Isle;
What would his death be but my own reward?
Then, mine, I will forego. It is foregone!
Let him escape with all my House's blood!
Ere he can reach land, Djabal disappears,
And Hakeem, Anael loved, shall, fresh as first,
Live in her memory, keeping her sublime
Above the world. She cannot touch that world
By ever knowing what I truly am,
Since Loys,—of mankind the only one
Able to link my present with my past,
My life in Europe with my Island life,
Thence, able to unmask me,—I've disposed
Safely at last at Rhodes, and . . .

Enter KHALIL.

Kha.   Loys greets thee!
Dja. Loys? To drag me back? It cannot be!
An. [*Aside.*] Loys! Ah, doubt may not be stifled so!
   Kha. Can I have erred that thou so gazest? Yes,
I told thee not, in the glad press of tidings
Of higher import, Loys is returned
Before the Prefect, with, if possible,
Twice the light-heartedness of old. As though
On some inauguration he expects,
To-day, the world's fate hung!
   Dja.   —And asks for me?
   Kha. Thou knowest all things! Thee in chief he greets,
But every Druse of us is to be happy
At his arrival, he declares: were Loys
Thou, Master, he could have no wider soul
To take us in with. How I love that Loys!
   Dja. [*Aside.*] Shame winds me with her tether round and
     round!
   An. [*Aside.*] Loys? I take the trial! it is meet,
The little I can do, be done; that faith,
All I can offer, want no perfecting

Which my own act may compass.   Aye, this way
All may go well, nor that ignoble doubt
Be chased by other aid than mine.   Advance
Close to my fear, weigh Loys with my Lord,
The mortal's with the more than mortal's gifts!

 Dja. [*Aside.*] Before, there were so few deceived! and now
There's doubtless not one least Druse in the Isle
But (having learned my superhuman claims,
And calling me his Khalif-God) will clash
The whole truth out from Loys at first word!
While Loys, for his part, will hold me up,
With a Frank's unimaginable scorn
Of such imposture, to my people's eyes!
Could I but hold him longer yet awhile
From them, amuse him here until I plan
How he and I at once may leave the Isle?
Khalil I cannot part with from my side—
My only help in this emergency:
There's Anael!

  An.   Please you?

  Dja.   (Anael—none but she!)
[*To* ANAEL.] I pass some minutes in the chamber there,
Ere I see Loys: you shall speak with him
Until I join you.   Khalil follows me.

 An. [*Aside.*] As I divined: he bids me save myself,
Offers me a probation—I accept!
Let me see Loys!

  Loys. [*without.*] Djabal!

  An. [*Aside.*]   'Tis his voice.
The smooth Frank trifler with our people's wrongs,
The self-complacent boy-inquirer, loud
On this and that inflicted tyranny,
—Aught serving to parade an ignorance
Of how wrong feels, inflicted! Let me close
With what I viewed at distance; let myself
Probe this delusion to the core!

  Dja.   He comes!
Khalil, along with me! while Anael waits
Till I return once more—and but once more!

ACT III

ANAEL *and* LOYS.

An. Here leave me! Here I wait another. 'Twas
For no mad protestation of a love
Like this you say possesses you, I came.

Loys. Love—how protest a love I dare not feel?
Mad words may doubtless have escaped me—you
Are here—I only feel you here!

An. No more!

Loys. But once again, whom could you love? I dare,
Alas, say nothing of myself, who am
A Knight now, for when Knighthood we embrace,
Love we abjure: so speak on safely—speak,
Lest I speak, and betray my faith so! Sure
To say your breathing passes thro' me, changes
My blood to spirit, and my spirit to you,
As Heaven the sacrificer's wine to it—
This is not to protest my love? You said
You could love one . . .

An. One only! We are bent
To earth—who raises up my tribe, I love;
The Prefect bows us—who removes him; we
Have ancient rights—who gives them back to us,
I love.—Forbear me! Let my hand go!

Loys. Him
You could love only? Where is Djabal? Stay!
[*Aside.*] Yet wherefore stay? Who does this but myself?
Had I apprized her that I come to do
Just this, what more could she acknowledge? No!
She sees into my heart's core: what is it
Feeds either cheek with red, as June some rose?
Why turns she from me? Ah fool, over-fond
To dream I could call up . . .

. . . What never dream
Yet feigned! 'Tis love! Oh Anael, speak to me!
Djabal!

An. Seek Djabal by the Prefect's chamber
At noon! [*She paces the room.*

Loys. [*Aside.*] And am I not the Prefect now?
Is it my fate to be the only one

Able to win her love, the only one
Unable to accept her love?   The Past
Breaks up beneath my footing: came I here
This morn as to a slave, to set her free
And take her thanks, and then spend day by day
Content beside her in the Isle?   What works
This knowledge in me now!   Her eye has broken
The faint disguise away; for Anael's sake
I left the Isle, for her espoused the cause
Of the Druses, all for her I thought, till now,
To live without!
    —As I must live!   To-day
Ordains me Knight, forbids me—never shall
Forbid me to possess myself, heart, arm,
Thy soldier!
  An.   Djabal you demanded, comes!
  Loys. [*Aside.*] What wouldst thou, Loys? See him?
   Nought beside
Is wanting: I have felt his voice a spell
From first to last.   He brought me here, made known
The Druses to me, drove me hence to seek
Redress for them; and shall I meet him now,
When nought is wanting but a word of his,
To—what?—induce me to spurn hope, faith, pride,
Honor away,—to cast my lot among
His tribe, become a proverb in men's mouths,
Breaking my high pact of companionship
With those who graciously bestowed on me
The very opportunities I turn
Against them.
    Let me not see Djabal now!
  An. The Prefect also comes!
  Loys. [*Aside.*]   Him let me see,
Not Djabal!   Him, degraded at a word,
To please me,—to attest belief in me—
And, after, Djabal!   Yes, ere I return
To her, the Nuncio's vow shall have destroyed
This heart's rebellion, and coerced this will
For ever.
    Anael, not before the vows
Irrevocably fix me . . .
      Let me fly!
The Prefect, or I lose myself for ever!   [*Goes.*

An. Yes, I am calm now; just one way remains—
One, to attest my faith in him: for, see,
I were quite lost else: Loys, Djabal, stand
On either side—two men! I balance looks
And words, give Djabal a man's preference,
No more. In Djabal, Hakeem is absorbed!
And for a love like this, the God who saves
My race, selects me for his bride! One way!—

Enter DJABAL.

Dja. [*to himself.*] No moment is to waste, then; 'tis
    resolved!
If Khalil may be trusted to lead back
The Druses, and if Loys can be lured
Out of the Isle—if I procure his silence,
Or promise never to return at least,—
All's over! Even now my bark awaits—
I reach the next wild islet and the next,
And lose myself beneath the sun for ever!
And now, to Anael!

An.   Djabal, I am thine!

Dja. Mine? Djabal's?—As if Hakeem had not been?

An. Not Djabal's? Say first, do you read my thoughts?
Why need I speak, if you can read my thoughts?

Dja. I do not, I have said a thousand times.

An. (My secret's safe, I shall surprise him yet!)
Djabal, I knew your secret from the first—
Djabal, when first I saw you . . . (by our porch
You leant, and pressed the tinkling veil away,
And one fringe fell behind your neck—I see!)
. . . I knew you were not human, for I said
" This dim secluded house where the sea beats
Is Heaven to me—my people's huts are Hell
To them; this august form will follow me,
Mix with the waves his voice will,—I have him;
And they, the Prefect; Oh, my happiness
Rounds to the full whether I choose or no!
His eyes met mine, he was about to speak,
His hand grew damp—surely he meant to say
He let me love him: in that moment's bliss
I shall forget my people pine for home—
They pass and repass with pallid eyes!"
I vowed at once a certain vow; this vow—
Not to embrace you till my tribe was saved.

Embrace me!

Dja. [*Apart.*] And she loved me! Nought remained
But that! Nay, Anael, is the Prefect dead?

An. Ah, you reproach me! True, his death crowns all,
I know—or should know—and I would do much,
Believe! but, death—Oh, you, who have known death,
Would never doom the Prefect, were death fearful
As we report!

          Death!—a fire curls within us
From the foot's palm, and fills up to the brain,
Up, out, then shatters the whole bubble-shell
Of flesh, perchance!

              Death!—witness, I would die,
Whate'er death be, would venture now to die
For Khalil—for Maani—what for thee?
Nay but embrace me, Djabal, in assurance
My vow will not be broken, for I must
Do something to attest my faith in you,
Be worthy of you!

Dja. [*avoiding her.*] I come for that—to say
Such an occasion is at hand: 'tis like
I leave you—that we part, my Anael,—part
For ever!

An.   We part? Just so! I have succumbed,—
I am, he thinks, unworthy—and nought less
Will serve than such approval of my faith!
Then, we part not! Remains there no way short
Of that? Oh, not that!

            Death!—Yet a hurt bird
Died in my hands—its eyes filmed—" Nay, it sleeps "
I said, " will wake to-morrow well "—'twas dead!

Dja. I stand here and time fleets. Anael—I come
To bid a last farewell to you: perhaps
We never meet again—but, ere the Prefect
Arrive . . .

           Enter KHALIL *breathlessly.*

Kha. He's here! The Prefect! Twenty guards,
No more—no sign he dreams of danger—all
Awaits thee only—Ayoob, Karshook, keep
Their posts—wait but the deed's accomplishment
To join us with thy Druses to a man!
Still holds his course the Nuncio—near and near

The fleet from Candia's steering!

Dja. [*Aside.*]   All is lost!
—Or won?

Kha.   And I have laid the sacred robes,
The sword, the head-tiar, at the porch—the place
Commanded—Thou wilt hear the Prefect's trumpet.

Dja.   Then I keep Anael,—him then, past recall,
I slay—'tis forced on me! As I began
I must conclude—so be it!

Kha.   For the rest
(Save Loys, our foe's solitary sword)
All is so safe that . . . I will ne'er entreat
Thy post again of thee—tho' danger's none,
There must be glory only meet for thee
In slaying the Prefect!

An. [*Aside.*]   And 'tis now that Djabal
Would leave me!—in the glory meet for him!

Dja.   As glory, I would yield the deed to you,
Or any one; what peril there may be,
I keep. [*Aside.*] All things conspire to hound me on!
Not now, my soul, draw back, at least! Not now!
The course is plain, howe'er obscure all else—
Once offer this tremendous sacrifice,
Prevent what else will be irreparable,
Secure these transcendental helps, regain
The Cedars—then let all dark clear itself!
I slay him!

Kha.   Anael, and no part for us!
[*To* DJA.] Hast thou possessed her with . . .

Dja. [*to* AN.]   Whom speak you to?
What is it you behold there? Nay, this smile
Turns stranger—shudder you? The man must die,
As thousands of our race have died thro' him.
One blow, and I discharge his weary soul
From the flesh that pollutes it—let him fill
Straight some new expiatory form, of earth
Or sea, the reptile, or some aëry thing—
What is there in his death?

An.   My brother said,
Is there no part in it for us?

Dja.   For Khalil,—
The trumpet will announce the Nuncio's entry;
Here, I shall find the Prefect hastening

In the Pavilion to receive him—here,
I slay the Prefect; meanwhile Ayoob leads
The Nuncio with his guards within—once these
Secured in the outer hall, bid Ayoob bar
Entry or egress till I give the sign
Which waits the landing of the argosies
You will announce to me; this double sign
That justice is performed and help arrived,
When Ayoob shall receive, but not before,
Let him throw ope the palace doors, admit
The Druses to behold their tyrant, ere
We leave for ever this detested spot.
Go, Khalil, hurry all—no pause—no pause!
Whirl on the dream, secure to wake anon!

   Kha.   What sign? and who the bearer?
   Dja.   Who shall show
My ring, admit to Ayoob—How she stands!
Have I not . . . I must have some task for her.
Anael! not that way! 'Tis the Prefect's chamber;
Anael, keep you the ring—give you the sign!
(It holds her safe amid the stir)—You will
Be faithful?
   An. [*taking the ring.*] I would fain be worthy of you!
                              [*Trumpet without.*

   Kha.   He comes!
   Dja.   And I too come!
   An.   One word, but one!
Say, shall you be exalted at the deed?
Then? On the instant?
   Dja.   I exalted? What?
He, there—we, thus—our wrongs revenged—our tribe
Set free—Oh, then shall I, assure yourself,
Shall you, shall each of us, be in his death
Exalted!
   Kha.   He is here!
   Dja.   Away—away!   [*They go.*

    Enter the PREFECT *with* Guards *and* Loys.

   The Prefect. [*to* Guards.] Back, I say, to the galley every
      guard!
That's my sole care now; see each bench retains
Its complement of rowers; I embark
O' the instant, since this Knight will have it so.

Alas me! Could you have the heart, my Loys?
[*To a* Guard *who whispers*.] Oh, bring the holy Nuncio here
    forthwith!   [*The* Guards *go*.
Loys, a rueful sight, confess, to see
The grey discarded Prefect leave his post,
With tears i' the eye! So you are Prefect now?
You depose me—you succeed me? Ha, ha!
    Loys. And dare you laugh, whom laughter less becomes
Than yesterday's forced meekness we beheld . . .
    Pref.   . . . When you so eloquently pleaded, Loys,
For my dismissal from the post?—Ah, meek
With cause enough, consult the Nuncio else!
And wish him the like meekness—for so staunch
A servant of the church can scarce have bought
His share in the Isle, and paid for it, hard pieces!
You've my successor to condole with, Nuncio!
I shall be safe by then i' the galley, Loys!
    Loys. You make as you would tell me you rejoice
To leave your scene of . . .
    Pref.   Trade in the dear Druses?
Blood and sweat traffic? Spare what yesterday
We had enough of! Drove I in the Isle
A profitable game? Learn wit, my son,
Which you'll need shortly! Did it never breed
Suspicion in you, all was not pure profit,
When I, the insatiate . . . and so forth . . . was bent
On having a partaker in my rule?
Why did I yield this Nuncio half the gain,
If not that I might also shift . . . what on him?
Half the peril, Loys!
    Loys.   Peril?
    Pref.   Hark you!
I'd love you if you'd let me—this for reason,
You save my life at price of . . . well, say risk
At least, of yours. I came a long time since
To the Isle; our Hospitallers bade me tame
These savage wizards, and reward myself—
    Loys. The Knights who so repudiate your crime?
    Pref. Loys, the Knights! we doubtless understood
Each other; as for trusting to reward
From any friend beside myself . . . No, no!
I clutched mine on the spot, when it was sweet,
And I had taste for it. I felt these wizards

Alive—was sure they were not on me, only
When I was on them: but with age comes caution:
And stinging pleasures please less and sting more.
Year by year, fear by fear! The girls were brighter,
Than ever ('faith there's yet one Anael left,
I set my heart upon—Oh, prithee, let
That brave new sword lie still!)—These joys looked brighter,
But silenter the town, too, as I passed.
With this alcove's delicious memories
Began to mingle visions of gaunt fathers,
Quick-eyed sons, fugitives from the mine, the oar,
Stealing to catch me: brief, when I began
To quake with fear—(I think I hear the Chapter
Solicited to let me leave, now all
Worth staying for was gained and gone!)—I say,
Just when for the remainder of my life
All methods of escape seemed lost—that then
Up should a young hot-headed Loys spring,
Talk very long and loud, in fine, compel
The Knights to break their whole arrangement, have me
Home for pure shame—from this safehold of mine
Where but ten thousand Druses seek my life,
To my wild place of banishment, San Gines
By Murcia, where my three fat manors lying,
Purchased by gains here and the Nuncio's gold,
Are all I have to guard me,—that such fortune
Should fall to me, I hardly could expect!
Therefore, I say, I'd love you!

 Loys.   Can it be?
I play into your hands then? Oh, no, no!
The Venerable Chapter, the Great Order
Sunk o' the sudden into fiends of the pit?
But I will back—will yet unveil you!

 Pref.   Me?
To whom?—perhaps Sir Galeas, who in Chapter
Shook his white head thrice—and some dozen times
My hand this morning shook, for value paid
To that Italian Saint, Sir Cosimo?—
Indignant at my wringing year by year
A thousand bezants from the coral-divers,
As you recounted; felt he not aggrieved?
Well might he—I allowed for his half-share
Merely one hundred! To Sir . . .

Loys.   See! you dare
Inculpate the whole Order; yet should I,
A youth, a sole voice, have the power to change
Their evil way, had they been firm in it?
Answer me!
    Pref.   Oh, the son of Bretagne's Duke,
And that son's wealth, the father's influence, too
And the young arm, we'll even say, my Loys,
—The fear of losing or diverting these
Into another channel, by gainsaying
A novice too abruptly, could not influence
The Order! You might join, for aught they cared,
Their red-cross rivals of the Temple! Well,
I thank you for my part, at all events!
Stay here till they withdraw you! You'll inhabit
This palace—sleep, perchance, in this alcove,
Where now I go to meet our holy friend:
Good! and now disbelieve me if you can:
This is the first time for long years I enter
Thus [*lifts the arras*] without feeling just as if I lifted
The lid up of my tomb!
    Loys.   They share his crime!
God's punishment will overtake you yet!
    Pref. Thank you it does not! Pardon this last flash:
I bear a sober visage presently
With the disinterested Nuncio here—
His purchase-money safe at Murcia too!
Let me repeat—for the first time, no draught
Coming as from a sepulchre salutes me.
When we next meet, this folly may have passed.
We'll hope—Ha, ha!   [*Goes thro' the arras.*
    Loys.   Assure me but . . . he's gone!
He could not lie! Then what have I escaped!
I, who have so nigh given up happiness
For ever, to be linked with him and them!
Oh, opportunest of discoveries! I
Their Knight? I utterly renounce them all!
Hark! What, he meets by this the Nuncio? yes
The same hyæna groan-like laughter! Quick—
To Djabal! I am one of them at last,
Those simple-hearted Druses—Anael's tribe!
Djabal! She's mine at last—Djabal, I say!—   [*Goes.*

ACT IV

Enter DJABAL.

   Dja.   Let me but slay the Prefect—The end now!
To-morrow will be time enough to pry
Into the means I took: suffice, they served,
Ignoble as they were, to hurl revenge
True to its object.   *[Seeing the robes, etc. disposed.*
         . . . Mine should never so
Have hurried to accomplishment! Thee, Djabal,
Far other moods befitted! Calm the Robe
Should clothe this doom's awarder!
[Taking the robe.]   Shall I dare
Assume my nation's Robe? I am at least
A Druse again, chill Europe's policy
Drops from me—I dare take the Robe.   Why not
The Tiar? I rule the Druses, and what more
Betokens it than rule?—yet—yet—   *[Lays down the Tiar.*
[Footsteps in the alcove.] He comes!   *[Taking the sword.*
If the sword serves, let the Tiar lie! So, feet
Clogged with the blood of twenty years can fall
Thus lightly! Round me, all ye ghosts! He'll lift . . .
Which arm to push the arras wide?—or both?
Stab from the neck down to the heart—there stay!
Near he comes—nearer—the next footstep! Now!
        [As he dashes aside the arras, ANAEL *is discovered.*
Ha! Anael! Nay, my Anael, can it be?
Heard you the trumpet? I must slay him here,
And here you ruin all.   Why speak you not?
Anael, the Prefect comes! *[*ANAEL *screams.]* So late to feel
'Tis not a sight for you to look upon?
A moment's work—but such work! Till you go,
I must be idle—idle, I risk all!   *[Pointing to her hair.*
Those locks are well, and you are beauteous thus,
But with the dagger 'tis, I have to do!
   An. With mine!
   Dja.   Blood—Anael?
   An.   Djabal—'tis thy deed!
It must be—I had hoped to claim it mine—
Be worthy thee—but I must needs confess
'Twas not I, but thyself . . . not I have . . . Djabal!

Speak to me!

  Dja.   Oh my punishment!

  An.   Speak to me!

While I can speak—touch me—despite the blood!

When the command passed from thy soul to mine,

I went, fire leading me, muttering of thee,

And the approaching exaltation,—make

One sacrifice! I said,—and he sate there,

Bade me approach; and, as I did approach,

Thy fire with music burst into my brain—

'Twas but a moment's work, thou saidst—perchance

It may have been so! well, it is thy deed!

  Dja.   It is my deed!

  An.   His blood, all this!—this! And . . .

And more—sustain me, Djabal—wait not—now—

Let flash thy glory! Change thyself and me!

It must be! Ere the Druses flock to us!

At least confirm me! Djabal—blood gushed forth—

He was our tyrant—but I looked he'd fall

Prone as asleep—why else is Death called sleep?

Sleep? He bent o'er his breast—'Tis sin, I know,

Punish me, Djabal, but wilt thou let him?

Be it thou that punishest, not he—who creeps

On his red breast—is here—'tis the small groan

Of a child—no worse! Bestow the new life, then!

Too swift it cannot be, too strange, surpassing!

                            [*Following him up and down.*

Now! Change us both! Change me and change thou!

  Dja. [*sinks on his knees.*]   Thus!

Behold my change! You have done nobly! I!—

  An. Can Hakeem kneel?

  Dja.   No Hakeem, but mere Djabal!

I have spoken falsely, and this woe is come.

No—hear me ere scorn blasts me! Once and ever,

The deed is mine . . . Oh think upon the Past!

  An. [*to herself.*] Did I strike once, or twice, or many times?

  Dja. . . . I came to lead my tribe where, bathed in glooms,

Doth Bahumid the Renovator sleep—

Anael, I saw my tribe—I said, "Without

A miracle this cannot be"—I said

" Be there a miracle! "—for I saw you!

An. His head lies south the portal!

Dja.   —Weighed with this
The general good, how could I choose my own,
What matter was my purity of soul?
Little by little I engaged myself—
Heaven would accept me for its instrument,
I hoped—I said, Heaven had accepted me!

An. Is it this blood breeds dreams in me!—Who said
You were not Hakeem? and your miracles—
The fire that plays innocuous round your form?

> [*Again changing her whole manner.*
Ah, thou wouldst try me—thou art Hakeem still!

Dja. Woe—woe! As if the Druses of the Mount
(Scarce Arabs even there—but here, in the Isle,
Beneath their former selves) should comprehend
The subtle lore of Europe! A few secrets
That would not easily affect the meanest
Of the crowd there, could wholly subjugate
The best of our poor tribe! Again that eye?

An. [*after a pause springs to his neck.*] Djabal, in this
        there can be no deceit!
Why, Djabal, were you human only,—think,
Maani is but human, Khalil human,
Loys is human even—did their words
Haunt me, their looks pursue me? Shame on you
So to have tried me! Rather, shame on me
So to need trying! Could I, with the Prefect
And the blood, there—could I see only you?
—Hang by your neck over this gulf of blood?
Speak, I am saved! Speak, Djabal! Am I saved?

> [*As* DJABAL *slowly unclasps her arms, and puts her
>   silently from him.*
Hakeem would save me! Thou art Djabal! Crouch!
Bow to the dust, thou basest of our kind!
The pile of thee, I reared up to the cloud—
Full, midway, of our Fathers' trophied tombs,
Based on the living rock, devoured not by
The unstable desert's jaws of sand,—falls prone!
Fire, music, quenched: and now thou liest there
A ruin, obscene creatures will moan thro'!
—Let us come, Djabal!

Dja.   Whither come?

An.   At once—

Lest so it grow intolerable. Come!
Will I not share it with thee? Best at once!
So feel less pain! Let them deride—thy tribe
Now trusting in thee,—Loys shall deride!
Come to them, hand in hand, with me!

Dja.   Where come?

An. Where?—to the Druses thou hast wronged! Confess,
Now that the end is gained—(I love thee now)
That thou hast so deceived them—(perchance love thee
Better than ever!) Come, receive their doom
Of infamy—(Oh, best of all I love thee!
Shame with the man, no triumph with the God,
Be mine!) Come!

Dja.   Never! more shame yet? and why?
Why? You have called this deed mine—it is mine!
And with it I accept its circumstance.
How can I longer strive with Fate? The Past
Is past—my false life shall henceforth show true—
Hear me: The argosies touch land by this;
They bear us to fresh scenes and happier skies;
What if we reign together?—if we keep
Our secret for the Druses' good?—by means
Of even their superstition, plant in them
New life? I learn from Europe: all who seek
Man's good must awe man, by such means as these.
We two will be divine to them—we are!
All great works in this world spring from the ruins
Of greater projects—ever, on our earth,
Men block out Babels, to build Babylons.
I wrest the weapon from your hand! I claim
The deed! Retire! You have my ring—you bar
All access to the Nuncio till the forces
From Venice land!

An.   Thou wilt feign Hakeem then?

Dja. [*putting the Tiar of Hakeem on his head.*] And from
   this moment that I dare ope wide
Eyes that till now refused to see, begins
My true dominion! for I know myself,
And what I am to personate. No word?   [ANAEL *goes.*
'Tis come on me at last! His blood on her——
What memories will follow that! Her eye,
Her fierce distorted lip and ploughed black brow——
Ah, fool! Has Europe then so poorly tamed

The Syrian blood from out thee?   Thou, presume
To work in this foul earth by means not foul?
Scheme, as for Heaven,—but, on the earth, be glad
If a least ray like Heaven's be left thee!

                                                    Thus
I shall be calm—in readiness—no way
Surprised.   [*A noise without.*
                    This should be Khalil and my Druses!
Venice is come then!   Thus I grasp thee, sword!
Druses, 'tis Hakeem saves you!   In!   Behold
Your Prefect!

    Enter LOYS.   DJABAL *hides the khandjar in his robe.*

  Loys.   Oh, well found, Djabal! but no time for words.
You know who waits there?   [*Pointing to the alcove.*
                              Well!—and that 'tis there
He meets the Nuncio?   Well!   Now, a surprise—
He there—
    Dja.   I know—
    Loys.   ——is now no mortal's lord.
Is absolutely powerless—call him, dead—
He is no longer Prefect—you are Prefect!
Oh, shrink not!   I do nothing in the dark,
Nothing unworthy Breton blood, believe!
I understood at once your urgency
That I should leave this isle for Rhodes; I felt
What you were loath to speak—your need of help;
I have fulfilled the task, that earnestness
Imposed on me; have, face to face, confronted
The Prefect in full Chapter, charged on him
The enormities of his long rule; he stood
Mute, offered no defence, no crime denied;
On which, I spoke of you, and of your tribe,
Your faith so like our own, and all you've urged
So oft to me—I spoke, too, of your goodness,
Your patience—brief, I hold henceforth the Isle
In charge, am nominally Prefect,—but you,
You are associated in my rule—
Are the true Prefect!   Ay, such faith had they
In my assurance of your loyalty
(For who insults an imbecile old man?)
That we assume the Prefecture this hour!
You gaze at me!   Hear greater wonders yet—

I throw down all this fabric I have built!
These Knights, I was prepared to worship . . . but
Of that, another time; what's now to say,
Is—I shall never be a Knight! Oh, Djabal,
Here first I throw all prejudice aside,
And call you brother! I am Druse like you!
My wealth, my friends, my power, are wholly yours,
Your people's, which is now my people—for
There is a maiden of your tribe, I love—
She loves me—Khalil's sister—

 Dja.   Anael?
 Loys.   Start you?
Seems what I say, unknightly? Thus it chanced:
When first I came, a novice, to the Isle . . .

 Enter one of the NUNCIO'S Guards *from the alcove.*

 Guard. Oh, horrible! Sir Loys! Here is Loys!
And here—   [*Others enter from the alcove.*
[*Pointing to* DJABAL.] Secure him, bind him—this is he!
          [*They surround* DJABAL.
 Loys. Madmen—what is't you do? Stand from my
   friend.
And tell me!
 Guard. Thou canst have no part in this—
Surely no part—but slay him not! The Nuncio
Commanded, Slay him not!
 Loys.   Speak, or . . .
 Guard.   The Prefect
Lies murdered there by him thou dost embrace.
 Loys. By Djabal? miserable fools! How Djabal?
  [*A Guard lifts* DJABAL'S *robe;* DJABAL *flings down the
   khandjar.*
 Loys. [*after a pause.*] Thou hast received some insult worse
   than all—
Some outrage not to be endured—
[*To the* Guards.]   Stand back!
He is my friend—more than my friend! Thou hast
Slain him upon that provocation!
 Guard.   No!
No provocation! 'Tis a long devised
Conspiracy: the whole tribe is involved:
He is their Khalif—'tis on that pretence—
Their mighty Khalif who died long ago,

And now is come to life and light again—
All is just now revealed, I know not how,
By one of his confederates—who, struck
With horror at this murder, first apprized
The Nuncio.   As 'twas said, we find this Djabal
Here where we take him.
   Dja. [*Aside.*]   Who broke faith with me?
   Loys. [*to* DJABAL.] Hear'st thou? Speak! Till thou
    speak, I keep off these,
Or die with thee.   Deny this story!   Thou
A Khalif, an impostor?   Thou, my friend,
Whose tale was of an inoffensive race,
With . . . but thou know'st—on that tale's truth I pledged
My faith before the Chapter: what art thou?
   Dja. Loys, I am as thou hast heard.   All's true!
No more concealment!   As these tell thee, all
Was long since planned.   Our Druses are enough
To crush this handful: the Venetians land
Even now in our behalf.   Loys, we part here!
Thou, serving much, would'st fain have served me more;
It might not be.   I thank thee.   As thou hearest,
We are a separated tribe: farewell!
   Loys. Oh, where will truth be found now? Canst thou so
Belie the Druses?   Do they share thy crime?
Those thou professedst of our Breton stock,
Are partners with thee?   Why, I saw but now
Khalil, my friend—he spoke with me—no word
Of this! and Anael—whom I love, and who
Loves me—she spoke no word of this!
   Dja.   Poor Boy!
Anael, who loves thee?   Khalil, fast thy friend?
We, offsets from a wandering Count of Dreux?
No—older than the oldest—princelier
Than Europe's princeliest tribe are we.—Enough
For thee, that on our simple faith we found
A monarchy to shame your monarchies
At their own trick and secret of success.
The child of this our tribe shall laugh upon
The palace-step of him whose life ere night
Is forfeit, as that child shall know, and yet
Shall laugh there!   What, we Druses wait forsooth
The kind interposition of a boy?
—Can only save ourselves when thou concedest?

—Khalil admire thee?   He is my right hand,
My delegate!—Anael accept thy love?
She is my Bride!
    Loys.   Thy Bride?   She one of them?
    Dja.   My Bride!
    Loys.   And she retains her glorious eyes!
She, with those eyes, has shared this miscreant's guilt!
Ah—who but she directed me to find
Djabal within the Prefect's chamber?   Khalil
Bade me seek Djabal there, too!   All is true!
What spoke the Prefect worse of them than this?
Did the Church ill to institute long since
Perpetual warfare with such serpentry
As these?   Have I desired to shift my part,
Evade my share in her design?   'Tis well!
    Dja.   Loys, I have wronged thee—but unwittingly;
I never thought there was in thee a virtue
That could attach itself to what thou deemest
A race below thine own.   I wronged thee, Loys,
But that is over: all is over now,
Save the protection I ensure against
My people's anger—by their Khalif's side,
Thou art secure and may'st depart: so, come!
    Loys.   Thy side?—I take protection at thy hand?

Enter other Guards.

    Guards.   Fly with him! fly, Sir Loys! 'tis too true!
And only by his side thou may'st escape!
The whole tribe is in full revolt—they flock
About the palace—will be here—on thee—
And there are twenty of us, we, the Guards
Of the Nuncio, to withstand them!   Even we
Had stayed to meet our death in ignorance,
But that one Druse, a single faithful Druse,
Made known the horror to the Nuncio!   Fly!
The Nuncio stands aghast.   At least let us
Escape their wrath, O Hakeem!   We are nought
In thy tribe's persecution! [*To* Loys.] Keep by him!
They hail him Hakeem, their dead Prince, returned—
He is their God, they shout, and at his beck
Are life and death!
    Loys. [*springing at the khandjar* Djabal *had thrown down,
    seizes him by the throat.*]

Thus by his side am I!
Thus I resume my knighthood and its warfare!
Thus end thee, miscreant, in thy pride of place!
Thus art thou caught! Without, thy dupes may cluster,
Friends aid thee, foes avoid thee,—thou art Hakeem,
How say they?—God art thou! but also here
Is the least, meanest, youngest the Church calls
Her servant, and his single arm avails
To aid her as she lists. I rise, and thou
Art crushed! Hordes of thy Druses flock without:
Here thou hast me, who represent the Cross,
Honour and Faith, 'gainst Hell, Mahound, and thee!
Die! [Djabal *remains calm.*] Implore my mercy, Hakeem,
        that my scorn
May help me! Nay—I cannot ply thy trade—
I am no Druse—no stabber—and thine eye,
Thy form, are too much as they were—my friend
Had such! Speak! Beg for mercy at my foot!

                                            [Djabal *still silent.*
Heaven could not ask so much of me—not, sure,
So much! I cannot kill him so!

                                    Thou art
Strong in thy cause, then! Dost outbrave us, then!
Heard'st thou that one of thine accomplices,
Thy very people, has accused thee? Meet
His charge! Thou hast not even slain the Prefect
As thy own vile creed warrants. Meet that Druse—
Come with me and disprove him—be thou tried
By him, nor seek appeal—promise me this—
Or I will do God's office! What, shalt thou
Boast of assassins at thy beck, yet Truth
Want even an executioner? Consent,
Or I will strike—look in my face—I will!
    Dja. Give me again my khandjar, if thou darest!

                                            [Loys *gives it.*
Let but one Druse accuse me, and I plunge
This home. A Druse betray me? Let us go!
[*Aside.*] Who has betrayed me?   [*Shouts without.*
                            Hearest thou? I hear
No plainer now than years ago I heard
That shout—but in no dream now! They Return!
Wilt thou be leader with me, Loys? Well!

ACT V

The Uninitiated Druses, *covering the stage tumultuously,* and *speaking together.*

Here flock we, obeying the summons. Lo, Hakeem hath appeared, and the Prefect is dead, and we return to Lebanon! My manufacture of goats' fleece must, I doubt, soon fall away there—Come, old Nasif—link thine arm in mine—we fight, if needs be—Come, what is a great fight-word? " Lebanon? " (My daughter—my daughter!)—But is Khalil to have the office of Hamza?—Nay, rather, if he be wise, the monopoly of henna and cloves—Where is Hakeem?—The only prophet I ever saw, prophesied at Cairo once, in my youth—a little black Copht, dressed all in black too, with a great stripe of yellow cloth flapping down behind him like the back-fin of a water-serpent—Is this he? Biamrallah! Biamreh! HAKEEM!

Enter the NUNCIO *with* Guards.

Nuncio. [*to his* Attendants.] Hold both, the sorcerer and
  this accomplice
Ye talk of, that accuseth him! And tell
Sir Loys he is mine, the Church's hope:
Bid him approve himself our Knight indeed!
Lo, this black disemboguing of the Isle!
[*To the* Druses.] Ah, children, what a sight for these old eyes
That kept themselves alive this voyage through
To smile their very last on you! I came
To gather one and all you wandering sheep
Into my fold, as tho' a father came . . .
As tho', in coming, a father should . . .
[*To his* Guards.] (Ten, twelve
—Twelve guards of you, and not an outlet? None?
The wizards stop each avenue? Keep close!)
[*To the* Druses.] As if one came to a son's house, I say,
So did I come—no guard with me—to find . . .
Alas—alas!
  A Druse. Who is the old man?
  Another. Oh, ye are to shout!
Children, he styles you.
  Druses. Ay, the Prefect's slain!
Glory to the Khalif, our Father!

Nuncio.   Even so!
I find, (ye prompt aright) your Father slain;
While most he plotted for your good, that father
(Alas! how kind, ye never knew)—lies slain!
[*Aside.*] (And Hell's worm gnaw the glozing knave—with me,
For being duped by his cajoleries!
Are these the Christians? These the docile crew
My bezants went to make me Bishop o'er?)
[*To his* Attendants, *who whisper.*] What say ye does this
    wizard style himself?
Hakeem? Biamrallah? The third Fatemite?
What is this jargon? He—the insane Khalif,
Dead near three hundred years ago, come back
In flesh and blood again?
    Druses.   He mutters! Hear ye?
He is blaspheming Hakeem. The old man
Is our dead Prefect's friend! Tear him!
    Nuncio.   Ye dare not!
I stand here with my five-and-seventy years,
The Patriarch's power behind, and God's above me!
Those years have witnessed sin enough; ere now
Misguided men arose against their lords,
And found excuse; but ye, to be enslaved
By sorceries—cheats;—alas! the same tricks, tried
On my poor children in this nook of the earth,
Could triumph,—that have been successively
Exploded, laughed to scorn, all nations thro'—
" *Romaioi, Ioudaioi te kai proselutoi,*
" Cretes and Arabians "—you are duped the last!
Said I, refrain from tearing me? I pray ye
Tear me! Shall I return to tell the Patriarch
That so much love was wasted—every gift
Rejected, from his benison I brought,
Down to the galley-full of bezants, sunk
An hour since at the harbour's mouth, by that . . .
That . . . never will I speak his hated name!
[*To his* Servants.] What was the name his fellow slip-fetter
Called their arch-wizard by? [*They whisper.*] Oh, Djabal was't?
    Druses. But how a sorcerer? false wherein?
    Nuncio.   (Ay, Djabal!)
How false? Ye know not, Djabal has confessed . . .
Nay, that by tokens found on him we learn . . .
What I sailed hither solely to divulge—

How by his spells the demons were allured
To seize you—not that these be aught save lies
And mere illusions. Is this clear? I say,
By measures such as these, he would have led you
Into a monstrous ruin: follow ye?
Say, shall ye perish for his sake, my sons?

 Druses. Hark ye!

 Nuncio.   —Be of one privilege amerced?
No! Infinite the Patriarch's mercies be!
No! With the Patriarch's licence, still I bid ye
Tear him to pieces who misled you! Haste!

 Druses. The old man's beard shakes, and his eyes are white
fire! After all, I know nothing of Djabal beyond what
Karshook says; he knows but what Khalil says; who knows
just what Djabal says himself—Now, the little Copht Prophet,
I saw at Cairo in my youth, began by promising each bystander
three full measures of wheat . . .

Enter KHALIL *and the Initiated* Druses.

 Kha. Venice and her deliverance are at hand!
Their fleet stands thro' the harbour! Hath he slain
The Prefect yet? Is Djabal's change come yet?

 Nuncio [*to* Attendants.] What's this of Venice? Who's
  this boy?

[Attendants *whisper.*] One Khalil?
Djabal's accomplice, Loys called, but now,
The only Druse, save Djabal's self, to fear?

[*To the* Druses.] I cannot hear ye with these aged ears:
Is it so? Ye would have my troops assist?
Doth he abet him in his sorceries?
Down with the cheat, guards, as my children bid!

    [*They spring at* KHALIL: *as he beats them back,*
Stay—no more bloodshed—spare deluded youth!
Whom seek'st thou? (I will teach him)—Whom, my child?
Thou knowest not what these know, have just told me.
I am an old man, as thou seest—have done
With earth, and what should move me but the truth?
Art thou the only fond one of thy tribe?
'Tis I interpret for thy tribe!—

 Kha.   Oh, this
Is the expected Nuncio! Druses, hear—
Endure ye this? Unworthy to partake
The glory Hakeem gains you! While I speak,

The ships touch land: who makes for Lebanon?
They'll plant the winged lion in these halls!
    Nuncio. [*Aside.*] If it be true! Venice?—Oh, never
    true!
Yet, Venice would so gladly thwart our Knights,
And fain get footing here, so close by Rhodes!
Oh, to be duped this way!
    Kha.   Ere he appears
To lead **you** gloriously, repent, I say!
    Nuncio. [*Aside.*] Oh, any way to stretch the arch-wizard
    stark
Ere the Venetians come! Were he cut off,
The rest were easily tamed. [*To the* Druses.] He? Bring
    him forth!
Since so you needs will have it, I assent!
You'd judge him, say you, on the spot? Confound
The sorcerer in his very circle? Where's
Our short black-bearded sallow friend who said
He'd earn the Patriarch's guerdon by one stab?
Bring Djabal forth at once!
    Druses.   Ay, bring him forth!
The Patriarch drives a trade in oil and silk—
And we're the Patriarch's children—true men, we!
Where is the glory? Show us all the glory!
    Kha. You dare not so insult him! What, not see . . .
(I tell thee, Nuncio, these are uninstructed,
Untrusted—they know nothing of our Khalif!)
—Not see that if he lets a doubt arise
'Tis but to give yourselves the chance of seeming
To have some influence in your own Return!
That all may say they would have trusted him
Without the all-convincing glory—ay,
And did! Embrace the occasion, friends! For, think—
What merit when his change takes place? But now,
For your sakes, he should not reveal himself!
No—could I ask and have, I would not ask
The change yet!

Enter DJABAL *and* LOYS.

                 Spite of all, reveal thyself!
I had said, pardon them for me—for Anael—
For our sakes pardon these besotted men—
Ay—for thine own—they hurt not thee! Yet now

One thought swells in me and keeps down all else!
This Nuncio couples shame with thee, has called
Imposture thy whole course, all bitter things
Has said—he is but an old fretful man!
Hakeem—nay, I must call thee Hakeem now—
Reveal thyself! See! Where is Anael?—See!
 Loys. [*to* DJA.] Here are thy people! Keep thy word to me!
 Dja. Who of my people hath accused me?
 Nuncio.   So!
So, this is Djabal, Hakeem, and what not?
A fit deed, Loys, for thy first Knight's day!
May it be augury of thy after life!
Ever be truncheon of the Church as now
That, Nuncio of the Patriarch, having charge
Of the Isle here, I claim thee [*turning to* DJA.] as these bid me,
Forfeit for murder on thy lawful prince,
Thou conjuror that peep'st and mutterest!
Why should I hold thee from their hands? (Spells, children?
But hear how I dispose of all his spells!)
Thou art a Prophet?—would'st entice thy tribe
Away?—thou workest miracles? (Attend!
Let him but move me with his spells!) I, Nuncio . . .
 Dja. . . . Which how thou cam'st to be, I say not now,
Though I have also been at Stamboul, Luke!
—Ply thee with spells, forsooth! What need of spells?
If Venice, in her Admiral's person, stoop
To ratify thy compact with her foes,
The Hospitallers, for this Isle—withdraw
Her warrant of the deed which reinstates
My people in their freedom, tricked away
By him I slew,—refuse to convoy us
To Lebanon and keep the Isle we leave—
—Then will be time to try what spells can do.
Dost thou dispute the Republic's power?
 Nuncio.   Lo ye!
He tempts me, too, the wily exorcist!
No! The renowned Republic was and is
The Patriarch's friend: 'tis not for courting Venice
That I—that these implore thy blood of me!
Lo ye, the subtle miscreant! Ha, so subtle?
Ye, Druses, hear him! Will ye be deceived?
How he evades me! Where's the miracle
He works? I bid him to the proof—fish up

Your galley-full of bezants that he sunk!
That were a miracle!   One miracle!
Enough of trifling, for it chafes my age—
I am the Nuncio, Druses!   I stand forth
To save you from the good Republic's rage
When she shall find her fleet was summoned here
To aid the mummeries of this crafty knave!

    [*As the* Druses *hesitate, his* Attendants *whisper.*
Ah, well suggested!   Why, we hold this while
One, who, his close confederate till now,
Confesses Djabal at the last a cheat,
And every miracle a cheat!   Who throws me
His head?   I make three offers, once I offer,—
And twice . . .

  Dja.   Let who moves perish at my foot!
  Kha. Thanks, Hakeem, thanks!   Oh, Anael, Maani,
Why tarry they?
  Druses [*to each other.*]   He can!   He can!   Live fire—
[*To the* Nuncio.] (I say he can, old man!   Thou know'st him
  not—)
Live fire like that thou seest now in his eyes,
Plays fawning round him—See!   The change begins!
All the brow lightens as he lifts his arm!
Look not at me!   It was not I!
  Dja.   What Druse
Accused me, as he saith?   I bid each bone
Crumble within that Druse!   None, Loys, none
Of my own people, as thou saidst, have raised
A voice against me.
  Nuncio.   [*Aside.*]   Venice to come!   Death!
  Dja. [*continuing.*]   Confess and go unscathed, however
  false!
Seest thou my Druses, Luke?   I would submit
To thy pure malice did one Druse confess!
How said I, Loys?
  Nuncio [*to his* Attendants, *who whisper.*]   Ah, ye counsel so?
[*Aloud.*]   Bring in the witness, then, who, first of all,
Disclosed the treason!   Now I have thee, wizard!
Ye hear that?   If one speaks, he bids you tear him
Joint after joint—well then, one does speak!   One,
Befooled by Djabal, even as yourselves,
But who hath voluntarily proposed
To expiate, by confessing thus, the fault

Of having trusted him.   [*They bring in a veiled* Druse.

   Loys.   Now, Djabal, now!

   Nuncio.   Friend, Djabal fronts you! (Make a ring, sons!)
—Speak!

Expose this Djabal; what he was, and how;

The wiles he used, the aims he cherished; all,

Explicitly as late you spoke to these

My servants—I absolve and pardon you.

   Loys.   Thou hast the dagger ready, Djabal?

   Dja.   Speak,

Recreant!

   Druses.   Stand back, fool! farther! Suddenly

You shall see some huge serpent glide from under

The empty vest—or down will thunder crash!

Back, Khalil!

   Kha.   I go back? Thus go I back!

[*To* An.] Unveil! Nay, thou shalt face the Khalif! Thus!

   [*He tears away* Anael's *veil :* Djabal *folds his arms and
bows his head : the* Druses *fall back :* Loys *springs from
the side of* Djabal *and the* Nuncio.

   Loys.   When she was true—she only of them all!

True to her eyes—may keep those glorious eyes,

And now be mine, once again mine!   Oh, Anael?

Dared I think thee a partner in his crime—

That blood could soil that hand? nay, 'tis mine—Anael,

—Not mine?—Who offer thee before all these

My heart, my sword, my name—so thou wilt say

That Djabal, who affirms thou art his bride,

Lies—say but that he lies!

   Dja.   Thou, Anael?

   Loys.   Nay, Djabal, nay, one chance for me—the last!

Thou hast had every other—thou hast spoken

Days, nights, what falsehood listed thee—let me

Speak first, now; I will speak, now!—

   Nuncio.   Loys, pause!

Thou art the Duke's son, Breton's choicest stock—

Loys of Dreux—God's sepulchre's first sword—

This wilt thou spit on, this degrade, this trample

To earth?

   Loys [*to* An.] Ah, who had foreseen, " One day, Loys

" Will stake these gifts against some other good

" In the whole world? "—I give them thee!   I would

My strong will might bestow real shape on them,

That I might see, with my own eyes, thy foot
Tread on their very neck! 'Tis not by gifts
I put aside this Djabal—we will stand—
We do stand—see—two men! Djabal, stand forth!
Who's worth her—I or thou? I—who for Anael
Kept, purely, uprightly my way, the long
True way—left thee each by-path—boldly lived
Without the lies and blood,—or thou, or thou?
I! Love me, Anael! Leave the blood and him!
[*To* DJA.] Now speak—now, quick on this that I have said,—
Thou with the blood, speak if thou art a man!

    Dja. [*to* AN.] And was it thou betrayedst me? 'Tis well!
I have deserved this of thee, and submit:
Nor 'tis much evil thou inflictest: life
Ends here. The cedars shall not wave for us—
For there was crime, and must be punishment.
See fate! By thee I was seduced—by thee
I perish—yet do I, can I repent?
I, with my Arab instinct, thwarted ever
By my Frank policy,—and, within turn,
My Frank brain, thwarted by my Arab heart—
While these remained in equipoise, I lived
—Nothing; had either been predominant,
As a Frank schemer or an Arab mystic,
I had been something;—now, each has destroyed
The other—and behold, from out their crash,
A third and better nature rises up—
My mere Man's-nature! And I yield to it—
I love thee—I—who did not love before!

    An. Djabal—

    Dja.   It seemed love, but true love it was not—
How could I love while thou adoredst me?
Now thou despisest, art above me so
Immeasurably—thou, no other, doomest
My death now—this my steel shall execute
Thy judgment—I shall feel thy hand in it!
Oh, luxury to worship, to submit,
Transcended, doomed to death by thee!

    An.   My Djabal!

    Dja. Dost hesitate? I force thee then! Approach,
Druses! for I am out of reach of fate;
No further evil waits me—Speak the truth!
Hear, Druses, and hear, Nuncio, and hear, Loys!

An. HAKEEM!   [*She falls dead.*

        [*The* Druses *scream, grovelling before him.*
         Ah, Hakeem!—not on me thy wrath!
Biamrallah, pardon—never doubted I!
Ah, dog, how sayest thou?

      [*They surround and seize the* NUNCIO *and his* Guards. LOYS
        flings himself upon the body of ANAEL, *on which* DJABAL
        continues to gaze as stupefied.

    Nuncio.   Caitives! Have ye eyes?
Whips, racks, should teach you! What, his fools? his dupes?
Leave me! unhand me!

    Kha. [*approaching* DJABAL *timidly.*] Save her for my sake!
She was already thine—she would have shared
To-day thine exaltation—think! this day
Her hair was plaited thus because of thee—
Yes, feel the soft bright hair—feel!

    Nuncio [*struggling with those who have seized him.*]
                            What, because
His leman dies for him? You think it hard
To die? Oh, would you were at Rhodes, and choice
Of deaths should suit you!

    Kha. [*bending over* ANAEL'S *body.*] Just restore her life!
So little does it—there—the eyelids tremble!
'Twas not my breath that made them—and the lips
Move of themselves—I could restore her life!
Hakeem, we have forgotten—have presumed
On our free converse—we are better taught.
See, I kiss—how I kiss thy garment's hem
For her! She kisses it—Oh, take her deed
In mine—Thou dost believe now, Anael?—See
She smiles! Were her lips open o'er the teeth
So, when I spoke first? She believes in thee!
Go not without her to the Cedars, Lord!
Or leave us both—I cannot go alone!
I have obeyed thee, if I dare say so—
Hath Hakeem thus forgot all Djabal knew?
Thou feelest then my tears fall hot and fast
Upon thy hand—and yet thou speakest not!
Ere the Venetian trumpet sound—ere thou
Exalt thyself, O Hakeem! save her—save her!

    Nuncio. And the accursed Republic will arrive
And find me in their toils—dead, very like,
Under their feet!

What way—not one way yet

To foil them?   None?   [*Observing* DJABAL'S *face.*

What ails the Khalif?   Ah,

That ghastly face—a way to foil them yet!
[*To the* Druses.] Look to your Khalif, Druses!   Is that face
God Hakeem's?   Where is triumph—where is . . . what
Said he of exaltation—hath he promised
So much to-day?   Why, then, exalt thyself!
Cast off that husk, thy form, set free thy soul
In splendour!   Now, bear witness—here I stand—
I challenge him exalt himself, and I
Become, for that, a Druse like all of you!

   The Druses.   Exalt thyself—exalt thyself—O Hakeem!
   Dja. [*advances.*] I can confess now all from first to last.
There is no longer shame for me!   I am . . .

[*Here the Venetian trumpet sounds—the* Druses *shout:
his eye catches the expression of those about him, and, as
the old dream comes back, he is again confident and inspired.*

. . . Am I *not* Hakeem?   And ye would have crawled
But yesterday within these impure courts
Where now ye stand erect!—Not grand enough?
—What more could be conceded to such beasts
As all of you, so sunk and base as you,
But a mere man?—A man among such beasts
Was miracle enough—yet him you doubt,
Him you forsake, him fain would you destroy—
With the Venetians at your gate, the Nuncio
Thus—(see the baffled hypocrite!) and best
The Prefect there!

   Druses.   No, Hakeem, ever thine!
   Nuncio.   He lies—and twice he lies—and thrice he lies!
Exalt thyself, Mahound!   Exalt thyself!
   Dja.   Druses! we shall henceforth be far away!
Out of mere mortal ken—above the Cedars—
But we shall see ye go, hear ye return,
Repeopling the old solitudes,—thro' thee,
My Khalil!   Thou art full of me—I fill
Thee full—my hands thus fill thee!   Yester eve,
—Nay, but this morn—I deemed thee ignorant
Of all to do, requiring words of mine
To teach it—now, thou hast all gifts in one,
With truth and purity go other gifts!

All gifts come clustering to that—go, lead
My People home whate'er betide!
[*Turning to the* Druses.]   Ye take
This Khalil for my delegate? To him
Bow as to me? He leads to Lebanon—
Ye follow?

   Druses. We follow! Now exalt thyself!

   Dja. [*raises* Loys.] Then to thee, Loys! How I wronged
    thee, Loys!
—Yet, wronged, no less thou shalt have full revenge,
Fit for thy noble self, revenge—and thus:
Thou, loaded with these wrongs, the princely soul,
The first sword of Christ's sepulchre—thou shalt
Guard Khalil and my Druses home again!
Justice, no less—God's justice and no more,
For those I leave!—to seeking this, devote
Some few days out of thy Knight's brilliant life,
And, this obtained them, leave their Lebanon,
My Druses' blessing in thine ears—(they shall
Bless thee with blessing sure to have its way)
—One cedar-blossom in thy Ducal cap,
One thought of Anael in thy heart—perchance,
One thought of him who thus, to bid thee speed,
His last word to the living speaks! This done,
Resume thy course, and, first amid the first
In Europe, take my heart along with thee!
Go boldly, go serenely, go augustly—
What can withstand thee then?
[*He bends over* ANAEL.]   And last to thee!
Ah, did I dream I was to have this day
Exalted thee? A vain dream—hast thou not
Won greater exaltation? What remains
But press to thee, exalt myself to thee?
Thus I exalt myself, set free my soul!

[*He stabs himself—as he falls, supported by* KHALIL *and*
    Loys, *the* Venetians *enter : the* ADMIRAL *advances.*

   Admiral. God and St. Mark for Venice! Plant the Lion!

[*At the clash of the planted standard, the* Druses *shout, and*
    move tumultuously forward, Loys *drawing his sword.*

   Dja. [*leading them a few steps between* KHALIL *and* Loys.]
On to the Mountain. At the Mountain, Druses!   [*Dies.*

A BLOT IN THE 'SCUTCHEON

A TRAGEDY

PERSONS

MILDRED TRESHAM.
GUENDOLEN TRESHAM.
THOROLD, Lord Tresham.
AUSTIN TRESHAM.
HENRY, Earl Mertoun.
GERARD.
Other Retainers of Lord Tresham.

TIME, 17—.

ACT I

SCENE I.—*The interior of a Lodge in* LORD TRESHAM'S *Park. Many* Retainers *crowded at the window, supposed to command a view of the entrance to his Mansion.* GERARD, *the Warrener, sitting alone, his back to a table on which are flagons, etc.*

 1st Ret. Ay—do—push, friends, and then you'll push
  down me.
—What for? Does any hear a runner's foot,
Or a steed's trample, or a coach-wheel's cry?
Is the Earl come or his least poursuivant?
But there's no breeding in a man of you
Save Gerard yonder: here's a half-place yet,
Old Gerard!
 Ger. Save your courtesies, my friend.
Here is my place.
 2nd Ret. Now, Gerard, out with it!
What makes you sullen, this of all the days
I' the year? To-day that, young, rich, bountiful,
Handsome Earl Mertoun, whom alone they match
With our Lord Tresham thro' the country-side,
Is coming here in utmost bravery
To ask our Master's Sister's hand?

Ger.   What then?

2nd Ret. What then? Why, you she speaks to, if she meets
Your worship, smiles on as you hold apart
The boughs to let her thro' her forest walks,
You, always favourite for your no-deserts,
You've heard, these three days, how Earl Mertoun sues
To lay his heart, and house, and broad lands too,
At Lady Mildred's feet—and while we squeeze
Ourselves into a mousehole lest we miss
One congee of the least page in his train,
You sit o' one side—" there's the Earl," say I—
" What then," say you!

3rd Ret.   I'll wager he has let
Both swans he tamed for Lady Mildred, swim
Over the falls and gain the river!

Ger.   Ralph,
Is not to-morrow my inspecting-day
For you and for your hawks?

4th Ret.   Let Gerard be!
He's coarse-grained, like his carved black cross-bow stock.
Ha, look now, while we squabble with him, look!
Well done, now—is not this beginning, now,
To purpose?

1st Ret.   Our retainers look as fine—
That's comfort! Lord, how Richard holds himself
With his white staff! Will not a knave behind
Prick him upright?

4th Ret.   He's only bowing, fool!
The Earl's man bent us lower by this much.

1st Ret. That's comfort. Here's a very cavalcade!

3rd Ret. I don't see wherefore Richard, and his troop
Of silk and silver varlets there, should find
Their perfumed selves so indispensable
On high days, holy-days! Would it so disgrace
Our Family, if I, for instance, stood—
In my right hand a cast of Swedish hawks,
A leash of greyhounds in my left?—

Ger.   —With Hugh
The logman for supporter—in his right
The bill-hook—in his left the brushwood-shears!

3rd Ret. Out on you, crab! What next, what next? The
   Earl!

1st Ret. Oh, Walter, groom, our horses, do they match

R 41

The Earl's? Alas, that first pair of the six—
They paw the ground—Ah, Walter! and that brute
Just on his haunches by the wheel!

6th Ret.   Ay—Ay!

You, Philip, are a special hand, I hear,
At soups and sauces—what's a horse to you?
D'ye mark that beast they've slid into the midst
So cunningly?—then, Philip, mark this further;
No leg has he to stand on!

1st Ret.   No? That's comfort.

2nd Ret. Peace, Cook! The Earl descends. — Well,
    Gerard, see
The Earl at least! Come, there's a proper man,
I hope! Why, Ralph, no falcon, Pole or Swede,
Has got a starrier eye—

3rd Ret.   His eyes are blue—
But leave my hawks alone!

4th Ret.   So young, and yet
So tall and shapely!

5th Ret.   Here's Lord Tresham's self!
There now—there's what a nobleman should be!
He's older, graver, loftier, he's more like
A House's Head!

2nd Ret.   But you'd not have a boy
—And what's the Earl beside?—possess too soon
That stateliness?

1st Ret.   Our Master takes his hand—
Richard and his white staff are on the move—
Back fall our people—(tsh!—there's Timothy
Sure to get tangled in his ribbon-ties—
And Peter's cursed rosette's a-coming off!)
—At last I see our Lord's back and his friend's—
And the whole beautiful bright company
Close round them—in they go! [*Jumping down from the
    window-bench, and making for the table and its jugs,
    etc.*]   Good health, long life,
Great joy to our Lord Tresham and his House!

6th Ret. My father drove his father first to court,
After his marriage-day—ay, did he!

2nd Ret.   God bless
Lord Tresham, Lady Mildred, and the Earl!
Here, Gerard, reach your beaker!

Ger.   Drink, my boys:

Don't mind me—all's not right about me—drink!
  2nd Ret. [*Aside.*] He's vexed, now, that he let the show
    escape!
[*To* GER.] Remember that the Earl returns this way—
  Ger. That way?
  2nd Ret.   Just so.
  Ger.   Then my way's here. [*Goes.*
  2nd Ret.   Old Gerard
Will die soon—mind, I said it! He was used
To care about the pitifullest thing
That touched the House's honour, not an eye
But his could see wherein—and on a cause
Of scarce a quarter this importance, Gerard
Fairly had fretted flesh and bone away
In cares that this was right, nor that was wrong,
Such a point decorous, and such by rule—
(He knew such niceties, no herald more)
And now—you see his humour: die he will!
  2nd Ret. God help him! Who's for the great servants'-
    hall
To hear what's going on inside? They'd follow
Lord Tresham into the saloon.
    3rd Ret.   I!—
    4th Ret.   I!—
Leave Frank alone for catching, at the door,
Some hint of how the parley goes inside!
Prosperity to the great House once more—
Here's the last drop!
    1st Ret.   Have at you! Boys, hurrah!

SCENE II.—*A Saloon in the Mansion.*

Enter LORD TRESHAM, LORD MERTOUN; AUSTIN, *and*
GUENDOLEN.

  Tresh. I welcome you, Lord Mertoun, yet once more,
To this ancestral roof of mine. Your name
—Noble among the noblest in itself,
Yet taking in your person, fame avers,
New price and lustre,—(as that gem you wear,
Transmitted from a hundred knightly breasts,
Fresh chased and set and fixed by its last lord,

Seems to re-kindle at the core)—your name
Would win you welcome!—

  Mer.   Thanks!
  Tresh.   —But add to that,
The worthiness and grace and dignity
Of your proposal for uniting both
Our Houses even closer than respect
Unites them now—add these, and you must grant
One favor more, nor that the least,—to think
The welcome I should give;—'tis given! My lord,
My only brother, Austin—he's the King's.
Our cousin, Lady Guendolen—betrothed
To Austin: all are yours.

  Mer.   I thank you—less
For the expressed commendings which your seal,
And only that, authenticates—forbids
My putting from me . . . to my heart I take
Your praise . . . but praise less claims my gratitude,
Than the indulgent insight it implies
Of what must needs be uppermost with one
Who comes, like me, with the bare leave to ask,
In weighed and measured unimpassioned words,
A gift, which, if as calmly 'tis denied,
He must withdraw, content upon his cheek,
Despair within his soul:—that I dare ask
Firmly, near boldly, near with confidence
That gift, I have to thank you.—Yes, Lord Tresham,
I love your sister—as you'd have one love
That lady . . . oh more, more I love her! Wealth,
Rank, all the world thinks *me*, they're yours, you know,
To hold or part with, at your choice—but grant
My true self, *me* without a rood of land,
A piece of gold, a name of yesterday,
Grant me that lady, and you . . . Death or life?

  Guen. [*apart to* Aus.] Why, this *is* loving, Austin!
  Aus.   He's so young!
  Guen. Young? Old enough, I think, to half surmise
He never had obtained an entrance here,
Were all this fear and trembling needed.
  Aus.   Hush!
He reddens.
  Guen.   Mark him, Austin; that's true love!
Ours must begin again.

Tresh.   We'll sit, my lord.
Ever with best desert goes diffidence.
I may speak plainly nor be misconceived.
That I am wholly satisfied with you
On this occasion, when a falcon's eye
Were dull compared with mine to search out faults,
Is somewhat.   Mildred's hand is hers to give
Or to refuse.
    Mer.   But you, you grant my suit?
I have your word if hers?
    Tresh.   My best of words
If hers encourage you.   I trust it will.
Have you seen Lady Mildred, by the way?
    Mer. I . . . I . . . our two demesnes, remember, touch—
I have been used to wander carelessly
After my stricken game—the heron roused
Deep in my woods, has trailed its broken wing
Thro' thicks and glades a mile in yours,—or else
Some eyass ill-reclaimed has taken flight
And lured me after her from tree to tree,
I marked not whither . . . I have come upon
The Lady's wondrous beauty unaware,
And—and then . . . I have seen her.
    Guen. [*aside to* AUS.]   Note that mode
Of faultering out that when a lady passed
He, having eyes, did see her! You had said—
" On such a day I scanned her, head to foot;
" Observed a red, where red should not have been,
" Outside her elbow; but was pleased enough
" Upon the whole."   Let such irreverent talk
Be lessoned for the future!
    Tresh.   What's to say
May be said briefly.   She has never known
A mother's care; I stand for father too.
Her beauty is not strange to you, it seems—
You cannot know the good and tender heart,
Its girl's trust and its woman's constancy,
How pure yet passionate, how calm yet kind,
How grave yet joyous, how reserved yet free
As light where friends are—how embued with lore
The world most prizes, yet the simplest, yet
The . . . one might know I talked of Mildred—thus
We brothers talk!

Mer.   I thank you.
Tresh.   In a word,
Control's not for this lady; but her wish
To please me outstrips in its subtlety
My power of being pleased—herself creates
The wants she means to satisfy. My heart
Prefers your suit to her as 'twere its own.
Can I say more?
    Mer.   No more—thanks, thanks—no more!
    Tresh. This matter then discussed . . .
    Mer.   . . . We'll waste no breath
On aught less precious—I'm beneath the roof
That holds her: while I thought of that, my speech
To you would wander—as it must not do,
Since as you favour me I stand or fall.
I pray you suffer that I take my leave!
    Tresh. With less regret 'tis suffered, that again
We meet, I hope, so shortly.
    Mer.   We? again?—
Ah yes, forgive me—when shall . . . you will crown
Your goodness by forthwith apprising me
When . . . if . . . the Lady will appoint a day
For me to wait on you—and her.
    Tresh.   So soon
As I am made acquainted with her thoughts
On your proposal—howsoe'er they lean—
A messenger shall bring you the result.
    Mer. You cannot bind me more to you, my lord.
Farewell till we renew . . . I trust, renew
A converse ne'er to disunite again.
    Tresh. So may it prove!
    Mer.   You, Lady, you, Sir, take
My humble salutation!
    Guen. and Aus.   Thanks!
    Tresh.   Within there!
[*Servants* enter. TRESHAM *conducts* MERTOUN *to the door.*
    Meantime AUSTIN *remarks,*

                                        Well,
Here I have an advantage of the Earl,
Confess now! *I'*d not think that all was safe
Because my lady's brother stood my friend.
Why, he makes sure of her—" do you say, yes—
" She'll not say, no "—what comes it to beside?

I should have prayed the brother, " speak this speech,
" For Heaven's sake urge this on her—put in this—
" Forget not, as you'd save me, t'other thing,—
" Then set down what she says, and how she looks,
" And if she smiles," and (in an under breath)
" Only let her accept me, and do you
" And all the world refuse me, if you dare ! "

   Guen. That way you'd take, friend Austin ? What a shame
I was your cousin, tamely from the first
Your bride, and all this fervour's run to waste !
Do you know you speak sensibly to-day ?
The Earl's a fool.

   Aus.   Here's Thorold. Tell him so !

   Tresh. [*returning.*] Now, voices, voices ! 'St ! the lady's
    first !
How seems he ?—seems he not . . . come, faith give fraud
The mercy-stroke whenever they engage !
Down with fraud—up with faith ! How seems the Earl ?
A name ! a blazon ! if you knew their worth,
As you will never ! come—the Earl ?

   Guen.   He's young.

   Tresh. What's she ? an infant save in heart and brain
Young ! Mildred is fourteen, remark ! And you . . .
Austin, how old is she ?

   Guen.   There's tact for you !
I meant that being young was good excuse
If one should tax him . . .

   Tresh.   Well ?

   Guen.   —With lacking wit.

   Tresh. He lacked wit ? Where might he lack wit, so
    please you ?

   Guen. In standing straiter than the steward's rod
And making you the tiresomest harangues,
Instead of slipping over to my side
And softly whispering in my ear, " Sweet lady,
" Your cousin there will do me detriment
" He little dreams of—he's absorbed, I see,
" In my old name and fame—be sure he'll leave
" My Mildred, when his best account of me
" Is ended, in full confidence I wear
" My grandsire's periwig down either cheek.
" I'm lost unless your gentleness vouchsafes " . . .

   Tresh. . . . " To give a best of best accounts, yourself,

" Of me and my demerits."   You are right!
He should have said what now I say for him.
You golden creature, will you help us all?
Here's Austin means to vouch for much, but you
—You are . . . what Austin only knows!   Come up,
All three of us—she's in the Library
No doubt, for the day's wearing fast.   Precede!

 Guen.   Austin, how we must—!
 Tresh.   Must what?   Must speak truth,
Malignant tongue!   Detect one fault in him!
I challenge you!

 Guen.   Witchcraft's a fault in him,
For you're bewitched.

 Tresh.   What's urgent we obtain
Is, that she soon receive him—say, to-morrow—
Next day at farthest.

 Guen.   Ne'er instruct me!
 Tresh.   Come!
—He's out of your good graces since, forsooth,
He stood not as he'd carry us by storm
With his perfections!   You're for the composed,
Manly, assured, becoming confidence!
—Get her to say, " to-morrow," and I'll give you . . .
I'll give you back Urganda, to be spoiled
With petting and snail-paces.   Will you?   Come!

SCENE III.—MILDRED'S *Chamber.   A painted window over-*
  looks the park.   MILDRED *and* GUENDOLEN.

 Guen.   Now, Mildred, spare those pains.   I have not left
Our talkers in the Library, and climbed
The wearisome ascent to this your bower
In company with you,—I have nor dared . . .
Nay, worked such prodigies as sparing you
Lord Mertoun's pedigree before the flood,
Which Thorold seemed in very act to tell—
—Or bringing Austin to pluck up that most
Firm-rooted heresy—your suitor's eyes,
He would maintain, were gray instead of blue—
I think I brought him to contrition!—Well,
I have not done such things, (all to deserve

A minute's quiet cousin's talk with you,)
To be dismissed so coolly!

   Mil.   Guendolen,
What have I done . . . what could suggest . . .

   Guen.   There, there!
Do I not comprehend you'd be alone
To throw those testimonies in a heap,
Thorold's enlargings, Austin's brevities,
With that poor, silly, heartless Guendolen's
Ill-timed, misplaced, attempted smartnesses—
And sift their sense out? now, I come to spare you
Nearly a whole night's labour. Ask and have!
Demand, be answered! Lack I ears and eyes?
Am I perplexed which side of the rock-table
The Conqueror dined on when he landed first,
Lord Mertoun's ancestor was bidden take—
The bow-hand or the arrow-hand's great meed?
Mildred, the Earl has soft blue eyes!

   Mil.   My brother—
Did he . . . you said that he received him well?

   Guen. If I said only " well " I said not much–
Oh, stay—which brother?

   Mil.   Thorold! who—who else?

   Guen. Thorold (a secret) is too proud by half,—
Nay, hear me out—with us he's even gentler
Than we are with our birds. Of this great House
The least retainer that e'er caught his glance
Would die for him, real dying—no mere talk:
And in the world, the court, if men would cite
The perfect spirit of honour, Thorold's name
Rises of its clear nature to their lips:
But he should take men's homage, trust in it,
And care no more about what drew it down.
He has desert, and that, acknowledgment;
Is he content?

   Mil.   You wrong him, Guendolen.

   Guen. He's proud, confess; so proud with brooding o'er
The light of his interminable line,
An ancestry with men all paladins,
And women all . . .

   Mil.   Dear Guendolen, 'tis late!
When yonder purple pane the climbing moon
Pierces, I know 'tis midnight.

Guen.   Well, that Thorold
Should rise up from such musings, and receive
One come audaciously to graft himself
Into this peerless stock, yet find no flaw,
No slightest spot in such an one. . . .
Mil.   Who finds
A spot in Mertoun?
Guen.   Not your brother; therefore,
Not the whole world.
Mil.   I'm weary, Guendolen.—
Bear with me!
Guen.   I am foolish.
Mil.   Oh, no, kind—
But I would rest.
Guen.   Good night and rest to you.
I said how gracefully his mantle lay
Beneath the rings of his light hair?
Mil.   Brown hair!
Guen. Brown? why it *is* brown—how could you know
    that?
Mil. How? did not you—Oh Austin 'twas, declared
His hair was light, not brown—my head!—and, look,
The moon-beam purpling the dark chamber! Sweet,
Good night!
Guen.   Forgive me—sleep the soundlier for me!
                    [*Going, she turns suddenly.*
                                        Mildred!
Perdition! all's discovered.—Thorold finds
—That the Earl's greatest of all grandmothers
Was grander daughter still—to that fair dame
Whose garter slipped down at the famous dance!   [*Goes.*
Mil. Is she—can she be really gone at last?
My heart—I shall not reach the window! Needs
Must I have sinned much, so to suffer!
    [*She lifts the small lamp which is suspended before the
    Virgin's image in the window, and places it by the purple
    pane.*]   There!
                    [*She returns to the seat in front.*
Mildred and Mertoun! Mildred, with consent
Of all the world and Thorold,—Mertoun's bride
Too late! 'Tis sweet to think of, sweeter still
To hope for, that this blessed end soothes up
The curse of the beginning; but I know

It comes too late—'twill sweetest be of all
To dream my soul away and die upon!   [*A noise without.*
The voice! Oh! why, why glided sin the snake
Into the Paradise Heaven meant us both?
        [*The window opens softly.—A low voice sings.*

There's a woman like a dew-drop, she's so purer than the purest;
And her noble heart's the noblest, yes, and her sure faith's the surest:
And her eyes are dark and humid, like the depth on depth of lustre
Hid i' the harebell, while her tresses, sunnier than the wild-grape cluster,
Gush in golden-tinted plenty down her neck's rose-misted marble:
Then her voice's music . . . call it the well's bubbling, the bird's
     warble!

       [*A figure wrapped in a mantle appears at the window.*

And this woman says, "My days were sunless and my nights were
     moonless,
"Parched the pleasant April herbage, and the lark's heart's outbreak
     tuneless,
"If you loved me not!" And I who—(ah, for words of flame!) adore
     her!
Who am mad to lay my spirit prostrate palpably before her—

       [*He enters—approaches her seat, and bends over her.*

I may enter at her portal soon, as now her lattice takes me,
And by noontide as by midnight make her mine, as hers she makes me!

       [*The* Earl *throws off his slouched hat and long cloak.*

My very heart sings, so I sing, beloved!
    Mil. Sit, Henry—do not take my hand.
    Mer.   'Tis mine!
The meeting that appalled us both so much
Is ended.
    Mil.   What begins now?
    Mer.   Happiness
Such as the world contains not.
    Mil.   That is it.
Our happiness would, as you say, exceed
The whole world's best of blisses: we—do we
Deserve that? Utter to your soul, what mine
Long since, beloved, has grown used to hear,
Like a death-knell, so much regarded once,
And so familiar now; this will not be!
    Mer. Oh, Mildred, have I met your brother's face,
Compelled myself—if not to speak untruth,
Yet to disguise, to shun, to put aside
The truth, as what had e'er prevailed on me

Save you, to venture?   Have I gained at last
Your brother, the one scarer of your dreams,
And waking thoughts' sole apprehension too?
Does a new life, like a young sunrise, break
On the strange unrest of our night, confused
With rain and stormy flaw—and will you see
No dripping blossoms, no fire-tinted drops
On each live spray, no vapour steaming up,
And no expressless glory in the east?
When I am by you, to be ever by you,
When I have won you and may worship you,
Oh, Mildred, can you say " this will not be? "
  Mil.   Sin has surprised us; so will punishment.
  Mer.   No—me alone, who sinned alone!
  Mil.   The night
You likened our past life to—was it storm
Throughout to you then, Henry?
  Mer.   Of your life
I spoke—what am I, what my life, to waste
A thought about when you are by me?—you
It was, I said my folly called the storm
And pulled the night upon.—'Twas day with me—
Perpetual dawn with me.
  Mil.   Come what, come will,
You have been happy—take my hand!
  Mer. [*after a pause.*]   How good
Your brother is! I figured him a cold—
Shall I say, haughty man?
  Mil.   They told me all.
I know all.
  Mer. It will soon be over.
  Mil.   Over?
Oh, what is over? what must I live thro'
And say, " 'tis over? "   Is our meeting over?
Have I received in presence of them all
The partner of my guilty love,—with brow
Trying to seem a maiden's brow—with lips
Which make believe that when they strive to form
Replies to you and tremble as they strive,
It is the nearest ever they approached
A stranger's . . . Henry, yours that stranger's . . . lip—
With cheek that looks a virgin's, and that *is* . . .
Ah, God! some prodigy of thine will stop

This planned piece of deliberate wickedness
In its birth even—some fierce leprous spot
Will mar the brow's dissimulating—I
Shall murmur no smooth speeches got by heart,
But, frenzied, pour forth all our woeful story,
The love, the shame, and the despair—with them
Round me aghast as men round some cursed fount
That should spirt water, and spouts blood. I'll not
. . . Henry, you do not wish that I should draw
This vengeance down? I'll not affect a grace
That's gone from me—gone once, and gone for ever!
    Mer. Mildred, my honour is your own. I'll share
Disgrace I cannot suffer by myself.
A word informs your brother I retract
This morning's offer; time will yet bring forth
Some better way of saving both of us.
    Mil. I'll meet their faces, Mertoun!
    Mer.   When? to-morrow?
Get done with it!
    Mil.   Oh, Henry, not to-morrow!
Next day! I never shall prepare my words
And looks and gestures sooner!—How you must
Despise me!
    Mer.   Mildred, break it if you choose,
A heart the love of you uplifted—still
Uplifts, thro' this protracted agony,
To Heaven! but, Mildred, answer me,—first pace
The chamber with me—once again—now, say
Calmly the part, the . . . what it is of me
You see contempt (for you did say contempt)
—Contempt for you in! I would pluck it off
And cast it from me!—but no—no, you'll not
Repeat that?—will you, Mildred, repeat that?
    Mil. Dear Henry—
    Mer.   I was scarce a boy—e'en now
What am I more? And you were infantine
When first I met you—why, your hair fell loose
On either side!—my fool's cheek reddens now
Only in the recalling how it burned
That morn to see the shape of many a dream
—You know we boys are prodigal of charms
To her we dream of—I had heard of one,
Had dreamed of her, and I was close to her,

Might speak to her, might live and die her own,
Who knew?—I spoke—Oh, Mildred, feel you not
That now, while I remember every glance
Of yours, each word of yours, with power to test
And weigh them in the diamond scales of Pride,
Resolved the treasure of a first and last
Heart's love shall have been bartered at its worth,
—That now I think upon your purity
And utter ignorance of guilt—your own
Or other's guilt—the girlish undisguised
Delight at a strange novel prize—(I talk
A silly language, but interpret, you!)
If I, with fancy at its full, and reason
Scarce in its germ, enjoined you secrecy,
If you had pity on my passion, pity
On my protested sickness of the soul
To sit beside you, hear you breathe, and watch
Your eyelids and the eyes beneath—if you
Accorded gifts and knew not they were gifts—
If I grew mad at last with enterprise
And must behold my beauty in her bower
Or perish—(I was ignorant of even
My own desires—what then were you?) if sorrow—
Sin—if the end came—must I now renounce
My reason, blind myself to light, say truth
Is false and lie to God and my own soul?
Contempt were all of this!

    Mil.   Do you believe . . .
Or, Henry, I'll not wrong you—you believe
That I was ignorant. I scarce grieve o'er
The past! We'll love on—you will love me still!

    Mer.   Oh, to love less what one has injured! Dove,
Whose opinion I have rashly hurt, my breast—
Shall my heart's warmth not nurse thee into strength?
Flower I have crushed, shall I not care for thee?
Bloom o'er my crest my fight-mark and device!
Mildred, I love you and you love me!

    Mil.   Go!
Be that your last word. I shall sleep to-night.

    Mer.   This is not our last meeting?

    Mil.   One night more.

    Mer.   And then—think, then!

    Mil.   Then, no sweet courtship-days

No dawning consciousness of love for us,
No strange and palpitating births of sense
From words and looks, no innocent fears and hopes,
Reserves and confidences: morning's over!
   Mer. How else should love's perfected noontide follow?
All the dawn promised shall the day perform.
   Mil. So may it be! but—
                        You are cautious, love?
Are sure that unobserved you scaled the walls?
   Mer. Oh, trust me! Then our final meeting's fixed?
To-morrow night?
   Mil.   Farewell! Stay, Henry . . . wherefore?
His foot is on the yew-tree bough—the turf
Receives him—now the moonlight as he runs
Embraces him—but he must go—is gone—
Ah, once again he turns—thanks, thanks, my love!
He's gone—Oh, I'll believe him every word!
I was so young—I loved him so—I had
No mother—God forgot me—and I fell.
There may be pardon yet—all's doubt beyond.
Surely the bitterness of death is past!

ACT II

Scene.—*The Library.*

Enter Lord Tresham *hastily.*

This way—In, Gerard, quick!
          [*As* Gerard *enters,* Tresham *secures the door.*
                    Now speak! or, wait—
I'll bid you speak directly.   [*Seats himself.*
                    Now repeat
Firmly and circumstantially the tale
You've just now told me; it eludes me; either
I did not listen, or the half is gone
Away from me—How long have you lived here?
Here in my house, your father kept our woods
Before you?
   Ger.   —As his father did, my lord.
I have been eating sixty years, almost,
Your bread.

Tresh.   Yes, yes—You ever were of all
The servants in my father's house, I know,
The trusted one. You'll speak the truth.
  Ger.   I'll speak
God's truth: night after night . . .
    Tresh.   Since when?
    Ger.   At least
A month—each midnight has some man access
To Lady Mildred's chamber.
    Tresh.   Tush, " access "—
No wide words like " access " to me!
    Ger.   He runs
Along the woodside, crosses to the south,
Takes the left tree that ends the avenue . . .
    Tresh. The last great yew-tree?
    Ger.   You might stand upon
The main boughs like a platform . . . Then he . . .
    Tresh.   Quick!
    Ger. . . . Climbs up, and, where they lessen at the top,
—I cannot see distinctly, but he throws,
I think—for this I do not vouch—a line
That reaches to the Lady's casement—
    Tresh.   —Which
He enters not! Gerard—some wretched fool
Dares pry into my sister's privacy!
When such are young, it seems a precious thing
To have approached,—to merely have approached,
Got sight of, the abode of her they set
Their frantic thoughts upon! He does not enter?
Gerard?
    Ger. There is a lamp that's full in the midst,
Under a red square in the painted glass
Of Lady Mildred's . . .
    Tresh.   Leave that name out! Well?
That lamp?
    Ger.   —Is moved at midnight higher up
To one pane—a small dark-blue pane—he waits
For that among the boughs; at sight of that,
I see him, plain as I see you, my lord,
Open the Lady's casement, enter there . . .
    Tresh. —And stay?
    Ger.   An hour, two hours.
    Tresh.   And this saw you

Once?—twice?—quick!

    Ger.   Twenty times.

    Tresh.   And what brings you

Under the yew-trees?

    Ger.   The first night I left

My range so far, to track the stranger stag

That broke the pale, I saw the man.

    Tresh.   Yet sent

No cross-bow shaft thro' the marauder?

    Ger.   But

He came, my lord, the first time he was seen,

In a great moonlight, light as any day,

From Lady Mildred's chamber.

    Tresh. [*after a pause.*]   You have no cause—

—Who could have cause to do my sister wrong?

    Ger.   Oh, my lord, only once—let me this once

Speak what is on my mind! Since first I noted

All this, I've groaned as if a fiery net

Plucked me this way and that—fire, if I turned

To her, fire if I turned to you, and fire,

If down I flung myself and strove to die.

The lady could not have been seven years old

When I was trusted to conduct her safe

Thro' the deer-herd to stroke the snow-white fawn

I brought to eat bread from her tiny hand

Within a month. She ever had a smile

To greet me with—she . . . if it could undo

What's done to lop each limb from off this trunk . . .

All that is foolish talk, not fit for you—

I mean, I could not speak and bring her hurt

For Heaven's compelling: but when I was fixed

To hold my peace, each morsel of your food

Eaten beneath your roof, my birth-place too,

Choked me. I wish I had grown mad in doubts

What it behoved me do. This morn it seemed

Either I must confess to you, or die:

Now it is done, I seem the vilest worm

That crawls, to have betrayed my Lady!

    Tresh.   No—

No—Gerard!

    Ger.   Let me go!

    Tresh.   A man, you say—

What man? Young? Not a vulgar hind? What dress?

Ger.   A slouched hat and a large dark foreign cloak
Wraps his whole form: even his face is hid;
But I should judge him young; no hind, be sure!
  Tresh.   Why?
  Ger.   He is ever armed: his sword projects
Beneath the cloak.
  Tresh.   Gerard,—I will not say
No word, no breath of this!
  Ger.   Thanks, thanks, my lord!

                                        [*Goes.*

    [TRESHAM *paces the room.   After a pause,*
Oh, thought's absurd!—as with some monstrous fact
That, when ill thoughts beset us, seems to give
Merciful God that made the sun and stars,
The waters and the green delights of earth,
The lie!   I apprehend the monstrous fact—
Yet know the Maker of all worlds is good,
And yield my reason up, inadequate
To reconcile what yet I do behold—
Blasting my sense!   There's cheerful day outside—
This is my library—and this the chair
My father used to sit in carelessly,
After his soldier-fashion, while I stood
Between his knees to question him—and here,
Gerard our gray retainer,—as he says,
Fed with our food from sire to son an age,—
Has told a story—I am to believe!
That Mildred . . . oh no, no! both tales are true,
Her pure cheek's story and the forester's!
Would she, or could she, err—much less, confound
All guilts of treachery, of craft, of . . . Heaven
Keep me within its hand!—I will sit here
Until thought settles and I see my course.
Avert, oh God, only this woe from me!
  [*As he sinks his head between his arms on the table,* GUEN-
    DOLEN'S *voice is heard at the door.*
Lord Tresham!   [*She knocks.*]   Is Lord Tresham there?
  [TRESHAM, *hastily turning, pulls down the first book above*
    him and opens it.
  Tresh.   Come in!   [*She enters.*
Ah, Guendolen—good morning.
  Guen.   Nothing more?
  Tresh.   What should I say more?

Guen.   Pleasant question! more?
This more! Did I besiege poor Mildred's brain
Last night till close on morning with " the Earl "—
" The Earl "—whose worth did I asseverate
Till I am very fain to hope that . . . Thorold,
What is all this? You are not well!
    Tresh.   Who, I?
You laugh at me.
    Guen.   Has what I'm fain to hope
Arrived, then? Does that huge tome show some blot
In the Earl's 'scutcheon come no longer back
Than Arthur's time?
    Tresh.   When left you Mildred's chamber?
    Guen. Oh late enough, I told you! The main thing
To ask is, how I left her chamber,—sure,
Content yourself, she'll grant this paragon
Of Earls no such ungracious . . .
    Tresh.   Send her here!
    Guen. Thorold?
    Tresh.   I mean—acquaint her, Guendolen,—
—But mildly!
    Guen.   Mildly?
    Tresh.   Ah, you guess'd aright!
I am not well—there is no hiding it,
But tell her I would see her at her leisure—
That is, at once! here in the Library!
The passage in that old Italian book
We hunted for so long is found, say,—found—
And if I let it slip again . . . you see,
That she must come—and instantly!
    Guen.   I'll die
Piecemeal, record that, if there have not gloomed
Some blot i' the 'scutcheon!
    Tresh.   Go! or, Guendolen,
Be you at call,—with Austin, if you choose,—
In the adjoining gallery—There, go! [GUENDOLEN *goes.*
Another lesson to me! you might bid
A child disguise his heart's sore, and conduct
Some sly investigation point by point
With a smooth brow, as well as bid me catch
The inquisitorial cleverness some praise!
If you had told me yesterday, " There's one
" You needs must circumvent and practise with,

" Entrap by policies, if you would worm
" The truth out—and that one is—Mildred!" There—
There—reasoning is thrown away on it!
Prove she's unchaste . . . why you may after prove
That she's a poisoner, traitress, what you will!
Where I can comprehend nought, nought's to say,
Or do, or think! Force on me but the first
Abomination,—then outpour all plagues,
And I shall ne'er make count of them!

Enter MILDRED.

Mil.   What book
Is it I wanted, Thorold? Guendolen
Thought you were pale—you are not pale! That book?
That's Latin surely!
   Tresh.   Mildred—here's a line—
(Don't lean on me—I'll English it for you)
" Love conquers all things." What love conquers them?
What love should you esteem—best love?
   Mil.   True love.
   Tresh. I mean, and should have said, whose love is best
Of all that love or that profess to love?
   Mil. The list's so long — there's father's, mother's,
    husband's . . .
   Tresh. Mildred, I do believe a brother's love
For a sole sister must exceed them all!
For see now, only see! there's no alloy
Of earth that creeps into the perfect'st gold
Of other loves—no gratitude to claim;
You never gave her life—not even aught
That keeps life—never tended her, instructed,
Enriched her—so your love can claim no right
O'er hers save pure love's claim—that's what I call
Freedom from earthliness. You'll never hope
To be such friends, for instance, she and you,
As when you hunted cowslips in the woods,
Or played together in the meadow hay.
Oh yes—with age, respect comes, and your worth
Is felt, there's growing sympathy of tastes,
There's ripened friendship, there's confirmed esteem,
—Much head these make against the new-comer!
The startling apparition—the strange youth—
Whom one half-hour's conversing with, or, say,

Mere gazing at, shall change (beyond all change
This Ovid ever sang about!) your soul
. . . *Her* soul, that is,—the sister's soul! With her
'Twas winter yesterday; now, all is warmth,
The green leaf's springing and the turtle's voice,
" Arise and come away!" Come whither?—far
Enough from the esteem, respect, and all
The brother's somewhat insignificant
Array of rights! all which he knows before—
Has calculated on so long ago!
I think such love, (apart from yours and mine,)
Contented with its little term of life,
Intending to retire betimes, aware
How soon the back-ground must be place for it,
I think, am sure, a brother's love exceeds
All the world's loves in its unworldliness.
    Mil. What is this for?
    Tresh.   This, Mildred, is it for!
Oh, no, I cannot go to it so soon!
That's one of many points my haste left out—
Each day, each hour throws forth its silk-slight film
Between the being tied to you by birth,
And you, until those slender threads compose
A web that shrouds her daily life of hopes
And fears and fancies, all her life, from yours—
So close you live and yet so far apart!
And must I rend this web, tear up, break down
The sweet and palpitating mystery
That makes her sacred? You—for you I mean,
Shall I speak—shall I not speak?
    Mil.   Speak!
    Tresh.   I will.
Is there a story men could—any man
Could tell of you, you would conceal from me?
I'll never think there's falsehood on that lip!
Say, " There is no such story men could tell,"
And I'll believe you, tho' I disbelieve
The world . . . the world of better men than I,
And women such as I suppose you—Speak!
[*After a pause.*] Not speak? Explain then! clear up, then!
    Move
Some of the miserable weight away
That presses lower than the grave! Not speak?

Some of the dead weight, Mildred!   Ah, if I
Could bring myself to plainly make their charge
Against you!   Must I, Mildred?   Silent still?
[*After a pause.*]   Is there a gallant that has night by night
Admittance to your chamber?
[*After a pause.*]   Then, his name!
Till now, I only had a thought for you—
But now,—his name!

    Mil.   Thorold, do you devise
Fit expiation for my guilt, if fit
There be!   'tis nought to say that I'll endure
And bless you,—that my spirit yearns to purge
Her stains off in the fierce renewing fire—
But do not plunge me into other guilt!
Oh, guilt enough!   I cannot tell his name.

    Tresh.   Then judge yourself! How should I act? Pronounce!

    Mil.   Oh, Thorold, you must never tempt me thus!
To die here in this chamber by that sword
Would seem like punishment—so should I glide,
Like an arch-cheat, into extremest bliss!
'Twere easily arranged for me! but you—
What would become of you?

    Tresh.   And what will now
Become of me?   I'll hide your shame and mine
From every eye: the dead must heave their hearts
Under the marble of our chapel-floor;
They cannot rise and blast you! You may wed
Your paramour above our mother's tomb;
Our mother cannot move from 'neath your foot.
We two will somehow wear this one day out:
But with to-morrow hastens here—the Earl!
The youth without suspicion that faces come
From Heaven, and hearts from . . . whence proceed such
    hearts?
I have despatched last night at your command
A missive bidding him present himself
To-morrow here—thus much is said—the rest
Is understood as if 'twere written down—
" His suit finds favour in your eyes,"—now dictate
This morning's letter that shall countermand
Last night's—do dictate that!

    Mil.   But, Thorold—it
I will receive him as I said?

Tresh.   *The Earl ?*
Mil.   I will receive him!
Tresh. [*Starting up.*]   Ho there! Guendolen!

GUENDOLEN *and* AUSTIN *enter.*

And, Austin, you are welcome too! Look there!
The woman there!
    Aus. and Guen.   How?   Mildred?
    Tresh.   Mildred once!
Now the receiver night by night, when sleep
Blesses the inmates of her father's house,
—I say, the soft sly wanton that receives
Her guilt's accomplice 'neath this roof which holds
You, Guendolen, you, Austin, and has held
A thousand Treshams—never one like her!
No lighter of the signal lamp her quick
Foul breath near quenches in hot eagerness
To mix with breath as foul! no loosener
Of the lattice, practised in the stealthy tread,
The low voice and the noiseless come-and-go!
Not one composer of the Bacchant's mien
Into—what you thought Mildred's, in a word!
Know her!
    Guen.   Oh, Mildred, look to me, at least!
Thorold—she's dead, I'd say, but that she stands
Rigid as stone and whiter!
    Tresh.   You have heard . . .
    Guen.   Too much! you must proceed no further!
    Mil.   Yes—
Proceed—All's truth! Go from me!
    Tresh.   All is truth,
She tells you! Well, you know, or ought to know,
All this I would forgive in her. I'd con
Each precept the harsh world enjoins, I'd take
Our ancestors' stern verdicts one by one,
I'd bind myself before them to exact
The prescribed vengeance—and one word of hers,
The sight of her, the bare least memory
Of Mildred, my one sister, my heart's pride
Above all prides, my all in all so long,
Had scattered every trace of my resolve!
What were it silently to waste away
And see her waste away from this day forth,

Two scathed things with leisure to repent,
And grow acquainted with the grave, and die,
Tired out if not at peace, and be forgotten?
It were not so impossible to bear!
But this—that, fresh from last night's pledge renewed
Of love with the successful gallant there,
She'll calmly bid me help her to entice,
Inveigle an unconscious trusting youth
Who thinks her all that's chaste, and good, and pure,
—Invite me to betray him . . . who so fit
As honor's self to cover shame's arch-deed?
—That she'll receive Lord Mertoun—(her own phrase)—
This, who could bear? Why, you have heard of thieves,
Stabbers, the earth's disgrace—who yet have laughed,
" Talk not of tortures to me—I'll betray
" No comrade I've pledged faith to! "—you have heard
Of wretched women—all but Mildreds—tied
By wild illicit ties to losels vile
You'd tempt them to forsake; and they'll reply
" Gold, friends, repute, I left for him, I have
" In him, why should I leave him then for gold,
" Repute, or friends? "—and you have felt your heart
Respond to such poor outcasts of the world
As to so many friends; bad as you please,
You've felt they were God's men and women still.
So not to be disowned by you! but she,
That stands there, calmly gives her lover up
As means to wed the Earl that she may hide
Their intercourse the surelier! and, for this,
I curse her to her face before you all!
Shame hunt her from the earth! Then Heaven do right
To both! It hears me now—shall judge her then!

      [*As* MILDRED *faints and falls,* TRESHAM *rushes out.*

  Aus. Stay, Tresham, we'll accompany you!
  Guen.   We?
What, and leave Mildred? We? why, where's my place
But by her side, and where's yours but by mine?
Mildred—one word—only look at me, then!
  Aus. No, Guendolen! I echo Thorold's voice!
She in unworthy to behold . . .
  Guen.   Us two?
If you spoke on reflection, and if I
Approved your speech—if you (to put the thing

At lowest) you, the soldier, bound to make
The King's cause yours, and fight for it, and throw
Regard to others of its right or wrong,
—If with a death-white woman you can help,
Let alone sister, let alone a Mildred,
You left her—or if I, her cousin, friend
This morning, playfellow but yesterday,
Who've said, or thought at least a thousand times,
" I'd serve you if I could," should now face round
And say, " Ah, that's to only signify
" I'd serve you while you're fit to serve yourself—
" So long as fifty eyes await the turn
" Of yours to forestall its yet half-formed wish,
" I'll proffer my assistance you'll not need—
" When every tongue is praising you, I'll join
" The praisers' chorus—when you're hemmed about
" With lives between you and detraction—lives
" To be laid down if a rude voice, rash eye,
" Rough hand should violate the sacred ring
" Their worship throws about you,—then indeed,
" Who'll stand up for you stout as I ? "   If so
We said and so we did,—not Mildred there
Would be unworthy to behold us both,
But we should be unworthy, both of us,
To be beheld by—by—your meanest dog,
Which, if that sword were broken in your face
Before a crowd, that badge torn off your breast,
And you cast out with hootings and contempt,
—Would push his way thro' all the hooters, gain
Your side, go off with you and all your shame
To the next ditch you choose to die in !   Austin,
Do you love me ?   Here's Austin, Mildred,—here's
Your brother says he does not believe half—
No, nor half that—of all he heard !   He says,
Look up and take his hand !

Aus.   Look up and take
My hand, dear Mildred !

Mil.   I—I was so young !
Beside, I loved him, Thorold—and I had
No mother—God forgot me—so I fell !

Guen.   Mildred !

Mil.   Require no further !   Did I dream
That I could palliate what is done ?   All's true.

Now, punish me!   A woman takes my hand!
Let go my hand!   You do not know, I see—
I thought that Thorold told you.
    Guen.   What is this?
Where start you to?
    Mil.   Oh Austin, loosen me!
You heard the whole of it—your eyes were worse,
In their surprise, than Thorold's!   Oh, unless
You stay to execute his sentence, loose
My hand!   Has Thorold gone, and are you here?
    Guen.   Here, Mildred, we two friends of yours will wait
Your bidding; be you silent, sleep or muse!
Only, when you shall want your bidding done,
How can we do it if we are not by?
Here's Austin waiting patiently your will!
One spirit to command, and one to love
And to believe in it and do its best,
Poor as that is, to help it—why, the world
Has been won many a time, its length and breadth,
By just such a beginning!
    Mil.   I believe
If once I threw my arms about your neck
And sunk my head upon your breast, that I
Should weep again!
    Guen.   Let go her hand now, Austin.
Wait for me.—Pace the gallery and think
On the world's seemings and realities
Until I call you.   [AUSTIN *goes.*
    Mil.   No—I cannot weep!
No more tears from this brain—no sleep—no tears!
O Guendolen, I love you!
    Guen.   Yes: and " love "
Is a short word that says so very much!
It says that you can confide in me.
    Mil.   Confide!
    Guen.   Your lover's name, then!   I've so much to learn,
Ere I can work in your behalf!
    Mil.   My friend,
You know I cannot tell his name.
    Guen.   At least
He *is* your lover? and you love him too?
    Mil.   Ah, do you ask me that?—but I am fallen
So low!

Guen.   You love him still, then?

Mil.   My sole prop
Against the guilt that crushes me!   I say,
Each night ere I lie down, " I was so young—
" I had no mother—and I loved him so! "
And then God seems indulgent, and I dare
Trust him my soul in sleep.

Guen.   How could you let us
E'en talk to you about Lord Mertoun then?

Mil.   There is a cloud around me.

Guen.   But you said
You would receive his suit in spite of this?

Mil.   I say there is a cloud . . .

Guen.   No cloud to me!
Lord Mertoun and your lover are the same!

Mil.   What maddest fancy . . .

Guen. [*calling aloud.*]   Austin! (Spare your pains—
When I have got a truth, that truth I keep)—

Mil.   By all you love, sweet Guendolen, forbear!
Have I confided in you . . .

Guen.   Just for this!
Austin!—Oh, not to guess it at the first!
But I *did* guess it—that is, I divined—
Felt by an instinct how it was—why else
Should I pronounce you free from all that heap
Of sins which had been irredeemable?
I felt they were not yours—what other way
Than this, not yours? The secret's wholly mine!

Mil.   If you would see me die before his face . . .

Guen.   I'd hold my peace! And if the Earl returns
To-night?

Mil.   Ah, Heaven, he's lost!

Guen.   I thought so! Austin!

Enter AUSTIN.

Oh, where have you been hiding?

Aus.   Thorold's gone,
I know not how, across the meadow-land.
I watched him till I lost him in the skirts
Of the beech-wood.

Guen.   Gone? All thwarts us!

Mil.   Thorold too?

Guen.   I have thought. First lead this Mildred to her room.

Go on the other side: and then we'll seek
Your brother; and I'll tell you, by the way,
The greatest comfort in the world.   You said
There was a clew to all.   Remember, sweet,
He said there was a clew!   I hold it.   Come!

ACT III

Scene I.—*The end of the Yew-tree Avenue under* Milred's
window.   A light seen through a central red pane.

Enter Tresham *through the trees.*

Again here!   But I cannot lose myself.
The heath—the orchard—I have traversed glades
And dells and bosky paths which used to lead
Into green wild-wood depths, bewildering
My boy's adventurous step; and now they tend
Hither or soon or late; the blackest shade
Breaks up, the thronged trunks of the trees ope wide,
And the dim turret I have fled from fronts
Again my step; the very river put
Its arm about me and conducted me
To this detested spot.   Why then, I'll shun
Their will no longer—do your will with me!
Oh, bitter!   To have reared a towering scheme
Of happiness, and to behold it razed,
Were nothing: all men hope, and see their hopes
Frustrate, and grieve awhile, and hope anew:
But I . . . to hope that from a line like ours
No horrid prodigy like this would spring,
Were just as though I hoped that from these old
Confederates against the sovereign day,
Children of older and yet older sires
(Whose living coral berries dropped, as now
On me, on many a baron's surcoat once,
On many a beauty's wimple) would proceed
No poison-tree, to thrust from Hell its root,
Hither and thither its strange snaky arms.
Why came I here?   What must I do?—[*A bell strikes.*]—A
    bell?
Midnight! and 'tis at midnight . . .   Ah, I catch

—Woods, river, plains, I catch your meaning now.
And I obey you! Hist! This tree will serve!

[*He retires behind one of the trees. After a pause enter*
MERTOUN *cloaked as before.*

Mer. Not time! Beat out thy last voluptuous beat
Of hope and fear, my heart! I thought the clock
In the chapel struck as I was pushing thro'
The ferns. And so I shall no more see rise
My love-star! Oh, no matter for the past!
So much the more delicious task to see
Mildred revive: to pluck out, thorn by thorn,
All traces of the rough forbidden path
My rash love lured her to! Each day must see
Some fear of hers effaced, some hope renewed!
Then there will be surprises, unforeseen
Delights in store. I'll not regret the past!

[*The light is placed above in the purple pane.*

And see, my signal rises! Mildred's star!
I never saw it lovelier than now
It rises for the last time! If it sets,
'Tis that the re-assuring sun may dawn!

[*As he prepares to ascend the last tree of the avenue,* TRESHAM
arrests his arm.

Unhand me—peasant, by your grasp! Here's gold.
'Twas a mad freak of mine. I said I'd pluck
A branch from the white-blossomed shrub beneath
The casement there! Take this, and hold your peace.
Tresh. Into the moonlight yonder, come with me!
—Out of the shadow!
Mer.   I am armed, fool!
Tresh.   Yes,
Or no?—You'll come into the light, or no?
My hand is on your throat—refuse!—
Mer.   That voice!
Where have I heard . . . no—that was mild and slow.
I'll come with you!   [*They advance.*
Tresh.   You're armed—that's well.
Your name—who are you?
Mer.   (Tresham!—she is lost!)
Tresh. Oh, silent? Do you know, you bear yourself
Exactly as, in curious dreams I've had

How felons, this wild earth is full of, look
When they're detected, still your kind has looked!
The bravo holds an assured countenance,
The thief is voluble and plausible,
But silently the slave of lust has crouched
When I have fancied it before a man!
Your name?

 Mer.   I do conjure Lord Tresham—ay,
Kissing his foot, if so I might prevail—
That he for his own sake forbear to ask
My name! As Heaven's above, his future weal
Or woe depends upon my silence! Vain!
I read your white inexorable face!
Know me, Lord Tresham!

         [He throws off his disguises.

 Tresh.   Mertoun!
[After a pause.]   Draw now!
 Mer.   Hear me
But speak first!

 Tresh.   Not one least word on your life!
Be sure that I will strangle in your throat
The least word that informs me how you live
And yet seem what you seem! No doubt 'twas you
Taught Mildred still to keep that face and sin!
We should join hands in frantic sympathy
If you once taught me the unteachable,
Explained how you can live so, and so lie!
With God's help, I retain, despite my sense,
The old belief—a life like yours is still
Impossible! Now draw!

 Mer.   Not for my sake,
Do I entreat a hearing—for your sake,
And most, for her sake!

 Tresh.   Ha, ha, what should I
Know of your ways? A miscreant like yourself,
How must one rouse his ire?—A blow?—that's pride
No doubt, to him! one spurns him, does one not?
Or sets the foot upon his mouth—or spits
Into his face! Come—which, or all of these?

 Mer. 'Twixt him, and me, and Mildred, Heaven be
   judge!
Can I avoid this? Have your will, my Lord!

    [He draws, and, after a few passes, falls.

Tresh.   You are not hurt?

Mer.   You'll hear me now!

Tresh.   But rise!

Mer.   Ah, Tresham, say I not " you'll hear me now!"
And what procures a man the right to speak
In his defence before his fellow-man,
But—I suppose—the thought that presently
He may have leave to speak before his God
His whole defence?

Tresh.   Not hurt?   It cannot be!
You made no effort to resist me.   Where
Did my sword reach you?   Why not have returned
My thrusts?   Hurt where?

Mer.   My lord—

Tresh.   How young he is!

Mer.   Lord Tresham, I am very young, and yet
I have entangled other lives with mine.
Do let me speak—and do believe my speech,
That when I die before you presently,—

Tresh.   Can you stay here till I return with help?

Mer.   Oh, stay by me! When I was less than boy
I did you grievous wrong, and knew it not—
Upon my honour, knew it not!   Once known,
I could not find what seemed a better way
To right you than I took: my life—you feel
How less than nothing had been giving you
The life you've taken! But I thought my way
The better—only for your sake and hers.
And as you have decided otherwise,
Would I had an infinity of lives
To offer you!—now say—instruct me—think!
Can you from out the minutes I have left
Eke out my reparation?   Oh—think—think!
For I must wring a partial—dare I say,
Forgiveness from you, ere I die?

Tresh.   I do
Forgive you.

Mer.   Wait and ponder that great word
Because, if you forgive, I shall hope
To speak to you of—Mildred!

Tresh.   Mertoun,—haste
And anger have undone us. 'Tis not you
Should tell me for a novelty you're young—

Thoughtless—unable to recall the past!
Be but your pardon ample as my own!

　　Mer.　Ah, Tresham, that a sword-stroke and a drop
Of blood or two, should bring all this about!
Why, 'twas my very fear of you—my love
Of you—(what passion's like a boy's for one
Like you?)—that ruined me! I dreamed of you—
You, all accomplished, courted everywhere,
The scholar and the gentleman. I burned
To knit myself to you—but I was young,
And your surpassing reputation kept me
So far aloof—oh, wherefore all that love?
With less of love, my glorious yesterday
Of praise and gentle words and kindest looks,
Had taken place perchance six months ago!
Even now—how happy we had been! And yet
I know the thought of this escaped you, Tresham!
Let me look up into your face—I feel
'Tis changed above me—yet my eyes are glazed.
Where? where?
　　　　[*As he endeavours to raise himself, his eye catches the lamp.*
　　　　　　　　Ah, Mildred! What will Mildred do?
Tresham, her life is bound up in the life
That's bleeding fast away!—I'll live—must live,
There! if you'll only turn me I shall live
And save her! Tresham—oh, had you but heard!
Had you but heard! What right have you to set
The thoughtless foot upon her life and mine,
And then say, as we perish, " Had I thought,
" All had gone otherwise." We've sinned and die:
Never you sin, Lord Tresham!—for you'll die,
And God will judge you.

　　Tresh.　　　　　　Yes, be satisfied—
That process is begun.

　　Mer.　　　　　　And she sits there
Waiting for me. Now, say you this to her—
You—not another—say, I saw him die
As he breathed this—" I love her "—(you don't know
What those three small words mean) say, loving her
Lowers me down the bloody slope to death
With memories . . . I speak to her—not you,
Who had no pity—will have no remorse,
Perchance intend her . . . Die along with me,

Dear Mildred!—'tis so easy—and you'll 'scape
So much unkindness! Can I lie at rest,
With rude speech spoken to you, ruder deeds
Done to you—heartless men to have my heart,
And I tied down with grave-clothes and the worm,
Aware, perhaps, of every blow—Oh God!—
Upon those lips—yet of no power to tear
The felon stripe by stripe? Die, Mildred! Leave
Their honorable world to them—for God
We're good enough, tho' the world casts us out!

                                             [A whistle is heard.

   Tresh. Ho, Gerard!

    Enter GERARD, AUSTIN, *and* GUENDOLEN, *with lights.*

                       No one speak! you see what's done!
I cannot bear another voice!
   Mer.   There's light—
Light all about me and I move to it.
Tresham, did I not tell you—did you not
Just promise to deliver words of mine
To Mildred?
   Tresh.   I will bear those words to her.
   Mer. Now?
   Tresh. Now! Lift you the body, Gerard, and leave me
The head.
     [As they have half raised MERTOUN, *he turns suddenly.*
   Mer. I knew they turned me—turn me not from her!
There! stay you! there!   *[Dies.*
   Guen. [*after a pause.*] Austin, remain you here
With Thorold until Gerard comes with help—
Then lead him to his chamber. I must go
To Mildred.
   Tresh.   Guendolen, I hear each word
You utter—did you hear him bid me give
His message? Did you hear my promise? I,
And only I, see Mildred!
   Guen.   She will die.
   Tresh. Oh no, she will not die! I dare not hope
She'll die. What ground have you to think she'll die?
Why, Austin's with you!
   Aus.   Had we but arrived
Before you fought!
   Tresh.   There was no fight at all!

He let me slaughter him—the boy!—I'll trust
The body there to you and Gerard—thus!
Now bear him on before me.

    Aus.   Whither bear him?

    Tresh.   Oh, to my chamber. When we meet there next,
We shall be friends.

                     [*They bear out the body of* MERTOUN.
                    Will he die, Guendolen?

    Guen.   Where are you taking me?

    Tresh.   He fell just here!
Now answer me. Shall you in your while life
—You who had nought to do with Mertoun's fate,
Now you have seen his breast upon the turf,
Shall you e'er walk this way if you can help?
When you and Austin wander arm in arm
Thro' our ancestral grounds, will not a shade
Be ever on the meadow and the waste—
Another kind of shade than when the night
Shuts the woodside with all its whispers up!
But will you ever so forget his breast
As willingly to cross this bloody turf
Under the black yew avenue? That's well!
You turn your head! and *I* then?—

    Guen.   What is done
Is done! My care is for the living.   Thorold,
Bear up against this burthen—more remains
To set the neck to!

    Tresh.   Dear and ancient trees
My fathers planted, and I loved so well!
What have I done that, like some fabled crime
Of yore, lets loose a fury leading thus
Her miserable dance amidst you all?
Oh, never more for me shall winds intone
With all your tops a vast antiphony,
Demanding and responding in God's praise!
Hers ye are now—not mine! Farewell—Farewell!

    SCENE II.—MILDRED'S *Chamber*. MILDRED *alone*.

He comes not! I have heard of those who seemed
Resourceless in prosperity,—you thought
Sorrow might slay them when she listed—yet
Did they so gather up their diffused strength
At her first menace, that they bade her strike,

And stood and laughed her subtlest skill to scorn.
Oh, 'tis not so with me! the first woe fell,
And the rest fall upon it, not on me:
Else should I bear that Henry comes not?—fails
Just this first night out of so many nights?
Loving is done with! Were he sitting now,
As so few hours since, on that seat, we'd love
No more—contrive no thousand happy ways
To hide love from the loveless, any more!
I think I might have urged some little point
In my defence, to Thorold; he was breathless
For the least hint of a defence; but no!
The first shame over, all that would might fall.
No Henry! Yet I merely sit and think
The morn's deed o'er and o'er. I must have crept
Out of myself. A Mildred that has lost
Her lover—oh, I dare not look upon
Such woe! I crouch away from it! 'Tis she,
Mildred, will break her heart, not I! The world
Forsakes me—only Henry's left me—left?
When I have lost him, for he does not come,
And I sit stupidly. . . . Oh Heaven, break up
This worse than anguish, this mad apathy,
By any means or any messenger!

    Tresh. [*without.*]   Mildred!
    Mil.   Come in! Heaven hears me!
[TRESHAM *enters.*]   You? alone?
Oh, no more cursing!
    Tresh.   Mildred, I must sit.
There—you sit!
    Mil.   Say it, Thorold—do not look
The curse—deliver all you come to say!
What must become of me? Oh speak that thought
Which makes your brow and cheek so pale!
    Tresh.   My thought?
    Mil. All of it!
    Tresh.   How we waded—years ago—
After those water-lilies, till the plash,
I know not how, surprised us; and you dared
Neither advance nor turn back, so we stood
Laughing and crying until Gerard came—
Once safe upon the turf, the loudest, too,
For once more reaching the relinquished prize!

How idle thoughts are—some men's—dying men's!
Mildred—
   Mil.   You call me kindlier by my name
Than even yesterday—what is in that?
   Tresh. It weighs so much upon my mind that I
This morning took an office not my own!
I might . . . of course, I must be glad or grieved,
Content or not, at every little thing
That touches you—I may with a wrung heart
Even reprove you, Mildred; I did more—
Will you forgive me?
   Mil.   Thorold? do you mock? . . .
Or no . . . and yet you bid me . . . say that word!
   Tresh. Forgive me, Mildred!—are you silent, sweet?
   Mil. [*starting up.*] Why does not Henry Mertoun come
    to-night?
Are *you*, too, silent?
   [*Dashing his mantle aside, and pointing to his scabbard,*
    which is empty.
                 Ah, this speaks for you!
You've murdered Henry Mertoun! now proceed!
What is it I must pardon? This and all?
Well, I do pardon you—I think I do.
Thorold, how very wretched you must be!
   Tresh. He bade me tell you. . . .
   Mil.   What I do forbid
Your utterance of! so much that you may tell
And will not—how you murdered him . . . but, no!
You'll tell me that he loved me, never more
Than bleeding out of his life there—must I say
" Indeed " to that? Enough! I pardon you!
   Tresh. You cannot, Mildred! for the harsh words, yes:
Of this last deed Another's Judge—whose doom
I wait in doubt, despondency, and fear.
   Mil. Oh true! there's nought for me to pardon! True!
You loosed my soul of all its cares at once—
Death makes me sure of him for ever! *You*
Tell me his last words? *He* shall tell me them,
And take my answer—not in words, but reading
Himself the heart I had to read him late,
Which death . . .
   Tresh.   Death? you are dying too? Well said
Of Guendolen! I dared not hope you'd die—

But she was sure of it.

   Mil.   Tell Guendolen
I loved her, and tell Austin . . .

   Tresh.   . . . Him you loved—
And me?

   Mil.   Ah, Thorold! was't not rashly done
To quench that blood, on fire with youth and hope
And love of me, whom you loved too, and yet
Suffered to sit here waiting his approach
While you were slaying him?   Oh, doubtlessly
You let him speak his poor confused boy's-speech
—Do his poor utmost to disarm your wrath
And respite me!—you let him try to give
The story of our loves, and ignorance,
And the brief madness, and the long despair—
You let him plead all this, because your code
Of honor bids you hear before you strike:
But at the end, as he looked up for life
Into your eyes—you struck him down!

   Tresh.   No! no!
Had I but heard him—had I let him speak
Half the truth—less—had I looked long on him,
I had desisted!   Why, as he lay there,
The moon on his flushed cheek, I gathered all
The story ere he told it!   I saw thro'
The troubled surface of his crime and yours
A depth of purity immovable!
Had I but glanced, where all seemed turbidest
Had gleamed some inlet to the calm beneath!
I would not glance—my punishment's at hand.
There, Mildred, is the truth! and you—say on—
You curse me?

   Mil.   As I dare approach that Heaven
Which has not bade a living thing despair,
Which needs no code to keep its grace from stain,
But bids the vilest worm that turns on it
Desist and be forgiven,—I—forgive not,
But bless you, Thorold, from my soul of souls!

                             [*Falls on his neck.*
There! do not think too much upon the past!
The cloud that's broke was all the same a cloud
While it stood up between my friend and you!
You hurt him 'neath its shadow—but is that

So past retrieve?   I have his heart, you know—
I may dispose of it—I give it you!
It loves you as mine loves!   Confirm me, Henry!

                                                            [*Dies.*

    Tresh.   I wish thee joy, beloved!   I am glad
In thy full gladness!
    Guen. [*without.*] Mildred!   Tresham!
[*Entering with* AUSTIN.]   Thorold,
I could desist no longer.   Ah, she swoons!
That's well—
    Tresh.   Oh! better far than that!
    Guen.   She's dead!
Let me unlock her arms!
    Tresh.   She threw them thus
About my neck, and blessed me, and then died.
—You'll let them stay now, Guendolen!
    Aus.   Leave her
And look to him!   What ails you, Thorold?
    Guen.   White
As she—and whiter!   Austin—quick—this side!
    Aus.   A froth is oozing thro' his clenched teeth—
Both lips, where they're not bitten thro', are black!
Speak, dearest Thorold!
    Tresh.   Something does weigh down
My neck beside her weight: thanks: I should fall
But for you, Austin, I believe!—there, there—
'Twill pass away soon!—ah, I had forgotten—
I am dying.
    Guen.   Thorold—Thorold—why was this?
    Tresh.   I said, just as I drank the poison off,
The earth would be no longer earth to me,
The life out of all life was gone from me!
There are blind ways provided, the foredone
Heart-weary player in this pageant-world
Drops out by, letting the main masque defile
By the conspicuous portal:—I am through—
Just through:—
    Guen.   Don't leave him, Austin! death is close.
    Tresh.   Already Mildred's face is peacefuller!
I see you, Austin—feel you—here's my hand,
Put yours in it—You, Guendolen, yours too!
You're Lord and Lady now—You're Treshams—Name
And fame are yours—You hold our 'Scutcheon up.

Austin, no Blot on it!   You see how blood
Must wash one blot away: the first blot came
And the first blood came.   To the vain world's eye
All's gules again—no care to the vain world,
From whence the red was drawn!

    Aus.   No blot shall come!

    Tresh.   I said that—yet it did come.   Should it come,
Vengeance is God's not man's.   Remember me!   [*Dies.*

    Guen. [*letting fall the pulseless arm.*]   Ah, Thorold, we can
    but—remember you!

COLOMBE'S BIRTHDAY

A PLAY

" Ivy and violet, what do ye here,
" With blossom and shoot in the warm spring-weather,
" Hiding the arms of Monchenci and Vere? "

HANMER.

DEDICATION :—NO ONE LOVES AND HONOURS BARRY CORNWALL MORE THAN ROBERT BROWNING DOES ; WHO, HAVING NOTHING BETTER THAN THIS PLAY TO GIVE HIM IN PROOF OF IT, MUST SAY SO.

LONDON: 1844.

PERSONS

COLOMBE OF RAVESTEIN, Duchess of Juliers and Cleves.
SABYNE } Her Attendants.
ADOLF
GUIBERT
GAUCELME } Courtiers.
MAUFROY
CLUGNET
VALENCE, Advocate of Cleves.
PRINCE BERTHOLD, Claimant of the Duchy.
MELCHIOR, his Confidant.

PLACE, *The Palace at Juliers.*

TIME, 16—.

ACT I

Morning. SCENE—*A corridor leading to the Audience-chamber.*

GAUCELME, CLUGNET, MAUFROY, *and other* Courtiers, *round* GUIBERT, *who is silently reading a paper : as he drops it at the end—*

Gui. That this should be her birthday; and the day
We all invested her, twelve months ago,
As the late Duke's true heiress and our liege;
And that this also must become the day . . .
Oh, miserable lady!
 1st Court.   Ay, indeed?
 2nd Court. Well, Guibert?
 3rd Court.   But your news, my friend, your news!
The sooner, friend, one learns Prince Berthold's pleasure,

The better for us all: how writes the Prince?
Give me—I'll read it for the common good—
   Gui. In time, sir—but, till time comes, pardon me!
Our old Duke just disclosed his child's retreat,
Declared her true succession to his rule,
And died: this birthday was the day, last year,
We convoyed her from Castle Ravestein—
That sleeps out trustfully its extreme age
On the Meuse' quiet bank, where she lived queen
Over the water-buds,—to Juliers' Court
With joy and bustle: here again we stand;
Sir Gaucelme's buckle's constant to his cap—
To-day's much such another sunny day!
   Gau. Come, Guibert—this outgrows a jest, I think!
You're hardly such a novice as to need
The lesson, you pretend.
   Gui.   What lesson, sir?
That everybody, if he'd thrive at court,
Should, first and last of all, look to himself?
Why, no: and therefore, with your good example,
(—Ho, Master Adolf!)—to myself I'll look.

                Enter ADOLF.

   Gui. The Prince's letter; why, of all men else,
Comes it to me?
   Adolf.   By virtue of your place,
Sir Guibert! 'Twas the Prince's express charge,
His envoy told us, that the missive there
Should only reach our lady by the hand
Of whosoever held your place.
   Gui.   Enough!   [ADOLF *retires.*
Then, gentles, who'll accept a certain poor
Indifferently honourable place,
My friends, I make no doubt, have gnashed their teeth
At leisure minutes these half-dozen years,
To find me never in the mood to quit?
—Who asks may have it, with my blessing, and—
This to present our lady. Who'll accept?
You,—you,—you? There it lies, and may, for me!
   Mau. [*a youth, picking up the paper, reads aloud.*]
" Prince Berthold, proved by titles following
" Undoubted Lord of Juliers, comes this day
" To claim his own, with licence from the Pope,

" The Emperor, the Kings of Spain and France " . . .

   Gau. Sufficient " titles following," I judge!
Don't read another! Well, —" to claim his own? "

   Mau. " And take possession of the Duchy held
" Since twelve months, to the true heir's prejudice,
" By " . . . Colombe, Juliers' Mistress, so she thinks,
And Ravestein's mere lady, as we find!
Who wants the place and paper? Guibert's right!
I hope to climb a little in the world,—
I'd push my fortunes,—but, no more than he,
Could tell her on this happy day of days,
That, save the nosegay in her hand, perhaps,
There's nothing left to call her own! Sir Clugnet,
You famish for promotion: what say you?

   Clug. [*an old man.*] To give this letter were a sort, I take it,
Of service: services ask recompence:
What kind of corner may be Ravestein?

   Gui. The castle?—Oh, you'd share her fortune? Good!
Three walls stand upright, full as good as four,
With no such bad remainder of a roof.

   Clug. Oh,—but the Town?

   Gui.   Five houses, fifteen huts;
A church whereto was once a spire, 'tis judged;
And half a dyke, except in time of thaw.

   Clug. Still, there's some revenue?

   Gui.   Else Heaven forfend!
You hang a beacon out, should fogs increase;
So when the Autumn floats of pine-wood steer
Safe 'mid the white confusion, thanks to you,
Their grateful raftsman flings a guilder in;
—That's if he means to pass your way next time.

   Clug. If not?

   Gui.   Hang guilders, then—he blesses you!

   Clug. What man do you suppose me? Keep your paper!
And let me say it shows no handsome spirit
To dally with misfortune: keep your place!

   Gau. Some one must tell her.

   Gui.   Some one may: you may!

   Gau. Sir Guibert, 'tis no trifle turns me sick
Of court-hypocrisy at years like mine,
But this goes near it. Where's there news at all?
Who'll have the face, for instance, to affirm
He never heard, e'en while we crowned the girl,

That Juliers' tenure was by Salic law;
That one, confessed her father's cousin's child,
And, she away, indisputable heir,
Against our choice protesting and the Duke's,
Claimed Juliers?—nor, as he preferred his claim,
That first this, then another potentate,
Inclined to its allowance?—I, or you,
Or any one except the lady's self?
Oh, it had been the direst cruelty
To break the business to her! Things might change—
At all events, we'd see next masque at end,
Next mummery over first: and so the edge
Was taken off sharp tidings as they came,
Till here's the Prince upon us, and there's she
—Wreathing her hair, a song between her lips,
With just the faintest notion possible
That some such claimant earns a livelihood
About the world, by feigning grievances
Few pay the story of, but grudge its price,
And fewer listen to, a second time.
Your method proves a failure; now try mine—
And, since this must be carried . . .
    Gui. [*snatching the paper from him.*] By your leave
Your zeal transports you! 'Twill not serve the Prince
So much as you expect, this course you'd take;
If she leaves quietly her palace,—well:
But if she died upon its threshold,—no:
He'd have the trouble of removing her!
Come, gentles, we're all—what the devil knows!
You, Gaucelme, won't lose character, beside—
You broke your father's heart superiorly
To gather his succession—never blush!
You're from my province, and, be comforted,
They tell of it with wonder to this day—
You can afford to let your talent sleep!
We'll take the very worst supposed, as true—
There, the old Duke knew, when he hid his child
Among the river-flowers at Ravestein,
With whom the right lay! Call the Prince our Duke!
There, she's no Duchess, she's no anything
More than a young maid with the bluest eyes—
And now, sirs, we'll not break this young maid's heart
Coolly as Gaucelme could and would! No haste!

His talent's full-blown, ours but in the bud—
We'll not advance to his perfection yet—
Will we, Sir Maufroy?   See, I've ruined Maufroy
For ever as a courtier!

 Gau.   Here's a coil—
And, count us, will you?   Count its residue,
This boasted convoy, this day last year's crowd!
A birthday, too—a gratulation-day!
I'm dumb: bid *that* keep silence!

 Mau. and others.   Eh, Sir Guibert?
He's right: that does say something: that's bare truth.
Ten—twelve, I make: a perilous dropping off!

 Gui. Pooh—is it audience-hour?   The vestibule
Swarms too, I wager, with the common sort
That want our privilege of entry here.

 Gau. Adolf! [*Re-enter* ADOLF.] Who's outside?

 Gui.   Oh, your looks suffice!
Nobody waiting?

 Mau. [*looking through the door-folds.*]   Scarce our number!

 Gui.   'Sdeath!
Nothing to beg for, to complain about?
It can't be!   Ill news spreads, but not so fast
As thus to frighten all the world!

 Gau.   The world
Lives out of doors, sir—not with you and me
By presence-chamber porches, state-room stairs,
Wherever warmth's perpetual: outside's free
To every wind from every compass-point,
And who may get nipped needs be weather-wise.
The Prince comes and the lady's People go;
The snow-goose settles down, the swallows flee—
Why should they wait for winter-time?   'Tis instinct;
Don't you feel somewhat chilly?

 Gui.   That's their craft?
And last year's crowders-round and criers-forth,
That strewed the garlands, overarched the roads,
Lit up the bonfires, sang the loyal songs!
Well, 'tis my comfort, you could never call me
The People's Friend!   The People keep their word—
I keep my place: don't doubt I'll entertain
The People when the Prince comes, and the People
Are talked of!—Then, their speeches—no one tongue
Found respite, not a pen had holiday

—For they wrote, too, as well as spoke, these knaves!
Now see: we tax and tithe them, pill and poll,
They wince and fret enough, but pay they must
—We manage that,—so pay with a good grace
They might as well, it costs so little more.
But when we've done with taxes, meet folk next
Outside the toll-booth and the rating-place,
In public—there they have us if they will,
We're at their mercy after that, you see—
For one tax not ten devils could extort;
Over and above necessity, a grace;
This prompt disbosoming of love, to wit—
Their vine-leaf-wrappage of our tribute-penny
And crowning attestation, all works well—
Yet this precisely do they thrust on us!
These cappings quick, and crook-and-cringings low,
Hand to the heart, and forehead to the knee,
With grin that shuts the eyes and opes the mouth—
So tender they their love; and tender made,
Go home to curse you, the first doit you ask;
As if their souls were any longer theirs!
As if they had not given ample warrant
To who should clap a collar on their neck,
Rings in their nose, a goad to either flank,
And take them for the brute they boast themselves!
—Stay—there's a bustle at the outer door—
And somebody entreating . . . that's my name!
Adolf,—I heard my name!

    Adolf.   'Twas probably
The Suitor.

    Gui.   Oh, there is one?

    Adolf.   With a suit
He'd fain enforce in person.

    Gui.   The good heart
—And the great fool! Just ope the mid-door's fold—
Is that a lappet of his cloak, I see?

    Adolf. If it bear plenteous signs of travel . . . ay,
The very cloak my comrades tore!

    Gui.   Why tore?

    Adolf. He seeks the Duchess' presence in that trim:
Since daybreak, was he posted hereabouts
Lest he should miss the moment.

    Gui.   Where's he now?

Adolf. Gone for a minute possibly, not more.
They have ado enough to thrust him back.
  Gui. Ay—but my name, I caught?
  Adolf. Oh, sir—he said
—What was it?—You had known him formerly,
And, he believed, would help him did you guess
He waited now—you promised him as much—
The old plea!—'Faith, he's back,—renews the charge!
[*Speaking at the door.*] So long as the man parleys, peace
    outside!
Nor be too ready with your halberts, there!
  Gau. My horse bespattered, as he blocked the path,
A thin sour man not unlike somebody.
  Adolf. He holds a paper in his breast, whereon
He glances when his cheeks flush and his brow
At each repulse—
  Gau. I noticed he'd a brow.
  Adolf. So glancing, he grows calmer, leans awhile
Over the balustrade, adjusts his dress,
And presently turns round, quiet again,
With some new pretext for admittance.—Back!
(*To* GUIBERT.)—Sir, he has seen you! Now cross halberts!
  Ha—
Pascal is prostrate—there lies Fabian too—
No passage! Whither would the madman press?
Close the doors quick on me!
  Gui. Too late—he's here.

Enter, hastily and with discomposed dress, VALENCE.

  Val. Sir Guibert, will you help me?—Me, that come
Charged by your townsmen, all who starve at Cleves,
To represent their heights and depths of woe
Before our Duchess and obtain relief!
Such errands barricade such doors, it seems:
But not a common hindrance drives me back
On all the sad yet hopeful faces, lit
With hope for the first time, which sent me forth!
Cleves, speak for me! Cleves' men and women, speak—
Who followed me—your strongest—many a mile
That I might go the fresher from their ranks,
—Who sit—your weakest—by the city-gates,
To take me fuller of what news I bring
As I return—for I must needs return!

—Can I? 'Twere hard, no listener for their wrongs,
To turn them back upon the old despair—
Harder, Sir Guibert, than imploring thus—
So I do—any way you please—implore!
If you . . . but how should you remember Cleves?
Yet they of Cleves remember you so well!
—Ay, comment on each trait of you they keep,
Your words and deeds caught up at second hand,—
Proud, I believe, at bottom of their hearts,
Of the very levity and recklessness
Which only prove that you forget their wrongs.
Cleves, the grand town, whose men and women starve,
Is Cleves forgotten?—Then remember me!
You promised me that you would help me once
For other purpose: will you keep your word?

   Gui. And who may you be, friend?
   Val.   Valence of Cleves.
   Gui. Valence of . . . not the Advocate of Cleves
I owed my whole estate to, three years back?
Ay, well may you keep silence! Why, my lords,
You've heard, I'm sure, how, Pentecost three years,
I was so nearly ousted of my land
By some knaves' pretext,—(eh? when you refused me
Your ugly daughter, Clugnet,)—and you've heard
How I recovered it by miracle
—(When I refused her)! Here's the very friend,
—Valence of Cleves, all parties have to thank!
Nay, Valence, this procedure's vile in you—
I'm no more grateful than a courtier should—
But politic am I—I bear a brain,
Can cast about a little, might require
Your services a second time! I tried
To tempt you with advancement here to court
—" No!"—well, for curiosity at least
To view our life here—" No!"—our Duchess, then,—
—A pretty woman's worth some pains to see,
Nor is she spoiled, I take it, if a crown
Completes the forehead pale and tresses pure. . . .

   Val. Our city trusted me its miseries,
And I am come.
   Gui.   So much for taste! But " come,"—
So may you be, for anything I know,
To beg the Pope's cross, or Sir Clugnet's daughter,

And with an equal chance you get all three!
If it was ever worth your while to come,
Was not the proper way worth finding too?
    Val.   Straight to the palace-portal, sir, I came—
    Gui.   —And said?—
    Val.   —That I had brought the miseries
Of a whole city to relieve.
    Gui.   —Which saying
Won your admittance?   You saw me, indeed,
And here, no doubt, you stand: as certainly,
My intervention, I shall not dispute,
Procures you audience; which, if I procure,
That paper's closely written—by Saint Paul,
Here flock the Wrongs, follow the Remedies,
Chapter and verse, One, Two, A, B, and C—
Perhaps you'd enter, make a reverence,
And launch these " miseries " from first to last?
    Val.   How should they let me pause or turn aside?
    Gau. [*ta* VALENCE.] My worthy sir, one question: you've
      come straight
From Cleves, you tell us: heard you any talk
At Cleves about our lady?
    Val.   Much.
    Gau.   And what?
    Val.   Her wish was to redress all wrongs she knew.
    Gau.   That, you believed?
    Val.   You see me, sir!
    Gau.   —Nor stopped
Upon the road from Cleves to Juliers here,
For any—rumours you might find afloat?
    Val.   I had my townsmen's wrongs to busy me.
    Gau.   This is the Lady's birthday, do you know?
—Her day of pleasure?
    Val.   —I know that the Great,
For Pleasure born, should still be on the watch
To exclude Pleasure when a Duty offers:
Even as, the Lowly too, for Duty born,
May ever snatch a Pleasure if in reach:
Both will have plenty of their birthright, sir!
    Gau. [*Aside to* GUIBERT.] Sir Guibert, here's your man!
    No scruples now—
You'll never find his like!   Time presses hard.
I've seen your drift and Adolf's too, this while,

But you can't keep the hour of audience back
Much longer, and at noon the Prince arrives.
[*Pointing to* VALENCE.] Entrust *him* with it—fool no chance
    away!
   Gui.—Him?
   Gau.   —With the missive! What's the man to her?
   Gui. No bad thought!—Yet, 'tis yours—who ever played
The tempting serpent—else, 'twere no bad thought!
I should—and do—mistrust it for your sake,
Or else . . .

     Enter an Official *who communicates with* ADOLF.

   Adolf. The Duchess will receive the Court!
   Gui. Give us a moment, Adolf! Valence, friend,
I'll help you: we of the service, you're to mark,
Have special entry, while the herd . . . the folks
Outside, get access through our help alone
—Well, it is so, was so, and I suppose
So ever will be—your natural lot is, therefore,
To wait your turn and opportunity,
And probably miss both. Now, I engage
To set you, here and in a minute's space,
Before the lady with full leave to plead
Chapter and verse, and A, and B, and C,
To heart's content.
   Val.   I grieve that I must ask,
This being, yourself admit, the custom here,
To what the price of such a favour mounts?
   Gui. Just so! You're not without a courtier's tact!
Little at court, as your quick instinct prompts,
Do such as we without a recompense.
   Val. Yours is?—
   Gui.   A trifle: here's a document
'Tis some one's duty to present her Grace—
I say, not mine—these say, not theirs—such points
Have weight at court. Will you relieve us all
And take it?—Just say, " I am bidden lay
" This paper at the Duchess' feet."
   Val.   No more?
I thank you, sir!
   Adolf.   Her Grace receives the Court!
   Gui. [*Aside.*] Now, *sursum corda*, quoth the mass-priest!
   Do—

Whoever's my kind saint, do let alone
These pushings to and fro, and pullings back;
Peaceably let me hang o' the devil's arm
The downward path, if you can't pluck me off
Completely!   Let me live quite his, or yours!
   [*The* Courtiers *begin to range themselves, and move towards
    the door.*
After me, Valence!   So our famous Cleves
Lacks bread?   Yet don't we gallants buy their lace?
And dear enough—it beggars me, I know,
To keep my very gloves fringed properly!
This, Valence, is our Great State Hall you cross:
Yon grey urn's veritable marcasite,
The Pope's gift; and those salvers testify
The Emperor.   Presently you'll set your foot
. . . But you don't speak, friend Valence!
   Val.   I shall speak.
   Gau. [*Aside to* GUIBERT.]   Guibert—it were no such un-
    graceful thing
If you and I, at first, seemed horrorstruck
With the bad news.   Look here, what you shall do!
Suppose you, first, clap hand to sword and cry
" Yield strangers our allegiance?   First I'll perish
" Beside your Grace " !—and so give me the cue
To . . .
   Gui.   Clap your hand to note-book and jot down
That to regale the Prince with?   I conceive!
[*To* VALENCE.]   Do, Valence, speak, or I shall half suspect
You're plotting to supplant us, me the first,
I' the Lady's favour: is't the grand harangue
You mean to make, that thus engrosses you?
—Which of her virtues you'll apostrophise?
Or is't the fashion you aspire to start,
Of that close-curled, not unbecoming hair?
—Or what else ponder you?
   Val.   My townsmen's wrongs!

ACT II

Noon. Scene.—*The Presence-chamber.*

The Duchess *and* Sabyne.

The D.   Announce that I am ready for the Court!
Sab.   'Tis scarcely audience-hour, I think—your Grace
May best consult your own relief, no doubt,
And shun the crowd; but few can have arrived . . .
The D.   Let those not yet arrived, then, keep away!
'Twas *me*, this day, last year at Ravestein,
You hurried.   It has been full time, beside,
This half-hour.   Do you hesitate?
Sab.   Forgive me!
The D.   Stay, Sabyne; let me hasten to make sure
Of one true thanker: here with you begins
My audience, claim you first its privilege!
It is my birth's event they celebrate—
You need not wish me more such happy days,
But—ask some favour!   Have you none to ask?
Has Adolf none, then?   this was far from least
Of much I waited for impatiently,
Assure yourself!   It seemed so natural
Your gift, beside this bunch of river-bells.
Should be the power and leave of doing good
To you, and greater pleasure to myself:
You ask my leave to-day to marry Adolf?
The rest is my concern.
Sab.   Your Grace is ever
Our Lady of dear Ravestein,—but, for Adolf . . .
The D.   "But"?   You have not, sure, changed in your
      regard
And purpose towards him?
Sab.   *We* change!
The D.   Well, then?   Well?
Sab.   How could we two be happy, and, most like,
Leave Juliers, when . . . when . . . but 'tis audience-time!
The D.   "When, if you left me, I were left indeed"—
Would you subjoin that?—Bid the Court approach!
—Why should we play thus with each other, Sabyne?
Do I not know, if courtiers prove remiss,
If friends detain me, and get blame for it,

There is a cause?   Of last year's fervid throng
Scarce one half comes now!

    Sab. [*Aside.*]   One half?   No, alas!

    The D.   So can the mere suspicion of a cloud
Over my fortunes strike each loyal heart.
They've heard of this Prince Berthold; and, forsooth,
Each foolish arrogant pretence he makes,
May grow more foolish and more arrogant,
They please to apprehend!   I thank their love!
Admit them!

    Sab. [*Aside.*]   How much has she really learned?

    The D.   Surely, whoever's absent, Tristan waits?
—Or at least Romuald, whom my father raised
From nothing—come, he's faithful to me, come!
(Sabyne, I should but be the prouder—yes,
And fitter to comport myself aright)
Not Romuald?   Xavier—what said he to that?
For Xavier hates a parasite, I know!   [SABYNE *goes out.*

    The D.   Well, sunshine's everywhere, and summer too;
Next year 'tis the old place again, perhaps—
The water-breeze again, the birds again
. . . It cannot be!   It is too late to be!
What part had I, or choice in all of it?
Hither they brought me;   I had not to think
Nor care, concern myself with doing good
Or ill, my task was just—to live,—to live,
And, answering ends there was no need explain,
To render Juliers happy—so they said.
All could not have been falsehood!   Some was love,
And wonder and obedience—I did all
They looked for!   Why then cease to do it now?
Yet this is to be calmly set aside,
And—ere next birthday's dawn, for aught I know,
Things change, a claimant may arrive, and I . . .
It cannot nor it shall not be!   His right?
Well then, he has the right, and I have not,
—But who bade all of you surround my life
And close its growth up with your Ducal crown
Which, plucked off rudely, leaves me perishing?
I could have been like one of you,—loved, hoped,
Feared, lived and died like one of you—but you
Would take that life away and give me this,
And I will keep this!   I will face you—Come!

Enter the Courtiers *and* VALENCE.

The Courtiers.   Many such happy mornings to your Grace!
The D. [*Aside, as they pay their devoir.*]   The same words
    —the same faces,—the same love!
I have been over-fearful.   These are few—
But these, at least, stand firmly—these are mine!
As many come as may, and if no more,
'Tis that these few suffice—they do suffice!
What succour may not next year bring me!   Plainly
I feared too soon! [*To the* Court.]   I thank you, sirs: all
    thanks!
    Val. [*Aside, as the* DUCHESS *passes from one group to
    another, conversing.*]
'Tis she—the vision this day last year brought,
When for a golden moment at our Cleves
She tarried in her progress hither.   Cleves
Chose me to speak its welcome, and I spoke
—Not that she could have noted the recluse
—Ungainly, old before his time—who gazed—
. . . Well, Heaven's gifts are not wasted, and that gaze
Kept, and shall keep me to the end, her own!
She was above it—but so would not sink
My gaze to earth!   The People caught it, hers—
Thenceforward, mine; but thus entirely mine,
Who shall affirm, had she not raised my soul
Ere she retired and left me—them?—She turns—
There's all her wondrous face at once!   The ground
Reels and . . . [*suddenly occupying himself with his paper.*]
                These wrongs of theirs I have to plead!
    The D. [*to the* Court.]   Nay, compliment enough! And
    kindness' self
Should pause before it wish me more such years.
'Twas fortunate that thus, ere youth escaped,
I tasted life's pure pleasure—one such, pure,
Is worth a thousand, mixed—and youth's for pleasure:
Mine is received; let my age pay for it.
    Gau.   So, pay, and pleasure paid for, thinks your Grace,
Should never go together?
    Gui.   How, Sir Gaucelme?
Hurry one's feast down unenjoyingly
At the snatched breathing-intervals of work?
As good you saved it till the dull day's-end

When, stiff and sleepy, appetite is gone!
Eat first, then work upon the strength of it!

   The D.   True: you enable me to risk my Future,
By giving me a Past beyond recall.
I lived, a girl, one happy leisure year:
Let me endeavour to be the Duchess now!
And so,—what news, Sir Guibert, spoke you of?

                              [As they advance a little, and GUIBERT *speaks.*
—That gentleman?

   Val. [*Aside.*]   I feel her eyes on me!

   Gui. [*to* VALENCE.]   The Duchess, sir, inclines to hear your
    suit!

Advance!   He is from Cleves.

   Val. [*coming forward.*] [*Aside.*] Their wrongs—their
    wrongs!

   The D.   And you, sir, are from Cleves? How fresh in
    mind,
The hour or two I passed at queenly Cleves!
She entertained me bravely, but the best
Of her good pageant seemed its standers-by,
With insuppressive joy on every face?
What says my ancient, famous, happy Cleves?

   Val.   Take the truth, lady—you are made for truth!
So think my friends: nor do they less deserve
The having you to take it, you shall think,
When you know all—nay, when you only know
How, on that day you recollect at Cleves,
When the poor acquiescing multitude
Who thrust themselves with all their woes apart
Into unnoticed corners, that the few
Their means sufficed to muster trappings for,
Might fill the foreground, occupy your sight
With joyous faces fit to bear away
And boast of as a sample of all Cleves
—How, when to daylight these crept out once more,
Clutching, unconscious, each his empty rags
Whence the scant coin, which had not half bought bread,
That morn he shook forth, counted piece by piece,
And, well-advisedly, on perfumes spent them
To burn, or flowers to strew, before your path
—How, when the golden flood of music and bliss
Ebbed, as their moon retreated, and again
Left the sharp black-point rocks of misery bare

—Then I, their friend, had only to suggest
" Saw she the horror as she saw the pomp! "—
And as one man they cried " He speaks the truth—
" Show her the horror! Take from our own mouths
" Our wrongs and show them, she will see them too! "
—This they cried, lady! I have brought the wrongs.

   The D. Wrongs? Cleves has wrongs—apparent now and
      thus?
I thank you—in that paper?—Give it me!

   Val. (There, Cleves!) In this! (What did I promise
      Cleves?)
Our weavers, clothiers, spinners are reduced
Since . . . Oh, I crave your pardon—I forget
I buy the privilege of this approach,
And promptly would discharge my debt. I lay
This paper humbly at the Duchess' feet!

                       [*Presenting* GUIBERT'S *paper.*

   Gui. Stay—for the present . . .

   The D.   Stay, sir? I take aught
That teaches me their wrongs with greater pride
That this your Ducal circlet. Thank you, sir!

  [*The* DUCHESS *reads hastily; then, turning to the* Courtiers—
What have I done to you? Your deed or mine
Was it, this crowning me? I gave myself
No more a title to your homage, no,
Than church-flowers, born this season, wrote the words
In the saint's-book that sanctified them first.
For such a flower, you plucked me—well, you erred—
Well, 'twas a weed—remove the eye-sore quick!
But should you not remember it has lain
Steeped in the candles' glory, palely shrined,
Nearer God's Mother than most earthly things?
—That if't be faded 'tis with prayer's sole breath—
That the one day it boasted was God's day?
Still, I do thank you—had you used respect
Here might I dwindle to my last white leaf,
Here lose life's latest freshness, which even yet
May yield some wandering insect rest and food:
So, fling me forth, and—all is best for all!

[*After a pause.*] Prince Berthold, who art Juliers' Duke, it
    seems—
The King's choice, and the Emperor's, and the Pope's—
Be mine, too! Take this people! Tell not me

Of rescripts, precedents, authorities,
—But take them, from a heart that yearns to give!
Find out their love,—I could not; find their fear,—
I would not; find their like,—I never shall,
Among the flowers!   [*Taking off her coronet.*
                    Colombe of Ravestein
Thanks God she is no longer Duchess here!

    Val. [*advancing to* GUIBERT.]   Sir Guibert,—knight, they
      call you—this of mine
Is the first step I ever set at court.
You dared make me your instrument, I find;
For that, so sure as you and I are men,
We reckon to the utmost presently:
But as you are a courtier and I none,
Your knowledge may instruct me.   I, already,
Have too far outraged, by my ignorance
Of courtier-ways, this lady, to proceed
A second step and risk addressing her
—I am degraded—you, let me address!
Out of her presence, all is plain enough
What I shall do—but in her presence, too,
Surely there's something proper to be done!
[*To the others.*]   You, gentles, tell me if I guess aright—
May I not strike this man to earth?

    The Courtiers. [*as* GUIBERT *springs forward, withholding*
      him.]   Let go!
—The Clothiers' spokesman, Guibert?   Grace a churl?

    The D. [*to* VALENCE.]   Oh, be acquainted with your party,
      sir!
He's of the oldest lineage Juliers boasts;
A lion crests him for a cognisance;
" Scorning to waver "—that's his scutcheon's word;
His office with the new Duke—probably
The same in honour as with me; or more,
By so much as this gallant turn deserves;
He's now, I dare say, of a thousand times
The rank and influence that remain with her
Whose part you take!   So, lest for taking it
You suffer . . .

    Val.   I may strike him then to earth?

    Gui. [*falling on his knee.*]   Great and dear lady, pardon
      me!   Hear once!
Believe me and be merciful—be just!

I could not bring myself to give that paper
Without a keener pang than I dared meet
—And so felt Clugnet here, and Maufroy here
—No one dared meet it. Protestation's cheap,—
But, if to die for you did any good,
[*To* GAUCELME.] Would not I die, sir? Say your worst
    of me!
But ıt does no good, that's the mournful truth.
And since the hint of a resistance, even,
Would just precipitate, on you the first,
A speedier ruin—I shall not deny,
Saving myself indubitable pain,
I thought to give you pleasure (who might say?)
By showing that your only subject found
To carry the sad notice, was the man
Precisely ignorant of its contents;
A nameless, mere provincial advocate;
One whom 'twas like you never saw before,
Never would see again. All has gone wrong;
But I meant right, God knows, and you, I trust!
    The D. A nameless advocate, this gentleman?—
—(I pardon you, Sir Guibert!)
    Gui. [*rising, to* VALENCE.]—Sir, and you?—
    Val. —Rejoice that you are lightened of a load.
Now, you have only me to reckon with!
    The D. One I have never seen, much less obliged?—
    Val. Dare I speak, lady?
    The D.   Dare you! Heard you not
I rule no longer?
    Val.   Lady, if your rule
Were based alone on such a ground as these
                  [*Pointing to the* Courtiers.
Could furnish you,—abjure it! They have hidden
A source of true dominion from your sight.
    The D. You hear them—no such source is left . . .
    Val.   Hear Cleves!
Whose haggard craftsmen rose to starve this day,
Starve now, and will lie down at night to starve,
Sure of a like to-morrow—but as sure
Of a most unlike morrow-after-that,
Since end things must, end howsoe'er things may.
What curbs the brute-force instinct in its hour?
What makes, instead of rising, all as one,

And teaching fingers, so expert to wield
Their tool, the broadsword's play or carbine's trick,
—What makes that there's an easier help, they think,
For you, whose name so few of them can spell,
Whose face scarce one in every hundred saw,
You simply have to understand their wrongs,
And wrongs will vanish—so, still trades are plied,
And swords lie rusting, and myself stand here?
There is a vision in the heart of each
Of justice, mercy, wisdom; tenderness
To wrong and pain, and knowledge of its cure—
And these, embodied in a woman's form
That best transmits them, pure as first received,
From God above her, to mankind below.
Will you derive your rule from such a ground,
Or rather hold it by the suffrage, say,
Of this man—this—and this?

 The D. [*after a pause.*] You come from Cleves—
How many are at Cleves of such a mind?

  Val. [*from his paper.*] " We, all the manufacturers of
  Cleves "—

 The D. Or stay, sir—lest I seem too covetous—
Are you my subject? such as you describe
Am I to you—though to no other man?

  Val. [*from his paper.*]—" Valence, ordained your Advocate at Cleves "—

 The D. [*replacing the coronet.*] Then I remain Cleves'
  Duchess! Take you note,
While Cleves but yields one subject of this stamp,
I stand her lady till she waves me off!
For her sake, all the Prince claims I withhold;
Laugh at each menace; and, his power defying,
Return his missive with its due contempt! [*Casting it away.*

  Gui. [*picking it up.*]—Which to the Prince I will deliver,
  Lady,
[Note it down, Gaucelme]—with your message too!

 The D. I think the office is a subject's, sir!
—Either . . . how style you him?—my special guarder
The Marshal's—for who knows but violence
May follow the delivery!—Or, perhaps,
My Chancellor's—for law may be to urge
On its receipt!—Or, even my Chamberlain's—
For I may violate established form!

[*To* VALENCE.] Sir,—for the half hour till this service ends,
Will you become all these to me?
 Val. [*falling on his knee.*] My Liege!
 The D. Give me!
      [*The* Courtiers *present their badges of office.*
[*Putting them by.*] —Whatever was their virtue once,
They need new consecration! [*Raising* VALENCE.] Are you
 mine?
—I will be Duchess yet!   [*She retires.*
 The Courtiers. Our Duchess yet!
A glorious lady! Worthy love and dread!
I'll stand by her,—and I, whate'er betide!
 Gui. [*to* VALENCE.] Well done, well done, sir! I care not
 who knows,
You have done nobly, and I envy you—
Tho' I am but unfairly used, I think:
For when one gets a place like this I hold,
One gets too the remark that its mere wages,
The pay and the preferment, make our prize—
Talk about zeal and faith apart from these,
We're laughed at—much would zeal and faith subsist
Without these also! Yet, let these be stopped,
Our wages discontinue,—then, indeed,
Our zeal and faith, we hear on every side,
Are not released—having been pledged away
I wonder with what zeal and faith in turn?
Hard money purchased me my place! No, no—
I'm right, sir—but your wrong is better still,
If I had time and skill to argue it.
Therefore, I say, I'll serve you, how you please—
If you like,—fight you, as you seem to wish—
(The kinder of me that, in sober truth,
I never dreamed I did you any harm)—
 Gau.—Or, kinder still, you'll introduce, no doubt,
His merits to the Prince who's just at hand,
And let no hint drop he's made Chancellor,
And Chamberlain, and Heaven knows what beside!
 Clug. [*to* VALENCE.] You stare, young sir, and threaten!
 Let me say,
That at your age, when first I came to court,
I was not much above a gentleman;
While now . . .
 Val. —You are Head-Lackey? With your office

I have not yet been graced, sir!

Other Courtiers to Clug.   Let him talk!

Fidelity—disinterestedness—

Excuse so much! Men claimed my worship ever

Who, stanch and steadfastly . . .

Enter ADOLF.

Adolf.   The Prince arrives!

Courtiers. Ha? How?

Adolf.   He leaves his guard a stage behind
At Aix, and enters almost by himself.

 1st Court. The Prince! This foolish business puts all out!

 2nd Court. Let Gaucelme speak first!

 3rd. Court.   Better I began
About the state of Juliers—should one say
All's prosperous and inviting him?

 4th Court.   —Or rather
All's prostrate and imploring him!

 5th Court.   That's best!
Where's the Cleves' paper, by the way?

 4th Court. [*to* VALENCE.]   Sir—sir—
If you'll but give that paper—trust it me,
I'll warrant . . .

 5th Court. Softly, sir—the Marshal's duty!

 Clug. Has not the Chamberlain a hearing first
By virtue of his patent?

 Gau.   Patents?—Duties?
All that, my masters, must begin again!
One word composes the whole controversy—
We're simply now—the Prince's!

 The Others.   Ay—the Prince's!

Enter SABYNE.

Sad. Adolf! Bid . . . Oh, no time for ceremony!
Where's whom our lady calls her only subject?
She needs him! Who is here the Duchess's?

 Val. [*starting from his reverie.*] Most gratefully I follow to
 her feet!

ACT III

Afternoon. SCENE.—*The Vestibule.*

Enter PRINCE BERTHOLD *and* MELCHIOR.

Berth. A thriving little burgh this Juliers looks.
[*Half-apart.*] Keep Juliers, and as good you kept Cologne:
Better try Aix, though!—
   Mel.   Please 't your Highness speak?
   Berth. [*as before.*] Aix, Cologne, Frankfort,—Milan;—
    Rome!—
   Mel.   —The Grave
—More weary seems your Highness, I remark,
Than sundry conquerors whose path I've watched
Through fire and blood to any prize they gain.
I could well wish you, for your proper sake,
Had met some shade of opposition here
—Found a blunt seneschal refuse unlock,
Or a scared usher lead your steps astray.
You must not look for next achievement's palm
So easy: this will hurt your conquering!
   Berth. My next? Ay—as you say, my next and next!
Well, I am tired, that's truth, and moody too,
This quiet entrance-morning; listen why!
Our little burgh, now, Juliers—'tis indeed
One link, however insignificant,
Of the great chain by which I reach my hope—
—A link I must secure; but otherwise,
You'd wonder I esteem'd it worth my grasp.
Just see what life is, with its shifts and turns!
It happens now—this very nook—to be
A place that once . . . but a short while since, neither—
When I lived an ambiguous hanger-on
Of foreign courts, and bore my claims about,
Discarded by one kinsman, and the other
A poor priest merely,—then, I say, this place
Shone my ambition's object; to be Duke—
Seemed then what to be Emperor seems now.
My rights were far from being judged as plain
In those days as of late, I promise you—
And 'twas my day-dream, Lady Colombe here

Might e'en compound the matter, pity me,
Be struck, say, with my chivalry and grace
(I was a boy!)—bestow her hand at length,
And make me Duke, in her right if not mine.
Here am I, Duke confessed, at Juliers now!
Hearken: if ever I be Emperor,
Remind me what I felt and said to-day!

    Mel.   All this consoles a bookish man like me!
—And so will weariness cling to you! Wrong—
Wrong! Had you sought the Lady's court yourself,—
Faced the redoubtables composing it,
Flattered this, threatened that man, bribed the other,—
Pleaded, by writ and word and deed, your cause,—
Conquered a footing inch by painful inch,—
And, after long years' struggle, pounced at last
On her for prize,—the right life had been lived,
And justice done to divers faculties
Shut in that brow: yourself were visible
As you stood victor, then! whom now—(your pardon!)
I am forced narrowly to search and see—
So are you hid by helps—this Pope, your uncle—
Your cousin, the other King! You are a Mind,—
They, Body: too much of mere legs-and-arms
Obstructs the mind so! Match these with their like—
Match mind with mind!

    Berth.   And where's your mind to match?
They show me legs-and-arms to cope withal!
I'd subjugate this city—where's its mind?

                       [*The* Courtiers *enter slowly.*

    Mel.   Got out of sight when you came troops and all!
And in its stead, here greets you flesh-and-blood—
A smug œconomy of both, this first!

                 [*As* CLUGNET *bows obsequiously.*
Well done, gout, all considered!—I may go?

    Berth.   Help me receive them!

    Mel.   Oh, they just will say
What yesterday at Aix their fellows said,—
At Treves, the day before!—Sir Prince, my friend,
Why do you let your life slip thus?—Mean time,
I have my little Juliers to achieve—
The understanding this tough Platonist,
Your holy uncle disinters, Amelius—
Lend me a company of horse and foot,

To help me through his tractate—gain my Duchy!
   Berth. And Empire, after that is gained, will be—?
   Mel.   To help me through your uncle's comment,
    Prince!   *[Goes.*
   Berth. Ah? Well! he o'er-refines—the scholar's fault!
How do I let my life slip? Say, this life,
I lead now, differs from the common life
Of other men in mere degree, not kind,
Of joys and griefs,—still there is such degree—
Mere largeness in a life is something, sure,—
Enough to care about and struggle for,
In this world: for this world, the Size of things;
The Sort of things, for that to come, no doubt!
A great is better than a little aim—
And when I wooed Priscilla's rosy mouth
And failed so, under that grey convent-wall,
Was I more happy than I should be now
       [By this time, the Courtiers *are ranged before him.*
If failing of my Empire? Not a whit!
—Here comes the Mind, it once had tasked me sore
To baffle, but for my advantages!
All's best as 'tis—these scholars talk and talk!
                        [Seats himself.
   The Courtiers. Welcome our Prince to Juliers!—to his
    Heritage!
Our dutifullest service proffer we!
   Clug. I, please your Highness, having exercised
The function of Grand Chamberlain at Court,
With much acceptance, as men testify . . .
   Berth. I cannot greatly thank you, gentlemen!
The Pope declares my claim to the Duchy founded
On strictest justice; if you concede it, therefore,
I do not wonder—and the kings my friends
Protesting they will see such claim enforced,
You easily may offer to assist us.
But there's a slight discretionary power
To serve me in the matter, you've had long,
Though late you use it. This is well to say—
But could you not have said it months ago?
I'm not denied my own Duke's truncheon, true—
'Tis flung me—I stoop down, and from the ground
Pick it, with all you placid standers-by—
And now I have it, gems and mire at once.

Grace go with it to my soiled hands, you say!

Gui. (By Paul, the Advocate our doughty friend
Cuts the best figure!)

Gau.   If our ignorance
May have offended, sure our loyalty . . .

Berth. Loyalty? Yours?—Oh—of yourselves you
    speak!
—*I* mean the Duchess all this time, I hope!
And since I have been forced repeat my claims
As if they never had been made before,
As I began, so must I end, it seems.
The formal answer to the grave demand—
What says the lady?

Courtiers [*one to another.*] *1st Court.* Marshal! *2nd
    Court.* Orator!

Gui. A variation of our mistress' way!
Wipe off his boots' dust, Clugnet?—that, he waits!

1st Court. Your place!

2nd Court. Just now it was your own!

Gui.   The devil's!

Berth. [*to* GUIBERT.] Come forward, friend—you with
    the paper, there!
Is Juliers the first city I've obtained?
By this time, I may boast proficiency
In each decorum of the circumstance!
Give it me as she gave it—the petition
(Demand, you style it)—what's required, in brief?
What title's reservation, appanage's
Allowance?—I heard all at Treves, last week!

Gau. [*to* GUIBERT.] "Give it him as she gave it!"

Gui.   And why not?
[*To* BERTHOLD.] The lady crushed your summons thus
    together,
And bade me, with the very greatest scorn
So fair a frame could hold, inform you . . .

Courtiers.   Stop—
Idiot!—

Gui. —Inform you she denied your claim,
Defied yourself! (I tread upon his heel,
The blustering Advocate!)

Berth.   By heaven and earth!
Dare you jest, sir?

Gui.   Did they at Treves, last week?

Berth. [*starting up.*]   Why then, I look much bolder than I
    knew,
And you prove better actors than I thought—
Since, as I live, I took you as you entered
For just so many dearest friends of mine,
Fled from the sinking to the rising power
—The sneaking'st crew, in short, I e'er despised!
Whereas, I am alone here for the moment—
With every soldier left behind at Aix!
Silence? That means the worst—I thought as much!
What follows next then?

    Courtiers.   Gracious Prince—he raves!

    Gui. He asked the truth and why not get the truth?

    Berth. Am I a prisoner? Speak, will somebody?
—But why stand paltering with imbeciles?
Let me see her, or . . .

    Gui.   Her, without her leave,
Shall no one see—she's Duchess yet!

    Courtiers. [*Footsteps without, as they are disputing.*] Good
    chance!
She's here—the Lady Colombe's self!

    Berth.   'Tis well!
[*Aside.*] Array a handful thus against my world?
Not ill done, truly! Were not this a mind
To match one's mind with? Colombe!—Let us wait!
I failed so, under that grey convent-wall!
She comes!

    Gui.   The Duchess! Strangers, range yourselves!
    [*As the* DUCHESS *enters in conversation with*
        VALENCE, BERTHOLD *and the* Courtiers *fall*
        back a little.

    The D. Presagefully it beats, presagefully,
My heart—the right is Berthold's and not mine!

    Val. Grant that he has the right, dare I mistrust
Your power to acquiesce so patiently
As you believe, in such a dream-like change
Of fortune—change abrupt, profound, complete?

    The D. Ah, the first bitterness is over now!
Bitter I may have felt it to confront
The truth, and ascertain those natures' value
I had so counted on—that was a pang—
But I did bear it, and the worst is over:
Let the Prince take them!

T 41

Val.   —And take Juliers too?
—Your People without crosses, wands, and chains—
Only with hearts?

The D.   There I feel guilty, sir!
I cannot give up what I never had:
For these I ruled, not them—these stood between.
Shall I confess, sir? I have heard by stealth
Of Berthold from the first: more news and more;
Closer and closer swam the thunder-cloud,
But I was safely housed with these, I knew!
At times, when to the casement I would turn,
At a bird's passage or a flower trail's play,
I caught the storm's red glimpses on its edge—
Yet I was sure some one of all these friends
Would interpose—I followed the bird's flight,
Or plucked the flower—some one would interpose!

Val. Not one thought on the People—and Cleves there!

The D. So, sadly conscious my real sway was missed,
Its shadow goes without so much regret:
Else could I not again thus calmly bid you,
Answer Prince Berthold!

Val.   Then you acquiesce?

The D. Remember over whom it was I ruled!

Gui. [*stepping forward.*] Prince Berthold, yonder, craves
an audience, Lady!

The D. [*to* VALENCE.] I only have to turn, and I shall face
Prince Berthold! Oh, my very heart is sick!
It is the daughter of a line of Dukes,
This scornful insolent adventurer
Will bid depart from my dead father's halls
I shall not answer him—dispute with him—
But, as he bids, depart! Prevent it, sir!
Sir—but a mere day's respite! Urge for me
—What I shall call to mind I should have urged
When time's gone by—'twill all be mine, you urge!
A day—an hour—that I myself may lay
My rule down! 'Tis too sudden—must not be!
The world's to hear of it! Once done—for ever!
How will it read, sir? How be sung about?
Prevent it!

Berth. [*approaching.*] Your frank indignation, Lady,
Cannot escape me! Overbold I seem—
But somewhat should be pardoned my surprise,

At this reception,—this defiance, rather.
And if, for their and your sakes, I rejoice
Your virtues could inspire a trusty few
To make such gallant stand in your behalf,
I cannot but be sorry, for my own,
Your friends should force me to retrace my steps,
Since I no longer am permitted speak
After the pleasant peaceful course prescribed
No less by courtesy than relationship
Which, if you once forgot, I still remember.
But never must attack pass unrepelled.
Suffer, that through you, I demand of these,
Who controverts my claim to Juliers?

  The D.   —Me,
You say, you do not speak to—

  Berth.   Of your subjects
I ask, then: whom do you accredit? Where
Stand those should answer?

  Val. [*advancing.*]   The Lady is alone!

  Berth. Alone, and thus? So weak and yet so bold?

  Val. I said she was alone—

  Berth.   —And weak, I said.

  Val. When is man strong until he feels alone?
It was some lonely strength at first, be sure,
Created organs, such as those you seek,
By which to give its varied purpose shape—
And, naming the selected ministrants,
Took sword, and shield, and sceptre,—each, a man!
That strength performed its work and passed its way:
You see our Lady: there, the old shapes stand!
—A Marshal, Chamberlain, and Chancellor—
" Be helped their way, into their death put life
" And find advantage! "—so you counsel us:
But let strength feel alone, seek help itself,—
And, as the inland-hatched sea-creature hunts
The sea's breast out,—as, littered 'mid the waves,
The desert-brute makes for the desert's joy,
So turns our lady to her true resource,
Passing o'er hollow fictions, worn-out types,
—So, I am first her instinct fastens on!
And prompt I say, so clear as heart can speak,
The people will not have you; nor shall have!
It is not merely I shall go bring Cleves

And fight you to the last,—though that does much,
And men and children,—ay, and women too,
Fighting for home, are rather to be feared
Than mercenaries fighting for their pay—
But, say you beat us, since such things have been,
And, where this Juliers laughed, you set your foot
Upon a streaming bloody plash—what then?
Stand you the more our Lord that there you stand?
Lord it o'er troops whose force you concentrate,
A pillared flame whereto all ardours tend—
Lord it 'mid priests whose schemes you amplify,
A cloud of smoke 'neath which all shadows brood—
But never, in this gentle spot of earth,
Can you become our Colombe, our play-queen,
For whom, to furnish lilies for her hair,
We'd pour our veins forth to enrich the soil!
—Our conqueror? Yes!—Our despot? Yes!—Our Duke?
Know yourself, know us!

    Berth. [*who has been in thought.*] Know your lady, also!
[*Very deferentially.*]—To whom I needs must exculpate myself
From having made a rash demand, at least.
Wherefore to you, sir, who appear to be
Her chief adviser, I submit my claims,   [*Giving papers.*
But, this step taken, take no further step,
Until the Duchess shall pronounce their worth.
Here be our meeting-place; at night, its time:
Till when I humbly take the Lady's leave!

    [*He withdraws. As the* DUCHESS *turns to* VALENCE, *the*
      Courtiers *interchange glances and come forward a little.*

    1st Court. So, this was their device!

    2nd Court. No bad device!

    3rd Court. You'd say they love each other, Guibert's friend
From Cleves, and she, the Duchess!

    4th Court.   —And moreover,
That all Prince Berthold comes for, is to help
Their loves!

    5th Court. Pray, Guibert, what is next to do?

    Gui. [*advancing.*] I laid my office at the Duchess' foot—

    Others. And I—and I—and I !

    The D.   I took them, sirs!

    Gui. [*Apart to* VALENCE.] And now, sir, I am simple
      knight again—
Guibert, of the great ancient house, as yet

That never bore affront: whate'er your birth,—
As things stand now, I recognise yourself
(If you'll accept experience of some date)
As like to be the leading man o' the time,
Therefore as much above me now, as I
Seemed above you this morning. Then, I offered
To fight you: will you be as generous
And now fight me?

 Val.   Ask when my life is mine!

 Gui.   ('Tis hers now!)

 Clug. [*Apart to* VALANCE, *as Guibert turns from him.*] You,
  sir, have insulted me
Grossly,—will grant me, too, the selfsame favour
You've granted him, just now, I make no question?

 Val.   I promise you, as him, sir!

 Clug.   Do you so?
Handsomely said! I hold you to it, sir!
You'll get me reinstated in my office
As you will Guibert!

 The D.   I would be alone!
[*They begin to retire slowly : as* VALENCE *is about to follow—*
Alone, sir—only with my heart,—you stay!

 Gau. You hear that? Ah, light breaks upon me! Cleves—
It was at Cleves some man harangued us all—
With great effect,—so those who listened said,
My thoughts being busy elsewhere: was this he?
Guibert,—your strange, disinterested man!
Your uncorrupted, if uncourtly friend!
The modest worth you mean to patronise!
He cares about no Duchesses, not he—
His sole contest is with the wrongs of Cleves!
What, Guibert? What, it breaks on you at last?

 Gui. Would this hall's floor were a mine's roof—I'd back
And in her very face . . .

 Gau.   Apply the match
That fired the train,—and where would you be, pray?

 Gui. With him!

 Gau.   Stand, rather, safe outside with me!
The mine's charged—shall I furnish you the match
And place you properly?—To the ante-chamber!

 Gui. Can you?

 Gau.   Try me!—Your friend's in fortune!

 Gui.   Quick—

To the ante-chamber!—He is pale with bliss!

Gau. No wonder!   Mark her eyes!

Gui.   To the ante-chamber!

[*The* Courtiers *retire.*

The D. Sir, could you know all you have done for me
You were content!   You spoke, and I am saved!

Val. Be not too sanguine, Lady!   Ere you dream,
That transient flush of generosity
Fades off, perchance!   The man, beside, is gone,—
Whom we might bend; but see the papers here—
Inalterably his requirement stays,
And cold hard words have we to deal with now.
In that large eye there seemed a latent pride,
To self-denial not incompetent,
But very like to hold itself dispensed
From such a grace—however, let us hope!
He is a noble spirit in noble form!
I wish he less had bent that brow to smile
As with the fancy how he could subject
Himself upon occasion to—himself!
From rudeness, violence, you rest secure;
But do not think your Duchy rescued yet!

The D. You,—who have opened a new world to me,
Will never take the faded language up
Of that I leave?   My Duchy—keeping it,
Or losing it—is that my sole world now?

Val. Ill have I spoken if you thence despise
Juliers; although the lowest, on true grounds,
Be worth more than the highest rule, on false:
Aspire to rule, on the true grounds!

The D.   Nay, hear—
False, I will never—rash, I would not be!
This is indeed my Birthday—soul and body,
Its hours have done on me the work of years.
You hold the Requisition: ponder it!
If I have right—my duty's plain: if He—
Say so—nor ever change a tone of voice!
At night you meet the Prince—meet me at eve;
Till when, farewell!   This discomposes you?
Believe in your own nature, and its force
Of renovating mine.   I take my stand
Only as under me the earth is firm—
So, prove the first step stable, all will be!

That first, I choose—[*laying her hand on his.*]—the next to
take, choose you! [*She withdraws.*
Val. [*after a pause.*] What drew down this on me! On
me—dead once—
She thus bids live,—since all I hitherto
Thought dead in me, youth's ardours and emprize,
Burst into life before her, as she bids
Who needs them!—Whither will this reach, where end?
Her hand's print burns on mine . . . Yet she's above—
So very far above me! All's too plain—
I served her when the others sank away,
And she rewards me as such souls reward—
The changed voice, the suffusion of the cheek,
The eye's acceptance, the expressive hand—
—Reward, that's little, in her generous thought,
Though all to me . . .
               I cannot so disclaim
Heaven's gift, nor call it other than it is!
She loves me!
[*Looking at the* Prince's *papers.*]—Which love, these, per-
chance, forbid!
Can I decide against myself—pronounce
She is the Duchess and no mate for me?
—Cleves, help me! Teach me,—every haggard face,—
To sorrow and endure! I will do right
Whatever be the issue—help me, Cleves!

ACT IV

Evening. SCENE.—*An Ante-chamber.*

Enter the Courtiers.

Mau. Now then, that we may speak—how spring this
mine?
Gau. Is Guibert ready for its match? He cools!
Not so friend Valence with the Duchess there!
" Stay, Valence—are not you my better self? "
And her cheek mantled—
    Gui.   Well, she loves him, sir—
And more,—since you will have it I grow cool,—
She's right: he's worth it.

Gau. For his deeds to-day?
Say so!
Gui. What should I say beside?
Gau. Not this—
For friendship's sake leave this for me to say—
That we're the dupes of an egregious cheat!
This plain, unpractised suitor, who found way
To the Duchess thro' the merest die's turn-up—
A year ago, had seen her and been seen,
Loved and been loved—
Gui. Impossible!
Gau. —Nor say,
How sly and exquisite a trick, moreover,
Was this which—taking not their stand on facts
Boldly, for that had been endurable,
But, worming in their way by craft, they choose
Resort to, rather,—and which you and we,
Sheep-like, assist them in the playing off!
The Duchess thus parades him as preferred,
Not on the honest ground of preference,
Seeing first, liking more, and there an end—
But as we all had started equally,
And at the close of a fair race he proved
The only valiant, sage, and loyal man.
And she, too, with the pretty fits and starts,—
The careless, winning, candid ignorance
Of what the Prince might challenge or forego—
She had a hero in reserve! What risk
Ran she? This deferential easy Prince
Who brings his claims for her to ratify
—He's just her puppet for the nonce! You'll see,—
Valence pronounces, as is equitable,
Against him: off goes the confederate:
As equitably, Valence takes her hand!
The Chancellor. You run too fast—her hand, no subject
takes!
Do not our Archives hold her father's Will?
That will provides against such accident,
And gives next heir, Prince Berthold, the reversion
Of Juliers, which she forfeits, wedding so.
Gau. I know that, well as you,—but does the Prince?
Knows Berthold, think you, that this plan, he helps,
For Valence's ennoblement,—would end,

If crowned with the success which seems its due,
In making him the very thing he plays,
The actual Duke of Juliers?   All agree
That Colombe's title waived or set aside,
He is next heir.

    The Chan.   Incontrovertibly!

    Gau. Guibert, your match, now, to the train!

    Gui.   Enough!
I'm with you—selfishness is best again!
I thought of turning honest—what a dream!
Let's wake now!

    Gau.   Selfish, friend, you never were—
'Twas but a series of revenges taken
On your unselfishness for prospering ill.
But now that you're grown wiser, what's our course?

    Gui. —Wait, I suppose, till Valence weds our Lady,
And then, if we must needs revenge ourselves,
Apprise the Prince—

    Gau. —The Prince, ere then dismissed
With thanks for playing his mock part so well?
Tell the Prince now, sir!   Ay, this very night—
Ere he accepts his dole and goes his way,
Explain how such a marriage makes him Duke,
Then trust his gratitude for the surprise!

    Gui. —Our Lady wedding Valence all the same
As if the penalty were undisclosed!
Good!   If she loves, she'll not disown her love,
Throw Valence up—I wonder you see that!

    Gau. The shame of it—the suddenness and shame!
Within her, the inclining heart—without,
A terrible array of witnesses—
With Valence by, to keep her to her word,
And Berthold's indignation or disgust—
We'll try it!—Not that we can venture much:
Her confidence we've lost for ever—Berthold's
Is all to gain!

    Gui.   To-night, then, venture we!
Yet—if lost confidence might be renewed?

    Gau. Never in noble natures!   With the base ones,—
Twist off the crab's claw, wait a smarting-while,
And something grows and grows and gets to be
A mimic of the lost joint, just so like
As keeps in mind it never, never will

Replace its predecessor! Crabs do that
But lop the Lion's foot—and—
    Gui.   To the Prince!
    Gau. [*Aside.*] And come what will to the lion's foot, I pay you,
My cat's-paw, as I long have yearned to pay!
[*Aloud.*] Footsteps . . Himself! 'Tis Valence breaks on us ι
Exulting that their scheme succeeds!—We'll hence—
And perfect ours! Consult the Archives, first—
Then, fortified with knowledge, seek the Hall!
    Clug. [*to* GAUCELME *as they retire.*] You have not smiled so
    since your father died!

As they retire, enter VALENCE *with papers.*

    Val. So must it be! I have examined these
With scarce a palpitating heart—so calm,
Keeping her image almost wholly off,
Setting upon myself determined watch,
Repelling to the uttermost his claims,
And the result is . . . all men would pronounce
And not I, only, the result to be—
Berthold is Heir; she has no shade of right
To the distinction which divided us,
But, suffered to rule first I know not why,
Her rule connived at by those Kings and Popes,
To serve some devil's purpose,—now 'tis gained,
Whate'er it was, the rule expires as well.
—Valence, this rupture . . selfish can it be?
Eject it from your heart, her home!—It stays '
Ah, the brave world that opens on us both!
. . . Do my poor townsmen so esteem it? Cleves,—
I need not your pale faces! This, reward
For service done to you? Too horrible!
I never served you—'twas myself I served!
Nay—served not—rather saved from punishment
Which, had I failed you then, would plague me now!
My life continues yours, and your life, mine—
But if, to take God's gift, I swerve no step—
Cleves!—if I breathe no prayer for it—if she,
                          [*Footsteps without.*
Colombe, that comes now, freely gives herself—
Will Cleves require, that, turning thus to her,
I . . .

Enter PRINCE BERTHOLD.

—Pardcn, sir,—I did not look for you
Till night, in the Hall; nor have as yet declared
My judgment to the Lady!

Berth.   So I hoped.

Val. And yet I scarcely know why that should check
The frank disclosure of it first to you—
What her right seems, and what, in consequence,
She will decide on—

Berth.   That I need not ask.

Val. You need not: I have proved the Lady's mind—
And, justice being to do, dare act for her.

Berth. Doubtless she has a very noble mind!

Val. Oh, never fear but she'll in each conjuncture
Bear herself bravely; she no whit depends
On circumstance; as she adorns a throne,
She had adorned . . .

Berth.   . . . A cottage—in what book
Have I read that, of every queen that lived?
A throne? You have not been instructed, sure,
To forestall my request?

Val.   'Tis granted, sir—
My heart instructs me. I have scrutinized
Your claims . . .

Berth. Ah—claims, you mean, at first preferred!
I come, before the hour appointed me,
To pray you let those claims at present rest—
In favour of a new and stronger one.

Val. You shall not need a stronger: on the part
Of the lady, all you offer I accept,
Since one clear right suffices: yours is clear.
Propose!

Berth. I offer her my hand.

Val.   Your hand?

Berth. A Duke's, yourself say: and, at no far time,
Something here whispers me—the Emperor's.
The Lady's mind is noble; which induced
This seizure of occasion ere my claims
Were—settled, let us amicably say!

Val. Your hand!

Berth.   (He will fall down and kiss it next!)
Sir, this astonishment's too flattering—

Nor must you hold your mistress' worth so cheap!
Enhance it, rather,—urge that blood is blood—
The daughter of the Burgraves, Landgraves, Markgraves,
Remains their daughter; I shall scarce gainsay!
Elsewhere or here, the Lady needs must rule:
Like the Imperial crown's great chrysoprase,
They talk of—somewhat out of keeping there,
And yet no jewel for a meaner cap!

    Val. You wed the Duchess?
    Berth.   Cry you mercy, friend!
Will the match influence many fortunes here?
A natural solicitude enough!
Be certain, no bad chance it proves for you!
However high you take your present stand,
There's prospect of a higher still remove—
For Juliers will not be my resting-place,
And, when I have to choose a substitute
To rule the little burgh, I'll think of you.
You need not give your mates a character!
And yet I doubt your fitness to supplant
The grey smooth Chamberlain—he'd hesitate
A doubt his lady could demean herself
So low as to accept me. Courage, sir!
I like your method better—feeling's play
Is franker much, and flatters me beside.

    Val. I am to say, you love her?
    Berth.   Say that too!
Love has no great concernment, thinks the world,
With a Duke's marriage—How go precedents
In Juliers' story—how use Juliers' Dukes?
I see you have them here in goodly row;
(Yon must be Luitpold,—ay, a stalwart sire!)
—Say, I have been arrested suddenly
In my ambition's course, its rocky course,
By this sweet flower—I fain would gather it
And then proceed—so say and speedily—
—(Nor stand there like Duke Luitpold's brazen self!)
Enough, sir: you possess my mind, I think.
This is my claim, the others being withdrawn,
And to this, be it that, in the Hall to-night,
Your Lady's answer comes; till when, farewell! [*He retires.*
    Val. [*after a pause.*] The heavens and earth stay as they
    were—my heart

Beats as it beat—the truth remains the truth!
What falls away, then, if not faith in her?
Was it my faith, that she could estimate
Love's value,—and, such faith still guiding me,
Dare I now test her?—or grew faith so strong
Solely because no power of test was mine?

Enter the DUCHESS.

   The. D.   My fate, sir! Ah, you turn away—all's over!
But you are sorry for me—be not so!
What I might have become, and never was,
Regret with me; what I have merely been,
Rejoice I am no longer; what I seem
Beginning now, in my new state, to be,
Hope that I am,—for, once my rights proved void,
This heavy roof seems easy to exchange
For the blue sky outside—my lot henceforth!
   Val.   And what a lot is Berthold's!
   The D.   How of him?
   Val.   He gathers earth's whole good into his arms,
Standing, as man, now, stately, strong and wise—
Marching to fortune, not surprised by her:
One great aim, like a guiding-star, above—
Which tasks strength, wisdom, stateliness, to lift
His manhood to the height that takes the prize;
A prize not near—lest overlooking earth
He rashly spring to seize it—nor remote,
So that he rests upon his path content:
But day by day, while shimmering grows shine,
And the faint circlet prophesies the orb,
He sees so much as, just evolving these,
The stateliness, the wisdom and the strength,
To due completion, will suffice this life,
And lead him at his grandest to the grave.
After this star, out of a night he springs;
A beggar's cradle for the throne of thrones
He quits, so, mounting, feels each step he mounts,
Nor, as from each to each exultingly
He passes, overleaps one grade of joy.
This, for his own good:—with the world, each gift
Of God and man,—Reality, Tradition,
Fancy and Fact—so well environ him,
That as a mystic panoply they serve—

Of force, untenanted, to awe mankind,
And work his purpose out with half the world,
While he, their master, dexterously slipt
From such encumbrance, is meantime employed
With his own prowess on the other half.
Thus shall he prosper, every day's success
Adding, to what is He, a solid strength—
An aëry might to what encircles him,
Till at the last, so life's routine lends help,
That as the Emperor only breathes and moves,
His shadow shall be watched, his step or stalk
Become a comfort or a portent; how
He trails his ermine take significance,—
Till even his power shall cease to be most power,
And men shall dread his weakness more, nor dare
Peril their earth its bravest, first and best,
Its typified invincibility.
So shall he go on, greatening, till he ends
The man of men, the spirit of all flesh,
The fiery centre of an earthy world!
    The D. Some such a fortune I had dreamed should rise
Out of my own—that is, above my power
Seemed other, greater potencies to stretch—
    Val. For you?
    The D.   It was not I moved there, I think:
But one I could,—though constantly beside,
And aye approaching,—still keep distant from,
And so adore. 'Twas a man moved there!
    Val.   Who?
    The D. I felt the spirit, never saw the face!
    Val. See it! 'Tis Berthold's! He enables you
To realise your vision!
    The D.   Berthold?
    Val.   Duke—
Emperor to be: he proffers you his hand.
    The D. Generous and princely!
    Val.   He is all of this.
    The D. Thanks, Berthold, for my father's sake — no
    hand
Degrades me!
    Val.   You accept the proffered hand?
    The D. That he should love me!
    Val.   "Loved" I did not say!

Had that been—love might so incline the Prince
To the world's good, the world that's at his foot,—
I do not know, this moment, I should dare
Desire that you refused the world—and Cleves—
The sacrifice he asks!

   The D.   Not love me, sir?

   Val.   He scarce affirmed it.

   The D.   May not deeds affirm?

   Val.   What does he? . . . Yes—yes—very much he does!
All the shame saved, he thinks, and sorrow saved—
Immitigable sorrow, so he thinks,—
Sorrow that's deeper than we dream, perchance!

   The D.   Is not this love?

   Val.   So very much he does!
For look, you can descend now gracefully—
All doubts are banished, that the world might have,
Or worst, the doubts yourself, in after-time,
May call up of your heart's sincereness now:
To such, reply, " I could have kept my rule—
" Increased it to the utmost of my dreams—
" Yet I abjured it! " This, he does for you:
It is munificently much!

   The D.   Still " much! "
But why is it not love, sir? Answer me?

   Val.   Because not one of Berthold's words and looks
Had gone with love's presentment of a flower
To the beloved: because bold confidence,
Open superiority, free pride—
Love owns not, yet were all that Berthold owned:
Because where reason, even, finds no flaw,
Unerringly a lover's instinct may.

   The D.   You reason, then, and doubt?

   Val.   I love, and know.

   The D.   You love?—How strange! I never cast a thought
On that! Just see our selfishness—you seemed
So much my own . . . I had no ground—and yet,
I never dreamed another might divide
My power with you, much less exceed it!

   Val.   Lady,
I am yours wholly!

   The D.   Oh, no, no, not mine!
'Tis not the same now, never more can be!
—Your first love, doubtless! Well, what's gone from me?

What have I lost in you?
   Val.   My heart replies—
No loss there! . . . So to Berthold back again!
This offer of his hand, he bids me make—
Its obvious magnitude is well to weigh!
   The D. She's . . . yes, she must be very fair for you!
   Val. I am a simple Advocate of Cleves.
   The D. You! With the heart and brain that so helped me,
I fancied them exclusively my own,
Yet find are subject to a stronger sway!
She must be . . . tell me, is she very fair?
   Val. Most fair, beyond conception or belief!
   The D. Black eyes?—no matter! Colombe, the world leads
Its life without you, whom your friends professed
The only woman—see how true they spoke!
One lived this while, who never saw your face,
Nor heard your voice—unless. . . . Is she from Cleves?
   Val. Cleves knows her well!
   The D.   Ah—just a fancy, now!
When you poured forth the wrongs of Cleves,—I said,
—Thought, that is, afterward . . .
   Val.   You thought of me?
   The D. Of what else? Only such great cause, I thought,
For such effect—see what true love can do!
Cleves is his love!—I almost fear to ask
. . . Nor will not! This is idling—to our work!
Admit before the Prince, without reserve,
My claims misgrounded; then may follow better
. . . When you poured out Cleves' wrongs impetuously,
Was she in your mind?
   Val.   All done was done for her—
—To humble me!
   The D.   She will be proud at least!
   Val. She?
   The D.   When you tell her!
   Val.   That will never be!
   The D. How—are there sweeter things you hope to tell?
No, sir! You counselled me,—I counsel you
In the one point I—any woman—can!
Your worth, the first thing; let her own come next—
Say what you did through her, and she through you—·
The praises of her beauty afterward!
Will you?

Val.   I dare not!

The D.   Dare not?

Val.   She I love
Suspects not such a love in me.

The D.   You jest!

Val.   The lady is above me and away!
Not only the brave form, and the bright mind,
And the great heart, combine to press me low—
But all the world calls rank divides us.

The D.   Rank?
Now grant me patience!   Here's a man declares
Oracularly in another's case—
Sees the true value and the false, for them—
Nay, bids them see it, and they straight do see!
You called my court's love worthless—so it turned:
I threw away as dross my heap of wealth,
And here you stickle for a piece or two!
First—has she seen you?

Val.   Yes!

The D.   She loves you, then.

Val.   One flash of hope burst—then succeeded night—
And all's at darkest now.   Impossible!

The D.   We'll try: you are—so to speak—my subject yet?

Val.   As ever—to the death!

The D.   Obey me, then!

Val.   I must!

The D.   Approach her, and . . . No!   First of all
Get more assurance; " my instructress," say,
" Was great, descended from a line of kings,
" And even fair "—(wait why I say this folly)—
" She said, of all men, none for eloquence,
" Courage, and (what cast even these to shade)
" The heart they sprung from,—none deserved like him
" Who saved her at her need—if she said this,
" What should not one I love, say? "

Val.   Heaven—this hope—
Oh, lady, you are filling me with fire!

The D.   Say this!—nor think I bid you cast aside
One touch of all that awe and reverence!
Nay—make her proud for once to heart's content
That all this wealth of heart and soul's her own!
Think you are all of this,—and, thinking it,
. . . (Obey!)

Val.   I cannot choose!

The D.   Then, kneel to her!

[VALENCE *sinks on his knee.*

I dream!

    Val.   Have mercy! Yours, unto the death,—
I have obeyed. Despise, and let me die.

    The D.   Alas, sir, is it to be ever thus?
Even with you as with the world? I know
This morning's service was no vulgar deed
Whose motive, once it dares avow itself,
Explains all done and infinitely more,
So takes the shelter of a nobler cause,
Your service named its true source,—loyalty!
The rest's unsaid again. The Duchess bids you,
Rise, sir! The Prince's words were in debate.

    Val. [*rising.*] Rise! Truth, as ever, Lady, comes from
    you!
I should rise—I that spoke for Cleves, can speak
For Man—yet tremble now, that stood firm then!
I laughed—for 'twas past tears—that Cleves should starve
With all hearts beating loud the infamy,
And no tongue daring trust as much to air!
Yet here, where all hearts speak, shall I be mute?
Oh lady, for your own sake look on me!
On all I am, and have, and do—heart, brain,
Body and soul,—this Valence and his gifts!
I was proud once—I saw you—and they sank,
So that each magnified a thousand times
Were nothing to you—but such nothingness
Would a crown gild it, or a sceptre prop,
A treasure speed, a laurel-wreath enhance?
What is my own desert? But should your love
Have . . . there's no language helps here . . . singled me,—
Then—Oh, that wild word "then!"—be just to love,
In generosity its attribute!
Love, since you pleased to love! All's cleared—a stage
For trial of the question kept so long
For you—Is Love or Vanity the best?
You, solve it for the world's sake—you, speak first
What all will shout one day—you, vindicate
Our earth and be its angel! All is said.
Lady, I offer nothing—I am yours,
But for the cause' sake, look on me and him

And speak!
 The D. I have received the Prince's message:
Say, I prepare my answer!
 Val.   Take me, Cleves!
            [He withdraws.
 The. D. Mournful—that nothing's what it calls itself!
Devotion, zeal, faith, loyalty—mere love!
And, love in question, what may Berthold's be?
I did ill to mistrust the world so soon—
Already was this Berthold at my side!
The valley-level has its hawks, no doubt:
May not the rock-top have its eagles, too?
Yet Valence . . . let me see his Rival then!

ACT V

Night. SCENE.—*The Hall.*

Enter BERTHOLD *and* MELCHIOR.

 Mel. And here you wait the matter's issue?
 Berth.   Here.
 Mel. I don't regret I shut Amelius, then!
But tell me, on this grand disclosure,—how
Behaved our spokesman with the forehead?
 Berth.   Oh,
Turned out no better than the foreheadless—
Was dazzled not so very soon—that's all!
For my part, this is scarce the hasty, showy,
Chivalrous measure you give me credit of!
Perhaps I had the fancy,—but 'tis gone—
—Let her commence the unfriended innocent,
And carry wrongs about from court to court?
No, truly! The least shake of Fortune's sand,
—My uncle-Pope chokes in a coughing-fit,
King Philip takes a fancy to blue eyes,—
And wondrously her claims would brighten up!
Forth comes a new gloss on the ancient law,
O'er-looked provisoes, past o'er premises,
Follow in plenty—No—'tis the safer step.
The hour beneath the convent-wall is lost—
Juliers and she, once mine, are ever mine.

Mel. Which is to say, you, losing heart already,
Elude the adventure!
  Berth.   Not so—or, if so—
Why not confess at once, that I advise
None of our kingly craft and guild just now
To lay, one moment, down their privilege
With the notion they can any time at pleasure
Retake it—that may turn out hazardous!
We seem, in Europe, pretty well at end
O' the night, with our great masque: those favoured few
Who keep the chamber's top, and honour's chance
Of the early evening, may retain their place
And figure as they list till out of breath.
But it is growing late; and I observe
A dim grim kind of tipstaves at the doorway
Not only bar new-comers entering now,
But caution those who left, for any cause,
And would return, that morning draws too near;
The ball must die off, shut itself up. We—
I think, may dance lights out and sunshine in,
And sleep off headache on our frippery—
But friend the other, who cunningly stole out,
And, after breathing the fresh air outside,
Means to re-enter with a new costume,
Will be advised go back to bed, I fear.
I stick to privilege, on second thoughts!
  Mel. Yes—you evade the adventure!—And, beside.
Give yourself out for colder than you are.
—King Philip, only, notes the lady's eyes?
Don't they come in for somewhat of the motive
With you too?
  Berth.   Yes—no: I am past that now!
Gone 'tis—I cannot shut my eyes to fact.
Of course, I might by forethought and contrivance
Reason myself into a rapture. Gone!
And something better's come instead, no doubt.
  Mel. So be it! Yet, all the same, proceed my way,
Though to our end; so shall you prosper best.
The lady,—to be won for selfish ends,—
Will be won easier my unselfish . . . call it,
Romantic way.
  Berth. Won easier?
  Mel.   Will not she?

Berth. There I profess humility without bound!
Ill cannot speed—not I—the Emperor!
  Mel. And I should think the Emperor best waived,
From your description of her mood and way!
You could look, if it pleased you, into hearts;
But are too indolent and fond of watching
Your own—you know that, for you study it!
  Berth. Had you but seen the orator her friend,
So bold and voluble an hour before,
Abashed to earth at aspect of the change!
Make her an Empress? Ah, that changed the case!
. . . Oh, I read hearts! And for my own behoof,
I court her with my true worth—see the event!
I learned my final lesson on that head
When years ago,—my first and last essay!
Before my uncle could obtain the ear
Of his superior, help me from the dirt—
Priscilla left me for a Brabant Duke
Whose cheek was like the topaz on his thumb.
I am past illusion on that score.
  Mel.   Here comes
The lady—
  Berth. —And there you go! But do not! Give me
Another chance to please you. Hear me plead!
  Mel. You'll keep, then, to the lover, to the man?

Enter the DUCHESS—*followed by* ADOLF *and* SABAYNE, *and,
        after an interval, by the* Courtiers.

  Berth. Good auspice to our meeting!
  The D.   May it prove!
—And you, sir, will be Emperor one day?
  Berth. (Ay—that's the point!) I may be Emperor.
  The D. 'Tis not for my sake only, I am proud
Of this you offer: I am prouder far
That from the highest state should duly spring
The highest, since most generous, of deeds.
  Berth. (Generous—still that!) You underrate yourself.
You are, what I, to be complete, must have—
Find now, and may not find, another time.
While I career on all the world for stage,
There needs at home my representative—
  The D. —Such, rather, would some warrior-woman be—
One dowered with lands and gold, or rich in friends—

One like yourself!

   Berth.   Lady, I am myself,
And have all these: I want what's not myself,
Nor has all these.   Why give one hand two swords?
Here's one already: be a friend's next gift
A silk glove, if you will—I have a sword!

   The D. You love me then?

   Berth.   Your lineage I revere—
Honour your virtue, in your truth believe,
Do homage to your intellect, and bow
Before your peerless beauty.

   The D.   But, for love—

   Berth. A further love I do not understand.
Our best course is to say these hideous truths,
And see them, once said, grow endurable.
Like waters shuddering from their central bed,
Black with the midnight bowels of the earth,
That, once up-spouted by an earthquake's throe,
A portent and a terror—soon subside,
Freshen apace, take gold and rainbow hues
In sunshine, sleep in shadow,—and, at last,
Grow common to the earth as hills or trees—
Accepted by all things they came to scare.

   The D. You cannot love, then?

   Berth.   —Charlemagne, perhaps!
Are you not over-curious in love-lore?

   The D. I have become so, very recently.
It seems, then, I shall best deserve esteem,
Respect, and all your candour promises,
By putting on a calculating mood—
Asking the terms of my becoming yours?

   Berth. Let me not do myself injustice, neither!
Because I will not condescend to fictions
That promise what my soul can ne'er acquit,
It does not follow that my guarded phrase
May not include far more of what you seek,
Than wide professions of less scrupulous men.
You will be Empress, once for all—with me
The Pope disputes supremacy—you stand
And none gainsays, the Earth's first woman!

   The D.   That—
Or simple Lady of Ravestein again?

   Berth. The matter's not in my arbitrement!

Now I have made my claims—which I regret—
Cede one, cede all!

 The D.   This claim then, you enforce?
 Berth.   The world looks on.
 The D.   And when must I decide?
 Berth.   " When," Lady? Have I said thus much so
  promptly
For nothing? Poured out, with such pains, at once
What I might else have suffered to ooze forth
Droplet by droplet in a life-time long,
For aught less than as prompt an answer, too?
All's fairly told now—who can teach you more?
 The D.   I do not see him!
 Berth.   I shall ne'er deceive!
This offer has been made befittingly
Would time allow the better setting forth
The good of it, with what is not so good,
Advantage, and disparagement as well—
But as it is, the sum of both must serve.
I am already weary of this place—
My thoughts are next stage on to Rome. Decide!
The Empire—or,—not even Juliers now!
Hail to the Empress—farewell to the Duchess!

  [*The* Courtiers, *who have been drawing nearer and nearer,*
   interpose.

 Courtiers. . . . " Farewell," Prince? when we break in at
  our risk—
 Clug. (Almost upon Court-licence trespassing)—
 Courtiers.—To point out how your claims are valid yet!
You know not, by the Duke her Father's will,
The lady, if she weds beneath her rank,
Forfeits her Duchy in the next heir's favour—
So 'tis expressly stipulate. And if
It can be shown 'tis her intent to wed
A subject, then yourself, next heir, by right
Succeed to Juliers.
 Berth.   What insanity? . . .
 Gui.   Sir, there's one Valence—the pale fiery man
You saw and heard, this morning—thought, no doubt,
Was of considerable standing here—
I put it to your penetration, Prince,
If aught save love, the truest love for her,
Had made him serve the lady as he did!

He's simply a poor advocate of Cleves
—Creeps here with difficulty, finds a place
With danger, gets in by a miracle,
And for the first time meets the Lady's face—
So runs the story—is that credible?
For, first—no sooner in, than he's apprised
Fortunes have changed; you are all-powerful here,
The Lady as powerless: he stands fast by her!
    The D. [*Aside.*] (And do such deeds spring up from love
      alone?)
    Gui. But here occurs the question, does the Lady
Love him again? I say, How else can she?
Can she forget how he stood singly forth
In her defence, dared outrage all of us,
Insult yourself—for what save love's reward?
    The D. (And is love then the sole reward of love?)
    Gui. But, love him as she may and must—you ask,
Means she to wed him? "Yes," both natures answer!
Both, in their pride, point out the sole result—
Nought less would he accept nor she propose!
For each conjecture was she great enough—
—Will be, for this!
    Clug.   Though, now that this is known,
Policy, doubtless, urges she deny . . .
    The D.— What, sir, and wherefore?— since I am not
      sure
That all is any other than you say?
You take this Valence, hold him close to me,
Him with his actions: can I choose but look?
I am not sure, love trulier shows itself
Than in this man, you hate and would degrade,
Yet, with your worst abatement, show me thus:
Nor am I—(thus made look within myself,
Ere I had dared,)—now that the look is dared—
Sure that I do not love him!
    Gui.   Hear you, Prince?
    Berth. And what, sirs, please you, may this prattle
      mean?
—Unless to prove with what alacrity
You give your Lady's secrets to the world—
—How much indebted, for discovering
That quality, you make me, will be found
When next a keeper for my own's to seek!

Courtiers. " Our Lady? "
Berth.   —She assuredly remains!
   The D.   Ah, Prince—and you too can be generous?
You could renounce your power, if this were so,
And let me, as these phrase it, wed my love
Yet keep my Duchy?   You perhaps exceed
Him, even, in disinterestedness!
   Berth.   How, Lady, should all this affect my purpose?
Your will and choice are still as ever, free!
Say, you have known a worthier than myself
In mind and heart, of happier form and face;
Others must have their birthright!   I have gifts,
To balance theirs, not blot them out of sight!
Against a hundred other qualities,
I lay the prize I offer.   I am nothing—
Wed you the Empire?
      The D.   And my heart away?
   Berth.   When have I made pretension to your heart?
I give none.   I shall keep your honour safe—
With mine I trust you, as the sculptor trusts
Yon marble woman with the marble rose,
Loose on her hand, she never will let fall,
In graceful, slight, silent security.
You will be proud of my world-wide career,
And I content in you the fair and good.
What were the use of planting a few seeds,
The thankless climate never would mature—
Affections all repelled by circumstance?
Enough: to these no credit I attach,—
To what you own, find nothing to object.
Write simply on my Requisition's face
What shall content my friends—that you admit,
As Colombe of Ravestein, the claims therein,
Or never need admit them, as my wife—
And either way, all's ended.
      The D.   Let all end!
   Berth.   The Requisition!
   Courtiers.   —Valence holds, of course!
   Berth.   Desire his presence!   [ADOLF *goes out.*
   Courtiers. [*to each other.*]   Out it all comes yet!
He'll have his word against the bargain still!
He's not the man to tamely acquiesce!
One passionate appeal—upbraiding even,

Might turn the tide again!   Despair not yet!
                                        [*They retire a little.*
  Berth. [*to* MELCHIOR.]   The Empire has its old success, my
   friend!
  Mel.   You've had your way: before the spokesman
   comes,
Let me, but this once, work a problem out,
And ever more be dumb!   The Empire wins?
To better purpose I have read my books!

     Enter VALENCE.

  Mel. [*to the* Courtiers.]   Apart, my masters!
[*To* VALENCE.]   Sir, one word with you!
I am a poor dependent of the Prince's—
Pitched on to speak, as of slight consequence:
You are no higher, I find—in other words,
We two, as probably the wisest here,
Need not hold diplomatic talk like fools:
Suppose I speak, divesting the plain fact
Of all their tortuous phrases, fit for them—
Do you reply so, and what trouble's saved!
The Prince, then—an embroiled strange heap of news
This moment reaches him—if true or false.
All dignity forbids he should enquire
In person, or by worthier deputy;
Yet somehow must enquire, lest slander come:
And so 'tis I am pitched on.   You have heard
His offer to your Lady?
  Val.   Yes.
  Mel.   —Conceive
Her joy thereat?—
  Val.   I cannot.
  Mel.   No one can:
All draws to a conclusion, therefore.
  Val. [*Aside.*]   So!
No after-judgment—no first thought revised—
Her first and last decision!—me, she leaves—
Takes him—a simple heart is flung aside,
The ermine o'er a heartless breast embraced!
Oh Heaven, this mockery has been played too oft!
Once, to surprise the angels—twice, that fiends
Recording, might be proud they chose not so—

Thrice, many thousand times, to teach the world
All men should pause, misdoubt their strength, since men
Could have such chance yet fail so signally,
—But ever—ever—this farewell to heaven.
Welcome to earth—this taking death for life—
This spurning love and kneeling to the world—
Oh Heaven, it is too often and too old!

    Mel. Well, on this point—what but an absurd rumour
Arises—these, its source—its subject, you!
Your faith and loyalty misconstruing,
They say, your service claims the lady's hand!
Of course, nor Prince nor Lady can respond—
Yet something must be said—for, were it true
You made such claim, the Prince would . . .

    Val.   Well, sir, would?

    Mel. —Not only probably withdraw his suit,
But, very like, the lady might be forced
Accept your own.—Oh, there are reasons why!
But you'll excuse at present all save this,—
I think so. What we want is, your own witness,
For, or against—her good, or yours: decide!

    Val. [*Aside.*] Be it her good if she accounts it so!
[*After a contest.*] For what am I but hers, to choose as she?
Who knows how far, beside, the light from her
May reach, and dwell with, what she looks upon?

    Mel. [*to the* Prince.] Now to him, you!

    Berth. [*to* VALENCE.] My friend acquaints you, sir,
The noise runs . . .

    Val.   . . . Prince, how fortunate are you,
Wedding her as you will, in spite of it,
To show belief in love! Let her but love you,
All else you disregard! What else can be?
You know how love is incompatible
With falsehood—purifies, assimilates
All other passions to itself.

    Mel.   Ay, sir:
But softly! Where in the object we select,
Such love is, perchance, wanting?

    Val.   Then, indeed,
What is it you can take?

    Mel.   Nay—ask the world!
Youth, beauty, virtue, an illustrious name,
An influence o'er mankind!

Val.   When man perceives ...
—Ah, I can only speak as for myself!
  The D.   Speak for yourself!
  Val.   May I?—no, I have spoken,
And time's gone by!—Had I seen such an one—
As I loved her—weighing thoroughly that word—
So should my task be to evolve her love—
If for myself!—if for another—well!
  Berth.   Heroic truly!   And your sole reward,—
The secret pride in yielding up your own?
  Val.   Who thought upon reward?   And yet how much
Comes after—Oh what amplest recompense!
Is the knowledge of her, nought? the memory, nought?
——Lady, should such an one have looked on you,
Ne'er wrong yourself so far as quote the world,
And say, love can go unrequited here!
You will have blessed him to his whole life's end—
Low passions hindered, baser cares kept back,
All goodness cherished where you dwelt—and dwell.
What would he have?   He holds you—you, both form,
And mind, in his,—where self-love makes such room
For love of you, he would not serve you now
The vulgar way,—repulse your enemies,
Win you new realms, or best, in saving you
Die blissfully—that's past so long ago!
He wishes you no need, thought, care of him—
Your good, by any means, himself unseen,
Away, forgotten!—He gives that life's task up,
As it were ... but this charge which I return—
                    [*Offers the Requisition, which she takes.*
Wishing your good!
  The D. [*having subscribed it.*]   And opportunely, sir—
Since at a birthday's close, like this of mine,
Good wishes gentle deeds reciprocate.
Most on a wedding day, as mine is too,
Should gifts be thought of: yours comes first by right.
Ask of me!
  Berth.   He shall have whate'er he asks,
For your sake and his own!
  Val. [*Aside.*]   If I should ask—
The withered bunch of flowers she wears—perhaps,
One last touch of her hand, I never more
Shall see!

[*After a pause, presenting his paper to the* Prince.
    Cleves' Prince, redress the wrongs of Cleves!
Berth. I will, sir!
The D. [*as* VALENCE *prepares to retire.*] Nay, do out
    your duty, first!
You bore this paper: I have registered
My answer to it: read it and have done! [VALENCE *reads it.*
—I take him—give up Juliers and the world!
This is my Birth-day.
Mel.   Berthold, my one hero
Of the world she gives up, one friend worth my books,
Sole man I think it pays the pains to watch,—
Speak, for I know you through your Popes and Kings!
   Berth. [*after a pause.*] Lady, well rewarded! Sir, as well
    deserved!
I could not imitate—I hardly envy—
I do admire you! All is for the best!
Too costly a flower were you, I see it now,
To pluck and set upon my barren helm
To wither—any garish plume will do!
I'll not insult you and refuse your Duchy—
You can so well afford to yield it me,
And I were left, without it, sadly off!
As it is—for me—if that will flatter you,
A somewhat wearier life seems to remain
Than I thought possible where . . . 'faith, their life
Begins already—they're too occupied
To listen—and few words content me best!
[*Abruptly to the* Courtiers.] I am your Duke, though! Who
    obey me here?
   The D. Adolf and Sabyne follow us—
   Gui. [*starting from the* Courtiers.]——And I?
Do I not follow them, if I mayn't you?
Shall not I get some little duties up
At Ravestein and emulate the rest?
God save you, Gaucelme! 'Tis my Birth-day, too!
   Berth. You happy handful that remain with me
. . . That is, with Dietrich the black Barnabite
I shall leave over you—will earn your wages,
Or Dietrich has forgot to ply his trade!
Meantime,—go copy me the precedents
Of every installation, proper styles,
And pedigrees of all your Juliers' Dukes—

While I prepare to go on my old **way**,
And somewhat wearily, I must confess!

The D. [with a light joyous laugh as she turns from them.] Come, Valence, to our friends—God's earth. . . .

Val. [as she falls into his arms.]—And thee!

END OF VOL. I.